The Cambridge Companion to
PLATO'S *REPUBLIC*

Edited by G. R. F. Ferrari
University of California, Berkeley

CAMBRIDGE
UNIVERSITY PRESS

CAMBRIDGE UNIVERSITY PRESS
Cambridge, New York, Melbourne, Madrid, Cape Town, Singapore, São Paulo, Delhi

Cambridge University Press
32 Avenue of the Americas, New York, NY 10013-2473, USA

www.cambridge.org
Information on this title: www.cambridge.org/9780521548427

First published 2007
Reprinted 2007, 2008, 2009

Printed in the United States of America

A catalog record for this publication is available from the British Library.

Library of Congress Cataloging in Publication Data

The Cambridge companion to Plato's Republic / [edited by] G. R. F. Ferrari.
    p. cm. – (Cambridge companions to philosophy)
Includes bibliographical references and index.
ISBN-13: 978-0-521-83963-1 (hardback)
ISBN-13: 978-0-521-54842-7 (pbk.)
1. Plato. Republic. I. Ferrari, G. R. F. (Giovanni R. F.) II. Title.
JC71.P6C36   2007
321'.07 – dc22   2006029156

ISBN 978-0-521-83963-1 hardback
ISBN 978-0-521-54842-7 paperback

CONTENTS

vii

CONTRIBUTORS

NORBERT BLÖSSNER is Privatdozent in Classical Philology at the Free University of Berlin and the author of a new commentary on Books 8–10 of Plato's *Republic*, to appear under the auspices of the Akademie der Wissenschaften und der Literatur, Mainz. Among his books are *Dialogform und Argument: Studien zu Platons "Politeia"* (Steiner Verlag, 1997), *Musenrede und "geometrische Zahl"* (Steiner Verlag, 1999), and *Cicero gegen die Philosophie* (Vandenhoeck & Ruprecht, 2001).

NICHOLAS DENYER is a Fellow of Trinity College, Cambridge, where he is a Senior Lecturer in Philosophy. He is also a Senior Lecturer in the Faculty of Classics, University of Cambridge. He is the author of *Time, Action and Necessity: A Proof of Free Will* (Duckworth, 1981); *Language, Thought and Falsehood in Ancient Greek Philosophy* (Routledge, 1991); *Plato: Alcibiades* (Cambridge University Press, 2001); and numerous articles, both on the history of ancient philosophy and on various questions in logic, ethics, and metaphysics. He is currently producing an edition of Plato's *Protagoras*.

G. R. F. ("JOHN") FERRARI is Professor of Classics at the University of California, Berkeley. He has edited a translation of Plato's *Republic* by Tom Griffith in the series Cambridge Texts in the History of Political Thought (Cambridge University Press, 2000). He is the author of *Listening to the Cicadas: A Study of Plato's* Phaedrus (Cambridge University Press, 1987) and *City and Soul in Plato's* Republic (Academia Verlag, 2003; rpt. University of Chicago Press, 2005).

STEPHEN HALLIWELL is Professor of Greek at the University of St. Andrews. His books include *Aristotle's Poetics* (Duckworth,

1986/98); *Plato*, Republic 10 (Aris & Phillips, 1988), and *The Aesthetics of Mimesis: Ancient Texts and Modern Problems* (Princeton University Press, 2002). He has published more than seventy articles on Greek literature, philosophy, and rhetoric; his next book, dealing with texts and issues from Homer to Christianity, will be entitled *Greek Laughter: Explorations in Cultural Psychology from Homer to Christianity*.

ARYEH KOSMAN was educated at the University of California at Berkeley, at Hebrew University, and at Harvard University. He has taught at various institutions in the United States and has been at Haverford College since 1962, where he is John Whitehead Professor of Philosophy. He is the author of a number of essays in the history of philosophy, primarily on Plato and Aristotle.

PAUL W. LUDWIG is Tutor at St. John's College, Annapolis. He is the author of *Eros and Polis: Desire and Community in Greek Political Theory* (Cambridge University Press, 2002) and articles on Plato, justice, the political passions in ancient thought, and existentialism. He is currently working on a book on friendship in ancient political philosophy and its relevance to recent political theory.

MITCHELL MILLER is Professor of Philosophy at Vassar College. He is the author of *The Philosopher in Plato's Statesman* (Nijhoff, 1980; rpt. Parmenides Publishing, 2004), and *Plato's Parmenides: The Conversion of the Soul* (Princeton University Press, 1986; rpt. Penn State University Press, 1991) as well as essays on a number of other dialogues and on Hesiod, Parmenides, and Hegel. He has a long-standing interest in the Platonic project of the "longer way" to the Good and the interplay this involves of harmonics, form theory, and the "so-called unwritten teachings."

DONALD R. MORRISON is Professor of Philosophy and Classical Studies at Rice University. He is the author of numerous articles on Plato, Socrates, and many other topics from a variety of fields within ancient philosophy. He is currently editing the *Cambridge Companion to Socrates* and is at work on two other projects: one on conceptions of analytic method in late Greek philosophy; the other on the good of the city in classical Greek political philosophy.

JESSICA MOSS is Assistant Professor of Philosophy at the University of Pittsburgh. She is the author of several articles on Plato's *Gorgias*,

Protagoras, and *Republic* and is at work on a book on appearances of goodness in the philosophy of Plato and Aristotle.

DAVID K. O'CONNOR has been teaching at the University of Notre Dame since 1985, where his work focuses on ancient philosophy, ethics, and philosophy and literature. He is a faculty member of the departments of Philosophy and Classics. He recently edited and introduced Percy Bysshe Shelley's 1818 translation of Plato's *Symposium* (St. Augustine's Press, 2002) and is working on *Romancing Plato: Shelley, Emerson, Yeats, Stevens*, a study of the influence of Plato and Shakespeare on the philosophical skepticism of four major poets in the Romantic tradition.

RICHARD D. PARRY is the Fuller E. Callaway Professor of Philosophy at Agnes Scott College. He is the author of *Plato's Craft of Justice* (State University of New York Press, 1996). He has published articles on Plato's ethics as well as on the physical theory in *Timaeus* and *Laws* 10.

CHRISTOPHER ROWE is Professor of Greek at Durham University, United Kingdom. He is the author of a new translation of Aristotle's *Nicomachean Ethics*, to accompany a full philosophical commentary by Sarah Broadie (Oxford University Press, 2002) and wrote (with Terry Penner) *Plato's* Lysis (Cambridge University Press, 2005). He edited (with Malcolm Schofield) *The Cambridge History of Greek and Roman Political Thought* (Cambridge University Press, 2000) and (with Julia Annas) *New Perspectives on Plato, Modern and Ancient* (Harvard University Press, 2002). He is currently completing a monograph for Cambridge University Press titled *Plato and the Art of Philosophical Writing*.

Following positions at Cornell University and Balliol College, Oxford, MALCOLM SCHOFIELD is Professor of Ancient Philosophy at Cambridge, where he has taught for close to thirty-five years. He is co-author (with G. S. Kirk and J. E. Raven) of *The Presocratic Philosophers*, 2nd ed. (Cambridge University Press, 1983), and has published widely on many areas and periods of Greek and Roman thought. He has been working mainly on ancient political thought since *The Stoic Idea of the City* (Cambridge University Press, 1991) and is co-editor (with Christopher Rowe) of *The Cambridge History of Political Thought* (Cambridge University Press, 2000). His latest book is *Plato: Political Philosophy* (Oxford University Press, 2006).

DAVID SEDLEY is Laurence Professor of Ancient Philosophy at the University of Cambridge, where he is also a Fellow of Christ's College. He is co-author (with A. A. Long) of *The Hellenistic Philosophers* (Cambridge University Press, 1987). He also wrote *Lucretius and the Transformation of Greek Wisdom* (Cambridge University Press, 1998), *Plato's Cratylus* (Cambridge University Press, 2003), and *The Midwife of Platonism: Text and Subtext in Plato's Theaetetus* (Oxford University Press, 2004). He also edits philosophical papyri. His recent and current work has been largely on the ancient debate about creationism and on philosophy in the first century B.C.

ROSLYN WEISS is Professor of Philosophy at Lehigh University. She is the author of *Socrates Dissatisfied: An Analysis of Plato's* Crito (Oxford University Press, 1998), *Virtue in the Cave: Moral Inquiry in Plato's* Meno (Oxford University Press, 2001), and *The Socratic Paradox and Its Enemies* (University of Chicago Press, 2006). She has published numerous articles on ancient and medieval philosophy.

HARVEY YUNIS is Andrew W. Mellon Professor of Humanities and Classics at Rice University. He is the author of *Taming Democracy: Models of Political Rhetoric in Classical Athens* (Cornell University Press, 1996) and a commentary on Demosthenes' speech, *On the Crown* (Cambridge University Press, 2001). He is currently working on an edition of and commentary on Plato's *Phaedrus*.

ABBREVIATIONS

I. PLATONIC TEXTS

Alc.	*Alcibiades*
Ap.	*Apology*
Chrm.	*Charmides*
Cra.	*Cratylus*
Cri.	*Crito*
Criti.	*Critias*
Epin.	*Epinomis*
Epist.	*Epistles (Letters)*
Euphr.	*Euthyphro*
Euthd.	*Euthydemus*
Grg.	*Gorgias*
H. Ma.	*Hippias Major*
H. Mi.	*Hippias Minor*
La.	*Laches*
Lys.	*Lysis*
Menex.	*Menexenus*
Phd.	*Phaedo*
Phdr.	*Phaedrus*
Phil.	*Philebus*
Pol.	*Politicus (Statesman)*
Prm.	*Parmenides*
Prt.	*Protagoras*
Rep.	*Republic*
Smp.	*Symposium*
Sph.	*Sophist*
Theag.	*Theages*

Tht.   *Theaetetus*
Ti.   *Timaeus*

II. MODERN TEXTS

DK   H. Diels, *Die Fragmente der Vorsokratiker*, 6th ed., rev.
       W. Kranz, 3 vols. (1906; Berlin, 1952).
LSJ   H. G. Liddell and R. Scott, *A Greek-English Lexicon*, rev.
       H. S. Jones, 9th ed. (Oxford, 1940), with new
       supplement (1843; Oxford, 1996).

Editor's Introduction

I

When is it that we choose to journey with companions? Most often, I suppose, when we want to make the journey fuller, more pleasant, more vivid. But we may also want a fellow traveler to point out landmarks we might be missing or perhaps to assure us we are headed along the best or safest route to our destination. The companion is not a scout; he does not strike out ahead in order to prepare us for a journey that we have not yet begun. This *Companion to Plato's* Republic, accordingly, is not a preparatory book; it is not written to be read in advance of Plato's *Republic*, still less instead of it. Scouting out the unread text to come is the purpose that introductions to translations or editions of that text legitimately serve; outright substitution for the text is the dubious offer of a thousand Web sites.[1]

This *Companion*, by contrast, seeks to walk with those who are already on the road: whether with first-time readers who want guidance as they read or with those second-time readers, third-time readers, or indeed fully seasoned readers of the *Republic* whose desire to deepen their appreciation of the work has not waned and who choose to deepen it in the company of more experienced readers or of their peers.

[1] The service of scout is one that I have myself performed with the introduction I wrote to Tom Griffith's translation of the *Republic* (Ferrari, ed. 2000). That introduction also contains biographical information about Plato that is potentially relevant to the *Republic* and that is not a topic in any of the chapters of this volume. The present introduction has the contents and aims of this *Companion* primarily in view – not the contents and aims of Plato's *Republic*.

Although the series *Cambridge Companions* now covers most major philosophers and philosophic movements as well as a plethora of other intellectual figures and movements, it has not been the practice to offer *Companions* to individual works. A *Cambridge Companion to Plato* has existed for some years;[2] why, now, a *Cambridge Companion to Plato's* Republic?

If I were to reach for a word that could explain why the *Republic* should be singled out for individual treatment among Plato's dialogues, I would say this: that although it is not the most technical or even perhaps the most philosophical of the dialogues (not for the most part displaying the muscular philosophic athleticism of a dialogue like the *Theaetetus*), although it does not ravish the reader in the manner of the *Symposium* or the *Phaedrus*, although it would be pointless to insist that it (and not the many other candidates that have been proposed) is Plato's "masterpiece," still, the *Republic* is, without a doubt, Plato's epic. In its scale, in its complexity, in the inexhaustible abundance of questions that it raises, both hermeneutic and more purely philosophic – above all, in its lissom gravity, the *Republic* is the one truly successful epic to which Plato stretched himself in his lifetime. Do not remind me of the *Laws* in this connection. The *Laws* does not stand to the *Republic* as *Odyssey* to *Iliad*; it stands to the *Republic* as *Finnegans Wake* to *Ulysses*. The *Republic* is Plato's philosophic *Iliad* and *Odyssey* combined.

II

At least since that fabled time when Odysseus held the court of King Alcinous spellbound with the story of his adventures (Homer, *Odyssey* 13.1–2), large audiences have been drawn to a long and epic tale well told. It is no surprise, then, that Socrates' narrative of his night out in the seamy port district of Athens – a night when his young companions coaxed so many strange and startling ideas from his lips – has taken pride of place among Plato's philosophic works in its popularity with the general reading public for as long as such a thing as the "general reading public" has existed. It has not, of course, existed for very long. Not until the nineteenth century, in fact, did the *Republic* truly explode in popularity, notably in the English-speaking world. It was then that Benjamin Jowett made it a

---

[2] Kraut 1992.

focus of the "Greats" curriculum at Oxford, and thereby a focus of the education of the English gentleman; it was then, too, that Bernard Bosanquet decided to key his *Companion to Plato's* Republic to a popular translation of the day on the grounds that this translation was "of a size and cost which make it universally accessible."[3] Bosanquet was tuning his work not to the ear of Jowett's Oxford but to that of the audience who took his university extension classes on Plato and who knew no Greek.[4]

The democratizing intent of those extension classes has since refashioned the university itself. Thus the *Companion* that the reader now holds in her hand, or in his hand, while it inherits that energizing burst of popularity from the nineteenth century, derives its raison d'être as much from the diffusion of the *Republic* to general audiences within the university as from its importance to a wider reading public in the university's ambit.

The very features that make for a classic with the educated public may also render that classic suspect to specialists. As a graduate student, I had the opportunity to weigh the solemn declaration made by a teacher of mine in secondary school, that "no man may call himself educated who has not read Plato's *Republic*," against the urgings of an adviser who dismissed the *Republic* as "Plato preaching." (The two remarks are not in fact incompatible, though at the time I felt them to be.) In the days before a general reading public existed, the *Republic*'s fate lay chiefly in the hands of scholars. (That is not to say that the *Republic* was written chiefly for an audience of scholars.)[5] Beginning with the first generation of Plato's successors and continuing through the Platonist commentators in the early centuries of our era, these specialists not unnaturally showed most interest either in the work's more abstruse or in its more controversial themes. They pondered its mathematical, metaphysical, and theological passages; they debated its apparent hostility to the poets, or its recommendation that women of the elite class should have political rights equal to those of the men. As a result, they did not accord the *Republic* that central position among Plato's dialogues which it later

---

[3] Bosanquet 1925 [1895], p. viii.

[4] For details of this history, see Glucker 1987, esp. pp. 190–98.

[5] Harvey Yunis in section II of his chapter for this volume considers the extent to which the new prose literature to which the *Republic* belongs was written for more than just a scholarly audience.

came to occupy; they treated it as one significant member of the corpus among others.

When Friedrich Schleiermacher (the nineteenth-century German theologian, philosopher, and translator of Plato) reconstrued the corpus of dialogues as a systematic structure, one that seats the *Republic* on a foundation consisting of the keystones to the arches formed by more basic and therefore preparatory dialogues,[6] or when in our own day Charles Kahn traces a pattern by which the aporetic dialogues (those that end with no satisfactory answer to the question investigated) anticipate and build toward a resolution that only the *Republic* provides,[7] both are responding to the *Republic*'s epic quality. It is this that can tempt a reader to seek evidence to show that in the interpretation of Plato, all roads (or most roads) lead to the *Republic*. And such a reader must treat the *Republic* as a unity. Proclus, by contrast, the fifth-century A.D. scholar of Plato, writes a commentary on the *Republic* (it is the major commentary to survive from antiquity) that is actually a series of essays – essays, moreover, of radically divergent length and focus. It is not that Proclus refuses to treat the dialogue as a unity – the unity of its theme is in fact one of the first things he sets out to prove. He is also a proponent of the thesis that Plato sees himself as rivaling Homer, but, typically, he treats this idea in a single massive essay (the sixth) that unearths Homeric motifs and styles in many dialogues other than the *Republic*. He fails, after all, to engage with the work as a unity; in that sense, he is not alive to its epic sweep.

The mid-twentieth-century standoffishness with regard to the *Republic*, the tendency to plunder the text for arguments, especially arguments about Platonic "Forms," leaving the sense of the whole to be given by books derived from sets of lectures or in any case intended for undergraduates, while turning in one's more serious work to Plato's more technical dialogues, has had the salutary effect of accelerating the retreat from nineteenth-century overreach. The way has been open for some time for scholars to reconsider the *Republic*: no longer insisting on its overall primacy among Plato's dialogues, but maintaining something of the romantic sense of its scope that the nineteenth century bequeathed.[8]

---

[6] Schleiermacher 1836, pp. 42–43. (The extended architectural metaphor is his.)

[7] Kahn 1996.

[8] Press 1996 provides an excellent capsule history of the *Republic*'s reception from antiquity to modern times. See also the other works listed in section IV.L of this

Nor have they failed to seize the opportunity. The journals abound with articles on the *Republic*. Perhaps drawn by the increased stature of moral and political philosophy and of action theory in philosophy as currently practiced, these articles often home in on questions not readily isolated from the *Republic*'s overall argument (or from the ambition to discern such an argument): questions about social justice; about the nature and value of the philosophic life; about the psychology on which the *Republic*'s various proposals depend; about whether the work has a utopian intention and, if so, how serious it is; and about whether the larger elements that structure the *Republic*'s argument are in fact coherent.

Then there are the several far-from-introductory monographs on the *Republic* that have appeared in English alone over the last fifteen years or so;[9] there is the ongoing multivolume and multiauthor commentary in Italian;[10] and just the two years preceding the appearance of this volume have seen the publication of a collection of new articles on the *Republic* in French and another in English.[11] And yet, even setting aside their evident differences of scale, format, and scholarly affiliation, there is little repetition among these books, so lively is the current discussion. In the ocean of the *Republic* there is room for all to swim.

The time is ripe, then, for a comprehensive book of essays on the *Republic*, essays that build on what the past two or three decades of scholarship have achieved but that do not assume this achievement will be familiar to their readers, essays that differ not only in topic but also in interpretive method, comprising thereby a book that can at least attempt to match the inexhaustibility of its subject.

III

If indeed a reader of the *Republic* who is true to its stature must approach the work as a unified argument, this is a unity that readers

volume's bibliography. For a view of the moral to be drawn from this history different from the one drawn here, see Annas 1999.

[9] The seminal work in this category was surely Reeve 1988.

[10] Vegetti 1998–.

[11] Dixsaut 2005; Santas 2006. Although both works arrived in time to be acknowledged and itemized in the general bibliography, their contents were for the most part not available to be considered by the authors of this volume – except by those few who had access to early versions of particular chapters, whether through contact with their authors or indeed identity with them.

of the present volume will quite properly construct for themselves. They will not find unanimity among the authors of these essays. They do not have here a book whose authors share a single paradigm and divide the task of presenting its ramifications.

Instead, within this book the same topics often reappear in different colors and are viewed in different lights. This occurs despite the fact that the order of chapters cleaves to the sequence in which topics are presented in the ten books of the *Republic* – or, rather, because of that fact. For since the *Republic* itself makes a point of interweaving its themes – since it is replete with anticipations, suspensions, echoes, and transformations of its leading ideas – the authors of these chapters often find themselves coming upon a common topic by a private route, the route afforded by the particular stretch of argument assigned to them. That they arrive from a different direction may then contribute to the divergence of their ideas.

Take, for example, the vexed question of what motivates the philosopher in the ideal society to return to the "cave" of political life and assume the duties of kingship. The most sustained discussion of the issue that this volume offers is to be found in David Sedley's essay (chapter 10, section II). Although his focus is the discussion of philosopher-kingship in Books 5–7, Sedley finds it necessary to return to Book 1, with its claim that decent men agree to rule in order to avoid being ruled by their inferiors, if he is to resolve the issue and render "the text of the *Republic* . . . entirely and unproblematically consistent in the matter."

Roslyn Weiss, working at the cusp of Books 1 and 2, looks forward rather than backward and meets Sedley (in chapter 4, section IV) coming from the opposite direction. Like him, she thinks Book 1 has provided the materials for a solution to our question; but she denies that the motive of the "decent men" in Book 1 serves as a template for that of the philosopher. For Weiss, "nothing but justice can obligate a philosopher to rule." The philosopher finds justice desirable in itself, which is just as well, given that the consequences of justice – as manifested, crucially, in the benefits of philosophic rule – are good for others, not for oneself.

Malcolm Schofield comes on this same problem while working on the "noble lie" in chapter 6 (section IV). His interest accordingly is kindled more by the rhetoric that persuades philosophers to rule than by the traditional crux of motivation. He notes that Socrates "moves into direct speech to address his argument direct to the philosophers. He appeals to the understanding *they* need to have of *their* existential situation." And he draws a lesson for the operations of the noble lie; for in both cases the problem is "how to *persuade* the individual to do something required by the good of the city."

Attention to a different kind of rhetoric, that of the discourse between the dialogue's fictional characters, marks Mitchell Miller's response to the issue. Throughout his chapter on the philosopher's education (chapter 12) Miller is at pains to tease out the parallels with the education that Socrates is offering his protégés Glaucon and Adeimantus. Rather than contest directly those accounts of the philosopher's reserve toward descending into the cave that remain "at the level of what Socrates says to Glaucon," he brings to the debate (see his note 27) "the performative tension of what Socrates does with what he says": the contrast between the reserve attributed to the philosopher and the "zest for teaching" that Socrates displays in what Miller regards as an equivalent "descent," his descent to the port district and his generous pedagogical engagement there.

Whereas David Sedley seeks to restore unproblematic consistency to the text, David O'Connor finds in it the expression of two moods that, while not inconsistent, are thought-provokingly at odds: an "active, reformist mood" and a "dismissive, escapist mood." O'Connor is concerned in chapter 3 with the kind of moral guidance that Socrates is providing for Glaucon and Adeimantus; hence his interest in the mood that Socrates might transmit to them. For Sedley, the idea that the only good ruler is a reluctant ruler is "Plato's great political insight." But O'Connor (who is skeptical of how wholeheartedly Plato endorses the idea: "this is still a popular cover story among academics seeking leadership positions") sets in the scales those passages that seem to him to treat ruling as an intrinsic good for the philosopher, arriving finally (this is in his section VII) at an uneasy balance of the two moods: "From this point of view [that which regards the growth a philosopher experiences by ruling as an intrinsic good], political leadership is surely not just the instrumental good of avoiding the rule of worse people. But it is a growth that cannot be pursued. We must await some divine chance to experience it. The dominant mood is resignation at unavoidable loss, lightened only by gratitude for extraordinary beauty."

Finally, let us give ear to Donald Morrison's caveat on the whole affair in chapter 9, section 1: "the great messy hairball of an issue which is the philosopher's return to the cave has no clear resolution without importing a great deal that is not explicit in the text, so that any answer should be put forward by its advocates as speculative."

Similar chains could be constructed between chapters for many of the *Republic*'s main themes. Readers will come upon them for themselves or may trace them through the index. Certainly, then, this book is no chorale for sixteen voices; nor yet is it a cacophony. The sixteen chapters with their divergent reprises surround the reader with a more natural, lively, and varied soundscape than any single source could provide, even one that includes a précis of others' opinions. And lest the reader despair of encountering unanimity in these pages, I mention two instances. The authors who deal at some length with Book 1 (and note that no single chapter is dedicated to that book) all agree to treat it not only as integral to the *Republic* but as anticipating its argument. (The authors are Rowe, Weiss, and Sedley.) Another example: those who directly address the time-honored question of whether the *Republic* is primarily a political or primarily a moral work all respond that it is both. (The question dates back to Proclus; the responses in this volume come from Rowe, Kosman, and Morrison.)

Our book begins with three chapters that introduce the *Republic* whole, although in a variety of connections. Harvey Yunis considers for whom Plato was likely to have been writing, what effect he sought to have on that audience, and what means he applied to bring the effect about. Christopher Rowe then situates the *Republic* in the larger context of Plato's political and (to the extent that the two cannot be separated) his moral thought as this emerges from other dialogues. David O'Connor reengages the reader with the writerly substance of the *Republic* by tracing Plato's activity as reader and rival of the epic poets Homer and Hesiod. O'Connor shows how Plato mythologizes key themes in the dialogue's argument, casting its characters in a variety of roles in the mythic drama; and how that symbolic transformation does not simply duplicate but develops and sustains the argument.

Justice is the theme of chapters 4 and 5: Roslyn Weiss examines Socrates' arguments for the desirability of justice in Book 1 and sets them in play against the challenges made by Glaucon and

Adeimantus in Book 2; while Aryeh Kosman's focus falls at first on the discussion of justice in society and individual in Books 2–4, then broadens to embrace Platonic metaphysics and the concept of "cosmic" justice. An element of the ideal society's setup that has struck many readers over the years as a violation of justice is Malcolm Schofield's topic in chapter 6: the noble lie. This chapter also broaches the themes of the education appropriate to rulers of the ideal society, and of the censorship of poetry and other media within that education.

Whereas Kosman's chapter considers, among other things, how the harmony of an individual's soul can make for its justice, my own chapter on the three-part soul (chapter 7) gives an account of the arguments in Book 4 that provide that soul with its harmonizable constituents, and makes much of the development between the psychology proposed in Book 4 and that which emerges in later books. Psychology remains one focus of chapter 8, in which Paul Ludwig explains why the management of erotic passion and of sexual mores, which dominates Book 5 and returns to haunt the analysis of the tyrannical individual in Book 9, is of crucial importance not only to the *Republic*'s larger moral argument, but also to its political argument. Hence another focus of his chapter is the *Republic*'s utopianism. Utopianism is the exclusive concern of chapter 9, in which Donald Morrison argues that the political program of the *Republic* is no mere utopia – which is to say that it is not proposed as an impossible ideal – and subjects to criticism not only the major alternative accounts of Plato's intentions in this regard, but also the sleight of hand that Morrison detects in Plato's own argument.

David Sedley inaugurates in chapter 10 a trio of chapters that collectively discuss the figure of the philosopher-king, the education he receives, and the issues of Platonic metaphysics that arise in this connection in Books 5–7, including the famous allegories of sun, divided line, and cave. Sedley's chapter has two themes: the nature of the philosopher's knowledge, particularly in relation to the art of ruling (here Sedley discusses the allegory of the cave), and what motivates the philosopher to accept the burden of rule. Nicholas Denyer contributes in chapter 11 an account of the divided line and the importance of mathematics in the education of the philosopher-king. This task involves him in explaining more broadly how Plato takes mathematical thought to operate and what role "the

Good" plays in those operations. Whereas Sedley puzzles over how a mathematical education can be applied to issues of justice, Denyer puzzles over how an apparently moral concept such as the good can be applied to mathematics. Mitchell Miller, too, has much to say in chapter 12 about mathematics and about the cave in his discussion of the philosopher-king's education, but his emphasis falls on the effects of this education within the philosopher's soul – on the "love of the whole" that intellectual purification by the mathematical disciplines can help to induce. Miller's philosopher returns to the cave in an intellectual sense, not just as a political matter: he returns to the sensible. (Miller here seems to join Aryeh Kosman, chapter 5, section VII, in treating the Forms primarily as principles of the intelligibility of this our one world, rather than as constituting a world of their own.)

With Norbert Blössner's and Richard Parry's chapters we return to psychological themes, especially those of Books 8 and 9. Blössner's goal in chapter 13 is to explain the analogy between society and the individual soul that is so important an element of the *Republic*'s argument to show that justice pays, and so pervasive a motif in the structure of the whole. His goal is both to show how the analogy works and how it fits within the *Republic*. To that end he draws our attention at every turn to those features of the analogy that seem designed rather to advance the argument of the character Socrates within the fiction than to convince the reader that these are the views of the philosopher Plato and that they are worthy of general acceptance. Among these features would be the tripartite psychology itself. Blössner's chapter thus offers the most radically "rhetorical" approach to the *Republic* of any in the book. For that reason I have allowed it to conclude with a general explanation of its method (section IX) – something that other chapters show rather than tell. Richard Parry follows with a chapter on the psychology of the tyrannical individual in Book 9, the proof of whose unhappiness is in a sense the culminating moment of the *Republic*. Several earlier themes other than the purely psychological come together in this fourteenth chapter: the formation of character by upbringing; the nature and importance of erotic passion; and how that which prevails within the properly structured soul is a kind of justice.

The final two chapters return, as the *Republic* does, to the poetic and mythological topics introduced in this book by O'Connor and by Schofield. Jessica Moss (chapter 15) analyzes the arguments in Book 10 that justify the expulsion of "imitative" poetry from the ideal city. She makes a point of understanding the charge that such poetry has a morally corrupting effect – an ethical argument – in the light of the charge that it is "imitative" in nature – a metaphysical argument. Book 10 concludes with a tale of judgment after death and of the soul's choice of a new life back on earth; this volume concludes with Stephen Halliwell's treatment of that myth, the "myth of Er." He does not miss the opportunity it affords to look back on the *Republic*'s argument as a whole (for that argument too concerns the soul's choice of good or evil), and he finds in the ambiguity of the myth's perch between the literal and the allegorical an invitation to the reader to hold the conclusions of the entire dialogue in a thoughtful suspense.

For convenience, each chapter includes at the end a list of works cited by author and date in its footnotes, and some chapters append a list of further reading. In some cases, but not all, the concluding citation lists could function as a basic bibliography for the chapter's theme. For fuller guidance on these matters, however, the reader should consult the general bibliography on the *Republic* that I have furnished at volume's end, in which entries are divided first by category (commentary, translation, comprehensive study, etc.) and then by topic (justice, psychology, politics, metaphysics, etc.).

IV

Once the roster had been set, I arranged a conference at Berkeley for the authors of this volume to present initial versions of their chapters and to try them out both with their fellow authors and with a public audience. (I am grateful to the Loeb Classical Library Foundation, administered by the classics department at Harvard University, and to my own department of classics at Berkeley for their support of this conference.) As my editorial work on the written drafts progressed I made efforts to put individual authors in contact with those expressing different views on shared themes. And most authors had their later drafts read by a group of their fellows.

Nevertheless, this volume would not be the book it is if its authors did not work in quite different ways. Some are cracking puzzles in Plato; some tend to think along with Plato and see the world at least experimentally through his eyes; and some are dismantling the machine he made, in order to understand its mechanism. And these authors *feel* differently about Plato, too: some are celebratory; others more coolly analytical. All, however, share the conviction that to engage philosophically with the *Republic* and to read its text with all the care one can muster is an activity that brings its own reward. Producing this volume in their company has been a satisfying labor.

WORKS CITED

Annas, J. 1999. *Platonic Ethics, Old and New.* Ithaca, N.Y. Chap. 4: "The Inner City: Ethics without politics in the *Republic.*"

Bosanquet, B. 1925 [1895]. *A Companion to Plato's* Republic. London.

Dixsaut, M., ed. 2005. *Études sur la* République *de Platon,* 2 vols. Paris.

Ferrari, G. R. F., ed. 2000. *Plato: The* Republic, trans. T. Griffith. Cambridge.

Glucker, J. 1987. "Plato in England: The Nineteenth Century and After." In *Utopie und Tradition: Platons Lehre vom Staat in der Moderne,* ed. H. Funke. Würzburg.

Kahn, C. H. 1996. *Plato and the Socratic Dialogue: The Philosophical Use of a Literary Form.* Cambridge.

Kraut, R., ed. 1992. *The Cambridge Companion to Plato.* Cambridge.

Press, G. A. 1996. "Continuities and Discontinuities in the History of *Republic* Interpretation." *International Studies in Philosophy* 28, no. 4: 61–78.

Reeve, C. D. C. 1988. *Philosopher-Kings: The Argument of Plato's* Republic. Princeton; rpt., Indianapolis, Ind., 2006.

Santas, G., ed. 2006. *The Blackwell Guide to Plato's* Republic. Oxford.

Schleiermacher, F. 1836. *Schleiermacher's Introductions to the Dialogues of Plato.* Trans. W. Dobson. Cambridge; rpt., Bristol, 1992.

Vegetti, M., ed. 1998–. *Platone: La* Repubblica. Multiple vols. Naples.

1   The Protreptic Rhetoric of the *Republic*

In the *Republic* Socrates and his interlocutors consider the question of how one should live (352d). As befits a work of philosophy, the question is answered by Socrates by means of arguments that are intended to be compelling because of their logical and rational qualities. The characters in the dialogue demonstrate a great interest in the question, and in the arguments brought to bear, because they perceive that what is said about it will matter for, and may well determine, how they live their own lives (621c). How is the student of the *Republic* to react to Socrates' arguments? Students of the *Republic* are free to examine Socrates' arguments without feeling that those arguments may have any impact on how they will live their lives. That is an option opened up by the autonomy of reading and bolstered by the disciplinary practice of academic philosophy, which requires indeed the examination of the arguments but not the implementation of the results of that examination in one's own life. By long practice, it has been found possible, and often intellectually advantageous, to keep life and the study of life separate.

In this chapter I argue that Plato's purpose as a philosophical writer was not merely to present compelling arguments about how one should live, but to present them in such a way that the reader would be most likely to be compelled by them to choose to live in a particular way. This is not an entirely original idea; the urgency of Plato's writing has been evident to many of his readers for a long time. But at a time when writing and reading have many multifarious purposes and disciplinary habits are entrenched, it is worth examining anew Plato's practice as a philosophical writer.

Over the course of the conversation narrated by Socrates in the *Republic*, his two main interlocutors, Glaucon and Adeimantus, undergo a change. There are three closely related respects in which the change takes place.

First, Glaucon and Adeimantus change with respect to their views on justice. At the start of the *Republic,* neither Glaucon nor Adeimantus shares Thrasymachus' view that it pays to be unjust; and they incline toward Socrates' view that it pays to be just. But they are unconvinced that Socrates has actually refuted Thrasymachus in Book 1, and in spite of their inclinations they lack complete confidence that Socrates is right about justice and Thrasymachus wrong. Desiring an argument in favor of justice that will wipe away all doubts about its unconditional utility, Glaucon eloquently presents a worst-case scenario that contrasts the lives of two men (358b–362c). One is just but deprived of all the goods of this world and burdened by all the evils; the other man is unjust but enjoys all the goods of this world and none of the evils. Adeimantus adds the condition that for both men the rewards and punishments of the gods and other men are to be ignored (363a–368c). If Socrates can show that this just man is better off than this unjust man, he will have demonstrated that it always pays to be just without regard for appearances and consequences.

Socrates' response to the challenge issued by Glaucon and Adeimantus, which extends to the end of Book 9, is successful: the brothers are led through precisely the sort of argument about justice that they wish to hear, and they acknowledge that Socrates has made the stringent case they requested (580b–d, 588b–592b). With respect to their views on justice, Glaucon and Adeimantus are changed: previously they were not confident that it always pays to be just under any and all conditions, but now, as a result of Socrates' argument, they have become confident that it does always pay to be just.

Second, the change that Glaucon and Adeimantus undergo in their views on justice can be traced back to a change in their values – which is at the heart of the *Republic*'s argument. To make his argument about justice in response to Glaucon's challenge, Socrates undertakes to show what justice is in and of itself, without regard for how it is viewed or what consequences it entails (358b). For only if justice is seen in this stark light, isolated from the good repute in which it is generally held, will it be possible to demonstrate that justice is a good that by itself outweighs all other goods. Socrates argues that justice is a condition of the soul akin to health in the body; it is the condition in which all the parts of the soul perform their proper function and the soul as a whole functions in its proper way (Book 4). Socrates then shows that the good that consists in the excellence of the soul outweighs all other goods by itself (Books 8–9).

From the beginning the brothers leaned toward justice and were not overly enamored of worldly, material, conventional goods. So we should not suppose that in the course of the *Republic* Glaucon and Adeimantus undergo a complete change in values, just as the change in their views on justice was essentially a matter of degree. But their values do change to some degree and in a particular direction. Whereas previously Glaucon and Adeimantus were not convinced that the good of the soul was absolutely superior to all other goods, they learn from Socrates' argument that the good of the soul is such that in comparison to it all other goods must always be deemed inferior. They learn to value the soul more than they did before, and they value worldly, material, conventional goods less.

Third, Glaucon and Adeimantus are indeed characters in a fictional work of literature, so on one level it makes no sense to talk about the lives of these characters outside what is represented in *Republic*.[1] But this work of literature, far from being fantastical, possesses verisimilitude to an extraordinary degree: the imagined world created by the author corresponds in vivid detail to the real world inhabited by the author and reader. This verisimilitude is a product of Plato's art.[2] By the act of imagination initiated by the author, the reader is encouraged to suppose that, as a result of the change in their values and their views of justice, Glaucon and Adeimantus will now tend to make the choices they face solely on the basis of justice and to disregard the consequences and other features of their actions.

---

[1] Like Socrates, Thrasymachus, and the rest of the characters in the *Republic*, Glaucon and Adeimantus were historical persons; in fact, Glaucon and Adeimantus were Plato's brothers. The point at issue here concerns solely how Plato represents them in the dialogue; see Ferrari 2003, pp. 11–36.

[2] The realistic style of the dialogue has had the consequence of inducing readers, among them some ancient and modern scholars, to suppose that the Socrates presented in Plato's dialogues is a historically reliable account of the actual Socrates and his views. Despite considerable effort and ingenuity on the part of its adherents, that supposition has never been convincingly demonstrated, and no particular version of it has ever won more than a passing endorsement from the scholarly community; see Nails 1995. On Plato's creation of a literary Socrates, see Michelini 2003.

In accord with Er's mythic tale of choices and fates that closes the *Republic* and illustrates the benefit of making choices based solely on justice (614b–621b), the reader is also encouraged to suppose that Glaucon and Adeimantus are better off now in their new, changed condition at the end of the *Republic* than they were at the beginning.

Plato's overarching purpose in writing the *Republic* was to effect a change in his readers similar to the change that Glaucon and Adeimantus undergo at Socrates' hands in the fictional world of the dialogue. This purpose can be summed up in the word protreptic, from the Greek *protrepein*, which means "turn (someone) forward," hence "propel," "urge on," "exhort." Plato uses literary art, which in his case includes but is not limited to philosophical argument, to move his reader toward a greater readiness to adopt a just way of life. The full acquisition of virtue involves a long and complex education, as can be seen, for instance, in the account of the education of philosophers (Books 6 and 7). Protreptic discourse is not educational discourse as a whole and does not by itself bring about education in virtue. Rather, protreptic addresses the initial or preparatory stages of education. It aims to get education in virtue under way, to get the reader or auditor turned and moving in the right direction, and to make the acquisition of virtue an urgent priority.

Protreptic is not the name of a particular genre of discourse of fourth-century Greece despite the fact that certain fourth-century discourses refer to their protreptic function explicitly. Rather, protreptic refers to a function of discourse without regard to the form in which the discourse is cast. Protreptic is explicit when the writer or speaker addresses the recipient of his discourse and discloses his protreptic purpose explicitly. This occurs, for instance, in Isocrates' letter *To Philip*, exhorting Philip to lead a panhellenic expedition against Persia (*protrepein*, 5.17, 116); in Plato's *Euthydemus*, where Socrates demonstrates what, in his view, an exhortation to pursue wisdom and virtue would be like (*protreptikoi logoi*, 282d); and in Aristotle's *Protrepticus*, a lost work addressed to Themison, king of Cyprus, exhorting him to take up philosophy. In the *Republic*, the protreptic function is implicit, because the author never addresses the reader in his own voice and never says what his purpose is.[3]

---

[3] See Slings 1999, pp. 58–164, for a survey of protreptic discourse in fourth-century Greek literature. On protreptic discourse in Plato, see Gaiser 1959; Festugière 1973;

This rest of this chapter is divided into four sections. First, what did it mean for Plato to write literature that was intended to change his readers' values and views of justice, and what were the parameters and premises that made this protreptic literary project worth undertaking? Second, who was Plato's audience in the *Republic*? Third, how does the view of the *Republic* as protreptic square with Plato's views on political and philosophical discourse? And fourth, how is Plato's protreptic purpose reflected in the text and argument of the *Republic*?

I. WHAT WERE THE PARAMETERS AND PREMISES OF PLATO'S PROTREPTIC ENDEAVOR?

The change that Plato sought to effect in his readers cannot have been as specific as that which Glaucon and Adeimantus are portrayed as undergoing. Whereas the fictional characters have specific, well-delineated views when the work opens and acknowledge their specific, new positions by the end, readers in real life would come to the *Republic* with a range of views on justice and the soul, and the extent to which the experience of reading the *Republic* might move them closer to Socrates' position would also vary. But this unavoidable range of views in an unknown readership was of no practical consequence for Plato.

Plato could bank on the fact that, at least outside his own circle, no potential reader of the *Republic* had as firm a conviction about the absolute utility of justice as that which Socrates secures for Glaucon and Adeimantus in the course of the *Republic*. Glaucon, who is well informed, claims never to have heard such an argument before (358d). But if there were such a reader, for him the *Republic* would merely be redundant. Rather, Plato was addressing readers who – for any reason whatsoever – were less than fully convinced that justice was always more profitable than injustice, and that category included virtually everyone. When Glaucon and Adeimantus issue their challenge to Socrates in Book 2, they formulate an extreme

---

Gallagher 2004. On Aristotle's *Protrepticus*, see Düring 1961. Only after the classical period did protreptic become a recognized genre for exhorting the reader to take up philosophy, as the *Protrepticus* of Iamblichus (late 3rd, early 4th century C.E.), or some other formal schooling, as the *Protrepticus* of Galen (2nd century C.E.), an exhortation to study medicine.

case: they pit justice against whatever other goods can possibly be conceived, and they do not presuppose that any particular objection to justice is more telling than any other. The result is that anyone who harbors any doubt about the absolute utility of justice can look forward to Socrates' response as a potential answer to his or her particular concerns about justice. Glaucon and Adeimantus speak for themselves and for any readers who, like them, are well-intentioned, intellectually honest inquirers into the value of justice. They speak for Thrasymachus, the professional sophist who rejects justice on the grounds that it is a sham and by itself does the just man no good. They speak for people of ordinary intellectual attainments who, like Cephalus and Polemarchus in Book 1, have some regard for justice, based on the good repute that it enjoys, but have never sorted out how justice ranks in comparison to other goods, especially the material and social goods that they pursue. And they speak for the many who view justice as indeed a good thing, but one acquired solely for the sake of other good things and of no inherent value itself (358a). In short, there is no one who could not see in the challenge presented by Glaucon and Adeimantus a basis for having his or her own qualms about justice answered, whatever those qualms might be. Plato thereby ensured that virtually anyone who read the *Republic* would have good reason to take it seriously and attend to his project of changing their values.

Yet Plato could not hope to control how readers would read his book and thus how they would be affected by it. He was aware that, whatever the author's purpose in writing a book, readers have their own purposes, many of which cannot be anticipated, let alone controlled, by authors. In the *Phaedrus* Socrates says (275e):

Once a thing is put into writing, the composition, whatever it may be, drifts all over the place, getting into the hands not only of those who understand it, but equally of those who have no business with it; it doesn't know to address the right people and not the address the wrong. And when it is ill-treated and unfairly abused it always needs the help of its parent [i.e., the author] to come to its help, being unable to defend or help itself.   (trans. Hackforth)

So Plato would scarcely expect that he could change the values of every reader who picked up the *Republic* or that even sympathetic readers would necessarily adopt Socrates' position on justice and the soul with all the enthusiasm demonstrated by Glaucon and

Adeimantus. As Polemarchus says at the opening of the *Republic* (327c): "Could you persuade us if we refused to listen?"

The situation Plato faced as author is a rhetorical situation: addressing an audience that is considering a particular issue, he wants to change the way the audience thinks about that issue, but the only means at his disposal to do so are the resources of language. Given the (inevitable) limitations of those resources, the basic principle of rhetorical art is to focus on what lies within the author's control – the artistic manipulation of literary resources – and to relinquish the contingent – the actual response of actual readers. Recall Aristotle's definition of rhetoric, which became the operative definition as rhetoric developed into an art: "Let rhetoric be defined as the ability to see in each case the available means of persuasion" (*Rhetoric* 1.2.1).[4] Thus Plato's strategy was to exploit the available literary resources in such a way that an unknown reader would most likely be moved as close to Socrates' position on justice and the soul as was possible. The function of protreptic being to guide the reader or listener to adopt some attitude, protreptic is a form of rhetoric because it acknowledges a division between the responsibility of the author or speaker and that of the reader or listener. The author or speaker does what he can to guide the recipient toward a particular course, but it is up to the reader or listener whether or not to follow the guidance that has been offered. Protreptic rhetoric focuses on making that guidance as forceful as it can be and concentrates on the effect of the discourse on the recipient of the discourse, but, pursuing the task as a matter of art, it is not essentially concerned with the outcome, that is, how the reader or listener will respond.

Plato's protreptic task in the *Republic* is in certain respects parallel to the task that, as Plato represents it, Socrates undertook among his fellow Athenians. In the *Apology*, Socrates describes the nature of his philosophical activity in Athens (29d–30b):

I shall never stop practicing philosophy and exhorting you and elucidating the truth for everyone that I meet. I shall go on saying, in my usual way, My very good friend, you are an Athenian and belong to a city which is the greatest and most famous in the world for its wisdom and strength. Are you not ashamed that you give your attention to acquiring as much money as

---

[4] On the intrinsic ends of rhetoric and its status as an art, see Garver 1994, pp. 18–51.

possible, and similarly with reputation and honor, and give no attention or thought to truth and understanding and the perfection of your soul? . . . I spend all my time going about trying to persuade you, young and old, to make your first and chief concern not for your bodies nor for your possessions, but for the highest welfare of your souls. . . .   (trans. Tredennick)

It is unlikely that Socrates' protreptic activity had much success in changing his fellow citizens' values. There is no sign that such a change took place. And it was that very protreptic activity that, as Plato portrays it in the *Apology*, contributed to their willingness to convict him of impiety and corrupting the youth.[5] Yet Socrates insists on his pure motives and on the inherent value of his protreptic activity among the Athenians. That activity is, he says, "what god commands and it is my belief that no greater good has ever befallen you in this city than my service to god" (*Ap.* 30a). By making Socrates into a civic philosophical hero Plato has endorsed the view that even though Socrates may have failed in his attempt to change his fellow citizens' values, his protreptic activity was nevertheless worthwhile.[6] So too Plato's protreptic endeavor in the *Republic* should be judged with respect not to its ultimate success in changing his readers' values (which cannot in any case be measured) but to its aims, purposes, and methods. We can presume that the same combination of diffidence and determination that Socrates expresses when he agrees to take up the challenge issued by Glaucon and Adeimantus – "the best thing is to aid justice as best I can," says Socrates (368c) – will also have informed Plato's work as author.

Nevertheless, it is important to consider what kind of change would have to count as success for Plato's endeavor. Even Thrasymachus, the thoroughgoing amoralist, shows interest in Socrates' conversation with Glaucon and Adeimantus (450a–b) and Socrates is keen to maintain that interest (498c–d). But there is no sign that Thrasymachus is ultimately changed and no reason to believe that

---

[5] Cf. especially *Ap.* 30b: "if I corrupt the youth by this message, the message would seem to be harmful, but if anyone says that my message is different from this, he is talking nonsense." For fuller discussion, see Yunis 1996, pp. 153–56; Burnyeat 1997.

[6] A similar endorsement can be seen in the *Gorgias*: Socrates claims that he is the only true political expert and the only (Athenian) citizen truly engaged in politics (521d), even as he admits that in the democracy he is helpless to change politics for the better (521e–522a).

Plato expected to convert followers of Thrasymachus among his contemporaries. Yet if, as a result of reading the *Republic*, individuals who are already inclined toward justice and the soul, like Glaucon and Adeimantus, have those inclinations deepened to the point of certainty and acquire an immunity to the amoralism of Thrasymachus, that would be a highly significant achievement and would amply justify philosophy's work in the public realm. But no matter how much or little any reader valued justice before he began reading the *Republic*, if Plato were to move that reader even slightly closer to Socrates' view of justice and the soul than he was before, that would not be an insignificant achievement. From Plato's perspective, insofar as a reader learned to care even slightly less about wealth, power, and prestige and slightly more about justice and perfecting his soul, he would be better off (472b–c): he would be more likely to make the choices he faced on the basis of justice than on any other criteria.

II. WHO WAS THE AUDIENCE THAT PLATO SOUGHT TO INFLUENCE WITH THE *REPUBLIC*?

The *Republic* belongs to a cultural development that began in Greece in the latter part of the fifth century B.C.E. and accelerated in the fourth – the rise of popular prose literature. "Popular" must be defined carefully because in this context it means something different from what it means today. As made evident above all by Athenian tragic poetry, a highly refined form of mass entertainment, it is not possible to draw a clear line between a sophisticated, highbrow culture of the elite and a crude, undemanding culture of the masses.[7] In the first half of the fourth century, when the *Republic* was written, most of the population in the stratified societies of the Greek world had neither the education nor the leisure to read and understand formal literature on their own. So the new prose literature was not popular in the sense that it offered entertainment or instruction to masses of unsophisticated readers in the manner of a modern bestseller.

---

[7] Halliwell 2002, pp. 90–91. Nevertheless, Aristotle divides the audience of the theater into educated spectators and vulgar spectators, and advises appropriate entertainment for both types (*Politics* 1342a16–27).

Yet whereas in previous centuries literacy had been monopolized by experts and aristocrats, in Athens around the mid-fifth century the opportunities for literacy and the uses of literacy among the populace at large began a period of dramatic growth, as did the production and distribution of books.[8] And beyond the highly literate individuals who belonged mostly to the upper classes, individuals without the skill to read formal literature on their own might gather in groups to hear works of written literature read aloud.[9] The circulation of texts and the number of readers now reached the point where authors, in their capacity as private individuals, began to address the public as a whole through written texts. Thus the new prose literature existed outside the state institutions of assembly, courts, and theater. Those were the arenas of the two traditional modes of popular communication, poetry and oratory, which reached their audiences strictly in live performances regulated by the state. Avoiding both the constraints of democratic competition and the religious scruples attached to public poetic performance, the new prose authors addressed the public with a freedom of expression that was unprecedented in the Greek world.[10] The new prose literature was popular in the sense that it bypassed the existing forms of mass, oral communication to address an anonymous, amorphous, growing audience of readers.

Surviving fragments of comic plays of Plato's day reveal that Plato was well known to the Athenian public as an intellectual, a stock figure in Athenian comedy. Some fragments contain jokes that presume at least a vague awareness of some of Plato's basic ideas and terminology.[11] Since he was a prolific writer and avoided any prominent role in Athenian public life, this evidence attests to the fact

---

[8] On literacy and the rise of literate culture in fifth- and fourth-century Athens, see Harris 1989; Thomas 1989; Thomas 1992; Yunis 2003b.

[9] We cannot trace the extent of this phenomenon, but we know that it took place. On reading aloud to groups in fourth-century Athens, see Usener 1994; Thomas 2003.

[10] On the new prose literature and freedom from democratic constraints, see Yunis 1998. On freedom of thought and expression in Athens, see Dover 1976; Wallace 1994.

[11] The evidence was collected and discussed first by Diogenes Laertius (3.26–28) (2nd–3rd century C.E.) and more recently by Webster 1953, pp. 50–55. The following fragments of Athenian Middle Comedy (ca. 400–325 B.C.E.) refer to Plato's ideas or terminology (cited from Kassel 1983): Alexis 98, 163; Amphis 6; Cratinus junior 10; Epicrates 10; Theopompus 16.

that Plato's written works were the main vehicle through which he and his ideas came to public attention. Even so, the evidence does not exist (and probably never did) that would indicate precisely who and how many in Plato's Athens and contemporary Greece actually read the *Republic* and what kinds of interest and expertise these readers brought to their reading. The authors of the new prose literature themselves must have had no firm idea of who would read their books. The longevity that their texts possessed right from the start indicates their writing for an open-ended audience, one that could be enlarged at any time by anyone who could rise to the occasion, so to speak, by picking up the book and reading it or having it read to him.[12] Even if, as a matter of fact, most of the readers belonged, like Glaucon and Adeimantus, to the upper class, because they were the ones who mostly had the appropriate skills and leisure, the audience of the new prose literature was defined not by social, economic, or professional status but by moral and political status: individuals who were responsible for both their personal welfare and common affairs, who had choices to make, individually and collectively. Though moral reflection and criticism were historically the prerogative of the elite, the prose literature of fourth-century Greece reflects the expansion of that capability beyond traditional circles.

It would also be wrong to assume that the reading audience of a classical prose author would consist of those contemporaries who would find that author's message most congenial, as if, for example, Plato wrote for an elite audience because they were likely to share his strongly antidemocratic views. The classical prose authors evidently wanted to reach as many readers as possible and to persuade them to their view, creating and expanding their audience by the very act of writing artistic prose for an anonymous public. Whoever the readers actually were, they were addressed not as aristocrats or upper-class gentry, but as autonomous, thinking individuals.[13]

As evidenced by its most eminent practitioners – Herodotus and Thucydides, Plato, Xenophon, and Isocrates, Lysias and Demosthenes – the new prose literature concerned topics of general interest,

---

[12] Plato implies as much in the passage from the *Phaedrus* (275e), quoted above (p. 6).

[13] A similar conclusion is reached on the basis of other considerations by Blondell 2002, p. 28. For a different view see Menn 2006.

such as the history of Greece and Athens, exemplary lives of famous men, current events, moral and political problems, and education.[14] Yet even though this literature presumes no specialized knowledge, it brought to public attention what hitherto would have been considered specialized knowledge. In a remarkable act of synthesis, which may have been fostered by the rudimentary conditions of publishing written texts, the new prose authors found ways to address specialists while simultaneously maintaining their overall appeal to the diverse Greek reading public. For example, Thucydides addresses the broad public in his speeches and other set pieces, and he fashions his year-by-year chronicle of events to be comprehensible to any reader. But he occasionally injects a detail or contentious comment that was aimed at other specialists, not the average reader; and the historical dialectic on power and politics carried out over the work as a whole offers access to readers at different levels of sophistication.[15] So in the *Republic* the overall structure of Socrates' argument in defense of justice is determined by the analogy of city and soul, a move that sacrifices some precision for the sake of making the essential points more conspicuous (368d–e). This is a concession to the nonspecialist reader.[16] But in certain passages of the *Republic* Plato challenges the patience of nonspecialist readers by arguing with a rigor and precision that must have been intended primarily for the experts. This is evident, for example, in the mathematically expressed law of procreation that explains the dissolution of the just city (546a–d), a highly technical passage. But it also occurs less conspicuously, as when Socrates distinguishes philosophers, just proclaimed as the city's appropriate rulers, from lovers of spectacles by means of the more

---

[14] On the rise of Socratic discourses within the context of fifth- and fourth-century literature, see Kahn 1996, pp. 1–35. Most of Plato's dialogues are popular prose literature of the kind described here; however, six dialogues (*Theaetetus, Parmenides, Sophist, Statesman, Philebus,* and *Timaeus*) are too technical in their content and language and too sophisticated in their argumentation to be considered works of popular literature. (The *Laws* is borderline.) The audience of these dialogues, composed late in Plato's career, must have been students of philosophy, other philosophers, and those (necessarily few) members of the general public with enough philosophical acumen to follow them.

[15] For example, Thucydides 1.20.3 corrects Herodotus, but he is not mentioned by name. On Thucydides' historical dialectic, see Romilly 1956; Parry 1981.

[16] Socrates' explanation for introducing the city-soul analogy – "since we are not clever" (368d) – politely but ironically includes himself in those who would benefit from the analogy.

fundamental, ontological distinction between objects of knowledge (Forms) and objects of experience (476a–480a).[17]

The hallmark of the new prose literature, and the surest sign of its quest for a broad audience, was literary rhetorical art, that is, a pervasive concern with form and its effect on the reader.[18] The prose authors devised idioms, styles, and literary techniques in the attempt to win readers over to a particular view of things, while imbuing their texts with the immediacy and compelling quality that mark the best of Greek poetry and oratory. This was neither fine art (or art for art's sake), a notion that had yet to develop, nor generic art, since the literary genres were only in the process of formation. Rather, this was art deployed for didactic or persuasive purposes, and it was the specific purpose of each author that dictated the shape of his art. Isocrates, for instance, criticized Plato for being abstruse and thus useless to the citizen in need of concrete advice on political engagement.[19] Isocrates may simply have been wrong about Plato's ability to appeal to a broad audience, but even if he was correct (which we cannot know and have no reason to believe), that does not alter the fact that Plato wrote in a manner that *he* thought would, or perhaps could, captivate and instruct the reading public.

To take the most fundamental example: before Plato, philosophers treated arcane subjects in technical treatises that had no appeal outside small circles of experts.[20] These writings, "on nature," "on truth," "on being," and so on, mostly in prose, some in verse, were demonstrative, not protreptic. Plato, on the other hand, broke away from the experts and sought to treat ethical problems of universal relevance and to make philosophy accessible to the public. Basing his Socrates on the historical figure in ways we cannot discover, he presents a literary hero who was resolutely nonprofessional, averse to writing himself (since writing was residually recognized as a token of expertise), and accustomed to speaking with ordinary citizens in their own language. Thus in Book 1 of the *Republic* Socrates treats

---

[17] On multiple audiences addressed by Plato, see Szlezák 1999, responding to Friedrich Schleiermacher, whose general introduction to his translation of Plato's dialogues is accessible in English in Schleiermacher 1836. On multiple audiences addressed by Plato and Isocrates, see Morgan 2003.

[18] On the rise of literary rhetorical art in the fourth century, see Cole 1991.

[19] Isocrates 10.1, 13, 15.261–85. See Nightingale 1995, pp. 13–59.

[20] On the forms of philosophical writing before Plato, see Kahn 2003.

the defense of injustice offered by Thrasymachus, the professional sophist, with the utmost seriousness, but he deprives the professional of any special authority. Socrates' initial refutation of Thrasymachus fails to convince Glaucon and Adeimantus, but it establishes the occasion and the tone for Glaucon and Adeimantus to raise their own, nonprofessional questions about justice and to carry on the conversation in their own, nonprofessional way.

Plato's dialogues are distinguished from traditional philosophical treatises not simply with respect to their dialogue form, but with respect to the artistry with which the dialogue form is executed: they are vivid, unpredictable, and peopled by complex characters who care strongly about their views and provoke strong reactions in the reader.[21] The artistry of the *Republic*, as in most of Plato's dialogues, lies in making philosophy an ordinary, but exciting task. To take a small but potent example, nowhere is that artistry more palpable than in the *Republic's* justly famed opening line: "I went down yesterday to Piraeus with Glaucon, the son of Ariston" (327a).[22] The line is utterly innocent, shockingly offhand. The effect of this line and the opening scene (327a–328e) is to lull the reader into accepting the momentous conversation on justice that follows as arising naturally in consequence of a chance, everyday encounter. Thus the *Republic* undertakes not so much an implicit protreptic, as described above, but a disguised protreptic: disarmed by the naturalness of the conversation and intrigued by its unfolding drama, the reader is tricked into following closely the very argument that may ultimately change his values.

The *Republic* is exceptional within contemporary prose literature not just for its artistry, but also for the difficulty of the protreptic task that it undertakes. Plato's contemporary prose authors typically sought to persuade their readers of something. Some, like Thucydides, criticized democracy and Athenian institutions; others, like Isocrates and Xenophon, adopted a protreptic stance to offer moral or political advice. But only Plato went so far as to encourage his

---

[21] On the characters of Plato's dialogues, see Blondell 2002.

[22] Ancient scholars discussed this line as an example of Plato's unceasing effort to perfect his literary art: Dionysius of Halicarnassus, *On Literary Composition* 25 (2.133 Usener-Radermacher); Demetrius, *On Style* 21; Diogenes Laertius 3.37; and Quintilian, *On Oratorical Education* 8.6.64. For a modern assessment, see Denniston 1952, p. 41.

readers to reject society's inherited norms entirely (regarding such basic matters as marriage, family life, private property, and religious belief) and to accept in their stead norms that were derived from an idiosyncratic, idealist vision of reality and articulated by an autocratic philosopher. In this respect the *Republic* represents the pinnacle of the protreptic effort that is evident throughout Plato's writings. All the dialogues, especially the shorter, aporetic ones, possess protreptic qualities, inasmuch as they contest conventional values, inculcate philosophical method, and offer Socrates as a model.[23] But the protreptic task of the *Republic* is blunter. Spelling out in full the consequences of putting oneself under philosophy's rule, the *Republic* pressures the reader to decide – right now, so to speak – how he or she stands with respect to philosophy.

III. HOW DOES THE VIEW OF THE *REPUBLIC* AS PROTREPTIC SQUARE WITH PLATO'S VIEWS ON POLITICAL AND PHILOSOPHICAL DISCOURSE?

Plato holds the view that the philosopher, as the expert in politics, has an obligation to convey his expertise to the public; they need that expertise if they are to prosper. This obligation is on a par with the physician's obligation to provide his medical expertise to those who are ill in body. Thus, against their natural inclination to enjoy the life of pure philosophy apart from the affairs of the just city, the philosopher-kings are required to return to the cave to direct the affairs of their fellow citizens, who depend for their welfare on the philosopher's political expertise (*Rep.* 519c–520e). Yet the philosopher's obligation to provide political expertise is not absolute, just as the physician's obligation to provide medical expertise is not absolute. Like the physician, the philosopher is obliged to provide expertise only when he can advise freely and without constraint or danger to himself. For only in those conditions can the expert's advice remain undistorted by extraneous factors (such as what the recipient of the advice may want or what competing, sham experts may advise) and thus have a chance of being effective. Since in Plato's view the philosopher is unable to speak freely in a democracy without

---

[23] On the protreptic qualities of Plato's aporetic dialogues, see Frede 1992; Yunis 2003a.

endangering himself and his friends, Plato counsels the philosopher in a democracy to take shelter from the storm, observe a public silence, and pursue philosophy in private (*Rep.* 496c–e). Minding his own business, the philosopher is rendered by circumstances useless to the masses.[24]

Recall the dilemma of political discourse faced by Socrates. On the one hand, Socrates will not cater to the untrammeled desires of the democratic beast.[25] On the other hand, though Socrates used his elenctic method to turn his fellow citizens toward philosophy, and though the attempt was entirely honorable (*Ap.* 29d–30b, quoted above), that endeavor failed and ultimately proved as destructive to him as he feared direct political engagement would have proved.[26] Written protreptic, circulated in the public domain, offered Plato an escape from both the Socratic dilemma of political discourse and the philosopher's democratic isolation. Plato's written protreptic has the same philosophical and political aim as Socrates' protreptic elenchus: it offers philosophical guidance to the public at large without compromising the philosopher's freedom of speech. But unlike Socrates' elenchus, Plato's written protreptic does not plunge the philosopher into perilous contact with the democratic masses. It allows him to conduct public philosophical discourse from the safety of his isolation and also does not intrude on his professional activities in his school. And though Plato's written protreptic is often rhetorical – in the sense that it uses form for effect in an artistic manner – it is not rhetorical in the sophistic sense condemned by Plato in the *Gorgias* and elsewhere, namely, that, like flattery, it caters to irrational desires.[27]

---

[24] On Plato's arguments (in *Apology, Gorgias, Republic,* and *Laws*) regarding the philosopher's political discourse and its limitations in a democracy, see Yunis 1996, pp. 117–71, 217–23. Cf. also Plato, *Seventh Letter* 330c–331d, for a succinct statement.

[25] *Ap.* 32e, *Grg.* 521d–522c. For the democratic "beast," see *Grg.* 516a–d, *Rep.* 493b–c.

[26] At *Ap.* 31c–32a, Socrates explains that he refrained from taking an active role in Athenian politics because to do so would have exposed him to great danger without the possibility of accomplishing any good. On Plato's argument in the *Gorgias* that the Socratic elenchus was incapable of improving the citizens of democratic Athens, see Ober 1998, pp. 190–213.

[27] The difference between the harmful, flattering rhetoric of the sophist and the beneficial, instructive rhetoric of the philosopher is considered in the *Phaedrus*; see Yunis 1996, pp. 172–210.

Plato was surely aware that his written protreptic could not be guaranteed to change his readers in the way he intended – a point mentioned above. But, like Socrates' elenchus, it was nevertheless an honorable thing for him to attempt. In fact, since at the time that Plato wrote and disseminated his texts written protreptic was experimental and had no track record, it would have been dishonorable not to attempt it. The *Republic* is Plato's most extensive, most direct attempt to explain to the public what philosophy is and why political power should be entirely vested in the philosophers. In that respect, the *Republic* constitutes an attempt – an improbable one, but nevertheless a serious one – to foster the very situation that would enable the just city to come into being, namely, the situation in which the public understood, and therefore accepted, that their welfare depends on handing political power over to philosophers like Plato.[28]

The protreptic features of the *Republic* also implement some of the particular innovations in political discourse that Plato broaches in the *Republic*. By utilizing an unprecedented array of stylistic, rhetorical, imagistic, narrative, and other artistic devices (discussed below), the *Republic* represents an expansion of Plato's literary art in comparison with his shorter, aporetic dialogues, which, for all their undeniable artistry, are more restrained in their use of nondialectical devices. This expansion of Plato's literary art has its justification in the *Republic*'s own arguments on education and mimetic art. First, in the account of the guardians' early education in Books 2 and 3, Plato recognizes, and seeks to control, a vast range of influences on the guardians' character (376c–402c): mythological tales, narrative

---

[28] Plato commits himself to this project, underpinned by the notion that everyone, philosopher or ordinary citizen, is better off ruled by reason in the just city (*Rep.* 590c–d), even though some may find it ludicrous to suppose that he could ever sell such an elitist constitution to the masses. In addition to the *Republic* itself, Plato represents how the philosopher would address the masses directly in an attempt to persuade them to accept philosophers as their rulers (*Rep.* 499d–502a); cf. Yunis 1996, pp. 167–71. In classical Greece sudden and drastic changes of regime, as from narrow oligarchy to radical democracy or the reverse, were mundane occurrences. Though Plato later came to doubt the feasibility of philosopher-kings (*Laws* 691c–d, 713c, 874e–875d), he never doubted the need to bring philosophy and political power together. On the other hand, none of this implies that Plato had an exaggerated view of the likelihood of implementing philosophical rule. On Plato's political theory and contemporary Greek politics, see Brunt 1993; Trampedach 1994. On the Straussian tradition of reading the *Republic* ironically as an attack on philosophical utopia, see Strauss 1964, pp. 50–138, esp. pp. 121–27; Ferrari 1997.

and dramatic poetry, particular rhythms, songs, diction, and even household furnishings and objects. Plato aims to control and shape every possible facet of the young guardians' environment in order to enhance their propensity for adopting philosophical values.[29] This comprehensive, artistic approach to childhood education is paralleled in the *Republic*'s expansive range of literary techniques. The *Republic*'s narrative plot, mythological tales, prose rhythms, diction, humor, and other literary devices amount to a comprehensive artistic assault that aims to shape the reception of the argument and make readers more susceptible to the basic protreptic project. The very diversity of these devices, no less than the variety of characters who participate in the conversation (beyond Socrates, chiefly Glaucon and Adeimantus), offers different kinds of readers access to the argument.[30]

Second, discussing mimetic (representational) art in book 10 and expanding his argument against Homer, Plato demonstrates the harm done to the city and the soul by the very process of poetic mimesis (595b–608b): poetic mimesis increases the soul's receptiveness to and its appetite for the destructive pleasures (602b–606d).[31] But this section of the argument also contains the suggestion that the philosopher has an interest in harnessing the affective power of mimetic art – in prose – for his own educational and protreptic purposes (608a):

> So long as [poetry] is unable to make good her defense [against our argument] we shall chant over to ourselves as we listen to her this argument that we have given [i.e., the *Republic* itself] as a countercharm to her spell, to preserve us from slipping back into the childish loves of the multitude.   (trans. adapted from Shorey)

With regard to its status as a countercharm to poetry's spell, the *Republic*, a mimetic work of art in its own right, can be seen as a philosophical prose epic: it rests not on poetic inspiration, but on philosophical knowledge and authority; it ties the pleasures of mimesis not to conventional values, but to philosophical ones; it

---

[29] Burnyeat 1999, esp. pp. 217–22, 236–63.

[30] Burnyeat, 1999, pp. 293–95; Blondell 2002, pp. 245–50.

[31] Burnyeat 1999, pp. 222–28, 276–324, esp. pp. 318–24. On Plato's view of mimetic art, see also Ferrari 1989, pp. 92–148; Halliwell 2002, pp. 37–147.

appeals not to the appetitive pleasures, but to those of reason;[32] it enters the public realm not to garner fame, but for the sake of the public good. The *Republic* challenges and aims to supplant Homer, the reigning master of affective art, popular imagery, and conventional values. In this respect the great, unprecedented length of the *Republic* suits the magnitude of its protreptic ambition, which is not only to provide a comprehensive defense of justice and to rectify deeply ingrained cultural values, but also to bring about the symbolic displacement of the massive body of poetry at the center of the inherited culture. Yet the *Republic* does not compete with Homer for public approval, a contest that it does not seek to win and never could win.

IV. HOW IS PLATO'S PROTREPTIC PURPOSE REFLECTED IN THE TEXT AND ARGUMENT OF THE *REPUBLIC*?

There is, first of all, the substance of Socrates' argument itself, on which everything ultimately depends. The argument on justice must be cogent if it is to convince. But the cogency of Socrates' argument will not be considered further here because not only will it receive due attention in other chapters, but the interesting question about what is protreptic in the *Republic* concerns not the argument itself, but the mode in which the argument is cast, or what Plato has done to make the argument, such as it is, as compelling to his readers as possible. Second, there is Plato's extraordinary clarity, liveliness, and verisimilitude, which lure the reader into paying close attention to Socrates' account of justice. Third, there are the imagistic and narrative devices dispersed throughout Socrates' argument: the just city that makes it possible to see the justice of the soul "writ large" (368c–e); the simile (*homoiotēs*) of the sun (506e–509c) and the simile of the divided line (509d–511e); the image (*eikōn*) of the ship of state (487e–488e), the image of the cave (514a–517b), and the image of the soul as conjoined man, lion, and many-headed beast (588b–589b); the vivid descriptions of the timocratic, oligarchic, democratic, and tyrannical men (Book 8), which by contrast palpably demonstrate the superiority of the just man; and the myth (*muthos*) of Er (614b–621b).

---

[32] See *Rep.* 580e–587e on the different desires of the different parts of the soul; cf. also Burnyeat 1999, pp. 227–28.

These devices either substitute for argument or supplement it. They are a shortcut for readers who are not up to the rigors of naked, unadulterated argument on abstract concepts. The image of the ship of state, for instance, offered in response to Adeimantus (487b–d), supplements the argument on what a true philosopher is, which is offered in response to the more sophisticated Glaucon (485b–487a). The simile of the sun substitutes for an argument on the good that Socrates cannot give now, but hopes to be able to give on another occasion (506e–507a).[33] These devices utilize the affective potential of mimetic art to inculcate not philosophical knowledge but philosophical values, and thus correspond to the sanitized myths, graceful rhythms, and noble lies that inculcate not philosophical knowledge but philosophical values in the young, future guardians of the just city. While these devices lack the necessity bestowed by reason, to compensate for that lack they are vivid, novel, and memorable and possess narrative resonance, qualities that do more to persuade non-philosophical readers than the tedium of an argument they could not comprehend.[34] These devices are also not without effect on philosophically sophisticated readers, who are presumably not immune to rhetorical literary art.

One protreptic moment in the *Republic* that goes beyond these conspicuous rhetorical devices is worth considering in detail. In Book 5 Socrates speaks of three "waves" (*kumata*) that he fears will overwhelm the interlocutors (457a–c, 472a, 473c–d): the common training of men and women, the holding of wives and children in common, and – the biggest "wave" – philosopher-kings. These features of the just city are entailed by the argument on the just city.[35] But they are "waves" because they are so "deeply contrary to belief" (473e) that even interlocutors as sympathetic and astute as Glaucon and Adeimantus will probably find them ridiculous and impossible to accept. Socrates' response to the challenge issued by

---

[33] Little is known of Plato's lecture "on the good" (Aristoxenus, *Elements of Harmony*, 2.39–30 Rios = Aristotle, *On the good*, testimonia, Ross); see Denyer, chapter 11 in this volume.

[34] On the protreptic purpose of Plato's myths, see Most 2002; Annas 1982.

[35] "It was the inquiry into the nature of justice and injustice that brought us to this pass" (472b). Socrates presents the particular arguments that demonstrate the utility of these features of the just city only after he warns the interlocutors that they will have the effect of waves: common training of men and women: 451d–457c; holding of wives and children in common: 457d–465d; and philosopher-kings: 474b–541b.

Glaucon and Adeimantus in Book 2 and indeed Plato's underlying protreptic project hang in the balance: if the just city is merely a fantasy that bears no resemblance to life as it is lived – no more than a "wish," as Socrates says (450d) – then how can Glaucon and Adeimantus expect to find in justice the good that outweighs all the other goods that clearly are available in this life? Socrates gives vent to his apprehension: beyond the metaphor of waves, which he embeds in an extended *prodiorthōsis* – the rhetorical figure used to anticipate an obstacle – Socrates and the interlocutors first go back and forth over his readiness to attack the crisis and theirs to withstand it (449b–451b, 453d, 457d), and then Socrates reveals the full force of the crisis only gradually, until he can delay no longer and finally announces the philosopher-kings in dramatic fashion (472a–473e).

The arrangements for women, children, and rulers required by the argument on justice are incompatible with conventional beliefs about human nature current in fourth-century Greece, and it is that incompatibility that creates the threat posed by the "waves." Now, Socrates is not subject to this threat. Convinced by the argument that the arrangements in question are appropriate for the just city, he will not doubt the wisdom of these arrangements, or hesitate to accept them, just because they conflict with prevailing conventions. But Socrates is unique in this respect: it is in his nature to follow the argument serenely wherever it leads and to react imperturbably to whatever the argument demands. Convention, no matter how deeply entrenched, means nothing to him.[36] It is otherwise for the interlocutors, who do not so easily discard prevailing conventions. Faced with a radical breach between the argument and their deep-seated beliefs, they may doubt the argument, no matter how compelling the argument is considered on its own.[37] It is appropriate for Plato to dress up

---

[36] This is evident throughout Plato's work but most strikingly in the *Apology, Crito,* and *Phaedo,* where it matters for Socrates' own life whether or not he believes his own argument that flies in the face of convention.

[37] The possibility that the interlocutors will doubt the argument is expressed at 450c–d, 457d, 473c. Gaiser 1959, pp. 150–96, examines a number of cases in Plato that exemplify what he terms the "*apistia*-Gefahr" ("the danger of doubting the argument"), a phenomenon that Plato portrays with a variety of causes, consequences, and remedies. Reluctance to embrace what appears to be a compelling argument is hardly unreasonable, least of all in Socrates' presence, where arguments often turn out not to be conclusive and are always subject to reconsideration, as Book 2 of the *Republic* reopens the argument against injustice offered in Book 1.

this moment with displays of emotion and dramatic tension because it raises a fundamental protreptic problem: if the interlocutors – and the reader – see the validity of Socrates' argument on justice but are reluctant to accept it because it strikes them as impossibly far-fetched, how can they – interlocutors and reader – be encouraged to overcome their reluctance and accept the argument anyway? After all, the point of the entire endeavor is not merely to know the truth about justice but to know it and to live it.[38] This is a problem of the will and is properly attacked by rhetoric.

Socrates' demonstration that the just city is not a fantasy but a real if necessarily remote possibility (473b–502c) is part of the answer to this problem. But only part: Socrates' anxiety about the "waves" and the nature of the metaphor itself indicate that what threatens the argument is a feeling, or perhaps an intuition, that philosopher-kings are simply preposterous. Among Plato's readers, that feeling would be tenacious and not entirely allayed by yet another argument. Glaucon mentions the violent opposition that Socrates' proposal will awaken (473e–474a). Adeimantus remarks that popular distrust of argument will render the public immune to even good arguments for the philosopher's political usefulness (487b–d).[39] Plato's task was to convey not just a counterargument, but also a counterfeeling, that philosopher-kings are, or at least could be, natural.[40] The image of the cave (514a–521a) contributes greatly to this task: it depicts conventional values (according to which philosopher-kings are preposterous) as unnatural, and it explains the fact that the unnaturalness of these values has generally gone unnoticed. The cave image also portrays the acquisition of philosophical values (according to which philosopher-kings are appropriate) as a natural process, akin to the healthy, if sometimes painful, physical process of rising to the light and air, of gaining mobility and sharpening the powers of perception.

But this protreptic moment has another dimension, which is directed not at the interlocutors, but just at the reader. The manner in which Glaucon and Adeimantus react to the "waves" and

---

[38] Cf. Socrates' comment on the myth of Er at the very end of the *Republic*: "it will save us if we believe it" (621c).

[39] A rough sense of how popular Athenian opinion would view philosopher-kings can also be gleaned from Aristophanes' *Clouds*, which relentlessly parodies Socrates as the prototypical useless philosopher and pseudo-scientist.

[40] Cf. the "countercharm" of *Rep.* 608a, discussed above (p. 18).

end up as true believers functions as what might be termed epideictic protreptic (from epideictic rhetoric, the rhetoric of display). The
very spectacle of these Athenian gentlemen coming to accept the
naturalness of philosopher-kings (along with the rest of philosophy's
unconventional values) allows the reader to feel, or at least imagine,
that perhaps he too can withstand the "waves" and come to accept
philosopher-kings as natural. The ground is prepared when Plato creates all the literary fuss – the wave metaphor, the raised tensions, the
calculated delay – that precedes the announcement of philosopher-
kings. The fuss assures the nonphilosophical reader that his own
highly skeptical reaction is not inappropriate and not being ignored.
Yet after Glaucon admits that many people will react violently to
the notion of philosopher-kings (473e–474a), it comes as a mild surprise that he and Adeimantus calmly listen to Socrates, follow the
argument, and ultimately embrace it with little difficulty.

Philosophically sophisticated readers of the *Republic* have often
found Glaucon and Adeimantus, here and elsewhere in the dialogue,
too deficient in critical faculties, too ready to accede to Socrates'
argument, and therefore ineffectual as partners in dialectic.[41] But
they serve a different purpose. Though they are interested in philosophy, Glaucon and Adeimantus are not philosophers themselves.
They are sufficiently conventional in their values that Socrates has
reason to worry about how they will react to the "waves." They display conventional attitudes on luxury (372d) and happiness (419a).
After Socrates has completed his argument that justice always pays
in and of itself (end of Book 9), he adds a demonstration of the good
consequences of justice (608c–614a), a line of reasoning that appeals
to Glaucon and Adeimantus not as philosophers but as men of the
world. Indeed, as demonstrated by their potent challenge to Socrates
in Book 2, Glaucon and Adeimantus are sufficiently critical to make
Socrates work to convert them and to give readers the impression
that their conversion is a significant accomplishment. But they are
neither so critical nor so recalcitrant that they will not be won over
to Socrates' view of things.

Contrast this with Plato's aporetic dialogues, in which Socrates'
interlocutors are left uncertain what, if anything, has been established with regard to whatever question is at hand. And in the

---

[41] Blondell 2002, p. 210.

Gorgias, for instance, though Callicles wavers for a moment (513c–d), he refuses to accept Socrates' radical views on justice even though those views have been secured, as Socrates says, "with arguments of iron and adamant" (508e–509a). Examples are easily multiplied: these dialogues demonstrate the critical faculty at work and nurture it in the reader, a clear philosophical priority. But it is not clear in these dialogues whether the gulf between philosophy and nonphilosophers can possibly be bridged. Some characters in these dialogues are intrigued by philosophy; some are repelled; none is, so to speak, converted. Whereas the sympathy for Socrates' project evinced by Glaucon and Adeimantus in the *Republic* hinders their critical faculties, it allows Plato to demonstrate that his protreptic endeavor is, like the just state itself, not a fantasy but entirely possible, however remote it may seem. Glaucon and Adeimantus are not and do not become philosophers in the course of the *Republic*. But they submit themselves to philosophy's rule, and they do so for the right reasons, thereby becoming exemplary for Plato's readers in the public domain.[42]

WORKS CITED

Annas, J. 1982. "Plato's Myths of Judgement." *Phronesis* 27: 119–43.
Blondell, R. 2002. *The Play of Character in Plato's Dialogues*. Cambridge.
Brunt, P. A. 1993. *Studies in Greek History and Thought*. Oxford. Chap. 10: "Plato's Academy and Politics."
Burnyeat, M. F. 1997. "The Impiety of Socrates." *Ancient Philosophy* 17: 1–12.
Burnyeat, M. F. 1999. "Culture and Society in Plato's *Republic*." *Tanner Lectures in Human Values* 20: 215–324.
Cole, T. 1991. *The Origins of Rhetoric in Ancient Greece*. Baltimore, Md.
Denniston, J. D. 1952. *Greek Prose Style*. Oxford.
Dover, K. J. 1976. "The Freedom of the Intellectual in Greek Society." *Talanta* 7: 24–54. Rpt., in K. J. Dover, *The Greeks and Their Legacy*. London.
Düring, I. 1961. *Aristotle's* Protrepticus: *An Attempt at Reconstruction*. Göteborg.

---

[42] For criticism I am indebted to the contributors to this volume, especially John Ferrari, and to Peter Mack, Rachel Zuckert, Jefferds Huyck, Ryan Balot, Chris Carey, and Chloe Balla.

Ferrari, G. R. F. 1989. "Plato and Poetry." In *The Cambridge History of Literary Criticism*, vol. 1: *Classical Criticism*, ed. G. A. Kennedy. Cambridge.

Ferrari, G. R. F. 1997. "Strauss's Plato." *Arion* 5: 36–65.

Ferrari, G. R. F. 2003. *City and Soul in Plato's* Republic. Sankt Augustin; rpt., Chicago, 2005.

Festugière, A. J. 1973. *Les Trois "Protreptiques" de Plato. Euthydème, Phédon, Epinomis*. Paris.

Frede, M. 1992. "Plato's Arguments and the Dialogue Form." In *Oxford Studies in Ancient Philosophy*, suppl. vol.: *Methods of Interpreting Plato and His Dialogues*, ed. J. C. Klagge and N. D. Smith. Oxford.

Gaiser, K. 1959. *Protreptik und Paränese bei Platon*. Stuttgart.

Gallagher, R. L. 2004. "Protreptic Aims of Plato's *Republic*." *Ancient Philosophy* 24: 293–319.

Garver, E. 1994. *Aristotle's Rhetoric: An Art of Character*. Chicago.

Halliwell, S. 2002. *The Aesthetics of Mimesis: Ancient Texts and Modern Problems*. Princeton.

Harris, W. V. 1989. *Ancient Literacy*. Cambridge, Mass.

Kahn, C. H. 1996. *Plato and the Socratic Dialogue: The Philosophical Use of a Literary Form*. Cambridge.

Kahn, C. H. 2003. "Writing Philosophy: Prose and Poetry from Thales to Plato." In Yunis 2003b.

Kassel, R., and C. Austin, eds. 1983–. *Poetae Comici Graeci*. Berlin.

Menn, S. 2006. "On Plato's *Politeia*." *Proceedings of the Boston Area Colloquium in Ancient Philosophy* 21: 1–55.

Michelini, A. N. 2003. "Plato's Socratic Mask." In *Plato as Author: The Rhetoric of Philosophy*, ed. A. N. Michelini. Cincinnati Classical Studies 8. Leiden.

Morgan, K. A. 2003. "The Tyranny of the Audience in Plato and Isocrates." In *Popular Tyranny: Sovereignty and Its Discontents in Ancient Greece*, ed. K. A. Morgan. Austin, Tex.

Most, G. W. 2002. "Platons exoterische Mythen." In *Platon als Mythologe. Neue Interpretationen zu den Mythen in Platons Dialogen*, ed. M. Janka and C. Schäfter. Darmstadt.

Nails, D. 1995. *Agora, Academy, and the Conduct of Philosophy*. Dordrecht.

Nightingale, A. W. 1995. *Genres in Dialogue: Plato and the Construct of Philosophy*. Cambridge.

Ober, J. 1998. *Political Dissent in Democratic Athens*. Princeton.

Parry, A. 1981. *Logos and Ergon in Thucydides*. New York.

Romilly, J. de. 1956. *Histoire et Raison chez Thucydide*. Paris.

Schleiermacher, F. 1836. *Schleiermacher's Introductions to the Dialogues of Plato*, trans. W. Dobson. Cambridge; rpt., New York, 1973.

Slings, S. R., ed. 1999. *Plato: Clitophon*. Cambridge.

Strauss, L. 1964. *The City and Man*. Chicago.

Szlezák, T. A. 1999. *Reading Plato*, trans. G. Zanker. London.

Thomas, R. 1989. *Oral Tradition and Written Record in Classical Athens*. Cambridge.

Thomas, R. 1992. *Literacy and Orality in Ancient Greece*. Cambridge.

Thomas, R. 2003. "Prose Performance Texts: *Epideixis* and Written Publication in the Late Fifth and Early Fourth Centuries." In Yunis 2003b.

Trampedach, K. 1994. *Platon, die Akademie und die zeitgenössische Politik*. Stuttgart.

Usener, S. 1994. *Isokrates, Platon und ihr Publikum. Hörer und Leser von Literatur im 4. Jahrhundert v. Chr.* Tübingen.

Wallace, R. W. 1994. "Private Lives and Public Enemies: Freedom of Thought in Classical Athens." In *Athenian Identity and Civic Ideology*, eds. A. L. Boegehold and A. C. Scafuro. Baltimore, Md.

Webster, T. B. L. 1953. *Studies in Later Greek Comedy*. Manchester.

Yunis, H. 1996. *Taming Democracy: Models of Political Rhetoric in Classical Athens*. Ithaca, N.Y.

Yunis, H. 1998. "The Constraints of Democracy and the Rise of the Art of Rhetoric." In *Democracy, Empire, and the Arts in Fifth-Century Athens*, ed. D. Boedeker and K. Raaflaub. Cambridge, Mass.

Yunis, H. 2003a. "Writing for Reading: Thucydides, Plato, and the Emergence of the Critical Reader." In Yunis 2003b.

Yunis, H., ed. 2003b. *Written Texts and the Rise of Literate Culture in Ancient Greece*. Cambridge.

2   The Place of the *Republic* in Plato's Political Thought

The project of this chapter is in outline simple. I first argue (section I) that somehow or other Socrates, and what I shall broadly call the "Socratic conception of philosophy," are fundamental to Plato's political thinking in all periods of his writing (however these are to be defined), and I try to explain both why that should be so and what the consequences are for our understanding of Plato's political thought. I then (section II) go on to discuss the relationship of this Socrates – the one who, as I shall propose, stands constantly behind Plato as he reflects politically – to Callipolis, the second city of the *Republic* (second, that is, after Socrates' "city of pigs," as Glaucon calls it). To put it in a more punchy way, in this second section of the chapter I ask about the precise relationship between Socrates, the main speaker throughout the *Republic*, and the philosopher-rulers of the second city he is made by the author to construct.

But first, a couple of preliminaries.

(A) The old, simplistic, late twentieth-century account of Plato's political philosophy is now, in my view, dead and buried: the sort of account that has him starting out (in the *Republic*) with the ideal of rule by philosophers, then (in *Politicus* and *Laws*) rethinking that ideal and becoming a constitutionalist, even if, as he rethinks, he still looks back wistfully to the earlier dream.[1] Closer readings have in my view demonstrated

---

[1] The origins of this reading of Platonic political philosophy – for a standard example, see, e.g., Klosko 1986 – probably go back much earlier (see Pradeau 2002, p. 135, referring to the work of Ada Netschke-Hentschke), and indeed it is a highly attractive reading, especially given the way that the *surface* of the text of the *Laws* may seem to marry up with what we seem to learn about Plato's biography, and the dis-

beyond all reasonable doubt that this account radically mis-interprets all three dialogues (i.e., *Republic*, *Politicus*, and *Laws*);[2] it will no doubt persist among the wider public for a time, but it will and should be replaced eventually by a more nuanced story of Plato's political thought and its evolution.[3]

(B) I presuppose that the *Republic* really is – among other things – a political work. Granted, if "politics" is a matter of reconciling opposing interests in the community, of finding ways in which different groups can scratch along beside each other, then the *Republic*, which imagines and argues for the possibility of eradicating political conflict altogether, is no truly "political" work. But at the same time there seems no good reason in principle why the construction of utopias should not legitimately be seen as a part of political theorizing; that is, if there is meant to be some way of *approximating* to what is depicted in utopian mode,[4] as there is surely meant to be some way of approximating to the Callipolis of the *Republic*.

I. SOCRATIC ELEMENTS IN PLATO'S POLITICAL THINKING

Which are Plato's "political" dialogues? Apart from the usual suspects – *Republic*, *Politicus*, and *Laws* – we need to take into account

appointments in his life, from the – probably spurious – *Seventh Letter*. (Pradeau, in trenchant fashion, declares such biographical interpretation as simply "false"; he is right.)

[2] See, above all, Laks 1990, and his ch. 12 in Rowe 2000; for *Politicus*, see, e.g., Rowe 1995 and 2001.

[3] Bobonich 2002 offers one alternative evolutionary narrative; as will soon emerge, a more unitarian account may also recommend itself. Pradeau 2002 has shown the way in this respect, although Pradeau has a notion somewhat different from my own of the core concerns of Platonic political thinking.

[4] Or indeed just insofar as utopias may have a critical intent. The *Republic*'s utopia may be in danger of cutting across all the categories of utopia listed by Ferrari 2003, pp. 117–18: i.e., "idealistic," "realistic," "ironic," and even "writerly." The suggestion that Callipolis is "an ideal intended primarily to motivate personal morality," so that the *Republic* as a whole becomes "primarily a moral rather than a political work" (ibid.), seems to me an intelligible reading, but nonetheless finally indefensible. I shall be content to leave my reasons for saying this to emerge by themselves in what follows. (To anticipate a little, my main reason has much to do with a conviction that we should not be too easily beguiled by Plato's pretense of starting afresh every time – or most times – that he starts a new dialogue.)

at least *Crito, Gorgias, Menexenus,* and *Protagoras,* possibly *Euthydemus* (because of one central passage, from 288 to 292), and certainly *Timaeus-Critias.* (I take *Cleitophon* and *Minos* as being by other hands than Plato's.) I take no particular view, in the present context, of the chronological relationship among all these dialogues, beyond supposing that *Politicus, Timaeus-Critias,* and *Laws* are all relatively or, in the case of *Laws,* very late – and one of the incidental outcomes of my argument is that at least for the most part dating issues are relatively unimportant, because all of them (so I claim) are, broadly speaking, saying things that are recognizably the same; only the *perspective* is different. (But note those qualifications: "for the most part," "broadly speaking." I suggest that there is at least one major shift in Plato's overall perspective on politics.) Clearly, I cannot hope, in the space of a single chapter, to give anything like a complete treatment of the dialogues in question; instead, I merely sketch the outlines of a reading.

I begin with the *Gorgias,* and Socrates' claim to be (perhaps) the only true statesman in existence, on the grounds that he alone has the true interests of his fellow-citizens at heart, and goes about helping them to secure those interests – by telling them what they need to hear rather than giving them pleasure, with Parthenons, walls, and dockyards (*Gorgias* 521d–522a, with 517b–521d). It is easy enough to take this claim as purely provocative, pure paradox; after all, is Plato's Socrates not simply *a*political? To call him "apolitical," however, is to say no more than that he attaches no great value to political *institutions* as such, beyond – as the *Crito* surely proposes – the city itself, citizenship, and certain basic responsibilities that citizenship brings with it.[5] Such a position clearly still leaves him free to criticize existing statesmen, their methods, and their goals, and to reflect, however ironically, that what *he* does is actually what they should be doing, the irony consisting merely in the fact that his own methods involve addressing small numbers of people, or single individuals, not the large numbers with which the politician necessarily has to deal. It still remains true that Socrates is the one who has, or is as close as anyone comes to having, the kind of expertise that is needed for ruling: the kind of expertise that, in the *Protagoras,* he finds

---

[5] Since Plato chooses not to raise it, I gloss over the question of whether Socrates' membership of the Council – adverted to at *Apology* 32b – would have been consistent with such a stance: a citizen evidently had to put his name forward to be selected for such membership.

absent from democratic Athens (*Protagoras* 319a–320b); the kind, too, that he is also looking for in the *Euthydemus* but claims not to be able to identify (*Euthydemus* 290d–292e). Here in the *Euthydemus* he makes rather heavy weather of things: it is the expertise of the king or statesman, he suggests, that knows how to put things to use, so that even generals hand over to it what they capture (as intelligent mathematicians and astronomers hand over what they find to the dialecticians)[6]; it makes all things useful; it makes other people wise and good – only we don't know what it will make them good at (292e). Yet this is (I claim) patently a false *aporia* or impasse: it arises only because Socrates insists that identifying the statesman's art with making people good leads to a regress, which is true – if at all – only because the argument back in *Euthydemus* 281 has already effectively dismissed the only alternative accounts of the art that are currently available, namely, making people wealthy and free and getting rid of faction. In fact, there is no regress if, as the whole context gives us reason to suppose, being good and being wise are the same thing. (This is what Socrates has up his sleeve, and does not articulate directly.) In short, the statesman's job is to make other people wise and knowledgeable: wise and knowledgeable, that is, about what is good, the possession of which will make them happy, which in turn is what all of them want (since that is what everyone wants). All of this fits snugly enough with that stunning claim in the *Gorgias* ("I, Socrates, am – perhaps – the only true statesman alive": 521d). It also fits with the criticisms of existing statesmen and the goals they set themselves, whether in the *Gorgias* itself, in the *Protagoras*, or in the *Menexenus*, which is a relentless parody of the Athenians' self-identity, their sense of their history and destiny.[7]

There is an objection that might immediately be raised to this brief treatment of the *Euthydemus*: if the statesman of the *Euthydemus* is the statesman of the *Gorgias*, he surely ought to be a dialectician (if Socrates is a dialectician: cf., e.g., *Cratylus* 390c); yet the

---

[6] *Euthydemus* 290c. A gloss on this curious suggestion may be provided by, e.g., *Timaeus* 91d–e, which proposes that current astronomers cannot be trusted to make a proper assessment of the value of their findings, and *Republic* 528d–530c, where Socrates tells Glaucon and Adeimantus that true astronomy is not about the physical heavens.

[7] See Malcolm Schofield on *Gorgias* and *Menexenus* in ch. 10 of Rowe 2000, pp. 192–99.

dialectician appears to be treated as a kind of expert different from the statesman – the sort to whom geometers, astronomers, and experts in calculation hand over their findings. On the other hand, there is nothing in the *Euthydemus* passage to rule out the possibility that the statesman himself will be a dialectician; and the obvious – albeit partial – parallel with the *Republic*, which makes dialecticians/philosophers the only people qualified to rule, positively suggests it.[8] Discussion of the *Republic*, however, will be postponed until section II below. For now, I propose to take it as read that there is a strong continuity between *Gorgias* and *Euthydemus*, along with *Protagoras* and *Menexenus*. All of these dialogues are strongly critical of existing politicians, and have nothing positive to say about their "achievements"; all propose that true statesmanship, or kingship, is something utterly different from statesmanship as currently conceived. *Gorgias* and *Euthydemus* give us a particular slant on what this true statesmanship will be: something either depending on, or identical with, wisdom, understood as philosophical or dialectical expertise. There is just one relevant difference between these two dialogues, which is that the *Gorgias* presents ideal statesmanship in the shape of an actual, living person (Socrates), who claims *not* to be wise, only to be in love with wisdom, while the *Euthydemus* presents ideal statesmanship in terms of a wisdom that is itself ideal. But that difference will be unimportant, provided that Plato supposes thinking about ideal solutions to be useful even when the ideal is unattainable; and the fact that he represents ideal statesmanship in both modes – in terms both of the attainable and of the unachievable – seems fairly good evidence that he does suppose that.[9]

I now turn to *Politicus*, *Timaeus-Critias*, and *Laws*. *Politicus*, itself an exercise in dialectics, takes as its main subject the nature of the ideal statesman. Once again, statesmanship is treated as a kind of knowledge or expertise; the closest parallel for the expertise involved

---

[8] The one thing that is clear from the *Euthydemus* passage is that it is not *ordinary* kingly/statesmanlike expertise (or "expertise") that fits the bill; and the reference at 291a to the presence of "some superior being" guiding the discussion may easily be taken to suggest that, in one way or another, important lessons are to be derived from the route to apparent impasse. (I owe this footnote partly to suggestions made by John Ferrari.)

[9] See note 4 above.

is medicine (as usual: see esp. *Politicus* 293a–e). That and other indications confirm that the *aims* of statesmanship are the same as in
Gorgias and *Euthydemus*, that is, improving the citizens; only in
this case the statesman is seen explicitly as acting on, "curing," the
citizens en masse. The reason given for this in the *Politicus* (see
immediately below) is that the statesman cannot be everywhere at
once, prescribing individually for everyone. Here, I suggest, we can
see Plato taking us on from that paradox of the *Gorgias*: Socrates as
statesman. Such a possibility is ruled out in real terms by the very
nature of Socrates' method, since that is adapted only to addressing
people in ones or twos. The ideal statesman will, all the same, possess that knowledge that Socrates aims at. But only a few can possess
it, so that even if he, the ideal statesman, *could* actually get round to
everyone, he would be unlikely to be able to pass his knowledge on
successfully. So he must prescribe, and since he cannot do that on
an individual basis, he must do it by setting down general prescriptions. At the same time, given the whole context of the *Politicus*,
and especially the fact that it – or the conversation it represents in
written form – defines itself as aimed at making the interlocutors
into better dialecticians (285d), we must surely be meant to suppose
that the basis of the prescriptions laid down by the ideal statesman
will be provided by dialectic. (At its simplest, the point is that no
other method of reaching truth and understanding is even hinted at.
The application of that understanding might be another thing; but
how else but by philosophical means will the practitioner of statesmanship get his grasp of the good, the fine, and the just?)

Let us suppose that the *Euthydemus* gives us the absolutely ideal
case: the true statesman, himself possessing full knowledge, and able
to make his fellow-citizens equally wise and good: not all of them
good at everything, and not wise about shoe making, carpentry, and
so on, or about what is neither good nor bad (money, freedom, etc.),
but – by implication – the kind of wisdom and goodness that matters
(292c–d) . The *Gorgias* points out that this is exactly what Socrates
aimed at, even while suggesting its impossibility. *Politicus*, for its
part, presupposes – and goes out of its way to emphasize – what
Socrates says in the *Protagoras*, that we should expect political expertise to be a very rare thing (292e) . We could even dream of a world
in which it was not needed at all, but in the conditions we actually
find ourselves in, we really do need it. This is a major part of the

point of the grand myth of the *Politicus*, which has the world alternating between an age of Cronus and an age of Zeus: an age in which
there are no cities, because there is no need for them – everything is
provided for human beings without their having to lift a finger, for
themselves or for anyone else, and nothing threatens their ideal (?)
existence; and an age – that of Zeus – when humans have to fend for
themselves, which will include cooperating with each other. (The
speaker who retails the myth, a visitor from Elea, home city of Parmenides, in fact leaves it open whether the age of Cronus really was –
and will be – ideal. The issue seems to depend on whether people
under Cronus do any philosophy, which the standard Platonic view
makes the key to successful living. Yet the role of philosophy is ultimately to help us make choices, and apparently there are no choices,
or no *hard* choices, to be made under Cronus. So humans in that
era seem to need philosophy no more than they do the art of the
statesman. In effect Plato here discreetly – wittily? – underlines the
fantastic nature of such an existence. We may compare *Lysis* 218a–b,
Symposium 204a: the gods, being wise, do no philosophy, and neither
would we if we were like them.)

So let us suppose that political expertise could be found: then, in
this best of all possible worlds, it would still have to work with a
population not itself endowed with the same expertise. What, then,
will substitute for the statesman's understanding, if that cannot be
made universally available? Answer: law – an imperfect but necessary instrument. It will be imperfect in two ways. First, it will be
imperfect because it will always be too general. As the Eleatic visitor says (294a–295a), the circumstances of human life are constantly
changing, so that any set of general rules can only make the right
prescription in any particular case "roughly, somehow, like *this*"
(295a5). But, second, and in part as a consequence of the first sort
of imperfection, law will be imperfect insofar as it cannot actually
make people good and wise. The ideal statesman will employ orators to persuade the masses "through story-telling and not through
teaching" (304d): in other words, he will not even try to pass on his
expertise, but will merely ensure that its broad outcomes are communicated to the majority. The result is that such people will do
roughly the things the wise person would do, but without themselves being wise (cf. *Charmides* 164b–c); for the proper functioning
of their own individual rational faculties is in effect substituted the

ratiocination of the statesman, mediated through the law. (We find a very similar idea at *Republic* 9, 590c–d.)

Nowhere in the *Politicus* is philosophy given an explicit role in the running of the state. Yet Socrates the philosopher, searcher after truth, does make a brief appearance. This is in the course of a *reductio ad absurdum* of constitutionalism, which takes place in 297d–300a: just imagine, says the Eleatic visitor – if we made laws and written rules the be-all and end-all, we'd have to propose outlawing research; we'd finish by *executing* anyone who showed themselves wiser than the law. The language that the visitor uses leaves little doubt that we are supposed to think here of the example of Socrates,[10] and unless we suppose that Plato now actually approves of Athens for killing the old man off (a supposition that, as I have argued elsewhere,[11] goes completely against the run of the argument in this context of the *Politicus*: that we should stick to the law at all cost is something the visitor is *against*), there is nothing for it but to conclude that any actual constitution that tried to follow the pattern of what the visitor calls the "truest" constitution (301e) would make room for research. (We must aim for the best, I take the implication to be, even if it is, in all its details, beyond our grasp.) Again, only the outcomes of any Socratic (re)search would be communicated to the mass of the people; for if the official orators should fail to persuade them (see above), then in principle, if the statesman should so decide, force could be used. What makes a constitution correct is the presence of expertise, "whether it rules with or without laws, over willing or unwilling subjects, and whether the rulers are poor or wealthy – there is no principle of correctness according to which any of these must be taken into any account at all" (293c–d). This uncompromising position may well be unpalatable, and indeed quite un-Socratic; what makes it possible for Plato to endorse it, as I suppose that he does, is just that, like Socrates, he regards the Socratic quest as actually uncompletable.

Uncompletable or not, that quest will – on the analysis proposed – be the key to political life, and to human life, even in the *Politicus*. Dialectic, that is, will be as central to the best or only constitution

---

[10] "[I]f anyone is found [doing research] . . ., in the first place one must . . . call him . . . a star-gazer, some babbling sophist," etc.

[11] Rowe 2001.

of the *Politicus* as it is to the form and (indirectly) declared aims of the dialogue itself.[12] If the dialectical exchanges between the visitor from Elea and the Young Socrates feel, and are, different from those of the *Gorgias*, the *Euthydemus*, or for that matter of the *Protagoras*, there is no good reason for treating this difference as a difference in kind. Question and answer, with a particular set of aims and in a particular sort of context,[13] are the fundamental features of dialectic; and these features are as evident in the *Politicus* as in those other dialogues – only now with the addition of a new kind of method, that of collection and division, which so far embodies the aims, and presupposes the conditions, of dialectic as actually to be identified with it. Dialectic in Plato was always about *getting clear about the way things are*, through the medium of conversation.

But now – someone might object – *Timaeus-Critias* and *Laws* surely *are* different? In the description of the two ideal cities of the *Timaeus-Critias* (i.e., prehistoric Athens, on the one hand, and the original, uncorrupted Atlantis, on the other), not only is there no direct reference to philosophical government of any description, but there is precious little dialectic even between the interlocutors;[14] and much the same seems to hold of the mammoth *Laws*. This is probably the main basis for the claim that in his latest period Plato's dream of a new role for philosophy, at the helm of the ship of state, finally dissipated. Yet if we take a closer look, even here things are not quite what they seem. The quality of the government of prehistoric Athens is due to the direct involvement of Athena and Hephaestus, who not only fashioned the original inhabitants but directly instructed them about the nature of good government (*Timaeus* 24c–d, *Critias* 109c–d), while the first kings of Atlantis are themselves partly divine (*Critias* 113c–114c). As soon as we ask about any possible lessons from these models for any actual human society, and strip out the fantasy of direct contact with the divine, there seems to be no alternative available to the familiar model of a state with its laws and

---

[12] "Indirectly declared" insofar as the conversation is said to be about making the interlocutors better dialecticians.

[13] Aiming at the discovery of truth, and (so) excluding competition, aggression, insincerity, etc. (One should notice in passing that such conditions might be especially easy to achieve in "dialogue" with oneself.)

[14] Worse still, the interlocutors may well not be philosophers, capable of dialectic *more Socratico* at all: see next page.

institutions grounded in philosophy, and no alternative model of philosophy beyond that of dialectic. The *Timaeus* itself teases us with indirect references to the *Republic*, while superficially leaving out what was apparently the main ingredient of Callipolis, philosophical rule; and actually, neither that ancient Athens nor the first Atlantis will have had any need for philosophers, since the wisdom sought by philosophy is already built into the foundations of both (if less securely in the case of the second, apparently because Atlantis' system of government depends on accident of birth – with the proportion of divine genes constantly being reduced – rather than on education). Atlantis and Athens disappeared together beneath the waves; whatever is to replace them needs to be put together by human expertise – statesmanship, which in the best of all possible worlds will try its hardest to mimic the wisdom of the gods. The reasons why Plato chose to downplay the role of philosophy in *Timaeus-Critias* have ultimately to do with the kind of *audience* he has in mind, which is reflected in his choice of main speakers for the two dialogues (or three, as it was to be in the original project): men of action rather than philosophers, thoughtful and reflective but no experts in dialectic.[15] (Timaeus' account of the physical cosmos carries with it the same sort of limitations – but that is another story.[16])

Audience and interlocutors similarly determine the flavor of the *Laws*. This dialogue is for the most part resolutely down to earth, with little or nothing by way of metaphysical or any other kind of theory, except perhaps legal – that is, little or nothing by way of *explicit* theory. But once again, one only has to ask where exactly the whole construction, with its mass of detailed legislation and clear-eyed conception of purpose, *comes from*, and there is still only one possible answer: philosophy, and especially the kind of philosophy that we typically find exemplified in the generality of Platonic dialogues (i.e., dialectic). This is not to say, of course, that that is where *Plato* got everything from – as if he would sign his name only to things that he thought he could establish dialectically. Rather, the point is that it is presumably dialectic to which the Athenian, the main speaker in the dialogue, would assign any authority for the laws he and his two interlocutors, Cleinias and Megillus – neither

---

[15] The argument of the preceding few sentences summarizes that of my 2004 essay.
[16] See Rowe 2003.

of whom knows anything about any sort of philosophy – propose for
the new city of Magnesia that they construct in the course of *Laws*.
Or, to put it more accurately, the Athenian would assign authority
for such laws to the gods, but to them only because they are wise,
and because the laws proposed, to the extent that they are correct,
will reflect that wisdom (so, at any rate, one might deduce from
the beginning of Book 1 and the long theological argument of Book
10). The best evidence for the claim that philosophy is still in the
driver's seat comes from the short description in Book 12 of the kind
of discussion that will go on in that engine of the city, the so-called
Nocturnal Council: a miniature version of what we have come to
think of as a typical "Socratic" dialogue, on the unity of the virtues
(963a–964b). Poor Cleinias fails to follow, and the Athenian cuts the
description short. But the point is made – *this* is the basis on which
the legal code of Magnesia rests: not common sense, not the law of
Athens (though there are plenty of correspondences between Mag-
nesian and Athenian law), not Plato's dreams, but an understanding
of the way the world is, and of the place of human beings within
that world. And it is, in effect, the results of this idealized dialectic that are fed to the general population of Magnesia in the famous
"preambles" to the laws, which set out to persuade and so avoid the
need for any sanctions; in the same way it is what *might* be established by dialectical means that is offered to readers of the *Laws*. (In
case this should be thought of in itself as some kind of retreat on
Plato's part from his agenda as a political philosopher, the following
points should be made: first, that Plato's commitment to direct rule
by philosophers is not clear even in the *Republic*; second, that his
commitment to philosophy, in the spheres of ethics and politics, is
because of philosophy's capacity to change human life and society;
and third, that the corpus of his writings shows a permanent commitment to addressing nonphilosophers as well as philosophers. The
Republic itself is designed to shock – and especially those who have
not thought beyond existing structures.)

My argument so far, then, is that Socratic dialectic, enthroned
in the *Gorgias*, is never dethroned. But there is also another, and
clearly more fundamental, aspect to this continuity among what I
have chosen to identify as Plato's "political" dialogues. This shows
up perhaps most illuminatingly in the way that the *Laws* still sticks
to the idea that *no one goes wrong willingly* (5.731c, 734b; 9.860d). If

anyone does go wrong, and gets what is bad or less good for him than he could have got, then the action in question is not what he wanted; and this will be true whether it was caused by simple miscalculation or ignorance or by the intervention of uneducated desires (itself involving a kind of ignorance). The function of law is once again to substitute, in the case of the nonphilosophical, for philosophy: that is, to supply the right *kind* of answer, about how to act, for those not in a position to work it out for themselves. The preambles to the laws of Magnesia are there in recognition of the oddity, not to say paradox, involved in merely compelling people to do what is in any case in their own best interests, and – more than that – what they actually want to do, because (according to the *Laws* as much as to the *Lysis*, or the *Symposium*, or any other Platonic dialogue one cares to mention) everyone wants what is best for him- or herself. True, the agent may have, or feel, desires for things that are not in fact best for him; but – if, as the Athenian insists, he goes for them *unwillingly* – they are actually not what he wants. (So: even actions that have their origin in the agent himself may be involuntary: a thoroughly un-Aristotelian position, and one that for most moderns too would probably be counterintuitive.)

The rest follows easily enough. In any ordinary context, we might be tempted to say "so much the worse for the individual, if he is unable to work things out for himself; let him make his own mistakes." But it is a constant, for Plato, that cities exist to provide the good life for their citizens, and that means their helping the citizens so far as possible to avoid making mistakes. The best city of the *Laws*, Magnesia, is a kind of machine, designed by philosophers, for creating a happiness that otherwise, without the city and its institutions, and in the absence of philosophy, would and could not exist at all. (In the primeval Athens of the *Timaeus-Critias*, the machine is set up and programmed by Athena and Hephaestus: see above.) But it is not enough, Plato suggests, simply to *impose* the right choices on people. Just as the doctor owes a free person an explanation of why in fact surgery, or cautery, or evacuation is good for him or her, so the statesman owes the governed an explanation of why the prescriptions of the law are good for those required to be governed by it (4.720a–e). In both cases the explanation offered will necessarily be partial, since a full explanation would involve making the patient into a doctor and the citizen into a statesman. In one way this looks like a betrayal of that stance of Socrates in the *Gorgias*, which makes him a statesman just insofar as he tries to do what ordinary "statesmen" fail to do, and make them "wise and good" (if I may here run the *Gorgias* and the *Euthydemus* together). The population of Magnesia is actually prevented from doing what Socrates' interlocutors are encouraged to do more than anything, and *challenge* what they are being told. Yet at the same time it is – in another way – no more than a logical extension of Socrates' position, given that he cannot get round to everyone, any more than can the ideal statesman of the *Politicus*.[17] Nor (and this is crucial) is there any mistaking the fact that the general values governing the city of Magnesia are those advocated by the *Gorgias* or the *Euthydemus*: what the laws propose as good – broadly speaking, a life that so far as possible exhibits all the virtues and treats nothing else as independently valuable – is quite in line with what the Socrates in those superficially quite different dialogues had in his sights. The main difference is that the emphasis is now on the putative *conclusions* of Socratic dialectic rather than on the process itself.[18]

II. SOCRATES IN THE *REPUBLIC*: A RELUCTANT POLITICAL THEORIST?

Now from some points of view this change of emphasis would make all the difference in the world; and especially from that point of view that identifies Socrates more with a particular *method* than with

---

[17] I gloss over for the moment the fact that the Athenian who is the main speaker in the *Laws* plainly presupposes that people differ widely in their intellectual capacities – which is in fact the chief reason why philosophy/dialectic plays so small a part (as small a part as in both *Politicus* and *Republic*) in the actual, day-to-day government of the city. By contrast the Socrates of the *Gorgias*, say, is in principle committed by his underlying assumptions, or so I claim, to the idea that, in principle, anyone and everyone needs to do some philosophy and is capable of doing it. In the present section it has been my business to underline the continuities in Plato's political thinking; in the following section I admit to one major discontinuity, or set of discontinuities – which I claim will nevertheless not put seriously in jeopardy what I called in note 3 above a "*more* unitarian" approach.

[18] There will in fact be mechanisms for changing the laws in Magnesia (up to a point), provided that reasons can be provided for doing so; cf. my inference above from the *reductio* of constitutionalism in the *Politicus* that anyone whose investigations made them "wiser than the laws" (*Politicus* 299) ought to be positively welcomed in any rationally constituted state.

a particular, systematic, set of ideas. But such a perspective fails to do full justice to Plato's Socrates. If this "Socrates" may stand, roughly and temporarily, for the Socrates of more or less any dialogue putatively written before the *Republic*, he has a *theory* – about the human good, and about how to explain human action – that is almost as well worked out as it is radical and provocative, and would have been provocative also to Greeks of the late fifth and early fourth century B.C. The theory, in rough outline, is as follows.[19] *All desire is for the good* – not for what merely appears or is thought good, but for the real good; good people are wise ones, or rather would be if there were any; there are no bad people either, only ignorant ones; wisdom makes us happy, indeed in a way *is* happiness; and the wisdom in question is (or would be, if anyone ever possessed it) an understanding of what is truly good (for us), or, to put it more informatively, an understanding of what course of action will at any point contribute maximally to our happiness, starting from where we are now.

It is, I claim, Plato's advocacy of this sort of theory that explains Socrates' comportment, and strategy, in a whole range of dialogues. Two things in particular – apart from the indirectness implicit in Plato's use of the dialogue form – combine to help obscure this fact from any superficial reading. The first is that Socrates typically addresses different *aspects* of the same set of ideas in different dialogues, so that the whole to which they belong is rarely, if ever, on display at the same moment. The second, and perhaps larger, obstacle to our seeing exactly where Socrates is going (and exactly how radical he is) is that he also typically starts from *other* points of view, *other people's* assumptions. It is easy to be drawn into thinking that he is speaking with his own voice when he is actually – or more often, simultaneously – borrowing someone else's. Here is one central example: for the Socrates in question, "good" is the same as "wise": that is, to be good is to be wise. Furthermore, what are normally taken as varieties of goodness in people – courage, justice, and the rest – will also be identifiable as wisdom, insofar as goodness and

---

[19] The best source for the theory is the *Lysis*: see Penner and Rowe 2005. The inspiration for much of the rest of the present paragraph, and for the whole of the succeeding one, comes from this source, and to that extent and more must be acknowledged as jointly owned.

wisdom are the same.[20] So, when talking about goodness, Socrates may make a move that is intelligible only if goodness is identified with wisdom; while the reader, lulled into supposing that Socrates takes courage to be something quite distinct from wisdom, naturally smells a rat, and is likely to declare Socrates to be going off on a strange tack, making mistakes in argument and/or mistreating his interlocutor. Meanwhile the interlocutor may himself be equally bemused by the course the argument has taken. Both reader and interlocutor suffer from the same problem, of thinking that Socrates will be talking, and will have been talking throughout, about goodness/virtue as *they* understand it and typically talk about it.

Considerations of this sort are immediately relevant to the reading of the *Republic*, and especially to a proper understanding of the relationship between Book 1 and the remaining nine books. Any reader of the *Republic* will be struck at once by the contrast between Book 1 and Books 2–10. The first book by itself resembles a "dialogue of definition" like the *Laches* or the *Euthyphro*: taking a single item, in this case justice (as *Laches* takes courage and *Euthyphro* "piety" or "holiness"), and trying but ultimately – or at least, so it seems – failing to define it. Not unnaturally, it has often been supposed that this first book of the *Republic* was in fact originally a separate dialogue, which was then incorporated into the larger work. What this tends to suggest is that it is detachable, perhaps dispensable. This is no doubt encouraged by the way the argument is constructed: Book 1, toward the end, turns from attempting to define justice into a defense of it against an attack mounted by the fierce and redoubtable theoretician of rhetoric, Thrasymachus; then, right at the end, Socrates reflects that he really needed to define it first, and Book 2 makes a new start, with Glaucon and Adeimantus restating the case for injustice, and Socrates embarking on a new and apparently more successful search for the nature of justice. But it is, I think, thoroughly misleading to suppose that Book 1 is completely left behind, superseded. Nor is it enough to point out that it adumbrates, and links directly to, many of the main themes of the rest of the *Republic*, as if it were a mere introduction. After all, Socrates himself claims, after Glaucon

---

[20] I leave aside the question of whether courage and the rest are different varieties or species of wisdom – what one might call the *Protagoras* problem (see *Protagoras* 329b–330b).

and Adeimantus have launched their new attack on justice, that *he* thought the defense he had already offered against Thrasymachus was sufficient (2.368b).

What particularly feeds the temptation to separate Book 1, however, is the sense that Books 2–10 announce the arrival of a new Plato, writing and thinking in a new way. Book 1, from this perspective, represents a kind of farewell appearance for the old Socrates before he gives way to the new, ambitious constructions that are the mark of the mature (or "middle") Plato. This, as my brief pilgrimage in section I above through the other political works is intended to suggest, is in many ways likely to be an unhelpful reading: Plato remains a Socratic in politics, even if a Socratic with a difference. That is, he at least continues to show allegiance to the idea that everything begins, and indeed ends, with a dialectic that is recognizably still the dialectic of a *Euthyphro*, a *Gorgias*, or a first book of the *Republic*; and even in the *Laws*, his very last work, his main character is still saying things that sound exactly like the things Socrates was saying in the pre-*Republic* dialogues. This seems to me by itself sufficient reason to reconsider *Republic* 2–10. If these books are bracketed, however one looks at it, by ideas with an indelibly Socratic mark on them (ideas that resurface wherever one looks outside the *Republic*), then perhaps the sense that they mark a new beginning is overdone. That, in brief, is the chief theme of the remainder of the present chapter.

Let me begin with the relationship of Book 1 to Books 2–10. Book 1 is replete with familiar Socratic theses: that a friend is someone useful (334e–335a: actually a premise volunteered by Polemarchus), that harming someone means making them worse (335b–c), that it does not belong to a just person to harm anyone (335e), that justice is a kind of cleverness or wisdom (350a–c), and that the unjust are at odds even with themselves (351e–352a).[21] What if we treated these not as a collection of theses to be noted and then set to one side, but rather as providing the basis for the rest of the argument of the dialogue? Given what I have said about Plato's methods, and what I have proposed is his habit of having Socrates argue from

---

[21] Cf. *Lysis* 214c–d. In fact, as I shall argue, the *Republic* passage refers to synchronic internal dissension, whereas the *Lysis* is referring to diachronic changes in individuals (see Penner and Rowe 2005: ch. 4).

his own, unusual assumptions even while engaging with more ordinary ones, that might already explain the statement just referred to (Book 2, 368b), to the effect that in his view he had already answered Thrasymachus: his own position, if fully spelled out, would be invulnerable to Thrasymachus or anyone else. But he understands that Glaucon and Adeimantus are not convinced; he cannot stand by and watch justice attacked from any front, and so he'll come to justice's aid. Thus the main part of the *Republic* starts from the need to convince others of something of which Socrates is himself already convinced and that he himself thinks he has already said enough to show. If we find the arguments of *Republic* 1 unsatisfactory, that is because we ourselves are in the same position as Glaucon and Adeimantus, or perhaps Thrasymachus: we do not accept Socrates' own premises, and so we just think his arguments bad ones. Fair enough, he says; I'll just have to try harder. But one thing that we should not miss in all of this is that the argument Socrates is embarking on is apparently not one he himself needs. And we shall see positive reason for supposing that its terms are broadly dictated by the requirements of his audience, even if in fact he never commits himself to anything he does not believe in.

To help him find justice, Socrates begins, in Book 2, to construct a good city, as an analogy for the good (and so just) individual or soul. The city he constructs first is one that Glaucon describes as a "city of pigs" because of the simple life Socrates envisages its citizens as living. Again, as in Book 1, Socrates marks the distance between himself and the others: *he* thinks this kind of city the "true" one. But he consents to discuss the "luxuriant" (or "self-indulgent": *truphōsa*), modern kind that Glaucon has in mind, "for by looking at this kind of city too we might perhaps see how it is that justice and injustice are engendered in cities," that is, presumably, what causes a city to be just and what causes it to cease to be so. The "true," "healthy" city, which satisfied itself with necessities, would itself have been a good and just one; in Glaucon's "fevered" city, by contrast, with its requirement for all sorts of luxuries, justice will require additional measures to cure, or check, the "fever." (All this is a virtual paraphrase of Book 2.372e.) Somehow or other, says Socrates, it is the pursuit of things beyond the bare necessities from which "most of all bad things come about for cities, on both the individual and the public level, when they do come about" (373e); even the need for soldiers ("guardians", or "guards": *phulakes*) – whether war is good or bad – comes about from the same source.

The "city of pigs" bears some resemblance to the city of Magnesia in the *Laws* or perhaps to that combined with the portrait of life in the age of Cronus in the myth of the *Politicus*, since as yet here in the *Republic* Socrates has not built in any human political institutions at all, or even an army. (Another comparable passage will be the rather briefer description of the age of Cronus in *Laws* 4.713c–714a.) One might hesitate to call it a truly "Socratic" community, since there has also been no mention of the inhabitants of the city doing any *philosophy*. But since Socrates approves of this city, it perhaps goes without saying that they will;[22] and its citizens do in fact seem to have the kind of attitude toward material "goods" that is a typical outcome of Socratic dialectic. (Socrates cannot actually *say* that the citizens do philosophy, because the "city of pigs" also has to serve as the basis for the "fevered" one – not that it spontaneously develops a fever; it is Socrates and his interlocutors who bring that about as part of the fiction.)[23] In any case, what Socrates moves on to, with apparent reluctance, is a city that already possesses things he has no use for – luxury and wealth, which he portrays as the original reason for having an army: the "guards." Next comes the education of these guards, through music, poetry, and physical exercise; a kind of conditioning, including the inculcation of true or at any rate useful beliefs. (Only true falsehoods are excluded, the ones we all hate – Socrates suggests – because they actually mislead us: 382a–c, and cf. 412–13.) If the city is going to have warriors, it has to have warriors of the right sort, and Socrates proposes that they will be produced by a kind of upbringing and education that in effect combines an ordinary wealthy Athenian boy's experience with a considerable number of Socratic (or Platonic) elements – including, as it happens, the elimination, in the physical regime of the guards, of precisely those

---

[22] If so, the comparison with the age of Cronus is strictly limited. The difference from the age of Cronus is that people in the "city of pigs" are having to provide for themselves and each other – so living together and forming a city. At the same time this city differs from any ordinary city in that the causes of conflict, and the things that cause the overdevelopment of our irrational desires, have not yet been introduced. See further below.

[23] Cf. the fate of Callipolis, which goes into decline because reason gradually loses hold of the city.

luxuries that Glaucon insisted on including in the city (404b ff.):
a point that is thoroughly underlined at the beginning of Book 4,
when Adeimantus interrupts to object that Socrates has robbed the
guards of everything that people think makes them happy. Socrates
responds, as we'd expect, that he wouldn't be surprised if they were
in fact happiest just like that. Thus, significantly, the quality of
the "feverish" city turns out to depend on assimilating it to the
"healthy" one, so mitigating and eventually purging the effects of
the "fever."

But then there is another crucial development, as Socrates separates a section of the guards – who will be the "complete" guards,
414b – as *rulers*; the others will, he says, henceforward be called
"auxiliaries," *epikouroi*, and helpers, *boēthoi*, for the *dogmata*, the
"decisions"[24] of the rulers. (As emerges over the next three books,
the rulers will be the only ones qualified to make decisions, because
they are philosophers, who have the deepest possible understanding
of what is good; so naturally the warriors, who lack any such understanding, and know only what they've been told, must concede any
decision making to the rulers.) Socrates is not sure that he and the
others have devised the right sort of education for the auxiliaries
(416b–c): I take it that his worry is of the same sort that is eventually expressed in the myth of Er at the end of the whole dialogue,
about whether "habit, without philosophy" (10.619c7–d1) is really
sufficient to ensure that we make the right choices. (That, however,
will be much what will guide the behavior of the main population
in both *Politicus* and *Laws*: see section I above.)

Some mechanism is needed, not only to repel external enemies
but to impose internal control if people are inclined to break the
laws (3.415d–e), and the auxiliaries will fulfill these roles – both of
which, one might add, would apparently have been unnecessary if
"fever" hadn't been let into the city in the first place. In this context we should also notice 414b, which suggests that it is the rulers
who provide the real security, both against external enemies and
when it comes to friendships inside the city: as I take it, not giving external enemies any reason for attacking the city, and making
sure that internal friendships and loyalties are rightly directed. Having a *rational* policy is what matters: getting priorities right. The

---

[24] Not "convictions," as Reeve has it in the Hackett translation.

position of the warrior class, I think, is ambiguous and precarious: so far as Socrates' argument goes they wouldn't actually be needed at all were it not for that lower group and its demands for luxuries (to be supplied by its own expansion); that is the source of both external and internal threats, and the demands in question were added only at Glaucon's request.[25] "Callipolis," it seems, is very much Glaucon's, rather than Socrates', city, insofar as the presence in it of one main part of its structure – the warrior "class"– is owed to him. And this is part of the reason why I have suggested, in the title of the present section, that Socrates may be a *reluctant* political theorist. Seeing no need for the things that cause war, dissent, disharmony, he sees no fundamental need for political institutions themselves – even if prevailing conditions might temporarily require them, they are not part, as it were, of the furniture of his world.

So, gradually, the construction of the city is completed. Being a good city, it will have all the virtues: wisdom (in the shape of the ruler-guards), courage (in the "auxiliary" guards, the fighters), and "self-control" (insofar as the rulers, the auxiliaries, and the rest, i.e., the producers, all agree about who should rule); it will also be just, in virtue of the fact that the rulers rule, the fighters fight, and the producers produce: each "does his (or her) own." Or, in other words, the city is just because wisdom is in charge, and not the rather different virtues of the warrior and producer classes. Next, in Book 4, Socrates turns, in accordance with the strategy he set up near the beginning of Book 2, to the soul. Does it fall into three analogous "parts"? If it does, then the results reached in relation to the virtues of the city can be directly transferred. And so it turns out: a series of arguments shows that the soul too consists of three parts or elements (rational, "spirited" or aggressive-competitive, and "appetitive"), each with its own qualities, and each capable in principle of lording it over the others. So, analogously with the city, the good soul will be wise if its reasoning part is in good condition, courageous if its "spirited" part is similarly in the condition appropriate to it, and self-controlled if the three parts "agree" with each other about which should be in charge;

---

[25] We should notice that the structure of the ideal cities of both *Timaeus-Critias* and *Laws* is different: the army in both appears to be coextensive with the citizen body (with producers excluded). In the *Politicus*, the function of soldiering appears not to be given any special status, in relation, e.g., to weaving or animal husbandry.

while the good soul will be *just* insofar as, and by virtue of the fact that, reason, and a reasoned view of proper ends, governs the whole, even as the other parts perform their own respective roles (providing the competitive and the more basic appetitive drives), under the control of reason.

Now here we do seem to have something new. When Socrates defines virtues elsewhere, his tendency – as I proposed in section I above – is to *identify* them with wisdom, whereas here in *Republic* 4 wisdom is said to be one thing, and justice, courage, and self-control are said to be other things. Not only that, but courage is made to belong (1) to a group whose members *lack* wisdom, and (2) to a part of the soul that lacks reason altogether; and self-control and justice both involve relationships between groups and parts, two of which are, in each case, actually irrational (which I take as *lacking even any calculating power*)[26]. As a matter of fact, the way Socrates is now taking courage and self-control seems to be close enough to ordinary conceptions of the two virtues: courage as a matter of having the right kind of spirited disposition, together with the right sorts of beliefs, self-control as a matter of keeping one's competitive and appetitive instincts in check. Contrast the treatment of self-control in the *Charmides*, which manages without a single reference anywhere to control of irrational desire and impulses; contrast the treatment of courage in the *Laches*, which has rather little time for the idea of it as any sort of irrational *disposition*; both dialogues, while ending formally in *aporia*, nevertheless must appear on any reading to favor some kind of treatment of the virtues (excellences) in terms of knowledge. And, again, the first book of the *Republic* has itself introduced an identity between justice and wisdom.

Now we could try treating the Book I argument as simply *ad hominem*, that is, as part of an *ad hominem* argument in response to Thrasymachus' attack on justice; and maybe we even must do that, insofar as Book 4 gives us good reasons for supposing that Socrates

---

[26] This, it should be said, is a controversial matter; some (see, e.g., Bobonich 2002) hold that Plato means the two lower parts to have some kind of rudimentary means-end reasoning. I can only say that in my view he never commits himself to this, and there is general agreement that it would get him into extreme difficulties if he did. Whichever view we take, in any case he certainly cannot mean to suggest that the counterparts of the two lower soul parts in the city, the warriors and the producers, are themselves irrational (any analogy will have its limits).

now thinks wisdom itself conditional on other factors: specifically, on our irrational parts being in good shape. (Book 4, in a nutshell, proposes that the irrational is capable of interfering with the operations of reason and of distorting them, even of preventing the decisions of reason from going through; the very activity of philosophizing, implying commitment to the truth, will presuppose having one's irrational desires under control.) In that case, we shall have to presume Socrates to prefer the account of justice in Book 4.

Yet on closer examination this account is certainly not different *in kind* from the one that made justice simply the same thing as wisdom.[27] At the end of Book 4, Socrates claims that the person whose soul parts all "do their own" will be least likely to do the things normally, or "vulgarly," considered unjust: embezzling money, robbing temples, and so on (442d–443b). We are not told in so many words what is supposed to justify this claim, but the earlier connection of the origins of justice and injustice with the "luxuriant," "feverish" city, and indeed the general implications of much of Books 2–4, suggest that Socrates thinks it unnecessary to make his reasoning explicit: it is the irrational parts and their desires that cause the trouble – so that if the irrational parts can be kept subordinate, laying claim to no more than their proper role, while the rational part rules, all will be well – provided also, that is, that the rational part is sufficiently strong in us.[28] But that in turn suggests (1) that the rational part is naturally oriented toward the good (apart from mere faulty reasoning, it will be the irrational parts that make it go wrong), (2) that the just thing – the conventionally just thing – is part of that good, and (3) that reason is capable of determining that it is. Reason's

---

[27] Nor, in fact, do we find an account of the virtues like the *Republic*'s in any other dialogue.

[28] In many people, Socrates proposes, it will be weak (9.590c). Wisdom is plainly not the human default mode, as it were; even those who are rationally best equipped will need to do a lot of hard work and hard philosophy. Here is the source of that important contrast that I picked out in note 17 above between the Socrates of what I take to be pre-*Republic* dialogues and (e.g.) the Athenian of the *Laws* (the one seeming to allow that anyone might do philosophy, and indeed that everyone needs to, the other making philosophizing the preserve of the few). Plato appears to have abandoned the idea proposed in the *Lysis*, that no one is *terminally* bad/ignorant, i.e., with ignorance as their permanent and irrevocable condition (see, esp., *Lysis* 217c–218a with 220d).

"rule" over the irrational parts will consist in, or at least include, the ability to establish to what extent the objects of the irrational desires will contribute to that good.

One must admit that none of this is actually spelled out. The alternative, however, is to suppose that Socrates, and so Plato, is content merely to assert (without justification), and to have Glaucon accept (without demanding any justification), a connection between the Platonic idea of justice in the soul and the "vulgar" idea of it, as consisting merely in certain actions; and that would be surprising, in a context that at least appears to be argumentative in form, and from an author and a character both of whom claim to specialize in argument. (The author, Plato, does so only indirectly, of course – through Socrates. That Plato is a philosopher ought not, however, to be a matter for controversy.) It seems altogether preferable to try to establish *on what grounds* Socrates and Glaucon might respectively assert and accept the connection in question. I have proposed, in the last paragraph, the sorts of premises that Socrates might think the move justified; whether Glaucon fully understands those premises is another matter, but there is no requirement that Socrates' interlocutors should travel at the same speed, or exactly on the same trajectory, as he does. Indeed, I have already suggested that it is not atypical of Platonic dialogue-writing that interlocutors fail to follow Socrates precisely, so that they come to require different strategies, which take into account their distance from the master. So here, I suggest: the very form of Socrates' question to Glaucon – "who do you think would think [the Platonically/Socratically just person] *more likely* to [embezzle, rob temples, etc.] than people not like him?" (442e–443a) – is designed to elicit an impressionistic answer from someone who has only an impressionistic notion of what is going on in the argument. (That is, the question does not indicate a sense on *Socrates'* part that the connection is merely probabilistic.)

There is another example of the same process only a few lines later, in the very climax of the argument of Books 2–4. Now that they are agreed about what justice is, the next task for Socrates and Glaucon is to consider whether it is justice or injustice that "pays" (*lusitelei*, 445a), that is, "is better [for the agent]" (2.368a, b), so providing the fuller answer to Thrasymachus that Socrates set himself to find back at the beginning of Book 2:

So what's left for us, it seems, is to inquire whether in turn it pays to do just things and practice fine ones and be just, whether our being so is noticed or not, or rather to behave unjustly and be unjust, provided that one doesn't pay a penalty for it, and become better by being punished.

(Socrates at 444e–445a)

But Glaucon has already been persuaded by the analogy, just produced by Socrates, between justice and health, injustice and disease (they have agreed just before that "fine practices lead to our acquiring goodness [and justice], shameful ways to that of badness [and injustice]," in the same way as "healthy things produce health [in the body], unhealthy things disease"):

But . . ., Socrates, this inquiry now seems ridiculous to me. Life seems unliveable when the natural state of the *body* is being destroyed, even if one has every kind of food and drink, complete wealth, and complete power. Will it really be worth living when the natural state of the very thing by virtue of which we are living creatures is being destroyed – if a person is doing anything other than what will allow him to rid himself of badness and injustice and acquire justice and goodness, both sets of things having actually shown up as being what we have described them as being? (445a–b)

Given that analogy between body and soul, Glaucon thinks the case for justice and "virtue" clinched: acting justly must be better than acting unjustly, because the one produces justice/goodness (i.e., "virtue", in the soul), and the other produces injustice/badness – and if life isn't worth living when the body is being ruined, however much one has by way of food, drink, money, and power, so much the less must it be worth living if the *soul* is ruined. This may be enough to persuade Glaucon, but it hardly looks a particularly powerful argument as it stands. Why should anyone, and why should a Thrasymachus, accept the analogy between justice/virtue and health in the first place? So, for example, both allegedly involve the right elements ruling and being ruled (444d): what exactly are these elements in the case of the body?

The shape of this argument deserves close attention, and especially in relation to the last argument Socrates offered Thrasymachus at the end of Book 1. That argument, in brief, was that in the soul and in everything (horses, eyes, ears, pruning knives), it is goodness (excellence, "virtue": *aretē*) rather than its badness (*kakia*) that enables it to perform its function well; the function of the soul is "taking care and ruling and deliberating and all such things" (353d) – and "living" (i.e., causing us to be alive); the goodness of soul is justice (previously argued); so the just soul will live well. The argument that we have been considering at the end of Book 4, in effect, gives us a new version of this Book 1 argument. It is a version that, in particular, adds an explanation – provided by the preceding pages – of *why* the person with a just soul will live better: namely, because the just soul is one in which the reasoning part rules, and the nonreasoning parts are ruled. Glaucon's reference to the soul as "the very thing by virtue of which we are living creatures" (or just "by which we live") is only the most striking of a number of echoes of the earlier argument. But actually there are also anticipations in Book 1 of the tripartition of the soul, presupposed by Book 4: most noticeably 351e–361a, where Socrates suggests – without further explanation – that the unjust person is in a state of internal dissension and civil war.[29]

This at first sight all looks rather unsatisfactory. Why write three more books, one might be inclined to ask (Books 2–4), only to end up hardly any further on – apart, that is, from an outline sketch of a different and supposedly better kind of city (or, actually, of *two* such cities, if we include the "city of pigs")? To make such a judgment, however, is to forget two things: first, that *Glaucon* is now persuaded, in a way that he was not before; and second, that Socrates was himself happy with the argument as he put it in Book 1 (so he said, at 2.368b). And in fact we seem to need exactly the same sorts of premises to give the arguments in either Book 1 or Book 4 any kind of substance. Here is a reminder of the premises I proposed were needed to justify the link between "Platonic" and "vulgar" justice: that the rational part of the soul is naturally oriented toward the good, that conventionally just behavior is part of that good, and that reason is capable of determining that it is. These are, I claim, exactly the sorts of ideas that are needed to give muscle, and substance, to

---

[29] One of the terms used is *stasiazein* (1.352a); cf. *stasis* at 4.444b (between the parts of the unjust soul). Cf. note 21 above on the apparently similar (but actually different) idea at *Lysis* 214c–d. Of course, the *Republic* 1 passage *could* be taken in the same way as the passage in the *Lysis*; it is more natural, however, to read *Republic* 1 in the light of what follows it (even if we might speculate that it was originally an independent work – when the interpretative choices would have been different).

the claims, in Book 1, that justice is the *aretē*, goodness, of the soul, that we need justice for good living, that justice is wisdom, and so on. In other words, Socrates' confidence in his argument there stems from certain views that he holds, though he does not express them fully, and that neither Thrasymachus nor Glaucon and Adeimantus hold, even if they are likely to be more sympathetic to them than is Thrasymachus. But by the end of Book 4, through the use, inter alia, of the analogy of the city, he has brought Glaucon round to his position – even though, as I have suggested, Glaucon still does not fully grasp what that position is. If he did, he would not have needed the new argument.[30]

The Book 4 treatment of the virtues is in fact quite explicitly qualified as provisional. At 6.504b Socrates tells us that "we said[31] that it was another longer way round to see [the virtues] as perfectly as possible"; since he also tells us that it is "by means of [the good that] both just things and the rest become useful and beneficial" (505a) and that a guard who doesn't know "how it is that just and fine things are good" will not be worth much (506a), it seems at least defensible to suppose that "the longer way" would involve spelling out the precise role of wisdom and knowledge in the "virtues." However that may be, the same passages certainly make it impossible that the auxiliary guards in Callipolis possess real courage, or that anybody except the guards proper, the rulers, will possess either real justice or real self-control (*sōphrosunē*) – and they will possess them, as they possess courage, in consequence of their wisdom (and of their training and

---

[30] John Ferrari at this point referred me to his own rejection of the idea that the Plato of the *Republic* regards the rational part as "naturally oriented towards the good" (as I suppose): "when the *Republic* does eventually come round to saying explicitly what the rational part is in fact oriented towards (in Book 9), it's not the good but wisdom and knowing where the truth lies (581b)." But (1) there is no inconsistency between saying that reason is oriented toward knowing the truth and saying that it is oriented toward the good (if indeed it is a seat both of cognition and of desire, as no one ought to dispute; it is in any case the true good that reason will wish to discern); and (2) I take it that it is his commitment to reason's orientation toward the good that allows Plato to continue – even to the end of his life (see section I above) with that notorious claim that no one goes wrong willingly/voluntarily. It is in virtue of reason's natural connection with the good that "every soul" (importantly, not the whole soul) " . . . does everything [it can] for the sake of [the good]" (6.505d–e).

[31] The reference appears to be to 4.435d; I propose to pass over here the difficulties of making sense of this reference.

education). From *Glaucon's* point of view things may look different. But whether he fully sees it or not, what the city-soul analogy leads to is a model of virtue that actually undermines that point of view.

III. CONCLUSION

If all this appears to take us a long way away from the *political* aspect of the *Republic*, that is an illusion. Once again, for Plato the sole function of the political art, properly conceived, is to make people as good as possible. In his post-*Republic* political dialogues, he sees this as a matter of finding a substitute for that individual wisdom that is, as he consistently holds, the condition of true goodness – so maintaining, insofar as the new psychology, introduced and argued for in Book 4, will allow him, the position of the Socrates of the pre-*Republic* dialogues:[32] a substitute that consists in the *imposition*, through laws and institutions, of the right kind of judgments on the majority of the citizens and in the embedding of those judgments in their souls through the education of the irrational desires. In the second section of this chapter, I have tried to show two things: first, that the *Republic* ultimately proposes much the same kind of solution as the dialogues that come after the *Republic*; and second, that that solution, despite appearances, is nevertheless still continuous with – if in the end it is not, and cannot be, wholly compatible with – the substantive views and positions of the pre-*Republic* Socrates. At the least, I hope to have indicated how Plato might have *thought* he was continuing in the Socratic mold (as his choice to go on using Socrates as main character suggests he did), even if, from some perspectives, he is profoundly modifying, or even abandoning, Socrates' original insights. The introduction of irrational soul parts is, in many respects, a massive change; one that proposes a wholly different, and fundamentally pessimistic, understanding of human nature. Yet at the same time Plato retains the basic Socratic view that, as rational beings, it is the *real good* that we desire, and the *real good* that it is in all our interests to discover; or else – so Plato adds – to enact, to

---

[32] I.e., the position that makes goodness actually *identical with* wisdom. That it cannot be, of course, after the arguments of Book 4; goodness will now also be conditional on the keeping down of the irrational parts (see immediately below, and cf. 9.571b–572b, on the presence "in everyone" of "a dangerous, wild, and lawless form of desire").

the highest degree of which we are capable, even if that is divorced from understanding.

WORKS CITED

Bobonich, C. 2002. *Plato's Utopia Recast: His Later Ethics and Politics.* Cambridge.

Ferrari, G. R. F. 2003. *City and Soul in Plato's* Republic. Sankt Augustin; rpt. Chicago, 2005.

Klosko, G. 1986. *Plato's Political Theory.* NewYork and London.

Laks, A. 1990. "Legislation and Demiurgy: On the Relationship between Plato's *Republic* and *Laws.*" *Classical Antiquity* 9: 209–29.

Penner, T., and C. J. Rowe. 2005. *Plato's Lysis. Cambridge Studies in the Dialogues of Plato.* Cambridge.

Pradeau, J.-F. 2002. *Plato and the City: A New Introduction to Plato's Political Thought.* Exeter.

Rowe, C. J. 1995. *Plato: Statesman.* Warminster.

Rowe, C. J. 2001. "Killing Socrates." *Journal of Hellenic Studies* 121: 63–76.

Rowe, C. J. 2003. "The Status of the 'Myth' in Plato's *Timaeus.*" In *Plato Physicus. Cosmologia e antropologia nel Timeo,* ed. C. Natali and S. Maso. Amsterdam.

Rowe, C. J. 2004. "The Case of the Missing Philosophers in Plato's *Timaeus-Critias.*" *Würzburger Jahrbücher für die Altertumswissenschaft,* N.F. Band 28b: 57–70.

Rowe, C. J., and M. Schofield, eds. 2000. *The Cambridge History of Greek and Roman Political Thought.* Cambridge.

3 Rewriting the Poets in Plato's Characters

Plato gives depth to character by writing in three dimensions. In the *Republic*'s main speakers – Socrates and his two younger friends Glaucon and Adeimantus, Plato's real-life brothers – Plato characterizes fully human beings. First to the reader's sight are arguers and arguments, so the logical dimension of character becomes most immediately visible. But these men are not mere talking heads or disembodied minds. They have about them the smell of mortality, with their individual histories, personalities, and commitments. It is not just a question of what arguments are made, but of what sort of man would make a particular argument, or accept it, or long for it. Indeed, Socrates virtually begins his conversation with the brothers by saying he would respond to their arguments differently if he had a different view of their character (368a–b). We catch something of this ethical and psychological dimension of Plato's writing when, for example, Socrates must playfully defend himself in a mock trial, reminding us that one day he will be tried in deadly earnest; when Glaucon lets slip an erotic streak he would prefer not to own; when Adeimantus' limitations are implicitly revealed by having Socrates go beyond them in conversation with his more brilliant brother.

So Plato's characters do more than reveal the explicit logic of an argument. The ethical dimension of the words puts us on the scent of secret motives and unacknowledged ironies. But what the characters mean goes beyond anything the mere individuals Socrates and Glaucon and Adeimantus could say, no matter how logically keen and psychologically apt Plato's writing may be. For in Plato's hand, Socrates and the rest are no longer just individuals. They become representatives and exemplars of human possibilities as such. Plato invests his characters with this further dimension of significance by projecting them onto the gigantic figures of myth.

The *Republic* depends for this projection primarily on one story from each of the two founders of the Greek tradition of epic poetry, Homer and Hesiod: Homer's story of Odysseus' descent to the underworld (*Odyssey* Book 11), known as "The Visit to the Dead" (in Greek, *Nekuia*); and Hesiod's story of "The Golden Age of Cronus and the Races of Metal" (*Works and Days* 109–201). Writers who show themselves this way in the act of reading often reveal something precious about how they hope to be read. We are never closer to Plato as writer than when we are reading Plato reading.

Plato's intimacy with myth is, to say the least, not trumpeted in the *Republic*. In its tenth and final book, Socrates reflects on the shortcomings of the poets who have been the educators of Greece, especially Homer and Hesiod (600d and 612b). He all but excludes them from his best city-in-speech. Socrates comes to this judgment with a sense of loss and an almost embarrassed reluctance. "A certain friendship for Homer, and shame before him, which has possessed me since childhood, prevents me from speaking," he says, yet "still and all, a man must not be honored before the truth" (595b–c). But it is a harsh truth nonetheless, and a little later Socrates suggests that if someone can give an argument showing the poets are good for the city, "we should be delighted to receive them back from exile, since we ourselves are charmed by them" (607c).

By this point, Plato's readers may think he has banished the friendship and enchantment of the poets for good. But if we keep our ears open, the *Republic* discreetly echoes with the tones of Homer and Hesiod. Plato's massive rewritings ring throughout the work. To hear the voice of Plato, reader of the poets, reverberate in the characters of Plato, writer of the *Republic*, opens us to the third, mythic dimension of this gigantic dialogue. When Plato describes Socrates and Glaucon reliving Homer's "Visit to the Dead" or Socrates and Adeimantus returning to Hesiod's "Golden Age of Cronus," he brings an undertone of mythic commentary to the dialogue's logical analysis and ethical drama, a commentary constructed from the echoes of his exiled predecessors in the education of Greece.

I

We have been prepared for Socrates' harsh judgment on the poets in Book 10 by his infamous discussion with Adeimantus of "censoring" poetry in Books 2 and 3 (376d–398b). If some great poet arises in the city we are founding, says Socrates, "we would send him to another city, . . . while we ourselves would use a more austere and less pleasing poet and maker of myths for the sake of benefit" (398a–b). Socrates has in mind the benefit for the education of the guardians (in Greek, *phulakes*) in his city-in-speech, and he focuses on the need to reform the content of "music" (which means especially the poetry of Homer and Hesiod) to make it a vehicle of civic virtue and patriotism. In the first passage scrutinized for the way it portrays humans, Socrates criticizes Homer's presentation of the fate of heroes who die in battle (386a–d):

"And what if [the guardians] are to be courageous?" [said Socrates]. "Mustn't they also be told things that will make them fear death least? . . . Do you suppose anyone who believes Hades' domain exists and is full of terror will be fearless in the face of death and choose death in battles above defeat and slavery?"

"Not at all," [said Adeimantus].

"Then, concerning these tales too, it seems we must supervise those who undertake to tell them and ask them not so utterly to disparage Hades' domain, but rather to praise it, because what they say is neither true nor beneficial for men who are to be fighters."

"Indeed, we must," he said.

"Then, we'll expunge all such things," I said, "beginning with this verse:
'*Better to be bound to the fields, serving*
A landless man with scanty means of life,
Than over all the wasting dead to rule.'"

Socrates is reciting here a passage of Homer's *Odyssey* (11.489–491), from the famous section called "The Visit to the Dead." To make his way home from Troy, Odysseus must descend into the underworld to receive guidance from the soul (in Greek, *psuchē*) of the blind prophet Teiresias. While there, he converses with the souls of various other dead heroes, including Achilles, the Greek champion in the Trojan War. When Odysseus tries to cheer up the gloomy Achilles – he is, after all, dead – by pointing out the great honor he now receives below, Achilles will have none of it. "About death, do not try to comfort me, bright Odysseus," laments this hero, "I would rather be the living slave of a peasant, than the king of all the dead."

Socrates criticizes this Homeric hell, not so much because Homer's account is false, but because it undermines the courage and patriotism of the city's soldiers. We will not teach public spirit, Socrates tells Adeimantus, if we let Achilles, the most glorious of all the heroes, declare that his self-sacrifice was a mistake, and that even the greatest life in Hades' domain, the life of political leadership, is not worth the smallest life on the green earth.

Some four books later, in the so-called "Allegory of the Cave" that begins Book 7, Socrates makes a comment with an oddly familiar ring to it, this time to Glaucon. Socrates has told Glaucon that the man who has ascended to gaze on true reality and then is forced back into politics is like a man who has climbed his way up from a cave and now is forced back down to find his way among its shadows (516d–e):

"In your opinion," [said Socrates], "would [the man who has been out of the cave] be desirous of [the honors the cave-dwellers give out], and envy those who are honored and hold power among these men? Or, rather, would he be affected as Homer says and prefer very much 'to be bound to the fields, serving a landless man,' and to undergo anything whatsoever rather than to opine about those things and live that way?"

"Yes," [Glaucon] said, "I suppose he would prefer to undergo anything rather than live that way.

This is Socrates' second recitation of the lament of Achilles' soul, and it presents us with a puzzle. For now Socrates uses Homer's words exactly to undermine the attachment of one particular man to political leadership and to the affairs of any city. These very words had been censored for their tendency to produce precisely the effect Socrates wants to produce here: they tend to undermine one's whole-hearted attachment to politics and the city. The guidance Socrates gives Glaucon now flatly contradicts the pedagogy he and Adeimantus had agreed to earlier.

Socrates criticized Homer's gloomy hell for disheartening the guardians on whom the city must rely for their courage. But does not Socrates' identification of politics with hell have the same effect, if for different reasons? Socrates seems to be as poor an educator of this particular man Glaucon as Homer was claimed to be of the guardians. Socrates quotes Homer to make the choice between philosophy and politics the choice between life and death. Does this not sit ill with the optimistic and radical ambition of founding a "pure" city, even if only in speech?

II

These are awkward questions. Are they also Platonic questions?

Some readers will doubt that they are. It could, after all, be a coincidence or a slip, a minor infelicity, that Plato created this Homeric echo across 130 pages of text. All of the arguments given, all of the positions defined, in short all of the logical complexity of the dialogue that has passed between these points may eclipse the significance of Homer's small voice, a whisper of myth lost in a whirlwind of philosophy.

But the whispers start very early, and the reader should not multiply accidents beyond necessity. "I descended to Piraeus yesterday with Glaucon," say the opening words of the *Republic*. This opening could be unremarkable; taking a friend down from the city of Athens to its port was not in itself a portentous event, though Socrates seems not to have done it very often. His host Cephalus, an old man obsessed with fears of the afterlife, complains, "Socrates, you don't descend to us in the Piraeus very often" (328c). These twice-repeated forms of the word "descent" (in Greek, *katabasis*) have mythological overtones. For *katabasis* is the word for a trip to the underworld. In particular, it is the word Odysseus himself uses when he recounts to his wife Penelope his "Visit to the Dead" (*Odyssey* 23.252).

This initiating descent, which by itself might be too faint for allusion, is recalled in "The Myth of Er," the *Republic*'s concluding myth of the afterlife. Socrates tells Glaucon how the souls of the dead ascend from punishment under the earth or descend from reward in heaven (614d) and prepare to choose a new life, which they will live when they are shortly reborn in a new incarnation. After drawing lots to determine the order of choice, the souls begin making their choices. Many choose unwisely; but not the last soul (620c–d):

"By chance," [said Socrates], "Odysseus' soul had drawn the last lot of all and went to choose. From memory of its former labors it had recovered from love of honor, and it went around for a long time looking for the life of an apolitical private man. With effort it found one lying somewhere, neglected by others. It said when it saw this life that it would have done the same even if it had drawn the first lot, and was delighted to choose it."

It is Socrates himself who seems to be projected onto this chastened Odysseus, who retires to private life from the hurly-burly of his "labors" (in Greek, *ponoi*) – the word for the adventures and tasks of the hero. The hero will ascend from the underworld back into life with a new understanding that keeps him pure from political ambition.

This is Plato's mythologizing of a previous conversation of Socrates with Adeimantus, which at the time seemed merely personal and ethical (496a–e):

"Only a tiny remnant are left, Adeimantus," [said Socrates,] "of those who could worthily associate with philosophy. . . . [The true philosopher] stays quiet and minds his own business. . . . Seeing others filled with lawlessness, he would be satisfied if somehow he could live for himself a pure life here, without injustice and impious deeds, and with fine hopes for his departure; and then depart with cheerfulness and good temper."

Socrates explicitly uses himself as an example of this private, retiring philosopher (496c). The *Republic*'s initiating descent and its consummating ascent provide the mythic commentary on Socrates' heroic life, and particularly on his absence from politics.

Socrates characterizes a "descent" four more times in the dialogue, and all four reinforce and embellish this Odyssean theme. Indeed, three are directly connected to Socrates' second recitation of the lament of Achilles' soul in the "Allegory of the Cave." (The fourth, at 511b, is part of the immediately preceding account of the divided line.) In all three, Socrates tells Glaucon that, even in the best city, the guardians who complete their philosophical training will want to flee from politics, finding it a dead-world compared with the life of the mind outside the cave. But, says Socrates, they must be compelled to "descend" back into the political world, and bother themselves with all its petty labors (*ponoi*) and honors (516e, 519b, 520d, 539e).

III

So far, we have been considering Socrates as Odysseus, the intrepid and intelligent sojourner here, displaced in this land of labors. (In their accounts of Socrates' defense speech at his trial, Plato and Xenophon both have Socrates project his examinations of his fellow citizens as heroic "labors" (*ponoi*); see Plato, *Apology* 22a, and Xenophon, *Apology* 17.) But Plato's appropriation of "The Visit to the Dead" is characteristically more ambiguous than this Odyssean Socrates would be. To see this ambiguity, it helps again to return to the passage where Socrates and Adeimantus "correct" Homer's account of the afterlife.

As it happens, after Socrates and Adeimantus censor the lament of Achilles' soul, the next passage from the *Odyssey* they disapprove (*Odyssey* 10.494–495) is Circe's advice to Odysseus to seek the soul of Teiresias, the Theban prophet who will be Odysseus' guide in the underworld, and his adviser on how to get home. Teiresias is distinguished from all the other souls by a special gift granted him by Persephone, the Queen of the Dead-World (Socrates quotes only the second line at 386d):

> In death, Persephone still grants him thought,
> And shrewdness; while they are fretting shadows.

This is the only passage where Homer directly calls the persons of the underworld "shadows" (in Greek, *skiai*). (Odysseus a little later says his mother Antikleia's soul was "like a shadow" when he tried to embrace her: *Odyssey* 11.207.) Plato, with his wonderful sensitivity as a reader as well as a writer, was struck by the word "shadows." In the "Allegory of the Cave," Socrates uses "shadow" eight times in three pages to characterize what the nonphilosophical prisoners see (515a–517d). This density of Platonic shadows chimes with Odysseus' conversation with Achilles, reinforcing Plato's appropriation of Homer's myth. (Socrates also uses "shadows" half a dozen times to characterize the lower levels of the divided line, at 509d–510d and 532b–c, much as he uses "descent" of the line as well as the cave.)

But these shadows also add a potentially discordant note to descent, by intruding Teiresias. Other dialogues exploit this projection of Socrates onto Homer's character of Teiresias guiding

Odysseus' descent, notably the *Protagoras* (315b9 and c8) and the *Meno* (100a5). When we conceive of Socrates himself as the hero descending and ascending, we have one mythic projection. But when we project him instead onto the blind and shrewd prophet, guiding someone else through a descent, and even more through an ascent he may not make himself, Socrates takes on a very different mythic character. "I descended," Socrates began; but "with Glaucon," he went on. This casting of Socrates as Glaucon's charismatic sidekick, rather than as himself the leading man, fits very well with the drama of the *Republic*'s opening. An older figure, distinguished by his wit and wisdom, leads a younger, brasher protagonist and helps him to find his way in a shady world. The plot requires the hero to climb the path back out again. But the blind guide may fall to the wayside, no matter how hard he leans on his staff.

Plato develops the Teiresias theme in the same section where he recapitulated Achilles' lament, in the "Allegory of the Cave." For this is not a story of some self-sufficient hero who, solely by his own efforts, escapes to the light. It is conceived primarily as a story of education (514a), of conversion (518b–d). This conversion is not pleasant, nor is it wholly voluntary. The prisoners in the cave are released only under the ungentle prodding of a guide who will "drag" them up (515e). This unpleasant guide operates by "forcing them to answer his questions" (514d). When the prisoners see how the guide discombobulates one of their own whom he is trying to "release and lead up," they will even want to kill him (515d, 517a). Like the recitation of Achilles' lament, this introduction by Glaucon and Socrates of the theme of an underworld guide adds a mythic dimension to an earlier conversation with Adeimantus. Suppose someone persuades a talented young man, Socrates had said to Adeimantus, to reject the corrupting influence of his friends and flunkies and "turns him and drags him toward philosophy." Won't these friends and flunkies do everything in their power to destroy such a persuader, "plotting against him in private and attacking him in public?" (495e). The trial and execution of Socrates for his influence on talented young men is foreseen with Adeimantus, then mythologized with Glaucon.

The drama of Socrates telling Glaucon the "Allegory of the Cave" enacts the very story of education the "Allegory" told. Socrates plays the role of Glaucon's guide in the ascent from the cave of political ambition. He emphasizes to Glaucon that one who has ascended to the light would never go back down into the cave's shadows, unless forced by some necessity. The world of politics takes on the mythic significance of being the dead-world, a world of mere souls. Socrates' identity as mentor takes on the added mythic significance of prophet, the guide of souls through the underworld, and he stakes out his implicit claim to a special discernment in a realm otherwise inhabited by thoughtless shadows.

IV

Suppose Socrates is playing Teiresias to Glaucon's Odysseus, as well as playing Odysseus himself. This doubling of mythic identities would be the *Republic*'s version of the fateful ambiguity at the heart of Socrates' avowals and disavowals of knowledge in so many of Plato's dialogues. Does Socrates himself have the sort of knowledge required for the ascent out of the cave, or can he only point the way out for someone else?

The closest the *Republic* comes to an answer is at the beginning of one of its most enigmatic sections, the discussion of the form of the Good. This absolute Good, Socrates tells Adeimantus, "is what every soul pursues and for the sake of which it does everything. The soul divines that this Good is something, but is in confusion about it, and does not grasp sufficiently what it is" (505e). This "confusion" (in Greek, *aporia*) is something that Adeimantus and the reader both expect Socrates to cure, with something more reliable than divination (a word with the same root as "prophet"). After all, "Will we say even those best men in the city, into whose control we put everything, have to remain in obscurity about a thing of this kind and importance?" (505e–506a). Readers share Adeimantus' expectation that Socrates' answer is "No," and naturally think he is about to remove the obscurity.

But it is not so. "I divine," Socrates goes on, "that no one will adequately know what is just or noble before knowing this Good" (506a). The repetition clangs; does Socrates also only "divine" what this absolute Good is? When Adeimantus and then Glaucon press him to explain this mysterious Good, Socrates puts them off. He tells Glaucon cryptically, "What my thinking is on these topics appears to me more than can be reached with the present effort," leaving in obscurity whether his refusal is prompted by his limitations or theirs (506e). His final demurral is just as discreet, when Glaucon asks him to leave behind the image of the cave and tell plainly how this saving knowledge is obtained. "What you wish to see," says Socrates, "would no longer be an image, but the truth itself, just as it appears to me. Whether or not it is really that way isn't worth insisting on further; but that there is some such thing to see, must be insisted on" (533a). Socrates discerns that there is something to see, but he will not say that he sees it.

Plato has contrived a most garrulous silence to suspend the satisfaction of his readers' curiosity. But how angry can we be, when both of Plato's brothers were treated no better by Socrates?

V

What sort of guide does Socrates become for Glaucon? This depends on where we take Glaucon to start. Plato characterizes Glaucon in considerable psychological detail. Socrates senses in him an extreme manliness (357a) and notes his military courage (368a), talent for music (398e), and strong erotic passion (402d–e, 468b–c, 474d–475a; see also 458d). Glaucon also displays a penetrating intellect throughout the dialogue, not to mention a sometimes sarcastic wit at Socrates' expense (e.g., 509c, 547a–b, 595c, and 596d). He combines the love of honor and victory characteristic of military excellence with more musical and erotic traits, a combination rarely found (see 375c–376c, 475a–b, 485b, 503c, and 548d–e).

This love of honor, rooted in the so-called spirited part of the soul (in Greek, *thumos*), presents a pedagogical problem. The ambition to be honored is a potent motive toward noble ends, such as care for the common good. But it also tends toward harshness and toward a desire to dominate (see 475a–b, 549a, and 581a). How philosophy can channel this energy of noble aspiration, without diminishing it, is one of the central questions of the *Republic*. The question is introduced comically, in the paradox of how there can be guardians who are both gentle (to citizens) and harsh (to enemies) (375b–c). Socrates resolves the paradox by suggesting the guardians must be like good dogs, possessed of a "philosophic" nature combining in the proper way gentleness (to those they know) and harshness (to those they don't know) (375e–376c). More generally, the entire educational scheme of the *Republic* is organized around two poles of virtue, a "soft" pole connected to music and a "hard" pole connected to gymnastic (see also *Statesman* 306e–307a). The ideal student will have a disposition neither too hard nor too soft, and so be wholly receptive to both aspects of education (410c–e).

In this respect, does Glaucon have an ideal disposition? Glaucon's interest in founding a city, if only in speech, hints to us of his very intense political ambition (a hint confirmed by Xenophon, Plato's contemporary, in *Memorabilia* 3.6). His brother Adeimantus immediately thinks of Glaucon when the discussion turns to an extreme spiritedness (548d) that would be tipped too far toward love of dominating and ruling (549a). But Socrates says the man of extreme spiritedness is distinguished from Glaucon by being "more stubborn and somewhat less apt at music," as well as less eloquent, harsher to slaves, and perhaps a bit too fond of sport and the hunt (548e–549a). It seems Glaucon has something close to the right mixture of music and gymnastic, of the hard and the soft. But it is terribly difficult to get this mixture right, as difficult as defining whether a man cares too little or too much for money, or for his wife's opinion (see 549d in light of *Statesman* 307e). Though the energy that comes from love of honor is indispensable, it always is in danger of becoming questionable (see *Statesman* 309e).

Allowing for this question about his love of honor, Glaucon seems to have just the natural endowments he and Socrates enumerate when they characterize the guardians and philosophers in their ideal city (485b–487a). Or perhaps more precisely, this description of the ideal philosophic nature is also an idealization of Glaucon, a focus for his aspiration rather than simply an analysis of his present self. It must be with some exhilaration, then, that at the end of this passage the actual Glaucon hears Socrates say of this potential Glaucon, "When such men are made perfect [*teleos*] by education and age, wouldn't you turn the city over to them alone?" (487a).

But before Glaucon can give the emphatic "Yes" to this question that must have been on his lips and in his heart, Adeimantus interrupts. This all sounds good in theory, says Adeimantus, but it isn't true in practice. When it comes to politics, philosophy makes those who "linger in it for any length of time" politically useless, or even vicious (487b–d). His challenge complicates the easy optimism of Socrates and Glaucon that a man might pass from his actual to his perfected self to become a philosopher-king. To the brothers'

surprise, Socrates does not try to refute this charge. "Each one of
the traits we praised in the philosophic nature," such as courage and
moderation, "has a part in destroying the soul that has them and
tearing it away from philosophy," says Socrates, and so do advantages such as wealth and good connections (491b, 495a). The same
natural endowments that are the necessary prerequisites for philosophy also expose a man to almost irresistible temptations toward
tyranny. The worst can only come from the corruption of the best
(491d–e), and the potential philosopher is also the potential tyrant.
We would expect to find Socrates associating with young men who
find something fascinating about tyranny, who are open to its seduc-
tions, to exactly the extent we would expect to find him consorting
with those with a talent for philosophy.

Glaucon wants to loathe tyrants, but he feels their fascination,
and he is the potent if reluctant heir of the conception of tyranny
proposed (in Book 1) by Thrasymachus and attacked by Socrates. The
sophist was too easily charmed, says Glaucon, like a snake (358b),
and he asks Socrates for a more convincing refutation of the tyrant's
life of unbridled desire. His own speech (at the beginning of Book 2)
brilliantly sets the snake free again. He protests, a bit too much, that
he "rejuvenates" tyranny only for the sake of clarity – "Of course,
Socrates, I myself don't think this way at all; though I am confused"
(358c; also 361e). This alleged "confusion" (aporia) has a rather rotten
smell, like a sweet perfume over a fetid sweat, and his rejuvenation
is pungent with the intimacy of his hidden passion.

Glaucon's manly vigor (see 359b with 357a and 359a with 361d)
in defending the tyrant is most on display in the thought-experiment
he composes of "The Ring of Gyges" (359c–360b). Once upon a time,
an ancestor of Gyges was tending sheep, where he was "bound to
the fields" (359d; the same word as Achilles used in his lament)
of the king. A great storm and earthquake broke open a chasm in
the earth, into which he descended. There he saw many wonderful
things worthy of a myth (359d) and retrieved a magical ring. When
he discovered this ring had the power to make its wearer invisible,
the shepherd used this power to murder the king, commit adultery
with his wife, and assume the throne.

Glaucon asks his audience to consider whether they would act any
differently if they put such a ring on their finger. Invisibility is revealing of hidden desire. The just man "would act no differently from the

unjust, but both would go the same way" (360c). This immoral moral, whatever its general applicability, surely tells us much about what Glaucon finds within himself. The reason he feels "confused" by arguments in praise of tyranny is that a part of him is in accord with these arguments. His thought-experiment uncovers what he would prefer to conceal and perhaps what he hopes Socrates will drag him away from (see 515d).

Glaucon's "confusion" is caused by a mixture of obsession and revulsion. He is unwilling to acknowledge his own manifestly erotic temperament. When Socrates cites him as an authority on what "an erotic man" would say, Glaucon gets defensive: "If you want to point to me while you speak about what erotic men do, I agree for the sake of the argument" (474d–475a). But his thought-experiment has been too successful for this dodge. Why, after all, does he lay such stress on adultery, and sexual license more generally (360b), in the story? It is for the same reason that, when Socrates suggests the young men and boys should reward the courageous soldier with crowns, handshakes, and kisses, Glaucon suggests going further: "No one whom [the courageous soldier] wants to kiss should be permitted to refuse, so that a man who happens to be erotically attracted to someone, male or female, would be more eager to win the rewards of valor" (468b–c). Erotic passion is as deep a part of Glaucon as anything could be. But when in Book 9 the erotic nature of the tyrant is laid bare, we understand his earlier defensiveness. Eros is what makes Glaucon the right man for philosophy (see, esp., 474c–d), and at the same time it is what threatens to unman him.

Glaucon might successfully avoid confronting his erotic self, were it not that he has bad dreams. Socrates and Adeimantus see our unguarded dreams as the proof of this hidden self, dreams that adumbrate the Greek classics of the tyrannical and the tragic: incest, patricide, and cannibalism (571c–d). "The laws and better desires, with the help of argument," can weaken these bad desires, but yet are they present, "even in some of us who seem to be ever so measured" (571b, 572b). The most we can do is to calm these desires in the hopes of rousing a different part of ourselves. Socrates calls this best part of us the "calculating" or "thinking" part. In waking life, surely, it is what makes of us philosophers. But the description of its work in sleep and dream associates it with prophecy rather than calculation: "The best part, alone and pure and by itself, is left to inquire, and *to strive to* perceive *something it does not know*, something past, present, or future. . . . And it is in such a person that the best part most *touches* the truth, and least then do those lawless dream visions appear" (572a–b, emphasis added). This characterization should ring a bell. Socrates earlier described our imperfect divination of the Good: "The soul divines that this Good is *something*, but is in confusion about it, and *is not able to grasp* sufficiently what it is" (505e, emphasis added). We strive for a knowledge we do not have, we reach for a truth we do not grasp. Especially does politics show itself such a dream-world, fit only for anxious navigation by the shadow light of prophecy, a sleepy life that provoked Achilles' disgust (516c–d). Our dream, and Glaucon's, is to be fully awake (520c).

Cephalus' prophetic faculties about the afterlife (330d–e) were roused only when he, like Sophocles, had gotten old enough to be sexually impotent, escaping the same "many mad masters" that enthrall the tyrant (329b–d and 573a–c). In Glaucon, too, the erotic self competes with the prophetic self, and he has not the wisdom to be old. No wonder, then, that in his confusion he needs a Teiresias.

VI

Suppose you descended out of storm and earthquake into a "chasm" (359d; see 614c–d) broken open in the earth, into the hushed magnificence of the tomb where the ring of invisibility resides. Where would you be?

Glaucon gets an explicit answer to this question toward the end of the dialogue (612a–b):

"In the argument," [Socrates] said, "haven't we both cleared away the other parts of the criticism and also not brought in the wages and reputations connected with justice as you [plural] said Hesiod and Homer do? But we found that justice by itself is best for soul itself, and that the soul must do the just things, whether it has Gyges' ring or not, and, in addition to such a ring, Hades' cap."

Hades' cap, like Gyges' ring, made its bearer invisible. (The name "Hades" means "invisible," a fact Plato exploits in the *Phaedo*, 79b.) Socrates is adding a mythic dimension to Glaucon's thought-experiment: If your invisibility would release the desires Glaucon has suggested, your ring and your cap may as well be gifts from hell.

By explicitly referring back to Hesiod and Homer here, Socrates follows the established pattern of giving a mythic resonance to an idea of Adeimantus when responding to Glaucon. For it was Adeimantus, not Glaucon, who complained that *Hesiod and Homer* praised only the wages of justice (363a); Glaucon had made this complaint only against "the many" (358a).

It is easy to hear, in the tyrannical shepherd's "descent" (359d) into a chasm, all the other descents and caves in the dialogue. The "storm and earthquake" that "break open the earth" (359d) beneath the shepherd have their echoes, too. Most obviously, at the end of the dialogue's concluding myth (621b), "thunder and earthquake" mark the ascent of the reincarnated souls from Plato's underworld. But a second, quieter echo of this phrase from Glaucon's story is another amusing example of how Glaucon appropriates as myth what Adeimantus disapproves as pedagogy. In addition to Achilles' lament, Socrates proposes for Adeimantus' disapproval six more Homeric passages depicting the afterlife (386c–387a). Of these seven passages, three concern underworld descents in the *Odyssey*, and three the death of Achilles' beloved friend Patroclus in the *Iliad*. Only one of the seven, the second (*Iliad* 20.64–65), seems isolated, where Hades worries lest "his house be revealed to mortals and immortals, dreadful, rotting, which even the gods abhor." But this passage will ring a bell with readers who recall the storm and earthquake that broke the earth open for Glaucon's shepherd. For it is contention between Zeus and Poseidon that makes Hades worry that hell itself will be broken open. Zeus thunders from above, while Poseidon shakes from below, which threatens "to break open the earth" (*Iliad* 20.63). Glaucon's "storm and earthquake" rewrites the very passage Adeimantus wants to censor.

VII

The tensions in Glaucon's eroticism leave the reader of two minds or, better, of two moods with regard to Socrates' guidance of Glaucon. Socrates promotes an active, reformist mood, which places a high value on a purified politics. This reaches its highest development just as Socrates is prevented by Adeimantus' interruption from turning over the city-in-speech to Glaucon (487b). From that point, Socrates promotes a dismissive, escapist mood that denigrates political leadership by comparing it to ruling in hell rather than living in the sun. When Socrates recites the lament of Achilles a second time, are we forced to put an ironic smile on his earlier nurturing of Glaucon's radical ambition?

I believe it is a mistake to let Plato's escapist mood eclipse his more positive valuing of politics. Though his moods may not believe in each other, they do not contradict each other either. But the native hue of the reformist mood is sicklied over with the pale cast of doubt, doubt that reform can ever expect to earn the name of action. At the dialogue's thematic center (473c–e), Socrates suggests that human ills will cease only when either philosophers become kings or kings philosophers. While it is just barely possible this blessing should come to pass – Socrates says it is "not entirely a mere prayer" (540d; see also 499b–c) – it is also nothing one could bring about merely through resolution. The greatest political blessing possible for human beings is a matter of coincidence (473d), chance (499b), or some divine happenstance (499c).

This brute resistance of the highest political goals to human control does not look so important when one is in the grip of the escapist mood. Indeed, to be deprived of any opportunity at all to be a ruler is merely to avoid a distraction, and the sense that this lack of political opportunity would involve a real loss is attenuated, or suppressed altogether. (Socrates first introduces this escapist mood when he tells Glaucon that decent people accept political leadership only to avoid being ruled by worse people (347a–c); this is still a popular cover story among academics seeking leadership positions.) But I also hear a kind of regret in the *Republic*, as for something beautiful that must be forgone. This regret is the product when the reformer realizes that reform is out of his control.

Socrates expresses the reformer's regret memorably when he discusses with Adeimantus the attitude of a true philosopher to politics, given its dangers and corruption (496d–497a):

"Seeing others filled with lawlessness, [the true philosopher] would be satisfied," [said Socrates], "if somehow he could live for himself a pure life here, without injustice and impious deeds, and with fine hopes for his departure; and then depart with cheerfulness and good temper."

"Well," [Adeimantus] said, "then he would depart after having accomplished no small thing."

"But not the greatest either," [Socrates] said, "unless he chanced upon a fitting regime, since in a fitting one, he would grow more himself, and save the common with the private."

Here a reformed politics is not some necessity to be happily escaped like a mad master. Socrates acknowledges that ruling a city well serves the private good of the ruler. As he says a little further on (499b, emphasis added), "A city or a regime, and *similarly even a man*, will never become perfect [*teleos*]," unless some chance forces philosophers to rule whether they want to or not or a passion for philosophy arises in those who already have access to political power. In these two passages, the "growth" a philosopher experiences by ruling is an intrinsic good, just as the further perfection that those in political power would reach, if they fell in love with philosophy, would be an intrinsic good. From this point of view, political leadership is surely not just the instrumental good of avoiding the rule of worse people. But it is a growth that cannot be pursued. We must await some divine chance to experience it. The dominant mood is resignation at unavoidable loss, lightened only by gratitude for extraordinary beauty.

The Teiresias motif in the *Republic*, then, casts a pall of regret and resignation over Glaucon's political ambition. Socrates will guide Glaucon to be too worldly to dismiss politics, and too otherworldly to be confident of reforming it. The erotic self has not been harmonized with the prophetic self. This is not Plato's only word on the relation between the prophetic and the erotic, and perhaps it is not his last word. For example, the *Symposium* (which invites a hundred comparisons, not least by beginning (172c) with a report of Glaucon's own intense interest in its subject matter) certainly suggests a much closer relationship between the erotic and the prophetic (see 192d and 202e). But it is the end of Glaucon's story in the *Republic*.

The famous "Allegory of the Cave" is many things. But prominent among them, it is a rewriting of Homer. Socrates has guided Glaucon to a new mythic identity, from an ambitious Achilles to a chastened Odysseus. But this rewriting has complicated and elaborated Socrates' own mythic projection onto the triumphant hero. The terms of the rewriting prohibit us from saying Socrates simply is or simply is not this prose epic's hero. Is he the intrepid Odysseus himself, hero of a philosophical epic with its own nostalgia for a heavenly home (see 592a–b), or is he Teiresias, the hero's guide, intelligent and prophetic, but still essentially blind, with only a divination of the hero's way? Plato's myth refuses us the satisfaction of Homer's *Odyssey*, since we cannot say whether the main character found his way through many labors at last to home, or remained stranded in that dead-world of politics and ambition, saving others though he could not save himself. It is hard to see an accident in an ambiguity so subtly composed.

VIII

Having trained the reader's ear with these two Homeric themes, Plato offers us an entertaining coda. Socrates and Adeimantus censor one last *Odyssey* passage for the disheartening way it presents the dead-world (387a). Odysseus returned home and took his revenge on the would-be suitors of his wife Penelope. When they were dead, Hermes the Psychagogue (Leader of Souls) summoned them down to hell. In the Homeric description of which Socrates and Adeimantus disapprove (*Odyssey* 24.6–7), the suitors fret and flutter behind the divine leader:

> *Falling, the suitors' souls go squeaking down,*
> *like bats in nooks of eerie echoed caves.*

This citation is as careful in its assonance as the previous two. As it was only in the Teiresias passage that Homer called souls "shadows," so is this the only passage in which he explicitly likens the underworld to a cave. But the passage also prefigures one last aspect of the mythic dimension of the underworldly Socrates. He too becomes a psychagogue (from *psuchē* "soul" and *agagein* "to lead"), the priest leading others in a ritual of initiation and purification, into the mysteries of the afterlife.

Such initiation rituals, most famously the Eleusinian Mysteries, were central to Greek religious life. They typically involved a ritual journey, during which the presiding priest taught secret doctrines to the initiates, to purify them and protect them in the underworld. (Participation also often involved considerable expense.) The initiation culminated in the sudden revealing of a cult object, a sacred vision to be gazed upon only by the purified. The *Republic* appropriates the spiritual depths of these religious ideas. This is obvious in the grand concluding myth, where the soul is led on a purifying journey (611c) culminating in a vision of a pure column of light at the deep heart's core of the world (616b). But equally striking is the way Plato rings the changes on the schema of a *leader* conducting an initiate to *gaze* (using Greek words based on the root *the-*, from which derive the English "theater" and "theory") on a *sudden vision*, reaching a crescendo in the "Allegory of the Cave."

This was clearly a myth Plato intended to nurture. In the *Phaedo*, philosophy itself is presented as a purification rite (69b and 82d; in Greek, *katharmoi*), and the dialogue's tone is set by Pythagorean religious lore. The *Symposium* is even closer to the *Republic*. In its central speech, the prophetess Diotima makes elaborate use of the vocabulary of an *initiation* into a *mystery* (209e–210a), conducted by a *leader* (210a, 210e), to a *sudden vision* (210e; in Greek, *exaiphnēs* "sudden" and *kathoran* "see intensely"). In the *Republic*, these themes receive their first statement in Socrates' opening sentences (327a–b, emphasis added): "I *descended* to Piraeus yesterday with Glaucon, son of Ariston, wanting to pray to the *goddess*, and to *gaze* on how they would put on the *cult celebration*, since they were *leading* it for the first time. . . . After we had prayed and *gazed on the spectacle*, we went off toward town." Polemarchus, Cephalus' son, interrupts their departure, and he and Adeimantus tempt Glaucon and Socrates to visit Cephalus' house with the promise of "something worth your *gaze*" (328a; see 619e). When they arrive, old Cephalus, fresh from making one *sacrifice*, chides Socrates for not *descending* more often, and soon leaves to *sacrifice* some more (328c and 331d). He speaks of his past like a man with a guilty conscience, in search of the sort of reassurance that can be bought and sold, and he claims a special *vision* of the things of the underworld, especially its punishments (330d–331b). How compactly this opening has introduced the initiation themes we fully appreciate only later, when we learn the identity of the deity honored in the new cult being led: Bendis, a Thracian deity probably associated with Persephone, queen of the underworld (354a).

These themes are taken up again with special emphasis by Adeimantus. After Glaucon rejuvenates Thrasymachus' praise of the tyrant with "The Ring of Gyges," a speech uncomfortably revealing of his own erotic ambivalence, it is his brother's turn. But the arguments Adeimantus longs to hear from Socrates respond to different anxieties. It is the ghost of Cephalus that Adeimantus remembers and the old man's fearful invocation of the torments in the afterlife. "The man who finds many unjust deeds in his life often even wakes from his sleep in a fright," says father Cephalus (330e), and at least a part of Adeimantus inherits this concern for what dreams may come. These disturbing stories – Cephalus calls them "myths" (330d) – are understood by Adeimantus to be literary in origin, and he ascribes them to the poets Orpheus, Musaeus, and Musaeus' son, apparently Eumolpus, the founder of the Eleusinian Mysteries (363c, 363e, 364e; for the Orphic theme in *Symposium*, see 179d).

Adeimantus is anxious about all this Orphic religious lore. He is especially critical of sacrifices in expiation of misdeeds (364b–e). This particular religious mistake, Adeimantus grumbles, though it has Homeric authority (364d–e, which quotes *Iliad* 9.497–501), corrupts bold young men, like himself, as we understand (365a–b). Why not hope to expiate the lusts and ambitions of our strong years in a wealthy retirement? It seems to be the very plan behind Cephalus' taste in old age for all the comforts of Homer. Adeimantus also disapproves of many more specifically Orphic practices: of being led (*agagein*; 363c) into Hades by initiations (365a, 366a), of purifications (364e), and of rituals of "release" from punishment (in Greek, *lusis*; 364e, 365a, 366a). Is this critique of "release" intended to recall Glaucon's fantasy of the power of the ring, which gave license to "release from bonds" anyone we want (360b)? With Adeimantus, the manipulation of "release" is a religious nightmare; with Glaucon, it is a political dream. At any rate, Adeimantus is like his brother in denying any personal attachment to the position he will so vigorously build up for Socrates to tear down. Others would make these arguments in earnest, he would have Socrates know, "but I, just because I desire to hear the refutation from you – after all, there's nothing I have to hide from you – I speak as vehemently as I can" (367a–b) . A man doesn't choke like this unless he has something to swallow.

Plato returns to Adeimantus' themes with his characteristic pattern of elaboration: What Adeimantus rejected becomes the cornerstone of a myth Socrates and Glaucon enact in the cave. The prisoners there are "released from their bonds" (*lusis*; 515c, 517a, 532b) by a mysterious "someone," obviously a Socrates figure (see, esp., 515d and 517a). This release requires them to be reoriented and turned around, or more literally to be "led to turn" (*agagein* "to lead" with *peri* "around"; 514a, 515c, 518c, 518d, 521c). Socrates invites Glaucon to consider "how someone will lead them up to the light, just as some are said to have gone from Hades up to the gods" and adds that this leading up will be "a turning around of a soul from a sort of nocturnal day to true day, the path up to being, which is indeed what we call true philosophy" (521c). So being turned around is at the same time a being led up, a forced ascent. This conversion from darkness to light, we learn, is at first blinding, when the released prisoners "suddenly" try to adjust their "vision" to what the light illumines above. Similarly, they will be just as blind if they try to descend back for a "sudden vision" in the shadows (515c, 515e, 516a, 516e, 518a). The passage repeatedly characterizes the freed prisoners by their "gaze," upon the heavenly (516a), the enlightened (516b), the intelligible (517b), the divine (517d), and the real (518c). The shadows of the cave are thick with echoes from Adeimantus and his old man.

Finally, the philosophical and mathematical education that follows the "Allegory of the Cave" continues the Orphic resonance. Socrates and Glaucon consider how we are "led to gaze" on the highest things by concerning ourselves with unity (524e), number (525c), geometry (526e), and astronomy (529a). "All this concern for these arts we've gone through," Socrates recapitulates, "has this power to *release* and *turn around*, and to *lead up* what is best in the soul to *gaze* upon what is best in what exists" (532b–c, emphasis added). After this long "prelude," Glaucon asks Socrates for "the song itself," an account of the true philosophical art, dialectic (532d), which would be the consummation of Glaucon's initiation. In response, Socrates again makes his own an image that earlier received Adeimantus' explicit censure. Adeimantus had complained that in their writings, the Orphic poets "bury the impious and unjust in mud in Hades" (363d). Now, it turns out, this is the same fate from which dialectic will win our release: "Since there really is a sort of 'barbarous mire' in which the eye of the soul is buried," says Socrates, "dialectic gently drags and leads it up above, using the arts we described as helpers and assistant leaders of the turning around" (533c–d). When Socrates says there is "really" or, literally, a "barbarous mire" that buries the soul's eye, he is surely recalling the same Orphic theme as Adeimantus, and perhaps the specific language of a particular text. Dialectic, the final mystery of philosophy, does the very work of "dragging," "leading," and "turning" that characterized the initiating priest.

IX

"I descended": eerie echoes indeed. The small bell tolled in the first word resounds like a carillon in a cave. Plato has rewritten Socrates in the character of priest, prophet, and hero.

X

Adeimantus' anxiety about the notion that initiation and sacrifice can buy off the gods is only half of his story. He is also bothered by what the poets, especially Hesiod, say about the difficulty of virtue. He complains that Hesiod makes the "easy" road of vice "short and smooth," in contrast to the "long, hard" road of virtue, which the poet says is "rough and steep" (364d, paraphrasing *Works and Days* 287–91). Hesiod immediately goes on to say the road is rough "only at first; but when one reaches the top, then it is easy to travel, though hard before" (291–92). But Adeimantus does not quote this part of the lesson; Adeimantus wants virtue to be simpler than this. He is remembering Socrates' opening words to Cephalus (328d–e, emphasis added): "Cephalus, I am really delighted to discuss with the very old. Since they are like men who have proceeded on a certain *road* that perhaps we too will have to take, one ought, in my opinion, to learn from them what sort of road it is –whether it is *rough* and *hard* or *easy* and *smooth*. . . . What *message* do you give of old age?" Cephalus has been, Adeimantus thinks, a most harrowing "messenger" (in Greek, *angelos*) from that unspeakable place, since for Cephalus it is full of terrors. Plato's second brother does not want to acknowledge such trials in his philosophy of heaven and earth.

Adeimantus' dream, that virtue's road not be so rough and steep, will not come true. Hesiod, not Adeimantus, will have the final word.

In the concluding "Myth of Er," Plato has retolled the message from the road of virtue. Er himself is the more adequate messenger, consummating what Cephalus began and Glaucon's shepherd-turned-underworld-messenger continued (see 359e–360a). Er is commanded to be a messenger of all his visions in the afterlife (614d), bringing back to us here the message from the gods' spokesman there (619b). Wonderful are the wonders Er sees, but most wonderful of all are the fateful choices of human souls. When souls arrive in the afterlife, they prepare for this choice of new lives with a thousand-year journey. If they are judged to have lived a blameless life, they are sent on a heavenly journey, and after experiencing indescribable beauty, they return for their choice pure and clean; but the others return parched and dusty from a laborious journey under the earth (614d–615e).

This much of Er's message has been everything for which Adeimantus longed. Be good, and you get pie in the sky when you die; be bad, and you sweat through the underground ascent. But the pie is a poisoned sweet. After they go through their purgatorial millennium, "there is an exchange of evils and goods for most of the souls." For when it comes to choosing a new life, many who came from heaven rush into imprudent new lives, trapping themselves in self-destroying self-indulgence, "because they were untrained in labors" (619d). Learning comes through suffering: the dirty souls choose better lives than the pure ones. This is the very path the soul of Odysseus is pursuing, having been cured of his ambition by his labors (620c). Hesiod's hard lesson is vindicated, and even in the afterlife, the "smooth" way, though heavenly, leads to vice, the "rough" and earthly way to virtue. Socrates agrees with the poet that the good way is not the smooth way. We are dragged from the cave, reluctantly and in pain, Socrates had told Glaucon. We journey from the comforting shadows into the burning sun "along the *rough* and *steep* ascent" (515e, emphasis added). Glaucon receives the very words Adeimantus rejects.

At first, Hesiod had said, virtue's road is hard, but smooth once one is on top. Does Socrates give any hope to Glaucon's devout wish to reach this consummation? The "message" of Er, Socrates does promise, is that someone who "always philosophizes in a healthy way" will find "the journey from this world to the other and back again not earthly and *rough*, but *smooth* and heavenly" (619e, emphasis added). But the example of Odysseus raises misgivings, since it shows how much laborious roughness it may cost to achieve this release from the snares of smooth imprudence. Will Glaucon's keenness for the ascent be blunted, if he divines he seeks a summit that awaits at a distance of a thousand years? So the dialogue rings its final change on this theme of Hesiod's. Introduced by Socrates' question to Cephalus, retold in Adeimantus' complaint, echoed in Glaucon's cave, at last it resounds in Er's underworld.

XI

Hesiod's complexities provoke Adeimantus' anxieties. Adeimantus demands a simpler, purer virtue, and he is willing to pay an inhumanly high price to get it. Not that Adeimantus is unintelligent; far from it. But he is a horizontal man. He lacks the erotic lift of his vertical brother. The potential tyrant bears the mark of eros, but the potential philosopher also springs up in this venereal soil. Untroubled by erotic passion himself, Adeimantus has no great patience for this intricate plot. His cropped humanity can countenance eradicating the tares of tyranny even at risk of the wheat.

Yet this desire, to make virtue simple and pure, is in its way as motive to philosophy as Glaucon's more musical and erotic desires. Plato mythologized these vertical desires through a rewriting of Homer. To read Adeimantus' horizontal desires, he has instead subscribed to Hesiod's story of "The Golden Age of Cronus and the Races of Metal" (*Work and Days* 109–201).

The basic structure of Hesiod's "The Races of Metal" divides human history into five ages. These ages seem to be arranged in pairs, roughly in a pattern of degeneration corresponding to the declining preciousness of the metals that characterize the ages. A golden race is followed by silver, then bronze is followed by a (rather anomalous) race of heroes, and finally there is our own iron race, with a hint that it too will have a paired successor. The whole series is cast as a temporal succession of five or six races, and so might most immediately be read diachronically, as mythical history. But the myth can also receive a plausible structural or synchronic reading, so that every pair of races would be related atemporally, as two complementary possibilities for human culture, one better and one worse.

Whatever Hesiod's intentions may have been, Plato, at any rate, rewrites the whole series of races both ways, as a temporal process of development and as an analysis of structures present at the same time. Socrates appropriates Hesiod's structure, first implicitly, in the "noble lie" or "Phoenician tale" that justifies and explains the class hierarchy of the best city (414c–415c), then explicitly, for the political and psychological analysis of degeneration in Books 8 and 9. Degeneration is the result of chaotic mixing of the different metals when the rulers are no longer "apt at testing Hesiod's races and yours," Socrates tells Glaucon, and "faction must always be said to be 'of this ancestry' whenever it happens to arise" (546e–547a).

Socrates' seemingly offhand Homeric tag, "of this ancestry," is another example of Plato's fine ear. During the Trojan War, Diomedes meets Glaucus on the battlefield. He asks Glaucus who he is, and Glaucus responds with the glorious story of his ancestors, concluding with the quoted phrase (*Iliad* 6.211). Diomedes then realizes he and Glaucus share an old family connection. So they do not fight, but decide to exchange armor in token of friendship. But in the punchline of the story, Glaucus foolishly exchanges his golden armor for Diomedes' bronze (*Iliad* 6.235–236). "To exchange gold for bronze" became proverbial for making a poor bargain; Socrates uses the phrase, for example, to reject Alcibiades' offer to exchange his sexual favors for Socrates' wisdom (*Symposium* 219a). Here, not finding a model for actually mixing up a base with a precious metal in Hesiod, Plato characterizes Socrates as discreetly insinuating one from Homer.

Socrates uses Hesiod, then, very broadly, to model four related but distinct aspects of politics: the *class structure* of regimes, especially in the ideal city-in-speech; the *process* of regime change; the variety of *personality types*; and the *development* of personality. Plato has written Hesiod's "The Races of Metal" as deeply into the bones of the *Republic* as Homer's "The Visit to the Dead." But as interesting as this schematic use of Hesiod's myth is, the *Republic* does not reveal its close reading and its detailed rewriting of Hesiod at this general level. As the "descent" theme proved a mythic commentary on logical and ethical dimensions of the dialogue, so does a mythic dimension of Adeimantus' longing for simplicity become audible when we listen to Socrates' echoes and elaborations of "The Golden Age of Cronus."

XII

Hesiod's first two races of men, the golden and the silver (*Works and Days* 109–42), were made by the immortals of Olympus, in the age when Cronus was king in heaven, before he was dethroned by Zeus. Both races are in a way still present in our age of Zeus, for they have become immortal "spirits" (in Greek, *daimones*; not connected to *thumos*, "spiritedness"). The golden spirits dwell on the earth, the silver under the earth. The golden spirits are active but disguised reformers among us, promoting justice as guardians (*phulakes*) and hidden kings (*Works and Days* 121–26):

> *But then this race were hidden under ground*:
> *They are called sacred spirits of the earth,*
> *Good guardians of death-suffering men,*
> *Keeping guard on lawsuits and evil deeds,*
> *Clothed in mist, roaming everywhere on earth,*
> *Granting wealth; they have this kingly power.*

In describing our own age of iron, Hesiod again notes the presence of these "guardians of death-suffering men, clothed in mist," adding the comforting detail that there are "three myriads" of them (*Works and Days* 253–55). These thirty thousand avatars from the simpler age of Cronus are joined in the age of Zeus by Justice herself, who also comes "clothed in mist" to avenge wrongdoing (*Works and Days* 223–24). "Clothed in mist": all three passages emphasize that these guardians are disguised.

The notion that human beings can be "spiritual" appealed to Plato in a number of different ways. For example, the notion that philosophy is essentially something spiritual is central to Socrates' speech in the *Symposium* (202e–203a) . But we hear the special resonance in Plato's imagination of this very passage from Hesiod in another dialogue, the *Cratylus*. Plato has Socrates read Hesiod so that men can be spirits, it seems, even before they die (*Cratylus* 397e–398c, emphasis added; Socrates quotes *Works and Days* 121–23, slightly inaccurately):

"Hesiod says at first there was a golden race of human beings, 'but then this race were hidden as fated: they are called sacred spirits under earth, good guardians of death-suffering men.' He called this race golden, not because it had sprung up from gold, but because it was good and noble, as he also says we are an iron race. But someone living now, if he is good, which means he is wise, belongs to that golden race. So I claim every man who is good is spiritual, *both when he is alive and when he is dead*, and is correctly called a spirit."

Hesiod made his good and golden men haunt our cities after they die. In Socrates' reading, good and wise men haunt us as spirits even while they live. Plato has reimagined Hesiod's myth to create an ambiguity, conflating the golden age of the past with its echoes in the present.

In the *Republic*, Socrates recites two of these same lines to Glaucon, to describe how the city-in-speech will honor soldiers who fall bravely in battle (468e–469a, quoting *Works and Days* 122–23, slightly inaccurately). We will say, says Socrates, such soldiers were "of the golden race," and we will "follow Hesiod in believing that '*They change to sacred spirits of the earth, good guardians of language-using men.*'" Following the pattern we have already seen so many times, Socrates uses with Glaucon a passage of which Adeimantus would have disapproved. For Adeimantus and Socrates agreed to remove passages of this sort of divine disguise. "Let none of the poets," Socrates had proposed to him, "tell us that '*The gods, looking like outlandish strangers, change to many shapes to visit cities*'" (381d, quoting *Odyssey* 17.485–86). Though here Socrates cites Homer talking about gods, Hesiod's use of the motif with spirits should surely fall under Adeimantus' purifying axe, too. And soon after, Socrates does casually include "spiritual beings" with the gods who do not change, in contrast to humans (382e). But when he summarizes this entire discussion a little later, he puts "spirits and heroes" together, separating both from "gods" (392a). In this context in the dialogue, what is at stake in associating spirits with humans rather than gods?

When Socrates suggested to Adeimantus that the gods do not change their looks or disguise themselves, he put the point by saying that gods are "simple" (380d). By stressing divine simplicity, Socrates was playing on an anxiety of Adeimantus, but the anxiety is not primarily theological. Adeimantus had never been bothered by the gods' changes before (380d, 381e). As with all the reform of the poets, his main concern is that stories of gods may serve as bad examples to the guardians. Adeimantus becomes worried only because the example of divine disguise may be taken to justify human lying. Adeimantus would like the simple gods to be emulated by simple men.

But Socrates is not so simple. The reasons he gives for why the gods never lie turn out to explain why humans sometimes must. Gods never lie, says Socrates to Adeimantus, for two reasons: they do not fear their enemies, and they do not have mad or foolish friends (382c–e). By contrast, humans may lie, or disguise themselves, for protection from enemies, or to help friends who cannot be reformed simply by unadorned arguments, say. Indeed, the very distinction between a clever enemy and a foolish friend is not so clear (see 334c–335b); the wise man will find much scope for his powers of indirection. Socrates introduces a simple disapproval of divine disguise with a view to this subtle approval of human lying.

When Socrates reclassifies spirits with heroes rather than with gods, then, he assimilates them to his own subtle guardians, rather than to Adeimantus' simple gods. This also has the effect of making Socrates' guardians more like the disguised spiritual guardians from Hesiod's golden age. But there is this difference between Socrates and Hesiod: Hesiod's golden race become disguised spirits only after death, while in the *Republic* as in the *Cratylus*, for Socrates the golden race are already here, disguised spirits even while they are alive. The good they do is limited, no doubt, and it would be greater if it could be accomplished in the open, on behalf of whole cities and peoples. But it is "no small thing" even if it must be accomplished "as if from behind a wall, out of a storm," by a man saved for philosophy exactly by being "spiritual" (see 496c,d, 497a). Are these spiritual men, perhaps, hidden philosopher-kings, promoting justice from the shelter of that unobtrusive private life we see Odysseus choosing at the dialogue's end?

When we are in the mood for this question, we hear the "disguised guardian" theme in an unexpected place: the larger context of the very passage from Homer that Socrates had quoted as his star example of what Adeimantus should censor (*Odyssey* 17.483–87). At this point in the *Odyssey*, Odysseus has returned home, but he is in disguise as a beggar, protecting himself from the corrupt suitors of his wife Penelope. They have colonized his household in his long absence, and he is discreetly biding his time until he can avenge their injustice. He is abused by the chief thug, one Antinous, whose name means something like "Countervailing Thought." Another suitor reprimands Antinous' unnecessary harshness and tries to put some fear of gods into this enemy of Odysseus' plans:

> *Antinous, don't strike this sad wanderer.*
> *Be cursed, if he be some god from heaven!*
> *The gods, looking like outlandish strangers,*
> *Change to many shapes to visit cities,*
> *Noticing men's hubris and their respect.*

The delicious undertones of this passage all but drown out Adeimantus' superficial disapproval of it. Odysseus himself is the disguised "god," noticing the hubris of the suitors. A man as well as a god may hide himself from the enemies of his thought when his safety is at stake. Adeimantus had wanted to exclude this passage for what it said about the gods, but for Socrates it is exemplary for what it says about humans.

Socrates had introduced this whole issue of disguise, or more pointedly of lying, when he suggested that Cephalus' view of truth telling was too "simple" once we take account of the madness or intemperance of those we want to help (331c). The echoes throughout the dialogue hint at the many turns there can be in the relationship between truth and justice. It is no surprise that intrepid Glaucon, not simplicity-seeking Adeimantus, gets the instruction when it comes time to apply Socrates' principles of subtle lying. The dialogue's two really big lies are, as it turns out, both connected with Plato's rewriting of "The Races of Metal," and both involve disguising the true nature of political necessities derived from erotic life. Glaucon and Socrates teach the citizens the noble lie that they have souls of gold, silver, bronze, and iron (414d–415c). This belief will help the citizens to accept the city's treating their children as public resources, to be assigned social roles on the basis of talent rather than family. More radically, Socrates explicitly refers back to the principles he established with Adeimantus to justify to Glaucon the "throng of lies" necessary to regulate the erotic couplings of the guardians (459c with 382c). These two erotic aspects of life, breeding and raising children, are exactly the topics under discussion when Socrates explicitly invokes Hesiod's myth near the beginning of Book 8 (546d–547a). Is this infusion of Glaucon's erotic heat into Hesiod's cold metal the most subtle of all that vertical man's ascendancies over his brother?

However this may be, Adeimantus' censoriousness is one measure of his aggressive simplicity. He wants motives undivided, and words univocal. In short, he is one kind of philosopher. No wonder, then, he accepts Socrates' proposal for their censorship of Homer and Hesiod: the poems will be considered only for their manifest meaning, "whether they are made with a hidden sense or without a hidden sense" (378d). This refusal to read the poets with any complexity appeals to every Adeimantus. But it is soon enough contradicted by Socrates' practice, who makes the *Republic* buzz with his fine falsehoods.

XIII

Adeimantus' interest in simplicity also shows itself in his affection for the rustic innocence of the age of Cronus. Hesiod's golden race lived like gods, "no sorrow in their heart," free from labor, in perpetual vigor. Their life was a feast, their death a falling asleep. The fields yielded every fruit spontaneously and lavishly, their flocks flourished, and they lived in quiet ease, friends of the blessed gods (*Works and Days* 111–20). Their simple life was like an idyll of childhood. By contrast, the silver race that succeeded the golden was not merely simple, but childish. They fell into hubris among themselves and were thoughtless of gods (*Works and Days* 130–37). The contrast between the childlike golden race and the childish silver race intimates that the simplicity and innocence before Zeus supplanted Cronus – before us – are ambiguous blessings. To be "innocent" may be noble, but it may also be stupid, as Thrasymachus' abuse of Socrates made clear (see 343a, 343d, and 348c). It all depends on what one does with one's simplicity in the Age of Cronus. This Hesiodic ambiguity, too, was important for Plato's imagination. In his most elaborate retelling of Hesiod's myth, in the *Statesman*, the goodness or badness of the age of Cronus depends on whether or not its inhabitants used their leisure and abundance for philosophy (272b–d).

Adeimantus' nostalgia for this bucolic life is comical, because he does not acknowledge the ambiguity of innocence. When he and Socrates first construct a city-in-speech, Socrates describes the idyllic existence of its inhabitants – one can hardly call them citizens, since they seem to have no political structures – as if he sees nothing lacking in a commune of naked, shoeless, hymning vegetarians (372a–b). When Glaucon protests that these people lead a meager existence, Socrates tweaks him by gushing over the simple pleasures of a diet of figs, chickpeas, beans, myrtle, and acorns (372c). This is intentionally provocative, in part because Socrates' praise of such simple fare is so hyperbolic, and in part because these plants are standard comic slang for the sexual organs (e.g., see Aristophanes' *Acharnians* 801–2). Glaucon is provoked to respond in kind (372d): "And if it were a city of pigs, Socrates, you were providing for, isn't this just how you would feed them?" Glaucon makes it clear the pigs he has in mind are sows, since he uses the feminine form of the pronoun "them" (*autas*). To the Greeks, the pig was a figure of ignorance (see 535e). Glaucon has taken aim at the silly innocence of Adeimantus' city. But he has also picked up Socrates' double entendres to hurl an obscene insult at this "true and healthy city," as Socrates calls it (372e). He makes the pigs sows because terms for pigs were vulgar slang for female genitalia (e.g., see Aristophanes' *Acharnians* 781–782 and *Lysistrata* 684). He charges this simplest city with failing to answer to the ambitions of a real man, a masculine prejudice Socrates must struggle to overcome in the later arguments for the political participation of women (note, esp., 540c).

Socrates calls the city of expanded desire that Glaucon seeks a "luxurious" and "feverish" city. But from this point on, he makes constructing the city-in-speech a matter of channeling Glaucon's expanded desire, rather than of preserving Adeimantus' simple paradise. It is all Glaucon's happy fault.

XIV

Can this life of fevered and restless desire be redeemed? Plato, it seems, imagined such a redemption as a return to Hesiod's golden age.

After Zeus dethroned Cronus, wrote Hesiod, he made a new pair of races, stronger than Cronus' golden and silver races, but also more warlike. The bronze race, "terrible and strong, devoted to Ares' dreadful works and to hubris," were succeeded by the fourth race, the race of heroes, "better and more just," but still involved in "evil war and terrible battle" (*Works and Days* 145–46, 158–61). The age of Zeus, then, is no childhood idyll, wise or stupid. But it is like the age of Cronus in having a lower and a higher potential. As the silver race is to the golden, the bronze is to the heroic race. The violence of the bronze race extinguished their very names (*Works and Days* 152–54), while the heroes, in the wars over Oedipus at Thebes and over Helen at Troy, remain a living memory (*Works and Days* 162–65). The heroes are, we might say, the poets' race, which is why they are anomalous in the myth, a race of words, not of metal. The heroes also have a special connection to the golden race. Zeus rewarded some of the heroes by sending them to live apart from other men, in the Isles of the Blessed at the ends of the earth. There Cronus is king again, the land gives three harvests a year, and like the golden race they have "no sorrow in their heart" (*Works and Days* 167–73).

Hesiod's heroes escape from their labors to the golden age of Cronus. But unlike the original golden race, they do not return to the age of Zeus as disguised spirits. Which is the pattern of redemption: first heroic labors, then escape to golden pleasures, or first golden pleasures, then return as reforming guardians? Socrates inscribes the tension between reform and escape into the very heart of the guardians, as he projects them onto both the original golden race and the race of heroes (540b–c):

"For the most part," [Socrates said to Glaucon], "each [guardian] spends his time in philosophy, but when his turn comes, he drudges in politics and rules for the city's sake, not as though he were doing a thing that is fine, but one that is necessary. And thus always educating other like men and leaving them behind in their places as guardians of the city, they go off to the Isles of the Blessed and dwell. The city makes public memorials and sacrifices to them as spirits, if the religious authorities approve; if not, as to happy-spirited and divine men."

The guardians are heroes who escape from drudgery to the Isles of the Blessed. But they are equally spirits who return to rule the city. Socrates conflates Hesiod's first and fourth races or, rather, he plays on both at once in a chord of unusual beauty.

Socrates completes his variations on Hesiodic themes of reform and escape by exploiting the analogy between "The Races of Metal" and the account of political degeneration in Book 8. After the regimes and individuals dominated by virtue, honor, and money are examined, the fourth regime is democracy. Both this regime and the corresponding type of individual come in for very harsh criticism from Socrates. Yet Plato has contrived to find something of the myth's fourth age, the age of the heroes, in democracy. Bad as the democratic regime might be in itself, Socrates tells Adeimantus, its freedom means "it contains all species of regimes," so that "the man who wishes to organize a city, *as we were just doing,* needs to go to a city under a democracy" (557d, emphasis added). In other words, democracy is the regime to be sought by someone in a reforming mood. The reformer can use democracy to improve on democracy and construct his own Isles of the Blessed. But the escapist mood of philosophy is present, too. The democratic individual, though he lives a disordered life, at least "sometimes spends his time involved with philosophy" (561d). That is, the license the democratic individual gives to every pleasure means philosophy can have a chance with him – not much of a chance, but some. The democratic individual is a bit like the student who takes an elective in philosophy: the student will probably forget all about philosophy when the semester is over, but some lucky few will form a lifelong attachment. Because the democratic regime does not require anyone to rule (557e), it leaves open the sort of escape from politics that Socrates had suggested accounts for those few true philosophers not corrupted by their surroundings (496b).

Democracies may be full of silly silver men and brutal men of bronze, but they also allow the escape of heroes back to the golden age, whether in reformed communities or as isolated individuals. This mythic praise of democracy is no less divine, and all the more elegant, for being delivered in a whisper.

SUGGESTED FURTHER READING

Blondell, R. 2002. *The Play of Character in Plato's Dialogues*. Cambridge. The long chapter on the *Republic* develops an especially stimulating account of the tension between the personal nature of the motives and interests of Glaucon and Adeimantus and the impersonal tendency of Socrates' view of virtue and justice.

Bloom, A. 1991 [1968]. *The* Republic *of Plato*, 2nd ed. New York. Bloom's translation has a long "Interpretive Essay" that, as Bloom says, "relies heavily on Leo Strauss's authoritative discussion ... in *The City and Man*." Bloom adds interesting details on particular passages, but stays very close to Strauss's central theme of the disconnection between the philosopher and the political community, and well as Strauss's attention to differences between Glaucon's and Adeimantus' understanding of Socrates.

Clay, D. 2000. *Platonic Questions: Dialogues with the Silent Philosopher*. University Park, Pa. The brief chapter on "Socrates Hērōs" is a very useful discussion of Plato's use of Hesiod and Homer to present philosophers as "spirits" (*daimones*).

Cavell, S. 2004. *Cities of Words: Pedagogical Letters on a Register of the Moral Life*. Cambridge, Mass. Cavell's title comes from *Republic* 592a–b, the conclusion of Book 9. The lecture "Plato" (along with the appendix "Themes of Moral Perfectionism in Plato's *Republic*"), though embedded in Cavell's larger discussion, is also a fine meditation on the "descent" theme and the links among the opening scene, the cave, and the myth of Er.

Edmonds, R. G. III. 2004. *Myths of the Underworld Journey: Plato, Aristo-phanes, and the "Orphic" Gold Tablets*. Cambridge. A very helpful account of Orphic initiation, and the ways Aristophanes and Plato take it up. Though focused on Plato's *Phaedo*, the book also will help the reader of the *Republic*. Edmonds has a particularly good general account in his first chapter of the competitive relationship Plato and other authors have to the myths they inherit and rewrite.

Empson, W. 1966 [1936]. *Seven Types of Ambiguity*. Revised ed., New York. Though about English poetry, not Plato, Empson's discussions in chs. 3 and 4, of how ambiguity allows a writer to convey complex thoughts, point to the sorts of complexity the *Republic* achieves in its appreciation and appropriation of myth.

Ferrari, G. R. F. 2003. *City and Soul in Plato's* Republic. Sankt Augustin; rpt. Chicago. The first chapter has an account of the political attitudes of Adeimantus and especially of Glaucon that is an important alternative to the one in this chapter.

Henderson, J. 1991. *The Maculate Muse: Obscene Language in Attic Comedy*, 2nd ed. Oxford. The standard reference on the vocabulary and social importance of sexual obscenity in the time of Plato, the book's larger discussions of sexuality and social criticism are thought-provoking for anyone considering "the city of pigs" and "the community of women and children."

Hobbs, A. 2000. *Plato and the Hero: Courage, Manliness, and the Imper-sonal Good*. Cambridge. Chapters 7 and 8 of this book have an unusu-ally detailed and perceptive account of the importance of Achilles in the *Republic*, including an alternative account of the significance of the recita-tion in the cave of Achilles' lament.

Howland, J. 2004 [1993]. *The* Republic: *The* Odyssey *of Philosophy*. Rpt., Philadelphia, Pa. A book-length commentary in the Strauss tradition, with an acute appreciation of the theme of "descent."

Morgan, K. A. 2000. *Myth and Philosophy from the Presocratics to Plato*. Cambridge. This book focuses only on the explicit myths told by Plato's characters, such as the Myth of Er, to the exclusion of implied myths, such as Homer's "Visit to the Dead," onto which Plato projects his characters. But its general discussions of the competitive relation between myth and philosophy (chs. 1 and 2) and of myth as a vehicle for speaking of what exceeds philosophical knowledge (ch. 6) are directly relevant.

Nightingale, A. 2004. *Spectacles of Truth in Classical Greek Philosophy: Theoria in its Cultural Context*. Cambridge. A study of the "gaze" on truth, chapter 3 is an excellent discussion of the themes that connect the *Republic*'s opening descent to "gaze" on the festival with the philosophi-cal "gaze" in the cave.

Roochnik, D. 2003. *Beautiful City: The Dialectical Character of Plato's Republic*. Ithaca, N.Y. A crisply written, novella-length essay in the Strauss tradition, with a view of the *Republic*'s appreciation of democracy more radical than the one defended in this chapter.

Strauss, L. 1964. *The City and Man*. Chicago. Strauss's essay is the most influential and controversial interpretation of the *Republic* in English, the starting point for hundreds of debates about how to understand the dramatic aspects of the dialogue. Indispensable whether you like it or not.

Vernant, J.-P. 1983. *Myth and Thought Among the Greeks*. London. The two opening essays on Hesiod's "Myth of the Races" are seminal discussions of the difference between seeing the myth diachronically, as a story of development, and synchronically, as a structural account of present society.

Vidal-Naquet, P. 1986. *The Black Hunter: Forms of Thought and Forms of Society in the Greek World*. Baltimore, Md. The short essay "Plato's Myth of the Statesman, the Ambiguities of the Golden Age and of History," taking off from Vernant, has a fine discussion of the ambiguous value of simplicity and innocence in Plato.

4 Wise Guys and Smart Alecks in *Republic* 1 and 2

A curious thing happens at the beginning of *Republic* 2. Socrates and Glaucon are seen to have sharply divergent opinions regarding Socrates' success in his preceding conversation with Thrasymachus. Socrates is sufficiently pleased with how things went that he is ready now to leave. He has made his argument against Thrasymachus who sought, first, to locate justice in the camp of vice and ignorance and, second, to claim for injustice greater profitability than justice (354b). To be sure, Socrates berates himself at the end of Book 1 for letting the question of the nature of justice get away and pursuing these lesser matters instead. And although he there insists – as he frequently does in Plato's dialogues – that until he has knowledge of the nature of a thing he can *know* nothing else about it,[1] he registers no real doubt about the outcome of his arguments. Indeed, at 368b he says to Glaucon and Adeimantus that "in what I said to Thrasymachus I thought I showed that justice is better than injustice." The only reason Socrates feels he must stay is because, as he observes, "you did not accept it from me." Glaucon, and apparently Adeimantus as well, are, then, far less sanguine about Socrates' performance than Socrates himself is. What Socrates regards as a done deal, Glaucon and Adeimantus make him see as a mere "prelude" (357a).

What is the source of Glaucon's and Adeimantus's dissatisfaction? Why do they not concede Thrasymachus's defeat (357a)? What both Glaucon and Adeimantus are unhappy with is not Socrates' conclusions but his arguments. As Glaucon not so subtly suggests, Socrates'

---

[1] Variations on the "priority of definition" principle may be found at *Grg.* 448e, 463c; *Euphr.* 7b–e; *H. Ma.* 286c; and *Meno* 71b.

arguments only *seem* persuasive; they are not really so.[2] Socrates, he contends, has "charmed" Thrasymachus "like a snake,"[3] but has offered no proof (*apodeixis*) regarding either justice or injustice (358b). In Glaucon's view, Socrates has failed to say what justice and injustice are and has failed to illuminate "what power each itself has by itself when it is in the soul, discounting its wages [*misthous*] and consequences [*gignomena*]" (358b). Adeimantus, too, criticizes Socrates' argument. As he formulates his complaint, twice – at 367b and 367e – in virtually identical language,[4] Socrates has not shown except *tōi logōi*, that is, except through (presumably specious *ad hominem*) argument, that "justice is superior [*kreitton*] to injustice." He has neglected to show what justice and injustice in themselves do to the man who has them such that justice counts as a good thing and injustice as a bad one.

Whose assessment is right? Has Socrates shown, as he believes he has, that justice is better than injustice? Or has he utterly failed to establish the superiority of the former to the latter? Has he considered what each is in itself? And has he done anything to show that justice is one of the "finest" goods, that is, the goods that belong in Glaucon's second category of good things, those that are "likable" (*agapēteon*) both in their own right and for their consequences (358a)? To be sure, Socrates knows he has not given a full-blown account of justice and injustice and of their respective consequences but, then again, that is not his way: he is no speechifier. Yet has he not perhaps, in his own way – that is, operating in refutation mode – said enough about justice and injustice and their consequences to

---

[2] Glaucon is registering his disappointment in light of his earlier brief exchange with Socrates in Book 1, in which Socrates had asked him whether he would want to persuade Thrasymachus that it is not true that the life of the unjust man is superior (*kreittōn*) to that of the just man, and Glaucon responded: "How could I not want to?" (348a).

[3] This is the sort of criticism that Socrates levels at sophists and rhetoricians. See *Prt.* 315b, where Protagoras is said to draw students from every city through which he passes, "charming them with a voice like Orpheus's – and they follow spellbound." See, too, the very beginning of the *Apology*, where Socrates says: "I do not know, men of Athens, how my accusers affected you; as for me, I was almost carried away in spite of myself, so persuasively did they speak" (17a).

[4] The only significant difference between the two instances is that the second time around Adeimantus adds the phrase, "whether it is noticed by gods and human beings or not" (367e), a phrase he used earlier at 366e, and which Socrates echoes at 580c.

indicate not only what he thinks they are but why the former is good and the latter bad both in themselves and in view of what comes from them?

Interestingly, for Glaucon's and Adeimantus's sake, Socrates is willing to depart from his normal course and say what he thinks. He consents to do for them what he was conspicuously unprepared to do for Thrasymachus: answer when he "does not know and does not profess to know" (337e). When pressed by Glaucon and Adeimantus to come to justice's defense, Socrates feels, though he is surely no wiser now than he was a moment ago, and though he can still, therefore, do no more than "speak my opinion" (368c), that he "cannot *not* help out" (368b).

Why, we must wonder, is Socrates willing to address Glaucon and Adeimantus in a way that he was unwilling to address Thrasymachus? Three possible answers suggest themselves: (1) because Glaucon and Adeimantus, if one takes them at their word, are on the *right* side: they are rooting for justice; (2) because they do not prevent Socrates from the outset from speaking in terms of the profitable; on the contrary, that is what they demand that he do – at least with respect to justice in itself (347e, 367d); and (3) because they really do want to hear what Socrates has to say.

Thrasymachus, by contrast, did not really want to hear what Socrates had to say; what he wanted was to be heard. As Socrates observes, "Thrasymachus clearly desired to speak in order to win a good reputation, since he believed he had a very fine answer. But he feigned wanting to prevail upon me to be the one to answer" (338a). In addition, Thrasymachus forbade Socrates to say that the just is "the requisite [*to deon*], or the beneficial, or the profitable, or the gainful, or the advantageous," calling all these "inanities" (*huthlous*, 336d), even though, as Socrates rightly points out, Thrasymachus himself defined the just in terms of advantage when he contended that justice is "the advantage of the stronger" (339a). And, most important, Thrasymachus is on the *wrong* side: he champions the cause of injustice.

If Glaucon and Adeimantus do in fact diverge from Thrasymachus in that they, unlike him, attack justice only out of the noblest of intentions, it is nevertheless the case that the arguments they advance in support of Thrasymachus's view are alarmingly forceful – even passionate. As Socrates remarks, if he were to judge Glaucon

and Adeimantus by the arguments they make and not by their character, he would not trust that they remain unpersuaded that injustice is
better than justice (368a–b). Indeed, as we shall see, their speeches on
behalf of injustice not only amplify but significantly modify Thrasymachus's view. Yet Socrates' strategy in responding to them is to
offer a rather general account of the superiority of justice over injustice – not to refute each of their new points. I argue in what follows
that the general account Socrates offers in response to Glaucon and
Adeimantus he has already offered, in its essentials, by the end of
Book 1: he has already explained both why justice is desirable for its
consequences and why it is desirable in itself for the soul (or city)
that has it. Although, to be sure, he later expands on the case for
justice he has made in Book 1, the early case contains the core of all
he can and will say in the *Republic* in defense of justice.

I. WISE GUYS

Thrasymachus is the quintessential wise guy. His view of justice is
that it consists of the rules that the strong, those who have political
power, impose on the weak, their subjects, who are then obliged to
obey the rules, thereby advancing the interests of the strong. His
formulations, "Justice is the advantage of the stronger," "Justice is
the advantage of the rulers," and "Justice is someone else's good," all
amount to the same thing. The just are suckers. They get the short
end of the stick. They advance the interests of those who compel
them to do their bidding. Justice is bad for those who are just, and
good only for others. Justice, according to Thrasymachus, has no
redeeming value for the just man himself.

Many readers of Plato think Thrasymachus is just the *Gorgias's*
Callicles by another name. To be sure, and both on the surface and
beneath, these characters are two of a kind. On the surface, there are
obvious similarities. Both burst into conversations of which they
were not initially a part (*Grg.* 481b; *Rep.* 336b); both berate Socrates
for his deviousness in argument (*Grg.* 483a; *Rep.* 341a–b) and for
his "irony" (*Grg.* 489e; *Rep.* 337a); and both are sore losers (*Grg.*
499b, 505c, 515b; *Rep.* 343a, 352b). And in their message as well,
they are strikingly alike. For both agree that the right way to live
is that to which convention gives the name "injustice." There are,
however, significant differences between them in the finer points of

their theory, if not in their basic message. Here are some of those differences.

(1) Callicles and Thrasymachus define "the stronger" differently. For Thrasymachus "stronger" is a political term: the stronger are those who are actually in power – whether the regime be a tyranny, an aristocracy, or a democracy. Those in power make the rules for the people they rule. These are the men who, therefore, determine what is "just." Although Socrates eventually corners Thrasymachus into differentiating between those who are rulers "in our manner of speaking" (340d) and those who are rulers "in precise speech" (340e, 341b, 342b, 341c, 342d), only the former being subject to error, it is clear, first, that Thrasymachus meant no such thing and, second, that he, unlike Callicles, has no notion that some men but not others rule "by right." Only Callicles holds that those who actually rule are not necessarily – and certainly not simply by virtue of the fact of their rule – stronger. For him, "stronger" is not a political term: those who are stronger or superior are more intelligent and courageous than others; they are the ones who rule "by right" – whether they rule in fact or not.[5]

(2) Thrasymachus, although he regards injustice as the best and therefore as the right way to live for those who can do so successfully, does not make the conceptual leap to regarding injustice as just. The truly distinctive feature of Callicles' thinking on the matter is his notion of the "just by nature." Whereas Thrasymachus regards injustice as virtue and even as beautiful (348e), it is Callicles who speaks of the injustice favored by nature as "justice." He advances the idea that the property of the weak belongs "by nature" to the strong, so that when the strong take that property they take what by nature belongs to them.[6] The strong cannot, then, according to

---

[5] Darius and Xerxes are Callicles' heroes. Callicles' seemingly counterproductive appeal to Darius's invasion of Scythia and Xerxes' invasion of Greece, both of which ended in defeat, is meant to show that Darius and Xerxes, even though they lost their battles, were, by virtue of their "superiority," within their rights to have fought them. What Callicles argues is that by nature one needs no justification for conducting an invasion other than the right of the strong to rule the weak and to have more. On the oddness of Callicles' using Darius and Xerxes to bolster his case, see Irwin 1979, p. 175; Fussi 1996, p. 122; and Nichols 1998, p. 74 n. 74.

[6] Heracles, Callicles recounts, drove off the oxen of Geryon though they were neither given to him nor paid for by him. But in Callicles' twisted view, the oxen actually belonged to Heracles (so that he is not really stealing them), because the possessions of the inferior and weaker belong to the superior and stronger (*Grg.* 484b–c).

Callicles, be strictly said to steal; they merely reappropriate what has been in effect stolen from them. Whereas Thrasymachus would say that it is good and beautiful and wise to do wrong, Callicles says that when strong and superior men do wrong they actually do right. I am not sure if Callicles' view that injustice is just by nature is more radical or less radical, more immoral or less immoral, than Thrasymachus's, Glaucon's, and Adeimantus's view that injustice is good, strong, and profitable – but not quite just. On the one hand, any position that would call the unjust just seems more horrific than a position that stops short of doing so. But, on the other hand, though perhaps somewhat perversely, such a position seems to accord more weight than the other does to the evil of taking what is not one's own. Whereas Thrasymachus, Glaucon, and Adeimantus will all extol the virtue of taking what is not one's own, Callicles will insist that the strong man has taken only what is his own. (There are also ways in which Callicles seems to endorse *conventional* morality. As early as *Grg.* 486b–c, Callicles calls Socrates' imagined accuser "very lowly" and "degenerate," and as late as 511b, he finds it most "infuriating" that a base man should be able to kill a noble and good one. See also 521c, where Callicles again characterizes as degenerate and lowly the person who would bring Socrates into court. Indeed, Callicles regards Socrates as having a good nature (486b; see also 485d) and as being a good and noble man (511b), and regards the accusation against him as one that charges him with "doing an injustice" that he did not do (486b)).

(3) Thrasymachus maintains that the source of justice is the rulers, the strong. They set down the laws that are to be obeyed by their subjects. There is for him no justice besides the laws and conventions that the ruled are required by the rulers to observe. For Callicles, however, the source of conventional justice is the weak, those who fear losing out to the strong and who protect themselves, at the expense of the strong, by dictating what is just and unjust, noble and shameful. Justice is the way in which the weak protect themselves from the strong who would, if left unrestrained, take more than others, leaving others with less. At the same time, justice is the way in which the weak eviscerate the strong, making them obey rules that are foreign to their nature and, indeed, foreign to nature herself.

Callicles' unique "conspiracy" theory of conventional law and justice, according to which the weak many scheme against the natural elite few to prop themselves up by bringing their natural superiors down, accounts for why it does not occur to those who link Nietzsche with Callicles to link him instead with Thrasymachus or even with Glaucon, who, as we shall see, also thinks justice is a way for the weak to protect themselves – but from one another.

For our purposes, it is the third difference between Thrasymachus and Callicles that is of critical importance. Since Callicles thinks the weak invent justice to suppress the strong, he must also think that manmade justice serves the interests of the weak, that it has good consequences for them. Conventional justice, as Callicles sees it, serves the interests of those who are resigned to having no more than their fair share and thus embrace equality, at the same time that it thwarts the interests of those who want and can get more than their fair share and thus have nothing but disdain for equality. For Thrasymachus, however, since justice is something the strong impose on the weak, it is not advantageous to the weak in any way. Although both views are cynical – both regard justice as a weapon wielded by some against others – only Thrasymachus's view makes justice unequivocally bad and unprofitable for those who are conventionally just.

Here, then, is Thrasymachus' view. Thrasymachus thinks that the strong should serve their own interests in two ways: (1) by way of justice, that is, by having others obey the self-serving laws that they, the strong, impose, and (2) by way of injustice, that is, by exploiting others, cheating others, "getting the better" of others, and taking from others what is not theirs to take. With respect to the first way, when Thrasymachus says that "justice is the advantage of the stronger" (338c, 341a), what he means is that the stronger advance their own interests by way of the justice of others. When he says that "justice is someone else's good" (343c), he means the same thing, namely, that when a person is just, his justice redounds to the benefit not of himself but of someone else. Were someone to object to Thrasymachus's view on the grounds that on those occasions when a ruler obeys the law or, in other words, does something just, he could not then be said to be furthering "someone else's" good but his own (since the laws advance the interests of the rulers), Thrasymachus would no doubt reply that at those times such a man will have ceased to be a ruler "in the precise sense." For Thrasymachus, since the true ruler operates above the law and outside justice, the ruler who obeys the law – even if it is of his own making – serves not his own interests but those of others, and no longer qualifies as a real ruler. (This is, of course, the strategy Thrasymachus employs in order to avoid admitting that when rulers mistakenly make laws that fail to reflect their advantage, justice turns out not to be "the advantage of the stronger.")

With respect to the second way in which the strong should advance their interests, namely, by the practice of *in*justice, Thrasymachus has nothing but good things to say. Injustice, he says, is goodness and prudence; the unjust man is the man who is good and wise, excellent and sagacious. For Thrasymachus, the better and smarter man will serve his own interests by shortchanging others. (Within a single speech Thrasymachus shifts, apparently unaware, from political justice, by which the ruler benefits from the obedience of the ruled, to interpersonal justice, in which "the just man everywhere has less than the unjust man" (343d). This is true even "when each [the just and unjust man] holds some ruling office" (343e).)

But Thrasymachus does more than describe justice and injustice, the just man and the unjust. He advocates the life of injustice, lauding it on the grounds that it is the more profitable. He points out that an unjust man gets more money and property, that he, unlike the just man, preserves the good will of friends and relatives, that he is thought by others to be blessed and happy, that he subjugates cities and men to himself. Yet none of these facts in themselves determines that injustice is more profitable than justice. One must make the claim, too, that having and doing such things makes one happy. Only if that is the case will *pleonexia*, rapaciousness, be to one's advantage.

And, indeed, this is the claim that Thrasymachus makes. Directing his attention to "the most perfect injustice," Thrasymachus considers whether it makes "the one who commits it most happy, and the one who suffers it and who is unwilling to commit it most wretched" (344a). For Thrasymachus, then, it is not simply that the unjust man gets more – money, reputation, power, property, profit – but that he is as a result most happy.

We note that it is not just any injustice that Thrasymachus (and similarly Glaucon and Adeimantus) thinks makes people exceedingly happy. The injustice that he applauds is injustice "in a big way" (341a1), injustice that is "perfect" or "the most perfect" whether in a person or in a city (344a, 348b, 351b), injustice "on a sufficient scale"

(344c), and injustice "entire" (344c). It is this kind of injustice that is "mightier, freer, and more masterful than justice" (344c). It is this kind of injustice that distinguishes the tyrant (344a), who not only takes the money of the citizens but also kidnaps and enslaves them. It is those who practice injustice on this level, that is, perfectly – and not simple cutpurses – whom everyone calls happy and blessed (348d); those who blame injustice do so only out of fear of suffering it (344c–d; see also *Grg.* 492a). Injustice on this scale renders a man invulnerable by virtue of his vast power.

(Although the man whom Thrasymachus extols is the one who succeeds in being *perfectly* unjust, he actually thinks that all injustice – on any scale – is desirable as long as one escapes punishment (348d). Of course, the less crafty and less powerful committers of injustice do get caught and, when they do, pay a hefty price (344b). But Thrasymachus is not one to do a cost-benefit analysis and determine as a result that justice is on occasion – viz., when the committer of injustice gets caught and punished – more profitable than injustice. The fact is that Thrasymachus simply has nothing good to say, anywhere, about justice; he sees the just man as a patsy, as someone who always loses out to the unjust man (343d–e). That the unjust man always gets the better of the just man is, according to Thrasymachus, no less true of the ordinary unjust man of 343d than it is of the perfectly just man of 343e–344a.)

Since Thrasymachus thinks so highly of injustice, it is hardly surprising that he is contemptuous of justice. The just man is "truly simple" (343c); so, therefore, is Socrates (343d). Although Thrasymachus cannot at first quite bring himself to call justice vice (348c; but cf. 348e),[7] he does say of it that it is genteel naïveté (348c), and he says of the just man that he is "urbane and naïve" (349b).[8] Since the just man has less and gets less than the unjust man (343d), since he is always the loser, how wise can the just man be?

Socrates is taken aback by the radical departure from conventional notions of justice and injustice that Thrasymachus espouses. Thrasymachus cannot, of course, as Thrasymachus himself realizes,

---

[7] At 348e Socrates gets Thrasymachus to confirm that he believes what he had earlier resisted saying, viz., that justice is a vice: "But I wondered about this, that you put injustice in the camp of virtue and wisdom, and justice in their opposites," to which Thrasymachus replies: "But I certainly do set them down thus" (348e).

[8] In the *Hippias Minor*, Hippias characterizes Achilles as *haplous*, simple, and it is clear that for Hippias this makes him less able, less skilled, than the wily Odysseus.

call justice virtue and injustice vice at the same time that he maintains that injustice is profitable and justice is not (348c). Nor, indeed,
can he call injustice a vicious tendency (*kakoētheia*, 348d), as he
should if he calls justice *euētheia* – simpleness. (Socrates engages
in word play here. When Socrates asks Thrasymachus, If injustice
is virtue, then isn't justice vice? Thrasymachus says no. So, when
Thrasymachus proposes that justice is *euētheia*, Socrates proposes
that injustice is its opposite, *kakoētheia*.)

Thrasymachus finally settles on calling justice good counsel
(*euboulia*, 348d).[9] Indeed, insofar as injustice belongs in the camp of
wisdom (349a), the unjust man is prudent (348d, 349d), and insofar as
it belongs in the camp of virtue (349a), the unjust man is good (348d,
349d). The just man, as the opposite of the unjust, is, for Thrasymachus, none of these things.

II. SMART ALECKS

Is the view that Glaucon espouses on behalf of the many a restatement of Thrasymachus's view? Do the many, too, believe that justice
has no redeeming value for the just? Are they, too, wise guys? Or is
Glaucon's view (a view he claims to be defending only as devil's
advocate) distinct from Thrasymachus's view?

Although Glaucon indeed presents the many's view as a reinstate-
ment and reinforcement of its Thrasymachean precursor (358b–c) (as
does Socrates at 358a), the fact is that Glaucon's analysis of justice
departs markedly from Thrasymachus's. As we saw, Thrasymachus
maintains that justice is wholly bad for those who are just. But the
many think that justice belongs in Glaucon's third category of good
things, the category containing things that are distasteful drudgery
in themselves but are pursued for the sake of their "wages" and for
the reputation and the other desirable things that result from them.[10]

---

[9] See *Prt.* 333d, where Socrates asks whether it is possible for the unjust to exhibit
good counsel, and Protagoras says yes. See also the *Hippias Minor*, where wiliness
as the mark of the liar (*ho pseudēs*) is aligned with ability, cunning, intelligence,
and wisdom (365d–366a) .

[10] Both *doxa* and *eudokimēsis* refer at times to seeming just and at times to the
reputation one gains, along with other rewards, *because* one seems just. Thus,
when Adeimantus tells Socrates to "take away the reputations, as Glaucon told
you to," he means the former (363a; see also 367b); when he links reputation with
"wages" (*misthous*), he means the latter, viz., that a good reputation is one of the
rewards, along with gifts and honors, of seeming just (358a, 367d).

So, unlike Thrasymachus, the many – with Glaucon as their spokesman – think there *is* something good about justice: not about justice in itself, to be sure, but about its consequences. Glaucon may
have "been talked deaf by Thrasymachus and myriads of others"
(358c6–7), but he is not Thrasymachus. Glaucon (if, for the sake of the
argument, we may identify him with the view he disavows but fer-
vently expresses) promotes his own brand of cynicism. To distinguish
him from the "wise guy" Thrasymachus, I shall call him a "smart
aleck."

How, then, does the "smart aleck" Glaucon differ from the "wise
guy" Thrasymachus? First, whereas Thrasymachus thinks justice
originates with the strong who impose it on the weak, Glaucon
thinks it originates with the weak who impose it on each other.
Second, whereas Thrasymachus recognizes no participation of the
ruled in the setting down of the laws and compacts that constitute
justice, Glaucon traces the origins of justice to a simple calculus
executed by the many, according to which it is more profitable – for
those, at any rate, who are not able to do injustice without suffering
it – to set down laws and compacts called just in order to prevent
both the suffering of injustice (the worst state) and its commission
(the best state). And, third, whereas Thrasymachus regards justice as
a source of unmitigated wretchedness for those who are just, Glaucon describes justice as "pleasing" (359a) and as "honored" (359b) as
a mean between the best (doing injustice without suffering it) and
the worst (suffering injustice without taking revenge) (359a–b).

In light of these differences, one might say that it is Glaucon and
not Thrasymachus who is a throwback to the *Gorgias*'s Callicles;
and even, perhaps, that it is the *Gorgias*'s Polus and not its Callicles
whom Thrasymachus most closely resembles. In Thrasymachus's
eyes, as in Polus's, nothing beats tyranny: the tyrant does whatever
he wants and takes whatever he wants with absolute impunity; he
is the envy of all other men despite their mealy-mouthed condem-
nations of him; moreover, as consummately unjust, he always gets
the better of those who are just. Yet Glaucon, like Callicles, regards
(conventional) justice as an invention of the weak. And although it
may appear as if Glaucon resists that aspect of Callicles' analysis
that sees justice as having been created by the weak for the express
purpose of domesticating the strong – on Glaucon's analysis, the
weak do not expressly conspire to control the strong by way of their

justice-compact – nevertheless, as we shall see, what Callicles' weak do by design, Glaucon's weak accomplish by default. Let us ask, then, what effect a justice forged by the weak for the weak has on the strong. Even if the strong are not partners to the justice-compact, are they not affected by it?

All people – weak or strong, just or unjust – are affected by the institution of justice devised by the weak. For with it a new dimension is introduced into the arena of social relations: the critical importance of appearance. Whereas Thrasymachus's strong man is not concerned in the least with appearances – he imposes justice on others without deception and without cunning – Glaucon's is. Whereas Thrasymachus's "craftsman in the precise sense" is merely one who knows his own advantage, the sense in which Glaucon's strong man is a "craftsman" is that he knows what is possible and what is not. Knowing that not everything is possible, he must employ a whole range of skills to gain the advantages he seeks: he must cultivate a good reputation, and, because he, unlike Thrasymachus's ruler, might "trip up" (361a, 361b), he must master the practice of persuasion, curry favor with others who will then be his "friends," and, on occasion, resort to brute force (361b). The fact is that when justice arises as a result of the many's taking matters into their own hands, even the strong, those who resist participation in the demeaning compact called "justice," have to play by the many's rules. Anyone, whether just or unjust, who *appears* unjust will not succeed. Once justice reigns, there are only two ways to avoid wretchedness: to be seen as just or, as in the case of the shepherd in possession of Gyges' ring, not to be seen at all. (It is noteworthy that even the basic benefit for the sake of which the weak invented justice, viz. to avoid suffering injustice, will not accrue to a man who is just but seems otherwise.)

And what of the just? For Thrasymachus, the just are simply those who behave justly: in their foolish naïveté, they do not even wish to commit injustice (344a). Moreover, Thrasymachus neither sees nor makes any distinction between those who merely seem just and those who are truly so. For Glaucon, by contrast, the man who is "simple and genteel" (361b) is one who wishes not to seem but to be just. Whether there could actually be such a man is, however, highly doubtful: no one, Glaucon thinks, is just willingly (358c, 359b–360d). For the sake of his argument, Glaucon nevertheless places side by

side the unjust man who seems just and the just man who seems
unjust to see how the two will fare. Is it even thinkable, he asks,
that the just man who seems unjust could be judged happier than
the unjust man who seems just? Will not the just man be whipped,
racked, bound, have his eyes burned out, and be crucified? The unjust
man, however, "because he pursues a thing dependent on truth and
does not live in the light of opinion (362a),"[11] will rule the city,
marry whomever he wants, enter into contracts and partnerships
with whomever he wants, and experience no qualms. He gets the better of his enemies in both private and public contests; he is wealthy
and hence does good to friends and harm to enemies. He offers sacrifices to the gods and thus cares for them far better than the just man
does. It is, therefore, appropriate that he be dearer to the gods than
the just man. So, any way one looks at it, the unjust man, *but only
as long as he appears just*, has a better life than the just man.

(We observe that many of the advantages that Glaucon sees in the
unjust life recall themes already taken up in Book 1. First, Glaucon
notes that the unjust man will be able to rule the city, yet Socrates
had contended in his exchange with Thrasymachus that no one
rules willingly (346e).[12] Second, Glaucon notes that the unjust can
enter into contracts and partnerships with whomever they want. But
Socrates had already challenged, in his conversation with Thrasymachus, the compatibility of partnerships with "perfect" injustice
(352c; see *Grg.* 507e for the same point). Third, what Polemarchus
had regarded in Book 1 as the mark of justice, namely, helping one's
friends and harming one's enemies (334b), Glaucon now associates
with injustice. And fourth, whereas Glaucon believes that the unjust,

[11] Cf. Antiphon, *On Truth*, in Pendrick 2002. Ironically, it is the unjust man who
operates under conventional constraints. For although he means to pursue the
things that are good by nature, wanting not to seem unjust but to be so, and although
in that sense Glaucon is right to say that he does not live "in the light of opinion"
(*pros doxan*), nevertheless, insofar as he must make a concerted effort to seem just,
he can hardly be said to be above *doxa*. By contrast, the just man, although he
pursues the things of which conventional opinion approves, is the man who lives
his life free of concern about appearances.

[12] It will become clear later on, particularly in Book 7, that Socrates knows full well
that everyone – with the exception of philosophers – clamors to rule. Indeed, in
the Book 1 passage itself, Socrates recognizes that men now do actually "fight over
ruling" (347d). What Socrates means, of course, is that no one wants to rule insofar
as ruling requires caring for others; what everyone "fights over" is the perquisites
that accompany ruling.

because of their greater wealth, are in a better position to offer pleasing sacrifices to the gods than are the poorer just men, Cephalus had regarded sacrificing to the gods as a manifestation of justice, of giving the gods their due (331b). Three of the good things, then, that were aligned with justice in Book 1 are aligned with injustice in Glaucon's speech in Book 2: sacrifices, helping friends and harming enemies, and partnerships. And ruling, which Socrates had in Book 1 characterized as neither good nor desirable, becomes for Glaucon in Book 2 one of the boons of well-disguised injustice.)

Although Glaucon praises injustice as superior by nature (358e) and as the course every man – just or unjust – would pursue were he able to get away with it, nevertheless, on his analysis of justice, justice has power, as do the weak. For once the weak are in charge, those who pay justice no heed will suffer dire consequences; both just and unjust must appear just if they are to live well. Since, however, the desired profits of justice attach not to being just but to seeming so, it follows that, in the end, the justice that is a third-category good is not being just but seeming so.

It is Glaucon's revelation of the overarching importance of seeming just that inspires Adeimantus to supplement his brother's argument. What really damns justice, Adeimantus contends, is not what those who praise injustice say against it but what those who praise justice say in its favor. He makes the smart-aleck observation that those who exhort to justice those in their care praise not being just but seeming just, since the good things they cite as inducements for being just – a good name, political power, and desirable marriages – attach not to the being but to the seeming (363a). Indeed, according to Adeimantus, even divine rewards are said to depend on reputation (363a). Furthermore, those who vilify injustice can find in it nothing unsavory; all they can say is that it brings divine punishment (363d–e).

There are, of course, praisers of justice (in prose and verse) who call it beautiful. But, Adeimantus points out, they acknowledge, too, that justice is hard and full of drudgery, while intemperance and injustice are sweet, easy to acquire, and shameful only by opinion and convention. Moreover, since they recognize that injustice is more profitable than justice, even these advocates of justice honor bad men who are wealthy and powerful and call them happy, and dishonor and dismiss better men who are weak and poor. Nor can they deny that many good men do not get from the gods the good lives they merit, nor the bad men bad lives. And, of course, gods can be bought off, and for that one needs money. Those who have no money, no matter how just, will not find themselves in the gods' good graces. If, then, the proponents of justice and detractors of injustice can offer no incentives to justice other than the rewards that come from seeming just, and no disincentives to injustice other than the bad things that come from gods who either do not exist or can be mollified, there are no good reasons to be just and not unjust.

Who is most vulnerable to the smart aleck message? According to Adeimantus, those most susceptible to this corrosive idea are young people "with good natures," those who are clever and not easily duped. These young men both see through the phony tributes to justice to which they are subjected from birth and recognize as more profitable the life that involves no compromise but contains instead the best of both worlds: doing injustice (without paying the price) while not suffering it (since they will seem just). These young men recognize the hypocrisy of their friends and relatives: they smell the lust for injustice on the breath of those who praise justice; they see through the pieties and proprieties of their elders.

Since these up-and-coming smart alecks see no advantage in justice for those who do not also seem just, and since they regard the life of justice as a hard one, they determine the life of appearing just to be by far the better. To be sure, even this life is not easy (365d), but since it is the happy one, it is worth the effort. To get away with injustice, one will have to form secret clubs and societies with others who are like-minded. One will become versed in the art of persuasion by learning from its teachers. When persuasive speech does not suffice, one will resort to force. And just in case the gods exist, one will offer lavish sacrifices to appease them. The most the just can hope for is not to be punished by the gods, but in the meanwhile they forfeit the profits of injustice. The unjust, however, will reap the rewards of injustice as they avoid punishment by offering up persuasive prayer.

Although Adeimantus, particularly in his description of these discerning young men and their shrewd calculation of their own advantage, echoes much of what Glaucon had said, he fails to appreciate the real difference between Thrasymachus's notion that justice is imposed by the strong on the weak, on the one hand, and Glaucon's idea that justice originates in the self-protective and therefore self-benefiting compact entered into by the weak. He recognizes, to be sure, as Thrasymachus did not, that the unjust will have to work to appear just, but since what he does not see is that in this way justice serves the weak and constrains the strong, he conflates the two views he has heard. He remarks that unless Socrates is willing to attach a bad reputation and its bad consequences to the just man and a good reputation and its good consequences to the unjust, and unless he can still identify something that makes justice good and injustice bad, he, too, will be seen to be, *like Thrasymachus*, a proponent of injustice, a man who believes "that the just is someone else's good, the advantage of the stronger, whereas the unjust is one's own advantage and profitable, but disadvantageous to the weaker" (367b–c). The notion that the weak serve the strong via justice is, however, strictly Thrasymachean; it is utterly foreign to Glaucon's way of thinking.

III. THE CHALLENGE

What both Glaucon and Adeimantus demand of Socrates is a defense of justice "in itself" and "apart from its wages and consequences." In other words, they want Socrates to demonstrate the desirability in itself of justice, to prove that justice is something one might choose to have for its own sake, something that one could actually take delight in and like (357b–c),[13] even if, insofar as one failed to seem just, none of the rewards of justice, none of its "honors and gifts," accrued to one (361c). What Glaucon would like to know is "what power it [justice] has all alone by itself when it is in the soul" (358b). What he would want to hear is justice extolled "itself by itself" (358d). And what Adeimantus, too, would like to know is "what each [injustice and justice] itself does with its own power when it is in the soul of a man who possesses it," "why the one [injustice] is the greatest of evils a soul can have in it, and justice the greatest good" (366e). Adeimantus is no more interested than Glaucon is in being assured that being just (and not just seeming just) has good

---

[13] Socrates recalls Glaucon's expression of 357c, "one we like [*agapōmen*] both for its own sake and for its consequences," when he says at 358a that justice belongs in the finest class, "which is to be liked [*agapēteon*, 358a], both for itself and for its consequences, by the man who is going to be blessed."

consequences. For even though he asks why justice is to be counted among things that are *fruitful* (*gonima*) by their own nature, and even though he asks of what *profit* (*oninēsin*) justice is to the man who possesses it (367d), what he means by these expressions is: why is it good for a man to have justice rather than injustice *in his soul*?[14] Indeed, when Adeimantus asks why Socrates locates justice in the class containing "the greatest goods" (367c), he characterizes these as goods "worth having for what comes from them but much more for themselves" (367c) and demands of Socrates that he "praise *this* aspect of justice" (367d). Adeimantus, like Glaucon, means for Socrates to "leave wages and reputations for others to praise" – things such as gifts, honors, and reputations attach, after all, to *seeming* just – and both men are far more interested in learning what justice and injustice are (358b), why being just is all by itself good for a man and injustice bad, why "in doing injustice [a man] would dwell with the greatest evil" (367a), and what injustice and justice *do to* the man who has them (367b and 367e) – as opposed to what they procure for him.

(It is not easy to articulate the difference between a thing's being good in itself and its being good for its consequences. Perhaps one way to see the difference is to pose the following question to oneself: is the thing before me pleasant and desirable, such that even if no other thing I regard as good results from my having this thing, I would still want it? If the answer is yes, one will have discovered something good in itself. Were one to pose this question with respect to seeing, Glaucon maintains, the answer would surely be yes; were one to pose it with respect to undergoing surgery, the answer would be no. An example of something good both in itself and for its consequences might be having in one's life a partner one loves. Insofar as just having such a partner is a joy and is life-enhancing, it is something good in itself. That one's economic situation improves as a result is an added bonus.)

---

[14] Glaucon also spoke, as we recall, of his belief that the just life is "more profitable" (*lusitelesteron*) and of his wanting Socrates to persuade Thrasymachus of that truth (347e–348a). For Glaucon, then, Socrates' showing that justice is "more profitable" than injustice is equivalent to his showing that the life of the just man is superior to (*kreittōn*) the life of the unjust man (347e) and, later on, to his showing "that it is in every way better [*ameinon*] to be just than unjust" (357b).

IV. SOCRATES' DEFENSE OF JUSTICE

Even before Glaucon and Adeimantus in Book 2 fully pose their challenge to Socrates, Socrates has, at least in his own estimation, gone a long way toward answering it. He believes he has already shown in Book 1 why justice is good in itself apart from its consequences, as well as why its consequences are good. Moreover, he has made no appeal, when identifying the consequences of justice in Book 1, to the "wages and consequences" – honors, gifts, reputation – that attach to seeming just. Whether arguing for justice's good consequences or for its goodness in itself, Socrates has had recourse to goods that attach only to *being* just. (The good consequences that Socrates brings back into the discussion in Book 10 at 612a–613e are not the benefits of justice itself but, quite explicitly, the benefits of seeming just, the benefits that Glaucon had asked Socrates to remove from the just man for the sake of argument. In Book 10 Socrates gives Glaucon reason to hope that the traditional "goods" will accrue to the just man who will, under normal circumstances, also appear just.)

The first defense of justice that Socrates offers in *Republic* 1 is a defense of justice in its political aspect. As was argued above, Thrasymachus conceives of justice primarily (or at least initially) in a political sense, first as the advantage of the stronger, and subsequently even more explicitly as the advantage of the rulers. In its political aspect, Socrates maintains, justice – that is, not seeming just but being just – brings great benefits.

Socrates, we note, is certainly sympathetic to the idea that justice is advantageous. It seems clear that, had he been given the chance to say what he thinks, he would have said, as Thrasymachus anticipates (336d), that the just *is* the advantageous. As Socrates puts it, to be forbidden in advance to say that justice is "the requisite, or the beneficial, or the profitable, or the gainful, or the advantageous" is like being forbidden to say that 12 is 2 × 6, or 3 × 4, or 6 × 2, or 4 × 3. Moreover, Socrates never challenges Thrasymachus's notion that justice is "someone else's good." The only thing he finds objectionable in Thrasymachus's definition is his identification of the beneficiary of justice as "the stronger." As Socrates points out, rulers "in the precise sense" always rule for the sake of the ruled, for the sake, that is, of the weak. Here, then, is what must be Socrates' definition of political justice: "Justice is the advantage of the weaker."[15] Political justice has great value, great profitability, because of its salutary effects on the ruled. Besides setting the city in order, political justice provides moral guidance to those who cannot or do not properly guide themselves (590c–d).[16] When Socrates says, then, in Book 2, "I, for my part, suppose that it [justice] belongs in the finest one, which is to be liked, both for itself and for its consequences, by the man who is going to be blessed," the consequences to which he refers are those that redound to the ruled when the rulers are just. Socrates thus defies the Thrasymachean contention that the consequences of justice are beneficial to the strong. If the *Republic* is a sustained argument for the value to the polis of having the men who are most just – philosophers – rule, what Socrates says in Book 1 anticipates what follows. The philosopher is suited to rule on account of his wisdom; but that he is not unwilling to rule, despite the fact that ruling is beneficial not to himself but to others, can be attributed only to his justice.[17] Since neither Glaucon nor Adeimantus means by the profitability of justice anything but what favorably affects the just man himself, it is hardly surprising that they fail to notice Socrates' hints at justice's good *political* consequences, namely, the benefits good rulers bestow on the ruled.

It is important to note that, according to the *Republic*, nothing but justice can obligate a philosopher to rule. Ruling, as it is described in Book 1 as well as in Book 7, is in itself an onerous task, laborious drudgery that is seen by the best men as not good (347c) and by philosophers as not fine (540b). Since ruling is in its essence caring for others and hence beneficial to *them*, even those who wish to rule, Socrates maintains, do not desire the ruling itself, but the rewards that ruling brings them: power, wealth, honor, and limitless freedom, as well as the things that power, wealth, honor, and limitless freedom secure. Even for the eager-to-rule ruler, then, ruling

---

[15] See Strauss 1964, pp. 127–28.

[16] Cf. *Grg.* 517b, where Socrates says that a good politician "leads the desires in a different direction, not yielding, but persuading and forcing them toward the condition in which the citizens would be better."

[17] We may contrast Plato's philosopher with Aristotle's (*Nicomachean Ethics* 10.7–8). Aristotle's philosopher does not rule and is, in that sense, quite useless. Like the gods, Aristotle's philosopher does what Plato's would like to do: transcend the realm of justice.

belongs in Glaucon's third category of good things, things that are desired not in themselves but only for their consequences for the agent.[18]

(It is true that in Book 6 Socrates claims that philosophers in a suitable regime would accomplish the "greatest of things" and would "grow more and save the common things along with the private" (497a). Let us note, however, first, that the context in which this is said is one in which Socrates seeks to prove to Adeimantus that philosophers need not be useless; they are useless only because their skills go underappreciated by nonphilosophers. Second, it is in comparison with the plight of philosophers in unsuitable regimes, where they can barely shield themselves from the injustice that surrounds them and are lucky if they can live their lives with their own justice and piety intact, that they surely would "grow more" were they to rule in a suitable regime. The passage gives us no reason to think that philosophers would "grow more" as rulers if the alternative to their ruling in a suitable regime were for them to live the philosophical life as described in Book 7. But third, and most important, Socrates says nothing to indicate that philosophers, even in a suitable regime, would want to rule or would find in ruling anything other than drudgery. Even if they would accomplish great things for the ruled, that hardly entails their wanting to rule. Indeed, within just two Stephanus pages Socrates rather broadly hints that philosophers will *not* want to rule: "before some necessity happens along to compel those few philosophers who are not base – the ones now called useless – to tend to a city, whether they want to or not." (499b).)

In addition to the compensations of money, power, honor, and freedom that appeal to the cruder sort of man, the *Republic* identifies two incentives that might motivate a better class of men to rule.[19] The first of these is identified in Book 1 as the consolation of not being ruled by worse men (347b–d); the second is identified in Book 7 as the obligation owed to the polis in return for the extensive education and nurture that make philosophy possible (520a–e). Of the

---

[18] See *Grg.* 466–468 where bad and intermediate things are not desired for themselves. In the *Republic*, unlike in the *Gorgias*, however, bad things that bring good or desired consequences are called, by Glaucon, good things. See Heinaman 2002.

[19] It is striking that Socrates does not mention the value to just men of not being surrounded by unjust men, as he does at *Ap.* 25e and *Prt.* 327b. See also *Laws* 728b–c.

two, only the second, the demand of justice, motivates the philosopher. Although the first motivation is said to sway men characterized as "decent," "most decent," "good," and even "best," these men are also described as caring about appearances: "they do not wish to take wages openly . . . and get called hirelings, nor secretly on their own to derive profit from their ruling and get called thieves" (347a–b).[20] No matter how decent and good such men are, they certainly are not philosophers. (Note that this "compensation" was clearly not sufficient to motivate Socrates to enter politics. Contrary to what is commonly believed, Socrates does not regard philosophers or anyone else as moved solely by considerations of "rational egoism." He does not see people simply as better and worse calculators of their own interests.)[21]

It is not until Book 7 that the philosophical motivation of justice comes to light. In Callipolis – and only in Callipolis – philosophers are justly compelled to rule (520a, 540a–b; cf. 500d), because only in a polis to which the philosopher is indebted to the citizenry does justice exert a claim on him.[22] Although even in Callipolis the philosopher will have to be "compelled" to rule – for, first, if he lusted after rule he would be no philosopher (520e–521b): his concept of ruling would be one of self-aggrandizement at the expense of the ruled; and, second, he has discovered a better place and a better way to live, away

---

[20] In Book 10 it is said of "decent men" that they, with rare exceptions, "enjoy" Homer and other tragedies (605e). What such men would not wish to be seen doing when they suffer their own personal grief they allow themselves to do in response to tragedy. The man who is philosophically just, that is, just even when no one is looking, is perhaps best described by Adeimantus at 366c–d: he finds injustice disgusting because of his divine nature, or he has attained the kind of knowledge that keeps him away from it.

[21] For a defense of this view, see Weiss 2006, pp. 47–68.

[22] That justice cannot be reduced to rules (as Socrates shows in his exchange with Cephalus in *Rep.* 1) in no way mitigates the general bindingness of the rules of justice. In the case he presents to Cephalus, Socrates provides the reason that ordinary moral rules must be suspended: adherence to them would cause harm (331c). There are strong indications in the *Crito* (49a–e) and in the *Apology* (41d–e; see also 37b–c), as well as in Socrates' extensive exchange with Polemarchus in the *Republic* (335a–e), that at the very core of justice lies a no-harm principle. Socrates' exchange with Polemarchus culminates in his declaring that "it is not the job of the just man to harm either a friend or anyone else" (335d) and that "it is never just to harm anyone." So, a moral rule such as "pay your debts" is for the most part morally binding; exceptions are made only when obedience to the rule brings harm in its wake.

from the affairs of human beings (517c7–9) – the compulsion takes the form of an argument from justice: "we will say just things to them, compelling them to care for and guard the others" (520a).[23] When philosophers hear the justice argument, they will surely not disobey us and will not "be unwilling to participate in the labors of the city, each in his turn. . . . For surely we shall be imposing just duties on just men" (520b–d).[24]

(Eric Brown has argued that "justice alone does not force the philosophers to opt for the lesser happiness of ruling. . . . Were there no law, the philosophers would act justly and achieve maximal happiness by refusing to rule."[25] Brown regards obedience to just law as a principle distinct from what he calls the "principle of reciprocity" and thinks that were it not for this supplementary principle, philosophers would not rule, and their not-ruling would not constitute injustice. This reading is not, in my view, supported by the text. According to the text, the only reason that the philosophers will obey the law is because of the justice (or reciprocity) argument. Nevertheless, that there is a law mandating philosophical rule does play a part in the justice argument. For justice cannot demand that philosophers rule unless the following *two* conditions hold: (1) that philosophers are indebted to the polis and (2) that the polis *wants* philosophers to rule. It is not, then, that obedience to law constitutes a separate principle that philosophers regard as binding, but rather that the existence of a law requiring philosophers to rule is an indication that philosophical rule is wanted. Philosophers have no obligation to rule where they are not wanted. They should no more beg to rule than doctors to heal. Just as it is appropriate is for the sick to beg to be healed, so is it fitting for those in need of rule to beg to be ruled (489b–c).)

To be sure, unless philosophers are perceived as selflessly taking on an undesirable task for the sake of others, the citizens would never be persuaded, first, to accept their rule and, second, to provide

---

[23] Not all compulsion takes place through violence or the threat of violence. At *Ap.* 35d, for example, we find the expression "to persuade and force you [*biazoimēn*] by begging."

[24] For the view that the compulsion to which the philosopher succumbs is not the justice argument of Book 7 but the consideration in Book 1 that unless the best men rule they will be ruled by their inferiors, see chapter 10, section II, of this volume.

[25] Brown 2000, p. 10.

for their education and sustenance. For nonphilosophers crave ruling; they want to be the rulers. To them the argument must be made that it is the general happiness, and not any one particular group's happiness, that is of paramount importance (420b, 519e). Indeed, from the founders' perspective, that, too, is the reason philosophers must rule. But for the philosophers themselves, only the justice argument compels. That is why the founders must supply it. It is justice in the form of repaying a debt – and not the beneficence of advancing the welfare of the polis – that motivates the philosopher to rule. Indeed, were the philosophers compelled to rule without respite, the justice argument would be invalidated: philosophers are indebted to the citizens of Callipolis only insofar as the citizens make it possible for the philosophers to live the philosophical life.

For the philosopher, the particular just act of ruling in Callipolis is as unwelcome in itself as most acts of justice are to other (especially unjust) people. Socrates never pretends that doing what justice demands is appealing to all people – even the most wise – on all occasions. It is *being* just, having the condition of justice in one's soul, that appeals. (The ambiguity in the term "justice," which can mean being just as well as doing acts that are just, has been with us since Glaucon placed justice – doing just acts – in the class of beneficial drudgery (358a), yet demanded a defense of justice, when it is "all alone in the soul" as good in itself.) But since in order to become just one must act justly, that is, refrain from acting unjustly, acting justly is "profitable" (445a, 588e, 589d, 591a): it "produces and preserves" justice in the soul (443e–445b, 588b–591c).[26] Like doing gymnastic exercise or undergoing medical treatment, acting justly belongs in Glaucon's third category of goods: it is not enjoyable or desirable in itself but brings good consequences. (For good reason Socrates keeps fairly well concealed his recognition that *doing* justice is not desirable in itself.) What belongs in the "finest" category is being just: it is

---

[26] It is significant that, for the most part, when Glaucon and Adeimantus ask Socrates to prove that justice is more profitable than injustice, they want to know how having justice or injustice in one's soul benefits or harms the one who has it, but whenever Socrates makes the point that justice is "profitable" (*lusitelei*) and injustice detrimental, he speaks not of the justice and injustice in the soul but of the just and unjust *actions* that bring about and maintain the conditions of justice and injustice in the soul. Socrates recognizes that it is *doing* justice that is "profitable" for oneself, but *being* just that is desirable and good in itself for oneself.

this condition that is like the condition of health, which is good and desirable in itself – a source of joy and pleasure to the person in that condition – and good for its consequences. Unlike physical health, however, whose good consequences benefit the agent himself, the good consequences of a healthy soul benefit primarily not the agent himself but others. For once a man is just he does not do wrong, and that he does no wrong serves the advantage of others – not only in ruling but in all things. Of course, refraining from injustice also does preserve the just condition of the just man's soul: were a just man to act unjustly, he would damage his soul as surely as a healthy man who lives unhealthily would destroy his body. But being just, unlike being healthy, changes a man's desires: "the just man will never wish to do injustice" (*Grg.* 460c). Just men can therefore be counted on to act justly. And philosophers, qua just men, can be counted on to rule when ruling is what justice demands, despite their view of it as onerous and undesirable. They will rule because refraining from injustice follows from the just condition already firmly rooted in their souls. In ruling, the philosopher will produce good – even great – consequences for others, namely, the orderliness of the city and the increased virtue of the citizens. And these consequences – if not the means by which they are achieved – are indeed desirable to him. That is why Socrates says of "the man who is going to be blessed" that justice, that is, the justice in his soul, is desirable to him not only for itself but for its consequences as well (358a).

The notion that justice is desirable in itself is one that Socrates introduces in Book 1 and develops in Book 4. He argues that justice is what brings harmony to a soul (or to a city); it is that without which the soul (or city) could not work well. The argument proceeds ad hominem, attacking the Thrasymachean claim that the way to be happy and blessed is by cultivating "perfect injustice." What Socrates' argument *shows* is that it is precisely the perfectly unjust who can accomplish nothing, for surely some measure of justice is needed if anything is to get done. But what the argument *implies* is that the more justice people have within, the more in harmony they are with themselves, with others, and with the gods. By introducing the idea that justice is harmony, Socrates challenges the Thrasymachean view that justice is of no value to the just man himself. Moreover, Socrates' conception of justice in Book 1 as internal harmony – whether in city, clan, army, or individual – prefigures his characterization of it in Book 4 as the healthy condition of the city (434c) or soul (445a–b).

Socrates' argument for the superiority of justice to injustice in Book 1 is not complete, however, until the soul is introduced. Having argued there, admittedly lamely, that justice is virtue and wisdom, and injustice vice and ignorance (350d), Socrates "reminds" Thrasymachus that he "agreed" that justice is the virtue of the soul (353e). Although this is actually the first mention of the soul (what Thrasymachus had actually agreed to was only that justice is virtue and wisdom, at 350d),[27] Thrasymachus says: "We did so agree." And now Socrates concludes that insofar as justice is the virtue of the soul it is the sine qua non of a good life, that is, of a life well lived. The particular argument Socrates offers for this last point is frivolous at best. It runs as follows: (1) there are certain tasks that a man cannot do without a soul; (2) the soul cannot do these tasks well without its proper virtue; (3) one of the soul's tasks is to live; (4) the soul's proper virtue is justice; hence, (5) a man cannot *live well* without justice.[28] Despite the dubiousness of this argument, its point could not be more serious. Indeed, the idea that a person cannot live well without the soul's proper virtue, justice, is the point that Socrates makes to Crito in the *Crito*, to Hippocrates at the beginning of the *Protagoras*, and to Polus and again to Callicles in the *Gorgias*. If what determines whether a life is well lived or not is the state of one's soul, then a just man necessarily lives well: his justice is something that is good in itself *for him*. Moreover, if a just man, because he is just, rules others, thereby improving their souls, then others live well: the just man's justice is thus desirable for its consequences. Justice, like the other things in Glaucon's second category of good things – thinking and seeing and being healthy – is desirable both for itself and for its consequences.

If Socrates is satisfied at the end of Book 1 that he has shown that justice is better than injustice, it is because he has said in justice's

---

[27] That justice is human virtue had already been agreed to by Polemarchus at 335c.

[28] We see in Book 4 that the connection Socrates sought to establish in Book 1 between having a just soul and living well made its mark on Glaucon. For Glaucon says: "If life does not seem worth living with the body's nature corrupted, not even with every manner of food and drink and every manner of wealth and every manner of rule, will it then be worth living when the nature of *the very thing by which we live* is confused and corrupted . . .?" (445a–b).

defense all that he could: justice as harmony is desirable in itself; and the consequences of justice are good for others. Socrates maintained against Thrasymachus that a just ruler will promote the advantage not of himself, the stronger, but of the ruled, the weaker. That his arguments against Thrasymachus are poor at best, egregiously flawed at worst, reflects his way of dealing with overconfident bullies who lack even a modicum of respect for ordinary decency. Indeed, he handles Thrasymachus in the *Republic* much as he handled Polus in the *Gorgias*.

In addressing the concerns of respectable and respectful men such as Glaucon and Adeimantus, however, men who want to hear justice praised and, moreover, want to hear Socrates do the praising, Socrates seizes the opportunity to lay out a vision of the just and beautiful city and man. In the *Republic* Plato provides Socrates the rare occasion to engage interlocutors who, while not by any means timid or reticent, nevertheless hang on his every word. It is here that Socrates is able to paint a picture of justice on a grand scale. In doing so, however, Socrates never ventures far from the themes of Book 1: justice is harmony in the city or soul; and acts of justice do indeed have good consequences – for others.[29]

WORKS CITED

Brown, E. 2000. "Justice and Compulsion for Plato's Philosopher-Rulers." *Ancient Philosophy* 20: 1–17.

Fussi, A. 1996. "Callicles' Examples of *nomos tēs phuseōs* in Plato's *Gorgias*." *Graduate Faculty Philosophy Journal* 19: 119–49.

Heinaman, R. 2002. "Plato's Division of Goods in the *Republic*." *Phronesis* 47: 309–35.

Irwin, T., trans. 1979. *Plato: Gorgias*. Oxford.

Nichols, J. H., Jr., trans. 1998. *Plato: Gorgias*. Ithaca, N.Y.

Pendrick, G. J., ed. 2002. *Antiphon the Sophist: The Fragments*. Cambridge.

Strauss, L. 1964. *The City and Man*. Chicago.

Weiss, R. 2006. *The Socratic Paradox and Its Enemies*. Chicago.

[29] I wish to thank Robert Heinaman and especially John Ferrari for reading and critiquing this chapter. Their incisive comments helped me to improve it.

5 Justice and Virtue

The *Republic's* Inquiry into Proper Difference

The *Republic* is traditionally subtitled "On Justice," and when we begin reading the dialogue, it seems clear that justice is to be its central topic. Book 1 in fact could be read as an independent dialogue specifically about justice, on the model of those Platonic dialogues devoted to the discussion of single topics, topics such as piety in the *Euthyphro*, the highly elusive *sōphrosunē* in the *Charmides*, or understanding in the *Theaetetus*. So we might imagine Book 1 as an aporetic dialogue with a central eponymous character and dedicated to an investigation of justice, a dialogue entitled perhaps "Thrasymachus" with the subtitle "On Justice," the subtitle that Thrasyllus in fact gave to the entire *Republic*.[1]

But as we read further into the dialogue, and particularly as the argument begins to develop in Book 2, the focus of the discussion appears to shift to a larger concern, a concern with the general topic of virtue, and specifically virtue in relation to individual happiness. When I was first introduced to the *Republic* as a student, I was told that it is about this question of the relation of virtue to happiness, either in the form of the question of the rewards of virtue or in the form of the cognate question of whether there is a conflict between duty and interest. It is in terms of this larger question that the dialogue is often presented; the surface question remains one concerning the nature of justice, but the larger question that is seen to emerge is some version of the question of whether virtue is sufficient for happiness.

In this respect the *Republic* may be thought to reflect a more general feature of Platonic dialogues: the complexity of their subject

[1] See Tarrant 2000.

matter. Often a dialogue's topic is unclear, and in dialogues that appear to have an overt topic that appearance often vanishes on a deeper reading of the conversation. Is the *Phaedrus* about love or about rhetoric? Is the *Gorgias* about rhetoric or about (in the words of one ancient critic) "the ethical principles we require for political happiness"?[2]

This is a fact that seems hardly worth mentioning in the case of the *Republic*, whose scope is so broad as to include virtually every important issue Plato discusses anywhere and which yet weaves them together, miraculously, in a work of seamless artistic genius. It is that seamlessness that makes debates about the dialogue's central focus seem at once endless and pointless: is the *Republic* a work about social philosophy or a work about individual virtue? Is the picture of the ideal city merely an allegory for the soul, or a self-standing political program? Are the long discussions about ontology and epistemology merely excursions in the service of the political and ethical force of the dialogue, or are they subjects for which the earlier discussions are preparatory? These questions seem to fade in the face of the integrity and coherence of Plato's artistry, and may divert us from seeing the connections and analogies that Plato invites us to see.

But in spite of all this, justice remains the thematic thread that weaves its way through the course of the dialogue's long discussion and that seems to stand as the paradigm of virtue insofar as that discussion is devoted to the question of virtue's rewards. In this chapter I propose to look at the two concepts of justice and virtue together, to see how they might reveal some aspects of Plato's thought in this rich and complex dialogue. Specifically, I want to show how attending to the question of the relationship in the dialogue between justice and virtue will reveal a central feature of Plato's theory of justice in the *Republic*, the respect in which justice is a principle of *appropriate difference*, a virtue that governs the articulation of right and proper division.

I

What, then, is the relationship between justice and virtue? Here's a simple place to begin: justice *is* virtue. An easy reading of the dialogue might lead us to identify justice and virtue, or at least to see justice

[2] Olympiodorus, in Westerink 1970, p. 4.

as a paradigmatic form of virtue. On such a view, the question that
begins in Book 2 may be read simply as a continuation of the discussion of Book 1. The initial concern with the nature of justice is
revealed on reflection to be a general concern with the nature of
virtue and specifically with the reasons for pursuing it, that is, with
the question of the rewards of a good life.

It's not difficult to see the attractiveness of such an identification
and to see why it is that we often tend to think of justice as a pivotally
necessary feature of virtue in general, not merely one aspect of a
virtuous life but a condition central to our very concept of a virtuous
life. Two reasons might be thought to lead us in this direction. First,
we tend to think of justice as a primary mode of *social* morality,
conceiving of it as the central condition of social or political virtue,
and we then, in turn, take social or political virtue as primary or
even essential to our notion of morality. Second, we are impressed
with the fact that justice concerns our relations to others; if we think
that our moral, in contrast to our prudential, concerns are essentially
about such relations to others, this fact might lend credence to the
centrality of justice in our moral repertory. On both of these views,
justice, precisely because it is seen to organize the moral habits and
modes of actions and institutions in which as individuals we are able
to flourish in our dealings in the political and social realm, comes
to be viewed as the cardinal social virtue. It is surely some such
reasoning that leads to John Rawls' claim at the beginning of his
Theory of Justice: "Justice," he writes, "is the first notion of social
institutions, as truth is of the system of thought."[3]

When we think of justice and virtue this way, we can perhaps
understand why justice was such a key concept in Greek moral
thought, and why the Greek *dikaion* – just – and *adikon* – unjust –
were standard adjectives describing right action and wrongdoing. To
feel comfortable with this connection and to recognize the respect
in which justice might name a larger sense of moral or political law-
fulness, recall Aristotle's remarks at the beginning of Book 5 of the
Nicomachean Ethics.

Justice and injustice appear to be said in several senses: A person who breaks
the law and a person who takes more than his share, that is, an unfair

___

[3] Rawls 1971, p. 3.

person, are both said to be "unjust." So "just" means both lawful and fair and "unjust" both unlawful and unfair.

(*Nicomachean Ethics* 5.1, 1129a27–35)[4]

Compare, in a contemporary setting, the fact that the United States Department of Justice is concerned not merely with those aspects of criminal activity and judicial response that have to do with fairness and equity or with people getting a proper share of the goods and services of society. The aim of the judicial system itself is often thought of as achieving justice. We are then led to reconcile the larger and the more specific senses of justice by thinking of the judicial as charged with seeing to it that criminals and sometimes victims receive "what they deserve."

II

The view that I've sketched, as well as depending on a broad understanding of *justice*, depends on a very broad understanding of *virtue*, an understanding in which "virtue" refers to a general state or condition of morality. But as we read the *Republic*, we very soon come to realize the infelicity of such a view as an interpretation of Plato. Recall the first introduction of the concept of virtue in our dialogue. Early in Book 1 of the *Republic* Socrates and Thrasymachus are discussing what happens when a horse is injured, and Socrates asks whether a horse, when injured, "becomes worse with respect to the virtue of dogs, or that of horses?" and answers: "the virtue of horses" (335b).

The context here makes clear that when Socrates speaks of the virtue of horses and of the virtue of dogs, what he has in mind are the characteristics that make horses good horses and that make dogs good dogs. Somewhat later, in a discussion with Thrasymachus, the notion of virtue is connected with that of function (*ergon*); Socrates asks Thrasymachus. "Does there seem to you to be a virtue for each thing that has some function assigned to it?" (353b). A function

---

[4] Compare the more recent remarks of John Adam in his commentary on the *Republic*, Adam 1963 [1902], vol. 1, p. 12: "By [justice], it should be noted, is here meant man's whole duty to his fellows, as [piety] is right conduct in relation to the gods. In this wide sense the word was commonly understood by the Greeks; and even in the scientific study of ethics, the word still retained the same wider connotation, side by side with its more specific meanings."

(as is made clear in Aristotle's subsequent account of the concept) is an activity that is characteristic of a being; it is what something is engaged in doing when it is most being itself. It is (as we hear in English cognates of the Greek *ergon*) the *work* specific to an entity under some particular description.

A *virtue*, as we come to see in the development of the argument, is in turn a quality that an entity has that enables it to perform its function well, that is, to be itself characteristically in a good fashion. It is for this reason that Socrates is able to discuss in the first place the virtue of a horse or of a dog. Understood in this way, a virtue is simply a good quality. We ought therefore to be less inclined, when speaking morally, to think of a general condition of virtue than to think of particular virtues; for a virtue, as is perhaps most obviously true in Aristotle's subsequent use of the concept, is a good state of character. It is, as becomes clear in Aristotle's treatment, the dispositional capacity of a moral subject for appropriate action, a disposition for agency that is at the same time brought about by action.

We might pause here for a moment to note the importance of this notion of virtue to questions of moral philosophy. When virtue is central to the enterprise of moral theory, as it was in much of ancient and medieval theory and as it has become in recent so-called virtue ethics, the effects on moral philosophy are deep. The central question of moral philosophy, rather than being the question of what I should or shouldn't do, becomes instead the question of what kind of person I should or shouldn't become. Emphasis accordingly is less on issues of licit and illicit actions or the rules governing such action than on virtues and vices understood as states of character or their lack.

States of character as virtues may be thought of on a model of the descriptions of desirable qualities that either are composite and determined in relation to the subject in question, as when we speak of the *virtue of a knife*, or are single and qualitatively determined, as when we speak of the *virtue of sharpness*. We may thus find ourselves speaking, on the one hand, of *human virtue* or, on the other, of *the virtue of temperance* or of any of the specific states of character in terms of which we praise one another as trustworthy, loyal, helpful, friendly, courteous, kind, obedient, cheerful, thrifty, brave, clean, or reverent.

In all these cases, of course, the disposition, as I mentioned, is a disposition for appropriate action. A virtue is to be understood (to use John McDowell's felicitous phrase) as a reliable sensitivity to the requirements that situations impose on behavior.[5] It is therefore important to stress, lest we lose sight of this fact in our enthusiasm for virtue ethics, that the answer to the question of what kind of person one should become is, on Plato's and Aristotle's view, alike: a person properly disposed to act in certain appropriate ways. How we are to negotiate the differing roles of character and action in the economy of our moral theories is a central issue with which moral philosophy is asked to deal, and one that often lies at the center of Plato's thinking.

In the argument of the *Republic*, that issue might seem particularly problematic. For Socrates proposes in the heart of the early books of the dialogue to convince Glaucon and Adeimantus that the just life is valuable in its own right, and the argument at the end of Book 4 is meant to register the success of that project. But as a number of readers have pointed out, the problem that Socrates addresses is set in terms of a conception of justice understood as just action and just behavior, whereas the account of justice that Socrates offers as an answer to that problem concerns justice as a state of character, as a certain harmony of the soul. But if the project is to justify doing just acts and refraining from unjust ones, and the justification instead offers a properly ordered soul, then the argument has missed the point unless we can show that the former behavior entails the latter condition. Where does Socrates show such entailment?[6]

But if we bracket this question, we should recognize that our discussion has led us to entertain a more sophisticated view of the relation between justice and virtue, for we can now say that justice is *a* virtue. This means simply that it is one among the states or qualities of an entity that in some sense enable that entity to do well what it characteristically does. And this recognition in turn should lead us to the question: which virtue specifically *is* justice? Notice that this is the very question that the *Republic* asks in Book 1 and again in Books 2 to 4. To which such quality do we refer when we term an entity such as an individual or a city just? Early in Book 2, Socrates proposes that (1) the answer to this question, because justice

---

[5] McDowell 1979, p. 332.

[6] This problem was most famously addressed in recent literature by David Sachs (see Sachs 1963). For other discussions, see Annas 1981, p. 169.

is a general attribute, will be constant over several different kinds of entity to which we might ascribe it and that (2) we would do well to look at justice in a political organization, where it might be easier to discern.

III

So: whatever it is to which we ascribe the virtue of justice (say of it, in other words, that it is just), justice is something (or one of the several things) that enables it to do well what its function is. What sort of thing? Following Socrates' proposal, let's talk first about the city, where this means a society or commonwealth, a "republic," – any kind of organization of individuals who come together for their common weal. To know what justice is in a commonwealth, we'll need to know what the characteristic activity of such an entity is, that is, we'll need to know what is the nature of a commonwealth. Socrates suggests that we address this question by imagining the origin of social collectivity. He finds this origin in the division of labor, the simple fact that none of us is self-sufficient. Thus Socrates at 369b: "I think that a city comes to be because none of us is self-sufficient, but we all need many things."

The argument with which he immediately follows this observation is simple but critical. Different folks being different, they are therefore able to do different things, and there will therefore be better and worse divisions of labor depending on who does what. Put this observation together with the claim that someone will do work best if she devotes the large part of her energies to that work, and there emerges the central argument of the early parts of the *Republic*: a society will work best if different people do different jobs, and if they do the jobs for which they are best suited.

It should be clear that this argument depends on several assumptions that we might find questionable. One is the notion that the differences among people are sufficiently determinate to make possible clear answers to the question of who is best qualified to do what. The other is that it will be clear how to determine who does what, or at least how to determine who decides who does what. These are interesting questions and questions that may justifiably trouble us about the political organization that's imagined in the course of the dialogue. But for these questions even to arise, we need first to understand the formal principle underlying that organization: that principle is the desirability of people doing work for which they're suited.

We have then, according to Socrates, the originating principle of a political organization, together with the recognition that anything will count as a virtue of such a commonwealth if it makes that system of organization work well. Note that this archeology and determination of virtue will apply to any kind of social organization that is devised for a common purpose. Consider, to use a perverse example, those ensembles in numerous heist movies that set out to rob financial institutions; imagine a group that proposes to rob the Cassa di Risparmio in Florence. There are a number of characteristics that such a group will need to cultivate or hope that it antecedently possessed if it wishes its venture to be successful. It will need intelligent planning, and it will need both as a group and individually not to be easily frightened. If it is to perform the robbery well, it will need furthermore to be able to practice a kind of self-restraint; our thieves must not seize the first piece of money they see nor become so greedy as to endanger the operation by overextending its duration.

It should be obvious that I've just mentioned three of the four cardinal virtues that Socrates invokes in the early books of the *Republic*, the virtues of wisdom, courage, and *sōphrosunē* – temperance or self-mastery. In addition, our band of thieves will need to be able to carry out a number of particular functions. Someone will need to be a driver, for example, and someone will need to deactivate the alarm systems; with the proper imagination, and assuming that we've watched the right movies, we can easily extend this list. Note furthermore that for each of these specific *functions* there will be an appropriate specific *virtue*. A group planning a heist will wish to have as a driver someone who knows how to drive, indeed, someone who is a *good* driver. Similarly, the person who is to deal with alarm systems must understand such systems, and the person who is to stand guard should be someone who is alert. In general, the several functions of a complexly organized project like a heist will be best carried out by people who have the skills to carry them out. It is this fact that is often behind the wit and verve of heist movies, which are in a sense the descendants of such fairy tales as Grimm's "The Six Servants," tales in which grotesqueries are fantastically transformed into virtues. And it is, as I shall suggest in a moment, a version of this fact (though less fantastical) that informs Plato's theory of justice.

I remarked that we have already mentioned wisdom, courage, and temperance as virtues integral to our project, and now we've noticed in addition specific virtues desirable to carry out particular functions necessary to the project. What about the virtue of justice? Is it similarly a characteristic that will appear in the list of qualities we will look for in a good band of thieves? If we think of the project of robbery itself as illicit and of justice simply on the model of a general principle of social morality, it would appear that justice is precisely something lacking from the enterprise we've imagined. But in fact, the justice of the *Republic* is indeed required for our project; it is precisely what we have been talking about in the previous paragraph. For it is the assignment of tasks according to the principle of giving to each person the job she is best able to do that results in the condition of justice. So our project will be just insofar as good drivers drive, skilled technicians handle the computer systems, and master minding is carried out by master minds.

This is essentially how justice is defined by Socrates in the conversation at 433a and b of the *Republic*:

Justice, I think, is exactly what we said must be established throughout the city when we were founding it. . . . We stated, if you remember, that everyone must practice one of the occupations in the city for which he is naturally best suited. Moreover, we've heard many people say and have often said ourselves that justice is doing one's own work and not meddling with what isn't one's own. . . .Then it turns out that this doing one's own work in a certain way may be presumed to be justice.

Here "one's own work" must be understood – this is the force of Socrates' addition "in a certain way" – to mean the work appropriate to one, that is, the work, as he has just pointed out, for which one is "naturally best suited." Justice is precisely this principle that functions are to be carried out by the citizens best suited to carry them out.

Recall that this account applies not simply to justice in the commonwealth, but to justice in the individual as well. Here's how Socrates puts it at 441d:

A person is just in the same way as a city . . . And the city was just because each of the three classes in it was doing its own work . . . . . Then each one of us in whom each part is doing its own work will himself be just.

Several things important for the understanding of our dialogue and for the understanding of other aspects of Plato's thinking follow from this account of justice; here I will mention four.

(1) In the first place, note that an individual is just *by analogy* with the global justice that characterizes the city, and not by virtue of contributing to that justice. It's tempting to suppose that because political justice is each person doing what she is best suited to do, justice for the individual is any given person so doing what she is best able to do. But that's wrong; individual justice is an analogue to political justice and not a shadow of it. It is the principle according to which each functionally differentiated element within the individual does what it is best able to do.

In one sense, this fact is simply an expression of the original strategy of Book 2, the strategy that leads Socrates to urge that their investigation begin with justice in the city, where things are larger and easier to see, and only then turn to the individual, attending to how the form is similar in the two (369a). In this recommendation, and in the subsequent playing out of Socrates' strategy, there is a constant intimation that justice in the individual, though perhaps more difficult to discern, is the true goal of their inquiry. This intimation might tempt us to read the entire political thrust of the dialogue as merely in the service of an individual moral psychology. Succumbing to this temptation, as I suggested earlier, would be a mistake, although it would be an equal mistake to read the dialogue as merely an essay in political imagination. But recalling this strategy reinforces our recognition that justice in the city and justice in the individual are said by Socrates to be formally equivalent, and thus structurally analogous in the sense I've just outlined.

But if this is true, we can't help but wonder what the relationship is between the justice that characterizes an individual citizen's soul and that citizen's contribution to social and political justice. Moreover, we may wonder how the isomorphism of justice in city and soul is connected to the claim of the later books that cities of a certain sort engender citizens that are like them.[7]

(2) A related, though parenthetical point, is this: it does not require a great feat of literary imagination to read the definition we are given in Book 4 as a variant of what was rejected in Book 1, when

---

[7] The problem is notably set by Bernard Williams in his classic essay, Williams 1973. See also Lear 1992 and Norbert Blössner's chapter 13 in this volume.

Polemarchus offers as an account of justice the saying of Simonides that it is just to render to each that which is his due (331e). Reflecting on the similarity of these accounts of justice should serve to remind us of the manner in which Plato's dialectic in its search for definition looks to the discovery not of some privileged formula but of the proper understanding of the several formulas that tradition supplies to the learned. In a sense, what has happened by Book 4 is only that the discourse has provided to its participants the proper sense of "render" and "his due", and therefore made possible the appropriation of a truth that otherwise could not be understood properly. At the same time, the similarity reinforces the necessity of recalling the conversation of Book 1 in the midst of our reading of the later books of the *Republic*, a recollection that must pose for any thoughtful reader one of the central interpretive questions for this dialogue: what is the relation between the ordinary accounts of justice that inform the discussion of Book 1 and the more technical and developed account of justice that governs the dialogue's subsequent discussion?

(3) More central to our narrative is the following point: it is not sufficient to say, as we sometimes do, that justice according to Plato is a matter of balance or harmony among the parts of the city or of the individual, not even if we add the clarification *proper* balance or harmony. It is of course important to realize that justice as a form of harmony is, like temperance, a sort of virtue different from wisdom and courage. Wisdom and courage belong to the whole because they belong to some part of the whole; justice and temperance, however, do not properly belong to any part at all, but only to the whole and only because of some global fact about the parts in their relation to one another or to the whole.

This distinction is not difficult to understand. A variously colored group of animals need not be a group of piebald animals; for the group to be variously colored does not require that each of the members of the group be variously colored. But a hungry group of animals is probably a group of hungry animals; in the former case but not in the latter, the global feature is the result of a relation among the features of the group's constituents rather than an additive enlargement of those features. But when we have pointed this fact out, we have not yet specified the nature of justice in a subject until we specify *what kind* of harmony or balance it is. I've suggested that the kind of harmony is that achieved when the differentiation of function is determined by what differentiated parts of the subject are best able to carry out the subject's several specific functions.

(4) Finally, it's not sufficient to characterize justice as a mere division of labor. If we are to recognize justice as a *virtue*, it is essential that we characterize the division of labor as carried out according to some normative principle. Socrates' archeology of the city posits the division of labor, or more technically, the division of function, as the origin of the polis, that is, the origin of political or social structure. But a good polis is one in which that structure is articulated according to a normative principle, and it's that normative principle that introduces the virtue of justice into the city. The principle I've pointed to is the principle that articulates differentiation of function by appealing to what different elements in the city are best suited to do.

IV

So we can now put simply the notion of justice that is developed in those sections of Books 2 to 4 that concern the city. A city is constructed on the principle of a division of function. That's because such a division is the fundamental feature of social life. Justice is the principle of a differentiation of function that is based on *natural ability*. If the question is: what should different groups of folks do? the answer is: what they're good at, that is to say, what they are best suited to do. That is, as we might say, only just.

Two points about virtue now follow, one that is clear in what we've said and one that remains to be made explicit. The first is simply that, as I've stressed, justice in this sense is said to be a *virtue*, and the reason this is understood to be a virtue is quite simple: it's good for people to do what they're good at. We need to parse this fact quite carefully: for people to do what they're good at is a good thing. It is, of course, a different question whether or not to do what they're good at is a good thing for those people. But properly parsed, the principle that it's good for people to do what they're good at is the principle of justice.

The second point about virtue is this: to say that justice is the principle of a differentiation of function that is based on *natural ability* is tantamount to saying that it is the principle of differentiation based on *virtue*. For a virtue just is, as we have seen, a quality that enables its subject to perform some function well. When, therefore, Socrates says that justice is the principle "that everyone must practice one of the occupations in the city for which he is naturally best suited," he is essentially saying that in a just city, each person practices the occupation *for which he has the appropriate virtue.*

The same type of analysis, as I indicated, yields an understanding of justice in the individual; justice is the harmony achieved when each functionally differentiated element of a person is given and performs a function for which it is best suited, that is, for which it has the virtue. Realizing this fact should lead us to reflect on the question of what is the virtue, say, of mind – that is, what is wisdom or *sophia* – in terms of the question: what is the appropriate function of mind? But we should also be led to ask about spirit: what is its appropriate function and its virtue? And what is it to desire and to desire appropriately?

Note that in the case of these questions, the *political* uncertainty I briefly referred to, about how best to determine who is qualified to do what, reveals itself differently. From the standpoint of a psychological theory based on a notion of faculties and their natural activities, the concern for appropriate differentiation of function relative to these different faculties seems more benign, and the cardinal principle that mind is to rule is dependent only on the connection of thought to action. For the contrary notion that one might do well to think, say, with one's heart should appear as odd as the notion that one might do well to watch carefully with one's ears or listen attentively with one's eyes.

To then recognize that the mind and not the desires are to think us through how we are to act is not to deny that we need to attend conscientiously to our desires, as to our emotions and spiritual urges. It is only to recognize that our appetitive faculties are not naturally endowed to direct our thoughtful action, however critical they may be to our grasp of the proper goals and directions of that action. But that fact is no more injurious to some vision of "psychic democracy" than the fact that in a properly organized psyche, mind does not desire, but through its rational powers enables a proper exercise of the desiderative faculties, that is, the desiring of the whole person. To be sure, Socrates is able, in the course of a discussion in Book 9 governed by the image of a soul fragmented and divided theoretically, to speak of the desires of all parts of the soul including the reasoning part (580d). But the discussion reveals that he intends that which each part loves, those objects to which it is by its nature directed (581b). And the ideal vision remains one of "the entire soul following without rebellion the part that loves wisdom, such that each part can do what is appropriate for it to do, that is, be just, and moreover, such that each part can enjoy the pleasure appropriate to it, the best and truest of which it is capable" (586e).

This recognition is essentially the realization, therefore, that in the ideal individual, as in the ideal city, that which rules rules not as a tyrant but as a "guardian," that is, as a just and loving protector. I take one central project of the *Republic* to be that of inviting us to imagine our lives in this way: governed by a reason whose mode of government is nontyrannical. In this dialogue, Plato offers as a proper model of governance for the living of our lives the vision of a commonwealth led by thoughtful rulers whose rule, as the dialogue never tires of reminding us, stands in sharp contrast to that of a tyrant.

V

An appropriate function, then, is the function for which a thing is best suited, and that in turn means the function for which it has the appropriate virtues. Justice, therefore, is a virtue of any complex and functionally differentiated entity in which function is determined on the basis of virtue. It turns out, therefore, that justice is, so to speak, a self-referring virtue. It is the virtue that characterizes those entities whose functional differentiation is in accordance with the principle of function following virtue. It is, to reveal again why we think of it as justice, the proper adjustment of function and virtue.

Justice may therefore be thought to be a quite general principle of a proper agreement between being and acting, or more precisely, between dispositional and active being: between the way things *are* and what it is that they are busy at work *being*. It is for this reason that justice is able to appear in the *Republic* not simply as a politically and morally grounded concept, but as a metaphysical and ontological concept as well; the forms and their connection to the Good are governed by such a concept. For the universe as a whole can be thought of as a functionally differentiated complex, and ideally each thing *is busy at work being* what it's appropriate for it *to be*, where the first being is analogous to the functioning of elements in the city and the second being, that of the forms, to the natures of such elements that makes them appropriate for such functioning.

It will help to recall in this connection earlier ontological invocations of justice; consider these two moments from the now fragmentary body of pre-Platonic philosophy. Anaximander speaks of generation as the appearance of things out of some indeterminate nature and corruption as their return to that nature when "of necessity they give to one another the just penalty [*dikēn tisin*] for their injustice [*adikia*]."[8] On Anaximander's view, coming into being is figured as a mode, so to speak, of ontological *pleonexia*, the greed and overreaching of one's due that violates proper justice; existent things overstep the primordial justice of equality represented in "the indeterminate" [*apeiron*]. Compare this view with the saying of Heraclitus that war is common and that justice is strife.[9] Heraclitus sees justice in the eristic struggle of difference found in being and in its deepest polemical structure.

We might describe the distinction between these two thinkers in anachronistic terms as the distinction between an ontological politics of equality and an ontological politics of difference. Plato situates himself in the midst of this dialectic, offering the allegiance of particular things to their essential natures, that is, to their forms, as a mode of justice. This ontological justice is determined by an equality of individuals under the forms, although the forms themselves are defined in their being by their essential difference from one another.

In a just cosmos, therefore, the forms must be governed by the same principles of right difference that I've suggested characterize a just society or a just individual. Socrates is thus able to speak of justice and injustice among the forms themselves, as he does in Book 6 (500c):

For surely, Adeimantus, there is little leisure for the person whose thought is truly on being to look down to human affairs, and by fighting with them come to be filled with envy and hatred; but by always looking at those things that are organized and always as they are, and realizing that they neither are unjust to nor are treated unjustly by one another, but all are in order according to reason, that's what he imitates and above all tries to be like.

[8] Anaximander, DK 12, B1.
[9] Heraclitus, DK 22, B80.

Think here, following the *Republic*'s spatial metaphors, of the divided line of Book 6 as having both a vertical and a horizontal dimension. The vertical dimension is made explicit in Socrates' discussion, but the horizontal dimension is implied by the plurality of entities at any given level of the line. Justice may then be thought of as the ideal principle that governs the *downward* vector along this vertical dimension, a vector of imaging, but also of dispersion and exemplification, producing the diaspora of being whose upward direction is governed by eros, by the love that the phenomenal world has for its own true nature. As the horizontal dimension of the divided line is governed by principles of multiplicity and unification, so the vertical dimension evokes the twin themes of justice and love that properly divide and hold together the commonwealth of being.

Thus the sense in which justice plays a role in the *ontology* of the *Republic* becomes clearer in light of the notion of justice I've urged is at work in that dialogue. Insofar as it is right for things to act out their nature, justice is once again some form of agreement between, on the one hand, proper *being*, figured in the dialogue as virtue, and, on the other, proper *action*, figured in this dialogue as function.

VI

As a study of justice, the *Republic* may then be seen as an inquiry into the ethics and metaphysics of *difference*, of the proper modes of being's articulation into differentiated parts. What I've suggested is that if a complex entity, a city, for example, is, as a city perforce must be, functionally differentiated, it makes sense to ask: what is the principle of right differentiation? And since that principle is justice, the inquiry into justice is an inquiry into that principle. The dialogue thus figures justice as a principle of difference, a principle in which function is determined by ability and differentiation follows the lines of virtue. In this sense, the *Republic*, insofar as it is an essay on justice, is an essay on the principle of appropriate *division*, an inquiry into the nature of *right difference*.

Several years ago, I had the occasion to read two books, both devoted in different ways to celebrating differences among people and urging greater respect and appreciation for those differences. I was struck by the fact that in both of these books, Plato appears as

a central arch-villain, repeatedly depicted as a relentless champion
of unity understood as uniformity, and therefore understood in such
a way as to undermine and establish impediments to what one of
the authors termed "the dignity of difference." What I've here tried
to show is that the account of justice as a regulatory principle of
difference ought to lead us to distrust such descriptions.[10]

The *Republic*'s foregrounding of justice as a regulatory principle of
difference may temporarily obscure our vision of the issue of appropriate *collection*. But it is an issue to which the dialogue urges us to
attend. What are the principles of right collection to which Plato's
discourse in this dialogue appeals? If a city is to be appropriately
organized, it must not only be differentiated in the right way, which
in the conceptual scheme of the *Republic* means that parts must be
given the functions for which they are best suited. It must also be
true, in the first place, that only differences that truly make a difference are honored. The city must be attentive to those accidental
differences that obscure an underlying equality. Justice must therefore attend to equality at a deeper level than that of mere equity. It
must also be true, in the second place, that the city is a whole, and
not merely a random cluster of parts. We might call this the platonic
virtue of integrity. It is not mentioned explicitly in the *Republic*, but
I take it to inform the discussion of that dialogue from its politics to
its ethics to its ontology. The integrity of being, as I've urged with
the differentiation of being, must characterize generally the complex
entities in the *Republic*'s purview, not only the city, but the individual soul as well, and the modes of being attended to in the ontology
of Book 6.

The requirement that complex entities if they are to be good must
exhibit integrity and wholeness as well as proper differentiation is
revealed in a number of ways in the dialogue's argument. At the
most obvious level, it is represented in the correspondent virtue of
sōphrosunē, which in the *Republic* matches justice as a global virtue,
that is, a virtue that characterizes complex beings such as cities or
persons by reason of global facts about them rather than facts about
one or another of their parts, in this case the global fact of proper
agreement rather than proper differentiation. It is thus the principle
of political friendship and psychic harmony.

[10] The books are Sacks 2002 and Boyarin 1994.

It is more subtly exhibited in two dimensions of the divided line. One is the lateral relation of items at the same level as one another, items that are given unity and integrity only in reference to the principle on the next level of the line, the principle at once of their commonness and of their integrity. The other is the vertical relation of those items to that principle, the ideal unity and integrity of the line itself. This latter unity corresponds to the most basic unity of the *Republic*, the ideal harmony of being and appearance. It is this harmony that in one sense is most fundamental to the dialogue's vision of justice. Recall the witty adumbration of this fact in Glaucon's remark in Book 2 (361a) that the paradigmatic form of injustice is the *discrepancy* between appearing and being: appearing to be just while actually being unjust.

Very early in Book 5, and therefore quite soon after the explicit account of justice as a principle of proper difference, the discussion turns, in a way that might seem accidental, to the question of women. Here Socrates mounts a notorious argument for the equal access of women to the role of guardian by means of the distressing premise that since women are inferior to men in *every* respect, there can be no significant difference between the two of them. Note that the issue in fact follows from the discussion we have been engaged in. For the question as Socrates articulates it is explicitly the question of whether all differences are differences that demand differentiation of the sort we've been talking about. Here is how he puts the issue (454b):

When we assigned different ways of life to different natures and the same ones to the same, we didn't at all examine the form of natural difference and sameness we had in mind or in what regard we were distinguishing them. . . . [So] we might ask ourselves whether the natures of bald and long-haired men are the same or opposite. And, when we agree that they are opposite, then, if the bald ones are cobblers, we ought to forbid the long-haired ones to be cobblers, and if the long-haired ones are cobblers, we ought to forbid this to the bald ones. . . . And aren't we in this ridiculous position because at that time we did not introduce every form of difference and sameness in nature, but focused on the one form of sameness and difference that was relevant to the particular ways of life themselves?

The question here is one that obviously arises from an inquiry into appropriate difference: granted that men and women are different from one another, are they different in a way that legitimates functional distinction? Are they, as we sometimes say, different in a way that makes a difference? For not every difference, as this example in the *Republic* shows, makes a difference.

Much of the rest of the dialogue concerns these conditions on difference. Some of them involve cases in which sameness trumps difference, as with men and women. Indeed, one way of thinking of philosophy, introduced by Socrates at this very moment in the dialogue, is as the ability to understand principles of sameness and difference.

More important, however, is the respect in which difference is the condition of proper unity. I said earlier that one pole of ontological justice is represented by an equality of individuals under the forms, but this is not quite accurate. For a form is a principle of structured wholeness, not merely of collective totality. The unity of instances under a form is, in the language of the *Theaetetus*, that of a *holon* and not simply a *pan*. The instances of a form are in turn not fungible, that is, they are not identical with one another and therefore not interchangeable. For they are equal only insofar as they are instances of that form; each of them is characterized by many other predicates that make them different from one another. So the unity of a form is permeated by a contrary and inescapable element of difference, a difference among individuals brought into harmony by the form that marks their common being. These individuals inhabit a field of difference that is organized insofar as a form is the principle of their being this or that.

It is because the form governs a field of difference, and not merely a plurality, that I'm led to speak of the horizontal vector of the divided line, the relation, that is, among the several images that are images of a single original, among the several instances of a kind that are instances of that single kind, or among the several accounts of a being that are various ways of revealing the single nature of that being.

Elsewhere I've argued that attention to the horizontal is critical to grasping Plato's theory of dialectic and understanding.[11] My purpose in introducing the issue here, however, is to make two points more restricted in scope. One is simply to stress the importance

---

[11] In the course of remarks on the *Statesman* in a different version of this essay, Kosman 2004.

of the lateral dimension in the spatial metaphors of Plato's ontology, an importance that I think would make little sense without the recognition of justice as a principle of difference that I have here been championing. The other is to invoke the strength of the lateral in order to remind us that the Platonic form is ideal; that is, it is a virtual and at the same time transcendent principle of the being of its many instances. These instances, as I've suggested, occupy a field of difference such that their unity must be achieved in integrity and not mere collection. Recall the just individual: precisely because he

> does not allow any part of himself to do the work of another part. . . he puts himself in order. . . and harmonizes the three parts of himself like three limiting notes in a musical scale. . . . He binds together those parts and any others there may be in between, and from having been many things he becomes one, moderate and harmonious. (443d)

This integrity of the individual and the corresponding integrity of the city are reproduced in the ontological register in the integrative harmony of the many in relation to the one. Ultimately, what governs this mode of integrity for Plato is the Good, but as the passage from Book 4 that we've just read makes clear, the recognition of integrity has its beginnings in a proper understanding of justice.[12]

Several traditions in antiquity attest to the story that in his esoteric lectures on the Good, Plato, in his account of the Good, invoked the One and the indefinite Dyad as the fundamental principles of being. The testimony invokes for us an interesting connection between the Good and these principles. The principles of the One and the Dyad are different from those either of cardinality or of ordinality. One and two are principles of cardinality, that is, of number, as first and second are of ordinality, of the number of sequential experience; but the One and the Dyad are principles of the opposition between collection and division, dynamic principles of unity and multiplicity. Thus they are not in a sense principles of number at all; the One and the indefinite Dyad, unity and teeming diversity, are principles of being, that is, principles of the modes of our understanding how it is that the manifold of experience presents itself to us in an organized fashion, both in our ability to organize elements of

[12] See Lachterman 1989–90.

our experience into units and in our ability to see similarities among the elements of our experience and organize things into their kinds.

It is this ability to understand the structure of our experience as involving the organization of things into their kinds that is part of the foundation of Plato's theory of forms. But that ability can be appreciated only against the background of our cognate ability to recognize difference and to understand it appropriately. My suggestion in this chapter is that the *Republic*'s attention to justice is grounded in this ability and that justice is best understood as a principle of appropriate differentiation.

As we've noted at several moments, questions concerning why this is an account of *justice* are unavoidable. What is the relationship between this rather technical sense of justice as appropriate difference and our general sense of justice as a social and political virtue? Or more specifically, how is justice, understood as a virtue of individual psychic organization, related to the notion of justice as a general principle of social and political well-being and to the individual's contribution to such justice? We can give a rudimentary answer to these questions by noting that no adequate theory of social justice can ignore the issue of how to accommodate difference and allow for proper and appropriate modes of distinction. But finally the *Republic* remains an aporetic dialogue by leaving us with these questions, questions that are perhaps part of the larger moral question that informs the dialogue. What is the relation between, on the one hand, virtue, broadly conceived as a state of soul or, as we would say, a state of character, an individual constitution characterized by proper desire, tranquillity, thoughtful courage, and self mastery, and, on the other, the happiness, well-being and political flourishing of individuals in the broad communal and social contexts of our collective lives?

At the same time, to recognize justice as a principle of appropriate differentiation is to recognize the centrality of issues of difference and similarity, division and collection, in the theoretical program of the *Republic*. Acknowledging that fact is also to acknowledge the importance of a proper understanding of the forms as principles of collection. We misread Plato disastrously when we read him in light of a Gnostic otherworldliness that pictures the forms as resident in a place far far away from ours, rather than as the principles of the intelligibility and being of this our sweet world. It is as disastrous a misreading to portray the forms as ontological tyrants designed to stamp out diversity, difference, and otherness. We need to remind ourselves often that, as I've urged, the *Republic* is an argument against tyranny, against the tyranny of the political ruler and the tyranny of reason alike, and against the tyranny of forms as well. It is indeed an argument for rational rule, but its rationality is one that can flourish only in the space of proper collection and division, only by the recognition of the true similarities and differences alike in the world. This is simply to say that in this dialogue, as throughout his writing, Plato is devoted to a philosophical vision designed to enable us to see things as they are.

WORK CITED

Adam, J., ed. 1963 [1902]. *The Republic of Plato*. Cambridge.

Annas, Julia. 1981. *An Introduction to Plato's* Republic. Oxford.

Boyarin, D. 1994. *A Radical Jew: Paul and the Politics of Identity*. Berkeley.

Kosman, A. 2004. "The Faces of Justice: Difference, Equality, and Integrity in Plato's *Republic*." *Proceedings of the Boston Area Colloquium in Ancient Philosophy* 20: 153–68.

Lachterman, D. 1989–90. "What Is 'The Good' of Plato's *Republic*?" *St. John's Review* 39: 139–71.

Lear, J. 1992. "Inside and Outside the *Republic*." *Phronesis* 37: 184–215. Rpt. in J. Lear, *Open Minded: Working Out the Logic of the Soul* (Cambridge, Mass., 1998).

McDowell, J. 1979. "Virtue and Reason." *Monist* 62: 331–50.

Rawls, J. 1971. *A Theory of Justice*. Cambridge, Mass.

Sachs, D. 1963. "A Fallacy in Plato's *Republic*." *Philosophical Review* 72: 141–58.

Sacks, J. 2002. *The Dignity of Difference: How to Avoid the Clash of Civilizations*. London and New York.

Tarrant, H. 2000. *Plato's First Interpreters*. Ithaca, N.Y.

Westerink, G. ed. 1970. *Olympiodorus: Commentaria in Platonis Gorgiam*. Leipzig.

Williams, B. A. O. 1973. "The Analogy of City and Soul in Plato's *Republic*." In *Exegesis and Argument* (*Phronesis* Supplementary vol. 1), ed. E. N. Lee, A. P. D. Mourelatos, and R. M. Rorty (Assen, 1973) Rpt. in *Plato 2: Ethics, Politics, Religion and the Soul*, ed. G. Fine (Oxford, 1999).

6 The Noble Lie

I. THE POLITICS OF LYING

Socrates' introduction of the *Republic*'s notorious "noble lie" comes near the end of Book 3 (414b–c). "We want one single, grand lie," he says, "which will be believed by everybody – including the rulers, ideally, but failing that the rest of the city." Grand lie? Noble lie? G. R. F. Ferrari has a good note on the issue:[1] "The lie is grand or noble (*gennaios*) by virtue of its civic purpose, but the Greek word can also be used colloquially, giving the meaning 'a true-blue lie,' i.e. a massive, no-doubt-about-it lie (compare the term 'grand larceny')." This is not the only point on which there might be argument about the translation. Some prefer to "lie" the more neutral "falsehood" (which need not imply deliberate deception), others "fiction" (perhaps trying to prescind from questions of truth and falsehood altogether). Cornford had "bold flight of invention."[2] I think "lie" is exactly right. But the argument for that will emerge later, in section II.

The noble lie is to serve as charter myth for Plato's good city: a myth of national or civic identity – or rather, two related myths, one grounding that identity in the natural brotherhood of the entire indigenous population (they are all autochthonous, literally born from the earth), the other making the city's differentiated class structure a matter of divine dispensation (the god who molds them puts different metals in their souls). If people can be made to believe it, they will be strongly motivated to care for the city and for each other.

By permission of Oxford University Press. This chapter includes material first published in chapter 7 of *Plato: Political Philosophy* (Oxford University Press, 2006).

[1] Ferrari 2000, p. 107 n. 63.
[2] Cornford 1941, p. 106.

The *Republic's* explicit reliance on such a mechanism to secure assent and commitment to the political arrangements it proposes still has the capacity to shock and offend. It makes the noble lie a natural focus for many of the major questions the dialogue provokes.

First and most obviously, the use of the noble lie is what more than anything may prompt the charge that the *Republic's* preoccupation with political unity is a recipe for "the collectivist, the tribal, the totalitarian theory of morality," to quote Popper's formulation – inasmuch as it licenses wholesale deception of individual citizens as the means to secure the good of "the state" (as Popper conceptualized Plato's city).[3] Such deception is quite incompatible with the assumption of modern liberal political philosophy since Locke that the only valid way of legitimating the political order is by appeal to reason: to *rational* considerations that have the power to motivate acceptance of a political authority by those who are to be subject to it. It is similarly and connectedly in conflict with the fundamental moral requirement, often associated above all with Kantian ethics, that people be treated as ends, not means. The noble lie seems an affront to human dignity, and something that undermines the human capacity for self-determination in particular. Our own time is seeing both an explosion in knowledge and the media by which it is communicated, and unprecedented levels of concern about standards of probity in public life and about lying and the manipulation and suppression of information in particular. Not that it would be reasonable to expect these ugly processes to stop. As John Dunn wrote back in 1979 (commenting on realization that moral and practical insight is not the preserve of any elite):[4]

If this realization dictates a hugely more democratic conception of political rights and capabilities than Plato favoured, it neither dictates nor indeed permits that ruthlessly evasive and disingenuous egalitarianism which pervades the ideologies of the modern world, capitalist and socialist alike, and pretends that the problems of power have been solved or would be solved if the power of human beings was rendered equal. And since the structural inequality of power in the societies of the modern world, however drastically reorganised these might be, is so intractably vast and since such power cannot be rendered safe, insulated from the capacity to harm, it is clear enough that one of the most widely deplored characteristics of the Platonic

---

[3] Popper 1966 [1945], p. 107.
[4] Dunn [1993] 1979, p. 116.

Republic, the noble lie, has at least as guaranteed a place in any possible structures for our world as it had in that of Plato.

Plato is in fact nowhere more our contemporary than in making similar preoccupations – knowledge, virtue, truth, deception – central to his own vision of what matters in politics.

Nor is that just a contemporary perspective. In having Socrates sanction lying as a basic ingredient in political discourse, Plato must have known he was breaching the norms of the democratic political ideology of his own time and place. It is true that Odysseus the trickster is held up as a figure commanding admiration from the readers of the *Odyssey*. That was a reflection of the archaic worldview symbolized by Hesiod when he made Zeus first marry Metis ("Resource") and then, when she is pregnant with Athena, turn her own powers against her, "deceiving her wits by trickery with wily words" and swallowing her whole (*Theogony* 886–91). *Metis* involves "flair, wisdom, forethought, subtlety of mind, deception, resourcefulness, vigilance, opportunism . . . and experience." It has to do with "the future seen from the point of view of its uncertainties" and is at a premium in "transient, shifting, disconcerting and ambiguous" situations. As Marcel Detienne and Jean-Pierre Vernant have shown, *metis* encapsulates a cluster of attributes and values that remained prized (although not characteristically by the philosophers) throughout Greek literature and thought down to Oppian's *Treatise on Fishing* in the second century A.D. and beyond.[5]

Odysseus was not always presented as he had been in the *Odyssey*. More pertinent for our purposes is Sophocles' *Philoctetes* of 409 B.C., a profound meditation – played out in the theater before the Athenian *demos* – on the moral corrosiveness and dubious political advantage of Odysseus' attempt to get the youthful Neoptolemos to hoodwink Philoctetes into what was to be an enforced return to the Greek camp at Troy. The Athenians generally thought of lying and deceit as the way not they but the Spartans conducted political life, as is testified above all by Pericles' antitheses on the subject in the funeral speech attributed to him by Thucydides (2.39.1). A democratic political culture, by contrast, required a general commitment on the part of speakers in the assembly to tell the truth. As Demosthenes put it on one occasion (19.184):

---

[5] Detienne and Vernant 1978. Quotations from pp. 3–4, 107.

There is no greater injustice anyone could commit against you than to speak falsehoods. For where the political system depends on speeches, how can political life be conducted securely if these are not true?

Hence the Athenians' intense resentment against speakers they suspected of manipulating them: the demagogues who figure so prominently in Aristophanic comedy and Thucydidean history. Hence too Diodotus' reflections during the debate on Mytilene of 427 B.C. (again as reconstructed by Thucydides) about the spiraling debasement of democracy and democratic rhetoric produced by widespread contravention of the norm of veracity (3.43.2–4):

It has become the rule also to treat good advice honestly given as being no less under suspicion than bad, so that a person who has something good to say must tell lies in order to be believed, just as someone who gives terrible advice must win over the people by deception. Because of these suspicions, ours is the only city that nobody can possibly benefit openly, without thoroughgoing deception, since if anyone does good openly to the city, his reward will be the suspicion that he had something secretly to gain from it.

What Diodotus sees as the ultimate degradation of political culture – an outcome where "a person who has something good to say must tell lies in order to be believed" – is apparently embraced by the Platonic Socrates as no more troubling than the white lies someone tells a child when getting it to take some medicine.[6]

"One *single*, grand lie" might suggest a possible line of defense on Plato's behalf. Did he perhaps think that relations among citizens in general and between rulers and ruled in particular should exhibit openness and candor, but that there had to be just one exception: the myth that spelled out the basis on which that relationship was founded? No, that is not what Plato thought. The noble lie might with luck be the one thing needed to induce in the citizens an overriding concern for the good of the city. But lying and falsehood are seen as pervasive necessities in the politics and culture of the good city, and in this regard there is an asymmetry between rulers and ruled. One particularly chilling remark on the subject occurs in Socrates' discussion in Book 5 of the mechanisms that will be needed to sustain belief in the eugenic system for controlling breeding. "It will be a necessity," he says (459c), "for the rulers to use many drugs." He then

---

[6] For an excellent treatment of the material surveyed in this paragraph (and of a great range of similar evidence), see J. Hesk, *Deception and Democracy in Classical Athens* (Cambridge, 2000).

explains what he has in mind (459c–d): "It looks as though the rulers are going to have to use a great deal of falsehood and deception for the benefit of those they are ruling." So in this instance the ruled (here not the economic class, but the young soldiers who are to support the rulers) will be told that the mating arrangements are simply the outcome of a lottery. The ruled, by contrast, should have nothing to do with lying. For an ordinary citizen to lie to the rulers is worse than for a patient or someone in training to lie to his doctor or trainer about his physical condition, or for a sailor not to tell the navigator the truth about the state of the ship and those sailing it. If a ruler catches any of the artisans lying like this, "he will punish him for introducing a practice which is as subversive and destructive in a city as it is in a ship" (3.389 b–d).[7]

Socrates' insistence on the need for lying to sustain the political order is all of a piece with his general treatment of culture and society more broadly. The cave analogy of Book 7 – the most striking and memorable image in the entire dialogue – represents uneducated humanity as imprisoned by illusions, feeding uncritically on third-hand images of reality (7.514a–515c, 516c–d, 517d–e). When Socrates subsequently argues that philosophers must be compelled to return to the cave to exercise their function as rulers, the implication is presumably that most of those they are to govern, although citizens of an ideal city, have very little ability to resist deception or to respond to anything better than images of truth (cf. 520b–c). That implication is not contradicted by the radical program of censorship of the poets that he works through in Books 2 and 3, in the context of his treatment of the upbringing of the "guardians" or "guards."[8]

Of course, there is an important sense in which the reason why Homer and Hesiod are attacked, and great tracts of their poetry

---

[7] In the prelude introducing legislation to govern sale and exchange of goods, the *Laws* construes adulteration of coinage as a form of lying and deceit, and treats someone who does it as in effect guilty of swearing a false oath. It pronounces that anyone who commits this sort of crime will be "most hateful to the gods" (cf. *Rep.* 2.382a) as well as liable to a flogging (*Laws* 11.916d–918a) .

[8] From now on I shall say "guards." Probably the principal associations of this word are nowadays on both sides of the Atlantic those conveyed, e.g., by "security guards" (who protect a company's property and employees from external dangers). This function closely parallels the prime function of Plato's *phulakes*, at least as originally articulated in the guard dog comparison (see, e.g., 2.375a–d), although "prison guard" is the association that may be conjured up by Socrates' remark that locating the guards in their own garrison will best enable them to "control [lit. "hold down"] those within, if any of them refuse to obey the laws" (3.415d–e) .

ruled unfit for consumption, is that they tell falsehoods. Sometimes Socrates seems to mean by this that gods or heroes are represented as doing things which they did *not* do: for example, it simply isn't the case (according to Socrates) that Kronos took revenge on his father Ouranos by castrating him (2.377e–378a) or that Achilles dragged Hector round the tomb of Patroclus and slaughtered prisoners taken alive on his funeral pyre (3.391b). But the reason why Socrates disputes what we might call the factual truth of these accounts is that they are at odds with the conceptions of god and of moral virtue that should inform the education of the guards. His real objection is that such stories are "not admirable" (2.377d–e) and "impious" (3.391b). In fact in the passage in which he first introduces the notion of lies as useful drugs, he concedes that with stories such as those told by Homer and Hesiod, we don't *know* where the truth lies so far as events long ago are concerned. In these circumstances the right thing is to "make falsehood as much like the truth as possible" (2.382b–c): that is, to tell a story that encapsulates *moral* truth even if – inevitably – it is fanciful if conceived as fact. Education *has* to begin with stories like this – "broadly speaking false, though there is some truth in them" (2.377a). In other words, the culture is and must be saturated with myths that are literally false, and deceptive if believed to be factually true. But the deception is legitimate if like the noble lie and the stories Socrates *wants* the young to hear, they are morally admirable fictions that drug people into sound convictions and lead them to virtue (2.377b–c, 378e–379a). What is wrong with Homer and Hesiod is not in the end that they lied, but that there was nothing morally admirable in most of the lies they told (2.377e).[9]

II. THE MORALITY OF LYING

So far we have been looking at ways in which the noble lie, and the whole conception of a well-ordered society it represents, conflict with the outlook of ancient Athenian ideology and modern liberal ethical and political thought alike – even if ideological mechanisms of this sort may be a political necessity. It could also be argued that some deep-seated tensions in the project of the *Republic* itself rise to the surface at this point. The Platonic Socrates is quite explicit that

---

[9] For fuller treatment of the topic covered in this paragraph, see, e.g., Ferrari 1989, pp. 92–148, at pp. 108–19; cf. also Burnyeat 1999.

his proposals for a role for the philosopher in government will be perceived as generally paradoxical (5.473c–e) and nothing "fine" or "good" so far as the philosophers for their part are concerned (7.540b; cf. 1.347c–d, 7.520d, 521a). The need to employ lies and deceit to maintain the social and political fabric is presumably itself one of the reasons why Plato has him attribute that view to them. Popper thought such lying and deceit by philosopher rulers actually incompatible with the *Republic*'s own definition of genuine philosophers as those who love truth and the contemplation of truth.[10] Getting to grips with this issue will take a little time.

In a key passage of Book 2 Socrates finds it helpful in his discussion of whether the gods lie or dissemble to distinguish between lies in the soul and lies in speech – between the true or real lie and a spoken imitation or image of it, something that is "not quite an unadulterated lie" (2.382b–c). He goes on at once to observe that the true lie is hated not only by gods but by humans, whereas lying in speech has uses (for humans, not gods) that don't merit hatred (2.382c–e). What does he mean by the "lie in the soul"? Nothing very exalted, he assures us. "All I am saying is that to lie, and to be deceived, and to be ignorant about reality in one's soul, to hold and possess the lie there, is the last thing anyone would want." And this – the true lie – is then defined as "the ignorance in the soul of the person who has been deceived" (2.382b).

Socrates' distinction is a simple one. It turns on the implicit thought that lying is such a profoundly disturbing thing that we ought to try to identify what it is that is so disturbing about it, and let that control our use of the expression "lie." What is disturbing about lying is not in the end saying something false out loud in words to someone else, nor deliberately trying to mislead them, but *saying something false in your own mind to yourself*, particularly something false about "the most important things" (2.382a). So we should adjust our use of the language of truth and falsehood accordingly. Saying something false to another with intent to deceive is certainly a lie (the "lie in words"), but the outcome lying in speech tries to achieve – belief in a falsehood – is what the real evil of lying consists in: the true lie (the "lie in the soul"), therefore. It's still appropriate (Socrates seems to think) to speak then of a *lie*, not just the

---

[10] Popper 1966 [1945], p. 138.

internal enunciation of a falsehood, because that falsehood expresses the state of mind of someone who is *deceived* into believing what they say to themselves. To put it differently, deception is an ambiguous notion. It can mean being deceived by oneself or by another (real deception), or it can mean trying to deceive someone else – which if the deceiver is not himself or herself deceived is "not unadulterated" deception, but a mere image of the real thing (the fact that you are saying something false makes it sound as though you are deceived, even though you aren't).

The Stoics seem to have built on this distinction in developing their own absolutist solution to the problem of reconciling philosophical love of truth and the expediency of lying for political and other prudential reasons. According to them, the wise person – that is, the person who is perfectly rational – will sometimes say things that are false (*deliberately* say such things, as the standard examples they recycled make clear). But there will be no intent to deceive, even if the speaker knows very well that the outcome will be deception. And the wise will say what is false "without assent." So they will not count as lying, "because they do not have their judgment assenting to what is false." This is as much as to say that the wise are not in the grip of what the *Republic* describes as the true lie, the lie in the soul. The difference is that the Stoics stick to common usage in reserving the word "lie" exclusively for speech acts. Of course, the upshot is an innovative conception of lying in speech: someone counts as lying only if they are *themselves* deceived in some way (although presumably not the same way as the person to whom their falsehood is uttered is deceived) – above all, no doubt, regarding what is good and bad. The root cause of such deception of soul would be a morally bad disposition, as emerges in the Stoics' treatment of examples of falsehoods that may legitimately be told. A doctor who tells his patient or a general who tells his troops something false does not lie provided his intention is not bad. Just so, the Stoics' wise person says false things from a morally good disposition. The implication of their radical conception of lying is the counterintuitive proposition that the Platonic Socrates' useful medicinal lies are not lies at all.[11]

---

[11] The relevant texts are Plutarch, *On Stoic Contradictions* 1055f–1056a, 1057a–b; Sextus Empiricus, *Adversus Mathematicos* 7.42–5; Stobaeus, *Eclogae* 2.111.10–17; and Quintilian, *Institutio* 12.1.38. For discussion, see Bobzien 1998, pp. 271–74.

Just because the lie in words (to revert now to Socrates' own categories) is a lie only in words, not in the speaker's soul also, and therefore "not quite an unadulterated lie," it obviously does not follow that there is any blanket justification for telling such lies. To say that they are "not quite unadulterated" suggests a shade of gray a lot closer to black than white. And it is not hard to think of reasons why Socrates might want to encourage general aversion to them: not least because a successful lie in words will be responsible for deception – a "true lie" – in the *hearer's* soul (although like the Stoics he might have wished to insist that principally and ultimately it is everyone's *own* responsibility whether they give their assent to a falsehood). Exceptions would always need a special defense, such as the argument that the telling of the right kind of myths to children induces not deception but *truth* in their souls in regard to "the most important things" (2.382a).

Nonetheless we should not be surprised that the *Republic* allows for such exceptions. It was Augustine, not Plato, who was the first notable champion of what we might call the absolutist position on the morality of lying: holding that all lying is wrong, and forbidden by God as sinful. Indeed Augustine represents a watershed between antiquity and modernity in the history of the moral philosophy of lying. The massive influence of his view on the matter was such that much subsequent discussion has felt obliged at least to grapple with the absolutist position, even though few have embraced it like Kant without qualification.[12] The questionability of the absolutist stance is brilliantly exhibited in the chapter entitled "Sincerity: Lying and Other Styles of Deceit" in Bernard Williams' last book, *Truth and Truthfulness*.[13] But in treatments of lying by Greek and Roman authors before Augustine there is not much to suggest that it even occurred to people that absolutism was a serious option. It is the Stoics who stand out as exceptions to the general rule, but exceptions only of the highly qualified kind we have just glanced at. The *Republic*, however, unquestionably envisages justifications for lying.

In the passage at the end of Book 2 we have been considering, Socrates lists a few types of occasion on which lying may be "useful,

---

[12] See Bok 1978, ch. 3. Although in the end absolutist, Augustine's treatment of the topic (primarily in *De mendacio* [late 390s A.D.] and *Contra mendacium* [422 A.D.]) is highly nuanced and extremely subtle: for an analysis, see Kirwan 1989, pp. 196–204.

[13] B. Williams, *Truth and Truthfulness* (Princeton, 2002), ch. 5.

so as not to be deserving of hatred" (2.382c). Stories about events long ago – the myths he subjects to censorship – constitute one category of useful lie. The other cases he mentions form a pair: lying to enemies and lying to one's so-called friends, if in derangement they are attempting to do something bad. These two sorts of useful lie are no less important for him. Their articulation as such is probably not due to Plato. I suspect that the category of the useful lie is one he took over from Socrates himself. In Xenophon's *Memorabilia*, for example, Socrates engages in rather more extended and pointed discussion of the topic of whether it is just to lie to one's friends as well as one's enemies, with permissible examples including lying to a depressed and indeed suicidal friend, lying to children to induce them to take medicine when they need it, and lying by a general to encourage his down-hearted troops (*Mem.* 4.2.14–18; the last of these examples is mentioned as a commonplace in a speech to the Athenian assembly by Andocides delivered in 391 B.C.: 3.34). This anticipates Socrates' initial characterization of useful lies in general as "taking the form of a drug [*pharmakon*]," the point being that just as only doctors – the experts – should administer drugs, so in the public sphere it is appropriate for the rulers alone to lie, for the benefit of the city, whether as regards enemies or citizens (3.389b–c).

The example of the deranged or depressed friend who needs to be lied to for his or her own good takes us right back to the beginning of the *Republic*. In the initial conversation between Cephalus and Socrates, the idea begins to emerge that justice might be a matter of telling the truth and repaying one's obligations. Socrates raises the case of the deranged friend by way of objection. Suppose such a person had lent you weapons when of sound mind and now asks for their return; then it *wouldn't* be the act of someone behaving justly to comply with the request, or to tell the whole truth. So "this isn't the definition of justice, speaking the truth and giving back what one takes" (1.331a–d). The issue of truth telling and indeed of its ambiguity is thereby marked out as something we may expect to figure on the agenda of the dialogue as a whole. Socrates' position – that there will always be cases where truth telling *wouldn't* be just – is later reinforced by epistemological and metaphysical considerations advanced at the end of Book 5. There he argues quite generally that *any* particular exemplification of beauty or justice or largeness or heaviness and so on may turn out to be an exemplification also of precisely the opposite: ugliness, injustice, smallness, lightness. So it would be a mistake to suggest that they could constitute part of the essence of beauty or justice and so on and qualify as objects of knowledge rather than opinion (5.479a–480a). An absolutist position on truth telling proves therefore to be incompatible with Platonism. In Platonism the realm of the absolute is the Forms, not the world of human experience and activity.

In his account at the beginning of the next book of the dispositions that must become second nature to the philosopher as one devoted to knowledge, Socrates early on lists "aversion to falsehood" (6.485c), which he explains as "not willingly accepting falsehood in any form – hating it, but loving truth." In the conversational exchange that then ensues, it is argued that this requirement simply follows from the philosopher's love of wisdom. Someone who genuinely loves learning things "must make every possible effort, right from earliest childhood, to reach out for truth of every kind" (6.485d). Adam in his great commentary on the Greek text of the *Republic* thought "truth" here meant "metaphysical truth" – of which someone whose soul harbored a lie about "the most important things" would be ignorant.[14] I'm not sure Plato meant to be so restrictive. "All truth" or "truth of every kind" sounds as though it might include truth in speech as well as truth in the soul.[15] Adam was right, however, in the main thing he wanted to deny. Plato cannot be tacitly withdrawing the claim that in their capacity as rulers philosophers will necessarily resort to deception in order to maintain the social and political fabric of the city. What does follow (on the more inclusive view of what "truth of every kind" encompasses) is that even as they tell politically expedient lies, philosopher rulers will hate doing it. There really is a tension at this point between their aspirations as philosophers and the constraints under which they must operate as rulers. A little later Socrates asks (6.486a): "Do you think, then, that the mind which can take a large view, and contemplate the whole of time and the whole

---

[14] Adam 1963 [1902], vol. 2, p. 4.

[15] Does 7.535d–e suggest otherwise? According to Socrates, a "crippled" soul hates telling or hearing a deliberate lie, and gets terribly cross about it, but puts up with the "unwilling lie," wallowing in ignorance and experiencing no distress when its ignorance is revealed for what it is. This is someone who has an inverted and perverted sense of the relative importance of the lie in words and the lie in the soul. It would be wrong to infer that lies in words are *not* to be viewed with distaste. But they are a minor matter compared with "true" lies.

of reality, is likely to regard human life as of any importance?" Everything to do with ruling – as preoccupied exclusively with the affairs of humans – must for a philosopher be irksome triviality, and that presumably includes the need to tell lies.

The once influential political philosopher Hannah Arendt wrote in 1967 as follows:[16]

> I hope no one will tell me any more that Plato was the inventor of the "noble lie." This belief rested on a misreading of a crucial passage (414c) in the *Republic*, where Plato speaks of one of his myths – a "Phoenician tale" – as a *pseudos*. Since the same Greek word signifies "fiction", "error", and "lie" according to context – if Plato wants to distinguish between error and lie, the Greek language forces him to speak of "involuntary" and "voluntary" *pseudos* – the text can be rendered with Cornford as "bold flight of invention" or be read with Eric Voegelin . . . as satirical in intention; under no circumstances can it be understood as a recommendation of lying as we understand it.

It will by now be evident that Arendt was simply wrong about the interpretation of *pseudos*. The noble lie is specifically introduced as one of the "falsehoods that get created as needed which we were talking about a little while back" (3.414b). Socrates is referring to the useful medicinal lies first exemplified in Book 1 by the case of the deranged friend's dagger, and then categorized near the end of Book 2. The noble lie, like the entire discussion of acceptable and unacceptable narratives in Books 2 and 3, is conceptualized in terms of the polarity of lying and truth telling, and resonates as such with discussions of political expediency in many other Athenian texts of the late fifth and fourth centuries, as well as with Plato's own metaphysical preoccupation with truth. Carl Page rightly comments on "how deeply woven into the fabric of the entire conversation" is his treatment of lying.[17] Nietzsche was a surer guide than Arendt when he congratulated Plato on "a real lie, a genuine, resolute, 'honest' lie" (*Genealogy of Morals* 3.19).

III. CARING FOR THE CITY

The first part of the myth of the noble lie concludes with its moral. The earth – their mother – releases her sons, "and now it is their

---

[16] Arendt 1968, ch. 7 ("Truth and Politics"), at p. 298 n. 5.
[17] Page 1991, p. 2.

duty to deliberate on behalf of the country they are in and defend it – just as they would their mother or nurse – and to regard the rest of the citizens as their brothers, born from the earth" (3.414e). When the whole narrative is over, and Glaucon and Socrates have finished their brief discussion of it, Socrates says (3.415d–e):

Our job now is to arm our earth-born, and lead them forth, with the rulers at their head. Let them go and look for the best place in the city to put their camp, a place from which they may best control those within, if any of them refuse to obey the laws, or repel those without, if any enemy comes down on them "like a wolf on the fold."

All the citizens are "earth-born," but these passages make it crystal clear that Socrates is focusing principally on the rulers (deliberation being their job) and the military (defense being theirs), just as he does in addressing the story to them in the first instance before the rest of the city, and endeavoring to persuade *them* to believe it. To understand why the noble lie is written this way we need to attend to the broader context.[18]

After nearly forty pages' discussion of the military class and its selection and education, Socrates asks almost casually which of them are to rule and which to be ruled (3.412b; not for him debate about whether monarchy, democracy, or some form of oligarchy or aristocracy is the right system, just the *assumption* that rulers will be drawn from the guards – who are now (414b) divided into guards proper and "auxiliaries" or "supporters"). In answering his own question, he specifies three principal qualifications those selected as rulers will need to possess. They are to be wise (*phronimoi*, Aristotle's word for *practical* understanding), able, and above all people who care for the city (412c). In the immediate sequel Socrates focuses exclusively on acquisition of the third and (as he represents it) most important of these attributes: the others are apparently reserved for later, when the rulers have been identified as philosophers. In launching his treatment of the third desideratum, his first move is to suggest that someone is most likely to care for something if he loves it (*philein*). And then he makes the following intriguing remark (412d):

And he would be most likely to love a thing when he believed that what is in its interest is the same as what is in his own, and when he supposed that if it did well, he would do well too, and if it didn't, neither would he.

---

[18] For a similar approach to the one adopted here, see Hahm 1969.

This formulation of perceived coincidence of interest as a key condition needing to be satisfied if a person is to love something might have led one to expect some argument next on why it *will* be in the interests of wise and capable guards to promote the interests of the city. That never happens. Why not?

It is not that the *Republic* is not concerned with that kind of issue. After all, Book 2 begins with Glaucon's articulation of the idea that a social contract prohibiting mutual wrong, and more generally institution of the rule of law, will be perceived as in the interests of the individual, assuming standard conditions of general "weakness when it comes to wronging others" (2.358e–359b), or mutually assured destructive capability, as they used to say during the Cold War. A train of thought in Book 1 may give us a clue as to why we get nothing like that here. There Socrates argues against Thrasymachus at some length that no art or skill (medicine and seamanship are the favorite examples) is practiced as such to secure what is best for the practitioner, but only for what is under its control and in its care. So if people are to be prepared to undertake political rule (conceived as a form of expertise), there has to be "payment" to induce them to do it – money, or prestige, or else some penalty for not ruling. Now the good, the sort of people who would make suitable rulers, aren't interested in money or prestige. So in their case a penalty will be required, to compel them to take it on. The main element in that, and the main reason why they will agree to exercise rule, is the prospect of being ruled by someone worse if they refuse to do it themselves. They undertake rule, therefore, not as something good, which will be a good experience for them, but as something unavoidable (1.346d–347d).[19] From this piece of reasoning there emerges an example where – to revert to the thesis in Book 3 that interests us – the interest of the city is indeed perceived to coincide with that of the person we would wish to be its ruler. It is in the interests of the city that such a person exercise rule, because that is its best chance of being well governed. And it is also in the interests of that kind of person, because otherwise they risk being ruled over by someone worse than themselves.

But this is hardly a recipe for securing rulers who will *love* their city. Coincidence of perceived interest may be a *necessary* condition

---

[19] I am grateful to Melissa Lane for emphasizing to me the importance of this passage in Book 1 for interpretation of the political philosophy of the *Republic*.

of such an outcome, but if the ruler perceives what is in his interest not as something positively good but as merely unavoidable (as is reiterated later in the dialogue, too, most explicitly at 7.540a–b; cf. 520d), it will not be *sufficient* to motivate love. Indeed, when Glaucon says (2.358c) that on the contractarian view of justice, people practice it *unwillingly*, as something unavoidable, not something good (exactly echoing Socrates' words at 1.347c–d), his formulation simply expresses what is implicit in Socrates' assessment of the attitude to ruling that the good person will form in the light of calculation of self-interest, not just in Book 1, but in the central books of the dialogue, too.[20]

It is therefore understandable that having introduced perceived coincidence of interest between city and ruler as a necessary condition of the ruler's loving the city in our Book 3 passage, Socrates says no more at this point to explain *why* rulers will believe that their interests coincide with those of the city. It is not that he could not give an answer. It is rather a problem about the kind of answer that might be forthcoming if he remained within the conceptual framework of rational egoism, within which the *Republic* invariably discusses questions of interest. An answer of that sort could not supply him with an adequate account of the motivation to care for the city that he is looking for here. So having stipulated that rulers will love the city only if they think its interests coincide with their own, Socrates moves on at once to conclude that the right members of the military class to select as potential rulers (or guards proper) are people who (1) throughout their lives are utterly determined to do what they think to be in the city's interests and refuse to act in any way whatsoever which they think would be against its interests and (2) throughout their lives guard unswervingly the conviction that it is their duty to do what at any time they judge best for the city (3.412d–e; cf. 413c). A whole page is then given over to the tests and trials they must be put through from earliest childhood to ensure that they do not involuntarily lose this true conviction (involuntarily, because it is only false beliefs that people give up voluntarily). Three areas of risk are identified, and three kinds of test proposed accordingly. They might be prone to forget their conviction or be persuaded out of it; pain or grief might cause them to abandon it; or

[20] See further David Sedley's chapter 10 in this volume.

they might be seduced out of it by pleasure or terrified out of it by danger. The person who under constant testing emerges unsullied should be appointed ruler and guard of the city (3.412e–414a).

So far there is nothing on *how* guards who come successfully through this process *acquired* their motivation and the conviction that underpins it in the first place. Enter the noble lie. In his closing comments on the myth, Socrates indicates that a main purpose in inculcating it in the minds of the citizens is precisely to bring them "to care more about the city and one another" (3.415d). This is the nearest he gets to an explicit statement on how guards develop commitment to the city: they will need to be persuaded by the noble lie or something like it. It is of course a paradox that the one specific mechanism he proposes for generating a motivation that is supposed to be rooted in unshakable true conviction is a lie – something explicitly labeled a "device" (3.414b). Yet once we set the noble lie in the context of education of the young (which I assume is the main context appropriate for it – more on this later), the paradoxicality is mitigated, and indeed a thoroughly sensible rationale begins to emerge.

Socrates does not explain in so many words why children have to be started off on stories whose truth is encased in falsehood, but various things he says in the first page or two of his critique of Homer and Hesiod make the rationale for this and the criteria he expects such stories to meet fairly clear. For example, he thinks the minds of children highly malleable (2.377b) and unsophisticated (they cannot judge what to take literally or otherwise, 378d), but at the same time the opinions they take on board at this early age tend to be difficult to wash out and unchangeable (378d–e). This is doubtless why fictive stories about a paradigmatic but inaccessible past rather than abstract arguments are the things to teach them – and it is extraordinarily important that from the outset these be "as beautiful as possible," to lead them toward virtue (378e). Here considerations of the good of the city must be paramount. If we want the people who are to protect our city to regard it as a crime to fall out with each other at the drop of a hat, stories about battles between giants and the many and varied enmities of gods and heroes toward family and kin must be off the agenda. If we want to convince them that no citizen has ever quarreled with another citizen – that such a thing is an impiety – then that's what old people must tell children from the word go, and poets must be made to compose stories to that effect for them as they grow older (378b–d). This is a job for poets, not philosophers – presumably because it is the poet, not the philosopher, who is skilled in exploiting cultural tradition to produce images and narratives with the requisite resonance and power and who is experienced in molding people's souls by such means (378e–379a). Hence when Plato tries his own hand at myth in the noble lie, he adapts well-known stories: the myth of Cadmus and the earthborn warriors sown from dragons' teeth, and Hesiod's myth of metals.[21]

IV. A QUESTION OF IDENTITY

The noble lie tells the guards (rulers and auxiliaries) and the rest of the citizens something quite different from all the other stories expurgated and wished for in Books 2 and 3. It instructs them about *themselves* – in fact, it tells them who they are. The territory their city occupies is literally mother to them all, and so the rulers in particular are to conceive their obligations as those of sons who must deliberate about the welfare of the mother who has nurtured them, and the military their obligations as those of sons who must defend her, regarding all the other citizens as brothers (3.414e). The implication is that they are *not* to identify themselves primarily as individuals, with interests defined in terms of rational egoism, but as parts or members of a whole, understood on the model of a family – something immediately intelligible to children, of course.

The second part of the myth – Plato's adaptation of Hesiod – complicates the picture. While all the citizens are brothers, god has used "gold" in creating those fit to be rulers, "silver" for the auxiliaries, "iron" and "bronze" for the farmers and artisans: not human, perishable gold (and so on), as we hear a little later, but pure divine gold, in their souls (3.415a, 416e–417a) . The focus of the narrative, however, is on the imperative god issues to the rulers. The first and most important instruction they are given as guards relates to the adulteration of these metals in the souls of the offspring produced in each of the classes. Precisely because all citizens are members of the same family and have the same genetic material, it will sometimes

---

21 There is a good deal more to say about the mythical discourse of the noble lie as such than I have room for here. For some further remarks on the subject, see my "The noble lie as Mythical Discourse," in Partenie 2008.

happen that gold parents will produce children with an admixture of iron or bronze: these have to be expelled into the ranks of artisans or farmers. Conversely, when farmers or artisans produce children with admixtures of gold or silver, they are to be promoted to guards or auxiliaries. The entire myth concludes dramatically, with ominous mention of an oracle predicting the destruction of the city should iron or bronze guards take charge (3.415a–c).

The story of the metals also says something about the citizens' identity or, rather, identities. Of course, it is a way of expressing the fundamental argument for the specialization of functions according to natural aptitude that Socrates has already articulated (2.369b–370c), and particularly of insisting on the consequential need for mobility between classes where appropriate (that will be reiterated in nonmythical terms a little later: 4.423c–d; cf. 4.434a–b, 5.468a). But the noble lie insinuates the thought that these political arrangements are not due at all to the *fiat* of human decision, but *simply* reflect the way people indeed are (that they are that way is in itself no falsehood, on Socrates' premises, and given his eugenic program). And it conveys the warning that resisting or neglecting the implications of that will be politically disastrous – because people cannot be what they really are not.

The metaphor of filial obligation, therefore, is what the noble lie makes underpin the overriding commitment to the good of the city required of its rulers, supported by its military. There is no nonmetaphorical piece of political theory developed elsewhere in Books 2 to 4 into which it can be translated (contrast the story of the metals). And crucial to it is an existential dimension untranslatable into theory. In effect it says to the rulers: "*This* – the city – is *your* mother, *you* must deliberate on her behalf and defend her." We have to wait until Book 5 for a nonmythical articulation of the relationship between city and citizens that could transform the metaphor into something more literal (though still an imaginative projection). The radical eugenic breeding provisions Socrates there proposes require a reconceptualizing of the family. All the young are to think of *anyone* else who was evidently conceived during the same mating festival as brothers or sisters, and parents are to treat *all* such children as their sons and daughters (5.461d–e). In fact every time one guard meets another, he or she will *assume* it is a brother or sister or mother or father, or the child or parent of one (5.463c). In such a city, more than in any other, the binding unity that Socrates calls the "foot-print" of the good will be apparent. Everyone will use "I" and "my" simultaneously. All will rejoice and grieve over exactly the same events (all saying with reference to the same thing "I'm really upset by that," etc.). They will behave like the parts of one body, which are all affected by pain or pleasure in any one of them (e.g., the fin-ger), so that we say, "The *person* feels pain *in* the finger" (5.462a–d, 463e–464b).

What this passage in Book 5 brings home is something of essential importance for an understanding of the noble lie. Plato evidently sees no way of developing the motivation to care for the city *independent* of the creation of what one might call a holistic political ideology. The metaphor of filial obligation or recompense is his favorite way of articulating such an ideology. Something like it recurs in the famous discussion in Book 7 of the return of philosophers from contempla-tion of eternal truth to the cave of human existence. At the end of the cave analogy, Socrates says that "the best natures" must not be allowed to avoid descending from their philosophical studies back into the cave – to fulfill their duty to take their turn as rulers over the other citizens. Glaucon objects (7.519d): "What? Are we going to do them an injustice, and make them live a worse life when a better is possible for them?" On the second point Socrates issues a reminder that their concern as legislators is the good of the whole city, not of any particular class within it. His reply on the first point does not (as some commentators would have preferred) invoke the metaphysics of the Forms, but turns on considerations of reciprocal obligation. Significantly, he moves into direct speech to address his argument direct to the philosophers. He appeals to the understanding *they* need to have of *their* existential situation.

Other cities, Socrates has remarked, do nothing to nurture the political potential of their philosophers. "But we have produced *you* as leaders and kings," he begins, "and have educated you accord-ingly, so that you can share in both the philosophical and the political life."[22] When his quite sustained speech to them is complete, he asks

---

[22] Whether their counterparts elsewhere would be regarded by Socrates as having any political obligations reciprocating for their education and upbringing is a moot point. If one supposed it legitimate to extend the argument made by the laws of Athens in the *Crito* to other cities generally, an affirmative answer might be inferred. But the *Republic* takes the view that in most actual or conceivable

Glaucon: "Then do you fancy those we have nurtured will disobey us after hearing this, and refuse to take their turn in sharing in the exertions of the city?" "Impossible," says Glaucon, now convinced: "It is a just instruction, and they are just." It is striking how he couches his verdict in terms of justice. The verdict is prepared for by reflection not on justice as it comes to be conceived in the main argument of the *Republic* but on justice as Simonides thought of it – paying back what you owe to somebody (1.331d–e).[23] Not that the dialogue in the end sees any necessary incompatibility between these two conceptions of justice. The first thing we are told about the characteristic behavior of the just person defined at the end of Book 4 is that he is someone who repays his debts (442e–443a). Such a person counts behavior in the political as in other spheres "just" when it preserves and promotes psychic harmony (443c–e, presumably a necessary, not a sufficient condition).[24]

There is a notable anticipation in the earlier *Crito* of the pattern of argument I am detecting in these passages of the *Republic*. In that dialogue the issue for Socrates' friend Crito is why the philosopher will not effect an escape from the prison to which he is confined, awaiting execution of the sentence of death passed on him by the Athenian court. The main body of the explanation Socrates offers him is contained in an extended piece of political rhetoric put in the mouths of the personified laws of Athens and addressed in the second person direct to Socrates himself and to his existential situation (compare the *Republic* contexts we have been considering). The laws appeal for the most part to Simonidean justice, and in the first instance to considerations with which we are now familiar. The laws and the city produced Socrates – it was under their auspices that his parents married and brought him to birth. They too are similarly responsible for his upbringing or nurturing and his education. So if the laws and the city now decide that Socrates must perish, the reciprocity of obligation dictates not that he should do what he can to

---

politeiai education and upbringing are so deficient that keeping one's hands free from impiety and injustice may often be the most one can reasonably expect of a philosopher (cf. 6.496a–e, 9.592a–b).

[23] For this reading of Socrates' argument as an appeal to justice as reciprocity, see, e.g., Gill 1996, pp. 287–307; Nightingale 2004, pp. 131–37.

[24] Here I glide past issues much debated in recent scholarship. See, e.g., Annas 1978; Dahl 1991.

destroy the laws and the city (which is what ignoring their jurisdiction would amount to) but that he should obey the decision out of filial respect (*Crito* 50d–51c).

The issues at stake in all three of these texts – the *Crito* passage, the treatment of the return to the cave in Book 7 of the *Republic*, and the noble lie – are closely comparable: how to *persuade* the individual to do something required by the good of the city. In each case the considerations put forward in favor are drawn not from the deeper resources of Socratic or Platonic philosophy but from more popular discourse. In the *Crito* and the return to the cave passage, the argument is presented as a piece of political rhetoric addressed in the second person to the philosopher, while in the noble lie Socrates has recourse in myth to another popular form, and again in its second part adopts a more urgent mode of expression by addressing the citizens in the second person. The second person is for the Platonic Socrates peculiarly appropriate to communication between members of a family about their obligations and commitments. "I was always concerned with you," he tells the Athenians at his trial (*Ap.* 31b), "approaching each one of you like a father or an elder brother to persuade you to care for virtue." When there is a need to move people to make particular commitments to a particular community, the arguments Plato produces for elevating the good of the city above that of the individual have nothing metaphysical about them.

V. BELIEVING THE LIE

"You seem reluctant to tell your story," says Glaucon (3.414c), having heard Socrates' prefatory remarks about it. "It's a very reasonable reluctance," replies Socrates, "as you'll find when I tell it." Socrates in fact hedges his narrative around with a good deal of commentary. Three elements in the commentary – obviously interconnected – stand out. First, the noble lie is presented with a show of considerable reluctance. Socrates claims to be at a loss to know how to present it, and indeed to pluck up the nerve to do so. Second, there is an implication that the Lie is somehow outrageous. After hearing the first Cadmeian part of it, Glaucon indicates that he now realizes why Socrates was ashamed to tell the Lie, and Socrates himself may be suggesting that his story sounds archaic – not the sort of thing that happens or could happen in the contemporary world. Little wonder. Apart from any other problem there may be with it, he envisages its recipients having to be persuaded that "the entire upbringing and education we gave them, their whole experience of it happening to them, was after all merely a dream, something they imagined, and that in reality they spent that time being formed and raised deep within the earth – themselves, their weapons, and the rest of the equipment which was made for them" (3.414d–e). Unsurprisingly (and finally), the interlocutors express little confidence that the rulers of the city could be made to believe such a myth. Socrates confesses that a great deal of persuasion would be needed. And when he asks Glaucon whether he can think of any device whereby the rulers *could* be persuaded of the story, Glaucon says: "No way" (3.415c). What he does concede – and I take the concession to be of the utmost importance – is that with their sons and in subsequent generations there would be more chance, presumably because the first rulers would tell it to their children at a stage in their development when they are impressionable and uncritical. Socrates replies (415d): "Even that" – I interpret, having children believe the Lie – "would help to make the rulers" – I suppose, the first rulers – "care more for the city and each other."

Let us take a step backward and reflect briefly on the complexities of what is going on in this extraordinary section of text. One thing at least must now be abundantly clear. The noble lie is very far from being simply a brazen piece of propaganda designed primarily to control the mass of the population of the ideal city (as usual, it is not the population at large that is uppermost in Plato's mind).[25] It is aimed at the rulers in the first instance, and its main purpose is to get them to be public-spirited. It is a lie because it attempts to persuade citizens of false things about their origin and upbringing, but noble because it communicates in symbolic form truths about the good city, its foundation in human nature, and the behavior it requires. And it is the subject of authorial commentary shot through with sophisticated intellectual embarrassment, and not with the Machiavellian blandness associated with the amoral manipulation of information typical of our own time or with its analogue in Diodotus's Athens. In short, it is a decidedly unstraightforward piece of writing.

---

[25] This was the interpretation of R. H. S. Crossman, in Crossman 1937, p. 130. A different view is in Dunn 1993 [1979], p. 116 n. 68.

The focus of the embarrassment is somewhat elusive. Perhaps it is Plato's way of signaling a mainly literary discomfort. Socrates and his interlocutors are imagining themselves as legislating for a city they are *founding* in some sense or other (cf. 7.519c), as new Greek cities had often in recent history been founded all over the Mediterranean and on the coast of the Black Sea. Yet if a city is to have a charter myth, its origins need to be represented as more than human and as rooted in a remote past. The credibility of the myth will depend on creating in the telling a psychological distance that ensures no conflict between present experience and the very different original condition being imagined. There is therefore a problem in trying to conceptualize what it would be like for citizens of a newly created community to believe a myth that will imply that it came into being very differently. Plato faces the problem head on. He has Socrates seize the bull by the horns and tell the citizens of his good city their charter myth without making the least attempt to generate the requisite psychological distance. The myth of the earthborn is about *them*, and they must be got – impossibly – to think that what they all know perfectly well about their real upbringing is a dream.

Plato *need* not have written the noble lie passage this way. He could from the outset have made it something the original citizens tell the *children* about the remote origins of the city (the scenario presumably envisaged by Glaucon when he pronounces his verdict, as likewise by Socrates when he speaks of it as something that will turn into a tradition or *phēmē*: 415d). That way the problem of nonexistent psychological distance would never have arisen in the first place. The very fact that this alternative was so obviously available to Plato suggests that the embarrassment he injects into the dialogue at this point has dimensions other than the one we have singled out so far. Socrates started by describing the myth – evidently with reference to the Cadmeian section – as having something Phoenician about it (hardly just because Cadmus came from that part of the world)[26] and as being the kind of thing usually said (and believed) about the past, not the present. This may suggest a modern and Greek disdain for such crudities, comparable with that implicit in Phaedrus's incredulity that Socrates might really believe the story of

---

[26] Cornford 1941, p. 106, has "Eastern tale," which I think gives the appropriate "orientalizing" flavor.

Boreas's abduction of Orithuia (*Phdr.* 228b–e). Socrates remarks that
the thing the story tells of – generation of human beings from the
earth – "has happened in many places, as the poets say and have succeeded in convincing people" (3.414c). This may be a sly reference to
the Athenians' own myth of autochthony.[27] They claimed to be the
only Greek people that had literally sprung from the soil they lived
off: "Alone of the Greeks," said Isocrates in a work of 380 B.C. (*Paneg.*
24, in words that parallel Socrates' at *Rep.* 3.414e), "we can call her
[Attica] not only native land but mother and nurse." Plato himself
had exploited the Athenian claim – investing it with strongly democratic and egalitarian commitments quite contrary to those of the
myth of the metals here – in his parody of Pericles' funeral speech
in the *Menexenus* (*Menex.* 237b–239a). No doubt he envisages for
the *Republic* a readership of urbane skeptics, to whom some sort of
apology is needed for advocating the use of such material. To a degree
Socrates had prepared the way, with his general theory of the use of
false stories in bringing children up. But this is the first actual example he presents of a myth whose employment he is recommending,
not criticizing, other than the flat retelling as narrative, not dramatic
representation, of the beginning of Book 1 of the *Iliad* earlier in Book
3 (393c–394b). This, we might conjecture, accounts for some at least
of the parade of nervousness at this juncture.

In Book 2 of Plato's *Laws* there occurs the following exchange
(2.663e–664a):

Cleinias: Truth is a fine thing, Visitor, and it has staying power. Yet it
    appears to be something not easy to persuade people about.
Visitor: I'll allow you that. Yet it proved easy to persuade people of the
    Sidonian [i.e., Phoenician] story, incredible though it was, and thousands
    of others.
Cleinias: What do you have in mind?
Visitor: The story of the teeth that were sown, and of how armed
    men grew from them. Here in fact is a notable example for a lawgiver, of
    how someone who tries can persuade the souls of the young of anything,
    so that the only question he has to consider in inventing such stories is
    what would do most good to the city, if it were believed. Then he must
    discover every possible device to ensure that the whole community

---

[27] For which see Loraux 1993, ch. 1.

speaks with one and the same voice about these subjects, constantly and throughout their lives, in their songs, their stories, and their speeches.

Like so many passages in the *Laws*, this one constitutes among other things a commentary on the *Republic*'s noble lie. It serves to reinforce a reading of the noble lie that relates it above all to the educational program of Books 2 and 3, and in particular to the question of motivating people to care for the city from their earliest years. Given Socrates' theory of the efficacy of myths in molding children's souls, it is highly plausible that the children of the rulers and of the other citizens could be persuaded of its charter myth – just as the Athenian visitor envisages. The hypothesis that Plato thinks they could is supported by – and helps in its turn to explain – the way Socrates argues in the Book 7 passage on the return of the philosophers to the cave. With a further look at that passage my argument will conclude.

Socrates there appeals to the philosophers' recognition that they are obliged to repay the city for the upbringing and nurture they have received (7.520a–d) . One might worry (scholars have worried a great deal) that this is an argument pitched at too superficial a level to be appropriate to thinkers who have been deeply immersed in study of the Form of the Good and all it entails.[28] But let us suppose that the philosophers had indeed been persuaded in childhood of the myths of the noble lie. And let us further suppose that they have never lost either the conviction thereby instilled in them that above all they must care for the city as a matter of reciprocal obligation or (yet more important) the motivation to do so that the conviction supports. What will have changed for them now that they have achieved philosophical understanding? First, they will no longer believe the myths as myths. They will have the sort of grasp of the rationale for the good city that is articulated in the philosophical argument of the *Republic* (cf. 6.497c–d). Second, they will have become only too aware that in the pursuit of knowledge of eternal truth they have discovered something incomparably more important than the city, and something also far more desirable as a good. They will consequently need to be *compelled* to take their turn at ruling. But patriotic conviction – "hard to wash out" and tested in every kind of trial – will

---

[28] For an excellent recent review of the debate about the issue, see Brown 2000; also Rosyln Weiss' chapter 4 and David Sedley's chapter 10 in this volume.

remain writ deep in their souls, something Socrates stresses once again after he has introduced the topic of an education fit for philosopher rulers, even as he allows that the discussion back in Book 3 glided past and veiled the difficulty that would be presented by that perspective (6.503a).[29]

On this supposition it should follow that, however clear and universal the philosophical vision they enjoy outside the cave, and however small human life appears from that perspective, or again however preoccupied they might be with the health and happiness of their own souls, nonetheless the philosophers' conviction of their political duty and the sense of their own identity that goes with it are so deeply entrenched that its unphilosophical and predialectical dictates will in the end trump all other considerations. The problem of adjusting perspective on reentry to the cave is alluded to and may mean that they need *reminding* of it – hence the argument about reciprocation Socrates imagines himself and the other interlocutors putting to them. But any lapse in recollection of what they have all along been committed to could be no more than temporary. And a reminder of their obligation, together with a statement of the contribution they are uniquely capable of making thanks to their philosophical grasp of truth, is all that will be necessary for them to recover themselves. In short, what Plato makes Socrates say, philosophically undemanding as it may be, turns out to be the appropriate thing to say, precisely because of the depth of the conviction and motivation it appeals to.[30]

WORKS CITED

Adam, J., ed. 1963 [1902]. *The* Republic *of Plato.* Cambridge
Annas, J. 1978. "Plato and Common Morality." *Classical Quarterly* 28: 437–51.
Arendt, H. 1968. *Between Past and Future: Eight Exercises in Political Thought.* New York.
Bobzien, S. 1998. *Determinism and Freedom in Stoic Philosophy.* Oxford.

[29] Adam has a good note on this point: see Adam 1963 [1902], vol. 2, p. 46.

[30] A first version of the argument of this chapter was delivered as the A. E. Taylor lecture in Edinburgh in March 2000, and in revised form later that year to gatherings in Oxford, Leiden, and Cambridge. The present version was presented in lecture form to an audience in Santiago de Chile in August 2004. I am grateful to those who commented on the material on these occasions and to John Ferrari, Geoffrey Lloyd, and David Sedley for written comments.

Bok, S. 1978. *Lying: Moral Choice in Public and Private Life*. New York.

Brown, E. 2000. "Justice and Compulsion for Plato's Philosopher-Rulers." *Ancient Philosophy* 20: 1–17.

Burnyeat, M. F. 1999. "Culture and Society in Plato's *Republic*." *Tanner Lectures in Human Values* 20: 215–324.

Cornford, F. M., trans. 1941. *The* Republic *of Plato*. Oxford.

Crossman, R. H. S. 1937. *Plato Today*. London.

Dahl, N. O. 1991. "Plato's Defence of Justice." *Philosophy and Phenomenological Research* 51: 809–34. Rpt. in *Plato 2: Ethics, Politics, Religion, and the Soul*, ed. G. Fine (Oxford, 1999).

Detienne, M., and J.-P. Vernant. 1978. *Cunning Intelligence in Greek Culture and Society*. London.

Dunn, J. 1993 [1979]. *Western Political Theory in the Face of the Future*. Cambridge.

Ferrari, G. R. F. 1989. "Plato on Poetry." In *The Cambridge History of Literary Criticism*, vol. 1, ed. G. A. Kennedy. Cambridge.

Ferrari, G. R. F., ed. 2000. *Plato: The* Republic, trans. T. Griffith. Cambridge.

Gill, C. 1996. *Personality in Greek Epic, Tragedy, and Philosophy: The Self in Dialogue*. Oxford.

Hahm, D. E. 1969. "Plato's 'Noble Lie' and Political Brotherhood." *Classica et Mediaevalia* 30: 211–27.

Hesk, J. 2000. *Deception and Democracy in Classical Athens*. Cambridge.

Kirwan, C. 1989. *Augustine*. London.

Loraux, N. 1993. *The Children of Athena*. Princeton.

Nightingale, A. W. 2004. *Spectacles of Truth in Classical Greek Philosophy: Theoria in its Cultural Context*. Cambridge.

Page, C. 1991. "The Truth about Lies in Plato's *Republic*." *Ancient Philosophy* 11: 1–33.

Partenie, C., ed. 2008. *Plato's Myths*. Cambridge.

Popper, K. R. 1966 [1945]. *The Open Society and Its Enemies, vol. 1: The Spell of Plato*. London.

Williams, B. 2002. *Truth and Truthfulness*. Princeton.

7 The Three-Part Soul

A full picture of the human soul emerges only gradually from the *Republic*. In Book 4 we come first upon a conventional enough distinction between calculation and desire, which under pressure from the correspondence between the microcosm of the just individual and the macrocosm of the just society, with its three different classes, is complicated by the addition of a third element, the element of "high spirit" (*thumos*). At this stage the three elements in the soul are distinguished principally by their functions: calculation calculates, desire desires, spirit gets spirited. If the text is pressed to assign them an object or goal as well as an activity, the indications would be that calculation is concerned with the good (i.e., with the best course of action); desire is concerned with pleasure; while spirit reacts to perceived slights or wrongs.

When we revisit these three elements in Books 8 and 9, however, they have taken on a different look. In Book 4 they seemed most like faculties; now they seem more like drives.[1] The desiring element is specified as the drive toward material satisfaction; spirit as the drive to win and to amount to something; calculation as the drive to discover truth. They have not shed their characteristic functions, but these have found a new context; and the biggest change is to the calculative element. Previously, it had been unclear whether this

---

[1] The collective terms chosen by Plato to refer to these elements seem deliberately vague. Most often, in fact, he uses no separate noun at all, but writes of "the calculative," "the spirited," "the desirous." When he does use a distinct noun, his most frequent choice is *eidos*, "form," "character," "kind of thing" (or its near synonym, *genos*). Least frequent is the noun *meros*, "part," which occurs seven times in this connection. "Element" has in English a vagueness that perhaps best matches the Greek.

element even had a goal of its own or was merely a supervisor that placed limits on the interests of the other elements in the interest of the individual as a whole. Now it is assigned an object of desire all its own, and that object is not the good, whether the good of the individual or the good *tout court*, but wisdom. Wisdom is a good, of course, arguably the highest good. But this element seeks wisdom because it is wisdom, not because it is good. It has turned out to be the philosophic element in the soul.[2]

For this reason we should not be content for the calculative element merely to supervise within us, not if we want to be happy. Its natural passion is directed at something different and better than this. Certainly, it is better that this element in each person should be supervisor than that it should fall under the control of the other elements of the soul and be reduced to a tool in their service, as described in Books 8 and 9. But although it is appropriate that the calculative element should supervise the others (441e), this is not what it loves to do. As the philosophic element in the soul, it takes on the job of ruling the soul with a reserve comparable in some respects to that with which philosophers take on the job of ruling the city. Even within the soul, ruling is *work*. (Philosophy, by contrast, though it takes exertion, is the finest and most serious play.) When he grants himself the license of myth, Plato gets the point across this way: the philosophic element is divine and immortal, the other elements are mortal and animal, and only the necessity of incarnation thrusts them together.

The philosophic element of the soul, then, is underdescribed in Book 4. This is at first sight surprising, since the pages of Book 4 in which the three elements of the soul are distinguished contain one of the most sustained and careful arguments in the *Republic*, and have accordingly attracted the sustained and careful attention of modern philosophers. It is disquieting to some of them that Socrates issues a warning in the preface to this argument not to expect a completely satisfactory outcome from it (435d). But the *Republic* never in fact supplies the "longer route" to resolving such matters that Socrates declares untaken in the Book 4 discussion. Although it

---

[2] Christopher Rowe (chapter 2 in this volume, n. 30) sees no inconsistency between reason's being oriented both toward the good and toward wisdom; indeed, there is none. The question (to be pursued in what follows) is why the text offers no evidence for this double orientation, and what the implications of its silence would be.

is a route that Socrates insists his philosopher-kings must be made to take (504a–d), he pointedly refuses to take it himself (506b–e, 533a); and no subsequent analysis of the divided soul in the *Republic* has the technicality and apparent rigor of this one in Book 4. So it is small wonder that some have been tempted to anticipate the fuller descriptions of the various elements, particularly of the philosophic element, grafting them retrospectively onto the Book 4 argument wherever they can be of service – as for example in the very exiguous description of the case of the thirsty man. In this way the various discussions of the soul in the *Republic* can be made to yield a unified psychology, whose apogee comes at its most technical point.[3]

This is a temptation worth resisting. Much of philosophic interest will go unremarked if we fail to ask ourselves why Plato chose to picture the three-part soul so differently at the different stages of his argument in the *Republic*.[4] In particular, we will fail to understand what it is about the philosopher that makes him the superior even of the just man described at the close of Book 4 – that seeming paragon of virtue.

I

In order to distinguish elements within the soul Socrates appeals in Book 4 to cases where a person experiences internal conflict over some action. There is the case of the thirsty man who holds himself back from quenching his thirst, the case of Leontius who is angry with himself for gawking at the corpses of executed criminals, and the case of Odysseus quieting his heart when it calls out for immediate vengeance on the suitors and their giggling servant girls. If one and the same person holds conflicting attitudes toward the same outcome, Socrates argues, it cannot be in respect of one and the same psychological element that he holds them.

It is a particular kind of mental conflict that the argument of Book 4 trains its eye on: not the dilemma arising from a mere coincidence of desires that cannot be simultaneously gratified, as when an invitation we would like to accept and a performance we would like to see

---

[3] The strategy is well developed in Cooper 1984; Kahn 1987; and in the third chapter of Bobonich 2002 (see esp. pp. 527–28, n. 11).

[4] The point is well appreciated in Blössner 1997 (the essence of which is distilled into English in his chapter 13 in this volume), and Roochnik 2003 (see esp. pp. 17–18).

fall on the same evening, but rather the wish to gratify a desire and, simultaneously, resistance to that wish; not two inclinations that happen to be incompatible but an inclination toward some action and a pulling back from that same action. If the general principle on which Socrates bases his division of the soul is at first expressed in language that seems as well suited to logical as to psychological application (436b) – language that may remind the modern reader of the logical principle of noncontradiction – it is in fact developed in terms of opposites, not of contradictories: in terms of assent and dissent, desiring and rejecting, pulling in and pushing away, rather than of assent and nonassent, desiring and not desiring, pulling in and not pulling in (437b–c). It would seem better described as a principle of conflict than of (non-) contradiction.[5] It is not merely through their differences but through their conflicts, then, that the parts of the soul are discovered.

An influential line of interpretation explains this fact as a striking development in Platonic psychology. That people do not want to be unhappy and will not choose a course of action they think will make them unhappy is a claim with much intuitive appeal; but Plato's Socrates in dialogues presumed by most to have been written before the *Republic* exploits this appeal in the cause of a quite counterintuitive insistence that people never act contrary to what they think is best. What actually happens to people who seem to themselves to be suffering weakness of the will, according to Socrates in these dialogues, is that they are mistaken about their good. His argument is helped by the thought that all desires are desires for the good. Accordingly, when our passage in Book 4 puts on Socrates' lips a warning not to be disturbed by the objection that everyone desires good things (438a), this line of interpretation takes Plato to be marking a break with the erstwhile paradox-monger. Here in the *Republic* Plato would be making room for a category of irrational desires that are blind to the good. That would be what Socrates is getting at when he treats thirst, hunger, and kindred appetites in isolation, specifying that we are not to consider whether the thirst is mild or strong or directed at a particular kind of drink, but that we should treat it as "thirst itself" or "thirst as such," which is directed at "drink itself." Just this is the move that prompts Socrates to anticipate the objection that everyone desires good things, with its apparent consequence

---

[5] Annas 1981, p. 137; Miller 1999, pp. 92–95; Smith 2001, pp. 118–19.

that thirst is not for drink alone but for good drink. By dispelling the objection he would be dispelling his former self. The soul whose elements are revealed by a principle of conflict turns out – not unnaturally, it may seem – to be a soul susceptible to the particular kind of inner conflict that is weakness of will, a phenomenon now understood not as the making of an intellectual mistake but, more realistically, as the defeat of one's better judgment when it comes into conflict with a desire that proves the more powerful motivator.[6]

The emphasis in this line of thinking falls on Plato's development and on his theory of action rather than on the purpose of the Book 4 discussion within the *Republic*. The position has been resisted by those who deny that Plato changed his mind on the question of weakness of the will,[7] as well as by those who deny that a divided soul is either necessary or sufficient to explain weakness of the will.[8] There are, moreover, several ways to understand the restriction of thirst to "thirst itself" without referring to the Socratic paradox about weakness of the will.[9] One scholar who accepts the role of a partite soul in the supposed development points out that we need not posit a category of blind, "good-independent" desires to achieve it;[10] another, that the considerations that drove Plato to divide the soul went well beyond weakness of will to embrace for the first time an entire theory of nonrational motivations.[11]

All should agree that it is the wider concept of mental conflict rather than the narrower concept of weakness of will that Book 4 in fact discusses. Neither Odysseus' thirst for vengeance nor the biological thirst of the thirsty man are permitted to overcome sober judgment; only Leontius is weak. Self-control and endurance are much in evidence in this passage on soul-division, both in its examples and in its generalizations (as at 440b–c). On the one hand, this casts an attractive light on the element that keeps both Odysseus and the thirsty man in check: the calculative part of the soul. On the other hand, it is a merely reflected light: the actions of the calculative part are attractive because the actions it resists are not (they

---

[6] Penner 1992, pp. 128–30, gives a concise and straightforward summary of this view. See also Reeve 1988, pp. 131–35; Irwin 1995, pp. 206–11.

[7] E.g., Ferrari 1990; Carone 2001; Weiss 2006, ch. 6.

[8] Shields 2001.

[9] E.g., Lesses 1987, pp. 156–57; Carone 2001, pp. 119–20; Hoffman 2003.

[10] Price 1995, pp. 49–50.

[11] Bobonich 2002, pp. 217–18.

are unhealthy, rash, or otherwise stupid). But are the actions of the calculative part attractive in themselves?

Odysseus' uncalculating anger, for example, is held back by that element in him "which has taken into consideration the better and the worse" (441c). The better and the worse being taken into consideration, however, are not the morally good and bad: this is clear from the fact that Odysseus' spirit, which is blind to the better and worse in this form, is intent on the same moral goal – justified revenge – that his calculation is advancing. What Odysseus is weighing against each other are better and worse strategies (the use of comparative adjectives is telling) for achieving this goal. He calculates that an immediate attack on the servant girls would break his cover at an inopportune moment and likely derail the vengeance he has planned for the following day against the whole gamut of his enemies: suitors, servant girls, and any others who are in league with them. (His deliberations are described in Homer, *Odyssey* 20.5–30, from which Socrates at 441b quotes one line, l.17.)

Socrates calls the reaction of Odysseus' spirit uncalculating (*alogistōs*, 441c); he does not call it unreasonable, for it is not unprovoked. The servant girls are brazenly contemptuous of his authority, of his house, of his family. Homer in the lines immediately preceding the one quoted by Socrates at 441b tells how the spirit within Odysseus barked like a dog – like a bitch defending her pups against an interloper. And if the quoted line describes Odysseus beating his chest and criticizing his heart, the discipline imposed on that dog-like organ is of a type that Plato has prepared the reader to see as sternly affectionate; for he had seen fit, less than a page earlier, to compare spirit's indignation at injustice and ardent pursuit of the noble to the behavior of a dog, albeit a dog that reason can restrain from its headstrong pursuit, and to remind us that the soldier-guardians of Callipolis were themselves compared to dogs in the service of ruler-shepherds (440c–d).

If Odysseus' calculative part is superior to his spirit, then, it is superior not morally but only to the extent that the thoughtful are superior to the headstrong. And the value of thoughtfulness depends on the direction of the thought. The thoughtfulness of the coolheaded criminal, Socrates will later point out, only increases the harm he can inflict (Book 7.518e–519a). At this stage, Socrates' argument has shown a distinctness between the parts, but it has not yet revealed what is at stake in their distinctness. His argument has not yet revealed that it is their goals, not merely their tactics, that are distinct.

II

The example of the thirsty man, too, is one in which the attractiveness of the calculative part comes to light only when we consider what it resists. In this case no affection attaches to the offending element, as it did to spirit. The thirsty man's appetite is compared to a beast dragging the resistant part to drink – or perhaps (for the text is uncertain) it treats the resistant element no better than a beast (439b).[12] Either way, this appetite is being a brute. Another of Socrates' comparisons makes it a thoughtless sybarite, "consorting with indulgence and pleasure" (439d). Its origins are described in words that smack of medical pathology: "It comes along through feelings/experiences/symptoms [pathēmata] and disorders/diseases [nosēmata]" (439d). The opposition to such an element would seem to be on the side of the angels.

But let us remind ourselves what it was that the principle of conflict, as subsequently developed, set in opposition to each other: an inclination toward some action and a pulling back from that same action. Nothing about this schema when considered abstractly puts the pulling back in a better light than the inclination resisted. (A boy might, for example, be inclined to do well at school but resist because he is reluctant to seem a teacher's pet.) Accordingly, when Socrates asks as a leading question whether it isn't the case that those who resist their thirst do so as the result of calculation, and Glaucon responds not with a decided affirmative but with a cagier "so it seems" (439d), the reader is invited to ponder how uncompelling an inference this is. For one thing, the resistance might derive from an aversion that is not only uncalculated but downright

---

[12] The genitive *thēriou* has the better manuscript support and is read by Slings 2003 *ad loc.* On this reading it is the thirst that is the beast, and one could compare the actions of the black horse dragging his charioteer in the *Phaedrus* (254) . On the reading *thērion*, familiar from earlier editions, the beast could be the resistant element (and one might then compare *Protagoras* 352b–c); but it could also, once again, be the thirst (if *thērion* were subject, not object, with its verb understood by ellipsis).

unreasonable. (Say, you are very thirsty, find soda generally thirst-quenching, but dislike the smell of Dr. Pepper because it reminds you of the dentist's – and Dr. Pepper is all there is to drink.) Or the resistance might not be unreasonable but nevertheless not be put up by the calculating part.

Consider in this connection how both a person who acknowledges himself to be in the wrong and one who on the contrary regards himself as having been wronged are described at 440c–d as willing to endure the deprivations of hunger and cold that might come their way, in the one case as punishment, in the other as ill treatment – ill treatment that must also be endured while retribution is sought. (The situation is not further specified but could be penal confinement or banishment to some inhospitable place without the means to support oneself.) These people are hungry but conquer their hunger; were they thirsty, too, as they presumably are, they would conquer their thirst. But their cases are intended to show what is characteristic of the spirited rather than of the calculative part.

True, spirit is said to be in alliance with reason here; still, the resistance to hunger and the like derives as much from the one as from the other – so much so that it now becomes unclear whether the spirited part is in fact distinct from the calculative at all (440e). It is in order to distinguish them that Socrates brings up the example of Odysseus quieting his heart; but this example, we saw, was notable for differentiating the conflicting elements not on moral but only on instrumental grounds. It is not well gauged to convince us that the two parts are fundamentally rather than superficially distinct – for their goals are not distinct.

What is more, when Glaucon suggests that some children never grow up to become capable of reasoning and that most attain it very late, remaining instead the spirited creatures they were from the first, and when Socrates adds that one can see the same thing in brute animals (441a–b), their observations open a space into which a counterexample to the account of the thirsty man's inner conflict could fit. (The gap only yawns the wider since these examples would not otherwise apply the principle of conflict at all, despite being brought in to distinguish the spirited and calculative parts.) For if these brutes and these children, small and big, were to endure pain and discomfort in order to fulfill some other need, their resistance could not come from a calculation of which they are, it is claimed, quite incapable. Socrates' addition of animals to Glaucon's list helps us to locate just such a counterexample in the nimbus of his citation from the *Odyssey*: the dog that shows fight against a man who has disturbed her whelps does not have her own safety and comfort in mind. (Compare the description of the spirited dog at 375b, "fearless in the face of everything.") So much for Socrates' proposal that those who suffer thirst and the like yet are unwilling to assuage themselves are acting in every case from calculation.

It is worth lingering to ask also why Glaucon responds so emphatically as he does when Socrates asks whether some thirsty people are sometimes unwilling to drink: "Yes indeed. Many of them. Often" (439c). Greek athletes in training might avoid wine and cold drinks (this is mentioned by Epictetus in his *Discourses* 3.15.2–4); Greek soldiers on campaign faced potentially unsafe water supplies (alluded to at 404b); but neither of these situations would be especially common. What stands behind Glaucon's emphatic response is likely the sentiment voiced by Socrates at 389e: that for most people self-discipline consists of two things, obedience to those in control of them, and personal control over the pleasures of drink, sex, and food. Socrates does not stop at this point to explain what enables most people to exercise this personal control, whether it is their own prudence or something different; he is far too busy excising what he regards as invitations to excess from the public poetry that the people of Callipolis will get to hear (389e–390d). (The lines in which Odysseus quiets his heart appear first here, as a text to be recommended rather than censored.) In other words, Socrates is constructing the framework for the social control that will endow his citizens with personal control (cf. 431c), and Plato thereby reveals the true nature of those citizens' personal control. It would be too simple, then, to describe these as cases in which an individual's calculative part is in control of his thirsts and hungers; the source of control is more diffuse.

For another widespread practice of resistance to drink we could look to the importance of dietetics in Greek medicine. This too has been a prominent topic in the *Republic* before Glaucon's emphatic response arrives at 439c. In a lengthy critique in Book 3 (405b–408c) Socrates had taken aim at health-faddists and hypochondriacs, with the aim of restricting medical care to the cure of disease and the treatment of injuries, and not allowing it to stray into the practice of dietetics and of other physical therapies embraced by those who are anxious about their health. Healthy people, he had suggested in the course of this argument, should not be unduly concerned about what they allow themselves to drink (408a–b). (Notice too that the allusion to unsafe water supplies for campaigning soldiers at 404b comes as part of a proposal that the guardian-soldiers of Callipolis, unlike Athenian soldiers, should be raised to have a physical constitution robust enough to cope easily with changes in their drinking water.) Glaucon had enthusiastically associated himself with this critique, asserting with an oath that excessive care of the body – anything beyond the normal exercises of the gymnasium – is one of the greatest impediments to appropriate participation in civic life (407b).

Here, then, is a realm of cases in which a person might resist drinking as a result of a well-calculated dietary plan, but where the cure would be worse than the disease. Once again we see that the actions of the calculative element are attractive only if they are attractively directed.

In short, Plato takes several opportunities to suggest that resistance to thirst might not be motivated by the best of reasons, and more generally to alert his readers to problems in the authority of the calculative part as presented so far in the *Republic*. Some factor other than one's calculative part may be in equally effective control. Alternatively, calculation may be in control, yet not working to a good end.

III

The calculative part needs a boost in the right direction, it seems; and at this stage of the argument it receives that boost entirely through socialization.

When Socrates begins to apply his threefold division of the soul to an analysis of the virtuous individual, he makes an important proviso. So long as both the calculative and the spirited elements have been properly educated and acculturated, he explains, they will work together to ensure that the desiring element does not grow strong through satisfying bodily pleasures and then attempt to usurp authority and enslave the other elements (442a–b). The young guardian acculturated to virtue will calculate, then, that moderation is the best course. His calculative part, being intelligent, is the locus of forethought on behalf of his entire soul (441e); it has knowledge of what is advantageous to each element and to the collective that they form (442c); and its conception of what is advantageous has been carefully formed by exposure to "fine words and studies" (442a).

The fact that Socrates needs to bring in the virtuous person's civic education in order to achieve this result shows the limitation of his argument at this point. The desiring element, he claims, is not the right "sort" to rule, is not suited by "birthright" to the task (*ou prosēkon . . . genei*, 442b). If it were to seize power it would not be "performing its proper role" and would have ceased to "know its place" – both these are meanings of the phrase *ta hautou prattēi* (442b). The social and political metaphors are thick on the ground here. Beyond what metaphor can do, it is only because the capacity for forethought and global deliberation belongs to the calculative element that the birthright to rule is given to it and denied to the others. But this being so, what is to prevent the calculative element choosing in favor of bodily pleasures on a regular basis? Socrates describes the appetite for such things, after all, as much the "largest" element in each person's soul (*pleiston*, 442a); does this not make it odd that in the same breath he should insist that for it to become "big" or "much" (*polu*) would be a breach of its station? A ruling element of a more populist bent might choose to award the appetites satisfaction in proportion to their numbers. In so doing, it could still be described as exercising forethought on behalf of the entire soul, however benighted its thinking might be. Only a particular acculturation, it seems, can prevent it from thinking this way.

The trouble here is caused by the fact that, to the extent that the calculative element as so far described has an interest at all, it is an interest that depends on the interests of the other elements, and depends on them intrinsically, not casually. Its interest is to adjust the interests of each against the other; it is a negotiator. But if it does not have a goal all its own – at least, no goal other than to occupy the negotiating role – the negotiation will in a sense be led by the other parties, despite the fact that the calculative element is in charge of the proceedings. It will be led by them in the sense that theirs are the interests to which it reacts, while it itself has no interest other than to react to theirs.

This gives the calculative part as described in Book 4 an inherently weak grip on power; that is why it needs careful bolstering by education if it is to command virtuous action. And this education must be of the type that trains the eye of the soul on the horizon of the social and the political rather than permitting it to rest on that of individual satisfaction. When describing this education in Book 3, Socrates tends to use terms that anticipate the emergence of the calculative element from its chrysalis: music and poetry will appeal to the "love of learning" (*philomathes*, 411d) that may be found in a guardian's soul and to his "philosophic nature" (410e, 411e). But their music and poetry, as is plain from the account Socrates gives of it in Books 2 and 3, will edify rather than educate their philosophic nature, to the extent that they are possessed of one. Its purpose is not to develop their philosophic nature for its own sake but to bend it to the requirements of the other elements in their character and ultimately to the needs of the city in which they must serve (411e–412a). As to the extent of their philosophic nature: we will take its measure when we consider once again the guardians' likeness to the dog.

A similarly teasing description of the calculative element as the "love(r) of learning" (*to philomathes*) occurs by implication at 435e, where it is attributed collectively to Athenian culture in order to suggest that it exists also in each Athenian. This epithet crops up here only to vanish for the remainder of Book 4, its hint of intellectual alacrity smothered by the long argument that has occupied us so far. In that argument the would-be lover of learning seems to operate only as a strategist. It is not, then, that the love of learning is never attributed to this part of the soul at this early stage of the *Republic*; the telling point is rather that its love of learning is not put to work. It is not directly involved in the control this element exercises over the others, whether, as we have seen, in contexts where this element's right to rule the others is what is described (441e) or in contexts where what is described is the manner in which it exercises power (442c). There the talk is not of its love of wisdom but of its forethought and ability to calculate what is advantageous to all. Just this is what will change in later books.

IV

It is at this point that a comparison with Freud's tripartite division of the soul into Ego, Id and Superego (or Ego-Ideal) can be especially illuminating. Comparisons between Freud and Plato come naturally because the two thinkers are close kin in some important respects, notably in their attention to the question of psychic health and in their analysis of psychic health in terms of a command structure of desires.[13]

Freud makes the very existence of a differentiated Id, Ego, and Superego depend on a history of the individual's development. (The account that follows has the Freud of *The Ego and the Id*, *Group Psychology and the Analysis of the Ego*, and *Civilization and Its Discontents* primarily in view.) Partitions are put up in the studio apartment of the soul as life becomes more complicated for it. A section of the originally undifferentiated Id develops into the Ego out of a confrontation with the restrictions imposed by the external world on the unrestricted needs of the Id. Later, at the Oedipal stage, the Ego manufactures the Superego in order to master Oedipal desires in the Id.

Equally important in this story is the fact that the partitions went up because of conflict and confrontation and that conflict is what keeps them up. If the tension is released, the walls may entirely collapse, as when the Ego and Superego fuse back together in the condition of mania, which is a complete absence of self-criticism. The pressure exerted on the partitions is inescapable, then; it is the condition of their existence.

Hence the tragic cast to even the ideal Freudian life, the life lived in self-knowledge. Freudian self-knowledge is a matter of accepting the results of our genesis – accepting that we are what we are through repression – and of managing the inevitable tensions between represser and repressed. The very terminology for the divisions of the soul shows this tragic cast: "Ego" and "Id" – or rather, "Ich" and "Es," "Me" and "It." To call the It "it" and oppose it to "me" is to withdraw it from identification with me, even though it – *the* "It" – is the locus of deep and authentic needs.

Freud's appeal to conflict in order to distinguish parts of the soul is comparable to the account we find in *Republic* 4. Not that Plato offers a genetic account of how the divisions arise – a fact that makes it easier for him eventually to transcend the Freudian pattern. But he does have Socrates use a principle of conflict as the tool to prise the

---

[13] The comparison between Plato and Freud is developed in Santas 1988 and Price 1990.

elements of the soul apart. So it interesting to discover that in Freud too the part that most closely resembles the calculative element in Plato, the Ego, also ends up being cast primarily as a negotiator or manager, without independent goals. To be sure, Freud is capable of describing the Ego as fulfilling a plan: he speaks of it seeking to bring the influence of the external world to bear upon the Id and endeavoring to substitute the reality principle for the pleasure principle that reigns unrestrictedly in the Id (see ch. 2 of *The Ego and the Id*). Later in that same work he will even say that the Ego strives to be moral (ch. 5) – although, since he equates "morality" there with "instinctual control," he must mean by this only that the Ego's task is to control the instincts of the Id.

These are in any case the strivings and endeavors of an element that Freud repeatedly describes also with metaphors of impotence: the Ego is a rider who is in the habit of guiding the horse of the Id where *the horse* wants to go and, unlike an actual rider, is using not its own strength but borrowed forces; or it is a servant of three masters: the external world, the libido of the Id, and the severity of the Superego; or it is a merely constitutional monarch. The Ego, like the calculative element of *Republic* 4, does not pursue independent interests; the Ego spends its time either acquiescing in or repressing desires derived from the Id.

v

The Freudian soul, then, is a soul that suffers unremitting internal pressure. And here a contrast rather than a similarity with Plato is immediately apparent. The presentation of the just man that comes as the grand finale to Book 4 (443c–e) is of an individual who is not only ruler of himself but also a friend to himself, whose soul is in perfect harmony, each element attuned to the other like the strings of a lyre or like the intervals of the musical scale to which those strings lent their names. If the Freudian "Ego" and Plato's "calculative part" are indeed comparable, the condition of the soul over which they preside seems quite different.

This contrast is real, but requires qualification. For if instead of contemplating the portrait of the ideally just man who corresponds to the ideally just city, as we do in Book 4, we lower our gaze a notch to the level of the thoroughly decent but still imperfect fellow described in Book 10, whose calculative part successfully restrains the urge to weep at his personal tragedies but lets it loose at performances of tragic drama, we shall encounter a soul closer to the Freudian model – its justice and self-control sustained by pressure. Let us examine this character, in order to locate the justice of the ideally just man with greater accuracy.

The relevance of the decent man's case to our inquiry into the three-part soul is clearly flagged by the recurrence of a version of the principle of conflict (603a) and an explicit backward reference to Book 4: Socrates recalls that their earlier discussion had adequately established that the soul is susceptible to opposition and struggle within itself (603d). The particular internal struggle that Socrates now considers is that of a "decent" or "respectable" man (the word is *epieikēs*, 603e) who loses someone dear to him. Such a man's reactions are conditioned above all by his sense of propriety. In attempting to restrain his feelings of grief and loss, he works hardest at not giving way to public lamentation. He would be ashamed to be seen or heard giving vent to such a display. Yet for that very reason he is likely to lose his grip on himself when alone, and say and do the things that "reason and custom" frown upon (604a).

We next encounter the decent man at the theater (he is again described as *epieikēs*, 605c). Here his inhibitions are removed; he no longer even attempts to restrain his feelings. He is prepared now to accept that real men *do* cry (605d–e), or at least he will not allow the disapproval he would normally feel at the sight of a man dissolved in grief to interfere with the pleasure he gets from sharing in the grief of the tragic hero (606b). So, too, at a comedy he is happy to indulge a delight in buffoonery that he would be ashamed to let govern his own behavior, for fear of the harm it would do to his good reputation (606c).

The key to the respectable man's emotional response in the theater is the likelihood that in his personal tragedies he will lose control of himself when left on his own. For this reveals that his is not true self-control at any time; it is rather a control imposed primarily from without, a pressure exerted on him by society. Reason in him requires the assistance of custom to prevail over his emotion, when it does prevail (604b–c). It is ready to follow custom's lead and give ear to a litany of sentiments on the value of keeping a stiff upper lip and on the ultimate insignificance of human beings, a litany that our respectable man will have heard in a variety of social contexts, not least among them the poetic performances at which he also finds emotional release from the inhibitions that those sentiments encourage.

Release from inhibitions – that is the pleasure the respectable man experiences in the theater and at other performances of poetry. It is more than just the pleasure of satisfying his appetite for tears, which may be supposed to be the experience of those in the audience more vulgar than he (as is suggested but not made explicit at 605a–b). Rather, he is satisfying an appetite that he has kept down by "force" (*bia*) in his regular life – a part of him that "has been hungry [*pepeinēkos*] for tears" and that he has deliberately starved (606a). In his regular life he is like a thirsty man who is nevertheless unwilling to drink; in the theater he receives temporary relief of a pressure that weighs on him at all other times. This is catharsis in the sense that the term has come to have in popular psychology: not the relief of a tension developed in the audience by the performance itself – say, by the suspense generated in the twists of its plot – but the relief of tensions that accrue in life and are brought to the performance fully formed. For once, our respectable man can allow himself to have a good cry and not feel bad about it.[14]

VI

Before applying this analysis to the topic of the ideally harmonious soul, let us consider the light it sheds on the one conflicted soul in Book 4 still to be scrutinized: Leontius (439e–440a). As he is walking to Athens and passing the place where the corpses of executed criminals were left to rot in public view, he feels the urge to take a closer look. At the same time he is disgusted and struggles against the urge, veiling his eyes. Finally, he gives in and runs up to the corpses, forcing his eyes wide open and cursing them: "There you are, you wretches! Take your fill of the beautiful spectacle!" The case proves that anger can fight against desires and so indicates that the spirited is distinct from the desiring part, as the case of Odysseus stilling his

---

[14] Although this conception of catharsis can be traced to Freud, who employed it in various forms as a therapeutic technique, Freud did not himself make the connection between catharsis and the reactions of a theatrical audience.

heart bears witness that the spirited is distinct from the calculative part.

With Leontius, it is as if the decent fellow of Book 10 lost his fight against grief not just when alone but also in public. When Leontius finally indulges the urge to feast his eyes, their satisfaction is the more extravagant for having been strongly resisted. The balance tips; where he was covering his eyes now suddenly he is jamming them open. His anger becomes public cursing as he makes a vain attempt to dissociate himself from his eyes, and thereby from his conduct, for the benefit of any who might witness it. (It is much too polished a piece of cursing to count as an involuntary outburst.) And many *did* witness it: not only does Socrates introduce the incident as an anecdote he once heard but Glaucon adds that he heard it independently himself (439e–440a). Leontius is making a spectacle of himself; so his behavior becomes a story.

His reputation would have been safe if only he had instead walked directly to Athens and into the theater of Dionysus, there to gaze to his heart's content upon the bloody corpses that result when tragic heroes perpetrate what they regard as justified revenge on criminal offenders. (Greek tragedy conducted its killings and mutilations offstage but was quite fond of the *coup de théâtre* afforded by the emergence of the grisly consequences into the light.) For these are not just any corpses by the roadside that Leontius hankers to look at. It is no traffic accident. It is the sight of justice wrought on criminals.[15]

Leontius is troubled by the "beautiful spectacle" when he encounters it in the flesh but would not have been had he encountered it in the theater (the word *theama*, like its English equivalent "spectacle," is often used of artistic events). Compare how Glaucon is squeamish about describing in explicit detail the punishments inflicted on criminals (361e–362a) but is perfectly happy to sit through a lengthy description of similarly horrible punishments inflicted on the souls of the criminal dead in a poetic tale, the myth of Er (614a–b, 615d–616a). (Socrates reminds him of his squeamishness just before broaching the myth, 613d–e.) Leontius' mistake, then, in contrast to the decent man whose tear-starved part longs to be "filled" when suffering any painful loss but is only allowed to get

---

[15] This point, which generally passes without notice, is appreciated and developed in other (not uncomplementary) ways in Benardete 1999, p. 102, and Allen 2000.

"filled" by the tragic poets (606a), is that he "fills" his eyes with reality, not fiction (440a).

(One sometimes encounters the suggestion that Leontius' interest in the corpses is sexual, on the grounds that a fragment of fourth century comedy ridicules a person of that name for being aroused by a boy as pale as a corpse. But the grounds are very insecure. The transmitted text neither contains Leontius' name nor makes the accusation described, but must be extensively emended to do so; and even if the emendation were correct, the joke might make better sense as a consequence of his gawking at corpses than as an explanation of it.)

In the theater Leontius could have lingered and thrilled with impunity over the corpses of offenders; in real life, when the dam of his inhibition finally breaks, it releases a burst of undignified and histrionic behavior. When Odysseus' nurse Eurycleia gets set to launch a triumphant ululation at the sight of the suitors' slain bodies littering the hall – another justified revenge haunting the *Republic*'s account of the spirited part – Odysseus "holds her back, eager though she was," and bids her exult only in her heart, as it is not right to crow openly over slain men (*Odyssey* 22.407–12). Odysseus here takes the role of Leontius' inhibition, Eurycleia that of his desire – with the difference that Odysseus is successful where Leontius' inhibition fails. Those, however, who attended a dramatic recital of this very revenge scene from the *Odyssey* – let us say it is the performance the rhapsode Ion describes himself giving of it in Plato's *Ion* (535b–e) – could permit themselves to be swept up unreservedly by its thrilling and gory details. (Ion declares he would count himself a failure if they did not, 535e.)

VII

Is the kind of internal pressure common to both Leontius and the decent man of Book 10 – as well as to the Freudian soul – quite absent from the man portrayed at the end of Book 4 as ideally just? He is the just man who has been educated in the just city – a guardian. The elements of his soul have been calibrated by the combination of literary, musical, and physical training peculiar to Callipolis (441e–442a). Of such a soul it would not be true to say, as Socrates says of the decent theatergoer in Book 10, that what is best in it has been inadequately educated "whether by argument or even by habit" (606a) – an important factor in the theatergoer's willingness to relax his guard over the urge to grieve. While the decent man's upbringing has imbued him with many a noble sentiment (rehearsed at 604b–c), it has also tempted him to find ersatz release from these strictures in the theater. But just these, we saw, are the temptations that Socrates rigorously excludes from the poetry, music, and other forms of art to which the guardians will be given access.

That the poetry to which the guardian is exposed does not tempt him to indulge the urge to grieve does not by itself prove that he fails even to feel the pressure of this urge in other circumstances. But Socrates argues that works of art, and cultural artefacts in general, when rigorously and globally controlled, have the power to shape one's character for all situations (395c–d, 401c, 425a). The ideal of freedom from grief at the death of a loved one presented to the young guardian in the course of his education (387d–388a) – the behavior that "decent" characters display in the poetry he is given (the word is *epieikeis*, again, 387d) – is notably more austere even than the behavior of the decent man in Book 10. In the later book Socrates introduces a note of realism: if, he says, he had been content previously not to inquire whether the man who takes such events most easily will feel grief at all, he now thinks it right to ask whether it is not more likely that the decent man will feel some grief, but be moderate in his emotion (603e). Perhaps, then, we are to suppose that by dint of continual exposure to the most austere of fictional models the young guardian will get as close to immunity from grief as is humanly possible and so escape the pressure experienced by the decent man who is raised in a less exceptional society.

But if grieving at the loss of a loved one is ruthlessly excised from the guardians' fiction, the spectacle of justified revenge that we imagined Leontius enjoying in the theater is not. These soldiers are being raised to defend their city fiercely against its enemies. Martial music, of a kind to accompany a character bravely enduring wounds and death in battle and in other forms of violence, will be required for their education (399a). After many pages listing poetic passages unsuitable for guardian ears, the first passages to be recommended for them to hear concern obedience in battle (389e). The only other passage that gets a positive recommendation is our old friend, the lines in which Odysseus restrains his anger (390d). Introducing them,

Socrates explains that not only words but also deeds of endurance in the face of everything should be presented to the guardians.

Is there any reason, then, why these soldiers who must learn to fight when outnumbered (422b–c) should not go on to hear the whole story of the punishment inflicted by Odysseus, his son, and his two loyal servants against the throng of offending suitors, the heroic combat of the few against the many, bloody though it was? The castration of Uranus by Cronus will be kept from them, not because of its violence but because it is parricide (378a–b); the ruthless castration of the disloyal goatheard Melanthius by Odysseus' henchmen need not. Nor need they be prevented from hearing how the servant girls were punished for their impudence: by Telemachus stringing them up on a rafter and hanging them. (The episodes are graphically described in *Odyssey* 22.457–477.)

It is not to be expected that a guardian of Callipolis would lose control of himself as Leontius does and exult over the corpses his fierceness has made. The guardian has been raised more strictly; also, his rules of engagement in war explicitly forbid him to continue to treat the bodies of slain enemies in a hostile fashion (469d–e). Nevertheless, the harmoniousness of his soul, genuine though it is, depends after all on the kind of inner tension exemplified in extreme form by Leontius. It is a tension peculiar to those whose spirited element waxes strong.

VIII

The name "Leontius" means "Lion-Man"; in the wax model of the three-part soul imagined by Socrates in Book 9, spirit is a lion (588d). Leontius' spirited anger against his ignoble desire is histrionically fierce.[16] Yet his spirit fails to conquer his desire. Why? Because his desire and his spirit are strangely close in this instance. To be fierce in the cause of just punishment is noble and beautiful in its way, but to succeed in this cause you must have an appetite for the ugliness, even the horror that your fierceness will bring about. Control this appetite, and you can make a soldier; let it control you, and the

---

[16] If Allen 2000, pp. 136–37, is correct in claiming that Leontius' squeamishness about the corpses is unusual in his society, the sensitivity of his spirited part would seem all the more pronounced.

result, if temporary, is a breakdown like that of Leontius. If permanent, it could become a madness like that of the tyrant in Book 9, who indulges throughout his life the horrific fantasies most people experience occasionally in dreams (571c–d, 574e).

In the guardian's case this tension is encapsulated in the reiterated comparison between guardians and dogs. The problem arises for the first time in Book 2 (375a–375e), after Socrates has likened the qualities required in a good soldier to those found in well-bred dogs: swiftness and alertness, strength of body, fierceness of spirit. He is immediately stymied by how to prevent men such as these from being aggressive with each other and with the citizens they are there to protect and should be mild toward, reserving their harshness for enemies in war. A fierce spirit would seem the opposite of gentleness; how can our guardians be possessed of both? Back to the rescue comes comparison with the dog. Dogs are notable not only for being spirited, but also for being as gentle as could be with those they are used to and recognize, while being the opposite with those they do not know.

How do they manage it? By being "philosophic" as well as spirited (375e–376c). For if dogs are hostile and friendly purely on the basis of whether they *know* the person they encounter, and regardless of whether the one they greet as friend has ever been kind to them or the one they reject as enemy has ever done them harm, they are creatures who put a high value on knowledge indeed. Born philosophers, clearly. So if the guardian is to be gentle to insiders as well as fierce to outsiders, he too must be philosophic as well as spirited.

The evident irony of this passage and the inappropriate application to animals of terms such as "lover of learning" (*philomathēs*) and "lover of wisdom" (*philosophos*) that will not find their true application until real philosophers have made their appearance in the *Republic*'s argument, at the end of Book 5, together indicate that the supposedly philosophic element in the guardian's soul is no more than the strategic, calculative faculty that we meet in Book 4. As in Book 4, it sets its sights no higher than does the spirited part: at marking the distinction between self and other, friend and foe. Its farthest horizon is social, not global.

The potential difficulty of this arrangement comes to light, however, in one further characteristic of the dog, which Socrates develops at the end of Book 3 (415e–416c): the dog's potential to turn on members of its own household if under stress or if improperly bred and raised. Our guardians will have the job of protecting the city from external enemies, who come on the city, says Socrates, like wolves on the fold. But we must take the greatest care to ensure that his own strength does not corrupt the guardian and make him too behave like a wolf to his fellow citizens, much as sheepdogs will sometimes turn on their own flocks. The sheepdog could be driven by malnutrition, by indiscipline, or by some bad habit (416a). It is not, then, the predatory instinct as such that is at fault, but the circumstances or the practice that brought about that instinct's release. The predatory instinct is present in all dogs; it is one of the very features that makes a dog amenable to discipline. Without that instinct the dog would be useless to its shepherd.

(When the passage in which Odysseus quiets his heart appears in our text for the first time, as a passage recommended for guardian ears at 390d, it is two lines, not one line long, and so includes the rationale that Odysseus gives to his heart: "You have endured filthier than this." A closer translation is: "You have endured more 'dog' than this" (*kunteron*). And the incident Odysseus has in mind is when the Cyclops devoured men from his crew, *Odyssey* 20.18–21.)

The transformation of the guardian from dog to wolf would be the easier because a complementary part of the guardian's job is to protect the city from internal rather than external enemies – from those who break the city's laws (415d). Such people are only so-called friends, and may be strategically deceived as one would deceive external enemies (382c). Nor is it always clear what counts as inside, what as outside: demonstrating this is one function of the long discussion in Book 5 on panhellenism in warfare, where Socrates argues for treating all Greeks as friends even if conflicts arise with them, leaving only non-Greeks to be treated as Greeks now treat other Greeks (470a–471c) .

We breed dogs for predatory aggression and then must raise them to be attached to their household if they are not also to be aggressive toward it. (Leontius makes it seem that his own predatory eyes are turning on him, and dogs are natural scavengers of corpses – a fact alluded to at 469d–e, the passage in which guardians are forbidden to despoil those they kill.) For similar reasons, the warlike guardians must be educated to identify their personal interest with the interest of the city (412c–d, 416b–c). This is how we must "guard against" (*phulakteon*, 416b) their turning on us – in effect, guarding against our own guardians. A few pages before this, in an exchange on the need for guardians to avoid the disorientation of drunkenness, Glaucon had remarked that it would be absurd for a guardian to need a guardian (403e). Now his joke has acquired a serious edge.

At this stage of his argument, then, Socrates has no better remedy for the propensity of the guardians to treat everyone, insider and outsider alike, as a possible enemy than to treat the guardians themselves as possible enemies, and work like the devil to make them friends.[17]

Within the guardian's soul the atmosphere is similarly watchful – courteous, but watchful. As the soldiers and their generals guarded against enemies both internal and external, so the spirited and strategic elements in the just man's soul not only "watch" (*tēreseton*, 442a) to ensure that the desiring element does not overstep its bounds and attempt to enslave them, but also "guard against" (*phulattoitēn*, 442b) the man's enemies in the outer world by lending him the wits and boldness to put up a successful fight. The desiring part, if it knows its place, is a friend; but it must always be watched as a potential enemy. The friendship is forever in need of preservation (443e).

Nor can the obedience of the spirited element be taken for granted. If Glaucon, obedient to Socrates' lead, insists with an oath that he has never seen spirit take the side of desire against reason either in himself or in anyone else (440b), that is because Glaucon has true nobility (368a, 548d–e). He is not one of those hypocritical noblemen of the Spartan type whose spirit "fiercely honors" money and the illicit pleasures money can buy, but honors them only in the dark, taking the side of desire against the law to which he pays lip service (548a–c). But Socrates himself is not so naïve: he acknowledges a spectrum in the behavior of spirit – the *nobler* a person is who knows himself to be in the wrong, the *less* his spirit will be aroused (440b–c) – and specifies that if the spirited part is indeed to be the ally

---

[17] This situation is reflected in a dispute over translation: should we translate the term *phulakes* as the more benign-sounding "guardians" (the traditional choice) or as the potentially more sinister "guards"? The reader who accepts the argument in this section should be less certain than Malcolm Schofield that either translation is quite satisfactory (see his discussion in chapter 6, n. 8).

of the calculative, it must have escaped corruption by poor upbringing (441a).

The harmony within the just man's soul is a lyre's harmony (443d): the strings that represent the parts of the soul are not in tension with each other but stand in mathematical relation to each other. A beautiful proportion pervades the whole. The relationship is not stable, however, but depends on tension at a second remove: on maintaining the correct tension in each string. Notice the difference between this analogy for the soul and that of the archer drawing his bow, an analogy that Socrates used at 439b to describe the conflict between the thirsty man's calculation and his thirst.[18] The tension represented by the drawn bow is a tension directly between parts of the soul: one part pulls and another resists. Nevertheless, the result is harmonious in its way: the archer's hands cooperate in their task.

The harmony of the Freudian soul and of the decent man in Book 10, both of them outwardly successful types, is the harmony of the bow. Conflict is the permanent condition of the Freudian soul: repression, acknowledged or unacknowledged, determines the soul's life – repression of an Id whose very nature is to resist repression. The conflict that determines the course of the decent man's life lies closer to the surface than this, in his constant habit of maintaining a stiff upper lip. Still, it is an experience of inner conflict that he can never escape; for his society finds ways to feed what in him resists inhibition, and to keep it active.

The just man described at the end of Book 4 seems to have succeeded in making the elements of his soul sufficiently friendly to each other that he experiences no actual conflicts within. His is the harmony of the lyre. Yet each individual string is under tension; the potential for inner conflict, if not its actuality, is ever present. As the lyre player must work constantly to keep each string tuned in proper relation to the others, so with the just man (443e–444a): each action that he chooses with a view to helping cement his inner condition is by the same token a conscious avoidance of one that could dissolve it.

---

[18] There may be a quiet development of Heraclitus here, who used bow and lyre indifferently to illustrate what he called a "backward-turning harmony": how something can agree with itself by the very fact of being at variance with itself (see DK fragment B51).

IX

That this cannot after all be the ideally just soul, the *Republic* will show its readers in Books 5–7, where genuine philosophers are introduced. This chapter has focused on the two key and interdependent factors that keep this soul from perfection: first, that it is based around its spirited part and, second, that its calculative part is not up to serving as an alternative base.

It is the spirited element in the soul, we saw, that both guards and must be guarded. This is the part that deals with enemies and that makes enemies. It is the "middle" tone (443d) standing between a highest and lowest tone that would otherwise form the unison of an octave.[19] A soul might have an easier job of being a unity without it. But in a human world, both city and man, however pacific, must expect to deal with those who will make enemies of them.[20] And if the guardian who is to become a judge of criminals cannot be permitted to experience criminality within his own soul but must be a "late-learner" of injustice, even at the cost of naïvete in his youth (409a–b), the same luxury is not permissible when it comes to war. The guardians who are to defend the city from violence must be taken to war as children and allowed, like puppies, to taste blood (537a). In this they would resemble a doctor who draws on his own experience of being ill in order to cure the sick (408d–e). At least half the young guardian's music is war music (399a–c).

(On the question of a soul's doing without its spirited part, it is worth considering why Plato has Socrates at 443d mention the intervening notes between the highest, middle, and lowest tones of the scale. He is sometimes understood to be opening the possibility that the soul, like a scale, may contain several more parts than these three.[21] But he may instead be conceding that a musical scale – *unlike* the soul – does, as it happens, contain more than three elements. He would be saying that a just man tunes the three parts of

[19] On the musical theory here, see West 1992, pp. 219–20. That Plato means the highest and lowest notes (*nēte* and *hypatē*) to cover a full octave, not merely a seventh, is supported by his explicit attribution of eight notes to the scale the Sirens sing as music of the spheres at 617b.

[20] For discussion of the possibility of a soul with no spirited element, see section IV of Paul Ludwig's chapter 8 in this volume. Fuller accounts of this element can be found in Gosling 1973, ch. 3, and Hobbs 2000, ch. 1.

[21] See, e.g., Murphy 1951, p. 30, and Smith 2001, pp. 127–28.

his soul as a musician tunes those three notes of the scale "and any others that as a matter of fact lie in between."[22] Plato's point in having him make this concession would not, however, be mere musical accuracy. It would instead be to suggest that as a musician must deal with however many notes there are in the scale or however many strings there are to his lyre, so the man who would be virtuous must deal with however many parts there are to his soul – even if there are fewer than three, not more. The suggestion is further developed when considering what form the soul might take in the afterlife, 612a.)

As for the calculative part, it stands in the same relation to the spirited part of the just man's soul as the rulers among the guardians do to the guardian-soldiers under their command. For as described in Books 2–4 these rulers are no philosophers but simply those who display to the highest degree the qualities of guardianship already canvassed for the guardian class as a whole (412c, 414b). They will be those who have demonstrated in the course of their training the greatest effectiveness – the greatest intelligence, endurance, and loyalty – when it comes to the task of keeping the city secure. That is why this chapter has so far spoken of "guardians" indifferently, without drawing the distinction between rulers and auxiliaries in the guardian class. For that distinction is a merely instrumental one; both sections of the guardian class are committed by their class membership to one and the same goal, and to no other. And this was the goal acquired by the guardian in his youth, when he was an auxiliary.

So it is too with the just man's soul in Book 4. If spirit must be the obedient assistant of the calculative part, this is only because the calculative part is better able to work out the steps required to maintain harmony, balance, peace in the soul. But if keeping the peace, punishing infractions, and righting wrongs are the goals of any of the soul's elements as so far described, they are the goals of spirit. As in the appropriately established city guardian-generals will emerge from the soldiery without losing the soldier's perspective, so in the appropriately educated soul the calculative part, by directing

---

[22] I owe this understanding of the sentence to David Sedley (who should not, however, be associated with the inference that I draw from it in the remainder of the paragraph – in particular, the inference that there may be an allusion to the soul's potentially having fewer than three parts).

the instincts of the spirited part, will in effect promote them. By guarding the guardian it will assist the assistant.

X

The figure of the philosopher overlays and disrupts this pattern in both city and soul. Once it has been revealed that the rulers of Callipolis are not to be mere guardian-generals but philosophers (473d–e), it can also be revealed that the calculative element in the soul is not in fact merely calculative but by nature philosophic (580d–581b). Chapters 10–12 in this volume consider in more detail the philosopher's character and education, and the nature of his understanding. This chapter concludes by giving some sense of how the harmony of the philosopher's soul differs from that of the just man's soul as described in Book 4, and of the extent to which it transcends the problems that were found lurking there.

Glaucon is sensitive to the difference between the two. When Socrates is casting about in Book 7 for the kind of study that would draw the soul toward understanding ultimate truth, Glaucon assures him that the musical and artistic education they gave to the guardians does not fit the bill, limited as it is to the achievement not of knowledge but of inner harmony through habituation (522a). And at the opening of Book 8 (543d) he volunteers the insight that when Socrates claimed previously (i.e., in Book 4) that the city he had described and the individual corresponding to that city were both good, he in fact had a still finer individual and city in mind to speak about.

Glaucon's sensitivity to this development is perhaps a consequence of his being not merely musical (398e), but also an erotic, passionate character (474d). For the development comes about because the calculative part has been recast as itself passionate; compared now to an eye of the soul that is naturally "kindled" by pure study (527e) and whose "flaming ray" (*augēn*, 540a) pure study will elevate and divert from its focus on the soul – for the whole soul must turn with it (518c).

No longer as in Book 4 is the task of the calculative part exhausted in "dragging" other parts or being "dragged" by them (*anthelkei*, 439b; *helkonta*, 439d), exhausted in this or in other managerial acts, even less forceful ones. Now what "drags" the calculative part is study (*helkei*, 533d; *holkon*, 521d), which draws it to higher levels of understanding. Now the person in whom the philosophic element is free to be itself, not enslaved by the other parts of the soul, is led by a true passion, a passion peculiar to this element and not intrinsically dependent on the others. The fundamental basis of its sway over the others is not its aptness for a supervisory role – though it has not lost this aptness – but the strength and nature of its passion. This manifests itself not through internal conflict but through the atrophy of the other elements in the face of an all-consuming interest, as when water is channeled to a single irrigation ditch and the others run relatively dry (485d). Far from focusing on the other elements, it transcends them. That the whole soul must turn with its eye indicates, certainly, that the civic mindfulness imbued either by a musical education of the sort the guardians receive or in some other way is still required to help effect the shift of focus, but it no longer delineates the eye's furthest horizon.

The metaphor of the irrigation ditches and the surrounding discussion of the philosopher's virtues in the opening pages of Book 6 constitute an analysis of the philosopher's nature rather than of his inevitable destiny. So far from there being any guarantee that a soul whose wisdom-loving part has sufficient potential will develop into that of a philosophic paragon, in the immediate aftermath of this analysis the several forms of danger and temptation that such a soul faces in life and that can prevent or distort its development are set forth at some length (489d–497a). The wrong sort of upbringing and education will spur such a character to excesses beyond the compass of a mediocre nature (491e); the wrong sort of political environment, the wrong sort of opportunities for public ambition will gather around a youth of such talent (494b–c) . The *Republic* is not starry-eyed about philosophy's capacity to save a soul. That is why in Callipolis the ideal is to combine – in modified versions, to be sure – what we might call a Spartan upbringing with an Athenian higher education.

A passage at the opening of Book 9 (571d–572a) evokes a new relationship between the three parts of the soul, in which the calculative element is described as coming into its own, "entering into meditation [*sunnoian*] with itself." Appropriately, it is a lyrical passage, which Socrates feels the need to excuse as an utterance he has been "carried away" to make (the verb he uses is *exagō*, 572b). The term *logistikon*, translated as "calculative" in this chapter in order to highlight its merely instrumental aspect, here turns its other face to the light and is better translated as "apt for reasoning" or the more familiar "rational."

The passage describes the proper regimen to use when preparing for sleep. Awaken your rational part and "feast" it (*hestiasas*, 571e) on fine discourse and inquiry; but put the other two parts to sleep, neither surfeiting nor shortchanging your material desires, nor dwelling on anything that might rouse the spirited part to anger. (The reader might note how different a feast this is for the eye of the soul than the feast that Leontius bid his eyes take their fill of.) In this way the rational part can be left in peace "to inquire and reach out, alone, pure, itself by itself, toward awareness of what it does not know."

This is neither the harmony of the bow nor the harmony of the lyre. It is no harmony at all. Yet it is evidently peaceful. Admittedly, it is a description of the meditative person's sleeping life only, not of his waking life. When it comes to planning a life that must contain days as well as nights, the wise man (in the final vignettes that the *Republic* draws of him, 591c–592b, 618b–619a) will make it his business to care for each element in his soul and to foster the best possible arrangement of those elements.

Indeed, it may seem that he will care for little else. He will choose even his studies with a view to how they affect the condition of his soul (591c). When that soul is between lives and must choose its next life, it will engage in furious "calculation" (*analogizomenon*, 618c; *sullogisamenon*, 618d) of all the possible factors that interact to make a better or worse life, and its ultimate criterion of judgment will be whether these factors produce justice or injustice within the soul.

How does such a soul differ from that of the just individual described in Book 4, who was eventually judged to fall short of perfection? Will the wise man's rational part too not engage itself with managing the other members of its community? How much difference does it make that this part now has a desire and a pursuit of its own – the pursuit of understanding for its own sake?

To the wise man's outward behavior it may make little or no difference. The philosopher who is a just man will show to the world a moderation, courage, and justice the equal but not obviously the superior of that shown by the virtuous man described in Book 4. With regard to his soul, however, he is working to establish and

preserve more than just the harmony of the whole; nor, as the virtuous man in Book 4 does, would he identify "wisdom" (*sophia*)
with the knowledge that supervises the preservation of this harmony
(443e). Within his soul there is now something worth preserving for
itself rather than simply because of its place in the whole, something
independently precious: the eye of the soul, whose power of thought
is inborn and can for that reason, if properly directed, become a virtue
of a different order (more "divine") than the moderation, justice, and
courage that can be imparted only through habit and practice (518e–
519a).

The wax model that represents the soul in Book 9 gives an image of
this new development by modeling the rational part as an inner man
within the outer man that the world gets to see (588d–e). Thus when
the person who believes that justice rather than injustice profits a
man is said to be promoting those words and actions "which will
make the man's inner man the strongest" (589a), the phrasing alerts
us to the fact that such a person is identifying with one element
within himself.

It is notable that in these final pages of Book 9 not only is the
rational part described in the familiar way as managing the other
elements (589b), but the whole person is also described as managing
the appropriate balance among all three elements of his soul. This
is not merely a loose way of talking; still less need it be a category
mistake. It is an excellent way to describe a choice of life. For readers
to puzzle over the relation between the outer and the inner man –
wondering, perhaps, who is really in charge here and whether the
outer man is something distinct from the sum of his parts – would
be for them to treat both outer and inner man as pawns in a theory of
action, game pieces whose moves on the board must follow a single
set of rules, on pain of failure to explain what human action is. If
instead we take the shift between the two kinds of description –
one where the inner man and one where the outer man controls the
whole – as a way of marking the distinction between choices that
determine particular actions and choices that embrace a pattern of
life, a metaphorical scheme emerges. For it is when Plato wishes
to describe one who is looking to the kind of person he will be,
not merely to what the situation demands (to drink or not to drink;
to approach the corpses or to pass them by), that images in which

an external agent controls the shape of some complex whole seem appropriate to him. So at the end of Book 9, in the context of the just man's intense focus on how he will live (591c), we read that he will watch over the "regime" within him (591e) or we recall that the just man of Book 4 was said to do everything he does as if he were a musician bringing into attunement three strings of his instrument – the three parts of his soul (443d–e).

(It is interesting that the opposite figure of speech crops up at a moment when a pattern of life is being set, but without conscious deliberation. When the decent man of Book 10 is weeping at the spectacle of tragedy in the theater, unaware of the long-term damage he is doing to his character, it is the best element within him, not he, that relaxes guard over the element that longs to grieve, reasoning that there is nothing shameful "for oneself" in doing so (606b). Rather than the outer man acting independently of the inner, here the inner man takes it upon himself to speak for the outer. It is doubly interesting that the same figure should occur also at 486a[23] in connection with the metaphor of the irrigation ditches, in a context where the philosopher's entire character is being imperceptibly molded by the strength of his rational part's desire to gaze on the spectacle of the cosmos.)

The choice of a less than perfect way of life, however unwise a choice it may be, is still a choice of life; accordingly, in those cases in Book 8 where a degenerate individual makes the decision to allow the desires of a particular element within his soul to shape his entire life (or in the case of the democrat man, to allow the desires of each element in turn to shape his life), Plato again speaks of the whole person as acting on the regime made up by the three elements of his soul. So the timocratic man "hands over political power" to his spirited element (550b), the very element that the oligarchic man then "kicks off the throne," installing his materialistic part as "Great King" in its place (553c–d). The democratic man, after too dissolute and chaotic a youth to permit true choice, brings certain of his better desires "back from exile" and "establishes his pleasures on an equal footing" (561b). (The tyrannical individual never emerges from the dissolute stage; he does not choose his way of life but descends into

[23] See Adam's notes to 486a4 and 606b8 in Adam 1963 [1902], vol. 2.

it, pushed by others; so he is never described as a man who acts on his inner regime.)[24]

The mistake these degenerate types make is to identify themselves with the wrong element or with the wrong combination of elements. As the imagery of the wax model implies, it is only when a man identifies himself with the goals of reason that the inner and outer man match and that natural integrity can be achieved.

XI

This shining image of integrity would be tarnished, however, if the outer man's identification with the inner entailed that any attention he paid to the other creatures within himself was merely instrumental, worthwhile only to the extent that it promoted the private interest the inner man takes in undisturbed pursuit of understanding. In that case the philosopher would seem to be living his whole life as he is when asleep and dreaming the finest of dreams. Or it would make Farmer Reason seem no better than Thrasymachus' shepherd in Book 1, who takes care of his sheep only to fleece them the more effectively (343b). Socrates has not forgotten that every art is concerned primarily for the interests of that on which it operates rather than for the interests of its practitioner (342a–e). The other elements of the philosopher's soul no more exist for the exclusive sake of its best part than the other classes in the city of Callipolis exist for the exclusive sake of its philosopher-rulers, despite the fact that philosophers are its best people and their activity its best activity.

To explain why reason should occupy itself with its companions in the soul out of more than merely the desire to minimize their disturbance, is it necessary to posit another type of desire that would be native to the rational part, in addition to its desire to understand: the desire to rule?[25] In fact, the desire to understand may suffice.

The philosopher, a person in whom reason rules of its own power, independent of social enforcement, makes all his choices in life with

---

[24] Instead it is the mad passion or "erōs" within him that brings about regime change (573b). See Ludwig's chapter 8 and Parry's chapter 14 in this volume.

[25] That the desire to rule in the soul must be native to the rational part and distinct from its desire to understand is argued by Cross and Woozley 1964, pp. 118–19, and by Cooper 1984, pp. 6–8. Klosko 1988 contests the claim with an argument different from the one attempted here.

a view to how they will affect the condition of his soul. (The virtuous man described in Book 4 is also said to make his choices on this basis, at 443e; but he does so, as we saw, from a different motive: because he has been acculturated to regard a self-disciplined, harmonious soul as the attribute of the best type of person, and because he wants – that is, his spirit wants – to make something of himself.) The philosopher does not look to the consequences of those actions in the larger world except to the extent that those consequences have an effect on his soul's good health. But in a soul where reason does indeed hold sway, this means that all the choices such a person makes are entirely within his power. No material inducement, no social ambition, no personal enemy can take that power from him. A better man cannot be harmed by a worse man, as Socrates puts it in the *Apology* (30d), and, by implication, will not be harmed by another good man. The good man is invulnerable.

But if this is so, then the philosopher's choices in life are in a way theoretical rather than practical – despite being effective, if the world will cooperate. He is in life as the disembodied soul is that in the myth of Er must ponder, in complete freedom of choice within the constraints of life's lottery (619b), how each mental and physical attribute, each circumstance of birth and social position, will affect a human being's condition in life, and therefore its own condition in the life on earth to come. Some things that the disembodied soul can directly choose, a living philosopher could not; but when the philosopher chooses, he chooses as freely and as directly as does the disembodied soul.

That some choice must be made is Necessity's decree, not the soul's desire; but the soul that responds to this decree by pondering its options with a philosopher's care is manifesting its desire to understand. It does not choose hastily, heedless of its prior existence, as does the soul that chooses a tyranny (619c); of its own accord, it seeks the best answer to a problem. It treats this problem as theoretical and general, as a study one might conduct at the feet of a master (618c), despite its awareness that much depends on a right answer.

Both this soul and that of the hasty chooser desire to be happy; for what was the hasty chooser grabbing at if not happiness? What distinguishes this soul from the hasty chooser is not the desire to be happy but the desire to understand: the pure desire to understand, which is for that reason also distinct from the profiteering thoughtfulness of the sharp-eyed criminal. And when the studious soul has chosen, its desire to understand will be ratified by the Fates as a happy life (619b, 620d).

So it is with the philosopher who lives that life. Within his soul, reason is compelled to rule, just as his soul was compelled to choose another life. The philosopher treats all pleasures other than the pleasure of understanding as "necessary in the true sense of the word, since if it were not for necessity he would have no need for them" (581e). Ruling the other parts is not reason's natural desire nor is it distinctive. Any part of the soul can rule the others, and to the extent that each part has a native desire that it seeks to fulfil, it also seeks to have its way within the soul.

If reason is going to have to rule – as it must, for the philosopher is a human being – it is going to rule right. Why? Because when it comes to this problem, as with any problem, it wants to know the best answer; because it desires to understand. Everyone seeks the good (505d–e), everyone wants to be happy; the philosopher strives harder than everyone else and is better equipped than everyone else to understand how.

Precisely because what the rational part of the soul naturally desires is to understand rather than to rule, it will not rule the other parts merely for its own benefit, as Thrasymachus' shepherd rules his sheep. And it is because those other parts lack this distinctive desire of reason that, should they come to power, they will treat the rational part as a mere tool of their private desires (as they are most clearly described doing within the oligarchic character's soul, 553d). The rational part is not seeking to prevail but to understand. And the problem that has been set for it to understand is not how to prevail over the other parts – a practical, merely instrumental problem – but how they all can best live together. This the philosopher will treat as a theoretical problem, one that can best be matched by a concern to discover, for its own sake, the best and most beautiful order of the whole – best and most beautiful because most rational.[26]

Let it be the case that, should push come to shove, reason will sacrifice the interest of the lower parts to its own interest; still its action in this case would not be selfish. It would be wise and global

---

[26] It is a concern to discover what Aryeh Kosman in chapter 5 in this volume calls "proper difference."

action performed under pressure, in recognition of how narrow the parameters of a good answer have become. If the situation demands that the interests of only one part can be satisfied, these had better be the interests of the best part. (Notice how compatible this way of describing reason's place in the soul remains with the descriptions of the calculative element in Book 4, whose capacity for forethought on behalf of the entire soul qualifies it to rule. The account of reason's workings in Book 4 was not false, then; it was only opaque. Book 4 does not permit us to appreciate the true basis of reason's capacity.)

The soul we are considering here is one in which reason is king. Any soul that falls short of this ideal falls short not only because the other parts are strong, but also because reason is correspondingly weak (549b; 560b; 573b).[27] Within this little city that the philosopher has founded for himself (591e), reason's word is law. Its thinking is effective; its "expoundings" are felt by the other parts as "commands" – both are meanings of the term *exēgētai* (586d), which occurs in an important passage describing the universal benefits of reason's rule. And this way of putting it provides a bridge between, on the one hand, the apparently automatic results within the philosopher's soul suggested by the image of the irrigation ditches at 485d (or by such a passage as 500c) and, on the other, the deliberate actions of Farmer Reason.

This activity of reason manifests itself at the level of the whole person as a choice. Of course, the world may be uncooperative and may prevent the choice from being effective beyond the confines of the philosopher's soul. But because his approach is in any case theoretical, not practical, this rebuff will not alter his happiness. The Fates give to each soul, just before birth, a "guardian spirit" (*daimona . . . phulaka*, 620d), whose job is to ratify in life the choice this soul has made outside it. The philosopher carries within him, as the "best of guardians," his reason (549b); in him it has the power to ratify happiness, a power it lacks in others. If this guardian is ruler of his little city, that is not because it desires to be, but because it was fated to be, and it was fated to be because, in the afterlife, too, this soul desired to understand.

---

[27] This schema leaves room for the possibility that the weakness of will to which such imperfect characters might be subject could continue to be traced to an intellectual mistake, to wrong thinking, as we found Socrates claiming in dialogues other than the *Republic*.

That the guardian rules is due also, let us not forget, to the fact that this soul chose not to drink the water of Lethe, and so remembered more in this life of the choice it had made (621a). It had come a long way across the desert and was very, very thirsty, but because it had pondered its choice and had desired to understand, because it was "saved by its intelligence" (*phronēsei*, 621a) and did not want to forget, it did not drink. Many are the occasions and many the people who, though thirsty, are unwilling to drink – so Glaucon had said. Perhaps his memory was stirring when he said it.

The philosopher's rational part seeks to order those realms whose order is entirely within its rational control. This is what it is to think theoretically. One such realm is his individual soul; another, in a way that everyone but the philosopher might think quite different, is the whole cosmos (486a). As for the human society that lies between these poles: unless it is Callipolis, it may have to wait.[28]

WORKS CITED

Adam, J., ed. 1963 [1902]. *The* Republic *of Plato*, 2 vols. Cambridge.
Allen, D. 2000. "Envisaging the Body of the Condemned: The Power of Platonic Symbols." *Classical Philology* 95: 133–50.
Annas, J. 1981. *An Introduction to Plato's* Republic. Oxford.
Benardete, S. 1999. *Socrates' Second Sailing: On Plato's* Republic. Chicago.
Blössner, N. 1997. *Dialogform und Argument: Studien zu Platons* "Politeia." Stuttgart.
Bobonich, C. 2002. *Plato's Utopia Recast: His Later Ethics and Politics.* Oxford.
Carone, G. 2001. "*Akrasia* in the *Republic*: Does Plato Change His Mind?" *Oxford Studies in Ancient Philosophy* 20: 107–48.
Cooper, J. 1984. "Plato's Theory of Human Motivation." *History of Philosophy Quarterly* 1: 3–21. Rpt. in *Plato 2: Ethics, Politics, Religion, and the Soul*, ed. G. Fine (Oxford, 1999), and in *Essays on Plato's Psychology*, ed. E. Wagner (Lanham, Md., 2001).
Cross, R. C., and A. D. Woozley. 1964. *Plato's* Republic: *A Philosophical Commentary*. London.
Ferrari, G. R. F. 1990. "*Akrasia* as Neurosis in Plato's *Protagoras*." *Proceedings of the Boston Area Colloquium in Ancient Philosophy* 6: 115–39.
Gosling, J. C. B. 1973. *Plato.* London.

[28] Special thanks go to Paul Ludwig, Mitchell Miller, David O'Connor, and Roslyn Weiss for the helpful comments they wrote on this chapter.

Hobbs, A. 2000. *Plato and the Hero: Courage, Manliness and the Impersonal Good*. Cambridge.

Hoffman, P. 2003. "Plato on Appetitive Desires in the *Republic*." *Apeiron* 36: 171–74.

Irwin, T. 1995. *Plato's Ethics*. Oxford.

Kahn, C. 1987. "Plato's Theory of Desire." *Review of Metaphysics* 41: 77–103.

Klosko, G. 1988. "The 'Rule' of Reason in Plato's Psychology." *History of Philosophy Quarterly* 5: 341–56.

Lesses, G. 1987. "Weakness, Reason, and the Divided Soul in Plato's *Republic*." *History of Philosophy Quarterly* 4: 147–61.

Miller, F. D., Jr. 1999. "Plato on Parts of the Soul." In *Plato and Platonism*, ed. J. M. van Ophuijsen Washington, D.C.

Murphy, N. R. 1951. *The Interpretation of Plato's Republic*. Oxford.

Penner, T. 1992. "Socrates and the Early Dialogues." In *The Cambridge Companion to Plato*, ed. R. Kraut (Cambridge).

Price, A. W. 1990. "Plato and Freud." In *The Person and the Human Mind: Issues in Ancient and Modern Philosophy*, ed. C. Gill (Oxford).

Price, A. W. 1995. *Mental Conflict*. London.

Reeve, C. D. C. 1998. *Philosopher-Kings: The Argument of Plato's Republic*. Princeton.

Roochnik, D. 2003. *Beautiful City: The Dialectical Character of Plato's Republic*. Ithaca, N.Y.

Santas, G. 1988. *Plato and Freud*. Oxford.

Shields, C. 2001. "Simple Souls," In *Essays on Plato's Pyschology*, ed. Ellen Wagner (Lanham, Md.).

Slings, S. R., ed. 2003. *Platonis Respublica*. Oxford.

Smith, N. D. 2001. "Plato's Analogy of Soul and State." *Journal of Ethics* 3: 31–49. Rpt. in *Essays on Plato's Psychology*, ed. E. Wagner (Lanham, Md., 2001).

Weiss, R. 2006. *The Socratic Paradox and Its Enemies*. Chicago.

West, M. L. 1992. *Ancient Greek Music*. Oxford.

8   Eros in the *Republic*

The *Republic* repeatedly treats eros as if it were unruly or bad and ought to be remade to be more congenial to good government. The illegality of choosing a mate for oneself, compulsory coed exercising in the nude, the imposition of eugenically determined match making, and the enforced discipline of having many sexual partners but no single partner to call "one's own" are decidedly strange institutions. Such attempts to coerce and mold eros to fit abstract justice imply a negative judgment about the political effects of ordinary erotic desire that is not in harmony with the liberated views about love and sex prevalent in most liberal democracies today. Nor are the coercive and legalistic stances toward sexual unions taken in the *Republic* and other political dialogues (e.g., *Pol.* 310bff.) in harmony with certain other dialogues of Plato, namely, the "erotic"[1] dialogues, which literally sing the praises of eros: in the *Symposium* and *Phaedrus*, eros is said to lead upward to pure beauty and goodness. In fact, the coercive parts of the *Republic* are not even in harmony with other parts of the *Republic* itself, for – just after the erotic regimen has been legally imposed – there follows a disquisition on eros that reads like a *Symposium* in miniature, with a profligate,

---

[1] English "eros" in this essay translates the Greek "*erōs*," which in the classical period referred primarily to passionate love or strong lust – with the proviso that the object need not be a human being, e.g., lust for learning in Plato. Classical *erōs* thus covered a much broader range than English eros (usually confined to sexual desire), but the fact that modern psychology has sometimes increased the range of eros by using it to mean sublimated desire for a multiplicity of objects justifies substituting the English term without italics. Two Greek passions that contrast with eros in this essay, *thumos* (spiritedness) and *philia* (familial affection and friendship), will initially be italicized but will lose their italics as their meanings emerge from the discussion.

promiscuous eros providing humanity's primary mode of access to the Forms.

This disparity is not the only sign of ambivalence toward eros in the *Republic*. The famous tripartite division of the soul introduced in the *Republic*, Book 4, is an insult to eros when considered in the context of the *Symposium*'s ladder of love. The tripartite division relegates eros to the lowest part of the soul, lumping eros together with other irrational desires, such as hunger and thirst (439d). All these desires, including eros, are said to be deaf to reason, unruly until policed by *thumos*, that is, the proud irascible "spirited" part (which can at least listen to reason). But in the erotic dialogues, and elsewhere in the *Republic* itself, reason and eros have a synergistic relationship. Most mysterious of all is the fact that elsewhere in the Platonic corpus, Socrates the exemplary philosopher is characterized as eros incarnate (e.g., *Tht.* 169c). By contrast eros is so corrupting in the *Republic*, Book 9, that the tyrannical man is characterized as eros incarnate. Eros is said to be the tyrant within the tyrant.

Harmonizing the *Republic* with the erotic dialogues and with itself involves sorting out the separate contributions of eros and *thumos*. Why should the tyrant be considered predominantly erotic – particularly in view of the fact that the *Republic* introduces the distinction between *thumos* and desire? Plato could have made *thumos* the chief characteristic of the tyrant if he had wanted to reserve eros for the chief characteristic of the philosopher: tyrants are characterized by pride and vengefulness (*thumos*) at least as much as they are characterized by acquisitiveness and luxuriousness (desire). Why make eros, and not *thumos*, guilty by association with tyranny? And what is the relationship between eros and that other prominent love believed to hold both families and cities together: *philia*, a love closely associated with *thumos*? How, more generally, is the strangeness of the *Republic*'s treatment of eros to be understood?

I. TENSION BETWEEN LOVE AND POLITICS?

Sexual communism and coed nudity in particular cry out for explanation. In the *Republic*'s regimen, natural attraction between lovers and beloveds must give way to a lottery system that ostensibly matches partners randomly and equally but in reality is a rigged lottery controlled by master eugenicists who make sure that individuals get matched with one another in keeping with the city's need for genetically superior citizens rather than with the individual's need for love or fulfillment. The couplings are monogamous only in the sense that they are serially monogamous. The private family based on love and affection is abolished, and the fundamental law against incest is breached, at least insofar as blue bloodlines are sometimes useful for producing better, swifter, smarter – if also more fragile and highstrung – thoroughbreds. Attributing these utopian – or dystopian – arrangements to a tension between love and politics has been a fruitful and influential interpretive strategy. An abbreviated chain of the reasoning through which certain types of love come into conflict with political justice might be the following: because private property is a source of injustice, communism of property is a necessity for the best regime. But inanimate property is not the only thing we call "ours": whatever we desire, including especially sexual partners such as spouses as well as the children produced through desire, we tend to consider as belonging to ourselves. Lest such "possessions" become sources of injustice (e.g., through favoritism and nepotism), the perfect regime would require that sexual partners and children, too, must be held in common (461e–462c; 464c–e). But then those desires that impel us toward some sexual partners and not others, as well as the possessiveness that drives us to hold on to them once we have them, must be remade to permit holding them in common – if legal arrangements can be found that will do so.

According to various interpretations based on the tension between love and politics, human nature and its passions are at odds with the imposition of communism, especially sexual communism.[2] The institution of sexual communism, on such "tension" readings, would be conceivable only as (at best) a thought-experiment that ignored or abstracted from the passions that would ordinarily lead couples to rebel against the system and establish their own secret

---

[2] Interpretations based on the tension between love and politics go back to Aristotle's *Politics* (2.1–5), which finds *philia*, rather than eros, incompatible with communism (see the subsequent discussion). "Tension" interpretations received a distinctively modern rendering at the hands of Leo Strauss, who thought that the *Republic* "abstracts from the body and from eros" (Strauss 1964, p. 138). Although tension interpretations can be derived from Strauss' overall hermeneutic approach, they are separable from that approach and are therefore available to scholars who have reservations about it. The general notion of "abstraction from eros" raises questions of how and with what aim the *Republic* abstracts from eros.

private realm, falling in love and producing the seedbed of a new family where families had been abolished. Coed nudity – that second strange institution – would likewise (on a "tension" reading) be possible only in the dialogic fiction, impossible in real life because real eros would be unable to handle the salacious sights without rearing its head, so to speak. This is certainly the way Allan Bloom in his commentary on the *Republic* understood the matter:

Men can be naked together because it is relatively easy to desexualize their relations with one another; but the preservation of the city requires the mutual attraction of men and women. The city can forbid homosexual relations. . . . But it cannot forbid heterosexual relations, and men and women could hardly be expected to be above attraction to one another at any particular moment. Hence the purpose of the gymnasia would be subverted. . . . This is part of Socrates' attempt . . . to act as though [eros] made no demands that cannot conform to the public life of the city. Once more, Socrates "forgets" the body. . . . [3]

Bloom assumes that the Greek homosexual attractions that were partly cultural in origin were susceptible of being modified by or for cultural institutions such as public nudity. Cultural or legal remedies can deeroticize relations between certain classes of citizens. This is a very big assumption and one that merits serious attention. For Bloom, however, there are natural limits to the efficacy of legal and cultural remedies. Heterosexual attraction is more difficult to suppress than homosexual attraction for two implicit reasons, both of which concern natural necessity: (1) human communities need heterosexual eros for replenishing the stock of citizens (a purposive claim of human nature on us), and (2) heterosexual attraction is so natural in so many people – it just springs up at the sight of a naked body – that its advent would destroy or make a mockery of the naked exercises (because eros is an irresistible efficient cause or "push," irrespective of purposiveness). The two different meanings of natural necessity implied in this reasoning, however, yield two very different results. Communities that were not underpopulated could temporarily ignore (1) and practice coed nudity for some time. If (2) is true, however, the coed nudity would be ruined practically on the first day. But as Natalie Bluestone in her criticism of Bloom

[3] Bloom 1991 [1968], p. 382. We can hear Strauss' phrase "abstracting from the body and eros" in Bloom's "forgetting the body."

points out, both males and females can and have exercised control in situations of coed nudity. Bluestone puts it pungently: "In the vaudeville review *Oh! Calcutta*, where nightly nude dancing of men and women was a theatrical spectacle, just such control was exercised for hundreds of performances. I cannot vouch for the rehearsals, of course."[4] One could multiply examples: men and women in coed nudist colonies and camps, for instance, coexist without eros falling upon them and destroying their volleyball games.

But if it is not the case that the institution of coed nudity is rendered impossible by eros, then it is also not the case that this part of the *Republic* simply ignores human passions or abstracts from them. Rather, we should follow up Bloom's other point that legal or cultural remedies can be found to deeroticize (partially or fully) relations among classes of citizens: Socrates could be intending to *use* nudity and communism to curb and control sexual love. If the nudity and serial relationships are intended to be corrosive of sexual shame and possessive attachment, respectively, then the passionate intensity and mystery that build up around sexual love as a result of these can be expected to be diminished. Elsewhere in Book 5, too, the guardians' eros seems meek and bovinely complacent,[5] all too easily at the beck and call of the regime. Why do they not rebel and choose the partner they desire – engaging in sex as an act of political rebellion, like the protagonists of Orwell's *1984*? Instead of attributing, with Bloom, this meekness to the fictional thought-experiment, we might consider whether the meekness is not the result of Socrates' instituting measures that themselves force eros into a meek and bovine mold. It would be in keeping with the erotic dialogues if Socrates intended for his guardians to expend only so much erotic attention on marriage and child production as was strictly necessary, while channeling the rest of their erotic energies into higher loves (e.g., 485d), such as their philosophical education.

Before pursuing this possibility, this juncture might be an appropriate moment to meet a significant objection to the foregoing: namely, the claim that Book 5 of the *Republic* is not about eros at all. Instead, Book 5 might seem to be principally about the family and

---

[4] Bluestone 1987, p. 220.
[5] Compare the overtones of herds and animals at *Republic* 451c–d, 459a–b, 460c–d, 466c.

about female equality, with love and sex being red herrings chased by modern readers. Clearly, Book 5 is about marriage and what becomes of it in the new regime: Polemarchus and Adeimantus ask to hear more about how the communism of property will be extended to include communism of women and children, too. But it might be a merely modern assumption that marriage necessarily entails eros. Historically, in Athens and many Greek cities, males seem to have had erotic experiences outside their marriages. The marriages themselves were mostly arranged rather than love matches. It might be anachronistic to say that replacing natural attraction between lover and beloved with a eugenics regime matching citizens who can produce good offspring is unnatural or unconventional, since natural attraction played a much smaller role in making ordinary Greek marriages successful than did the production of legal offspring. The *Republic* does not depart as violently from Greek contemporary practice as modern sensibility might assume. Add to these historical considerations Plato's disdainful attitude toward child production found in the erotic dialogues (e.g., *Smp.* 208e–209e; *Phdr.* 250e–251a), and it becomes plausible that Plato simply did not conceive of marriage and family as being especially erotic. Precisely because the elite philosophic life is so erotic for Plato, it follows that the household life of the masses is less so.

This strong objection is almost certainly a mistake. With regard to its historical component, plenty of evidence exists to show that Greeks assumed marriages with erotic content.[6] The declared purpose of Socrates' eugenically arranged marriages is to prevent "erotic necessities" from joining the wrong people (458d–e). Hence marriage – at least as redefined by Socrates – clearly concerns eros in the assumptions of the discourse itself. The reader need not be hot-blooded him- or herself to perceive the sexual interest behind the young interlocutors' question of how the guardians will hold their women and children in common (449c). Behind that question lies, at the very least, the thought: How will it be possible when everyone wants his own? Most probably, the young men have thought further and anticipate the pleasures that would await them if they were guardians: Now I can sleep with whomever I want – they're all mine! They do not initially appreciate the full implication of

[6] See Redfield 2003, pp. 48–54, and Calame 1999, pp. 116–29.

sexual communism: namely, that just as all the women belong to every man, so all the men belong to every woman. The addition of "and children" in the communism of women and children, and the issue of how children will be brought up (449d), make it clear that eros is not the only love under consideration in Book 5. Marriage is a *philia* relationship at least as much as it is an erotic relationship. Crucially, *philia* wants exclusive property rights as much as – perhaps much more than – eros does. As a preliminary way of distinguishing these two loves, we can say that nothing in Book 5 contradicts the notion that eros is an intense, questing passion, while *philia* is an enduring, lower-key passion: eros acquires but *philia* maintains.[7] *Philia* is a feeling of attachment to what one already possesses (or once possessed), that is, a love of one's own.[8] In lieu of discussing *philia* thematically, however, the *Republic* focuses attention directly on "one's own" (*oikeion*). We will subsequently argue that such love or affection for one's own finds its source in the *thumos* or spirited part of the soul.

The textual component of the above objection might wish to insist that Socrates in Book 5 speaks primarily of how females will share tasks equally with the males, while he speaks of eros only secondarily. The first wave of laughter (about training naked) is a sexual issue that arises only out of the equal-task issue. Yet it is precisely male eros that is prohibiting female task equality. Here again, the reader need not be a feminist to see the feminist relevance of Socrates' ideas: if female achievement were erotogenic for males, then eros would not be standing in the way of full female participation. But instead, men prefer their sexual objects, whether female or male, to be dependent and weak (*Phdr.* 239a). It is hard to see where the laughter at coed nudity comes from if eros is not the subtext of equality-as-coeducation, a subtext always threatening to break out

---

[7] On eros and *philia* together, see *Symposium* 179b–c, 182c; cf. *Lysis* 221b–d. Eros was popularly thought to destroy the status quo of *philia* relationships but also to lead the way to new *philia* relationships; see Faraone 1999, pp. 30, 86–88.

[8] In Greek, *to oikeion*. The definition is entertained at a dramatic moment in the *Lysis* (221e–222a); cf. *Symposium* 192c, 193a–d, 205d–206a with Aristotle's *Politics* 2.4. See also Price 1989, pp. 1–14. Proprietary feeling must not be thought to exhaust the higher potentialities of *philia*; rather, the politically relevant meaning of *philia* involves this sense of "one's own."

and become the primary text again. Eros is, in fact, the thread linking Book 5's topics together: the erotic philosopher-kings, who represent the third wave of laughter, otherwise have little to do with the first two waves: naked exercises and sexual communism. If we do not blind ourselves to the erotic theme of these first two waves (449c–472a), we can see how they fit together with the intense discussion of (the more recognizably Platonic) elite philosophical eros that immediately follows the third wave (474bff.). But even if we temporarily restrict ourselves to the female drama, eros emerges as an obstacle (if not *the* obstacle) to full female equality and thus an obstacle to justice. Eros will either thwart the perfecting of the political regime, or the political regime must change eros.

But in our earlier look at what created tension between eros and justice, the culprit seemed to be precisely the possessive element in eros – the desire for exclusive property rights. Hence our preliminary account of philia (namely, that philia is related to holding on to what is already one's own) becomes immediately relevant. What offends justice is not the erotic desire itself, but rather the possessiveness that tends to accompany or follow erotic desire. If an erotic desire without any sense of belonging could be imagined, such desire would never give rise to injustice. But philia in this politically relevant sense is precisely that feeling of belonging or "attachment." If the guardians can purge their eros of the love of their own – give up feeling any attachment – then they will accordingly be left to enjoy sexual intercourse in their brief couplings, albeit without philia. It is the absence of philia in their couplings that strikes modern readers as "loveless." But if a couple's eros were to produce philia as well, then the specter of a private household's putting its own interests ahead of the polity's interests arises once more.

Eros without attachment – without permanent belonging – is what the elite philosophers feel toward their subject matter in the third-wave discussion that now ensues. The philosophic eros is profligate and promiscuous: the philosophers in their quest for knowledge move from one erotic object to the next. The guardians are being asked to conduct their sex lives after the same fashion. Each guardian's eros is purged of its connection to the love of his or her own (or else the sense of "one's own" is radically expanded). It is correct, then, to distinguish the common or vulgar heterosexual eros, assumed to motivate many of the guardians after the integration of women, from the elite pederastic eros considered from 474b on. But it is a mistake to drive too deep a wedge between the two forms of eros. We argue that the sexual innovations (community of partners and coed nudity) are intended to transform heterosexual eros in ways that would enable it to enjoy as much as possible the political and philosophic advantages Socrates claims for elite pederasty. Accordingly, section 2 is devoted to the political purposes behind the transformation of eros. Section 3 is devoted to the philosophical purposes.

II. PLATO'S TREATMENT OF GREEK CITIES AND CIVIC IDEOLOGIES

Pursuing now the possibility that the *Republic*'s sexual legislation is intended to transform eros politically – rendering eros more pliable for the regime – we find the preponderance of historical evidence on the side of the *Republic*'s treating heterosexual eros in conscious imitation of the way actual cities in the Greek world treated homosexual eros. Or more accurately: we find the *Republic* basing its sexual legislation on interpretations of the historical evidence that Plato puts forward in the erotic dialogues (esp. *Smp.* 178d–179a, 182a–d). In the latter, Plato entertains (or makes his characters entertain) theses from a variety of civic ideologies in which both eros and philia were considered political principles creating supports on which oligarchical and (to a lesser extent) democratic regimes could be, in part, based. That Sparta was a model for the best regime has often been noted. But the Spartan model has not often been applied to the *Republic*'s sexual legislation. Socrates in the *Republic* seizes upon the Spartans' political use of pederasty, their common meals and sleeping arrangements (as well as male nudity) and expands them into coed nudity, common arrangements for everything (including sex), and a political use of eros between both sexes, not merely between males. Plato makes Socrates perfect or take to their logical conclusion tendencies inherent in Sparta but also found in greater or lesser degrees of institutionalization among the Cretans, among aristocrats in Athens, in the stories and ideology surrounding the Sacred Band of Thebes (which Plato knew and made his characters anachronistically refer to), as well as in several other Greek cities.[9] A variety of ideologies considered it good to have citizens who loved one another, all other things being equal, because they formed tighter bonds and fought harder on each other's behalf. Offshoots of such traditions asserted that male citizens who were erotically involved with one another were freedom-loving and anti-tyrannical (as for example in the Athenians' political myth of the homoerotic tyrannicides Harmodius and Aristogeiton): tyrants outlaw pederasty because they fear the strong bonds it creates among subjects whom they would prefer to keep weak and disunited.[10] The *Republic* makes use of these models, in which homoeroticism was thought to provide social cohesion between citizens and military cohesion between warriors. The *Republic* extrapolates from homoeroticism to include heterosexual eros as a glue cementing male-female pairs of citizen-warriors (instead of cementing families) in order to capitalize on the same alleged power of eros in political harness. Let us then examine sexual communism in light of the way Plato uses the historical and ideological precedents.

On erotic military tactics and the question of whether Sparta actually stationed lovers and beloveds side by side in the ranks in order to make them fight harder, the historical sources are ambiguous; but Plato was willing to interpret Theban and perhaps Spartan practice in this way.[11] Traditionally, armies were organized by tribe and hence were family affairs: grandfather, father, and son might all fight within sight of one another. In the heat of battle, soldiers fight not for their country or an abstract cause but for each other: they protect their comrades. All the more so if their comrades are friends and relatives (*philoi*). The traditional military arrangement thus relied on philia to motivate unit cohesion. Aristotle (*Politics* 2.4) asserts that philia among citizens was commonly thought to be the greatest good for cities. Cohesiveness or solidarity, literally "being one," was thought to be the work of philia. Militarily, Sparta and Thebes were thought to have innovated by substituting erotic love in place of philia (eros being more volatile than philia but perhaps for that reason a more

---

[9] Xenophon, *Constitution of the Lacedaemonians* 2.12–14; Ephorus in Strabo, *Geography* 10.4.21; Plato, *Laws* 636a–d. See also Cartledge 1981; Figueira and Nagy 1985; Ludwig 2002, pp. 173–78.

[10] *Symposium* 182a–d; Thucydides 1.20, 6.53–59; cf. 2.43.

[11] *Symposium* 178d–179a; cf. Xenophon, *Symposium* 8.32–35; *Hellenica* 4.8.39.

powerful passion on which to ground solidarity). This is only one among several ways in which Sparta was believed to have structured its incentives so that private passions would not conflict with – but would instead bolster – public concerns.

Going to war with someone you love, even with a sexual partner, was hence thinkable within contemporary discourses and provided a prototype for the *Republic* to use and develop. The move to include female sexual partners continues a pattern. Homoerotic cohesion between pairs of soldiers is widened to include heterosexual cohesion. Glaucon enthuses about how "it won't be permitted to refuse anyone who wants to kiss someone, so that if he happens to be in love, either with a male or with a female, he will be more zealous to win the prize for prowess" (*Rep.* 468b–c). Socrates agrees that marriages will be more easily obtainable for the brave than for others (in part because eugenics also dictates such legislation). Sexual success is harnessed to success in war.

Socrates imagines great numbers of guardians bonding together the way that family members previously did. Insofar as all citizens are to share in the joys and pains of possessing the same things, a form of philia is to be the prime mover in Socrates' larger project to make the city entirely unified. "*Philoi* hold possessions in common" (cf. *Rep.* 424a and 449c with 462a–b). Socrates wants to revolutionize the meaning of "one's own" (*oikeion*): all are to share "one belief about their own" (464c–d). If there is a child or a woman about whom any one guardian says "mine," all guardians should say "mine" about the same person. Again, philia is the type of love associated with one's one. The philia that used to help create private families is to go into making the city into one great public "family."

Historically, such ideas were not without example. Sparta weakened families by taking boys away at age seven, when the boys were formed into herds.[12] Adult males were also kept away from their families. Spartan communism in meals and sleeping arrangements for adult males deprived private homes of their titular heads, presumably so that the men would put the public good ahead of their narrower family interests. Spartans could thus be thought to have already undergone a partial revolution regarding "one's own." An erotic

---

[12] See note 5 and the separation of children at *Republic* 541a. Cf. *Laws* 666e–667a, 684d–685a; *Constitution of the Lacedaemonians* 2.1–14.

component – Spartan pederasty – played a central role in these severe arrangements. Socially esteemed, legally encouraged pederasty gave adult males a sexual interest outside the home, and the boys were available because they had been taken away from the control of their families. The erotic lover-beloved bond partially replaced the father-son philia relationship, with the older lover taking over the functions of parenting in his surrogate-father role toward the younger beloved. The stranglehold over the education of children exercised by parental pride was thus overcome. Here, as in the military arrangements, eros can be said to have replaced philia. The family was weakened, and its resistance to republicanism – for example, resistance in the form of nepotism and clannishness – was neutralized. In the space ceded by the family, the city could then construct a male collective, a kind of men's club or garrison within the city that effectually was the real city.

If Spartan homoeroticism contributed to the creation of a male collective, Socrates' polymorphous, incestuous eroticism radicalizes the Spartan project in order to create a unisex collective. Socrates expands the pool of citizens whom each individual can view sexually, that is, as potential erotic partners: he adds family members such as brothers and sisters previously considered off-limits to the pool (461e). Such encroachment by eros into the territory traditionally reserved for philia has the effect of ironing out differences within the citizen body, creating civic homogeneity. As Aristotle points out, family structure differentiates the citizen body into diverse roles. Family relations imply multiple roles for each individual: "the same man is addressed as son by one, as brother by another, and as cousin by a third" (*Politics* 2.3). Socrates' city is more unified if every guardian in a certain age group is actually or potentially the sexual partner of everyone else, rather than exclusively the spouse of one, daughter of another, cousin of a third. Serial sexual partners are far more interchangeable than family members in their exclusive roles could ever be. Detachable and homogeneous (i.e., "modular") citizens more easily fit together to form a uniform and unified whole. Spartan pederasty pried men and boys away from the family, giving them new roles more useful to the city. Socrates' polymorphous sexual communism finishes the job, prying women, girls, and everyone else away from the family and giving each one a single role: that of guardian.

Socrates veers away from total homogeneity by outlawing parent-child incest (461b–d). Presumably, Socrates wishes to capitalize on the social cohesion and civic obedience to be had from the belief that all older men are one's fathers: a citizen must treat a thousand or more seniors with the reverence ordinarily reserved for a single father and likewise with mothers. Had Socrates permitted sexual relationships between the generations to erode the parent-child philia relationship, he would have pitted the incentive structure of eros against the incentive structure of philia. Instead, he ostensibly preserves the best of both.

Yet this incentive strategy of Socrates' redefines and expands the philia it intends to harness. While abolishing family roles to achieve unity and homogeneity, Socrates simultaneously derives political incentives from philia by preserving family roles in new, expanded forms. The structuring of incentives so that private passions bolster public concerns is somewhat at odds with removing privacy and destroying the private sphere altogether. In the limit (and the limit appears to be where Socrates is taking this), there could conceivably be no private passion left to harness. How much philia can a guardian really feel for one thousand fathers, or for one thousand children? Will each guardian really fight harder under the gaze of the whole batch of the city's children born within ten months after the copulations in each of his or her serial marriages, that is, the vast array of children that biologically could be, and therefore politically are considered to be, his or her offspring (*Rep.* 467a–b, 461d; cf. *Smp.* 178d–179a, 207a–b with 208c–d)? Why care about those children more than the city's other children? At worst, Socrates would dilute the passions on which he intends to rely.

This reading of the *Republic*'s sexual communism as employing love to bring about unification and homogeneity goes back to Aristotle. "We think that philia is the greatest good for cities . . . and Socrates praises the city's being unified, [alleging that it is] the work of philia to unify" (*Politics* 2.4). Aristotle, stressing the heterogeneity of roles necessary to create a city ("a city does not come into being from members who are the same"; *Politics* 2.2), severely criticizes Plato's Socrates for overhomogenizing, overemphasizing sameness and unity. The alleged good of unification actually destroys cities, according to Aristotle. He imagines the unifying philia as produced by eros, comparing the *Republic* to Plato's "speeches on eros" (i.e., to the *Symposium*), in particular to Aristophanes' speech. Aristophanes' two lovers who desire to grow together and become one (*Smp.* 192b–e) necessarily desire their own destruction, says Aristotle (*Politics* 2.4), because one will be subsumed into the other, or else both together will become some third entity, not identical to either of the original two. Analogously, if a city were to become totally unified through love, such a city, too, would be destroyed. Excessive unity would collapse the city into a household or even, with further homogenization, into an individual (*Politics* 2.2). Something has to give: either the city collapses like a neutron star, or the philia that was supposed to unite it must break or snap. Real ties that bind cannot be spread thin over a thousand sons or a thousand daughters without losing their attractive force (*Politics* 2.4).

If philia is the object, Aristotle argues, better to make the ruled (not the rulers), that is, the farmers (not the guardians), hold their women and children in common. For those who practice sexual communism will feel no philia. Precisely if philia is the greatest good for cities, then the guardians need families and heterogeneous roles in order to experience philia (*Politics* 2.4). The implication is that philia will always be private or, at best, semi-private. Citizens should be differentiated and interdependent rather than homogeneous and modular. Thus Aristotle understands only the negative side of Socrates' sexual communism to be practicable. Sexual communism sweeps away clannishness and factionalism but without achieving the positive goal of creating one great family, every citizen bonded together through philia. Citizens cannot avoid loving their families or their factions more than their city except at the cost of not loving anything at all. It is impracticable to require every citizen to love every other citizen as strongly as he today loves his family. Socrates thus burns the candle at both ends, diluting the philia he hopes to channel into public avenues. If we agree with Aristotle's analysis – as I do – then the expansion of philia seems to lose its political raison d'être. But we said earlier that sexual communism was intended to transform eros in such a way that the philia that accompanies eros was either expanded or purged. That expansion project having failed, we are left with an eros from which philia has been purged, in effect a philia-less eros.

The case with coed nudity is similar in many respects to the foregoing account of sexual communism, and treating it at length would retrace much of the same ground.[13] Briefly, female nakedness radicalizes and completes a historical trend of civic rationalism about what is truly shameful (*Rep.* 452a–b). Socrates intends a revolution in shame just as he intends a revolution in "one's own." Through nudity, he encourages a shameless eros along parallel lines with his encouragement through sexual communism of a philia-less eros.

Of the three political aims for sexual communism – justice, unification, and eugenics – unification has been seen to fall short. Justice is partially implicated in the failure to create a unified collective, or communism: the things of friends are common, but the citizens cannot all be friends. Perfect justice will be destroyed if attachments are permitted; but bonding into a collective requires attachments. (The third political goal, eugenics, meets with failure only eventually, with ignorance of the "nuptial number"; 546a–547b.) We are thus led to look beyond the political for other purposes behind the transformation of eros. Educational and philosophic purposes also govern the transformation of eros, which seems to aim at purifying eros of extraneous elements, such as shame and philia. For example, removing the mystery of clothing can be seen to rationalize the guardians' response to beauty and ugliness (452d–e). But rationalizing the erotic response to beauty and removing the shame that prevents the guardians from seeing are goals analogous to the projects of the *Symposium* and the other erotic dialogues. Likewise, purging eros of philia enables eros to seek a wider pool of objects. Engaging in impersonal sexual unions is propaedeutic to seeking impersonal erotic objects, such as wisdom. A shameless eros that forms no attachments is ripe for the philosophic transformations discussed from 474b onward. The political purposes point beyond themselves. In short, having many partners constitutes part of the depersonalization of the erotic object that takes place in Plato's erotic theory more generally. This would definitively link Book 5's sexual legislation with the disquisition on eros from 474b onward.

Perhaps it is unsurprising that educational and philosophical motives should trump political motives in Plato. Whether Plato intended for the failure of unification to be deliberate on Socrates' part or (as Aristotle implies) a mistake is less important for the present argument than the fact that the sexual legislation perfects

---

[13] See Ludwig 2002, pp. 261–318.

several tendencies already inherent in Greek cities and ideologies. Socrates perfects the available politics by identifying tendencies and pushing them conceptually to their logical extremes. He thus shows the limiting case toward which the imperfect poleis existing in the world were – consciously or unconsciously – striving. He reveals the essence of the polis by showing it in its fullest, perfected form. The *Republic* thus continues to offer a political science even if it disappoints our expectation that it offers a political blueprint. Expanding male nudity and common meals to include female nakedness and common arrangements for everything was one of Socrates' ways of perfecting the politics of those cities, even – it should be added – at the cost of distorting love. He perfects politics not because a perfect politics is necessarily good, but because a perfect politics is perfectly revelatory of what politics is.

III. FROM THE SEXUAL LEGISLATION TO THE PHILOSOPHIC EROS

Earlier we suggested that the coercive erotic institutions of the *Republic* seem alien to the spirit of the *Symposium* and *Phaedrus* and indeed alien to at least one major passage in the *Republic* itself, a kind of "*Symposium* in miniature" beginning at 474b, directly following the imposition of the erotic regimen. Now an analogy between these two diverse stances on eros has been suggested. The transformation that eros undergoes in the *Republic*'s erotic regimen is analogous to what takes place on the initial rungs of the ladder of love in the *Symposium*. As we saw, detaching the guardians' sexual unions from family concerns and child rearing corrects the political problem of injustice arising from possessiveness only at the great, perhaps unacceptable, cost of removing the basis for affectionate love. However, the same detachment from family and child rearing incidentally also corrects the philosophic deficiencies of narrow closedness and lack of ambition associated with the heterosexual, child-producing eros in the erotic dialogues (*Smp.* 208e–209a and context; cf. *Smp.* 191c with *Phdr.* 256a–e).

Through the many marriages of sexual communism, the heterosexual unions of the guardians are forced to share in the transience that historically characterized pederasty but not marriage. Having many partners forces eros to become open and flexible rather than focused on one exclusive love. An open, flexible eros is educable, and philosophic education is the theme from 474b onward. The guardians' enforced shamelessness about appearing naked in front of the opposite sex and about consorting with many partners constitute a preparation for philosophic shamelessness about baring one's ideas (cf. *Tht.* 169a–b) and consorting with many ideas. Philosophy is a realm in which the parochial attachments to family and the philia felt exclusively for one's personal "own" are detrimental to progress. In permitting the education of the philosopher-kings to trump the sexual legislation's more strictly political motives, however, the dialogue raises the questions of whether and how its philosophic purposes fit together with its political purposes. The mini-*Symposium* within the *Republic* must now be examined.

Starting at 474b, the *Republic* duplicates some of the major topics of the *Symposium* speech of Diotima. In the *Symposium*, Diotima recommends that the young Socrates frequent many beautiful bodies, an activity that looks like promiscuity from a legal-political perspective. Yet if Socrates were to fall in love with one person and wish to remain permanently with that one (establishing a philia-relationship), he would also doom himself to remaining permanently at that level on the erotic ladder: his eros would never be permitted to climb the ladder of love to higher, impersonal objects of eros. Instead of seeking permanency, young Socrates must become an eroticist, beginning while still a young man to go to many beautiful bodies. First he must love the body of one person, but then he must recognize that the beauty in any one body is akin to the beauty in another. Realizing that it is foolish not to believe that the beauty in all bodies is one and the same, he must establish himself as a lover of *all* beautiful bodies (*Smp.* 210a–b).

The *Republic* duplicates this line of thought from the *Symposium*: Socrates places young Glaucon in the role of the young Socrates. He calls Glaucon an erotic man and a boy lover (474b). In place of the young Socrates' going from body to body in the *Symposium*, Glaucon allegedly loves the body parts of many different boys. (Diotima's discourse is normative advice, while Socrates' discourse to Glaucon is descriptive, but we shall see that this difference does not affect the argument.) A real lover, Socrates argues, never loves only one part and not another, but desires the whole (474c). He goes on to apply this principle to the whole class of boys: the eroticist Glaucon calls snub-nosed boys "charming," eagle-beaked boys "regal," and boys in between these extremes "well proportioned." He furthermore calls dark-skinned boys "masculine" and light-skinned boys "children of the gods." Pale or sallow boys he denominates "honey-green," seizing upon any excuse to find beauty in every single boy (474b–475a). Glaucon's eros leads him to do naturally and as a matter of course what Diotima encourages the young Socrates to do on the lower rungs of the ladder.

This whole disquisition linking elite pederastic eros to philosophy, which begins in Book 5 and carries over into Book 6 (474b–487a), is motivated by the third wave of paradox, following the first wave (coed nudity) and the second wave (sexual communism). The third wave is the paradox that philosophers must become kings. To determine who the real philosophers (and hence future kings) are, Socrates compares them to eroticists (and thereby to Glaucon). Just as eroticists love all parts of all boys, young philosophic natures love all branches of all learning. They are not picky. Unbeknownst to themselves, both the eroticist and the young philosophic nature dimly divine the intimations of the Forms: the eroticist sees beauty itself in his many beloveds, and the young philosophic nature sees wisdom glistening weakly amid the dross in the many branches of learning. Otherwise they would not be insatiable for the *whole* class of boys and the *whole* of learning, respectively: if they were capable of limiting themselves to monogamy or to, say, astronomy, then some illiberal motive other than pure beauty or wisdom, respectively, would be motivating their behavior. It is their very indiscriminateness – the promiscuity of their attractions – that marks them out as possessing natural potential.

But is their expansiveness simply natural? Societal influences, as well as nature, play a role in encouraging and discouraging the kind of erotic expansiveness that Glaucon experiences. Glaucon's tastes are hard to imagine apart from the transience inherent in the normal conventions of Greek pederasty (boys soon grew into men and became off-limits), together with the convention of athletic nudity – with its many bodies – in the gymnasiums and palaestras. As we saw earlier, the sexual legislation is essentially an extension of such pederastic conventions and practices to heterosexual unions. The regimen of many partners creates a field-bed from which an expansive, impersonal eros can emerge. The *Republic* is intensely interested in the contribution that political institutions can make to philosophic education. Socrates simply legislates that all the guardians shall be forced into an opportunity to develop tastes as expansive as Glaucon's. Glaucon, in turn, by loving all parts of all boys, has already gone far down the path Diotima recommends to Socrates: instead of settling down and becoming tied down to one exclusive beloved, Glaucon is attracted to them all. His eros is not currently leading him to find his other half, not leading him to "his own" (*Smp.* 193d, 205d–206a). Instead, he is ripe for higher rungs on the ladder. Analogously, the *Republic* prevents the eros of the guardians from leading them to "their own"; the institutions push them toward the ladder.

As if rehabilitated by the coercions and exertions it has undergone, erotic desire finally begins to be treated as a good thing late in Book 5. Desire, which in Book 4 needed *thumos* to stand guard over it (in consultation with reason) and eros, which earlier in Book 5 needed the schooling of coed nudity and sexual communism, now come into their own as the attractive urges to philosophize. "The philosopher is a desirer of wisdom" (475b); nothing is said about philosophic *thumos*, if indeed such a thing exists at all. Like the *Symposium*, the *Republic* explicitly deflects eros away from sexual intercourse and toward learning. "In proportion as the desires incline vehemently toward some one thing, we know that they are weaker toward the rest, like a stream that has been channeled away in that direction" (485d). Once the desires "have flowed toward learning," the citizen will "abandon those pleasures that come via the body."

Like the *Symposium*, the *Republic* forms a hierarchy out of the lower physical loves (e.g., for bodies and wine), the middle-level love of honor (*philotimia*), and the highest or culminating level: *philosophia* (*Rep.* 475a–b; cf. 581a–c). As we know from Diotima's *Symposium* speech just before her ladder of love (*Smp.* 208c–209e), she describes lovers pregnant in body who beget children; lovers pregnant in soul who engage in *philotimia*; and finally lovers pregnant in soul who engage in *philosophia*. The three are positioned hierarchically. The same hierarchy from sexual love to *philotimia* and from there to *philosophia* is also observed at *Phaedrus* 256a–e: there are couples who consider blessed the act of which quadrupeds are capable, then there are *philotimic* couples who only occasionally slip and permit themselves sexual intercourse, followed by philosophic couples who do not engage in bodily congress at all.[14] This hierarchy from the erotic dialogues represents the erotic parting of the ways among the three classes of the *Republic*. Child production alone characterizes the eros of the lowest class, the farmers and artisans. Child production is kept (as far as possible) from weighing down the guardians, whose eros will include love of honor and jealous protectiveness of the city. Emerging out of the guardian class will be the kings whose eros is oriented toward philosophy.

But this coincidence of philosophical aims with the more strictly political aims of the *Republic* may appear as the tail wagging the dog. Socrates shows us the whole class of guardians undergoing extraordinary erotic rigors so that a few might go on to become philosopher-kings. The nonphilosophic guardians cannot partake of the philosophical goals set for the philosopher-kings (except vicariously through having philosophically educated rulers). They can partake only of the political goals such as unification (which do not meet with success). The nonphilosophic guardians now seem to exist totally for the sake of the philosophers. More and more aspects of the *Republic* begin to point beyond the political. Socrates reverses a common charge against philosophers, that is, that they do not live up to moral and political standards (487c–d): he complains rather that no constitution of any current city lives up to the potential of the young philosophic nature (that is why philosophic types often go bad). Greek cities are not helping philosophers to realize their full growth (497a–b). Politics is for the sake of philosophy, not the other way around. Even justice, which initially motivated the inquiry into politics (to view justice writ large), now finds its fulfillment not in the political order but in the soul of the philosopher. True philosophers fulfill the promise of communism simply owing to the nature of the objects they desire: the ideas they traffic in are common property for anyone who wants them and has the capacity. Philosophers (qua philosophers) therefore lack possessiveness, wanting only to behold, not to own. Justice would still find fulfillment in philosophic souls, according to Socrates, even if the best regime never existed (592b). We gradually realize that Socrates has constructed an

---

[14] The *Republic* also parallels these erotic dialogues in what it has to say about the top of the "ladder" (*Rep.* 476c with *Smp.* 211b–e; *Rep.* 490b with *Smp.* 206e and 212a).

entire city in which his own activity is the very definition of justice. Callipolis mirrors the philosophic soul to the greatest extent possible.

On this reading, Socrates would be showing us a distorted image of political life reflected in the mirror of the philosophic life. That is, he shows what ordinary citizens' eros would look like if they consorted with bodies the way philosophers consort with ideas. Citizen life is assimilated as closely as possible to philosophic life (and is turned inside out by that assimilation). As we saw earlier, however, it was the city's own aspirations to justice that required coercing the citizens' eros into these strange, philosophic molds. Civic justice demands a perfection that goes beyond the limits of civic possibility and is available only in philosophy. Of all thinkable cities, Callipolis fails the least or comes closest to realizing the goal of mirroring philosophy. This is instructive because it represents the limits of politics. Politics points beyond itself. With the main focus of the dialogue shifting to philosophical education, the characters and aspirations of Socrates' young pupils come to the fore. Speeches about eros are themselves erotic, and vicarious participation in the sights and spectacle of the sexual institutions has operated on the desire of Glaucon and Adeimantus in such a way as to encourage them to talk about previously unmentionable topics, such as incest. Socrates loosens up the young men's conventional morality by appealing to their erotic desires, allowing their eros for thinking to come partly out of the box, to lose its habitual sense of shame. That shameless, polymorphous eros so useful for philosophizing will in turn have important political implications for the study of tyranny, particularly in the case of Glaucon, who (qua eroticist) is flattered to consider himself one of the young philosophic natures and a potential philosopher-king.

IV. THE EROS OF THE TYRANT AND GLAUCON'S AMBITION

There still remains the last, most mysterious eros of the *Republic* to be explored: the tyrant's eros of Book 9.[15] Why, after rehabilitating eros, should the dialogue turn around again and make eros the prime suspect in the psychology of tyranny? Why should eros take

---

[15] See also Richard Parry's chapter 14 in this volume.

precedence over *thumos* – with its aspects of pride, self-assertion and vengefulness – in motivating the tyrannical personality? Part of the answer is that the rehabilitation undergone by eros involved separating eros from *thumos*. The lack of possessiveness in the philosophic eros and the lack of attachment (philia) in the sexual unions of the guardians were examples of *thumos*-free eros. If, as we have argued, philia in this politically relevant sense is associated with possessiveness and one's own (*oikeion*), *thumos* has a vital connection to both. In the anecdote of Leontius, his *thumos* polices and maintains his self-respect against bad desires that threaten to make him a worse person (439e–440a).[16] Likewise, *thumos* will fight to the death to vindicate the self's rights against injustice imposed from without (440c–d). *Thumos* in these two examples, by opposing enemies both internal and external, asserts the self. In Homeric Greek and in various classical texts, the word *thumos* sometimes meant the whole self.[17] In Book 4 of the *Republic*, *thumos* is at the very center of the soul, between reason and desire. One's sense of self can apparently be enlarged so as to infuse itself into people and things beyond the self, which then become one's own. *Thumos* is capable both of savagery toward its own (*tous oikeious*) fellow citizens (destroying them along with the enemy when first introduced in Book 2, 375b–c) and of mildness toward its own, recognizing a face that is dear (*philēn*) to it and protecting the familiar in opposition to the alien and strange (376b). The key seems to be educating *thumos* (like a noble dog, 375e) to consider those citizens as belonging to it (and to consider itself as belonging to them). The familiar or status quo (like the family of owners whom a dog also "owns" as his) will then receive the affection. This seems to be the connection between philia and *thumos*.[18]

Having shown us the rarefied heights of thumos-free eros in the best regime, the dialogue in its portrayal of the decline of the regime now descends to eros that seeks exclusive possession. The souls of

---

[16] See also the subsequent discussion. For the punitive function of *thumos*, see *Laws* 731b.

[17] Ludwig 2002, pp. 194–97.

[18] Aristotle (*Politics* 7.7) makes explicit what he regards as only confusedly present in the *Republic*: "*thumos* creates the disposition to love [*to philētikon*], for *thumos* is the faculty of soul by which we feel philia." Hereafter we remove the italics from thumos, as we did previously with philia.

those declining human types that belong to the declining regimes can no longer maintain the separation of eros from thumos. But the portrait of the tyrant is complicated by the fact that Socrates gives only small indications that thumos is even partly responsible (571c–572b, 586a–587b); instead, he deliberately readopts the partial, merely political view of eros that obtained before 474b. Eros is said to cause tyranny. We are back to the nonphilosophic vantage point from which Cephalus expressed relief that old age had taken away his sexual desires (329a–d) and from which Glaucon assumed that the first things anyone would do upon discovering Gyges' invisibility ring would be to commit adultery and seize political power (360a–b). We must follow this strand that runs throughout the dialogue: the political "ambition" of Glaucon.[19] The political perspective on eros that Glaucon shares with most of his fellow citizens holds that eros is naturally possessive and selfish and so must be restrained. But as we have seen, the philosophical perspective on eros is that pure eros desires no exclusive possession; indeed, the objects of thought cannot be exclusively possessed. The admixture of thumos within eros was to blame for the philia that stood in the way of perfect justice; thumos seems to be at the root of all possessiveness. Why does Socrates continue to adhere to the lower, political view? How are we to understand the separate contributions of eros and thumos in the tyrant's desires?

The potential tyrant's handlers and hangers-on conspire to instill an eros in him that will organize all his other desires around it (572e–573a). The madness of this eros drives him over the edge, and he becomes actually tyrannical. This "drone" may be a sexual eros oriented toward a single individual: the tyrant engages in violence against his parents in order to get money for a girlfriend or boyfriend (574b–c), whom he apparently wishes to gratify and impress. His beloved is only a catalyst, however, and the handlers seem to know it. The synergy – personal desire and political desire working together – is in keeping with stories of other tyrants and potential tyrants in Plato and elsewhere. Callicles is lover to a boy named Demos but is also said to feel eros for the masses (dēmos), and his political ambition is characterized as wanting the masses to feel philia toward

---

[19] Xenophon attributes actual political ambition, including speechifying in public, to Glaucon (Memorabilia 3.6).

him in return (*Grg.* 481d, 513a–b). In Xenophon's *Hiero* (1.26–38), sexual desire is thought to lead the tyrant Hiero to desire tyranny, but he complains that political power prevents tyrants from knowing for sure whether their beloveds reciprocate genuine philia. In both cases, the tyrannical personality's eros is ordinary insofar as it wants secure attachment and belonging. The philosophic eros, by contrast, is unreciprocated: philosophers do not need to be loved back by the ideas they contemplate. Likewise, the serial unions of sexual communism were intended to preclude proprietary feelings. The tyrant's sexual eros is mixed up with his thumos. If he desired without hoping to possess exclusively, no amount or intensity of desire that the handlers instilled in him could make him commit to tyranny.

If to Glaucon's ambition we add his eroticism, Glaucon would seem to be in more danger than most of wanting to become a tyrant. Glaucon is both attracted to and repulsed by Thrasymachus' tough-talking denigration of justice. On the one hand, Glaucon is manly and spirited (357a, 548d with 581b) and therefore chafes under the irritating possibility that Thrasymachus may be right. On the other hand, there is hope that Glaucon will remain a solid citizen because he is more ambivalent than Callicles and Polus (*Grg.* 470c–471d), who openly confess their admiration for bloody tyrants such as Archelaus and the Great King and are attracted to the rhetorician Gorgias because they imagine that his art promises to help them subdue the masses. As we shall see, constraints arising from the ongoing education that Socrates is giving Glaucon dictate that Socrates continue to flatter his thumos, giving it more than its due.

Sorting out the separate contributions of eros and thumos in the tyrant's desires requires that we begin with the least distorting of cities – that "truest" and most natural "city of pigs" – and the role it plays in the psychology of Glaucon. In Book 2, Socrates constructs a small, basic city based on need. The denizens of this city feast on simple foods, are convivial and happy. They are in a sense the most erotically normal citizens in the *Republic*, having pleasant intercourse (an ambiguous term until the sequel): producing children but not too many (372b–c). But Glaucon rebels against their rustic simplicity, pejoratively calling this a "city of pigs." Citizens worthy of the name should have "relishes" (372c). He apparently despises the inhabitants for not enjoying the finer things in life. Socrates gives

Glaucon what he desires, allowing the basic city to transform itself into a luxurious, feverish city. He allows this on the grounds that justice and injustice will be more obvious in a bloated city full of unnecessary luxuries: relishes, courtesans, servants and many others (372e–373c). Wanting these luxury items leads directly to the necessity of seizing a neighbor-city's land – and therefore leads to war (373d–e). The whole need for a "guardian" class of warriors thus arises out of a concession to Glaucon's desire for relishes, a desire that has more to do with ambition (a desire that the citizens make something of themselves) than with simple hunger or the pleasure to be derived from eating the relishes. Ambition in fact combines with the pleasure of eating: if the relishes were not tasty, ambition would not claim that one "ought" to have them. Ambition uses desires and pleasures as counters (what in modern parlance would be called "perquisites").

The advent of the guardians will indirectly lead Socrates to introduce thumos into the soul as well, in order to preserve the one-to-one correspondence between parts of soul and classes of city (e.g., 440e–441a). In the city of pigs, thumos was scarcely necessary. In the feverish, bloated city (perhaps in all actual cities) thumos will be the lynchpin of the soul, just as the guardian class (i.e., the class with the most thumos) will be the lynchpin of the city. But it is not clear that matters had to be this way. Adeimantus was happy with the city of pigs. The move to a less "natural" city was motivated by Glaucon's thumos, which says, in effect: "My city deserves better." Likewise, Leontius in Socrates' anecdote gets angry at himself and his own eyes for being drawn to look at the sordid sight of executed criminals' corpses. He does not want to be the kind of person who enjoys seeing punishment. Leontius' thumos says, in effect: "I ought to be better than that." The fact that Glaucon's thumos manifests itself in pride or disdain, while Leontius' manifests itself in anger, shows the link between the two: prouder people, people with pretensions, are more likely to get angry if their self-image is violated either by others or by their own moral slip-ups. The denizens of the city of pigs had needs but no pretensions; they hence had no need of a military. They essentially had nothing to defend. Socrates has accommodated thumos in his city because Glaucon has a lot of thumos. The whole discussion of the tripartite scheme of the soul thus seems to grow out of an accommodation of the fact that Glaucon has thumos (in addition to mind and desire), that is, an accommodation of the fact that Glaucon's soul – like most souls – is tripartite.

But could there be a soul without thumos? Desire and mind would be together, with no third entity coming between them. Thumos is what separates the one from the other in Glaucon and most of the rest of us. Thumos seems natural: children exhibit thumos from a young age. Thumos of small children is activated mainly in aid of desires. When a desire is thwarted, thumos flares up and the child gets an additional impetus toward fulfilling the desire. Later, however, a very different use of thumos comes on the scene. Slightly older children learn to use thumos to squelch desires they know should not be fulfilled; their thumos reins in desires that are not in accordance with their self-image. Attempting to squelch desires by angrily and pridefully beating them down predictably leads to self-conflict, as it did for Leontius. While perilous, learning to use thumos to squelch desires seems indispensable if people are to live in society. Not all desires can be met.

Nevertheless, people in most or all societies could conceivably require a second education to liberate them from this first education they inevitably undergo. Undoing the damage wrought by thumos' repression of desires would entail substituting reasons why certain desires cannot be fulfilled in place of irrational anger (i.e., understanding why they cannot be met) and substituting rational desires in place of irrational desires. This second education would thus entail learning to let go of one's own when it was necessary to do so, that is, would entail "practicing dying" (*Phd.* 67e, 80e–81a).[20] This philosophical education would aim not only at making desire rational but, especially, at making reason desirous. This bipartite philosopher's soul cannot be natural in the sense of what springs up ordinarily ("nature naturing"). Humans "naturally" have thumos and therefore have tripartite souls. Besides, had thumos not been introduced as a third part, eros would never have been diverted from the low, unphilosophic desires of the city of pigs in the first place. Nevertheless, the bipartite soul could be seen as more fully natured ("nature natured"). Such a natural condition would be something like

---

[20] Given the association between thumos and one type of philia, the possibility of a philosophic soul without thumos raises the question of what the psychological basis of philosophic friendship is.

Aristotle's description of choice as "desirous mind" (*orektikos nous*) or "mindful desire" (*orexis dianoētikē*; *Nicomachean Ethics* 6.2). The interchangeable formulations hint at healing the bipartition much as the tripartition was healed: the fusion of mind and desire holds out the prospect of a unified soul.

Possibly the worst consequence of thumos' necessary collaboration with political society in separating mind from desire is the tendency to consider most desires as unruly or lower. This seems to be the origin of the political perspective on eros, a distortion in society's account of desire that is one consequence of the tension between love and politics. With the best of intentions, thumos relegates desires to the basement and sends the mind upstairs where, stripped of its desires, mind can do nothing but calculate. This political view is the very image of the tripartite soul.[21] Socrates flatters the thumos-centered view and pays lip service to it because of Glaucon's soul and because the philosophic soul is so rare as to be politically irrelevant. Yet a good politics would at least not remove the conditions for the emergence of the philosophic soul. The morality of using thumos to control desires may be the closest practicable approximation to the truth, but it remains a compromise. Socrates' interlocutors (and Plato's readers) could do far worse than to believe that political decline is caused by letting desires get out of control. But there is a tragic paradox, since the thumos that enables citizen virtue also prevents the ascent to philosophic virtue.

Socrates finally admits in Book 9, shortly after the discussion of the tyrant's eros, that – within the tripartite soul – not only the "desirous" part but also the other two parts have "desires." Thumos loves victory and honor, while the mind loves learning and wisdom (581a–b). But if desire is now distributed over the whole, how can the desirous part any longer be a part? Reading this new account of the soul back on the discussion of the tyrant would mean that "desire" should no longer be automatically construed in opposition to

---

[21] On political and moral reasons for adding thumos to the soul, see (from very different perspectives) Penner 1971 and Benardete 1989, pp. 203–10, 224–25. Cf. also Burger 2004–5. Stanley Rosen's otherwise very similar account contains an important difference: he characterizes Glaucon's wish for relishes to be primarily erotic rather than stemming from thumos; cf. Rosen 2005, pp. 75–76, 81, with pp. 394–96, 154. Rosen's earlier interpretation had implied that thumos was primarily responsible for Glaucon's wish, while the philosophic eros, in contrast, was gentle rather than spirited; see Rosen 1988 [1965], pp. 102–18 of the reprint, esp. pp. 111, 115.

thumos. Thumos has its desires. Indeed, the new scheme for the soul, in which desire informs each part,[22] seems motivated by the need to explain how mind and desire can combine in the philosopher's soul and how thumos and desire can combine in the tyrant's soul.

The tyrant satisfies in waking life the bad desires that occasionally afflict most people only in dreams: for incest, murders, and "terrible food," probably referring to cannibalism (571a–d, 574d–575a). Such desires are called unnecessary and against law (*paranomoi*). This distinction between unnecessary and necessary desires was first introduced in Book 8 during the slide from oligarchic to democratic personalities (558d–559a). Yet "unnecessary" is inadequate (if not euphemistic) for the horror of the desires that come in dreams: cannibalism would be wrong for no other reason than too much chocolate is wrong – people can do without it (cf. 559b–c). The distinction between necessary and unnecessary in fact assumes that thumos never makes desire seek "a pleasure alien [to it]" (587a). In what can hardly be a coincidence, Socrates signals the inadequacy of the distinction for capturing the synergy between thumos and desire by alleging that the desire for relishes is "necessary" (559b). We remember relishes were unnecessary in the truest and natural city, and were rather a concession to Glaucon's thumos. Relishes represent not desire alone but thumos acting through desire.

The contrariness to law (*paranomia*) of the tyrant's desires also requires scrutiny (571b; cf. *anomia*, 575a). Socrates' latter word choice implies that the tyrant seeks objects that just happen to put him beyond the law, while the former choice could mean the tyrant seeks out laws to break. We said earlier that thumos functions in two different ways: adding force to desires and restricting desires not in one's self-image. The tyrant's anger, for example, at running short of money (573e), probably helps push him to transgress the law. The question of greatest interest concerns the second function of thumos and whether the tyrant simply stops deriving his self-image from the conventional just opinions or whether he constructs a new self-image as a breaker of those conventions. Socrates asserts that the new opinions (clustered around eros) that used to come only in

---

[22] This desiring soul answers more closely to the *Phaedrus'* image of the soul as a charioteer and two horses. While the dark horse seems to monopolize sexual desire, the white horse is an erotic lover (*erastēs*) of honor, and the charioteer also experiences longing (*pothos*; 253c–254b).

dreams simply master the old opinions from the time when he was under the laws and his father (574d–e). Bad desires get out of control. Yet only the opinions based on those bad desires are new: Socrates concedes that the bad desires themselves came in dreams while still under the law. Nothing prevents us from wondering whether the bad desires originate partly with the laws themselves, perhaps acquiring their fascination from the prohibition. Only by comparison with his erotic counterpart, the philosopher, does the extent to which the tyrant is governed by thumos and convention become clear. Unlike the philosopher, the tyrant does not rationally ignore convention and proceed to fulfill natural desires. The tyrant is not merely anomian but antinomian. He wishes to flout convention. Why else, for example, should he wish to partake of "terrible food"? A murder could at least be construed as removing someone who prevented the tyrant from fulfilling a natural desire. But eating bad food can hardly be a pleasure; rather, his cannibalism implies vengefulness against an enemy, or else a reaction against the convention that previously restrained him, that is, a desire to commit an act merely because the act was previously forbidden. Conventionality,[23] in the latter case, is still remotely governing the tyrant in his embrace of the unconventional; thumos is still policing his soul, asserting a new self that is a breaker of laws. In both cases, thumos informs the desire.

In this way the *Republic* highlights the effectual, political truth that eros is almost always mixed together with thumos, while remaining true to the possibility of a philosophic eros unadulterated by thumos. The political account of eros, with its need to restrain desire, partially mirrors but in the end radically departs from the philosophical account of eros, in which desire is liberated along with reason. At the risk of some distortion to each, Plato combines the two accounts in the *Republic*, demonstrating the extent to which the political and the philosophic may be brought together. The closeness of the two accounts and yet the remaining gap between them reflect at once the need to base politics on thumos and the moral imperative of preserving the potential for philosophic eros in a good political order.

---

[23] Compare how Glaucon lets convention (nomos, in nomizetai; 372d) tell him the finer things that the city of pigs "ought" to have.

WORKS CITED

Benardete, S. 1989. *Socrates' Second Sailing: On Plato's* Republic. Chicago.

Bloom, A., trans. 1991 [1968]. *The* Republic *of Plato.* New York.

Bluestone, N. H. 1987. *Women and the Ideal Society: Plato's* Republic *and Modern Myths of Gender.* Amherst, Mass.

Burger, R. 2004–5. "The Thumotic and the Erotic Soul: Seth Benardete on Platonic Psychology." *Interpretation* 32: 57–76.

Calame, C. 1999. *The Poetics of Eros in Ancient Greece.* Princeton.

Cartledge, P. 1981. "The Politics of Spartan Pederasty." *Proceedings of the Cambridge Philological Society* 207: 17–36.

Dover, K. J. 1989 [1978]. *Greek Homosexuality.* Cambridge, Mass.

Faraone, C. 1999. *Ancient Greek Love Magic.* Cambridge, Mass.

Figueira, T. J., and G. Nagy, eds. 1985. *Theognis of Megara: Poetry and the Polis.* Baltimore, Md.

Ludwig, P. 2002. *Eros and Polis: Desire and Community in Greek Political Theory.* Cambridge.

Penner, T. 1971. "Thought and Desire in Plato." In *Plato 2: Ethics, Politics, and Philosophy of Art and Religion,* ed. G. Vlastos (Garden City, N.Y.). Rpt., Notre Dame, 1978.

Price, A. W. 1989. *Love and Friendship in Plato and Aristotle.* Oxford.

Redfield, J. 2003. *The Locrian Maidens: Love and Death in Greek Italy.* Princeton.

Rosen, S. 1988 [1965]. "The Role of Eros in Plato's *Republic.*" *Review of Metaphysics* 18: 452–75. Rpt. in S. Rosen, *The Quarrel between Philosophy and Poetry: Studies in Ancient Thought* (New York, 1988).

Rosen, S. 2005. *Plato's* Republic: *A Study.* New Haven, Conn.

Shorey, P., trans. 1982 [1937]. *The* Republic, 2 vols. Loeb Classical Library. Cambridge, Mass.

Strauss, L. 1964. *The City and Man.* Chicago.

9 The Utopian Character of Plato's Ideal City

Whether or to what degree Plato's *Republic* is a utopian work depends on what one means by "utopia," a word with a notoriously wide range of meanings. I shall simply stipulate that by "utopia" I mean a description of an imagined society put forward by its author as better than any existing society, past or present. The limiting case (relevant to the *Republic*) is the portrayal not just of a *better* society but of the *best* society. I call a "mere utopia" a description of an ideal society meant or recognized by its author to be an impossible society – a society in some sense better than any historical society, but which could never actually exist.[1]

Socrates calls his ideal city "Callipolis." Did Plato think Callipolis was realizable? Did he really believe that the city he portrays in the *Republic* is the best human society? As with so much else in Plato, scholars disagree. One mainstream interpretation, which fits most easily the surface of the text and which I share, is that Plato intends the society described in the *Republic* to be a utopia that is not a mere utopia.[2] Socrates paints a picture in words of the *best* human society, one difficult but not impossible to realize.

Compared with classical Athens, or indeed with any society existing today, the conditions in Callipolis are extraordinary. Communism of property, abolition of the family, tight control of every aspect of life by the philosophical ruling class, maximal "unity" of thought

---

[1] An outstanding survey article on utopianism in the *Republic* is Vegetti 2000, pp. 107–49. For background reading, the classic general account of utopian thought through history is Manuel and Manuel 1979. A useful survey of ancient Greek utopianism is Dawson 1992. A classic essay by a great ancient historian is Finley 1975.

[2] The best recent defense of this view is Burnyeat 1992.

and feeling among the citizens – features such as these have led critics from Aristotle onward to criticize Callipolis as so contrary to human nature as to be *both* impossible *and* undesirable. Aristotle does treat Plato's ideal society as a serious proposal, meant by Plato to be both realizable and good. But Aristotle thinks Plato is wrong on both counts.[3]

Some important scholars argue that Plato knew very well that Callipolis is neither possible nor desirable, and intended his readers (or anyway the more careful among them) to realize this. Socrates' remarks that Callipolis is both realizable and ideal are therefore *ironic*. An influential defender of this approach was Leo Strauss.[4]

Socrates acknowledges in the dialogue that Callipolis would be extremely difficult to bring about. He primarily has in mind the difficulty of ensuring that philosophers rule. But many readers of the *Republic* find other aspects of Socrates' Callipolis implausible. Within the guardian class, the strict control of sex, the sharing of spouses, and the communal raising of children seem to stretch human nature beyond its limits. The strict censorship and, more broadly, tight social control over thought and opinion throughout the society may be unachievable.

The extreme difficulty of realizing Callipolis raises questions about its relevance to ordinary political circumstances. Did Plato intend Callipolis to serve as the foundation of a political program, which could be used, for example, in reforming Athens or in founding a new Greek colony? A distinguished line of interpreters have argued that he did.[5] Others have taken an opposite position: that Plato's motive in writing the *Republic* was not primarily political but *ethical*. On this view, Callipolis is not intended as a guide to designing a better society. Instead, Plato'political utopia is a metaphorical device for clarifying justice and virtue in the individual soul.[6]

---

[3] Aristotle, *Politics*, 2.1–5.

[4] Strauss 1964; Bloom 1991 [1968].

[5] For a recent advocate of this view, see the introduction to an important French translation of the *Republic*, Leroux 2002. Distinguished earlier proponents include Barker 1918, p. 239, and Popper 1945. Popper's passionate attack on Plato provoked an enormous reaction. See, e.g., Bambrough 1967.

[6] The most prominent recent defender of this view is Julia Annas, e.g., in Annas 1999, ch. 4. See also Blössner 1997, pp. 190ff. (together with his chapter 13 in this volume); and Isnardi-Parente 1987.

My own view is that Plato's intention in the *Republic* is to present a utopia that is not a mere utopia. Evidence for this interpretation can be quickly sketched. In Book 2 Socrates sets out to describe the just city (368d–369a). In accord with the philosophical semantics of the *Republic*, what Socrates means by this is not a city that meets certain minimal or basic standards of justice, but rather a city that is *fully* just, which is in every way just and in no way unjust. Eventually, it will turn out that the perfectly *just* city is also the *best* city. So Socrates is not changing the subject when he says that in establishing his city his goal is to make it as happy – that is, as good, as well-off – as possible (420b). Socrates declares that this utopia is not a *mere* utopia when at 540d he asks rhetorically, "Don't you agree that the things we've said about the city and its constitution aren't wishful thinking, that it is hard for them to come about but not impossible?"[7]

The claim that Callipolis is realizable must be qualified. Socrates' description of the best city is a model (*paradeigma*). The material world imposes limits on perfection. No actual object can ever match its blueprint *exactly*. Socrates says:

> But if we discover what justice is like, will we also maintain that the just man is in no way different from the just itself, so that he is like justice in every respect? Or will we be satisfied if he comes as close to it as possible and participates in it far more than anyone else? . . . Then it was in order to have a model that we were trying to discover what justice itself is like and what the completely just man would be like, if he came into being, and what kind of man he'd be if he did. . . . . So don't keep trying to compel me to demonstrate that the sort of thing we have described in a theoretical way can also be fully realized in practice. If we turn out to be capable of finding how a city can be run in a way pretty close to the way you have described, then you can say that we have discovered how what you are asking for can be put into practice.   (472c–473b)

Thus a more precise and defensible version of the claim that Callipolis is realizable would be: Socrates depicts in words an ideal human society that may not be realizable in every detail, but may be closely approximated.

"Utopia as a paradigm": this motto is the key to understanding Plato's utopianism. A paradigm can be useful without being realized.

---

[7] The demand that Socrates show how Callipolis is possible structures much of the discussion in Books 5–7. See, e.g., 458c, 466d, 499–502.

For example, we can strive to approximate it, even if we are destined not to achieve our goal perfectly. Paradigms are abstract; a real city will be full of material messiness that the city in words can leave out; it is unrealistic to expect a perfect embodiment of utopia.

But we must not go too far and think that approximate realizability does not matter. Proof of approximate realizability is what protects us from a change of subject. Suppose we think that Mark Rothko's abstract painting *Earth and Green* is the most perfect expression of beauty in the history of art. Pointing to the painting, I say: "you want to know what a beautiful woman looks like – she looks like *that*." Well, no. The beauty expressed by the painting is not an ideal of *human* beauty. It is too abstract, and perhaps too beautiful, for that.

Socrates in 472 does not deny that approximate realizability is important, because only this guarantees that his ideal city is an ideal city *of human beings*. His repeated claims that his proposals about women do not conflict with "nature" go to the same point (453a ff., 466d). Over the centuries the main source of doubt about the feasibility of Plato's Callipolis is the thought that it violates human nature – real human beings could not live like that.

Central to any utopian project is its conception of the plasticity of human nature. How different could human beings be, when placed under the right circumstances, and still be human beings – members of our biological species? Socrates in the *Republic* commits himself to the idea that human nature is extremely plastic in some ways: we, or anyway an entire social class of us, could accept community of spouses and children. But in other ways human nature is not so plastic: for example, no ideal educational system could transform a majority of the population into philosophers. That is unattainable; nature is just too fond of dolts.

I. IF PHILOSOPHERS ARE KINGS . . .

After agreeing to show how his ideal city may be approximately possible, Socrates proceeds to declare his famous "greatest wave of paradox": it will be possible only if philosophers are kings or kings philosophize (473d).

Socrates had promised to show "how and under what conditions it would be most possible" (472d) to found this city. This phrase is somewhat unclear, leaving the status of the condition "if philosophers are kings" also unclear. Is Socrates merely proposing that "making philosophers kings" is the easiest way to realize the city? Or the way that, however easy or hard it is, will result in the closest approximation of the ideal? Is he presenting a necessary or a sufficient condition?

At 473b Socrates promises to show the smallest change that could produce an approximation of the ideal city. This sounds like he is offering a "minimal sufficient condition." If a city made this change, it alone (together with its consequences) would produce a city close to ideal.[8]

With his next breath Socrates calls it a "necessary condition": unless philosophers rule, this constitution will never be born to possibility or see the light of the sun (473d7).

Taking these remarks together, we see that Socrates is claiming that rule by philosophers is *both* necessary and sufficient to produce the happy city. The initial change may be small – making a philosopher the king or the king a philosopher – but this catalyst transforms society.

To understand just how "utopian" in the colloquial sense, how difficult of realization and under conditions how different from our own, Socrates' proposal is, we need to explore what he means by "a true and adequate philosopher" (473c). For it makes a huge difference which of two possibilities he has in mind: (1) A true philosopher is a lover of wisdom, one who aspires to knowledge but does not (necessarily) have it yet, or (2) the true philosopher whose rule is key to the approximation of heaven on earth does not just *love* wisdom, but *has* it; not just *aspires* to knowledge of the just, the beautiful, and the good, but *has* that knowledge.

I first point out the opposing advantages and disadvantages of these two conceptions for Socrates' project, and then confront the question of which one he means. Suppose the philosopher ruler who is key to

---

[8] We should not interpret Socrates as making the extreme statement that putting a philosopher in power *infallibly guarantees* the coming into being of a just city. Install a philosopher as king under conditions of war and famine and pervasive vice, and even he will fail. Socrates must implicitly be assuming here something like a "standard conditions" clause. Under favorable conditions, installing a philosopher as king is sufficient. At 540e–541a, Socrates suggests that the exile of all adults might be required.

the realization of the polis is a wise man, a philosopher who *knows*. It is then easy to imagine how such a ruler could make a city happy, since all of his decisions will be the right ones – guided as they are by knowledge of the good. On the other hand, this conception does pose an extra problem of practicability. One problem of practicability is how to get the wise man into power and induce him to rule. But the other, equally great problem is how to find or produce or educate a truly wise person in the first place. After all, Socrates spent a lifetime seeking wisdom, and failed.

The other conception of a true philosopher poses only a small problem of practicability. Socrates and his close associates were "philosophers" in this sense, as were Plato and his students and associates in the Academy. Here the big problem is to see how rulers who are merely lovers of wisdom, but are not wise, are sufficient to make a city happy.

Socrates spends the remainder of Book 5 defining "who the philosophers are that we dare to say must rule" (474b). Socrates' implicit answer in Book 5 is clear, that the true philosopher is a lover of wisdom, but not necessarily wise. He concludes Book 5 by saying that philosophers are "those who love and welcome the things of which there is knowledge" (479e–480a; cf. 376b).[9]

But right away at the beginning of Book 6, Socrates slides over to the other conception: "Since philosophers are those who are able to grasp what is always the same in all respects" (484b), clearly they should rule. The contrast is no longer between those who love sights and sounds and those who love true realities, but between the blind and those who "*know* each thing that is, and are not inferior to the others, either in experience or in any other part of virtue" (484d).

With these remarks, Socrates' argument shifts decisively. In Books 6 and 7, Socrates continues to equivocate between the two senses of "philosopher," but generally maintains that the rulers of the best city must be philosophers who are wise. A good example of Socrates' continuing equivocation comes at 499b–501c. He starts out by saying that a city cannot reach perfection (*telos*), unless philosophers rule and are obeyed or unless tyrants acquire love of wisdom (499b).

[9] In this passage Socrates does mention "those who contemplate true realities" and thus have knowledge. But he goes on to say not that the philosopher (i.e., the person of whom he has been speaking) *knows* these true realities, but rather that he loves and welcomes them.

In other words, a necessary condition of bringing about *Callipolis* is rule by wisdom-lovers.[10] But his conclusion is that "there is no way the city can be happy until it is designed by artists using the divine pattern [of the Forms]" (500e). An artist who can do this is no beginner, but a master craftsman. The philosopher who can do this job becomes "as ordered and divine" (500d) and as "perfectly good" (501d) as it is possible for a human being to be.

The philosophical grounds for Plato's shift from wisdom-lovers to the wise are easy to see. The rulers of the *best* city must make the *best* decisions, and those who have the power to make the best decisions are the *wise*. Suppose the city were run by a bunch of mere learners, of genuine truth-lovers who do not yet know very much. Such rulers will, out of ignorance, frequently make wrong decisions. Wrong decisions create injustice and instability. A city run by such people cannot be the best city; it cannot be Callipolis.

The idea that rule by wisdom-lovers is sufficient to bring about the best city faces another, perhaps deeper problem. Nothing guarantees that wisdom-loving rulers will have a correct conception of the best city. A fact notorious among philosophers is that loving the truth is compatible with being wrong about almost anything! (Consider the enormous variety of views held by talented, truth-loving philosophers throughout history.) Wisdom-loving rulers may think that democracy is better, others that oligarchy is. They may believe in controlling prices or in letting prices run free. They may encourage sexual continence or license. The one belief that wisdom-loving rulers will presumably have in common is that the city should support and encourage philosophy. But nothing prevents such rulers from having badly mistaken views about which policies (including fundamental constitutional policies) will in fact be effective in promoting that goal. Therefore, one important way in which a wisdom-loving philosopher-ruler can fail to create a good city, and even make a decent city worse, is by energetically and in all sincerity striving after a false conception of the good.

This helps to explain why Socrates' description of the philosopher's education (502–19) is so crucial to the argument of the *Republic*. The city must be run by people who have had that education, in

---

[10] A necessary condition, and perhaps also sufficient. "It will not happen until" is in this way ambiguous.

order for it to succeed. The ruling class of the best city must be led by wise people over fifty who have had a secure vision of the Form of the Good. Otherwise, too many errors of aim and execution will be made.

In Book 5 Socrates claims that a necessary and sufficient condition of the coming-into-being of Callipolis is that philosophers – that is, wisdom-lovers – rule. Socrates later shifts ground, assuming that the rulers of Callipolis are not just wisdom-lovers but wise. Plato's slide from one conception of philosophy to another is a deep problem. In tacitly moving from one conception of philosopher to another, Plato makes the happy city seem more possible than it is.

I can think of two ideas that might help to bridge the gap between Socrates' two conceptions of the philosopher. One is that wisdom is easy to come by for those who truly want it. But Socrates' life and Socrates' remarks in the *Republic* about his own limitations rule this out. The other solution is subtler. Plato might reasonably think, and Socrates hints in Book 5, that true philosophers, who love and are so welcoming of knowledge, are easily educable. Thus, *if* there is a wise person around to teach them, wisdom-lovers will readily become wise, and the conceptual gap between the two kinds of philosopher has little practical importance.

This second thought leaves untouched the most important hidden obstacle to the realization of Plato's happy city: how do we come by even *one* perfectly wise person, to begin the process?

The difficulty of this obstacle may depend in part on the character of Socrates. How wise was Socrates? This question is deeply controversial, and has been since antiquity. Suppose you think that Socrates was wise, or anyway that Plato's portrayal of Socrates portrays him as wise. Then you might claim that the existence of one wise philosopher is not *such* a difficult condition. Socrates was wise, and he emerged more or less spontaneously in classical Athens. Wise philosophers may be uncommon, but they are not impossible.

At the other extreme is the view that Socrates was ignorant, or anyway that he is portrayed that way by Plato. In the *Apology* Socrates denies that he is wise and claims to "know nothing fine" (21d). In the *Republic* Socrates has sufficient grasp of justice and human nature and other matters to spin out a theory of the best city. But this does not mean that Socrates actually *knows* what justice is or *knows* what the best city is like. Socrates describes a path of philosophical education. How far along that path are we meant to think that Socrates himself has traveled? Perhaps not very far. Socrates has had a lot of practice at dialectic. But his mathematical education probably falls short of the *Republic's* requirement. And Socrates surely lacks the firm grasp of the Form of the Good that is the capstone of philosophical education in Callipolis.[11]

There is an important indirect argument to the conclusion that Socrates was not wise. Socrates was helpless at politics (*Ap.* 31c–32a). The problem is not just that he was unable to persuade the many to listen to his views. The deeper problem is that Socrates was unable to function effectively at the level of the city. If Socrates – either the historical figure or the Platonic character – were made tyrant, he would make a mess of things straightaway.

Thus my own view is that Socrates was not wise.[12] Since not even Socrates is wise enough for him to be a philosopher whose rule makes Callipolis feasible, what reason does the *Republic* give us to think that such a person is possible at all? Socrates claims that the educational system of Callipolis will produce wise philosophers. But outside of Callipolis, before Callipolis is founded, how will such people come to be?

One speculative answer to this question immediately suggests itself. Perhaps Plato thought that his own school, the Academy, was capable of providing the philosophical education described in the *Republic*. Perhaps Plato thought that he himself was wise. Did Plato believe that if only he himself were allowed to rule, or act as effective adviser to a king, he could create something close to Callipolis? We will never know.[13]

If Plato did think that he was wise enough to rule a Callipolis, Plato was wrong. The wisdom required to rule an almost-perfect city is almost-perfect wisdom. Plato was not so wise as that; perhaps

---

[11] 506c–e, 354c, 450e–451a, 533a.
[12] This holds for both the historical figure and the Platonic character. Xenophon did portray Socrates as wise in his *Memorabilia*.
[13] The work that has come down to us as Plato's *Seventh Letter* is a fascinating source of potential evidence about both Plato's political ambitions and his views on the relation of philosophy to politics. Unfortunately, whether Plato himself wrote the letter is a difficult and disputed question: see Edelstein 1966. The letter may provide valuable clues, even if it is inauthentic: Sayre 2002 [1988].

no one is. Philosophically, one of the strongest objections to the possibility of Plato's Callipolis is that the wisdom required of its rulers is inhumanly great.

One thing I am *not* inclined to do here is to argue that since Callipolis is possible only if rulers are perfectly wise, and Socrates fails to argue that perfect wisdom is possible, Plato ironically intends the opposite of what is on the surface of the text, so that he means us to see that Callipolis is impossible after all. I don't think that Plato is ironic here – I think he cheats. Plato illegitimately exploits an ambiguity in the term "philosopher," by having Socrates slide silently from the wisdom-seeking philosopher of Book 5 to the fully wise philosopher of the "Return to the Cave."

Notoriously, one school of thought does hold that Plato's depiction of the ideal city is deeply ironic, and he means us to see that Callipolis is an impossibility, even an anti-utopia. For convenience I'll call this the Straussian interpretation,[14] to which I now turn.

First, a word about the hermeneutics of irony. As a student, I was attracted to ancient philosophy in part due to the allure of technical philology. "Philology as a rigorous science" was my motto, to paraphrase Husserl. But the literary device of irony completely undercuts that aspiration. There is no algorithm, no amount of brute force philology that will demonstrate the presence of irony to someone who doesn't see it, or the reverse. This difficulty runs deep. I'll illustrate it by quoting an eminent contributor to this volume, Christopher Rowe:

[H]owever low an opinion of Plato we may hold, we can scarcely suppose him to be deaf to the irony of the suggestion that the "quickest and easiest" way of achieving a "happy" city is to get rid of the majority of its original inhabitants.[15]

But I see no irony in that suggestion, and don't believe Plato did either. Evidently, on this point either Rowe or I has a tin ear. But there is no proving which of us it is. Scholars who display anger, and

---

[14] Although the label is convenient, it must be stressed that not all interpreters who take an ironizing approach are followers of Strauss. See, e.g., Gadamer 1980. Strauss and his close colleagues and students have important disagreements among themselves. See, e.g., Benardete 1989 and Nichols 1987.

[15] Rowe 1999, p. 268.

even contempt, for those on the opposite side of an "irony/no irony" debate are making a mistake.[16]

Scholars who treat Plato's utopian proposals as ironic agree with Plato's critics that Callipolis is impossible. Unlike the tradition of Plato's critics, however, these interpreters hold that Plato realized that his proposals are impossible, and even absurd, and that Plato intended alert and intelligent readers to see this. Thus Plato's true message is the opposite of the surface message of the text: Callipolis is incoherent and impossible.

Straussian interpreters give a variety of reasons why Callipolis is impossible.[17] Some are traditional criticisms, such as that communism of spouses and children is incompatible with human nature. But one distinctive line of argument has attracted considerable attention and debate.[18] At the end of the famous metaphor of the cave, Socrates explains that, after learning about the world outside the cave, philosophers must be "compelled" to return to the cave and employ their wisdom to benefit those who have been left behind (520a). The implication of the metaphor is that after having received a full philosophical education, up to and including a vision of the Form of the Good, philosophers in Callipolis must not be allowed to devote their lives entirely to the joys of contemplation. Instead, they must be required to make use of their wisdom in ruling the city.

The core of the Straussian argument is this: for the philosopher to reenter the cave, that is, to leave the life of contemplation for the grubby business of improving the lives of nonphilosophers, is bad for him. (It reduces his happiness or well-being.) Since it is irrational to choose what is worse for oneself, and the philosopher knows this, the philosopher will not return to the cave. What this implies for Callipolis is that the philosophical ruling class will not agree to perform their municipal duties. But without effective philosophical rule, Callipolis is impossible.

A few remarks on high points of this debate. First, the great messy hairball of the issue that is the philosopher's return to the cave has

---

[16] Of course, to say that there is no proving the matter does not imply that discussion is closed. Plenty of room for explanation and honest argument remains.

[17] There is a nice quick list in Strauss 1964, pp. 127–28.

[18] Strauss 1964, pp. 124–27; Strauss 1963; Bloom 1991 [1968], p. 407; Hall 1977; Bloom 1977.

no clear resolution without importing a great deal that is not explicit in the text, so any answer that is put forward by its advocates is speculative.[19] More particularly, it is true that, taken intrinsically, for a philosopher in Callipolis to turn from contemplation to city administration results in diminished well-being. Plato scholarship does not adequately emphasize that in Plato, welfare depends *not* just on the state of one's soul, *but also* (as in Aristotle) on activity. In the context of the ideal city, however, for a philosopher to refuse the "draft" into administration might be worse, from the point of view of self-interest, than accepting it, if, for example, justice requires obedience and having committed injustice is even worse than laboring in the bureaucracy. But defenders of the Straussian approach will rightfully reply that what justice requires is precisely at issue. They may say: it is unjust to require the philosopher to sacrifice himself, and Socrates' argument to the contrary is meant ironically.

An important response to the Straussian approach takes a different tack.[20] On this view, the philosopher, who has had cognitive contact with the Form of the Good, is motivated by his love of the good to do what he can to increase goodness in the world, however he can. Instead of psychological egoism, this version of Plato's philosopher-king is motivated by universal benevolence. He is a good-maniac.

There are hints in the text on which this interpretation can draw, but it is speculative. Against it one can argue that the philosopher-kings are patriots: they are motivated by loyalty above all toward their own city, and perhaps in a lesser way to all Greeks.

The issue of egoism versus altruism in Plato is a deep and difficult issue, and despite the devotion of much ink to it, it is poorly understood.[21] What is clear is that in the *Republic* the rulers are selected and educated to be profoundly loyal to the city (375c, 412e, 413c, 414de.) They are neither egoists nor universal altruists, but patriots. Both the Straussian and the universal benevolence interpretations require that the patriotic motivation of the ruling class is

[19] Two valuable recent articles devoted to this topic are Mahoney 1992 and Brown 2000. Brown's article provides an extensive bibliography.

[20] See Hall 1977; Kraut 1991, 1992. Cf. also Parry 1996, and his chapter 14 in this volume.

[21] A useful recent book on egoism vs. altruism in Greek ethics, including Plato, is White 2002. My own contribution to this debate, focusing on early Plato, is Morrison 2003.

transformed due to philosophical enlightenment. I'm not convinced; and if (Plato believes that) philosophers can be patriots, then any need for philosophers' self-sacrifice is no obstacle to the realization of Plato's ideal city.

II. FOR WHOM IS THE *REPUBLIC* USEFUL, AND HOW?

Our examination of the question of whether and how the *Republic* may be realizable has implications for another topic raised at the beginning, that is, whether the *Republic* is "primarily" political or "primarily" ethical. Is the *Republic* useful as a guide to political or individual action, and how?

If Plato's ideal city can be realized only with difficulty and under special conditions, then Plato cannot have intended it to provide "a political program." First, the conditions necessary for realizing Callipolis are not under anyone's control: they depend heavily on luck. If there is no wise man about, and it is not practical to banish all adults, then realizing Callipolis, as such, is not a sensible political program.

Well, one might reply, even if realizing Plato's ideal city is not a sensible political program, it still can be a guide to political action, giving political actors a goal to aim at approximating. The problem with this thought is that the precondition for Callipolis is so dramatic, and the revolution it requires so total, that this utopian vision cannot be approached gradually. Either there is a wise person available and the concrete conditions exist for putting him in power, or not. If not, the *Republic* seems to give one no guidance for political action. It rather suggests that nothing useful can be done. In this way the *Republic* is dangerously quietist.

Another way out of this criticism is provided by the account of degenerating constitutions in Books 8 and 9. Here Plato seems to regard his theoretically best city as holding the top place on a scale occupied at lower levels by more common forms of government. In this way, perhaps, using the theoretically best city as an orientation point can help one to decide to work toward oligarchy rather than democracy.

Insight into the issue can be gained by asking: what use would Socrates' portrait of the ideal city be to the philosopher-rulers of that city? My answer is that it will be of no use whatever. For these philosopher-rulers, Socrates' account would be superfluous. In crafting their city, the philosopher-ruler would look directly to the Forms – to justice itself, courage itself, beauty itself – as models. The verbal portrait given by Socrates in the dialogue is a mere imitation of these True Realities. Plato's philosopher-rulers will have direct access to the originals. As for the more concrete details present in Socrates's account, such as which mode of music to favor, and the content of the noble lie – the philosopher-rulers will not only be able to derive those details themselves, they will do it better and more accurately than Socrates, since their level of philosophical understanding surpasses his. [22]

Think of the hierarchy of Platonically good items. Fill it in how you wish. At the top is the Form of the Good. Up high there is the Form of justice. Also up there is the Form of the polis. (If you think there is such a thing. I suppose that Plato supposed that there is, though Socrates' story in the *Republic* is both too concrete and too partial to be a proper philosophical account of that form.) Superior in goodness to Callipolis is (I suppose) the divine craftsman of the *Timaeus*. Whatever your personal Platonic list is of really good items, there will be several that are superior to Callipolis. If what is needed to guide action is a paradigm, an idea of a very, very good thing that can provide a standard for judging, how does this particular middling paradigm, Socrates' theoretical city in the *Republic*, fit the bill? And for whom is it intended?

Naturally, nonphilosophers don't profit from the portrait. (Or do they? How much do students in undergraduate General Studies courses profit from reading Plato's *Republic*?)

One obvious answer is Glaucon and Adeimantus, Socrates's sympathetic interlocutors in the dialogue. Glaucon and Adeimantus are not wise, but are true philosophers in the broad sense of "wisdom-lovers" that includes the unwise. How might Socrates' description of the ideal city be useful to them? Perhaps it will provide them with a political program and motivation to take power. Glaucon and Adeimantus were real people.[23] If the issue is whether Plato intended the *Republic* to be useful to them, or to young Athenians

---

[22] 540a: "when [the philosophers] have thus beheld the Good itself, they shall use it as a pattern for ordering [*kosmein*] the city and its citizens and themselves."

[23] For biographical information on Glaucon and Adeimantus and other people mentioned in Plato's dialogues, see Nails 2002.

like them, this speculation leads us back into the cave of ancient biography and to Plato's personal political ambitions, where I decline to go.

More important philosophically is the general question of the usefulness of Plato's *Republic* to wisdom-lovers as such. Again, this question has an obvious answer: if the *Republic* contains wisdom, then it provides just what wisdom-lovers want and need. Wisdomlovers are the perfect audience for a book of wisdom.

But there are complications. Consider first the case of the wisdomlover who has just acquired power in the city. This person does not have wisdom, but desires it and is open and receptive to it. To this kind of ruler, Plato's portrayal of the ideal city could provide a useful model. The wisdom-loving ruler wants to make the city as good as possible, but lacks the intellectual and spiritual development needed to work out the goal for himself. Plato's portrayal of the ideal city provides that goal. Callipolis can be used by the wisdom-loving ruler as a model for his project of civic reform.

Of course, Plato's portrait of the ideal city is truly useful to the wisdom-loving ruler only if it is *true*. This is the sort of portrait that a truly wise philosopher would compose. This brings us back to the difficulty of finding even one wise philosopher in the first place. Though Plato may have thought otherwise, the wisdom required to write a (nearly) true description of the ideal city is not identical to the wisdom required to exercise effective rule. We can imagine the following sequence: A wise philosopher writes a utopian work, which a wisdom-loving ruler uses as a guide for civic reform. Following Plato's *Republic* as a guide, a crucial part of that project will be to develop an educational system that will produce philosophers who are wise with (as I, but not Plato, would put it) both practical and theoretical wisdom. These wise philosophers will rule better than the founding, merely wisdom-loving generation. Thus the process of civic improvement continues.

This scenario is, in its way, plausible. But Plato's portrait of the ideal city is *truly* useful to the wisdom-loving ruler only to the extent that it is *true*. And this brings us back to the necessity and difficulty of finding even one wise philosopher in the first place.

Rule by wisdom-lovers is not sufficient to bring about the best city, because wisdom-loving rulers may be led astray by a false conception of the good. Providing the wisdom-loving ruler with a dependable blueprint of goodness in the soul and in the city has the great benefit of solving that problem.

This does not, however, guarantee that wisdom-loving rulers will rule well. To begin with, there is the inevitable problem of correctly understanding the blueprint. Wisdom-loving rulers will make many errors of execution. Even if provided with an ideal goal to aim at, nothing prevents wisdom-lovers from steering a city into food shortages or invasion or internal strife.

We have discussed the case of wisdom-lovers who are also rulers. How might Plato's description of the ideal city be useful to wisdom-lovers who do not rule? This is important, because it is the normal situation. Plato, his students, and almost every philosopher since have lacked political power.

Plato's *Republic* may be useful to wisdom-lovers in ordinary circumstances – that is (one hopes), to us – in ways other than in its description of Callipolis. The *Republic* offers a philosophical psychology and an account of virtue and goodness in the soul, which can provide a guide for becoming good and living well. It offers an explanation of human cognition and an account of the world of Forms, knowledge of which may be intrinsically valuable. But what about the distinctively political core of the *Republic*, its description of Callipolis? Of what use is this to a wisdom-lover who is powerless to affect the overall structure of his society?

One small but important way in which the political theory of the *Republic* offers guidance to philosophers in ordinary circumstances is this: it gives them a *political* reason to promote the cause of philosophy within their own society, in order to hasten or make more likely the day when philosophers rule.

A famous text at the end of Book 9 is trumpeted by those who argue that Plato's aim in the *Republic* is ethical, and not (or only incidentally) political:

Perhaps there is a model of it in heaven, for anyone who wants to look at it and make himself its citizen on the strength of what he sees. It makes no difference whether it is or ever will be somewhere, for he would take part in the practical affairs of that city and no other.   (592b)

Socrates here declares that Plato's description of the ideal city makes a difference to the lives of philosophers in ordinary circumstances, because they should regard themselves as citizens of

Callipolis. He gives Plato's utopia a job to do in guiding our everyday lives. He shows a way to use politics in the service of ethics. Thus Socrates intends his portrait of Callipolis to help people like Glaucon and Adeimantus in the here and now, by giving them a paradigm for living their lives as individuals.

The problem is that Socrates' advice is very unclear. What does it mean to "regard yourself as a citizen-inhabitant [katoikizein]" of a city in words? How do you engage in the politics (politika prattein) of a theoretical entity? How do you concern yourself with its affairs? You can't vote in it, perform a liturgy, help run the warehouses.

It may be impossible to find a plausible interpretation of this passage that preserves its political character.[24] Plato famously says in the Gorgias that a physician who does not practice medicine is still a physician, because he possesses the skill. Perhaps here Plato is making the similar point that a philosopher in ordinary circumstances should regard himself as a member of "the community of philosophers."

This approach fails, for two reasons. The parallel case of the physician may explain why a wise philosopher deprived of power may still regard himself as a statesman. He has the skill. But it leaves unexplained how Socrates can talk of "engaging in the politics" of that city. A physician locked in jail may still be a physician, but he is unable to practice medicine. Second, Socrates' advice is directed at people like Glaucon and Adeimantus, at wisdom-lovers as well as the wise (591c). But "physician" corresponds to "wise philosopher." Socrates' advice also applies to those who lack the skill.

The problems with Socrates' appeal to the "heavenly city" can be highlighted by comparison with Stoic ideas. One suggestion is that what Socrates has in mind with his appeal to the "heavenly city" is something like the later Stoic idea of the true city as a community of all the wise, wherever on earth they may live. The Stoic wise man conducts his daily life as member of the community of the wise, just as Glaucon and Adeimantus are to conduct themselves as members of the heavenly city. But this comparison is unhelpful, in part because

---

24 Another unclarity in this passage is what Socrates means by "model in heaven." Myles Burnyeat argues for a nonpolitical reading of this phrase. According to Burnyeat, it refers not to the ideal city but to the heavens, i.e., the starry skies above (Burnyeat 1992, p. 177). Convincing arguments against Burnyeat's interpretation are given in Vegetti 2000, p. 139.

the point of the Stoic "true city" is to exclude mere wisdom-lovers like Glaucon and Adeimantus. Moreover, this idea of the true city faces the same philosophical difficulty as Socrates' suggestion: it is not at all clear what "engaging in political affairs" would consist in for a community of people who are isolated from contact with each other.

In fact, this supposed Stoic idea is probably not historically accurate.[25] We can learn something valuable about Plato's utopia in the *Republic* by comparing it with the two distinct ancient Stoic ideas of the ideal city. Neither Stoic conception is subject to the philosophical objections I have raised against Socrates' heavenly city.

One Stoic idea is that of Zeno's *Republic*, which is a utopian project similar to Plato's (Diogenes Laertius, *Lives of Eminent Philosophers*, 7.32–33). Zeno proposes an ideal communistic city, all of whose citizens are wise. But like the philosopher-rulers in Callipolis, the wise citizens in Zeno's ideal city live in a single territory and share a communal life together.

The other Stoic idea is that the entire cosmos is a city.[26] In this city all rational creatures, both gods and men, are citizens. This city includes both wisdom-lovers and the wise among its citizens. It also includes the vicious and the stupid. The inhabitants of this city are *not* unconnected, because the cosmos is united into of a single living being. Zeus's rationality is a single stuff that extends into and is part of every rational being. Every deliberate action of each rational being contributes to "the affairs of the cosmic city" as a constituent part of the life of cosmos.

Suppose we give up on making sense of citizenship and political action in Socrates' appeal to the heavenly city. There remains a more modest reading, according to which Socrates' point in this passage is that we should use the ideal city as a model for our own lives, by internalizing its structure in our souls.[27] This interpretation is supported by Socrates' remark at 591e that a sensible person will care for "the republic [*politeia*] within himself." This phrase is clearly a metaphorical reference to the state of one's soul (591a–b).

[25] Schofield 1999 [1991], pp. 57–92.
[26] See Arius Didymus, in Eusebius, *Preparatio Evangelica*, 15.15.3–5; Clement, *Stromateis*, 4.26.
[27] Annas 1999, p. 81.

Surely, this is at least *part* of Socrates' point in the passage. But we must ask again our earlier question about the appropriate level of abstraction. What does the paradigm of the ideal city offer to the wisdom-lover's project of caring for his own soul that other paradigms do not? Probably nothing. The model of the ideal city was useful in Socrates' project in the *Republic* as a means to get clear about justice and goodness in the soul (368d–369a). But once Socrates has accomplished this, the paradigm that is useful for self-cultivation is not Callipolis, but Socrates' account of justice and goodness in the soul.

All in all, despite its magnificent rhetoric, Socrates' appeal to the heavenly city in 592 is not very successful.

III. OTHER UTOPIAS IN PLATO

Plato's dialogues contain four other utopias: (1) the "city of pigs" in Book 2 of the *Republic*, (2) the proposed colony of Magnesia, in the *Laws*, and the two legendary cities of the *Timaeus/Critias*, (3) Atlantis and (4) ancient Athens. Each of these utopias has something to teach us, by comparison, about Callipolis. Here I focus on the "city of pigs."

After Socrates proposes in Book 2 of the *Republic* to look at "justice in a city" (368e–369a), he begins by describing a simple city whose citizens are brought together by need. Glaucon complains that the lifestyle of the inhabitants, as described by Socrates, is too primitive. Their diet is fit for pigs! (372d) Socrates wryly concludes that what Glaucon wants is the description of a *luxurious* city. Although Socrates insists that the simple city is "true" and "healthy" (372e), he gives in and switches his exposition to a luxurious city. Socrates continues describing this luxurious city through Book 7. Suitably tamed, structured, and ruled by philosophy, this luxurious city turns out to be Callipolis.

Socrates' "first city," or "city of pigs," is deeply puzzling. Why the false start? Does Socrates abandon this first city because it has some fatal flaw? Yet he calls it true and healthy. A true and healthy city is a good city. Is the city of pigs also a utopia, different from and perhaps in competition with Callipolis?

The principles that animate the first city are (1) that people are not self-sufficient and (2) that people do jobs better if they specialize. Socrates enumerates the required occupations: farmer, builder, weaver, cobbler, doctor, carpenter, shepherd, mechanic, and so on. Socrates describes the inhabitants' way of life:

> They'll produce bread, wine, clothes, and shoes, won't they? They'll build houses, work naked and barefoot in the summer, and wear adequate clothing and shoes in the winter. For food, they'll knead and cook the flour and meal they've made from wheat and barley. . . . They'll enjoy sex with one another but bear no more children than their resources allow, lest they fall into either poverty or war. . . . And so they'll live in peace and good health, and when they die at a ripe old age, they'll bequeath a similar life to their children.
>
> (372a–d)

Some scholars dismiss the city of pigs, arguing that it contributes little or nothing to the argument.[28] A plausible interpretation that gives the city of pigs a more positive role argues that the problem with the city of pigs is its falsity to human nature. The peaceful, simple life of Socrates' first city is possible only if people's wants do not go beyond their needs. But human beings are not like that. It is natural and inevitable that whatever people have, they will desire more; and whatever their neighbors have, they will desire more than their neighbors. Socrates' simple city ignores these facts. An ideal city *for human beings* must acknowledge these inevitable luxurious desires and carefully construct social mechanisms to control them. These social structures are present in *Callipolis* but absent in the city of pigs.[29]

Another line of interpretation is that the city of pigs is seriously intended as a utopia, as a city that is both good and possible. But the city of pigs is a second-best utopia. On this view, the city of pigs is an ideal city that is better than any existing city, but less good than Callipolis. In a recent defense of this line, Catherine McKeen[30] points out that in the city of pigs, people's desires are not uncontrolled. Desires are successfully controlled by accurate calculation of enlightened self-interest. In McKeen's view, the city of pigs is less good than Callipolis in several ways. The city of pigs is a mutual benefit society.[31] In the city of pigs, people act justly because they

---

[28] Crombie 1962, vol. 1, pp. 89–90; Annas 1981, p. 78.
[29] Reeve 1988, p. 171.
[30] McKeen 2004; Bloom [1991] 1968, pp. 344–46.
[31] Cf. Glaucon at 358e–359b.

perceive it to be in their self-interest. Callipolis is more unified and better, because its citizens value the welfare of the city as such. The city of pigs functions smoothly, as long as the individual interests of the inhabitants do not conflict with the interest of the city as a whole. But these interests can easily diverge, so that the city of pigs is unstable. The features of Callipolis are carefully designed to ensure that the interests of individuals coincide, both with each other and with the whole. As a result Callipolis, though mortal, is much more unified and stable than the city of pigs.

The interpretation I propose is even *more* favorable to Socrates' first city. On this reading, the city of pigs is perhaps as stable as Callipolis, but even more unified and better than Callipolis. Socrates' initial choice, his praise of the first city as "true" and "healthy" and his denigration of the second city that becomes Callipolis as "luxurious," receive a straightforward explanation: the city of pigs is the *Republic*'s ultimate utopia, its best city. Callipolis, though better than any existing city, ranks second.

Let us begin by noticing that the city of pigs satisfies the standard of justice Socrates develops later in the *Republic* (433–34): in the city of pigs, as in Callipolis, each person does his own job. The city of pigs is a just city, and therefore a good city.

We must keep in mind that Socrates' description of the city of pigs is seriously incomplete. He has been talking about the first city for only a few minutes when Glaucon's interruption puts an end to the topic. By contrast, Socrates' description of the luxurious city – the city that, when purged of luxury, becomes Callipolis – stretches over more than five books! If Socrates' description of the first city had been allowed to continue, surely he would have had many details to add. Scholars who argue that the city of pigs is *impossible* because of some *lack* – for example, lack of a mechanism to keep intemperate desires in check – commit the error of assuming that Socrates' description of the first city is complete.

In the middle books of the *Republic*, when pressed by his interlocutors, Socrates asks and answers the question, "Under what conditions is Callipolis possible?" Let us ask the same question about Socrates' first city: "Under what conditions is the city of pigs possible?"

The correct answer to this question, I propose, is: "If all the inhabitants are like Socrates." The outstanding characteristic of the first city is its temperance. Critics complain that this temperance is contrary to human nature. But Plato gives us a model of temperance in Socrates. Socrates is not prey to luxurious impulses. The city of pigs is a realizable utopia if it is possible to have a city whose citizens are like Socrates.

A city whose citizens are like Socrates will be a city full of philosophers. Plato's description of the occupations and activities in the city of pigs does not include philosophy. But nothing in Plato's description excludes philosophy, either.

The Glaucons among my readers will immediately respond: "But how is it possible to have a city all of whose inhabitants – farmers, masons, and merchants – have the character of Socrates?" The answer to that question would be a long and complicated story, long enough to extend over several papyrus rolls. But Plato says nothing in the *Republic* or elsewhere that implies that a city composed of people like Socrates is impossible.[32] For example, here is one way in which Socrates' first city might come about: the ruling class of Callipolis departs to found a colony on Mt. Athos. Having left the nonphilosophers behind, all inhabitants are virtuous philosophers: they have the character of Socrates. How this city will maintain and reproduce itself is, of course, a further question. One problem is that not all of the philosophers' children will be apt for philosophy (nature loves dolts); so those children must be sent away.

A city whose inhabitants are like Socrates is better than Callipolis because its inhabitants are better people. The lower classes in Callipolis do not have Socrates' virtues: temperance and justice must be imposed on them "from the outside."[33]

The question of the philosopher descending into the cave gains a new significance when we realize that the philosophers in Callipolis might have a choice of founding a colony consisting of only their

---

[32] The division into classes and the mechanisms of social control in Callipolis are necessitated by the assumption of luxurious desires. These desires make a city "feverish" (372e) and are "the sources of the worst evils for cities and individuals" at 373e. Socrates' description of Callipolis implies nothing about the possibility or impossibility of a city for which that assumption does not hold.

[33] The reliance by members of the lower classes on the virtue and reason of others is used by Christopher Bobonich as an important ground to deny that they are happy (Bobonich 2002, esp. pp. 51–57). A city in which the majority of inhabitants are not happy (*eudaimones*) is, insofar forth, worse than a city all of whose inhabitants are happy.

own class. Of course, in this city where all of the citizens are approximately equal in virtue, the farming and carpentry would need to be done by philosophers. Is the life of a philosopher in the city of pigs better than the life of a philosopher-ruler in Callipolis, or not? It seems to me that this "philosophical commune" would be a better city than Callipolis *and* that its inhabitants would lead slightly worse lives than they could have had ruling Callipolis. This implication is surprising, but not a contradiction.

WORKS CITED

Annas, J. 1981. *An Introduction to Plato's* Republic. Oxford.

Annas, J. 1999. *Platonic Ethics, Old and New.* Ithaca, N.Y.

Bambrough, R., ed. 1967. *Plato, Popper and Politics.* Cambridge.

Barker, E. 1918. *Greek Political Theory: Plato and His Predecessors.* London.

Benardete, S. 1989. *Socrates' Second Sailing.* Chicago.

Bloom, A. 1977. "Response to Hall." *Political Theory* 5: 315–30.

Bloom, A., trans. 1991 [1968]. *The* Republic *of Plato.* New York.

Blössner, N. 1997. *Dialogform und Argument: Studien zu Platons "Politeia."* Stuttgart.

Bobonich, C. 2002. *Plato's Utopia Recast: His Later Ethics and Politics.* Cambridge.

Brown, E. 2000. "Justice and Compulsion for Plato's Philosopher-Rulers." *Ancient Philosophy* 20: 1–17.

Burnyeat, M. F. 1992. "Utopia and Fantasy: The Practicability of Plato's Ideally Just City." In *Psychoanalysis, Mind, and Art,* ed. J. Hopkins and A. Savile (Oxford). Rpt. in G. Fine, ed., *Plato 2: Ethics, Politics, Religion and the Soul* (Oxford, 1999).

Crombie, I. M. 1962. *An Examination of Plato's Doctrines.* 2 vols. London.

Dawson, D. 1992. *Cities of the Gods: Communist Utopias in Greek Thought.* Oxford.

Edelstein, L. 1966. *Plato's Seventh Letter.* Leiden.

Finley, M. 1975. *The Use and Abuse of History.* London. Ch. 11: "Utopianism Ancient and Modern."

Gadamer, H.-G. 1980. *Dialogue and Dialectic.* New Haven. Ch. 4: "Plato's Educational State."

Hall, D. 1977. "The *Republic* and 'The Limits of Politics.'" *Political Theory* 5: 193–313.

Isnardi-Parente, M. 1987. "Motivi utopistici – ma non utopia – in Platone." In *La Città Ideale nella Tradizione Classica e Biblico-cristiana,* ed. R. Uglione (Turin).

Kraut, R. 1991. "Return to the Cave: *Republic* 519–521," *Boston Area Colloquium in Ancient Philosophy* 7: 43–62.

Kraut, R. 1992. "The Defense of Justice in Plato's *Republic*." In *The Cambridge Companion to Plato*, ed. R. Kraut (Cambridge).

Leroux, G., trans. 2002. *Platon: La* République. Paris.

Mahoney, T. 1992. "Do Plato's Philosopher-Rulers Sacrifice Self-interest to Justice?" *Phronesis* 38: 265–82.

Manuel, F., and F. Manuel. 1979. *Utopian Thought in the Western World.* Cambridge, Mass.

McKeen, C. 2004. "Swillsburgh City Limits (the "City of Pigs": *Republic* 370c–372d)." *Polis* 21: 70–92.

Morrison, D. 2003. "Happiness, Rationality, and Egoism in Plato's Socrates." In *Rationality and Happiness: From the Ancients to the Early Medievals*, ed. J. Yu, and J. Gracia (Rochester).

Nails, D. 2002. *The People of Plato: A Prosopography of Plato and Other Socratics.* Indianapolis, Ind.

Nichols, M. P. 1987. *Socrates and the Political Community: An Ancient Debate.* Albany, N.Y.

Parry, R. 1996. *Plato's Craft of Justice.* Albany, N.Y.

Popper, K. R. 1945. *The Open Society and Its Enemies, vol. 1: The Spell of Plato.* London.

Reeve, C. D. C. 1988. *Philosopher-Kings: The Argument of Plato's Republic.* Princeton.

Rowe, C. J. 1999. "Myth History, and Dialectic in Plato's *Republic* and *Timaeus-Critias*." In *From Myth to Reason?* ed. R. Buxton (Oxford).

Sayre, K. 2002 [1988]. "Plato's Dialogues in the Light of the Seventh Letter." In *Platonic Writings, Platonic Readings*, ed. C. Griswold, 2nd ed. (University Park, Pa.). New York, 1988.

Schofield, M. 1999 [1991]. *The Stoic Idea of the City*, 2nd ed. Chicago.

Strauss, L. 1963. "Plato." In *History of Political Philosophy*, ed. L. Strauss and J. Cropsey (Chicago).

Strauss, L. 1964. *The City and Man.* Chicago.

Vegetti, M., trans. and ed. 2000. *Platone: La* Repubblica, vol. 4, essay A: "*Beltista eiper dunata.* Lo statuto dell'utopia nella *Repubblica*." Naples.

White, N. 2002. *Individual and Conflict in Greek Ethics.* Oxford.

10 Philosophy, the Forms, and the Art of Ruling

I. WHY PHILOSOPHERS ARE EQUIPPED TO RULE

In his blueprint for an ideal society, the Socrates of Plato's *Republic* emphasizes three especially daring political proposals: first, inclusion of women in the guardian class, on fully equal terms with men; second, abolition of the family for this same elite class; and third, that philosophers should be kings. He speaks of these as three "waves" (5.457b–d, 472a, 473c–d), with the final proposal, that of philosopher-kings, heralded as the third and biggest wave within the "triple wave" (*trikumia*, 5.472a).

Quite how destabilizing these proposals are meant to sound can be appreciated only when we realize that Socrates is referring here not just to stormy waves but to a veritable tsunami of change. Not only have tsunamis been a familiar feature of Mediterranean history in both ancient and modern times, but eyewitness accounts of tsunamis – including the massive one in the Indian Ocean on December 26, 2004 – again and again describe a sequence of *three* waves, an indication that it is this specific phenomenon that Plato is calling to mind.[1] When Socrates speaks of a third and final wave as liable to "drown us in a deluge [*katakluzein*] of mockery and unbelievability" (5.473c), his reference is, if I am not mistaken, to a philosophical tsunami, a veritable cataclysm of incredulity that threatens to wash away his entire political agenda.

---

[1] Two passages from Athenian tragedy suggest to me an audience familiar with the tsunami phenomenon: (1) a giant wave ("with *trikumia*") preceded by an earthquake (Eur. *Hippolytus* 1198–214) and (2) a triple wave preceded by the sucking down of the sea (Aesch. *Septem* 758–61). Both these phenomena regularly precede a tsunami. I develop the theme in Sedley 2005.

We should bear in mind too that a tsunami could, like that at Helike on the Gulf of Corinth in 373 B.C.,[2] be sufficiently powerful to wipe out an existing city and require its wholesale re-creation. In advocating the institution of philosopher-kings, Socrates shows himself well aware (7.540d–541a) that he is doing nothing less revolutionary than that.

Why then, despite the expected incredulity, *should* philosophers rule? Why, in Plato's Callipolis, does their privileged acquaintance with the transcendent Forms uniquely equip philosophers for the tasks of government? Socrates' answer is conveyed by one formal argument, followed up by a series of images. I start with a brief look at the argument, a famous and controversial one located at the very end of Book 5 (476d–480a).[3]

This argument is envisaged as addressed not to the *Republic*'s philosophical interlocutors or readership but to an imaginary group of unphilosophical although culturally informed citizens who might well pride themselves on possessing knowledge, in an effort to persuade them that they have no such thing and should for this very reason put their welfare in the hands of philosopher-kings, who do. Characterized as "lovers of sights and sounds," they are in effect cultured individuals who seek to fill their lives with all manner of beautiful things, yet lack any understanding of the unitary essence of beauty, an essence that Platonically informed readers will equate with the Form of beauty, or "the Beautiful itself." Since members of this nonphilosophical intelligentsia have no awareness of any such transcendent entity, they are unlikely to accept initially that the philosophers have a stronger claim to knowledge than they themselves have. Nevertheless, they might yet be convinced, by a highly schematic mapping out of the relation of cognitive states to ontological realms that Socrates proceeds to develop. Beauty here will serve as no more than an example: the lessons about its understanding, when they emerge, will be readily extended to such concepts[4] as

---

[2] Strabo 8.7.1.55–2.4, 8.7.2.21–38; Pausanias 7.24.12.1–10.

[3] There is a large literature on this passage. For a reading radically different from the one adopted here, see Fine 1978, summarized and updated in Fine 1999a. Both articles are reprinted in Fine 2003.

[4] I use "concept," here and elsewhere, to indicate the object or content of a conception. By calling a Form a concept, I do not mean to imply that it is *merely* that, i.e., that it has no being independently of being conceived.

justice and goodness, which lie even closer to the core of the dialogue's argument. For even goodness, the very highest item in the *Republic's* metaphysical scheme and said to be "beyond being" (6.509b), is for the philosopher a bona fide object of knowledge and definition (7.533b–c).

Knowledge, the nonphilosophers are first asked to agree, is of *what is*. There has been much scholarly dispute about the precise meaning of this last phrase, but for present purposes suffice it to say that in classical Greek usage "what is" typically expands into "what is something or other" (and not, for example, into "what exists"). Hence knowledge is of *what is* simply because, for any given subject X and predicate F, you can know X to be F if and only if X *is* F. The same will apply even if the ". . . is . . ." proposition is not an ordinary predication but, for example, a statement of definitional identity. Hence knowing the definition of some Form, for instance, that (as argued in Book 4) justice *is* a certain interrelation of three parts, would be an excellent illustration of how and why knowledge is of "what is." (That this unqualified mode of being entails the subject's existence is not doubted by Plato, but that entailment is not enough to make the "be" in question existential in sense.)

Second, the nonphilosophers are expected to agree that "knowledge", an infallible power, is a cognitive faculty different from mere fallible "opinion" (*doxa*). Other cognitive faculties are distinguished from each other by having distinct objects – vision being of color, hearing of sound, and so on – and the same is taken to apply to knowledge and opinion. Hence knowledge and opinion are agreed to have different objects.

Although the inferential moves here (5.477c–478a) have rightly been regarded with some suspicion, the argument voices a deep-seated conviction of Plato's. Since knowledge can by its very definition never become false, its object must be such as to be incapable of falsifying it, as it would threaten to do if it could undergo change. Therefore the object of knowledge is something incapable of change. Opinion, by contrast, being variably true and false, is inherently subject to revision, a feature that implies that its objects are, correspondingly, items that are liable to change.

What then are their respective objects? Since knowledge has already been agreed to be of *what is*, and since opinion cannot be plausibly correlated to *what is not* (which would correspond rather to a cognitive faculty or quasi-faculty that systematically achieves falsehood, "ignorance" as Socrates chooses to call it), the object of opinion must lie between these two extremes. Opinion, thus, has as its object whatever it is that "fluctuates between what completely is not and what completely is" (5.479d).

So far this is no doubt too abstract and schematic to shed much light on anything. But what the nonphilosophical aesthetes are meant to be now better placed to understand is the following. The kind of beauty that they pursue – that of beautiful songs, paintings, statues, and so on – is of an irremediably fluctuating kind. The same things that count as beautiful in one context, perspective, aspect, or historical period[5] count as ugly in others. The aesthetes' evaluations are therefore subject to constant revision. Or, in the idiom of the current argument, "the many beautiful things" that they prize in fact fluctuate between *being* and *not being* beautiful. In other words, what "fluctuates between what completely is not and what completely is," the ontological class they have agreed to be the object of mere unstable opinion rather than of knowledge, turns out to match perfectly the very kind of object with whose pursuit they themselves are most concerned. Any aspiration they may have had to knowledge must be relinquished. Their chosen realm is one of shifting, perspectival opinion.

If only they understood the Form of beauty as well, they would appreciate that true cognition of it, in total contrast, is immune to such revision. When you come to know the essence or definition of beauty, you acquire understanding of an unchangeable truth that no more invites later revision than (Plato might say) your understanding of the properties of the number 2 could ever become out of date or inapplicable. What beauty itself is, it simply and unequivocally *is*. It is precisely by their detachment from the here and now, and their intellectual gravitation to the realm occupied by the changeless Forms, that philosophers gain cognitive access to Being, thus exercising the only faculty that can correctly be called "knowledge." The nonphilosophers do not know what they are missing, since they have

---

[5] At 5.479a–b the argument fails to specify these and other ways in which opposites are liable to be compresent, but readers were no doubt expected to be familiar with them from other dialogues, notably, from *Symposium* 211a. There again the example is beauty, for whose cultural instability cf. 4.424b (quoting Homer, *Odyssey* 1.351–52) with Adam 1963 [1902] *ad loc.*, 452c, *Laws* 660b.

never themselves distinguished Forms from their sensible instances. Nevertheless, the formal argument is meant to be sufficient to persuade them that they do not after all possess knowledge.

But why would this knowledge of unchanging Forms be the relevant kind of understanding required for administration of an entity, such as the city, that is inherently subject to change? The problem is exacerbated if the argument is taken to imply that, since knowledge's objects are limited to things incapable of change, the city's affairs are not even in principle capable of being "known." On such a reading, you can "know" what justice is, but no one, not even a philosopher, can comparably "know" that this or that policy is just, given only that in some circumstances or from some point of view that same policy is also unjust. This restriction of "know" may sound like a merely linguistic reform on Plato's part, but it is in reality much more than that, for it underwrites Plato's enterprise, central to the *Republic*, of radically reconceiving who or what a real political expert is.

Hence, although it is understandable that scholars have sometimes sought to rescue Plato from commitment to the implication that particulars cannot be known,[6] it will prove not only safer but also ultimately more enlightening to embrace that implication. For in both reflecting and developing Plato's two-world metaphysics, such a thesis throws light on a tension in Plato's thought that will take center stage in the second half of the present chapter: on the one hand, knowledge is essentially unworldly, and is best exercised and enjoyed by philosophers operating altogether outside civic structures; on the other hand, the proper running of the civic structures themselves vitally depends on those who possess the

---

[6] This alternative has been best defended by Fine (references in note 3). She opposes the "two worlds" interpretation that I am assuming and according to which knowledge and opinion are distinguished primarily by their *objects*, and instead holds that they are distinguished by their *contents*: knowledge's contents are always true, opinion's can be true or false. It seems to me that the objects analysis is strongly supported by the ensuing cave simile, where cognitive states are in effect defined by their objects. Fine and others have pointed out that at 520c the philosophers returning to the cave are told "you will *know* what the individual images are and what they are of," but this is weak evidence because Socrates is here engaged in using the idiom of the cave simile (cf. an immediately preceding reference to "darkness"), and not his preferred epistemological vocabulary. In a more technical passage such as 484c–d, one that capitalizes directly on the Book 5 argument, he seems careful to limit the good politician's "knowledge" to that of Forms.

knowledge being willing to apply it to the city's administration. For despite the fact, noted above, that in Plato's eyes you cannot, even in principle, "know" that a given policy is just, your ability to arrive at the (temporarily) correct "opinion" that in current circumstances such a policy is the most just will depend on prior knowledge, namely, your knowledge of what justice itself is.

Exactly *how* philosophical knowledge is meant to inform political activity is illuminated only when we move on to the celebrated similes in Books 6 and 7, of which I focus on two in particular.

Take first the simile of the Ship of State (6.487e–489c). The philosopher in existing society – exemplified here by a thoroughly Athenian-sounding democracy – is compared to an expert navigator trying in vain to make his voice heard on a ship where the crew (representing demagogues) have taken control, after drugging the rather deaf and short-sighted captain (the "people" or *demos*). These sailors flatly deny that navigation is an expertise, and they deride the expert when he insists that knowledge of winds and stars is required if one is to sail a ship correctly. They dismiss him as a mere "sky-watcher and chatterbox" (488e–489a, 489c). This derisive description echoes a phraseology that Plato's Socrates elsewhere uses with implicit approval (*Crat.* 401b7–9, *Phdr.* 270a1; cf. also its use at *Pol.* 299b), thus appropriating and turning to his own advantage the charges that were to be brought against him at his trial (cf. *Apol.* 18b). We are thereby invited to recognize in the expert navigator a thoroughly Socrates-like figure.

This expert's understanding of the stars, contrasted with the sailors' scornful ignorance of them, represents a gulf in communication between philosophers and the rest of society that Plato in the *Republic* seeks to display at its starkest, as a first step toward its eventual bridging. There can be no possible doubt that the stars in the Ship of State simile symbolize the Forms. And just as the stars with their unfailing regularities are, unbeknown to the crew, vital to the navigation of the ship, so too in Plato's eyes it is only by reference to absolute and unvarying values, equated as usual with Forms, that an intrinsically unstable entity like the city can be well regulated.[7]

The same point is further elucidated by the cave simile that opens Book 7. Its main epistemological lesson lies in the following contrast.

---

[7] Cf. 7.521a on the need for "a single aim" in those who govern a city.

On the one hand, there are the bound prisoners in the cave, whose exclusive reliance on shadows cast by statues and other manufactured objects that are themselves artificial images of beings in the outside world represents the level of understanding found in ordinary citizens not only of a nonideal city like Athens, but also of the hypothesized Callipolis. On the other hand, there is the philosopher who, following his release, has absorbed the reality of the outside world before returning to the cave. Although (a point I shall develop shortly) this returning philosopher is initially portrayed as a Socratic figure, uniquely achieving enlightenment in a nonideal city and rewarded for his pains by the uncomprehending hostility of his fellow citizens, he becomes in due course emblematic of the class of philosophers whose education the ideal city promotes, orchestrates, and values.

First, why are the chained prisoners described by Socrates as "like us" (515a)? Their epistemological state unmistakably matches the one Socrates has earlier called "conjecture," "fancy," or "imagination" (*eikasia*, 509d–511e), which amounts to basing one's experience on mere images of sensible particulars that are themselves mere images of Forms. Why are "we" like that? Don't we have innumerable daily experiences of sensible objects themselves, unmediated by their images? The answer to this old puzzle[8] lies, I believe, in the first sentence of Book 7: the cave is to be an allegory, not of our general cognitive state but of our *educational* state ("our nature as regards education and lack of education," 514a). It is educationally, then, that we all are, or at any rate start out, like the prisoners. Our woeful distance from fundamental truths could be illustrated in terms of mathematical education, as the mathematical focus of the ensuing educational program encourages us to do – see especially 7.532b–d, which insists that the entire process from the prisoner's first release to his looking up to the objects casting shadows outside the cave describes mathematical education. Nothing in the text suggests that such a reading exhausts the simile's meaning, and the references to education in general as its scope (7.514a) and to shadows of statues of justice (7.517d) are among many pointers that suggest

---

8 An outstanding recent study of the cave, Wilberding 2004, uses the need to solve this puzzle as a starting point for a radically new interpretation of the entire image. I cannot here address his interpretation, but I believe that the very simple solution I offer to the puzzle makes the reinterpretation at any rate unnecessary.

the contrary. Nevertheless, mathematical education is undoubtedly one of the image's applications.[9] Our distance from fundamental truths could also be illustrated in terms of society's dependence on poets like Homer as the source of all wisdom, as Socrates will show in Book 10 when he ranks poetry at two removes from reality, closely mimicking the cave's ontological and epistemological hierarchy.

But for our present inquiry it is more appropriate to concentrate on another educational topic suggested by the *Republic* itself, namely, education about justice.

That the cave is to be interpreted as illustrating, among other things, the abysmal incomprehension of justice among nonphilosophers becomes clear when the returning philosopher, dazzled by the outside light, can no longer see properly, and anyway no longer takes seriously the guessing games that the prisoners play about the sequence in which the shadows will appear. As a result he looks ridiculous and incompetent to the prisoners, who warn against anyone else following the example he has set and who would kill him if only they could get their hands on him (7.516e–517a). That is, a philosopher in an ordinary city will inevitably look dangerously unworldly, because his mind is on higher things. And where does he manifest this apparent unworldliness? Socrates describes him as cutting a poor figure "when forced, in the law courts and elsewhere, to contend about the shadows of what is just or about the statues whose shadows they are, and to enter debates about this [i.e., about what is just] using the assumptions about these things made by people who have never seen Justice itself" (7.517d–e). It is clear that a democratic city like Athens is envisaged, in which both in the law courts "and elsewhere" –meaning such political contexts as the assembly and council – the citizens engage in debates about what decisions will be just. The special focus on the law courts is explained by the oblique authorial allusion to Socrates' own future trial and condemnation. For Socrates was not known as a regular participant in

[9] Briefly, I take it that the prisoner's turning round to look at the statues and other manufactured images would represent the sensory pursuit of mathematics, as illustrated in the *Meno*; that the shadows and reflections outside the cave represent mathematical intermediates, that is, perfect intelligible images of mathematical Forms; and, of course, that the objects casting those reflections symbolize the mathematical Forms themselves.

discussions at the assembly or council. It is natural that Plato should want to put the focus instead on the Athenian law courts, where Socrates, for all his intellectual brilliance, was unable to secure himself an acquittal and where his fellow citizens, or in the language of the allegory his fellow prisoners, did indeed manage to get their hands on him and kill him. The parable thus represents, among other things, the Athenian democracy's treatment of the paradigmatic philosopher.

But I have jumped ahead to the story of the returning philosopher. Let me go back and ask about his original release from the cave. In the courts and assembly, we have seen, they argue about "the shadows of what is just or about the statues whose shadows they are." If the shadows constitute the whole of their experience, how can the prisoners argue about the objects casting them as well? To see why it is put this way, we must ask what the statues and shadows represent in the case of justice. The relevant statues in this part of the allegory are those depicting whatever item outside the cave symbolizes the Form of justice. In which case what these man-made statues stand for more specifically are human acts or decisions that mimic the true nature of justice with sufficient success to merit the predicate "just," albeit still incompletely, as Plato's metaphysics requires. The regular guessing games about which shadow will come along next might symbolize, for example, a debate in the assembly as to whether a proposed decree is just. Behind the prisoners are one or more statues representing the genuinely just decision to take in this situation; but all that the prisoners see are the shadows, or inadequate pretenses, of it that are danced in front of them by unscrupulous orators.[10] Normally, then, in both the assembly and the courts, the

---

[10] In saying this, I do not mean to identify these orators, demagogues, sophists, and other manipulators with any individuals portrayed in the cave simile. They cannot easily be equated with either (1) bound prisoners (if they were, how could they control the shadows?) or (2) the mysterious people carrying the manufactured images (or they would turn out to be, contrary to Plato's conviction, the most enlightened people in the city, uniquely able to tell real instances of justice from their fraudulent imitations). If (2) have any secure identity, they might be gods or daimons, conveying to us dependable guidance that we choose to ignore, or more plausibly the established laws of the city, which from *Crito* to *Laws* Plato tended to credit with an at least semi-authoritative status (an authority linked at *Laws* 713c–714a to that of daimons). As for orators and their ilk, it is safer to conclude that the imagery does not specifically cater to them.

arguments must be limited to being about the shadows. If the debate might sometimes extend to talk about the statues too, as Socrates indicates, the natural explanation is that this represents an attempt by an enlightened speaker, like the returning philosopher, to raise the level of discussion above the rhetorical fictions that are jostling for attention. If so, this talk will, sadly, fall on uncomprehending ears.

How the future philosopher is first released is left mysterious in the cave simile. This silence is understandable, because the answer would be very different in an ideal and a nonideal city, both of which are represented by the simile at different points. In an ideal city, the education system itself will bring about the release of the suitably gifted. In a nonideal city, there is nothing about the civic conditions as such that can account for the emergence of a philosopher (7.519a–b), so Plato is wise not to supply any symbolism for it. But we may guess that this incipient philosopher is already, while still tied up, refusing to play the games about justice that the assembly and law courts encourage, and instead insists on working out for himself what is just in each situation. By doing so, that is, by looking for the genuinely just act or decision behind the oratorical façade, he is already inserting into the talk about shadows some hypothetical reference to the objects that may be casting them. What, then, would be more natural than that, if he finds a way, he should force himself to turn round and look at those objects? Insofar as Socrates' own life is the model for the prisoner's escape, we may think once more of his characteristic insistence, when confronted with unlawful pressures, on making his own independent assessment of what action was just.[11]

At this stage of his release, although now free, our emerging philosopher is still inside the cave, that is, operating within the confines of the sensible world, dealing only with the merits of particular cases of justice and injustice.[12] But it is almost inevitable that he

---

[11] Notably, *Ap.* 32a–e.

[12] Although, within the ideal city, this phase bears some resemblance to the fifteen years of practical administrative experience scheduled for the trainee rulers (7.539e–540a), it differs in coming before, rather than after, their fifteen years of higher education. It therefore corresponds rather to their initial education, up to the age of twenty, as described in Books 2 and 3, an education designed to maximize their exposure through reformed cultural media to genuinely good models and other influences.

should next, however painful the transition may be, drag himself up into the outside world. For that world represents the world of Forms, and there alone can he seek the answer to the question that is now at the top of his agenda: what is justice?

Once in the intelligible world, we are told, he is at first so dazzled that he cannot look at the objects around him, one of which represents justice. All that he can manage is to look down at its reflection in a pool or its shadow on the ground. Only later will he be able to raise his eyes and look at the object casting this shadow or reflection, in other words, in our chosen example, to study the Form of justice directly in its own right.

What is represented by this intermediate stage, when shadows and reflections are all that he can directly contemplate? The shadows and reflections obviously enough symbolize images of Forms, but, since the region outside the cave represents the intelligible world, these will be intelligible images of Forms, not sensible images such as the statues and other manufactured replicas inside the cave must stand for. The shadows' ontological superiority to the statues is conveyed not only by this difference, but also by the fact that they are depicted as natural rather than merely artificial images. Admittedly, the manufactured images in the cave and the shadows and reflections outside are alike to the extent that both represent direct images of Forms; and the mathematical fact – never explicitly mentioned, but surely known to Plato[13] – that the two middle sections of the line (*pistis*, "trust," and *dianoia*, "thought") must be equal reflects this partial metaphysical parity between their respective objects, I suggest. Nevertheless, the escaped prisoner's upward move from sensible to intelligible images of Forms undoubtedly represents intellectual progress, and our next task is to work out what that consists in.

Now a sensible image of the Form of justice would be exemplified by a person, like Aristides, or a city, such as Sparta, judged to deserve the epithet "just," but still with an unavoidable compresence of injustice.[14] For according to Platonic metaphysics *all* sensible particulars suffer from this deficiency, whereby they never participate

---

[13] On this point, and for an account of the Line, see N. Denyer's chapter 11 in this volume.

[14] Cf. 5.479a–b.

in one Form without also participating, in some respect, in the opposite Form. That is precisely the reason why, in Plato's eyes, no study of particular cases of a given property can ever lead all the way to knowledge of that property in its own right.

We can infer, then, that the reason why the progression from seeing statues inside the cave to seeing shadows and reflections outside it represents an advance in understanding is that it corresponds to progress from studying justice through sensible instances, for example, by investigating an individual imperfectly just state like Sparta, to studying it through an *intelligible* instance. What could this latter be? A satisfying answer is provided by the procedure that has already been followed in *Republic* 2–4 for arriving at a definition of justice. For that definition was sought and found by first constructing and examining an idealized exemplar of justice: a perfect image of the Form of justice, namely, the ideal city. The ideal city is not itself the Form of justice,[15] and indeed it manifests justice no more than it does all the other cardinal virtues. However, thanks to not being a sensible exemplar, and thus not restricted by the usual limitations of sensible instantiations of Forms, it is *perfectly* just, as well as *perfectly* wise, and so on (4.427e; cf. 501d). Because of this perfection, it proved possible in Book 4 for Socrates and his interlocutors to read off from it the definitions of those virtues in a way that would have been impossible when looking at, for example, a Sparta or an Athens and seeking to disentangle its just aspects from its unjust aspects. When our escaped prisoner finally raises his eyes from the shadow or reflection of justice to the Form itself, he is making exactly that move, working from a perfect intelligible model in order to arrive at the definition of the Form of justice.

He has still not finished his education about justice, however. The escaped prisoner lets his eyes, now used to the light, travel further, not only over the beings all around him, but up to the heavenly bodies, until finally he can look at the sun (representing the Form of Good), in the light of which he now fully understands the new world around him for the first time.

Actually, it seems a credible conjecture that a value Form like justice, being so closely akin to goodness (the sun) itself, is represented

---

[15] See Burnyeat 1992. He argues, rightly, that the *Republic*'s ideal city is not a Form at all (pp. 298–99 of the reprint).

by one of the heavenly bodies (cf. 516a–b), rather than by one of the terrestrial beings populating the region outside the cave. If so, the ship simile and the cave simile come together at this point: in both, the heavenly bodies symbolize those entities – the moral Forms – by reference to which the philosopher alone would be able to govern the city.

There has been much debate and uncertainty as to why the Good is supposed by Plato to have the role of making the other Forms intelligible. The majority of scholars believe that goodness is a concept presupposed by, and therefore required for understanding, the "ideal" properties that the Forms possess qua Forms, in particular, their perfection.[16] I doubt whether this is either linguistically or philosophically the best answer. Linguistically, it is questionable whether "good" (*agathos*) – rather than, say, "perfect" (*teleios*), "pure" (*eilikrinēs*), or "correct" (*orthos*) – is a natural Greek word for the kind of perfection with which Forms exhibit the properties they stand for. Philosophically, the progress of the prisoner escaping the cave has given us reason to think not only that an ideal exemplar is as good or perfect a model of F-ness as the Form is, but that it can be grasped in its perfection even by someone who does not yet know the Good itself. Besides, Forms have other, equally important ideal properties, such as unity and eternal being, leaving it even less clear why perfection in particular should be singled out.[17]

Rather, I take it[18] that goodness stands over other Forms because it accounts for the proper concept specific to each Form, be it justice,

---

[16] This idea is much too widely advocated (or, in many cases, assumed) in the modern literature for me to document it here. The fullest articulations of it that I know are by G. Santas – see Santas 1980 and 2001, ch. 5. It is particularly well developed by M. Miller (chapter 12 in this volume), and I am aware that in the space available I am doing less than justice to his account.

[17] See note 21 below against the view that goodness *is* unity. If it were, then the view I am opposing might have to hold that goodness is what enables us to understand the uniqueness, rather than the perfection, of each Form. It is hard, however, to believe that Plato thinks the ultimate purpose of five years of dialectic lies in the need to understand what makes each Form one, especially when arithmetic already has unity as its special focus. For a more nuanced discussion of how goodness might relate to unity, see M. Miller's chapter 12 in this volume.

[18] My views on this have something in common with those of R. Patterson (Patterson 1985) and of N. Denyer (chapter 11 in this volume), both of whom give a more richly teleological account of the Forms' goodness than the majority of interpreters.

largeness, oddness, or (possibly even) man. Take justice first. Even if you have successfully formulated a definition of justice, you don't fully understand it until you have worked out what makes justice good.[19] Since justice is a value, the point is a readily intelligible one: no one, it might be said, could fully understand any given value without even knowing what goodness itself is. Although *Republic* 4 has already formulated a definition of justice, we were there told by Socrates that his route to it was a shortcut (435c–d), and in Book 6 (504b–d) he made it explicit that the "longer route" which was thus avoided would have been one via the Good. Thus the dialogue's definitional task regarding justice was not really completed in Book 4, and could not be completed by anyone who had not first reached an understanding of the Good itself – a task that according to Socrates requires ten years of preparatory mathematical studies, followed by five years of dialectic, culminating in a fully defended analysis of the Good. Only people with that level of education – an elite to which Socrates protests that he does not himself belong (6.506b–c) – could expect to understand not only what justice is, but, given that justice is as the definition says it is, precisely how it reflects or embodies goodness.

Seeing why justice should be thought to be fully intelligible only in the light of goodness is in fact a relatively easy task. Seeing why the same is true of man (if there is such a Form) should also not prove too problematic: if a human being is to be understood in terms of a divinely ordained function, as Plato holds, and if that function *is*, in effect, the Form of man, the Form will be understood fully only by someone who has internalized the lessons of the *Timaeus* sufficiently to understand the good served by the existence of human beings. Similar conclusions may be drawn even about the Forms of artefacts, introduced in Book 10 (596a–b), assuming that these have functions subordinate to the human good.

What has proved much more puzzling is why mathematical Forms, such as odd and even, are likewise assumed to be intelligible only in the light of goodness. The most promising solution, in my view, has been to recognize that Plato's account of the Good would itself have been a highly mathematical one.[20] This is attested by the

---

[19] Cf. 6.506a.

[20] E.g., Cooper 1977, p. 144 of the reprint.

near-contemporary accounts of his public lecture on the Good, in which he was said to have disappointed his audience by speaking largely of mathematics, and ended up saying something reminiscent of the *Philebus* account of the good in terms of limit and measure, probably that "the Good is a unification of limit."[21] If discussions in the Academy viewed the Good as something like an ideal proportionality, intelligible only through the conceptual framework of a high-level mathematics, many things are explained, among them (1) how Good might be the ultimate explanatory principle even for mathematical entities, while (2) also accounting for such values as Justice (which, appropriately, Socrates at 4.443c–444a has represented as itself a kind of harmony), (3) why he takes it as read that understanding of the Good would require a preliminary ten-year period of mathematical study, culminating in harmonics (7.522b–531c), and (4) why no definition of the Good was ever going to be formulated in an essentially nontechnical dialogue such as the *Republic* is.[22]

We are now in a better position to clarify what kind of knowledge Plato's philosophers bring to the art of government, and how radically it distinguishes them from the benighted prisoners in the cave. In its essential character it is mathematical knowledge, albeit at a level higher than any of the individual mathematical sciences. Its focus is the mathematical principles of proportionality on which all lower values ultimately depend. I suspect that, but for the dominant imagery of the cave, the mathematical content of these values would have been seen to extend much further down the chain of

[21] Aristoxenus, *Harm.* II 1, pp. 31.20–31.2 Meibom: *kai to peras hoti agathon estin hen*: like some others (e.g., Popper 1966 [1945], p. 146; Guthrie 1978, p. 424), I take *to peras* ("limit") to be part of what Plato said, and not just an adverbial expression meaning "to cap it all." For the definition of good as a unification of items previously identified with *peras*, see esp. *Phil.* 65a1–5. Although I have learned much from Burnyeat 2000, I doubt the specific view he and others defend that in *Rep.* the Good is identifiable with unity. I do not believe that Plato would have written about "the One itself" as a special object of arithmetic (7.524d–525a) if he had at the time of writing identified something of that same name with the unhypothetical first principle whose study stands above all the mathematical sciences. Undoubtedly, the unity of the city is, as Burnyeat rightly emphasizes, of paramount importance to its well-being, but proportionality is itself in turn the proper basis of a thing's unity; cf. *Tim.* 31c, "The finest of bonds is whichever does most to unify itself and the things it binds, and proportionality [*analogia*] is the naturally finest producer of this."

[22] Likewise, the *Philebus*, whose main focus is on an ideal exemplar of goodness, the good life, rather than on the Good itself.

transmission than the text of the *Republic* makes explicit. For example, an understanding of justice informed by a prior understanding of the Good would be far more technical and mathematical than the broad-brush sketches of civic and psychic harmony developed in Book 4.[23] As early as the *Gorgias* Plato's Socrates had attributed Callicles' moral ignorance to his neglect of mathematics, there explained as his failure to appreciate the power of "geometrical equality," a principle of just distribution in proportion to individual deserts that might well be expected to enter into the detailed decision-making of Callipolis.[24]

With due caution, we might compare economic science and its acknowledged indispensability to good government in the modern world. Comparably, in Platonic ethics mathematical thinking is not just a propaedeutic training for philosophical dialectic about values, but stands at the very heart of the discipline's methodology. This is by no means to suggest that all the detailed decision-making in the ideal city will be mathematical in form. But there is good reason to assume that the first principles invoked and applied in the course of decision-making would regularly exhibit mathematical features.[25]

Plato's Socrates never suggests that theoretical understanding of the value-Forms is sufficient to make his philosophers successful rulers. For that they need an appropriate all-round physical, cultural, and military education (Books 2 and 3), and a great deal of practical administrative experience as well (7.539e–540a). The thesis we have been examining up to this point is only that a high-level theoretical understanding of values is a *necessary* condition of skill in government. That, however, is already enough to generate the well-known problem to which I devote the second half of the chapter: why, given that they must possess this high-level theoretical understanding before becoming rulers, should philosophers want to spend their time on the practicalities of government?

---

[23] The only hint of this in *Rep.* is at 9.587b–e, the half-serious calculation that the just life is precisely 729 times pleasanter than the unjust.

[24] *Grg.* 508a, with the note *ad loc.* of Dodds 1959; cf. *Laws* 757b–c. How Plato might envisage proportional equality at work in his ideal city can be glimpsed, albeit without the mathematics, by comparing the randomly equal distributions characteristic of a democracy, at 8.558c, with the proportionate principles of distribution assumed at 4.433e–434b.

[25] For judicious discussions of the role of mathematics in the philosophers' training, see esp. Ferrari 2000, pp. xxix–xxxi, and Burnyeat 2000.

II. WHY PHILOSOPHERS WILL UNDERTAKE TO RULE

In Book 1, long before the idea of designing Callipolis has even been broached, Socrates' conversation with Thrasymachus is interrupted by an exchange with Glaucon. The exchange eloquently anticipates the conversation in the later books where the education of a ruling elite is worked out in detail by these same two, Socrates and Glaucon.

In the Book 1 passage, Socrates remarks to Thrasymachus that ruling, like any expertise, is essentially altruistic, and that this is why those who undertake it have to be rewarded either with money or with honor, or compelled by the threat of a penalty. Glaucon butts in to ask for an explanation of this third option, compulsion by threat of penalty. Socrates replies that money and honor are not motivations for the very best people, and continues (1.347b–d):

> For this reason, neither for money nor for honour are good people willing to rule. For they don't want either to exact payment for their office openly, so as to be called mercenary, or to get it furtively from the office they hold and to be called thieves. Nor do they rule for the sake of honour, not being honour-lovers (*philotimoi*). So they have to have compulsion (*ananke*) and penalties applied, if they are going to be willing (*ethelein*) to rule. That's why voluntarily taking on office without waiting to be compelled is liable to be considered unworthy. The greatest penalty is that of being ruled by one's inferior, if one is not willing to rule. This is the penalty that decent people seem to me to be afraid of when they discharge the offices of government, and when that happens they enter into government not as if they are embarking on something good or are destined to find it a good experience, but as something they are compelled to do and on the ground that they don't have equals or superiors to entrust with the task. For the probability is that, if a city of good men were to come into being, they would vie with each other *not* to govern, just as at present people vie to govern, and that it would then become plain that it is not in the nature of a real ruler to look to his own advantage, but rather to that of his subject.

It is extraordinary how intricately this exchange showcases the later developments of the dialogue.[26] The question of what could possibly motivate the best people in a city to undertake government is broached in a way that already draws on the three-class structure that is developed in the later books, where the lowest or mercenary class is motivated by the money-loving part of the soul, the

[26] Cf. Kahn 1993, p. 138.

military class by the honor-loving part. This psychology will leave no puzzle at all as to what might motivate members of the two lower classes to take on political office, should the opportunity arise: there is after all plenty of cash and plenty of honor to be earned by ruling. But, Socrates is arguing, there is no analogous reward on offer to the best people, since nothing that they want is provided by the activities of government. And since no possible enticement could persuade them to rule, they would instead have to be compelled by threats. Fortunately, however, the most effective such threat is one that imposes itself more or less automatically: it consists in the fact that, being *ex hypothesi* the best people in the city, if they decline to rule, they will have to put up with being ruled by others worse than themselves.

It is worthwhile to pause on the assumptions underlying these remarks.

First, although the ideas here map fairly accurately onto later developments in the *Republic*, Socrates' argument relies at this stage on appeals to experience and to received views. Whereas in later books, once the "best" people have been unmasked as philosophers, it will be judged problematic how their fellow citizens could actually want them to rule, at the present stage they are characterized with sufficient looseness to keep any such difficulty hidden. Socrates' claim is the ostensibly empirical one that in existing societies, when good people take on office, their motivation is the selfish one of avoiding subordination to their inferiors. We are, to this extent, not yet in the theory-driven world of an ideal city. Nevertheless, it is in the lines I have quoted that that celebrated thought-experiment gets its very first airing,[27] when Socrates envisages an imaginary city of good men, who are pictured as competing *not* to govern. From Socrates' passing utopian remark, combined with the anticipatory intervention of Glaucon, the passage gains a pronounced proleptic force.[28] My plan, partly for this reason, is to use the passage as a lens through which to investigate the dialogue's later provisions concerning philosophical government.

---

[27] Thus, e.g., Adam 1963 [1902], *ad loc.*: "the first express allusion to an Ideal City in the *Republic*"; his wording "*an* Ideal City" rightly allows for the fact that the ideal city depicted in later books differs in not consisting entirely of uniformly good individuals.

[28] Cf. Kahn 1993, and, more generally, Kahn 1996.

But as well as being forward-looking, the passage is also a vital bridge from Socratic to Platonic thought. Quite apart from its location in the highly Socratic opening book, when it identifies as a "penalty" the prospect of being ruled by one's own inferiors it is building on a distinctively Socratic theme. For the Socrates of the *Apology* very uncharacteristically claims *knowledge* of a closely related thesis, namely, that it is wrong to disobey one's superior, man or god (29b). Although the grounds of this knowledge claim have become a subject of controversy, I am inclined to assume that Socrates takes it as guaranteed true by the meaning of its own terms: if someone is better than you, it goes without saying that that person's judgment as to how you should conduct yourself outweighs your own. However construed, the grounds for the *Apology* thesis that it is bad to disobey your superior are likely to be identical to those of the *Republic* thesis, that it is bad to have to obey your inferior.

My next question is what, in this essentially Socratic approach to the art of ruling, is the role played by altruism? On the one hand, Socrates is emphatic (1.346d–347a) that any expertise (*technē*), be it ruling, medicine, or building, is essentially altruistic in character and purpose. On the other, he does not trace that altruism back to any moral or other feature of the art's practitioner qua human being. If you become a ruler, you are ipso facto committing yourself to promoting the good of your subjects; but, as the above quoted passage makes plain, absolutely nothing commits you to becoming a ruler. On the contrary, if you do choose to become a ruler, that will be because you have calculated that, at least by comparison with your other options, it is in your own best interests. And this self-interested calculation is envisaged as incorporating the assumption that ruling is not per se the best activity a good person could engage in. What better activity ruling might come second to is not indicated, but the silence is one that Book 7 will amply rectify.

What seems to me most significant, in view of later developments, is the following. That there should be something better to do than rule is not at this early stage in the discourse introduced as an inconvenient contingency that somehow has to be catered for. On the contrary, Socrates' point is that, in the interests of good government itself, things have to be so set up that there *is* something better that the ruler could have been doing.[29] For – so Plato's great political insight runs – the only good ruler is a reluctant one.

This reluctance is expressed in terms that deserve careful note: "so they have to have *compulsion* and penalties applied, if they are going to be *willing* to rule" (1.347c). On the one hand, good people will need to have "compulsion" (*anankē*) applied to them in order to get them to rule. On the other hand, as a result of this compulsion they will "be willing" (*ethelein*) to rule. The envisaged compulsion, that is, is not brute force operating against their better judgment, but the force of circumstances that makes the decision to rule, although not their preferred choice, one into which after weighing up their options they enter freely. Likewise the envisaged willingness does not express their absolute preference, but their acceptance of the compulsion that circumstances are exerting.

It is in Book 7 that these same concerns most recognizably return to the surface. The citizens equipped to rule best have by now been identified as philosophers. And thanks to the elaborate depiction of the philosophers' education we by this stage know a great deal about the skills and interests that will ensure that, on the one hand, they are uniquely equipped to rule but, on the other, they would have preferred not to. Their ruling skill depends primarily on their acquaintance with the Forms, thanks to which they alone understand and can impose the values that make for a just society. But their true passion is for a purely contemplative life devoted to dialectical reasoning about the Forms, undiluted by the less fulfilling political activity of applying the fruits of that knowledge to the merely human society in which they live.

The notorious puzzle that this gives rise to is why Socrates appears confident that the philosophers in his ideal city will actually agree to rule. He has compared their dialectical activity, dealing with Forms alone, to life outside the cave, their ruling activity to a return to the murky depths to order the lives of those less fortunate than themselves; and this has made it obvious to Glaucon that the political life is less fulfilling for them than the contemplative. Glaucon

---

[29] Thus ruling is, in terms of Glaucon's threefold division of goods (2.357a–d), best treated as a type (3) good, one like medical treatment, valued only for its consequences and not for its own sake. For the relation of Glaucon's schema to the current question, cf. R. Weiss's chapter 4 in this volume, section 4.

accepts Socrates' prediction that they will nevertheless obey the command to participate in government, citing by way of explanation the fact that they are just (7.520e). But the problem is that justice has in Books 2–4 been recommended as preferable because in the agent's own interest, whereas here we have a case where the philosophers' just act is conceded *not* to be in their best interest. The just act involves choosing a less happy life in place of a supremely happy one. Yet, it is predicted, they will choose it.

This has become a celebrated crux, one on whose solution entire reinterpretations of the *Republic* have been founded. I propose to lean on its antecedent in Book 1 in order to narrow down the possible solutions, before developing what I take to be the correct one. If the solution I shall advocate is right, the text of the *Republic* is entirely and unproblematically consistent in the matter.

First, we may doubt any interpretation according to which sheer moral goodness or understanding is sufficient to motivate the philosophers to take on office.[30] Certainly, the starting position in Book 1, as we have seen, discounted that option, it being only when one has already undertaken a craft, be it that of medicine or of ruling, that its altruistic practice becomes an actual commitment. Has anything changed relevantly since then? It seems not,[31] because the same terms are used systematically to describe the philosophers' predicament in Book 7 as we encountered in Book 1. Their preference for a nonpolitical life is, far from being a disqualification, the reason *par excellence* in favor of requiring them to rule (1.347d; 7.520d, 521b). Getting them to rule will require compulsion (1.347c–d; 6.499b–c, 500d; 7.519e, 520a, e, 521b, 539e, 540a, b), but in the circumstances they will nevertheless "be willing" (1.347c; 7.520d) to make the sacrifice.

---

[30] E.g., Irwin 1995, sec. 213; Kraut 1991.

[31] In Book 4 the trainee guardians are selected partly for their belief that the city's interests are identical to their own (412d–413d). Has this not, then, separated the ideal city's rulers from the self-serving potential rulers considered in Book 1, and ensured that they are single-mindedly motivated to undertake government? It seems not. Although their belief about identity of interest made their initial training much easier, it was never said to be *true*, let alone knowledge, but repeatedly just a "belief"; and their eventual preference for philosophy over ruling, as this emerges in Book 7, seems enough to show that the belief was not one that they could still be expected to hold by the time they were fully educated.

What some interpreters believe to be a relevant change between the two passages is the introduction of moral Forms in Books 5–7. These, it is suggested, provide new motivating factors for those few – the philosophers – who have cognitive access to them. In particular, use has been made of 6.500b–d, where the philosophers are described as naturally inclined to imitate the intrinsic orderliness of the Forms so far as they are able, explicitly including the imposition of demotic virtue on the souls of the citizens. But the passage is carefully cast in the same terms of "compulsion" that we have already repeatedly met: the philosopher is indeed bound to imitate *in his own soul* the orderliness of the Forms, but as for his imposition of some semblance of that same order on the souls of ordinary citizens, this is described as what he will aim to do "*if* some compulsion [*anankē*] arises" for him to apply his knowledge of Forms to others, and not simply to himself (500d).

An alternative, or complementary, way of securing the desired result, albeit this time without any very specific textual support, has been to point to the Form of the Good as the new motivating factor that transforms philosophers into pure altruists. In particular, it is sometimes remarked that the Form of the Good is absolute good, not someone or other's good. Correspondingly, it is argued, the philosophers' supreme desire can no longer be for their own good, but simply for the maximization of good wherever the opportunity presents itself.[32] I do not think there is adequate evidence anywhere in the *Republic* for this account of moral motivation.[33] True, the Good itself is an absolute value, not anyone's individual or collective good. But that is simply because it is a Form. Likewise, the large itself is pure largeness, not anything's largeness and not largeness relative to this or that comparand. Nevertheless, largeness itself can never be imposed on the world other than as something's largeness

---

[32] Mahoney 1992 (esp. p. 280, "the desire for the unrestricted good"); Cooper 1977; Annas 1981, ch. 10; Miller 1985; Parry 1996, esp. ch. 4.

[33] Even at 540a–e, a passage rightly given special emphasis by Parry 1996, pp. 211–13, the motivating force of the Good is subordinated to the familiar need to "compel" the philosophers to act with it as their model (540a). Better evidence might seem to lie in the *Timaeus*, where the Demiurge's motivation is simply his wish for *everything* to be good (29e–30a, cf. Parry 1996, pp. 202–3). But that is a very special case, in that the entire universe is already the object or domain of his craftsmanship. It therefore holds no implications for the domain that a lesser expert, such as the human philosopher, would be likely to choose.

relative to one or more other things. And exactly the equivalent goes for goodness itself as well. Thus there is no reason to suspect that the philosophers' acquaintance with goodness as a pure Form changes the parameters for its imposition on the sensible world or, in particular, that it erases whatever initial preference they may have for their own good.

There remains the fact that the philosophers are just and that their justice is cited as a motivating factor for their agreement to govern. However – a point too often overlooked – the fact that they are just is mentioned by Glaucon not as a reason why they will *want* to rule, but why they will *be willing*, that is, why they will not actually *disobey* the order to do so. The lesson of Book 1, that willingness is a notion that for Socrates can operate even when acting under compulsion, crucially helps in clarifying this. At 520d–e the following exchange takes place:

"Will our protégés disobey us, do you think, when they hear this, and not be willing to take their own individual turns at sharing in the city's work, despite most of the time dwelling with each other in purity?"

"Impossible," said Glaucon, "since we will be giving just orders to just people. But the main point is that each of them will approach ruling as a necessity – the very opposite of those who currently rule in each city."

Thus the philosophers' justice contributes to the explanation of their decision only to the extent that it throws light on the precise notion of compulsion that is being deployed. And I suggest that the missing assumption is the following. Just people could never be compelled to perform an unjust act, because they would sooner face death, as Socrates' conduct testified when he was ordered to take part in an unjust arrest (*Ap.* 32c–e). They can, on the other hand, be compelled to perform just acts. And that alone is the point on which Socrates and Glaucon are agreeing.

Nor should we worry that an alien notion of justice has somehow intruded, when the philosophers of Callipolis are told (520a–c) that, unlike self-taught philosophers in nonideal cities, they owe a debt to their city for their education and that their repaying it is therefore just. True, there is a strong resemblance to Simonides' notion of justice as repaying what you owe, discussed in Book 1 and rejected there with the counterexample of unjustly returning a weapon owed to someone who has in the meantime gone mad (1.331c, 331e–332a).

But what is being invoked is actually a revised version of that view, and one accommodated to the Book 4 definition of justice as psychic harmony. For when testing the Book 4 definition, Socrates gave a list of "vulgar" examples (4.442e4–443a11), the first and most elaborately worded of which was that someone with psychic harmony would be *unlikely* to refuse to return a deposit (though not explicitly that he would *never* do this):

> For example, if we had to agree about that city, and about the man with a nature and nurture that compare with it, whether someone like that seems the sort who after receiving a deposit of gold or silver would withhold it, who do you think would expect him, more than they would expect those who are not of his kind, to behave that way?[34]

This picks up the example of returning a "deposit" used in the Simonides critique (1.331e–332a) and takes account of that early discussion by being formulated cautiously enough to allow for special circumstances in which even the Platonically just person would refuse to repay what he owes. In this it also anticipates the serious possibility that philosophers in Callipolis might, while remaining just, find reasons not to repay their education.[35] But reminding them of the intrinsic Platonic justice of the act – its being the characteristic behavior of a Platonically just soul – is at least sufficient to ensure that they won't *resist* compulsion, as they would if the act were unjust.

Admittedly, it is notoriously unclear exactly why Socrates and Glaucon so readily agree in Book 4 that the Platonically just person

[34] The translation "more than they would expect" is what underlies my paraphrase "*unlikely* to refuse"; indeed, many translators so render the passage as to make degrees of likelihood explicit, e.g., Griffith in Ferrari, 2000: "Could anyone . . . imagine such a man to be more likely to do this than people who were different from him?" (similarly, Jowett, Shorey, Reeve, and others). An alternative rendition, "rather than those who are not of his kind" (e.g., Leroux, Grube and Reeve, Bloom), would make the assertion less qualified, allowing the possibility that the Platonically just man would *never* withhold a deposit; but even then the degree of expectation conveyed by "who do you think would expect him . . . ?" would remain considerably weaker than in the examples that follow at 443a.

[35] When at 7.520e Glaucon called it "impossible" that the philosophers would refuse to rule, that was explicitly the impossibility of just people refusing to obey a just order. The possibility that in other circumstances they might refuse to repay a debt would have to represent a case where doing so was unjust, as in the example of returning a knife whose owner has gone berserk.

would typically repay a deposit.[36] But that is a problem for the interpretation of Book 4, and should not be allowed to cast doubt on the
fact that the justice that in Book 7 plays this subordinate role in
inducing the philosophers to return to the cave is Platonic justice as
analyzed in Book 4.

We are thus brought back to the dominant and constantly repeated
notion of compulsion as the key to understanding why the philosophers agree to rule. And here once more we can hope to gain illumination from Book 1's anticipation. The references to compulsion
in Book 7 indicate that "we" – Socrates and his fellow utopian theorists – will "compel" the philosophers to rule.[37] But what form will
the compulsion take in Callipolis itself? Who or what will replace
these external legislators? Here, where Book 7 is silent, Book 1 is
eloquent. The compulsion that drives the best men to rule is there
explained, not as a coercion institutionally applied by threats and
other forms of political leverage, but as consisting in the stark nature
of the choice that faces them. For if they decline to govern, they will
suffer the worse fate of having to be ruled by their inferiors. And
therein lies the real compulsion. Once we recognize that the Book 1
preview has not been superseded but is still operative in Book 7, we
may usefully draw on it to inform our reading of the "compulsion"
emphasized in the latter book.[38] What really makes it inevitable
that the philosophers will shoulder the unwelcome duty of government is their recognition that, were they not to do so, they would no
longer live in an ideal city, and would instead be subject to the rule of
nonphilosophers, their own inferiors. That compulsion by circumstances, operative since Book 1, is not in Book 7 replaced by some
new motivation for undertaking to rule; all that Book 7 adds is the
reason why the philosophers will not resist the coercion that they
face, as in other circumstances they might have done.[39]

[36] The classic formulation of this problem is that of Sachs 1963.
[37] Hence at 7.519e it is by "law" that philosophers are required to rule.
[38] Brown 2000, pp. 8–9, puts all the emphasis on compulsion by the external legislators, but his list of passages on "compulsion" (both there and at pp. 5–6) lacks
the crucial Book 1 passage. Despite this particular disagreement, I am largely in
sympathy with Brown's findings.
[39] For example, the Socrates-like philosophers described at 7.520b, who do not owe
their education to their cities, by implication choose to accept rule by their inferiors
rather than govern. But why was the threat of rule by their inferiors not sufficient
to compel them? The reason may well be the impossibility of their participating

Is this too reductive an interpretation of "compulsion" to project forward into Book 7? It does not, for one thing, yet deal with the danger that any *one* philosopher might become a free rider, opting out of government but still enjoying the benefits of rule by his or her equals.[40] Here at least it may seem preferable for the "compulsion" to be understood as a constraint legally enforced by the constitution, and not as in effect reducible to the force exerted by a reasoned choice between alternatives. In reply, we might borrow another sound bite from the Book 1 passage: in a city of good men, Socrates maintained there, there would be a *competition* to get out of ruling, just as there is now to rule (347d). It is easy enough to envisage the system described by Socrates in Book 7, whereby the philosophers take it in turns to govern, but also not to govern, as the rational settlement they come to among themselves.

In ways such as this, we can narrow if not eliminate the gap between the two interpretations of "compulsion": the coercive sense in which it designates the apparently external enforcement of structures on the ideal state and the more benign one signifying the rational choices that its citizens make and abide by, given all the factors and circumstances that constrain their options. Compulsion is a notion that is called for above all when *creating* an ideal city out of a preexistent nonideal community. But internally to the running of such a city, compulsion in this strong sense becomes largely redundant, and easily gives way to its weaker but more benign counterpart advertised in Book 1, namely, enforcement by the dictates of prudential reason.[41]

---

effectively in the local form of government without committing injustice. If so, considerations of justice – the absence of a debt to repay, added to the danger of acting unjustly in government – can on occasion motivate philosophers to resist the compulsion, whereas in the ideal city it motivates them on the contrary to accede to it.

[40] Cf. White 1986, p. 25.

[41] My thanks to many participants in the September 2004 Berkeley conference for helpful discussion, to Mitch Miller, John Ferrari, Malcolm Schofield, and Nick Denyer for an extremely rich array of subsequent written comments, and to Harry Adamson for discussion of the issues addressed in the second half of the chapter. I also presented papers with much of the same content at a conference held at Aoyama Gakuin University, Tokyo, in April 2004, and to an audience at UNC Chapel Hill in March 2006; I am grateful for the valuable discussions on those occasions too.

282   DAVID SEDLEY

Adam, J., ed. 1963 [1902]. *The* Republic *of Plato*. Cambridge.

Annas, J. 1981. *An Introduction to Plato's* Republic. Oxford.

Brown, E. 2000. "Justice and Compulsion for Plato's Philosopher-Rulers." *Ancient Philosophy* 20: 1–17.

Burnyeat, M. F. 1992. "Utopia and Fantasy: The Practicability of Plato's Ideally Just City." In *Psychoanalysis, Mind, and Art*, ed. J. Hopkins and A. Savile (Oxford). Rpt. in Fine 1999c.

Burnyeat, M. F. 2000. "Plato on Why Mathematics Is Good for the Soul." *Proceedings of the British Academy* 103: 1–82. Rpt. in *Mathematics and Necessity*, ed. T. Smiley (Oxford, 2001).

Cooper, J. M. 1977. "The Psychology of Justice in Plato." *American Philosophical Quarterly* 14: 151–57. Rpt. in Cooper 1999.

Cooper, J. M. 1999. *Reason and Emotion*. Princeton.

Dodds, E. R. 1959. *Plato: Gorgias*. Oxford.

Ferrari, G. R. F., ed. 2000. *Plato: The* Republic, trans. T. Griffith. Cambridge.

Fine, G. 1978. "Knowledge and Belief in *Republic* V." *Archiv für Geschichte der Philosophie* 60: 121–39.

Fine, G. 1999a. "Knowledge and Belief in *Republic* 5–7." In Fine 1999b.

Fine, G., ed. 1999b. *Plato 1: Metaphysics and Epistemology*. Oxford.

Fine, G., ed. 1999c. *Plato 2: Ethics, Politics, Religion and the Soul*. Oxford.

Fine, G. 2003. *Plato on Knowledge and Forms*. Oxford.

Guthrie, W. K. C. 1978. *A History of Greek Philosophy*, vol. 5. Cambridge.

Irwin, T. 1995. *Plato's Ethics*. Oxford.

Kahn, C. H. 1993. "Proleptic Composition in the *Republic*, or Why Book 1 Was Never a Separate Dialogue." *Classical Quarterly* 43: 131–42.

Kahn, C. H. 1996. *Plato and the Socratic Dialogue*. Cambridge.

Kraut, R. 1991. "Return to the Cave: *Republic* 519–521." *Boston Area Colloquium in Ancient Philosophy* 7: 43–62.

Mahoney, T. 1992. "Do Plato's Philosopher-Rulers Sacrifice Self-interest to Justice?" *Phronesis* 38: 265–82.

Miller, M. 1985. "Platonic Provocations: Reflections on the Soul and the Good in the *Republic*." In *Platonic Investigations*, ed. D. J. O'Meara (Washington, D.C.).

Parry, R. D. 1996. *Plato's Craft of Justice*. Albany, N.Y.

Patterson, R. 1985. *Image and Reality in Plato's Metaphysics*. Indianapolis Ind.

Popper, K. R. 1966 [1945]. *The Open Society and Its Enemies*, vol. 1: *The Spell of Plato*. London.

Sachs, D. 1963. "A Fallacy in Plato's *Republic*." *Philosophical Review* 72: 141–58.

Santas, G. 1980. "The Form of the Good in Plato's *Republic.*" *Philosophical Inquiry* (Winter): 374–403. Rpt. in *Essays in Greek Philosophy 2*, ed. J. Anton and A. Preus (Albany, N.Y., 1983), and in Fine 1999b.

Santas, G. 2001. *Goodness and Justice.* Oxford.

Sedley, D. 2005. "Plato's Tsunami." *Hyperboreus* 11, no. 2: 205–14.

White, N. 1986. "The Ruler's Choice." *Archiv für Geschichte der Philosophie* 68: 22–46.

Wilberding, J. 2004. "Prisoners and Puppeteers in the Cave." *Oxford Studies in Ancient Philosophy* 27: 117–39.

11 Sun and Line
The Role of the Good

"I understand that less than I understand the Good of Plato," says a slave in comedy.[1] The slave's understanding of the Good would not have been much helped by attending Plato's own public lecture on the subject: the majority of the audience "came in the expectation of acquiring some of those things that conventionally count as human goods, such as health, wealth, strength, and in general some wonderful happiness; but when the discussion turned out to be on the mathematical sciences – numbers, geometry, astronomy – and the conclusion to be that good is one, this struck them as utterly paradoxical; whereupon some came to despise the business, and others started to make complaints."[2] Nevertheless, in one respect at least, it is actually quite easy to grasp what Plato has to say about the Good.

If for the moment we confine our attention to Forms of artifacts, it is easy to understand and accept the *Republic*'s claim that the Good has the privileged position of being what accounts for the existence and intelligibility of Forms, much as the Sun has the privileged position of being what accounts for the growth and visibility of plants (508b–e, 509b). For the claim will then be that everything about an ideal artifact is teleologically explicable. The ideal wheel is circular, and it has its axle in its center. These things are so because that is the best way for a wheel to be: a buckled wheel, or for that matter a

---

[1] Amphis, *Amphicrates* fr. 6, in Kassel 1983–.

[2] Aristoxenus, *Harmonics* 39.8–40.4 Rios, relaying a favorite anecdote of Aristotle's. An alternative translation of the words here translated as "and the conclusion to be that good is one" would be "and that the Limit is good, a single thing." For some discussion of these and other alternatives, see David Sedley's chapter 10 in this volume, note 21.

circular wheel with its axle off-center, would give a bumpy ride. And the Good accounts in this way for every aspect of the ideal wheel: if, for example, we ask about the color of the ideal wheel, then the only answer is that it has no particular color; and that is because there is no one color that is the best one for a wheel to have. Moreover, in appreciating these facts about the ideal wheel we come to understand why it is as it is. And that is how the Good accounts not only for the ideal wheel's existence but also for its intelligibility.

We can appreciate quite how thorough is the teleological explanation of the ideal wheel if we compare it with the teleological explanation of ordinary wheels. First, some ordinary wheels are actually defective, and such defects (missing spokes, flat tires) would not be defects if they could be explained as contributing to the good that wheels are there to achieve. Second, every ordinary wheel has many features that, even though they are not defects, are nevertheless not explicable teleologically: for example, some ordinary wheels are lubricated by an odd number of molecules of lubricant, and the rest are lubricated by an even number; there is nothing bad about either of these; nor however is there anything good, by reference to which we might explain why the number of molecules of lubricant lubricating an ordinary wheel is odd rather than even, or even rather than odd. Third, even when there is a teleological explanation of some aspect of an ordinary wheel, that explanation will not be the full explanation: we can say, for example, that the wheel is lubricated in order for it to spin freely, as any good wheel must; but even here there will always be more to say, about why this wheel is properly lubricated, when others are not.

When, in the light of the Good, we come to understand a Form, we must, claims the analogy with the Sun, use our minds, not our senses (507b). This claim too is easy to understand and accept if we confine our attention to Forms of artifacts. Think of the history of bad design. Until quite recently, electric kettles had broad bases; they were made of metal; and they had their handles at the top. In an electric kettle, these features are vices: the broad base means that even if you wish to boil only a cupful of water, you must put in much more than that, to cover the electric element safely; metal conducts heat so well that the outside rapidly reaches the dangerous temperature of the water boiling within; and handles at the top catch more heat than handles at the side would do. These features, vices in an electric kettle, are virtues in a kettle that is to be boiled on a fire. The kettle's broad base means that it will catch more of the available heat; being made of metal, it will rapidly conduct that heat to the water within; and the handle at the top will catch less heat than one at the side. This accounts for the design of kettles in the era when the most convenient way to boil a kettle was by placing it on a fire. When, however, the era of electricity dawned, then instead of focusing their minds on what a kettle is, on the Form of a kettle, the designers of the first electric kettles simply copied what they could perceive of earlier kettles, and added an electric element.

In thinking about ideal artifacts, and understanding them in the light of the Good that makes them be as they are, we are not thinking directly about the Good, any more than we look at the sun when, by its light, we see the plants that its light causes to grow. Indeed, much as we would bedazzle our eyes in attempting to look directly at the Sun, we are likely to befuddle our minds in attempting to think directly about the Good. The ease with which we appreciated that the ideal wheel is circular, with its axle at the center, has no counterpart when we ask what the Form of Good itself is like. Nevertheless, we can say some things about the Form of Good. As the audience at Plato's lecture on the subject learned to their disappointment, the Form of Good is not going to be any of the things that conventionally count as human goods, such as health or wealth or strength. Nor, for that matter, is the Form of Good going to be knowledge or pleasure (505b–d). For what the ideal wheel and the ideal kettle have in common is obviously not health, wealth, strength, knowledge, or pleasure, but something far more abstract. And anything that makes ordinary ideal objects so clearly comprehensible, while remaining so obscure itself, cannot itself be any ordinary ideal object. It must be altogether more grand (509b).

These points about our teleological understanding of ideal artifacts are too obvious to be seriously contested. It is therefore important to see how they might fall short of more contestable aspects of the theory of Forms.

First, the sort of eternity that, in the light of teleological considerations, we can attach to ideal artifacts is not perhaps the full eternity that Plato would attach to Forms. In no case can we set a date to the beginning or end of an ideal artifact: we cannot say that the ideal car was built in 1999 – and that is not because it was built in some other year. In all cases, the truths about ideal artifacts that we can discern by the light of the Good are everlastingly and unshakably true: it is, for example, everlastingly and unshakably true that the ideal kettle boils water, whereas no such thing holds everlastingly and unshakably of any perceptible kettle. Moreover, in many cases, the truths that hold changelessly about ideal artifacts are themselves truths about immunity to change: the ideal kettle does not corrode; the ideal knife never goes blunt. But this is not so in all cases. Sometimes the unchangeable truth about an ideal artifact requires that the artifact change: since the ideal clock always gives the right time, the time that it gives must always be changing. Sometimes, indeed, the unchangeable truth about an ideal artifact will speak of how the artifact perishes: in the light of teleological considerations about what it takes to make a good bomb, we can and must say that the ideal bomb explodes when, and only when, it is detonated. However, this fact about the ideal bomb is itself a timeless fact; and neither this, nor any other fact about the ideal bomb that we can discern in the light of the Good, enables us to name the date when the ideal bomb exploded, or even to attach any sense to the claim that, for example, the ideal bomb will explode at noon on New Year's Day 2009. And it may be that this is all that is needed for the ideal bomb to have the sort of eternity that Plato would wish to ascribe to his Forms. After all, *Republic* 597c–d speaks of another ideal artifact, the ideal bed, as made by the ideal artificer, God. But some have felt this passage to be an aberration, out of keeping with the general tendency of the theory of Forms; indeed, Aristotle tells us of Platonists, very close to Plato himself, who denied outright that there are Forms of artifacts (*Metaphysics* 991b6–7, 1080a5–6), and it would be hard to prove that they were wholly unfaithful to Plato.

There is a second respect in which our teleological understanding of ideal artifacts may fall short of the full theory of Forms. The theory seems to claim more than just that, for example, the ideal sword is perfectly sharp and free from corrosion, and therefore not to be identified with any of the many perceptible swords, such as Arthur's sword Excalibur and Roland's sword Durendal. For the theory seems to make the further claim that such a thing is true because there exists, in addition to Excalibur and Durendal, another sword that, unlike them, is precisely as we know the ideal sword to be. And that this is a further claim is clear when we reflect on the age of the average undergraduate. The age of any perceptible undergraduate increases at the rate of one year for every twelve months. No perceptible undergraduate could therefore be identical with the average undergraduate, whose age has remained roughly stable over the past century, and whose age actually decreases when young students are admitted at the start of the academic year, and again when the oldest students graduate. But none of this requires us to posit an imperceptible undergraduate who, unlike perceptible undergraduates, does not age at the standard rate. The reason is obvious: "The average undergraduate is 19.8 years old" does not say of some extraordinary undergraduate what "Clara is 19.8 years old" says of an ordinary one; instead, it speaks of ordinary undergraduates, but in an extraordinary way. It may be that something similar is true of our talk about ideal artifacts. Or again, it may not. For to reformulate "The ideal sword is perfectly sharp" as a statement about Excalibur and Durendal and the like, rather than as saying truly about an imperceptible sword what "Excalibur is perfectly sharp" says falsely about Excalibur, would be, to put it mildly, harder than reformulating talk about the age of the average undergraduate as talk about the ages of the many undergraduates that we can perceive. And perhaps one of the claims of the full theory of Forms is that ideal artifacts are not in any such way reducible to their perceptible counterparts. Or again, perhaps not. For contrast the ideal sword with, for example, the ideal artifact whose name begins with an S. The trouble with this is not simply that there is no further artifact whose name begins with an S, over and above the various perceptible artifacts with such a name, like perceptible staplers and swords and saucepans; for the ideal artifact whose name begins with an S suffers from the graver trouble that it was a nonsense right from the start, and that there never was any such thing in the first place to be reduced to perceptible ones. The ideal sword, by contrast, whether or not it is a further sword, in addition to perceptible swords, is free from the graver trouble; and it may be that this is all that the theory of Forms requires.

Third, ideal artifacts are not the only ideal objects, distinct from perceptible objects that also bear their names. There is, for example, the ideally flat surface, by comparison with which any visible thing to which we apply the term "flat surface," salt pan or croquet lawn or billiard table, is to some degree rough. We cannot lightly deny the existence of ideal objects of this kind. Geometry teems with talk of such things as ideally flat surfaces; and we have our work cut out if we want to maintain that there are no such things, on the grounds that no visible thing is quite like the planes of geometry. We would have to find some alternative way of recording the difference between flat and rough that we could otherwise record by saying that there is such a thing as the ideally flat surface, whereas there is no such thing as the ideally rough one, a surface so rough that none could possibly be rougher, a surface by comparison with which all visible rough surfaces are flat. Moreover, we would have to find some explanation for why geometry should seem so impressive a branch of knowledge if the objects of which it speaks are no more real than those spoken of in fairy tales.[3] The ideal objects of the mathematicized sciences are therefore no less well established than ideal artifacts. But, unlike ideal artifacts, they are not to be explained teleologically. Or so, at least, it seems.

Plato suggests that appearances here mislead: the way that we usually do geometry is imperfect, and because of this imperfection, we fail to appreciate that geometrical objects too must be seen in the light of the Good. Plato makes this suggestion as part of a string of comparisons, describing both the internal structure of the intelligible realm that is governed by the Good, and its connection with the visible realm that is governed by the Sun. In each case, the description is by a comparison with the internal structure of the visible realm. This is because the descriptions are addressed to people like us, people who, for the moment at least, feel more at home in the visible realm than elsewhere.

Within the visible realm, Socrates points out, Glaucon may observe a contrast between, on the one hand, solid objects such as plants, animals, and artifacts, and, on the other, their shadows and reflections "and everything else of that sort" (509d–510a). These days, we have mirrors of silvered glass that are of a far higher quality than the polished bronze mirrors of antiquity. In consequence, we are accustomed to think of some reflections ("mirror images") as exact counterparts of their originals, differing only by the interchange of left with right. We need to forget such thoughts if we are to appreciate Socrates' comparisons. We need instead to join the ancients, and think of reflections generally as partial and distorted likenesses that

[3] For the start of such an explanation, see Quine 1960, pp. 248–57.

are – the phrase is hard to resist – no more than shadows of their originals.[4] This contrast between solids and their shadowy semblances is, continues Socrates, correlated with a contrast between two kinds of mental state or event (511d): "trust" (*pistis*), and "fancy" (*eikasia*). The contrast is, we are told, that trust has more clarity (*saphēneia*) than fancy, just as the solids that are the objects of trust have more truth (*alētheia*) than the shadows and reflections that are the objects of fancy (511e; cf. 509d, 510a). The idea is not that absolutely every sighting of a shadow or a reflection amounts to no more than fancy, as if, merely by observing the earth's shadow during a lunar eclipse, astronomers fall into the most degraded of cognitive states. The idea is rather that fancy is the state of mind in which one is looking at some shadow or reflection, without appreciating that it is only a shadow or reflection. It is the state of mind of a kitten whom I once saw arch her back, fluff her fur, and hiss and spit at her own image in a mirror: she took the image to be another kitten, and responded accordingly.[5] Trust, by contrast, is the state of mind of one who appreciates that shadows and reflections are only shadows and reflections, imperfect likenesses of solid objects, but who makes about the visible realm the sort of mistake that the kitten made about her image in the mirror, the mistake of not appreciating that the visible realm itself is only an imperfect likeness of the intelligible realm that is governed by the Good.

Fancy and trust amount collectively to "opinion" (*doxa*), and as fancy is related to trust, so too, says Socrates, opinion as a whole is related to "knowledge" (*noēsis* is the term used in 534a; 510a suggests that Plato would also be happy with the term *gnōsis*): opinion is less clear than knowledge, and the objects of opinion are less true than the objects of knowledge (509d–510a, 534a).

We can understand this contrast between knowledge and opinion if we recollect the classic proof of the incommensurability of the

---

[4] See, e.g., Aeschylus, *Agamemnon* 839; Sophocles, *Ajax* 126, *Philoctetes* 946–47, for other ancient talk of reflections and shadows in the same breath.

[5] Don't just laugh at the kitten. Her state may well be yours too, if the analogy of the cave is right to suggest that *eikasia* is or is analogous to something that pervades the life of all human beings from childhood onward, unless and until they receive a proper education (514a–515b). For more on what this pervasive *eikasia* might be, see section I of David Sedley's chapter 10 in this volume.

diagonal of a square with its side.[6] Assume, for the moment, that the diagonal of a square is commensurable with its side; assume, in other words, that the side can be divided into exactly S equal units, and that the diagonal is exactly D of those units. If your choice of unit makes both S and D even, then double the length of the unit, and keep doubling it until at least one of them is odd. Now since, as we can remind ourselves by reading *Meno* 82b–85b, the square on the diagonal of a given square is double the area of the original square, $D \times D = 2(S \times S)$. So $D \times D$ is even. And so D is even too; in which case, since we have so chosen our unit that D and S are not both even, S would have to be odd. Now since D is even, there is an E such that $D = 2E$. So $4(E \times E) = 2(S \times S)$. So $2(E \times E) = S \times S$. So $S \times S$ is even. So the odd number S is also even. Which is absurd. So the diagonal of a square cannot be, as we earlier assumed, commensurable with its side.

The knowledge that we get from this proof has a clarity that we could never achieve from a perceptible square. Even the daintiest techniques of measuring perceptible squares will have their margin of error. They cannot make us certain of anything precise. A technique accurate to within one part in a thousand cannot make us certain of anything more precise than that the diagonal is somewhere between 1,413 and 1,415 thousandths of the side. And being certain of such a measurement will leave entirely unsettled many questions settled definitively by our mathematical proof, such as whether the diagonal of a square is or is not exactly 1,414,213 millionths of the side. Moreover this lack of clarity in the opinions that we can form about a perceptible square corresponds to a deficiency in perceptible squares themselves. No two sides of a perceptible square are exactly 1,000,000 millionths of one another; indeed, not even one side is so precisely bounded as to have an utterly determinate length. This deficiency in perceptible squares means that they are not truly squares, any more than the kitten in the mirror was truly a kitten. Because of this deficiency, our knowledge that the diagonal of a square is incommensurable with its side is not, in any obvious way, knowledge about perceptible squares. The natural inference is

[6] See Euclid, *Elements* Book 10, Appendix 27. This proof is apparently alluded to in 510d; certainly, 534d and 546c allude to related results about incommensurability.

that it can only be knowledge about something else, whose degree of truth matches the degree of clarity of the knowledge.

Furthermore, adds Socrates, there is, within knowledge, a distinction that corresponds to the distinction within opinion between fancy and trust. For knowledge has the two subspecies of "thought" and "intellect" (*dianoia* and *noēsis* in 511c–e, *dianoia* and *epistēmē* in 533e); and thought is, in respect of clarity and truth, inferior to intellect, as fancy was inferior in those respects to trust. It is in the region of thought that we will be able to locate mathematics and its objects, or – to be more precise – the imperfect sort of mathematics that does not appreciate the dependence of its objects on the Good.

Socrates sums up these comparisons in a mathematical object, the divided line. Divide a line, he instructs Glaucon, into two segments of unequal length. One segment represents opinion, the other represents knowledge, and their difference in length represents the way that opinion and knowledge differ in clarity, and their associated objects differ in truth. Then, in order to represent fancy, trust, thought, and intellect, their relative clarity, and the relative truth of their associated objects, subdivide each of these two segments into two subsegments, one of which stands to the other in the same ratio as the two segments of the original line (509d; Euclid *Elements* Book 6, Proposition 10 gives a procedure for making such divisions).

In obeying these instructions about ratios, Glaucon is faced with various arbitrary choices. For example, is he to make the line horizontal or not? And which subsegment is he to place at which end? As it happens, the line that he constructs is vertical, and its four subsegments for intellect, thought, trust, and fancy come in that order from top to bottom (511d–e, 533e–534a). Thus Glaucon might have constructed his line as in this diagram (the divided line according to Proclus):

But he might instead have constructed it as in this diagram (the divided line according to Plutarch):

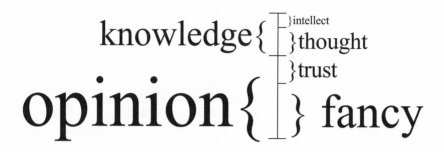

For when we obey Socrates' instruction to have the segment for opinion unequal to the segment for knowledge, we have to make also an arbitrary choice about which is to be the longer.

Some commentators claim that the choice here is not arbitrary. Proclus (*Commentaries on the* Republic *of Plato* 1.289.6–18 Kroll) says that a greater length represents a greater clarity, on the grounds that the intelligible is superior to and encompasses the visible and that what encompasses something is always greater than what it encompasses; while Plutarch (*Platonic Questions* 1001d–e) says that a greater length represents a greater obscurity, on the grounds that the divisibility, indefiniteness, and multiplicity of what is visible should be represented by a greater length. This wrangle between Plutarch and Proclus serves only to confirm the arbitrariness of our choice.

Why have us make such an arbitrary choice? When we draw a diagram in obedience to Socrates' instructions, we are producing a visible representation. Such a representation inevitably contains irrelevant features, features that correspond to nothing in the reality represented, features that in consequence cannot be explained by reference to the purpose of the representation. The proper response to such features is of course to ignore them, to abstract from irrelevant clutter, and think beyond the representation to the reality that it represents. Sometimes, such things are easily done: we all find it easy to realize that a foot-long picture of a snake need not be a picture of a foot-long snake. And it is, of course, because of our universal ease with interpreting visible images of visible things that Plato uses our dealings with such images to expound to us the intelligible realm. It is however not so easy to abstract from a diagram that we have drawn in obedience to Socrates' instructions. And this is not merely because we will have to abstract from the visible diagram to a geometrical object, a perfectly straight line, of no breadth, of no particular color, bounded and divided by perfectly sharp points. For even then, we will have to abstract further. We will need to realize that, however striking the difference between a line that has the opinion segment half the length of the knowledge segment, and one that has it forty-seven times the length instead, nevertheless, this difference too is altogether insignificant. We must abstract even from these mathematical features, in just the way that we had to abstract from the smudginess of the lines and points in our original diagram. We need to ignore everything about the diagram, save only the fact that it represents segments and subsegments related to one another in the complex series of proportions specified by Socrates. When we treat in this way a diagram that we have drawn, we are getting some practice in the kind of strenuously abstract thought that is needed to take us from the visible to the intelligible realm. And to give us such practice was no doubt the purpose of having us choose arbitrarily between making the opinion segment longer than the knowledge segment and making it shorter instead. The wrangle between Proclus and Plutarch shows how much we need that practice.

The divided line that we represent in our visible diagram has one surprising feature. Without ever affirming so outright, Plato leads us to expect that the four subsegments of the line, the subsegments for intellect, thought, trust, and fancy, will each differ in length. For the fact that they are arranged in that order from top to bottom of the line (511d–e, 533e–534a) seems to correlate with an order of merit among the mental states that they represent, and we are not told of any differences in merit other than those indicated by differences in length. Indeed, when Socrates says that geometers treat as images of geometrical objects those things that are imitated by shadows and reflections (510b, 510d–e, 511a), he comes close to implying not only that thought and trust have unequal subsegments, but also that the subsegment for thought has to that for trust the ratio that the subsegment for trust has to that for fancy. In fact, however, the subsegments for thought and for trust will turn out to be equal in length. And this is inevitably so, no matter how the line is divided, so long as it is divided as Socrates instructs.[7]

This surprising equality between the subsegments for trust and for intellect can hardly be accidental. Plato associated with two men who could have taught him far greater subtleties about the theory of proportion: Archytas of Tarentum, a friend (Plato *Epist.* 338c–d) whose remark that the various mathematicized sciences are all sisters (DK 47 B 1) is alluded to with approval in 530d (cf. 511b), and Eudoxus of Cnidus, a "pupil" (Cicero *De Divinatione* 2.42.87, *De Republica* 1.14.22) whose theory of planetary motions was the first great achievement in the mathematicized astronomy programmatically described at 528b–530c. Archytas showed how, given two straight lines A and B, we may construct two more straight lines X and Y, so that the ratios of A to X, of X to Y, and of Y to B are all equal; he showed also that, if A, B, and C are positive whole numbers such that the ratio of A to B is the same as that of C to C + 1, then there is no positive whole number X such that the ratio of A to X is the same as that of X to B.[8] Eudoxus originated the general theory of proportion expounded in Euclid *Elements* Book 5 (see Book V, Scholia 1 and 3): earlier thinkers had proved only piecemeal, by one proof for proportions among lines, another for proportions among positive whole numbers, and so on, results that Eudoxus was able to formulate and prove quite generally, for proportions among magnitudes of an arbitrary kind (cf. Aristotle *Posterior Analytics* 74a17–25). And there is direct evidence in the *Republic* itself that, whether or not he had learned it from Archytas and Eudoxus, Plato had knowledge of one slight but relevant subtlety within the theory of proportion. For in the passage of recapitulation at 534a, he has Socrates say that "as knowledge is to opinion, so intellect is to trust and thought is to fancy." These things are consequences of what Socrates said earlier, when first explaining the divided line, but not obviously so. They are much less obviously consequences than, for example, "as knowledge is to opinion, so intellect is to thought and trust is to fancy." And anyone who makes one of his characters infer the less obvious

[7] Exercise for the reader: prove this using the techniques of the theory of proportion set out in Euclid, *Elements* Book 5.

[8] DK 47 A 14, and DK 47 A 19. English translations of these passages can be found in Thomas 1939, pp. 131–33, 285–90.

consequence that "as knowledge is to opinion, so intellect is to trust" would have little difficulty in himself inferring the more obvious consequence that "as knowledge is to opinion, so intellect is to thought," and then putting these two together and himself inferring that thought is equal to trust. It is therefore hard to doubt that Plato chose the image of the divided line in full awareness that its subsegment for thought is inevitably equal to its subsegment for trust.

There are several reasons why Plato might have made such a choice. On the one hand, if the divided line does have the immediate purpose of expounding the superiority of thought over trust, then its very defectiveness for that immediate purpose would fit it to serve Plato's purposes in the longer term. It is central to Plato's thought about images that an image always falls short of the original of which it is an image. That is why he finds it so appropriate to describe the relationship between perceptible and intelligible as a relationship between image and original. The divided line is itself another image. So if it too is defective, that would be all to the good. On the other hand, perhaps the divided line is meant instead to hint that, in itself, thought is not after all superior to trust, that if we make the transition from trust to thought, but then go no further, we have not in fact improved ourselves cognitively, and that thought is superior to trust only in that thought is adjacent to, whereas trust is one step further removed from, the finest of all cognitive states, intellect. In this case, the fact that the divided line inevitably has equal subsegments to represent both trust and thought would be no defect at all. Finally, it may be that the divided line was chosen because it allows both these incompatible interpretations. For if images were not puzzlingly contradictory, then we would be liable to rest content with images, rather than be provoked to go beyond them to the reality from which they derive. Recall the discussion of fingers and size in 523b–524d: the senses unambiguously report fingers as fingers, and that does nothing to provoke the mind to think about what a finger is; but the mind is provoked to wonder what big and small might be, when the senses report that a single finger is both these things.

When you are engaged in thought, you treat physical objects as images of an intelligible reality. You appreciate that they are derivative and inferior copies of something more real and more clear than themselves, and you use them only as a device to help you think about the reality that they represent. Your cognitive state is therefore superior to mine, at my first encounter with geometry. My primary school teacher had told us of Pythagoras' Theorem. I therefore set out to test the theorem, by cutting a right-angled triangle out of colored card, and measuring its sides. I then did my sums, and concluded, with disappointment and indignation, that Pythagoras was wrong. But it was of course I who was wrong. Any mismatch between Pythagoras' Theorem and my right-angled triangle was to be blamed on my triangle, not on the theorem. For the right-angled triangle that I had cut from colored card was, in a crucial sense, no more a right-angled triangle than the kitten in the mirror was a kitten. Geometrizing about the bit of colored card was therefore as mistaken as hissing and spitting at the reflection. But, once you realize that a reflection is only a reflection, you may let it guide you in your dealings with what it reflects: you see that your image in the mirror has untidy hair, and you may use this to help you in tidying your own. Likewise, provided that you appreciate the difference between bits of colored card and the shapes spoken of in geometry, you may use the former to guide your thought about the latter.

Using physical objects as images of an intelligible reality is both a merit and a defect in the kind of intellectual activity that we have been labeling "thought." It is a merit, in that it makes thought superior to trust, which has no notion that physical objects are only images. It is a defect, in that it makes thought inferior to intellect, which has no need of such images (510b, 511c). And it is not the only defect in thought. Besides using physical objects as images, thought also, complains Socrates, conducts its enquiries on the basis of hypotheses, without being able to go beyond them to anything higher (510c, 511a, 511c–d). What exactly is this complaint? And how does thought's use of hypotheses relate to its use of images?

Look at this pair of diagrams:

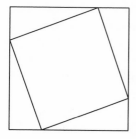 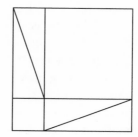

and consider how they are used in this proof of Pythagoras' Theorem: "The big square on the left is formed by fitting four copies of a right-angled triangle together with the square on its hypotenuse. The big square on the right is formed by fitting another four copies of the same right-angled triangle together with the squares on its other two sides. The big square on the left is equal to the big square on the right. But equals taken from equals leaves equals. So take away the four copies of the right-angled triangle from each of the big squares, and you will still be left with equals. So the square on the hypotenuse is equal to the sum of the squares on the other two sides." In our proof, we make all sorts of assumptions about how shapes can be fitted together to form other shapes, for no better reason than that these assumptions are suggested by the diagrams. But making such assumptions, for such a reason, is a hazardous enterprise. For look at this pair of diagrams (Lewis Carroll's Theorem from Fisher 1975, p. 92):

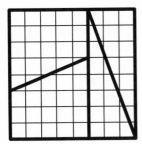 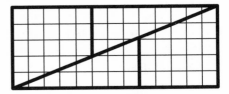

and consider this piece of reasoning that relies on assumptions suggested by these diagrams: "The big square on the left is formed by fitting two copies of a right-angled triangle together with two copies of a lopsided quadrilateral. The big rectangle on the right is formed by fitting another two copies of that same right-angled triangle together with another two copies of that same lopsided quadrilateral. But equals added to equals gives equals. So the eight-by-eight square on the left is equal to the five-by-thirteen rectangle on the right. So sixty-four is equal to sixty-five."

Both pieces of reasoning make apparently similar appeals to diagrams. The second piece of reasoning has evidently gone wrong somewhere. In consequence, we cannot treat the first piece of reasoning, in its current state, as a rigorous proof of Pythagoras' Theorem.

Nevertheless, the two pieces of reasoning are not equally bad. We can distinguish between them by subjecting them to the further discussions that, in *Meno* 85c–d, Socrates suggests for someone who has just been persuaded by a diagram of a special case of Pythagoras' Theorem. We can do little to elaborate on our argument that the eight-by-eight square is equal to the five-by-thirteen rectangle. We will soon get bogged down in muddle and contradiction if we attempt to argue that the pieces into which the square is cut can be assembled into a rectangle without the slightest gap on what looks to be its diagonal. We can however elaborate on the argument for Pythagoras' Theorem, to say much more about how the various shapes in the diagrams really do fit neatly together, just as they seem to, without any funny business by way of stretching or shrinking or gaps or overlaps or bulges or indentations. For example, we can show that right-angled triangles and regular quadrilaterals really do fit together, just as our diagrams suggest, once we have shown that each interior angle of a regular quadrilateral is a right angle, and that in any triangle containing a right angle the other two angles sum to one right angle. We can show these things, once we have shown that the interior angles of a triangle sum to two right angles. And we can argue for this in its turn by, for example, this argument that Eudemus ascribed to "the Pythagoreans," and that was therefore presumably already familiar to Plato. The Pythagoreans' proof comes from Proclus, *Commentary on Book 1 of the* Elements *of Euclid*, 379.2–16:

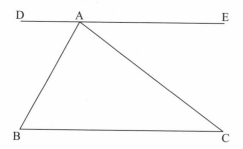

"Let ABC be a triangle, and let DE be drawn through A parallel to BC. So since BC and DE are parallel, the alternate angles are equal. So the angle DAB is equal to the angle ABC and the angle EAC is equal to the angle ACB. Let the angle BAC be added in common. So the angles DAB, BAC and CAE, that is, the angles DAB and BAE, that is, two right angles, are equal to the three angles in the triangle ABC. So the three angles of the triangle are equal to two right angles." We might even set out our entire argument in the axiomatic fashion familiar to us from the *Elements* of Euclid, and presumably familiar to Plato from the now lost books of *Elements* by his predecessor Hippocrates, and by his colleagues in the Academy Leon and Theudius (Proclus, *Commentary on Book 1 of the* Elements *of Euclid* 66.7–8, 66.20–21, 67.12–15). We can thus elaborate our earlier argument for Pythagoras' Theorem into something that will better deserve the name of "proof," for it will avoid reckless reliance on diagrams.

Nevertheless, avoiding reckless reliance on diagrams is not the same as avoiding all reliance on diagrams. For consider the Pythagoreans' proof that the angles of a triangle sum to two right angles: its instruction "let DE be drawn through A parallel to BC" is futile unless there is a line through A parallel to BC; and its inference "since BC and DE are parallel, the alternate angles are equal" is wrong if there is more than one line parallel to BC that passes through A. The proof then relies on the assumption that for any straight line and any point not on that line, exactly one parallel to that line passes through that point. And any proof of Pythagoras' Theorem will have to rely, if not on this assumption so formulated, at least on some equivalent thereof. But why accept this assumption? People did attempt to derive it from more basic geometrical principles. However, as Aristotle in *Prior Analytics* 65a1–9 observed, all their attempted derivations unwittingly argued in circles; and more recent developments have shown why no better argument is possible.[9] We therefore fall back on the diagram. This perhaps confirms our assumption, in that, for example, we can't add to the diagram a line that looks straight, that looks parallel to BC, that looks to pass through A, and that also looks distinct from DE. But this confirmation is a curious one. For the diagram would not look any different if several lines through A were parallel to BC, and all of them were, for a few million miles on either side of A, too close together for perception to tell them apart. Nor would the diagram look any different if every straight line through A met BC sooner or later, in some cases so much later that, for a few million miles on either side of A, the line through A did not get perceptibly closer to BC. So the diagram

---

[9] For a fairly untechnical account, see Sklar 1997, pp. 13–25.

confirms our assumption that there is a parallel to BC through A only in that DE does not look as if it has to meet BC sooner or later. Moreover, in giving us this curious confirmation that there is exactly one parallel to BC through A, the diagram gives us at most an assurance of this fact; it gives us no explanation. It tells us, at best, that this is so; it does not begin to tell us why.

Or again, consider how, in our elaborated proof of Pythagoras' Theorem, we would assume that each angle belongs to just one of three entirely distinct kinds: either it is a right angle, or it is smaller than some right angle and so acute, or it is bigger than some right angle and so obtuse. An alternative version of the assumption would be that "all right angles are equal to one another" (Euclid *Elements*, Book I, Postulate 4). We would rely on this assumption in reasoning that when four angles are assembled around a point, and each is equal to some right angle, then the four angles fit together snugly. Why make this assumption? A right angle is defined thus: "whenever a straight line standing on a straight line makes the adjacent angles equal to one another, then each of the adjacent angles is right" (Euclid *Elements* Book I, Definition 10). This definition requires that each right angle is one of a pair of right angles, each equal to the other of the pair; this definition says nothing about whether either is equal to any third right angle. Will diagrams help where the definition does not? Diagrams seem to indicate that all right angles are equal, in that we cannot draw a diagram that makes the alternative look possible. For look at this diagram

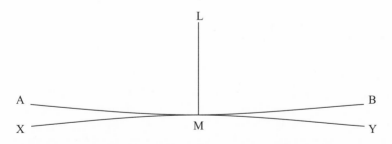

and try to imagine that LM is a straight line standing on the straight line AMB, making the adjacent angles AML and LMB equal to one another and therefore right; that LM also stands on the straight line XMY, making the adjacent angles XML and LMY also equal to one another and therefore also right; and finally that the right angle XML is bigger than the right angle AML, since it consists of the right angle AML, together with the angle AMX. The obvious retort is that the lines AMB and XMY do not even look straight, and could not look straight if they were in other respects to look as they are imagined to be. And this retort would be perfectly true. But it does nothing to rule out the idea that there are straight lines like AMB and XMY, kissing at a point and elsewhere diverging, but diverging so slowly that, for a few million miles on either side of the point at which they kiss, they look to be the same. And if this idea is correct, then our right angles could be different in size, while still looking all the same. Thus for right angles, as for parallels, we assumed something with only a curious confirmation, and with no explanation at all.

In short, even if we elaborate our argument into the best proof that geometry can manage, we are still like the mathematicians with whom Glaucon was familiar: "when people deal with geometry and arithmetic and the like, they hypothesize odd and even numbers, and the shapes, and three kinds of angle, and related things, depending on the subject. They act as if they know these things, once they have hypothesized them; and do not see fit to give any account of them either to themselves, or to anybody else, as if these things were obvious to everybody. Instead, they treat them as starting points, and go through the subsequent steps until they conclude, by consensus, at the thing they have set out to investigate" (510c–d). As Socrates asks at 533c: "How on earth could this sort of consensus ever amount to understanding?" Can we do any better than geometrical thought?

According to the divided line, geometrical thought is analogous to fancy, and we can do better than fancy by appreciating that reflections and shadows and the like – the objects that fancy accepts uncritically – are in fact only reflections and shadows, derivative from the three-dimensional visible objects that are their originals. We should therefore be able to do better than geometrical thought by appreciating that what it hypothesises is in fact only derivative from something else. But what exactly does geometry hypothesize? And what is the something else from which that is derivative?

According to Aristotle *Metaphysics* 987b14–18 (cf. 1028b19–21), Plato "says that, in addition to perceptible objects and Forms, things include also mathematical objects: they are intermediate, distinct from the perceptibles in that they are eternal and unchangeable, and distinct from the Forms in that there are several mathematicals of a kind, whereas each Form is unique." The idea is, for example, that since there are three straight lines in a triangle, then, if there is even one perfect triangle, there must be several perfectly straight lines; and so there must be other straight lines besides the perceptible ones (which are imperfect) and the Form of the straight line itself (which is unique). In what we have of Plato, he never says this in quite so many words. But he does come close to doing so in our passage from the *Republic*. At 511d, Glaucon describes mathematical thought as "something intermediate between opinion and intellect." Because mathematical thought does not have quite the clarity of intellect, the objects of mathematical thought, intelligible though they are, cannot have quite the truth of the objects of intellect (511e). Intellect and mathematical thought must therefore have distinct objects. Since the objects of intellect are "Forms themselves" (510b), the objects of mathematical thought must therefore be other than Forms. Nevertheless, the objects of mathematical thought will be as eternal and unchangeable as any Form: geometers talk of "squaring" and "applying" and "adding," as if they are engaged in activities; but they are well aware that the aim of geometry is "knowledge of what exists forever, not of what at some particular time comes into and goes out of existence" (Socrates at 527a–b; Glaucon, less cautiously, says at 527b that geometry is such knowledge, and not merely that it has such knowledge for its aim). As for the thought that "there are several mathematicals of a kind," this has its counterpart at 526a: the mathematicians are asked, "What kind of number can you be talking about, where the unit meets your requirements: each equal, every one to every one, not different in the slightest, and containing no part within it?"; and they reply that they are talking about intelligible numbers. The idea is that mathematicians might illustrate the mathematical truth that two threes make six by laying out two rows each of three pebbles; they will ignore as irrelevant the fact that some of the pebbles are rounder than others, and the fact that each one of the pebbles is also two half-pebbles; that is, they will pretend that each of the six pebbles is a perfect unit, perfectly interchangeable with any other; and they will treat the mathematical truth illustrated by the pebbles as a truth about pairs of trios, where the many units actually are as the mathematicians only pretended the pebbles to be.[10]

Against all these indications that the divided line represents mathematical thought as dealing with mathematical intermediates, some scholars set 510d–e, which describes mathematicians as "presenting their arguments with a view to the square itself, and to a diagonal itself, rather than to the one that they draw." This, some say, means that mathematical thought deals not with intermediates but with Forms.[11] Certainly, such "so-and-so itself" locutions can be used to indicate Forms. But that is not their only use. Thus when 363a speaks of people who fail to praise justice itself, the point is not that they fail to praise the Form of justice, but that they commend justice, not for any intrinsic merits, but for the good reputation that can be its consequence; when 394c speaks of stories told by the utterances of the poet himself, it does not mean the works of the Form of poet, but stories narrated by a poet speaking entirely *in propria persona*, without any of the speeches that form part of epic and the whole of drama; when 404c speaks of cooking things with fire itself, it does not mean cooking them with the Form of fire, but barbecuing them, by contrast with cooking them in pots; when 454a speaks of people wrangling over the name itself, the point is not that they wrangle over the Form of name, but that they wrangle just over words, rather than over what they mean; when 525e speaks of the unit itself, it means, not the Form of unit, but the multiple units, "each equal, every one to every one, not different in the slightest, and containing no part within it," that compose the intelligible numbers studied by mathematicians, as contrasted with the divisible and heterogeneous things that stand in for units in mathematicians' visual aids; when 604a speaks of how the experience itself can make us grieve, it does not mean the Form of experience, but particular experiences in the mind of someone who is not sufficiently rational and law-abiding to resist them. In general, then, Plato uses "so-and-so itself" locutions for any so-and-so free of some kind of clutter (consequences, actors, cooking pots, or whatever) that is indicated in the context;

---

[10] The idea may now look grotesque, but it has looked so only since Frege 1978 [1884], ch. 3. Not even this immediately persuaded every mathematician: see Frege 1979, pp. 72–86, for an entertaining restatement, provoked by work published in 1887, "as though the third section of my *Grundlagen* had never been written."

[11] See, e.g., Robinson 1953, p. 197, and Annas 1981, p. 251.

and when he uses such a locution for the Form of so-and-so, that is only because the Form is an uncluttered so-and-so. Hence, when mathematicians are described as "presenting their arguments with a view to the square itself and to a diagonal itself, rather than to the one that they draw," this means only that they are talking about geometrical objects free of something that clutters their diagram, free of what makes the diagram only an imperfect illustration of the fact that the diagonal of a square is incommensurable with its side. But "mathematical intermediates" would be such objects. We may therefore accept the indications that mathematical thought is concerned neither with perceptibles nor with Forms, but with things intermediate between the two. We may therefore accept also that, when we go beyond mathematical thought to intellect, we come to see mathematical intermediates as derivative from Forms, and to focus our minds directly on Forms themselves.

But why should intellect be an improvement on thought? What is it about Forms that means that, when thinking about them, our reasoning can be something other than just yet more deductions from peremptory and unexplained assumptions? According to Plato, intellect reasons dialectically (511b–c, 533c–535a), and proficiency in dialectic requires a maturity, and a prior education, that even under the best of circumstances few will have (536d–540b). So we should not expect it to be easy to understand why intellect is an improvement on thought. Let us do what we can.

It is easy enough to take a generalization about mathematical intermediates of some kind and derive it from the corresponding singular statement about the corresponding Form. For example, "In any isosceles triangle, the two equal sides subtend two equal angles" can be derived from "The ideal isosceles triangle has two equal sides, subtending two equal angles." We can do this also with generalizations that geometers would treat as the unexplained starting points of their proofs. Thus Euclid, in *Elements* Book 1, Definition 22, defines a square as "Among quadrilateral figures, one that is both equilateral and right-angled is a square." This is trivially derivable from "The ideal square is a figure with right angles and four straight and equal sides." Again, Euclid, in *Elements* Book 1, Postulate 4, postulates "All right angles are equal to one another." It is only slightly less trivial to derive this from "The ideal right angle is the universal standard by which angles are to be measured." Such derivations do not, in themselves, mark any great advance. Even if they explain what geometers can only hypothesize, they do so by affirming things that are no less in need of explanation. If such derivations are any advance, that is for two reasons. First, their affirmations about Forms are so tentative that we will see them as the hypotheses that they are, and not treat them as underivative and self-explanatory starting points (511b). Second, we can work our way up from these hypotheses to something that genuinely is an unhypothetical and self-explanatory starting point of the lot (510b, 511b).

Given what we were told in the image of the Sun, the unhypothetical starting point can only be the Good. But how might the Good be the unhypothetical starting point of mathematics? Plato, we may hope, does not envisage a novel axiomatization, where from axioms about the Good we deduce theorems about mathematics, and include among those theorems mathematical propositions that are currently taken as axiomatic. For if the novel axioms told us only about the Good, and did not also mention either squares or triangles, then we could deduce from them no conclusion about the triangle that would not apply just as well to the square; while if the novel axioms told us not only about the Good, but also about squares and triangles and all their distinctive features, then these axioms would hardly give the Good its unique place as the unhypothetical starting point of all the rest. And in any case, why should presenting mathematics by deduction from axioms that describe the Good, whether as well as or instead of "odd and even numbers, and the shapes, and three kinds of angle" (510c), be any more satisfactory than presenting mathematics in the style with which Glaucon was familiar? After all, Glaucon's dissatisfaction at 510c–d comes close to a dissatisfaction with the axiomatic style generally, and its habit of giving no further explanation of what seems so obviously true that it can be asserted without proof. Glaucon's dissatisfaction with mathematics as customarily presented would therefore be resolved not by replacing customary axioms with new ones that mention the Good but by supplementing customary axioms with some explanation of the facts that they so peremptorily assert.

Plato's idea seems to be that the Good will provide such an explanation and that we are to explain the existence and character of mathematical Forms teleologically, in something like the way that we explained teleologically the shape of the ideal wheel and the position of its axle. For there is an obvious sense in which the Good is the unhypothetical starting point of all teleological explanation: if something is explained as being there in order to achieve some goal, then the explanation is correct only to the extent that achieving the goal is good, and the explanation is completed when, and only when, we appreciate that and how the goal is good. For example, if you say that the wheels of your car have some tread on their tires in order to increase friction, and some oil on their bearings in order to reduce friction, then both explanations can be correct, but only because it is good to have lots of friction between a wheel and the road, and good also to have little friction between a wheel and its axle; and once we appreciate what is good about those various amounts of friction in those various contexts, we will have finished our teleological explanations of the tread and of the oil. In short, having a teleological explanation of something means seeing what is good about it; and it will be for this reason that the Good is the unhypothetical starting point of all that is teleologically explicable. Hence, if mathematical Forms are, like ideal artifacts, teleologically explicable in their entirety, then the Good will be the unhypothetical starting point of the whole of mathematics.

So how might we give a teleological explanation of mathematical Forms? The idea seems to be that mathematical Forms are as they are because of a certain sort of orderly beauty that this makes possible. Suppose, for example, that the ideal square is not right-angled. To be more precise, and to avoid quibbles that a square is right-angled "by definition," suppose that the ideally regular (i.e., equilateral and equiangular) quadrilateral has for its interior angles something other than right angles. (This is tantamount to denying the proposition about parallels that lay behind the Pythagoreans' proof that the interior angles of a triangle sum to two right angles.) In that case, it will not be possible to assemble four equal regular quadrilaterals to make a larger regular quadrilateral. Indeed, quite generally, there will be no two figures identical in shape but different in size, and space will not be uniform from one scale to another. This would be like the idea scorned in *Timaeus* 62c–63a (cf. *Phaedo* 108e–109a) that space is not uniform in different directions and that there is a cosmically privileged downward: if either idea were right, there would be an ugly arbitrariness to the world. Or again, suppose that the ideal right angle does not provide a universal standard by which angles are to be measured and that two right angles can be of different sizes, just as two obtuse or two acute angles can. On this supposition too, space would not be uniform. It would vary from one region to another: there could be two right-angled triangles, each with its right angle enclosed by sides of unit length, that could not be superimposed. The world would be messy and disordered, much as *Timaeus* 37c–39e suggests that the world would be a mess without the universal standard for the measurement of time provided by the regular motions of the heavenly bodies. None of this shows that these suppositions are self-contradictory. Nor could such teleological considerations demonstrate in any other way that these suppositions are mistaken. For sometimes, as 519d–e illustrates, one good thing must be forgone if another is to be secured; and it might turn out that the truth of these ugly suppositions is the price that must be paid if the Forms are to be, all things considered, as good as they can be. (The fact that teleological considerations can be set against one another in this way is of course one of the things that distinguishes teleological explanation from deduction; for a valid deduction can never be invalidated by adding new premises, not even if they contradict the old.) These teleological considerations do, however, show that these suppositions offend our sense of beauty, order, and even perhaps fairness. If we are inclined to reject these suppositions on such grounds, that is a modest venture into the upmost part of the divided line, where we see Forms in the light of the Good.[12]

WORKS CITED

Annas, J. 1981. *An Introduction to Plato's* Republic. Oxford.

Fisher, J. 1975. *The Magic of Lewis Carroll*. Harmondsworth.

Frege, G. 1978 [1884]. *The Foundations of Arithmetic*, trans. J. L. Austin. Oxford. Originally *Die Grundlagen der Arithmetik* (Breslau, 1884).

Frege, G. 1979. *Posthumous Writings*, ed. H. Hermes, F. Kambartel, and F. Kaulbach, trans. P. Long and R. White (Chicago).

Kassel, R., and C. Austin eds. 1983–. *Poetae Comici Graeci*. Berlin.

Quine, W. V. O. 1960. *Word and Object*. Cambridge, Mass.

Robinson, R. 1953. *Plato's Earlier Dialectic*, 2nd ed. Oxford.

---

[12] I am grateful to my fellow contributors, and above all to John Ferrari and Mitch Miller, for their attempts to force me to clarify this chapter. If their attempts were not wholly successful, that is not their fault, but mine.

Sklar, L. 1997. *Space, Time and Space-Time*. Berkeley.

Thomas, I., ed. 1939. *Greek Mathematical Works*, vol. 1: *Thales to Euclid*. London and Cambridge, Mass.

FURTHER READING

Burnyeat, M. F. 2000. "Plato on Why Mathematics Is Good for the Soul." *Proceedings of the British Academy* 103: 1–82. Rpt. in *Mathematics and Necessity*, ed. T. Smiley (Oxford, 2001).

Mueller, I. 1992. "Mathematical Method and Philosophical Truth." In *The Cambridge Companion to Plato*, ed. R. Kraut (Cambridge).

Santas G. 1980. "The Form of the Good in Plato's *Republic*." *Philosophical Inquiry* (Winter): 374–403. Rpt. in *Essays in Greek Philosophy* 2, ed. J. Anton and A. Preus (Albany, N.Y., 1983), and in G. Fine, ed., *Plato 1: Metaphysics and Epistemology* (Oxford, 1999).

Smith, N. D. 1996. "Plato's Divided Line." *Ancient Philosophy* 16: 25–46.

12 Beginning the "Longer Way"

I don't know yet. But we have set sail, and wherever the
argument, like the wind, should bear us, there we must
go.[1]

Republic 394d

At 435c–d and again at 504b ff., Socrates indicates that there is a
"longer and fuller way" that one must take in order to get "the best
possible view" of the soul and its virtues. But in neither passage does
Socrates take this "longer way." At 435c–d he accepts Glaucon's plea
to continue with the "methods" they have used so far, giving arguments "at that level." In the text that follows his reminder at 504b ff.
he restricts himself to an indirect indication of its goals by his images
of sun, line, and cave and to a programmatic outline of its first phase,
the five mathematical studies. If we stay within the dramatic context of the dialogue, we can see why Socrates offers such a partial
and incomplete characterization. As keen and receptive as they are
on political and ethical matters, Glaucon and Adeimantus are limited interlocutors on metaphysical issues; they have not undergone
the mathematical education Socrates prescribes, and they are not in
a position to raise critical questions about the Forms or the structure
the Forms imply for city and soul. Accordingly, in his initial willingness to forgo the "longer way" (435d) and in his later very introductory account of it, Socrates measures his words to what Glaucon
and Adeimantus are prepared to understand.

---

[1] The translations in this essay are my own, but I have benefited from comparisons
with the translations of Tom Griffith, Alan Bloom, and G. M. A. Grube and C. D. C.
Reeve.

But should we be content to stay within the dramatic context of the dialogue? By the way he frames Socrates' conversation with Glaucon and Adeimantus, Plato seems to invite us to step back and take a more critical perspective. By presenting the *Republic* as Socrates' narrative report the next day and by leaving Socrates' auditor unidentified, he makes it natural for us to take on that role and hear ourselves directly addressed. And if we do, we will find ourselves in a two-fold relationship to Socrates and what he tells us. On the one hand, his repeated narrative cues – every "I said, 'O Glaucon,'" and "he said, 'O Socrates,'" that punctuates the text – remind us that we are not the audience of the words that Socrates reports himself to have spoken; rather, he spoke those words *to Glaucon and Adeimantus*. On the other hand, we *are* the audience of Socrates' present report; we sit together with this present Socrates, aware that there is a distinction between the position from which he spoke to the brothers and the position from which he now speaks to us. Thus Plato puts us in an optimal position to recognize the limits that Glaucon and Adeimantus, in their very eagerness to hear him out, impose on Socrates and to feel the potential difference between what he said to them and what, if we could somehow interrupt him now with well-aimed questions, he might say to us.

The catalyzing idea of this chapter is that *Plato* intends the shortfall of Socrates' presentation of the "longer way" as a pointed provocation *to us*, aimed at moving us to speak up and ask Socrates for a deeper introduction. Of course, it will be up to us, mining the text as responsibly as possible, to discover this deeper Socratic position for ourselves. Our project, accordingly, is to take up this challenge, marking and drawing on the best resources Socrates gives us – above all but not only his provisional account of the five mathematical studies – in order to identify and begin to travel the "longer way."

I. CLIMAX AND ANTICLIMAX – ACHIEVEMENTS AND PROVOCATIONS

As Socrates presents it at 504c ff. the "longer way" is the educational process that will perfect the guardian of the city, raising him to the status of a philosopher-king. In its external phases it divides into ten years of mathematics, five years of dialectic, and fifteen years of practical-political experience, all consummated at about age fifty by the "vision" of the Good and the subsequent turn to the work of ruling. Socrates' presentation of this "longer way" is at once the philosophical climax and anticlimax of the *Republic* as a whole. This ambiguity is, I suggest, the key to the text's own deepest educational work. To begin to see how and why this might be so, consider each aspect in turn.

The presentation of the "longer way" promises to complete the two-fold project of constructing the just city so as to bring to view justice in the soul. The just city, Socrates has argued, requires the most perfect harmony of its parts, and this requires that the deliberations of the rulers be based on the most radical identification of their interests with the well-being of the city as a whole. The anticonventional depth of this identification is brought home by the first two "waves" of paradox (457b–c, 472a with 473c): the equality of women and men as guardians and, with the abolition of private families, the extension throughout the guardian class of the unity of feeling that binds parents with children and siblings with one another require of the rulers a detachment from the customary prestige of being male and well-born. Thus the third "wave" of paradox, an absurdity in any actual Greek city, makes good sense in Callipolis. Who in his or her self-understanding is freer from the narrowing concerns of the body and of social status – and, so, more genuinely capable of ruling on the basis of a care for the city as a whole – than the philosopher? In now showing Glaucon and Adeimantus the education that will make him a philosopher in the first place, moreover, Socrates offers his deepest exhibition of the justice of the soul. At the end of Book 4, psychic justice was both clarified and obscured by its relations to wisdom and moderation. For "each of the [parts] within [the soul] to do its own work" (443b) implies, for "the reasoning [part]," that it will cultivate wisdom; but moderation, as the "agreement" among the three that "the reasoning [part] should rule" (442c–d), focuses attention on its policy-making in coordinating the soul as a whole, and this leaves unfocused what its "ownmost work" – the work of reasoning, as such, that makes it wise – consists in. Now, by introducing the "longer way," Socrates begins to open this up for Glaucon and Adeimantus.

This "ownmost work" necessarily transcends – but also, as we'll observe, reappropriates and completes – the "music" and gymnastic of the prerational young guardians. Whereas the latter is an external "shaping" that "imprints" the "malleable" young soul with "opinions" that it would otherwise lack (377b–c), philosophical education is the quickening of a "capacity" for insight that is "in the soul" (518c) from the beginning. Again, whereas the goal of "music" and gymnastic is the formation of good character (518e, 522a), the goal of philosophical education is direct "understanding" of the Good *itself*. Socrates describes the spiritual transformation this involves by three memorable metaphors: the philosopher-to-be seeks to *awaken to reality* (476c–d), distinguishing for the first time Beauty itself from the many "beautiful things" at hand as the unique original of which they are "likenesses" (476c–d). Again, the philosopher-to-be *ascends from the cave* of sense perception and authoritative cultural heritage, the whole of which he at first presumes to be all there is, *into "the light"* of "the intelligible place" and to the intellectual recognition of "things themselves," that is, of the Forms and the Good (515e–516c, 517b–c). And still again, the intellect and, with it, "the whole soul" undergoes a *"conversion from a day that is like night to a true day"* (521c), that is, from "that which becomes" to "that which is and [to] the brightest [part] of that which is, . . . [namely,] the Good" (518c).

In at least two ways the philosopher's education also preserves the "music" and gymnastic that it transcends. The formation of character and disposition that these accomplish turns out to be a "trimming" of the soul's ties to becoming (519a) – one thinks especially of Socrates' aims to diminish the terror of death (386a–387e) and to achieve inward rule over the appetites (389d–390d) – and, as such, key preparation for its rise to "understanding" of the Forms. And this "understanding," since Forms are the originals of which particulars are "images" (520c), enables the philosopher to raise the keen perceptual awareness (401e) cultivated by "music" to the level, now, of the "know[ledge] of each image for what it is" (520c); it is this at once heightened and refounded grasp of all that becomes that particularly qualifies the philosopher to rule.[2]

In what way, then, is Socrates' presentation of the philosopher's education *anti*climactic? We have noted Glaucon's willingness – even eagerness – to forgo the "longer way" when Socrates first alludes to it at 435c–d. Though they have great good will toward

---

[2] See section I of David Sedley's chapter 10 in this volume.

Socrates and are as eager as any interlocutors in the dialogues to hear him out, Glaucon and Adeimantus have not made the "conversion" Socrates calls for, and as a consequence – as he indicates at several key places – Socrates must limit what he says and how he speaks to them. The result is that his presentation of philosophical education leaves its substance and character and, indeed, the character of the philosopher-king pointedly obscure. I count at least four basic places or ways in which Plato has Socrates say much less than, listening to his report the next day, we might wish.

1. *The obscurity of "the Good."* Understanding the Form of the Good is the key goal for the philosopher-king-to-be. But, Socrates tells Glaucon at 506e, "it appears to me beyond our present thrust to reach the views I now hold about it." Accordingly, he keeps these to himself and offers instead what he deems Glaucon and Adeimantus ready to receive, the simile of the sun. To state its two claims, epistemic and ontological, respectively: first, as the sun is the source of light and thereby enables the eye to see and enables visible "things"[3] to be seen, so the Good is the source of "truth" (*tēn alētheian*, 508e) and thereby enables the soul to know and enables knowable "things" to be known; and second, as the sun is the cause of the "coming-to-be, growth, and nourishment" of visible "things," so the Good is the cause of "the to-be and the being" (*to einai te kai tēn ousian*, of the "things" known; 509b). Alas, for all the precision with which, by his careful correlations, Socrates makes use of what is familiar to introduce Glaucon and Adeimantus to what is strange, the effect of the simile is to leave deeply obscure the Good as it is in and of itself. Socrates offers the simile as a means of first coming to think the Good – but if we try to turn from thinking of it in terms of the sun to thinking of it in terms proper to its own prior intelligibility, we find ourselves facing very difficult questions. What belongs to the category of "knowable things"? How are we to understand "the to-be and the being" of these "knowables"? What is the sense Socrates intends for *alētheia*, "truth," and how is it that truth in this sense

---

[3] There is no word in the Greek that corresponds to my word "things." Plato uses the definite article with the plural adjective, e.g., *ta horōmena*, "the seen" or, to convey the plural at the cost of the article, "what are seen" (508a, c, cf. 509b), and *ta nooumena*, literally, "the intellecteds" (508c). The sole function of my insertion of "things" is to convey the plural.

enables the soul to know and the "knowables" to be known? And at the heart of these obscurities, what is the sense Socrates intends for *agathon*, "good," and how is it that it belongs to the Good in this sense to be the ultimate cause both of the soul's knowing and of the very "to-be" and "being" of the "knowables" themselves?

2. *Socrates' reticence with regard to dialectic.* The highest stage of intellectual work short of the understanding of the Good is the dialectical study of Forms. What little Socrates reveals of it, he offers by way of two distinctions in his closing reflections on the divided line, at 510b–511c: whereas in the mathematical disciplines of "geometry, calculation, and the like" the mathematician uses sensibles as images in order to think not about these but rather about the nonsensibles of which they are images (510d–e), the dialectician "avails himself of nothing sensible but only of Forms, going by way of Forms to Forms and ending in Forms" (511c); and, second, whereas the mathematician begins from "hypotheses," that is, from claims about his subject matter that he presumes to be "manifest to all" (510d), and reasons from them to conclusions, the dialectician subjects his "hypotheses" to inquiry, seeking thereby to first discover what stands prior to them and, so, can serve as a genuine basis for them and for his subsequent reasoning from them (510b, 511b). Needless to say, these are difficult lines, as elusive as they are rich, and so we welcome Glaucon's request at 532d–e that Socrates "tell the character of the power of dialectic and what sorts of modes it divides into and, again, what its paths are." Socrates, however, refuses to say more, telling Glaucon that he has not achieved the freedom from sense perception and sensible imagery that understanding dialectic requires: "'You would no longer be able to follow,' I said, 'even though there is no lack of desire on my part [to explain]; but you would no longer be seeing an image of what we are speaking of but rather the true itself'" (533a).

3. *Sensible simile, intelligible content.* These points of obscurity reflect a pervasive substantive limitation – and, as I suggest at the close of this section, a pedagogical strength – of Platonic/Socratic discourse in the *Republic*. It is a requirement of the conversation as Socrates reports it that he construct sensible similes like the sun and the cave; to lead Glaucon and Adeimantus, since they have not undertaken anything equivalent to the ten years of mathematics needed for the "conversion" from becoming to being, Socrates

must find language that keys from the senses. But what he seeks to convey is the experience of that which precedes sensibles and, indeed, is itself the basis for whatever intelligibility and being sensibles have. This paradox reaches a paradigmatic intensity in Socrates' handling of the pivotal moment of the divided line passage: "as the opinable," he proposes, "is to the knowable, so the likeness is to that which it is like" (510a). By "the likeness" and "that which it is like," Socrates refers Glaucon to the relation between the sorts of things that belong to the two sections of the visible, the relation of, for example, shadows or reflections in water to the individual things of which they are shadows, and so on. Thus he conveys the thought that "the knowable" – most obviously, the Forms (recall 475e–480a) – are the originals of which "the opinable" – most obviously, sensible individuals – are "likenesses." This brilliant communication of *the* fundamental ontological relationship in Platonic thought risks, at the same time, betraying it. It is a pedagogical master stroke to find among sensibles an analogue to that relation by which the Forms stand as different in kind from and prior to sensibles; Socrates allows Glaucon and Adeimantus to proceed to the strange by way of the familiar. But precisely this is also the danger: the analogy tempts one to rely on the familiar, to let the relation of sensible model and likeness stand in for that of Form to sensible. This is at once an error of commission and an error of omission. One inadvertently thinks the Forms on the model of sensible things, missing their difference in kind, and so fails to take up the essential task of seeking new concepts by which to do justice to the Forms in their own distinct and prior kind of being. This problem should complicate our reception of the sun, the line, and the cave. Even as we appreciate the deftness with which Socrates constructs pictures for that which, according to the meaning the pictures convey, defies picturing, we must part from Glaucon and Adeimantus, who accept the limits Socrates draws, and, in *our* reception of Socrates' report, object. We will not really have received Socrates' content until we liberate it – and liberate ourselves for a genuine understanding of it – from its form.[4]

---

[4] Recall Aristotle's complaint that to invoke the notion of "models" (*paradeigmata*) is to rely on "empty discourse and poetical metaphors," *Metaphysics* A.9, 991a21–22. But Plato himself, through the dramatic *persona* of "Parmenides," was the first to expose the danger, in the *Parmenides*, esp. 132c12–133a6. For a powerful defense of the model/likeness analogy, see Patterson 1985. For an account of the hypotheses

4. *The philosopher's reluctance to "descend," Socrates' zest.* We turn, finally, to the notorious question of the philosopher's disinclination to break off from the theoretical life of studying the Forms and the Good to take up the political responsibility of ruling the city. Socrates' very act of explaining this to Glaucon and Adeimantus constitutes a striking performative tension. *On the one hand*, Socrates makes very understandable the philosopher's reluctance to abandon the satisfactions of contemplation (516c, 519c) for the difficult "drudgery" (540b) of politics; he shows why the philosopher, knowing that the esteem that his fellow citizens exchange is based on a fundamental misunderstanding of reality, finds no value in it (516c–d); he explains that the philosopher's lack of interest in ruling is actually a benefit for the city (520d, 521b), and he lays out the argument by which the philosopher must and will be persuaded of the "necessity" (519c, 520a, 540a) that he rule, namely, that by contrast with the situation in "other cities," in which a philosopher comes into being "against the will of the constitution," in Callipolis he owes his very education into philosophy to the city (520a–b). *On the other hand*, it is Socrates who presents all this, Socrates who has himself come to philosophy in spite of rather than with the support of Athens and who has himself willingly "descended" (327a)[5] into the Piraeus to spend this long dialogical night leading Glaucon and Adeimantus as close to the opening of the cave as they are able to go – and always, his "characteristic irony" (337a) notwithstanding, with an inexhaustible generosity and zest. His very presence in the Piraeus – doubled "now," a fictional day later, by his indefatigable narration of the night's events to us – stands strikingly at odds with his account of the philosopher's reluctance to "descend." Is this tension significant? If we take Plato to be serious about the performative dimension of the text, we must think that it is. And this should lead us to wonder whether there is something internal

---

in the *Parmenides* as a systematic rethinking of the forms in their own proper being, see Miller 1986.

[5] On the playful banter about the use of force at the very beginning of the dialogue, see Miller 1985, n. 9. I take this episode to be but the first of many moments in which Socrates plays hard to get in order to motivate others to pursue him. The point cannot be that Socrates wants to avoid teaching and return to contemplation; after all, he is returning with Glaucon to Athens proper. For more on Socrates' descent into the Piraeus, see David O'Connor's chapter 3 in this volume.

to Socrates' own philosophical experience, as Plato understands it, that, because not yet comprehensible to Glaucon and Adeimantus, he leaves pointedly unspoken. Does the dramatic fact of Socrates' own comportment itself express, behind the external "necessity" of which he speaks, an internal necessity of which he does not speak?

In these ways, Socrates falls away from the very height that he seems to be reaching, leaving us discontent and eager to pursue a new round of questions. Our situation is oddly reminiscent of Glaucon's and Adeimantus' at the end of Book I: as the insufficiency of Socrates' response to Thrasymachus moved them to ask that he do deeper justice to justice itself, so the insufficiency of his response to them moves us to ask that he speak more truly of the Forms and Good.

II. THE FIVE MATHEMATICAL STUDIES: THE "CONVERSION" OF THE SOUL

We turn now to the five mathematical disciplines: calculation and arithmetic,[6] plane geometry, solid geometry, astronomy, and harmonic theory. Socrates credits these with the "power" to "release [the cave dweller's soul] from its bonds and turn it around from the shadows to the statues and the firelight and lead it up from the cave into the sunlight" (532b); hence he sets aside ten full years for the philosopher-king-to-be to study the five disciplines, and he characterizes this work as the "prelude" (531d) to the dialectical study of the Forms.

If mathematical study has the power to alert the soul to the statues borne along the wall, that is, to the culturally authoritative interpretations by poets, law givers, and other opinion makers that inform our understanding of experience, this is presumably because, in sharp contrast, it does not itself depend on such authority[7] and, so, sets it in relief.

---

[6] *Logistikē te kai arithmētikē,* 525a. Cf. *arithmon te kai logismon,* 522c. In the *Gorgias,* Socrates distinguishes "calculation" and "arithmetic" as, respectively, computation and number theory. But in the *Republic* he pairs them and "refers [to them] indifferently." The phrase is Ian Robins', in his excellent article Robins 1995, p. 363.

[7] I readily acknowledge that in our postmodern context this is controversial. For the kind of analysis of the historical specificity of Greek mathematics that pursuing the question of the presence and absence of authority in it requires, see Klein 1968; Lachterman 1989.

That, further, mathematics has the power to lead the soul out of the cave lies in the way in which, in each of the five studies, the soul is required to turn its attention from sensibles to purely intelligible objects. These are not themselves Forms[8] (though, as we'll consider in section III below, Forms are close at hand, present not as objects but as functions constitutive of objects). Socrates indicates this limitation when he characterizes the soul as mathematics first brings it out of the cave as "still unable to look at animals and plants and the light of the sun – [it is able to look only] at divine appearances in water and shadows of that which *is*" (532b–c). The objects of mathematics are not "things themselves" (516a), that is, Forms; but they are also not mere "appearances," to be included among the "shadows" and "statues" within the cave. Rather, as intelligible, not sensible, they exist in the sunlight, and as disclosive of Forms with a truth that surpasses anything available inside the cave, they are "divine" and images "of that which *is*." Here are the specific turns from the sensible to the intelligible that, "making use of visibles . . . but thinking not about them but about those others that these are like" (510d), the five disciplines occasion. In calculation and arithmetic, thought turns from figured "arrangements" (522d, 525b) of pebbles to *the triangular, square, and oblong arrays of homogeneous and partless units* (526a) by which the series of integers, of odds, and of evens, respectively, are ordered.[9] In plane and solid geometry and in that part of astronomy that focuses on the trajectories of the celestial bodies, thought turns from imprecise (529d) and "deviant" (530b) sensible figures, "drawn and molded" (510e) or found in the sky (529b–e), to *the perfect figures*, impossible to achieve in anything "that has body and is visible" (530b), that these sensibles represent. And in that part of astronomy that focuses on relative velocities and in harmonic theory, thought turns from the visible motions we see in the sky (again 529b–e) and from the audible motions (530d) we hear as musical tones, motions that are "imperfect and [that, in their different media,] fail to arrive at the point where they ought to"

---

[8] This distinction, made already in his commentary on the ambiguous language at 510d7–8 by James Adam (Adam 1963 [1902], vol. 2, p. 68), was forcefully argued by M. F. Burnyeat in Burnyeat 1987, and again in Burnyeat 2001; see also Miller 1999, and David Sedley's chapter 10 and Nicholas Denyer's chapter 11 in this volume.

[9] See, e.g., Knorr 1975, pp. 142–61.

(530e), to *the pure ratios*, concords of number with number (531c), that these sensible motions fall short of.

To see how *each* of the five disciplines contributes to the ascent from the sensible, however, is not yet to see how they collaborate. Socrates stresses the importance of this, going so far as to conclude by declaring that mathematical study will be "profitless labor" (531d) unless the philosopher-to-be reaches an understanding of "the community and kinship" of the five. Thus he leaves Glaucon – and, now, the next day, us – with a major reflection to make. In the limited space at hand, let me make a start by offering four closely related (and, I hope, seminal) remarks.

1. *The sequence.* Our point of departure should be the sequence of the five studies. Socrates stresses this by numbering them (see "second," 527c, "third," 527d, "fourth," 528e) and, in correcting his initial omission of solid geometry, by making a point of explaining that they stand in a definite serial order (see 528a, d). If we look to this order as the expression of a motion, we find ourselves confronted with two contrary aspects. Thus Socrates provides in the series as a whole a philosophical analogue to the "thought"-"summoning" (523b-525a) mixtures of contraries by which he first introduces the study of numbers. Responding accordingly, let me first distinguish each of the contrary aspects, then consider their fit.

2. *First aspect: the purgative ascent to the threshold of the Forms.* On the one hand, the five studies, taken as a sequence, lead us gradually from experience oriented by the sensible to experience oriented by the intelligible. First, as we have already noted, by "calculation and arithmetic" Socrates has in mind[10] the study of number as figured arrays of units, with the use of pebbles and the like to signify the nonempirical arrays of units that are the study's true intentional objects. Second, plane and solid geometry stand together as the study of pure figure; number is now represented, and thought to be, not aggregates of discrete units but as the relative lengths and areas and volumes, all continuous quantities, that belong to figures. Third, what Socrates calls "astronomy" – but which, when he explains its nonempirical cast, is better understood as the general study of solids in motion or pure kinematics – is transitional

---

[10] On the way Socrates' language implies this, see Miller 1999, pp. 79–80.

between plane and solid geometry, on the one hand, and harmonic theory, on the other. For while it works with figures (above all, the homocentric circles and spheres by which Eudoxus interpreted the motions of the planets[11]), it focuses on the correlations of spatial and temporal relations, expressing these as ratios of distance and velocity. Thus it prepares the way for the exclusive focus on ratio in harmonic theory.

These observations position us to recognize the overall trajectory of the five disciplines: they constitute a series of purgations by which, bringing out in each later phase what is essential but inconspicuous in the earlier, thought leaves the visible and the spatial behind and arrives at the most purely intelligible referent short of the Forms themselves. In calculation and arithmetic, the pebbles in our sensible models and the pure units they represent are conspicuous, but it is by means of their spatial arrangements – in expanding triangles, squares, and oblongs – that their defining kinds, the series of integers and of odds and of evens, are collected and distinguished for thought. In the turn to plane and solid geometry, we drop the pebbles and the units they represent in order to let the figures that they compose emerge in their own right and come to stand as our proper objects. And next, in the turn by way of astronomy to harmonics, we make a second, precisely analogous purgation: now we drop these figures in order to let the ratios that they express emerge in *their* own right and come to stand as our proper objects. But ratios, in and for themselves, are neither visible nor spatial. Thus we move step by step to a mode of thought that, in taking what transcends spatiality as its object, readies us to make the turn to dialectic, that pure thinking that "avails [it]self of nothing sensible but only of Forms, going by way of Forms to Forms and ending in Forms" (511c).

3. *Second aspect: the reconstitution, within the intelligible, of the sensible. On the other hand*, even as the sequence of the five leads thought toward the Forms, it also turns back – but within the medium of pure intelligibility – to the sensible. We position ourselves to see this contrary motion if we focus on Socrates' reordering of the middle three disciplines. Correcting his own mistake, Socrates tells Glaucon,

---

[11] Mourelatos 1981 makes this connection and cites *Laws* 893c–d for a supportive exhibition.

After [the study of the] planar, . . . we went right on to [the] solid in circular motion, before taking it up in and for itself. But the right way is to take up the third dimension [as] next in order after the second.   (528a–b)

Thus the sequence proceeds from the two-dimensional to the three-dimensional to the three-dimensional in motion, hence in time. And this is to recover, albeit in its pure intelligibility, the full dimensional structure of the corporeal. Nor is this all. The further turn to harmonic theory leads us on to the very core of this structure and in the process extends the reach of thought beyond the specifically corporeal to all that is subject to becoming. Ratio, as we noted in (2), is expressed in space as figure; but as defining for musical pitch, it is also the inner structure of that which exists only in time, not in space. With the turn from the geometrical disciplines to harmonics, then, we recover in its pure intelligibility the innermost structure of all that becomes, both the corporeal *and* the incorporeal.

4. *The fit of purgation and reconstitution: the "conversion from becoming to being."* As brief and initial as these thoughts may be, they prompt a key insight into the idea of the "conversion from becoming to being" (518c). Just insofar as the purgative ascent via the five disciplines is the first phase of the conversion, the point of the latter will not be to abandon the sensible for the intelligible, exchanging one one-sidedness for another; on the contrary, the abstraction from the sensible that thought achieves in harmonic theory is at once, as well, thought's recovery of the sensible in its intelligible structure. Philosophical education, thus conceived, is moved by a love of the whole. The point of the conversion is to free ourselves from dependence on sense perception and its presumption that the spatio-temporally determinate is all there is – but the point, in turn, of this liberation is that we become able, by grasping the purely intelligible, to understand the world in its totality. Hence, even as the five studies expand our sense of reality to include the intelligible in its difference in kind from and priority to the sensible, they also bring us to understand the intelligible as the very *structure of* the sensible. Or, in Socrates' ontological terms, even as we come to understand "being" in its irreducible difference from and priority to "becoming," we also come to understand it as the very *being of* that which becomes. Accordingly, the "conversion" should be understood as a process not just of departure but, rather, of departure that is also return; in bringing the soul to the pure "understanding" of

being, philosophical education will bring it to the "understanding" of becoming as well, in its dependence on being.[12]

III. POINTS OF DEPARTURE: ON THE GOOD, DIALECTIC, SOCRATES

If these last reflections are well taken, they show how the philosopher-to-be's study of the five mathematical disciplines brings him to the very threshold of the Forms. This brings *us*, in turn, a long way toward an adequate response to the third of the four problems (as we listed them in section I) that Socrates leaves us with: just insofar as the study of figure and ratio shows us, now in purely mathematical terms, the relation of mathematicals to sensibles, it frees us from reliance on the sensible for an understanding of this relation. This is an important advance in the level of our understanding. But we are still only at the threshold of the Forms. How do we now "ascend" beyond mathematicals to their "models," to "that of which," as "divine appearances in water and shadows of what *is*" (532c), they are "likenesses"? That is, how do we now reach the Forms and the Good *in* their *own terms* – and, so, free ourselves from dependence on these very notions of "appearances in water" and "shadows"? Can we find concepts at the level of the Forms themselves by which to make properly intelligible the nature of the Forms and the Good and their priority to sensibles and mathematicals alike? With this task, we come back to the first and second of our four problems, the obscurity of Socrates' characterization of the Good and his silence on dialectic. While Socrates says nothing explicit, his remarks about geometry and harmonic theory, respectively, give us interesting points of departure for responding to these problems. These responses, in turn, provide an interesting point of departure for responding to the fourth problem, the tension between the reluctance to "descend" that Socrates imputes to the philosopher and the zest that he himself shows. Let me offer the following three sets of exploratory reflections.

   1. *The obscurity of the Good reconsidered: the practice of geometry and the functions of perfection.* If we pause to examine the geometer's use of "visible forms" (510d), we may glimpse a way in which

---

[12] For discussion of this notion of the "conversion," see Lee 1972, esp. p. 276 n. 14, and Miller 1986, passim.

the practice of geometry provides occasion for "catching sight of the Form of the Good" (526e). "A man experienced in geometry" (529c), Socrates says, would not confuse even the "most beautiful and most exact" of sensibles, the motions of the stars (529d–e), much less the figures he "draws" and the three-dimensional models he "molds" (510d–e), with the intelligible structures that are his true intentional objects. If we ask for the basis of this implicit knowledge, Socrates will reply in the geometer's behalf that anything "that has body and is visible" must "deviate from" (530b) the symmetry and regularity of the purely intelligible and, so, "fall far short" of it (529d) and be "something imperfect" (530e). But this presupposes that the geometer already has before him both some "visible form" – for instance, this ▽ that he "draws" – and the purely intelligible triangle that this ▽ represents. Suppose we ask how he is able to bring the purely intelligible triangle to mind in the first place. Now, strikingly, we'll find four distinct terms – only two of which are explicit objects, as we'll see – in a complex interplay. Consider: The geometer begins with (1) this sensible ▽ that he draws. But even as he considers it, he turns away from it, looking to (2) the perfection that it lacks; and in the context of pure intelligibility that the consideration of perfection opens up, he "sees," that is, conceives, (3) the perfectly triangular triangle that this ▽ only approaches or, as Socrates says, "falls short of." Nor is this all: even as the perfectly triangular triangle presents itself in thought, he knows of it that it is – and that the visible ▽ is not – a perfect triangle; hence there is also in play, though not as an object but as the tacit standard by reference to which he identifies and assesses the two triangles that *are* objects, (4) the Form that these instantiate, triangularity as such.

There is no doubt that Socrates distinguishes (1) the sensible ▽ that one draws from (4) the Form triangularity that it imperfectly instantiates. But what of the further distinctions we have marked? Is it right to distinguish (2) perfection from (3) the perfect exemplar, that is, the intelligible triangle? Is it right, further, to distinguish (3) that perfect exemplar from (4) the Form that it exemplifies?[13] And,

---

[13] With this distinction, the particular textual basis for which is 532c1–2 (recall n. 8), we break step both with the main line of scholarly commentary on the so-called middle period Forms, which has taken its bearings from Vlastos 1954, and in particular with Santas 1980. Vlastos argued that Plato treated the Forms as self-predicative, and Santas, taking Plato to conceive them as "ideal exemplars"

finally, if we are indeed right to draw these distinctions, how do (2) perfection and (4) the Form relate?

A Form and its perfect exemplar. That Plato has Socrates require us to distinguish (3) the perfectly triangular triangle, the perfect exemplar, from (4) the Form that it instantiates, triangularity, is implied by his characterization of the class of mathematical objects as – in the scheme of the cave – "divine appearances in water and shadows of what *is*" (532c). We have marked this distinction earlier; what remains to be added here is the observation that one cannot identify reflections and shadows for what they are without also in some sense knowing, along with them, what they are reflections and shadows *of*.[14] Socrates' metaphor implies not only the distinction of mathematicals from Forms but also, in the mathematician's explicit recognition of what each mathematical object is, an implicit or tacit knowledge of the Form that this object instantiates. That this knowledge is only tacit is implied by Socrates' characterization of those just emerging from the cave as "still unable to look at" (*pros . . . blepein*) things themselves in the sunlit world (532b–c); it belongs to the further passage from mathematics to dialectic to look from the "divine appearances and shadows" to the things reflected, from, for example, perfect figures to the Forms they instantiate. But a perfect triangle can be recognized *as* a perfect triangle only insofar as it exemplifies the form triangularity and this exemplarity guides the recognition. Hence the Forms are present for the mathematician, albeit not as objects in their own right but as defining for his objects

(p. 255ff. of the 1999 reprint), took this as a key assumption in his interpretation of the Good. If, however, Plato has Socrates *distinguish* the Forms from the perfect figures – that is, "ideal exemplars" – that instantiate them, this assumption becomes problematic. (For an interpretation of the numerous self-predicative statements in the dialogues that is substantively compatible with this distinction, see Nehamas 1979.) Our reflections to come will differ from Santas' interpretation of the Good in two further, equally important respects as well: we will find in the understanding of the Good as perfection as such the key to understanding Socrates' claim that the Good is the source of "truth," a point that Santas only mentions and then leaves unaddressed; and, as will become clear in what follows, we will find in Socrates' turn from the perfect figures of geometry to the pure ratios of harmonics a Platonic provocation to complicate our interpretation of goodness in terms of perfection by the distinct interpretation of it in terms of unity.

[14] See, for thoughtful development of this idea, Jacob Klein's discussion of "dianoetic *eikasia*" in Klein 1965, pp. 112–25, and Eva Brann's fascinating practice of it in the title essay of Brann 2004.

and, so, as orienting for his knowledge of them. It is these constitutive activities of defining and orienting, ontological and epistemic, respectively, that I meant to indicate earlier when I said that Forms are present in mathematical knowledge not as objects but as functions constitutive of them.[15]

Perfection as such, sensible particulars, and perfect exemplars: Does not (2), perfection, have a similar status? For the geometer to look to the perfection that (1) the visible particular lacks is not, or not yet, for him to bring an object to mind; rather, it is for him to orient himself toward the sensible particular in a way that first allows (3) the perfect figure that the sensible particular "falls short of" to present itself. Perfection, accordingly, is like the Forms in having the character of a function, not an object – now, however, it is the function of *providing the context in which* the purely intelligible perfect figure can first come to mind. Of course, once one notices this function, one can go on to reflect explicitly on it and, so, objectify it; indeed, that is just what we are now doing. But this is dangerous. If, when we reflect on perfection, we mistake for its own way of being a character – that of being a determinate object – that it first acquires only as a result of this very reflection, we lose rather than gain access to it. In its own way of being, perfection differs in kind from both the visible figure that it points beyond and the intelligible figure that it lets come to mind instead.

We may mark this difference in kind by three more pointed observations. First, it is only by considering the perfection the drawn ▽ lacks that the mathematician *first comes to* the perfect figure; hence it must be distinguished from the latter. Conflating perfection as such with, for example, the perfectly triangular triangle would leave us begging the question of how the geometer turns from the sensible to the mathematical. Second, in this bridging role, perfection is not determinate – it is an open question for the mathematician what specific perfection he will bring to mind when he first looks beyond this drawn ▽. (Keeping this in mind allows us – indeed, requires us – to think of it not as an object but rather as the provider of the context for objects.) And third, a distinct but related point, perfection as such transcends, and so is differently manifest in, the various specifically different exemplars, both imperfect and perfect, that the geometer

---

[15] For a kindred approach, see Wieland 1982, esp. ch. 2, sec 8.

may consider: this $\triangledown$ and this $\bigcirc$ and this $\diamondsuit$ all lack it, even as the perfect triangle that this $\triangledown$ "falls short of" and the perfect circle that this $\bigcirc$ "falls short of" and the perfect diamond that this $\diamondsuit$ "falls short of" each, but in each case with its own distinctive specificity, puts it on display for the mind's eye.

Perfection as such, Forms, and perfect exemplars. This indeterminateness of (2) perfection as such is the key, finally, to what is otherwise the most elusive of the distinctions that the practice of geometry gives us occasion to draw. Perfection as such and the Forms are alike in the inexplicitness of their presence to the geometer just emerging from the cave: each in its own way defers to the perfect exemplars, the purely intelligible figures, that the geometer brings to mind; perfection as such provides the context that first enables this thinking, while the Forms both define the figures he thinks and orient his identifying recognitions of them. In this collaboration, note, perfection as such and the Forms differ in kind from one another. Each Form is *an itself determinate way of determining* perfection as such; triangularity, for instance, and circularity have as their intelligible instantiations equally perfect but, of course, specifically different exemplars. Perfection as such, on the other hand, is *in and of itself indeterminate*; hence it both transcends and lends itself to the host of ways of determining it that the Forms just *are* and that their intelligible instantiations exemplify.

Implications for understanding the Good. If these distinctions are well taken, then the practice of geometry seems to offer resources for a first reply to our question about the sense of "good" in the notion of "the Good." And this provides a point of departure for rethinking the simile of the sun. If we understand the Good as perfection as such, then Socrates' two claims in its behalf gain a conceptual transparency that, at least in the context of geometry, frees us from depending on the perceptual content of the simile.

Consider first the epistemic causality Socrates claims for the Good. As perfection as such, the Good is the source of "the truth" (*tēn alētheian,* 508e ff.) that enables the soul to know and "knowable things" to be known in the sense that it provides the context in which the perfect figures of geometry first present themselves for thought. It is when the soul considers visible figures with respect to perfection that these perfect figures, purely intelligible, first "emerge from concealment,"[16] presenting themselves as the normative structures the visibles "fall short of." "Truth" just *is* this emergence from concealment, this disclosure, that occurs when we consider a visible figure with respect to perfection. The "knowables," in turn, are in the first instance these perfect structures. But these bring along with themselves, so to speak, the Forms they instantiate, making these implicitly present and, so, available for the explicit knowledge that the dialectician will seek.

Understanding the goodness of the Good as perfection as such also provides a starting point for seeing why Socrates claims ontological causality for it. The Good, he claims, is responsible for "the to-be and the being" (*to einai te kai tēn ousian*, 509b) of the "knowables." If there were no perfection as such, neither would there "be" a plurality of specifically different ways of determining it – that is, there would *exist* no Forms – nor would the Forms have their "being," that is, their basic nature, as these different ways of determining it. And since, to state the obvious, there could be no perfect instantiations of Forms if there were no Forms, the Good's responsibility for Forms implies its ultimate responsibility as well for their perfect instantiations, the purely intelligible objects of mathematics. Accordingly, as perfection as such, the Good is responsible for both the existence and the basic nature of Forms and mathematicals, the whole class of "knowables."

2. *Socrates' reticence with regard to dialectic – and, again, the obscurity of the Good – reconsidered: proleptic implications of the study of harmonic theory.* Socrates' remarks on harmonic theory are even more terse and compressed than those on geometry. Nonetheless, read in the larger context of our reflections on the five studies, they may provide a starting point for thinking about dialectic and, in that connection, for opening a second perspective on the Good. As with astronomy, so with harmonics; Socrates stresses that the appropriation of it for philosophical education requires setting aside the empirical interest that guides its usual practice. Even

---

[16] This phrase plays on the etymology of *alētheia* made a philosophical theme by Heidegger. (See, e.g., Heidegger 1998 [1931/32, 1940]. For a discussion that both appreciates Heidegger's insight and criticizes his failure to read Plato in light of it, see Hyland 1995, ch. 6). "Concealment" renders the stem *-lēth-*; "from" renders the negative force of the privative *a-*; and "emerge" renders the verbal force, suggesting an event or activity, of the *-e-*, vestige of the *-eu-* in the verb *alētheuein*.

the Pythagoreans, Socrates explains, "seek the numbers in heard concords and do not rise to problems, investigating [as, by contrast, the philosopher-to-be must do] which numbers are concordant [with each other] and which are not and in each case why" (531c1–4). Such study, he adds, will be "valuable for the search for the beautiful and good but without value if pursued for any other purpose" (531c).

Evidently, Plato has Socrates "predict [the] birth"[17] of Archytas' theory of means and proportions. In the years after the dramatic date[18] of the *Republic* but before its composition, Archytas had distinguished on purely mathematical grounds the geometric, arithmetic, and harmonic means, and he had shown how their combination yields the basic mathematical structure of the musical modes.[19] Briefly, the simplest case of the geometric mean and proportion is 1:2:4, and its key ratio, 1:2, defines the span of an octave. Between the extremes of the octave (1 and 2, raised to 6 and 12), the arithmetic and harmonic means are 9 and 8, respectively; the arithmetic mean divides the octave into the intervals of a fifth (6:9, i.e., 2:3) and a fourth (9:12, i.e., 3:4), and the harmonic mean divides it into the intervals of a fourth (6:8, i.e., 3:4) and a fifth (8:12, i.e., 2:3). Taken together, the three means yield the complex proportion 6:8:9:12, and thus pick out the fixed boundary notes, outer and inner, of each musical mode, articulating it as an octave differentiated into a fourth, the

[17] Barker 1989, p. 52. This is the second major anachronism in Socrates' presentation of the five studies; the first was his inclusion of solid geometry, which, as Plato, referring to seminal work with regular solids done by Theaetetus and others, has Glaucon point out, "doesn't seem to have been discovered yet" (528b). (On the difficulties with the conventional dating of Theaetetus' death and, so, the crediting to him of the discovery of the five regular solids, see Nails 2002, pp. 274–78.)

[18] On the obscurity of the dramatic date, see Nails 2002, pp. 324–26.

[19] "Modes," *harmoniai*, were the sets of notes, roughly analogous to our scales, that were heard as harmonious with one another and, so, as fit to provide the tones in a melody; musical instruments were tuned accordingly. Pythagorean musical theorists studied modes systematically and with special interest in the ratios that determined the intervals that defined their member notes – see esp. Barker 1989, pp. 46–52. The following is key background information for a first appreciation of the context Socrates presumes: each mode spanned an octave and consisted of two four-note subsets or "tetrachords." These, each spanning the interval of a fourth, were divided from one another by the interval of a whole tone. Only the two outer notes of each tetrachord were fixed; there were a host of locations possible for the two inner notes of each tetrachord, yielding different "genera" and "colorings" of the modes. For a general exegesis, see West 1992, esp. chs. 6–8.

interval of a whole tone, and a fourth:

```
|--------|---|--------|--------------|
geometric mean and proportion  1         :         2         :         4
arithmetic mean and proportion 2    :         3    :    4
harmonic mean and proportion   3  :    4         :    6
                               6  :    8 : 9      :    12
```

What does this have to do with dialectic? To see this requires bringing together two distinct reflections. First, we have already observed that even while the five mathematical studies turn thought from the sensible to purely intelligible structure, the sequence of the five reveals this as the intelligible structure *of the sensible*. To this we can now add, keying from Socrates' remark at 531c, that it is the *normative* structure of the sensible. If, in the case of music, sound is to be "beautiful and good,"[20] it must conform to the ratios by which Archytas' means structure the octave. Second, this normative order is the mathematical expression of a complex set of *relations between forms*. Though it is the work of the philosopher, not the harmonic theorist, to recognize and make this explicit, it is nonetheless implicit all along that the normative ratios that structure musical "modes" answer to the requirements of the Form of pitch. We get a first glimpse of these requirements if we ask: what are the conditions a musical sound must meet if it is to be on pitch? Minimally, each note must be some proportion of high to low; hence the Form pitch implies the Forms high and low and their instantiation as the tone continuum, which, since the notions of high and low are internally related as reciprocal relatives, ranges from some extreme predominance of high over low to a correspondingly extreme preponderance of low over high. Beyond this, no musical sound is ever "on pitch" in isolation; rather, it must belong to a set of pitches that stand at the right intervals to one another to be harmonious. Hence the Form pitch also implies, in addition to high and low, a set of Forms of notes that, in turn, pick out that definite set of proportions of high to low that stand at appropriate intervals to one another on the tone continuum. And these, now to invoke the first reflection, are

[20] Note that Socrates says *tou kalou te kai agathou*, not *tou kalou te kai tou agathou*. The latter would have referred to a conjunction of the two forms, "the Beautiful" and "*the* Good"; the lack of the second article implies, by contrast, reference to the combination of beauty and goodness and, so, a reference to the immanent characters that make for excellence, not to the forms of these characters.

precisely the intervals determined by Archytas' three means. The eidetic-mathematical structure – that is, the definite ensemble of Forms and mathematicals – thus constituted might be represented, using the technical Greek names of musical notes, roughly thus:

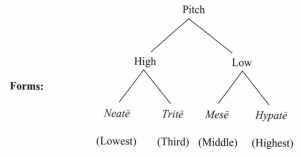

Is it right to project a field of eidetic-mathematical structure of this sort as what awaits the philosopher-to-be when he turns from mathematics to dialectic? Or have we read too much into Socrates' brief comments on harmonic theory? Mathematics, we have stressed, stops at the threshold of the Forms, and these reflections certainly lead us across that threshold. I would offer two closing reflections that in different ways should encourage us to take this risk.

First, Socrates pointedly leaves the journey along the "longer way" as a task for the future. For the philosopher-to-be who will go on to attempt it, he projects not only the practice of dialectic and the attainment of understanding of the Good but also a "precise grasp" (435d, also 504b, e) of the structure and virtues of the individual soul. He says nothing of the structure and virtues of the city, but if the analogy of city and soul holds, a "precise grasp" of the city would also, somehow, be in the offing. Given these anticipations, it is more than striking that when, much later, Plato in the *Philebus* has Socrates again take up the question of the Good, he has Socrates offer as a paradigm of dialectical analysis just the sort of account of the eidetic-mathematical structure of music that we have just laid out. What is more – and of course this claim requires its own exegesis and defense – in the second part of the *Philebus* Socrates provides the resources for an application of this mode of dialectic to the embodied soul.[21] And, still more, in the penultimate section of the *Statesman* Plato has the Eleatic visitor apply this same mode of dialectic to the city.[22] These contents of the *Philebus* and the *Statesman* appear to bring into the open what we have found to be implicit in Socrates' comments on harmonic theory and to put it to work in order finally to reach "the best possible view" (504b) of the soul and the city.

Second, the thought that the Form pitch implies normative requirements for actual musical sound – requirements for what is to be "beautiful and good" – both fits well with and expands our tentative reflections on the Good. It is no surprise that the perfect instantiations of the Forms, precisely as exemplifications of specific ways of determining perfection as such, should have normative status. But whereas the study of geometry, focused on intelligible figures, makes the perfection of these the most conspicuous aspect of that status, the study of harmonics brings to the fore the complex unity that makes for wholeness and harmony. This is striking both at each level and in the structural integrity by which the levels themselves are related. To see this, consider our preceding diagram. At the purely mathematical level, Archytas' means interlock and articulate the continuum of possible proportions of high and low as a repeating series of bounded intervals. At the eidetic level, each of the Forms of notes that make up a "mode" calls for each of the others, and this manifold complementarity makes the mode a harmonious whole. And in the way these levels themselves fit together, with the Archytan means giving mathematical expression to the Forms of notes by marking the select proportions of high and low that these Forms pick out on the continuum, there is a transparent fit of the mathematical with the eidetic. Prior to this whole structure, in turn, stands pitch,

---

[21] For the use of the account of the Form structure of musical modes to exhibit dialectical method, see 17c–e with reference to 16c–17a. The key concepts, first introduced in the third hypothesis of the *Parmenides* and then explicated at *Philebus* 23c–27c (with reference back to 16c), are *peras* and *apeiron*, "limit" and "unlimited." For the resources for the application of dialectic to the question of the right order of the embodied soul, see 31b–55c and 55c–59d, noting esp. 64b6–8. For exegesis, see Miller forthcoming.

[22] See esp. 287b–291a, 303d–305e. For explication, see my "Dialectical Education and Unwritten Teachings in Plato's *Statesman*," now included in Miller 2004.

the Form whose instantiation first calls for these coordinated ensembles of Forms of notes and of proportions, and prior to pitch, which, of course, is only one specific determination of it, stands the Good. Thus the Good emerges, by way of its exemplary determination by the Form pitch, as the source of the complex unity of Forms and of proportions that sets the preconditions for "beautiful and good" musical sound.

In the context of the *Republic* as a whole, the theme of the normative status of complex unity has deep and manifold resonance. As Socrates indicates in a host of ways, for both the city and the soul the decisive criterion of goodness is the proper distinction and harmonious fit of their parts; for both, it is the breakdown of this unity that is the mark of the decline from goodness. More particularly, the inward mark of the "gracefulness" that "music" instills in the young guardians is a critical eye for "what is lacking" and "what is not beautifully made" (401e), that is, to inflect from the negative to the positive, a keen appreciation for what is whole and harmonious. And in considering the turn from mathematics to dialectic Socrates sets as "the greatest test for [whether a young guardian has] a dialectical nature or not" whether he can raise that keen appreciation to the higher level of a "synoptic understanding of the kinship of the [five] mathematical studies with one another and with the nature of what *is*" (537c).

At the same time, this expansion of our sense of the Good opens up a still deeper task of synoptic understanding for one pursuing the "longer way": how do perfection as such and the requiring of appropriate unity – that is, the requiring of the fits that make for wholeness and harmony – *themselves fit together at the eidetic level?* At issue is nothing less than the nature of "the source of the whole" (*tēn tou pantos archēn*, 511b). Are perfection and unity two aspects of a single Form (and, if so, of the Good or of the One or of some higher third), or are they two distinct Forms (the Good and the One) in a harmonious relation of their own, or are they themselves, in some sense that is prior to the distinction our terms presuppose, identical?[23]

---

[23] One thinks here of Aristoxenus' ever-riddling report in the *Harmonics* of the crux of Plato's lecture(s?) on the Good, which might be translated as follows: "in the final analysis *good* is *one*" (*kai to peras hoti agathon esti hen*, 122.13–14). For

3. *The philosopher's reluctance to rule, Socrates' zest, reconsidered: assimilating oneself to the Good?* We should begin with a qualification: the tension between the Callipolitan philosopher's disinclination to "go down into the common dwelling place of the others" (520c) and Socrates' unconstrained and zestful will to "go down" to the Piraeus (327a) lacks the precise focus of a contradiction, for whereas the former descends to *rule*, Socrates descends to *teach*. But this is to distinguish terms that converge. On the one side, the crux of the philosophers' ruling activity, Socrates says at 540a, is "using the Good as a paradigm, to order city, [the] individuals within it, and themselves," and a core part[24] of this "order[ing]," he goes on to say, is "teaching":

> when [his] turn comes, each [philosopher] labors in service of the citizens and rules for the sake of the city, doing this not as something impressive but, rather, as necessary; and thus always educating[25] others of his sort and leaving them behind in his place as guardians of the city, [he] departs to dwell in the Isles of the Blessed.

On the other side, a primary goal of Socrates' pedagogy is to bring his fellow Athenians to the deepest possible recognition of the normative order of the soul, in order that they might structure their public and private lives accordingly. This is the task he pursues with Glaucon, culminating in their shared affirmation of the status of Callipolis as "a paradigm laid up in heaven" (592b), and we see

other translations, see chapter 10, note 21, and chapter 11, note 2, in this volume. For seminal discussion, see Sayre 1983; also Miller 1995.

24 Indeed, Socrates leaves unspecified what part of the philosophers' rule is *not* teaching. Although there are passing allusions to law making at 484d and 501a, in the *Statesman* and the *Laws* that will itself be interpreted as an educational activity. On the true statesman's special focus on education, see *Statesman* 308d–311c.

25 Does the *aei* ("always") in *aei paideusantas* at 540b5 accentuate the aorist significance of the participle or characterize the activity signified by its stem? That is, is it Socrates' point that the philosophers always make sure to have educated someone to take their place when they depart (that is Griffith's reading, accomplished by treating *paideusantas* and *antikatalipontas* as a conjunct and then taking *aei* with *antikatalipontas*, hence "after educating a *continuous succession*")? Or is the point that the philosophers are, as ruling, "always educating" (Bloom's reading and translation)? In helpful correspondence, John Ferrari, who as editor of Griffith's translation (recall n. 1) supports his reading, notes that the difference between Griffith and Bloom at the level of grammar need not imply a significant substantive difference; on both readings "educating future rulers is indeed a constant task for the philosopher kings, year in year out."

Socrates pursuing it in a variety of ways and with varying degrees of success in many other dialogues as well. It is the closest approximation to genuine "rule" that he can achieve in the corrupt culture of commercial and imperialistic Athenian democracy. Hence his famous claim in the *Gorgias* to be "one of a very few Athenians – and among those now living, the sole one – to attempt the true art and practice of politics" (521d).

Accordingly, what Socrates says of the Callipolitan philosopher's disinclination to rule and what he reveals of himself by his actions, his inexhaustible will to teach, stand in striking tension. We should not ignore this tension any more than we should fail to wonder at his reticence and self-constraint on the topics of the Good and dialectic. On the contrary, his silence on his own desire to "go down" and what accounts for it should be felt and met as, like that reticence, a Platonic-Socratic provocation to us, an invitation to seek out for ourselves what Socrates feels it is inappropriate to say to Glaucon and Adeimantus. And his reason for reticence – that Glaucon and Adeimantus have not yet undertaken the "longer way" – should focus our inquiry. Does the "longer way" lead to an experience that could explain Socrates' zest for descent?

In fact, another famous passage, if read in the light of our preceding reflections, gives us a promising point of departure for considering this. In this passage Socrates asserts a surprising continuity between "musical" and philosophical education. Recall first that throughout his presentation of "musical" education Socrates stressed the way the young soul "assimilates itself to" (377b)[26] the models it is presented with; this, he warned, is both potentially beneficial and potentially subversive, depending on the models, for "such imitations . . . [can] establish themselves as habits and [second] nature in body, speech, and thought" (395d). Now, at 500c–d Socrates claims that the philosopher too is subject to this sort of formative power. At this point he has not yet singled out the Good or introduced the issue of philosophical education; he speaks of the Forms generally,

---

[26] This verb, *enduetai*, is followed by the construction, *tupon . . . ensēmēnasthai*, signifying the act of making an impression in soft material with a stamp or seal. The whole expression might be translated more literally as "[the young soul] takes into itself" or "lets sink into itself whatever impression someone might want to press into it."

envisaging them as a plurality in timeless good order, and he reflects on the effect the philosopher's study of them has on the development of his character.

"[B]ecause he sees and contemplates entities that are set in a regular array and are always in the same condition, that neither do wrong to nor are wronged by one another but remain all in order according to reason, he imitates them and as much as possible makes himself like them [*mimeisthai to kai hoti malista aphomoiousthai*]. Or do you think there is any way of keeping someone from imitating that which he admires and so keeps company with?"

"It's not possible," [Adeimantus] said.

"Then the philosopher at least, keeping company with what is divine and in good order, will become as orderly and divine as it is possible for a man to be – though there is plenty of slander about."

"By all means, yes."

"Well then, if some necessity were to arise, requiring him to try to realize what he sees there in the characters of men, both in individuals and in the community, rather than just forming himself, do you suppose he'd turn out to be a poor craftsman of moderation and justice and the whole of popular virtue?"

"Least of all," he said.   (500c–d)

On its face, this passage is consistent with what Socrates says of the philosopher's disinclination to "descend." The philosopher's "imitation" and "making himself like" the forms moves him to become "orderly," to "form *himself*" – but it seems that he will not be moved to try to produce the same order in others. "Some necessity," Socrates implies, will be required to move him to do that. But what might such a "necessity" be?[27] It is precisely in connection with this question that it is important that Socrates has not yet

---

[27] For one answer, true to the level of what Socrates says to Glaucon, see Sedley's chapter 10 in this volume. For an approach akin to Sedley's, see Brown 2000. (See also Brown 2004, in which he argues that the impact of Callipolitan education suffices to predispose the philosopher to heed the arguments of the founders that he take up the responsibility to rule.) Neither Sedley nor Brown discusses the performative tension of what Socrates does with what he says. Both do discuss 500c–d and the philosopher's experience of the Good; but neither they nor the major commentators they rebut in their arguments against the relevance of this experience (see, e.g. Kraut 1991) bring together a recognition of the Good's "imitation"-provoking power with a conceptual articulation of its character. I have also learned from an early version of Singpurwalla 2006.

singled out the Good. As he will make emphatically clear, it is the Good above all that is the ultimate aim of philosophical education, hence the Good above all that the philosopher "admires" and seeks to "keep company with." And we have begun to articulate conceptually the aspects the Good will present to him as he works through the first phases of philosophical education, the study of geometry and harmonic theory. Hence we are now in position to distinguish what Socrates says about the formative power of the object of the philosopher's study and bring it together with what we have discerned about the Good. And this opens up a new path of reflection into Socrates' striking zest for teaching. Do we not find in Socrates' treatments of geometry and harmonic theory an indication of his own – that is, of what Plato dramatically projects as Socrates' own – "keeping company with" and "admiring of" the Good? And "is there any way" that he can have had this experience without being moved to "imitate" and "make himself like" the Good? But, then, should we understand his pedagogical generosity with others as a "habit" and "[second] nature" – and, so, an *internal* necessity – that he has acquired from this "imitation"?

With these thoughts in mind, let me gather the main elements of the newly conceptual understanding of the Good that our reflections on geometry and harmonic theory have begun to yield. The objects of geometry, first of all, give us occasion to think the goodness of the Good as perfection. Even as he "draws" and "molds" sensible figures, the geometer's thought is turned from these to perfection, and to his turning attention, so to speak, perfection makes a three-fold epistemic gift: it provides the enabling context – "truth" as the "coming out of concealment" – within which there first become present for thought both the perfect figures the sensibles fall short of and, with the same inexplicitness as that of the context itself, the Forms that these figures instantiate. What is more, perfection also makes the ontological gift that lets there first *be* Forms to be instantiated and known. Perfection as such, we saw, is indeterminate; in and of itself, it transcends any specific way of being determined. But what is indeterminate requires, for its own being, that it be determined. Hence, in its very transcendence perfection as such invites and lends itself to – or, more precisely put, implicates as its possible complements – all of the specific ways it might be determined. But this, the manifold of different ways of determining perfection, is just what the Forms are. Thus, perfection as such – the Good – is responsible for the existence and basic character of the Forms. Harmonic theory, in turn, redirects our attention from figures to the ratios they express, now, however, letting these stand as objects in their own right. But the ratios it first brings to view, the three means of Archytas' theory of proportions, occupy an intermediate status between, on the one hand, the Form of pitch and the subordinate Forms it implies and, on the other hand, the sensible sounds of actual music. Thus harmonic theory introduces us to a second aspect of the Good: as expressed in its determination as pitch and in the instantiation, in turn, of pitch as the eidetic-mathematical structure of the musical "modes," the Good now emerges as the source of the normative order – or, again, as the requiring of the harmonious fit of each balance of high and low with each of the others in a "mode" – that makes for the beauty and goodness of musical tones.

Even without resolving the perplexing questions we articulated earlier regarding the eidetic relations between goodness and unity, we can see the promise of bringing Socrates' comments at 500c–d into relation with these first conceptualizing reflections on the Good. In each of its three metaphysical functions, the Good is at work as a *giving* – and, in that it reemerges under some determinate aspect in what it gives, it is at work as a giving *of itself*.[28] If we now turn back to Socrates, his comportment as a teacher seems in key ways to constitute, at the level of human action and motivation, a "likeness" or analogue to the Good. Here, at least, are three points of prima facie correspondence to ponder. Whereas it is perfection as such that provides the epistemic context – the "truth" – within which the Forms first become accessible to thought, doesn't Socrates by his questions and provocations provide the pedagogical context within which his conversation partner can first "catch sight of" (526e) perfection as such and the Forms? Again, whereas it is perfection as such that, by requiring the being of the various specific ways it may be determined, is responsible both for the being of the Forms and for the setting of the normative conditions of their instantiation, doesn't Socrates, by providing his partner that pedagogical context, come as close as one person can to being responsible for another's existential achievement, within his limits, of the normative order for his

---

[28] For some initial reflections on the semantic connection between goodness and self-giving, see Miller 1985, esp. pp. 189–191.

own flourishing? Finally, doesn't Socrates' will to teach in its freedom from external necessity and ulterior motives seem similar to the Good in the root character – the *giving of itself* – of its causal functioning? By his own argument (520b), Socrates is under no obligation to Athens to "go down" into the "cave" of Athenian culture, nor does he seem in any discernible way to need or be selfishly desirous of anything that Glaucon and Adeimantus, much less Cephalus or Polemarchus or Thrasymachus, might offer him. (This unforced initiative and generosity is of course even more simply displayed by Socrates' relation to us, the unnamed recipients of his narration.) Accordingly, as the Good expresses its own nature in its giving of itself, doesn't Socrates express *his* own "nature," "doing" (to invoke his formula for justice) the "work" that he finds most truly "his own" (433d ff., 443c ff.), in his "descent" into Athens to teach?

Whence comes this extraordinary "nature"? Isn't this precisely that sort of "[second] nature" that "imitation" of the Good will "establish in body, speech, and thought"? Accordingly, don't we now have occasion to recognize a deep connection between the two kinds of education that Socrates prescribes for Callipolis, the external "shaping" of character by models and the quickening of the soul's internal "capacity" for insight? It is in the culminating experience of the latter, the "understanding" of the Good, that the philosophical soul receives its ultimate model; and it is through its "assimilating itself" to this model, in turn, that the philosopher is moved to "rule," that is, "to educate others like himself." If this is well attuned, then there is indeed an internal necessity that moves Socrates to give of himself by his descent into the Piraeus – and, too, that moves Plato to imitate Socrates' narration of this descent in the first place. And a crucial part of what Plato and his Socrates give us consists in their putting us in position to recognize this very giving as the human-existential "likeness" of the Good, a "likeness" that we too are challenged to let take form by "keeping company" with the Good along the "longer way."

IV. POSTSCRIPT: PROJECTED TASKS ON THE "LONGER WAY"

In its projected trajectory, the "longer and fuller way" stretches well beyond (to borrow Socrates' language for our own purposes) "the reach of our present thrust." This we recognize by the pointed incompleteness of what we have suggested, which yields not conclusions but further tasks. It seems appropriate to close by marking the most important of these. Together they make up a kind of philosophical agenda that, happily, anticipates and fits with much of what Plato gives us in the great successors to the *Republic*[29] – above all, the *Parmenides*, the *Sophist* and *Statesman*, the *Timaeus*, and the *Philebus*. The following are six proleptic titles.[30]

1. *Conceiving the Forms in their proper being* as *Forms.* In drawing on geometry and harmonic theory to gain a conceptual grasp of the Forms, we have been keying from what is implied about them by the kinds of purely intelligible intermediates – namely, perfect figures and normative proportions – that perfectly instantiate them. Forms, we have seen, are specific ways of determining perfection as such. To complete this ascent from mathematicals to Forms, we need to press further in our effort to grasp the being of the Forms *as* Forms. By what concepts may we understand what kind of entity it is that is a way of determining perfection? How may we conceptualize what it is, in the very being of this kind of entity, that lets it be the source of the normative proportions of its instantiations?

2. *Understanding the interrelations of the Forms.* In beginning to reflect on harmonic theory, we have seen a specimen case of the intricate interrelations of Forms, both the vertical relations (to invoke our diagrammatic schematization) by which a single Form implicates a plurality of Forms and the horizontal relations by which these many Forms relate to one another. Just insofar as Forms are different in kind from both their sensible and intelligible instantiations, these relations are different in kind from relations among sensibles and relations among mathematicals. But we have not yet found distinctive concepts for identifying and distinguishing these eidetic relations in their own proper character.

3. *Identifying the modes and processes of dialectic.* Nor, for all our reflection on Forms as its objects, have we identified and

---

[29] These dialogues are "successors" in the sense that each is given a dramatic context that invites the reader to hear it as (among other things) a revisiting of issues in the *Republic*.

[30] These titles correlate only very roughly with the five dialogues and with the issue of the so-called unwritten teachings that Aristotle credits to Plato in *Metaphysics* A6. For a synoptic sketch of the itinerary, see Miller 2003, esp. pp. 23–25.

distinguished the various ways in which dialectic moves among them. We have not yet begun to answer Glaucon's question at 532e: "what sorts of modes does dialectic divide into and . . . what are its paths?"

4. *Figures, ratios, Forms.* The turn from geometry to harmonics showed us, in retrospect, how spatial figures can be understood as the expression of ratios, and our reflections on the status of Archytas' means as intermediates between Forms and actual musical sounds showed us that ratios can be understood as the expression of Forms. This brings us to a daunting set of challenges. These might be formulated as three interrelated questions. First, in speaking of the way in which one sort of being is the expression of another, our understanding of the causal powers of Forms takes its bearings from their effects. Can we articulate the character of these causal powers at the level of the Forms themselves? Second, can we actually give the sort of full and determinate account of the intelligible structure of the sensible world that the sequence of the five mathematical studies implies? And, third, can we base this latter account on the former? That is, can we ground a mathematical physics on a fully and adequately articulated metaphysics of Forms as causes?

5. *The breadth of the "longer way."* Socrates introduces the five mathematical studies as a help in turning the soul to *all* of being – not just to those Forms that lend themselves to mathematical expression but also to the many others that would seem to resist it. The more deeply our path is illuminated by mathematics, the more urgently we want to understand whether we can extend our insight to, for example, the spheres of the ethical, the political, and the religious. To cite the most obvious case, can Socrates – or, on the basis of what Plato gives us, can we – make good on Socrates' claim that by traveling the "longer way" we will come to the "best possible view" of the soul and its virtues?[31]

6. *The Good.* Socrates tells Glaucon *both* that "every soul pursues the Good . . . and divines that it is something" (505d–e) *and* that in the ascent from the cave into the sunlight – that is, in the journey along the "longer way" – the Good will be "the last thing to

---

[31] See Miller forthcoming. For initial exegeses of analogous eidetic-mathematical order in the city, see my "Dialectical Education in the *Statesman*" in Miller 2004, and in cosmology and (in the broadest sense) zoology, see Miller 2003.

be seen, and with great difficulty" (517b). This implies that whatever glimpses we may now have must be held open for rethinking as we proceed. This should be welcome, for our reflections on geometry and harmonic theory have left us with an incomplete understanding, divided between the notions of perfection and unity and lacking the focus that, we may hope, a fully dialectical grasp of the Forms, still ahead of us, will provide. But this acknowledgment may not be open enough. Socrates' words at 394d, quoted at the very beginning of this chapter, should continue to resonate. Might crossing the eidetic threshold and taking up the work of dialectic, rather than merely providing integration and focus for what we have achieved so far, instead expand and further decenter our understanding, requiring yet another reorientation, one as radical in its own way as that which our reflections on geometry and harmonic theory have already occasioned?[32]

WORKS CITED

Adam, J., ed. 1963 [1902]. *The* Republic *of Plato*. Cambridge.

Barker, A. 1989. *Greek Musical Writings*, vol. 2. Cambridge.

Brann, E. 2004. *The Music of Plato's* Republic: *Socrates' Conversations and Plato's Writings*. Philadelphia.

Brown, E. 2000. "Justice and Compulsion for Plato's Philosopher-Rulers." *Ancient Philosophy* 20: 1–17.

Brown, E. 2004. "Minding the Gap in Plato's *Republic*." *Philosophical Studies* 117: 275–302.

Burnyeat, M. F. 1987. "Platonism and Mathematics: A Prelude to Discussion." In *Mathematics and Metaphysics in Aristotle*, ed. A. Graeser (Stuttgart).

Burnyeat, M. F. 2001. "Plato on Why Mathematics Is Good for the Soul." In *Mathematics and Necessity*, ed. T. Smiley (Oxford).

Heidegger, M. 1998 [1931/32, 1940]. "Plato's Doctrine of Truth." In *Pathmarks*, trans. T. Sheehan, ed. William McNeill (Cambridge).

---

[32] My thanks especially to John Ferrari for criticism and advice, to my fellow contributors to this anthology for the stimulation of our conference in Berkeley in September 2004, to Richard Mohr for his thoughtful reading, and to a number of my colleagues at Vassar, especially Rachel Kitzinger, Jeff Seidman, Uma Narayan, Jesse Kalin, Michael McCarthy, Giovanna Borradori, Michael Murray, and, many years ago, David Lachterman, for probing dialogue from surprisingly different perspectives along the way. I have learned a great deal, if not yet nearly enough, from all of them.

Hyland, D. 1995. *Finitude and Transcendence in the Platonic Dialogues.* Albany, N.Y.

Klein, J. 1965. *A Commentary on Plato's* Meno. Chapel Hill, N.C.

Klein, J. 1968. *Greek Mathematical Thought and the Origin of Algebra,* trans. E. Brann. Cambridge, Mass.

Knorr, W. 1975. *The Evolution of the Euclidean Elements.* Dordrecht.

Kraut, R. 1991. "Return to the Cave: *Republic* 519–521." *Boston Area Colloquium in Ancient Philosophy* 7: 43–62.

Lachterman, D. 1989. *The Ethics of Geometry.* New York.

Lee, E. N. 1972. "Plato on Negation and Not-Being in the *Sophist.*" *Philosophical Review* 81: 267–304.

Miller, M. 1985. "Platonic Provocations: Reflections on the Soul and the Good in the *Republic.*" In *Platonic Investigations,* ed. D. J. O'Meara (Washington, D.C.).

Miller, M. 1986. *Plato's* Parmenides: *The Conversion of the Soul.* Princeton. Rpt. University Park, Pa., 1991.

Miller, M. 1995. "'Unwritten Teachings' in the *Parmenides.*" *Review of Metaphysics* 48: 591–633.

Miller, M. 1999. "Figure, Ratio, Form: Plato's Five Mathematical Studies." In *Recognition, Remembrance, and Reality,* ed. M. McPherran. *Apeiron* 32.

Miller, M. 2003. "The *Timaeus* and the 'Longer Way': Godly Method and the Constitution of Elements and Animals." In *Plato's Timaeus as Cultural Icon,* ed. G. Reydams-Schils (Notre Dame, Ind.).

Miller, M. 2004. *The Philosopher in Plato's* Statesman. Las Vegas, Nev.

Miller, M. Forthcoming. "A More 'Exact Grasp' of the Soul? Tripartition in *Republic* 4 and Dialectic in the *Philebus.*" in *Truth,* ed. K. Pritzl (Washington, D.C.).

Mourelatos, A. P. D. 1981. "Astronomy and Kinematics in Plato's Project of Rationalist Explanation." *Studies in the History and Philosophy of Science* 12: 1–32.

Nails, D. 2002. *The People of Plato.* Indianapolis, Ind.

Nehamas, A. 1979. "Self-Predication and Plato's Theory of Forms." *American Philosophical Quarterly* 16: 93–103. Rpt. in A. Nehamas, *Virtues of Authenticity* (Princeton, 1999).

Patterson, R. 1985. *Image and Reality in Plato's Metaphysics.* Indianapolis, Ind.

Robins, I. 1995. "Mathematics and the Conversion of the Mind, *Republic* 7. 522c1–531e3." *Ancient Philosophy* 15: 359–91.

Santas, G. 1980. "The Form of the Good in Plato's *Republic.*" *Philosophical Inquiry* (Winter): 374–403. Rpt. in *Essays in Greek Philosophy* 2, ed.

J. Anton and A. Preus (Albany, N.Y., 1983), and in *Plato 1: Metaphysics and Epistemology*, ed. G. Fine. (Oxford 1999).

Sayre, K. 1983. *Plato's Late Ontology: A Riddle Resolved*. Princeton. Rpt. Las Vegas, 2005.

Singpurwalla, R. 2006. "Plato's Defense of Justice in the *Republic*." In *The Blackwell Guide to Plato's* Republic, ed. G. Santas (Oxford).

Vlastos, G. 1954. "The Third Man Argument in the *Parmenides*." *Philosophical Review* 63: 319–49. Rpt. in *Studies in Plato's Metaphysics*, ed. R. E Allen (London, 1965).

West, M. L. 1992. *Ancient Greek Music*. Oxford.

Wieland, W. 1982. *Platon und die Formen des Wissens*. Göttingen.

13 The City-Soul Analogy

Translated from the German by G. R. F. Ferrari

In the *Republic* Plato's fictional character Socrates develops an elaborate argument to support the thesis that justice pays, because only the just, not the unjust, have access to happiness. The procedure that Socrates adopts in order to make this argument is of a special sort. He derives claims about the human soul from claims that he makes about human society – the *polis* or "city." It is a procedure of crucial importance within the work as a whole.

Where and how is the comparison between city and soul introduced (section I)? What developments does it subsequently undergo (section II)? In which passages of the dialogue are characteristics of the soul derived from characteristics of the city, and what are these characteristics (section III)? How far does the similarity between city and soul extend, and what does Socrates do when he comes up against its limits (section IV)? How does the fact that the procedure is analogical influence the conception of the soul (section V) and of the city (section VI) in this dialogue? What role do causal relations between city and soul have to play – city coming to be formed by soul (section VII), and soul coming to be formed by city (section VIII)?

The interpretation presented in this chapter is one that I have elsewhere substantiated against the background of the extensive scholarly literature on the topic. I can do no more than allude to this debate here.[1] Often, where I differ from the (older) scholarly

---

[1] See Blössner 1997, which came about as a by-product of my work on a new commentary on *Republic* 8–10. The commentary is to appear in the series *Platons Werke: Übersetzungen und Kommentare*, ed. E. Heitsch and C. W. Müller (Mainzer

consensus, those points of difference result from a broader difference of methodology. Accordingly, I offer a brief account of my methodology in section IX. The chapter concludes with a summary of its results (section X).

I. THE ANALOGY INTRODUCED

That a similarity holds between city and soul is a proposal first mooted in Book 2 (368c–369a). Socrates is faced there with the task of determining the nature and the effects of justice in the soul, and of doing so in such a way that his interlocutors will be convinced of the truth of his standard claim that being just is advantageous to the just individual. To that end he introduces the following consideration: Justice is a quality that not only an individual but also the city as a whole can possess, and may be easier to recognize in the city, because the city is larger. (The contrast shows that by "city" (polis) Socrates understands a social group, which he opposes to the individual. Elsewhere too in the Republic the concept of the city or polis mostly designates not the state but rather the citizenry – not, then a legal "person" but a community of persons: see below, section VI). It would therefore make sense, claims Socrates, to determine what justice is in the city before turning in an analogous way to the individual – an investigation that would involve examining the similarity between the two, the larger and the smaller.

There are four points to notice here.

(1) Consideration of the city – which is to say, the political aspect of the dialogue – is in the service of and subordinate to the ethical goal of consideration of the individual. Socrates makes this quite explicit.

(2) Talk of the city as "larger" and of the individual as "smaller" conceals the fundamental distinction between the two, which is that while the city is visible, the soul is invisible. Attributes of the city can be directly observed, those of the soul at best inferred from other observations (see section III below).

(3) The similarity in question relates to one attribute, and one alone: that of being just. Nothing is said here at the outset about

Akademie der Wissenschaften). For convenience, I have added many cross-references between this chapter and the fuller discussion in my book of 1997.

other attributes shared by city and soul; still less are we given any reason at this point to suppose that city and soul are similar in their structure. (Groups can possess attributes that individual members of the group do not. A military corps of the United Nations can be multinational although each U.N. soldier is not. Likewise, a city can be structured oligarchically without the same being true of each of its citizens. See below, section VII.)

(4) That city and soul are similar is put forward as a hypothesis, as a supposition that must be put to the test; otherwise the comparison with larger and smaller letters that precedes it (368c–d) would make no sense. For if, after reading the big letters, a person could be sure that the small ones comprise the same text, he could spare himself the trouble of reading them. The comparison makes sense only if he must first examine *whether* the small letters comprise the same text as the big. Plato's formulations leave no doubt about this. (So at 368d he explicitly uses the term "whether", *ei*; and 369a too suggests that one must *examine whether* the similarity in fact holds.)

II. THE ANALOGY DEVELOPED

Socrates does not return to the topic of the similarity between city and soul until Book 4 (434d–435a). Much has been discussed since the topic was first broached at 368c–369a, and the result is that modern interpreters, no less than Socrates' interlocutors, may fail to notice that Socrates now alters his conception of that similarity in two significant ways.[2] These changes relate to the last two of the four points just listed. It is not going too far to assert that the whole of the subsequent argument hangs on them.

(On point 4): That a relation of similarity holds between city and soul, for one thing, is no longer treated in Book 4 as a hypothesis in need of proof but as assured fact. Socrates makes it quite plain that were he to fail to establish a similarity, this would prompt him to revise only the arguments that led to this result; he does not suggest that he would revise the hypothesis of similarity itself (434e–435a). Accordingly, at 435a–b he acts as if he is licensed to assume without

---

[2] Even in the most recent German "companion" to the *Republic* (Höffe 1997), these two passages are dealt with in two separate chapters, by two different authors, neither of whom notes the development between them.

further argument that if we can apply the same predicate ("just") to city and to soul, these two are similar in that respect. By 441c–d, after Socrates has argued that the soul has at least three parts, the structural similarity between virtues of the city and virtues of the soul has become outright "compelling" (441c *anankaion*; 441d *anankē, pasa anankē*); and it is this conviction that then determines what the virtues of the soul actually are.

(The term *aretē*, often translated as "virtue," functions in Greek as a substantive, "goodness," that corresponds to the adjective *agathos*, "good." This "goodness" is not a moral quality but an outstanding capacity or excellence – as when we say "a good logician." The question of whether, and why, human excellence, which makes happiness possible, also entails moral qualities, is a question that lies at the heart of Plato's *Republic*, and which that work makes controversial.)[3]

To understand the displacement that has occurred since Book 2, consider what would happen if we were to take the model of the large and small letters, which was used to introduce the hypothesis of a similarity in the first place, and apply it to the statements in 434d–435a. The observer would first read the big letters, doing so, unlike before, in the full conviction that the big and small letters are alike. In the event that his subsequent perusal of the small letters revealed that their text was not identical to that of the larger letters, rather than doubt the similarity between them, as we might expect, he would doubt his reading of the larger letters! Clearly, the model that in Book 2 was adequate to the situation yields outright nonsense in the altered conditions of Book 4.

(On point 3): Just as significant is how the scope of the analogy has been enlarged. In 435b–c Socrates brings up two considerations: the presence of justice in both city and soul, and the fact that justice in the city was found to be a matter of how the city's components behaved. He then draws the conclusion that the soul too must not only consist of parts, but must even have the same number and kinds of parts as the city does! Examination of the question of whether the analogy can be confirmed turns instead into an examination of the question of whether one can discover in the soul precisely three

---

[3] The best conceptual analysis of *aretē* known to me is Stemmer 1998.

elements or forces that would correspond to the three classes in the city (435c).

(If points 3 and 4 are both taken into account, 434d–435c contains an adequate explanation of why Socrates must postulate precisely *three* parts of the soul. Given these two claims, Socrates' argument could not proceed unless he were already assuming that the soul contains just this number of parts. See below, section III, where the development of the *Republic*'s psychology is discussed.)

The logic of extending the analogy in this way is fallacious. From the fact that city and soul are both just and that the city's justice is a matter of its parts (its classes) "doing their own" (e.g., 432b–434c), it does not inevitably follow that the just soul too must consist of parts, each doing its own. It could just as well be that justice in the individual soul is a matter of that individual doing his own, while the justice of the civic community consists in the fact that all of the members of that community are doing their own. Let Socrates be perfectly correct to define justice as "doing one's own"; still, he would be wrong to conclude that the soul consists of parts.[4]

The conclusion that those parts are of the same number and kinds as in the city is still less legitimate. Just because the justice of X consists in X's having parts that do their own, the conclusion does not follow that if A and B are just, each must have as many parts as the other, and the same kinds of parts. Although Socrates frames his procedure here as following on from what has already been granted, in reality he is dramatically extending the boundaries of the analogy.[5]

As a result of this extension – a move that Socrates rhetorically masks – the similarity of city and soul in a single aspect, the capacity of both to be just or unjust, becomes a comprehensive similarity in their structure. That city and soul are "alike" is something

---

[4] The phrase "doing one's own" is applied to quite different states of affairs in different parts of the *Republic*, each of which invites comment: see Blössner 1997, p. 258 n. 726.

[5] Cf. Ferrari 2003, pp. 37–42. (Can it be just coincidence that it is precisely at this point in the dialogue, and at no other, that Socrates confesses that if they continue using methods such as those they are currently employing, it will not be possible to investigate in a truly reliable way the question of whether the soul contains three parts corresponding to the three classes in the city?)

one can say from Book 4 onward, not before. It is an assertion that determines the discussion for the first time in 442e–449a, occurs a second time at 541b,[6] and becomes ubiquitous in Books 8 and 9.[7]

III. THE ANALOGY AT WORK

The analogy between city and soul is put to work not once but twice: first in Book 4, and again in Books 8 and 9.[8]

In Book 4 (425c–434c) Socrates gives an account of the "virtues" (*aretai*) of the city: wisdom (428b–429a), courage (429a–430c), self-control (430e–432b), and justice (432b–434d). Shortly after, on the assumption – now a premise confidently expressed – that the virtues of the city and those of the soul are analogous (441c–d), he applies this account to the virtues of the soul: justice, first at 441d–442a and again at 442d; courage (442b-c); wisdom (442c); and self-control (442c–d). Socrates' account of these virtues is at the same time a sketch of the structure of the just man's soul. We learn which force or element it is that "rules" in his soul, and acquire a first rough impression of how things are in his soul overall.

In Books 5–7 the analogy is put to no work. A relevant statement that occurs at the very end of Book 7, as a transition to Book 8, can be read as a straightforward reference back to the opening of Book 5 (449a) – although it could also be taken as a suggestion of Plato's to the reader, implicitly inviting him to fill a lacuna for himself.[9]

The most far-reaching application of the analogy is to be found in Books 8 and 9. Socrates there describes four inferior types of regime, to which he gives the names "timocracy," "oligarchy," "democracy," and "tyranny" (see section VI below). He sets them in order of rank, and in a kind of thought-experiment imagines each emerging from its predecessor. What principle might lie behind the choice and ranking of these constitutions is not made explicit; nor does the reader learn

---

[6] 472b–d does not count, since there it is not the similarity between city and soul that we find but the similarity between an imagined model of justice and the real world.

[7] E.g., 543c–d, 544a, e, 545a, b-c, 548d, 549b, 553a, 553e, 554a, b, 577d, 580d.

[8] The instances are fully collected in Andersson 1971.

[9] This is how it is taken by Ferrari 2003, pp. 85–116, who also attempts to gauge the results at which a reader who attempts to fill the lacuna might arrive.

why it is that Socrates represents one constitution as transforming itself into another rather than just describing them successively. Other, less significant positions that Socrates adopts he often justifies in detail; yet these highly consequential positions, which give shape to the entire argument that follows, he adopts without remark and with no explicit justification at all. Socrates, and Plato with him, keeps his thoughts on these matters to himself.[10] A further problem, quite a significant one, arises from the assertion that the good regime will degenerate into an inferior one; for can any regime that falls apart have truly been the good regime?[11]

Alongside the description of the four types of regime in 543c–576b we find a systematically analogous description of four types of individual soul or character, each taking its name from the corresponding regime. So there is both a timocratic city (545c–548d) and a timocratic man (548d–550c), an oligarchic city (550c–553a) and an oligarchic man (553a–555b), a democratic city (555b–558c) and a democratic man (558c–562a), and a tyrannical city (562a–569c) and a tyrannical man (571a–576b). (Only in the passage between 553e–554b and 555a–b is the thesis of similarity once again supported by argument. Everywhere else its validity is simply assumed.)

Each of these eight descriptive passages is further subdivided into a section describing the origins or development of the city or man in question and a section describing them in their fully developed condition (vice-versa in the case of the timocratic man), yielding sixteen sections in all, set out in corresponding pairs. This is followed by a proof of the tyrant's unhappiness, an argument that at least in its first part (576b–578b) depends on and explicitly hearkens back to the similarity between city and soul.

In its actual application, both in Book 4 and in Books 8 and 9, the analogy between city and soul is directed toward describing types of soul and furnishing each type with a range of traits. The claim that city and soul are analogous is to be resolved into the following three more particular claims.

---

[10] For an attempt to reconstruct Plato's thoughts and intentions here, see Blössner 1997, pp. 46–151.

[11] The curious "speech of the Muses" about the "marriage number" that Plato offers at this point is doubtless connected with this problem. For an attempt at explaining the connection, see Blössner 1999.

(a) City and soul should be constructed in an analogous way and out of analogous elements. It follows, in addition, that the number of possible arrangements of city and soul should be equal.

(b) The merits and defects of city and of soul should be such as can be described and explained in an analogous way, or in a way that at least seems analogous.

(c) These merits and defects of city and of soul should bring about human happiness and unhappiness in an analogous (or analogously describable) way.

Elaboration of (a): City and soul are to have the same number and the same kinds of parts. In the good city, three classes collaborate – philosophers, soldiers or guards, and producers. Correspondingly, in the good soul there is an interplay of three forces: the rational (*logistikon*), the spirited (*thumoeides*), and the appetitive (*epithumētikon*) (e.g., 435b–c). Each arrangement of elements in city and in soul is to be specified in terms of the dominance of precisely one social group or soul part; no provision is to be made in this scheme for coalitions of forces. (This, at least, is the principle that underlies Plato's account; the case of the democratic man is more complicated.) In Books 8 and 9 the appetitive part is split into three, raising the total number of forces in the soul to five (558c–d; 571a–572b); as a result, Plato now has five different arrangements of city and of soul to construct (544e, anticipated at 445c–d). (Both the unexpected introduction of this fivefold division as well as the choice and ranking of the inferior arrangements of city and of soul raise questions about Plato's criteria here that need to be explained if we are to understand his intentions but that are not explicitly addressed in his text.)[12] The ascendancy of a particular social group or soul part is to be linked to the dominance of a particular kind of striving or desire: with the rational element goes a striving for knowledge; with the spirited a striving after distinction and prestige; with the three subtypes of the appetitive a striving for money, freedom, and power, respectively (see 580d–581e; also 547b, 548c, 550b, 553b–d, 555b–c, 556c, 562b–c; etc.).

Elaboration of (b): Socrates attributes various merits (*aretai*) to what he calls the good and correct arrangement of city and soul (e.g.,

---

12 For an attempt at explanation, see Blössner 1997, pp. 46–151.

449a), and various defects (*kakiai*) to the bad and mistaken arrangements. The basis for this evaluation seems to be that only one of the forces within city and soul has the capacity to form a correct conception of the good and to attain knowledge of it. Its rule is the only sort, according to Socrates, that aims at the well-being of the entire city or of the entire person, ensuring a beneficial outcome for the social groups or soul parts other than itself. In other words, only its rule has the potential to be viewed by all as justified rule.

The claim, then, is that there is a "natural hierarchy" in city and in soul, and that where it exists, it creates merits or virtues (*aretai*), such as justice, wisdom, courage, and self-control (432b–434c, 441c–442b). By contrast, any falling off from the natural hierarchy produces injustice and so conflict (444b–c). These intially somewhat amorphous claims are concretely filled out in the description of the unjust types of city and soul (Books 8 and 9).

Elaboration of (c): Socrates' aim in the *Republic* is to show that only the good and correct arrangement of city and of soul produces genuine happiness. Now, it is clear on its face that communities derive benefit from the just behavior of their members – an intuition on which Glaucon based his social-contract theory of justice back at 358e–359b. By conceiving of the soul as a "community" of soul parts, along the lines of a civic community, Socrates transfers this intuition from the context of the city to that of the soul. It is a suggestive move. Indeed, it is from this move that the thesis that justice is advantageous to the just derives a good portion of its plausibility.

The idea is this: whether in city or in soul, the rule of that element that is preordained to rule should aim at attaining benefits that bring happiness to all. In this way what is advantageous to one element is by the same token advantageous to all – a "win-win" situation. As a result, when the appropriate element rules, it is able to rule through persuasion; other rulers must use force. Rule by the appropriate element guarantees a balance among interests and creates harmonious unity in city or in soul; all other regimes produce wretched conflict. And these mechanisms work to the same effect in city as in soul. That at least is the general scheme; as we shall see, its application is a complex matter and deviations from the scheme are allowed to accrue.

It is when he turns to the topic of tyranny that Socrates' derivation of the unhappiness of the defectively governed soul from that of the defectively governed city becomes most explicit. The condition of the tyrannical man's soul – who at his worst is an actual ruling tyrant (575b–d; 578b–c) – is explicitly compared to the condition of a tyrannized city, that is, an oppressed city, and not, let us notice, that of a tyrannizing or oppressive city (577c–d). When the terms of comparison are set out in this way, the wretchedness of the tyrannical soul follows almost automatically. The tyrant, that archetype of power exercised without constraints, instead appears in the *Republic* as an impotent slave to his own drives (574d–575a, 577b–578b, etc.). In the case of the other three faulty systems the corresponding derivation is less explicit but still clear enough. In all instances – this at least is what Socrates gives his interlocutors to understand – unjust and selfish striving, for all that it may achieve its superficial goals, fails to achieve its own truest goal: happiness (see sections V and VI below).

How does the city-soul analogy relate to Platonic psychology? Is it a device for inserting a preexistent Platonic psychology into the *Republic*, or has Plato in the *Republic* developed a special psychological theory in concert with the analogy? While no answer to this far-reaching question is likely to gain universal acceptance, the indications seem to me to point in a single direction.

(i) Where else could we look for the basis of the *Republic*'s psychology, if not in the analogy itself? The soul is invisible; neither its structure nor its operations are directly observable. Analysis of human behavior permits us to draw conclusions, but no more than that, about the nature of the soul. The fact that many different models of the soul can and have been constructed over time should sap our confidence in the reliability of these conclusions – not to mention that an entire research paradigm in psychology, behaviorism, claims to be able to dispense entirely with appeals to the nature of the soul. (Behaviorist psychology attends simply to the connection between "stimulus" and "response," leaving the soul deliberately out of account as an unknowable "black box.") But even if the behaviorist approach were wrong, it remains the case that there are no facts of human nature that could support an inference to the existence of three drives in the soul.

(The psychologist H. Heckhausen offers the following explanation at the level of principle to show why it is not possible to infer a threefold division of the soul from empirical data: "How many fundamental tendencies, drives, or needs should we distinguish? Obviously, this depends on the chosen level of generality and is for that reason an arbitrary matter that cannot be decisively settled. Freud thought he could manage with two drives, the sexual drive and the death drive. His student Adler attempted to derive everything from the drive to power. McDougall . . . distinguished 18 principal tendencies . . .; Murray . . . drew up a list of 27 needs, etc."[13])

If this is correct, then it simply cannot be from an analysis of human behavior that the psychology of the *Republic* derives. (If Plato thought that it could, then we would have to conclude that Platonic psychology is based on a fundamental error. But there is evidence that he was well aware of the facts, as subsequent sections will show.) Many readers of this work seem to have allowed themselves to be taken in by Plato's Socrates here, whose consummate skill in padding all those novel claims of his with appeals to the empirical realm works very suggestively. Some examples: (a) When Socrates has produced his novel definition of justice as the rule of reason in the soul (441d–442b), he tests its plausibility by checking that it is in agreement with conventional conceptions of that virtue (442d–443b). (b) In 573b Socrates' surprising assertion that the tyrannical character is ruled by "eros" is supported by appeal to longstanding literary expressions. (c) In 575e–576b the analysis of the tyrannical character culminates in precisely those qualities that have in any case always been ascribed to the unjust. (d) In 589c–591b Socrates attempts to show that ideas similar to those he has been developing (with his new conception of the soul) underlie longstanding ethical concepts in the shared culture.

Socrates appeals to the empirical realm not only when the soul is in question, but also in political matters. Consider, for example, his suggestion that the so-called timocracy is identical to the "Cretan or Spartan regime" – when in fact the Spartan regime would rank as a mixed constitution or as an oligarchy.[14] Or consider, in general, the many "realistic" traits that crop up in the descriptions of the inferior regimes, on account of which scholars have (wrongly) accorded them political or historical value (see below, section VI). And yet it

[13] In Weinert 1974, p. 136.
[14] See Blössner 1997, pp. 79–85.

is clear – although often overlooked – that in many cases Socrates brings the empirical evidence into harmony with his argument only by dint of an adroit choice and suggestive presentation of examples. The reader, and doubtless Plato himself, could readily discover counterexamples.

If the model of the soul that we find in the *Republic* does not derive from analysis of human behavior, neither does it emerge from a tradition. Plato would have found no consistent model of the soul in the variety of psychological forces that epic and drama represented now as cooperating, now as conflicting with each other. In particular, there is no credible pre-Platonic evidence for the notion that the soul is to be divided into three. Early Greek epic and lyric present a rich and highly complex psychology, many functional aspects of which live on in Plato's account; they do not, however, lead to a threefold division of the soul.[15]

(ii) Imagine if Plato's analysis of the soul's attributes were indeed independent of his analysis of those of the city: then it would be no more than a happy coincidence that city and soul should turn out to be analogous. The reason for this is that the city, unlike the soul, presented itself to Plato as an entity that he had no very great freedom to define. The basic givens of the city are there for all to see. The city must provide for basic material needs, assure security, organize a government. Its citizens will have a variety of jobs, divide labor between them, and have interests that conflict or coincide in an interplay of unity, discord, and power. No analyst of political life can dispense with such givens as these. But when it comes to portraying the soul, there is more room for play.

(iii) Following on from what is said at 434d–435a, Socrates' argument could not proceed unless it had already been established that the soul, no less than the city, consisted of three parts (see above, section II). This proviso on the argument is highly specific; so specific, indeed, that one can hardly believe Plato's ideas about the soul to have developed with such perfect timing as to provide Socrates with precisely the proof he needs at this precise moment.

---

[15] On this issue, and on the purported evidence for a threefold division of the soul in early Pythagoreanism, see further Blössner 1997, pp. 214–19 (and 169–76). On a tradition of comparison between the city and the *body*, see Ferrari 2003, pp. 62–65.

That Plato's thought developed is the consideration commonly adduced to explain why the Socrates of the *Phaedo* employs a different and simpler model of the soul than appears in the *Republic*. But such developmentalism fails to explain either the timing or the direction of the imagined progress. Why should it be that precisely in the period in which he was writing the *Republic* (and not before or after) Plato made a theoretical advance in precisely this direction (and not in a different one)? This remains unexplained. And when one bears in mind that the psychology of the *Phaedo* does not harmonize with the argument of the *Republic* nor the psychology of the *Republic* with the argument of the *Phaedo*, it must seem a positively miraculous coincidence that Plato's ideas about the soul should have developed at just the time and in just the way that would permit his character Socrates to achieve every one of the argumentative goals specific to this particular dialogue.[16]

Considerations such as these make it very probable that Plato developed the psychology of the *Republic* with the city-soul analogy in mind. The mere fact that the threefold division of the soul is maintained in later dialogues is no counterargument to this position. Besides, the persistence of this theory, as could readily be shown, offered advantages both of economy of argument and of rhetorical design. Appeal to a familiar model spared Plato the explanatory moves that any new model would have demanded. Simple literary economy, then, spoke for its retention. In addition, by formally retaining the old model, Plato was able to downplay alterations of its content.[17]

On other grounds too it would be advisable to surrender the assumption that Plato wrote his dialogues above all for the purpose of informing a broad audience about his actual philosophic views at the time (see section IX). And once we have done so, we are left with no reason to go looking for Plato's own theory of the soul in the arguments of his character Socrates in the *Republic*. This Socrates neither

---

[16] See further Blössner 2001, esp. pp. 129–34.

[17] A tripartite soul appears in the *Phaedrus* too (in its allegory of the soul chariot); the result has been that many scholars even now overlook the fact that the division of the soul in this dialogue is based on quite different criteria than in the *Republic* (see Blössner 1997, pp. 183ff. and 240ff.). Retaining the model at a formal level had its rhetorical advantages, then. See further Blössner 2001.

bears witness to nor asserts Platonic doctrine. Rather, he conducts a conversation conditioned by the requirements of its result – conditioned by the need to construct an argument that can demonstrate that justice pays.

IV. THE RHETORIC OF THE ANALOGY

Socrates misses no opportunity to develop the structural similarity of city and soul in its every detail. Metaphor is an important tool for this purpose.

Thus there are "drone-like desires" in the soul (554b–c) that correspond to the "drones" in the city (552a–d); desires that act as "allied troops" (559e–560a), corresponding to military allies of the city (556e); and, corresponding to the tyrant's bodyguard (567d–e), a "bodyguard" for the "tyrant of the soul," Eros (e.g., 573e). Socrates even finds an analogue within the soul for so particular a distinction as that between foreign mercenaries and freed slaves (575a). Often these metaphors form entire systems. So the drone-like desires "propagate themselves" (560b), "overtake" the "Acropolis" of the soul (560b), slam shut the "gates" and "forbid ambassadors access" (560c–d), carry out a revaluation of moral values (modeled on that described in Thucydides 3.82.4), and "banish" their opponents (560d–561a).

This rich panoply of metaphor brings to life the portrayal of the soul's inner workings, and at the same time gives the impression of confirming the structural similarity of city and soul, despite the problems that we saw attend its introduction (above, section II). As a result, Socrates is able to invoke the analogy without qualms wherever this serves his argument (as, for example, at 577b–c).

In fact the analogy of city and soul is based to a significant degree on rhetorical suggestion. This should become clear if we bring to mind some of the concrete facts that limit its validity.

Members of the city can change their group allegiance, but parts of the soul cannot. Those designated for the military class can become producers (415b–c), timocratic types can become oligarchic (551a), but within the soul, spirit never becomes appetite. All philosopher-kings began as members of the military class, but the rational part of the soul does not begin its existence as a spirited part. The rational and the aggressive elements seem to have disappeared from the oligarchic city (see 547e, 551a), but must remain present in the oligarchic soul, because the desire that rules this soul continues to require their capacities (see 553b7–d7; 554b7–e6). The oligarchic city is divided into rich and poor (551d); the oligarchic soul, by contrast, into better and worse desires (554d–e). In the democratic city, anarchy reigns (557a–558c); in the democratic soul, not anarchy, but *isonomia*, "equal rights." Moreover, the general principle of strict separation between political power and private property that is so central to the ideal city has no real analogue in the soul. (This list could be extended.)

And here is a more crucial point: the behavior of the city, if we can put it that way, is identical with the behavior of its members; but the behavior of an individual is not identical with that of his soul parts. For alongside the soul parts the individual himself stands as a distinct figure. He appears as the ruler of his "soul polity" (e.g., 554c–d, 558d), hands over rule of his soul to a particular part (e.g., 550b, 553b–d), supervises his inner system, and takes responsibility for it (e.g., 561b, 591e). When the tyrannical man fails to exercise this supervision and becomes an impotent slave to his desires, this is exceptional, and appears by comparison to be a failure of responsibility (573e–574a, 574e–575a, etc.). It is precisely the fact that the individual is responsible for the forces in his soul that gives sense in the first place to Socrates' argument urging the establishment of correct order among them. The city offers no analogue for this fact.

Two further and equally important points: First, the central question in the dialogue, whether it is justice or injustice that brings happiness, is a question that poses itself only for individuals, not for soul parts. Soul parts are neither happy nor unhappy; only the individual is happy or unhapppy. Nor are soul parts just or unjust – not if to be just is to have several parts within oneself, each of which "does its own." Otherwise an infinite regress would result.[18] But this premise about justice is necessary if Socrates' inference that the just soul has parts (435b–c) is not to be fallacious, disrupting the analogy at its outset. Second (and this objection targets what is perhaps the most fundamental claim made by the analogy): ruling in the city, whatever the identity of terminology might suggest, is naturally a

---

[18] For discussion of problems of this sort in the analogy see Bernard Williams' seminal article, Williams 1973.

quite different matter from "ruling in the soul" (the metaphor is traditional in Greek culture). Rule of men over men is achieved by means other than the "mastery" of forces in the soul; and it naturally requires also a different kind of legitimation. (While it may be convenient for Socrates to skate over this difference, it can scarcely serve the purposes of interpretation for us to follow him uncritically in this regard).

These limitations of the analogy do not merely affect details but go to the heart of the supposed structural similarity between city and soul. Can they have escaped Plato's notice? Was he so naïve as to have become the victim of his own metaphors? And is it just coincidence that Socrates should so purposefully and carefully skirt all the limitations we have considered?

Rhetorical suggestion, however, will not by itself achieve the impression of a comprehensive isomorphism between city and soul and get it to fly. A particular conception of the city and of the soul is also required.

V. THE CONCEPTION OF THE SOUL

The task of making city and soul appear analogous imposes its own constraints. They cannot be described in any way one pleases, if the task is to succeed. When portraying the city, even before the soul has come into view, the qualities that need to be brought front and center are those that can be transposed (albeit metaphorically) onto the soul. How far this constraint interferes with the task of political analysis in the proper sense remains to be investigated (see below, section VI). But similar constraints apply to the psychology of the *Republic*, and this is reason enough to doubt optimistic attempts to treat it as if it represented Plato's own conception of the soul.

The analogy imposes two different types of constraint on the individual soul. Looked at from one angle, the individual soul is the analogue of the city. So for instance when we read that the timocratic man "is like" or "is similar to" or "corresponds to" the timocratic city, we are to think of his soul as a "city writ small," which reproduces the pattern specific to the timocratic city. Plato gets this across by postulating the existence of forces in the soul that interact with each other as people in the city do: pursuing similar or contrasting interests, controlling each other, struggling with, or, as it may be, cooperating with each other. Each corresponding city/soul pair is marked by an equivalent drive or desire: In the timocratic city (548c) and soul (548d–e), it is the desire for prestige that dominates; in the oligarchic city (551a, 555b–c, 562a–b) and soul (e.g., 553c, 554a), the desire for wealth; in the democratic city (562b–563e) and soul (561a–562a), the desire to be free; in the tyrannical city (567d–569c) and soul (571a–576b), the desire for unlimited power.

Looked at from the opposite angle, people in the city are analogues for the drives or desires in the soul. It must be stressed, however, that it is not the individual citizen that satisfies the analogy but rather the social group to which he belongs, for example, the producers, the military, or the philosophers. So for example it is the dominant social class in the timocracy that corresponds to the dominant drive in the timocratic soul (spirit, the *thumoeides*). This social class creates the timocratic system and shapes its ruling values, norms, and goals, just as the spirited part that rules in the soul of the timocratic man establishes a "timocratic" structure there and shapes that individual's values, norms, and goals.[19]

It would seem obvious that a connection of some sort must hold between the type of individual who is analogous to a city, on the one hand, and the social group that shapes this city, on the other – for example, between the timocratic man and the men who make up the ruling class of the timocratic city. And it would seem equally obvious that this connection should have something to do with the drive or desire that is common to city and to soul. Yet how the relationship works, exactly, is far from clear. The straightforward idea that those who rule the city impose their own dominant desire on that city (see 544d–e and section VII below) has to be excluded in the cases of oligarchy and democracy, since in those cities the ruling class includes men of different character types. Socrates fails to explain the actual mechanism by which the desire peculiar to a certain type of person imposes itself on a city, or by which the desire peculiar to a part of the soul imposes itself on an individual person.

---

[19] Cf. 548c, "which comes from the spirited element that dominates there," *hupo tou thumoeidous kratountos*. While the expression "the spirited element" can be understood as an abstraction representing the military class, no reader of the Greek text could fail to associate it also with the part of the soul that goes by the same designation.

Evidently, this mechanism is not an essential element of Socrates' argument.[20]

The analogy has important effects on how city and soul are represented. Conceiving the soul as analogous to a city leads to the soul parts being portrayed as distinct living beings with distinct aspirations and impulses. Conceiving each part of the soul as driven always by one and the same desire, as Socrates does, leads by analogy to a one-dimensional view of how social classes act and of what their aspirations are. The result is that what Socrates describes are *types* of cities rather than realistic cities (cf. 544c–d). On the other side of the analogy, it leads to a one-dimensional view of the soul, too. It creates not individuals but, precisely, human *types*, who could never exist in the flesh – at least not without further specification. Just as the parts of the soul are driven always by one and the same desire, so the timocratic, oligarchic, democratic, and tyrannical types have only one overriding and constant drive, which is at the same time the primary trait that distinguishes these types from each other (cf. 580d–583a). All other traits ascribed to them by Socrates remain quite secondary by comparison.

The condition of being driven by one constant and overriding desire is traced back to the domination of a particular part of the soul. As described by Socrates in the *Republic*, the parts of the soul have the combined quality of capacities or faculties, on the one hand, and drives, on the other. That the parts of the soul are always also drives is already apparent at 439a–d; for how could a motivational conflict break out between the rational and the appetitive parts unless the rational part (*logistikon*) stands for a certain type of willing or wanting? (This is later made explicit: 580d–581c.) The traditional translation "rational part" or "reason" tends to obscure this fact. As drives, they either instigate particular actions or craft long-term orientations on life. These two situations should be sharply distinguished.[21]

---

[20] For an account of earlier attempts to elucidate this issue, see Blössner 1997, pp. 179–81. Ferrari 2003, pp. 37–119, offers a fresh and perceptive analysis of the topic, with partly different results from those presented here.

[21] In addition to Kraut 1973 and Irwin 1977, pp. 226–33, George Klosko has been a prime mover in bringing out this distinction (see, e.g., Klosko 1988, pp. 341–56). For a critical assessment of Klosko's view, see Blössner 1997, pp. 227–29. See also Ferrari's chapter 7 and Parry's chapter 14 in this volume.

(a) The description of the parts of the soul as instigators of particular actions is confined to 439a–441c, the passage in which they are first introduced. The basic situation underlying the various examples is that soul part X "wants" to bring about action A, while soul part Y "wants" to bring about action not-A. Each soul part can bring about various actions, with the result that there are (very many) more actions than soul parts. An individual's decision to engage in action A is described as the "victory" of soul part X (this rather than the "rule" of X) in a "contest" of desires.

(b) For the rest of the dialogue, beginning already at 441c, the parts of the soul bring about the pursuit of long-term goals. In this context, each soul part is tightly associated with a single goal, so that there are only as many goals as there are parts. An individual's decision to pursue the goal associated with soul part X is described as the "rule" of X in the person's soul (e.g., 550b, 553b–c, 559e–561a, 572d–573b). The rule of particular parts of the soul is correlated with the long-term goals of individuals and is the primary criterion by which individuals are divided into types. The capacities of the nondominant parts of the soul remain active (see, e.g., 553b7–d7); it is only as life-forming drives that they cease to operate. (Thus the distinction between an individual who is ruled by his rational part and one who is ruled by his spirited part is not a difference of intelligence, nor would the rule of philosophers be that of an intellectual elite over the intellectually less gifted. Rather, it would be the "rule" of the right goals in life over false ones.) These long-term goals of individuals are not just any goals, however; each is the *summum bonum*, the individual's ultimate goal in life and source of happiness. The fact that in the *Republic*'s psychological scheme only one soul part can rule means that these different ideas of happiness are exclusive alternatives. (This explains why Glaucon is not in fact a timocratic character, despite 548d.[22] Prestige is not Glaucon's dominant goal in life. What the discussion indicates is rather that a dominant goal in life is not something Glaucon and Adeimantus have yet discovered.)

Whereas the first of these conceptions of the soul parts, conception (a), serves only to introduce the parts of the soul into the dialogue,[23]

---

[22] Ferrari 2003, pp. 69ff., correctly sees this point.

[23] From the mere fact that individuals pursue different goals in life, the conclusion would not have followed, as 435e–436b shows, that the soul is divided into several

conception (b) is the one that determines the pattern and outcome of the remainder of the dialogue, generating the types of man that correspond to the types of city, distinguishing their goals and ways of life, as well as furnishing the grounds for proof of the tyrant's unhappiness (576b–578b; cf. 580c–581e). The transition between the two conceptions (between 439b–441c and 441d–442b) is made without fanfare. At no point does Socrates explicitly thematize this important shift. This is a clear example, then, of a rhetorical maneuver on his part. Also, the relative weighting of the two suggests that conception (a) was invented purely for the occasion (see below, section IX).

The fundamental distinction between the five types of individual in the *Republic* rests on their connection to distinct goals in life: the philosophic type aspires to knowledge, the timocratic type to preeminence (including honor), the oligarchic to wealth, the democratic to freedom, and the tyrannical to power. Given that each type of individual is also striving for happiness, these distinct aspirations entail distinct conceptions of happiness. "Happiness" (*eudaimonia*) is to the Greek way of thinking not merely a "good feeling" but a formal and, in principle, an objectifiable state of affairs: that is, the formal goal of "happiness" must be furnished with a particular content if our strivings are to be given a direction.[24] The five types of individual, then, represent five distinct conceptions of happiness, as either increase of knowledge, or preeminence and prestige, or material possessions, or the satisfaction of spontaneous moods and whims, or the exercise of power. But whereas the philosopher's conception of happiness is just and unselfish, those maintained by the four unjust types of individual are correspondingly unjust and egoistic.

The reason for this is that the goods sought by these four unjust types cannot be shared. The unjust individuals engage in a zero-sum game, in which personal advantage can be gained only at another's expense (cf. 349b–d). A man cannot be preeminent and superior unless others are inferior; one man's unlimited striving for wealth impoverishes others (e.g., 555c–d); the uninhibited freedom of the young and vigorous to satisfy their moods deprives the older

parts (see Blössner 1997, pp. 225–30). Most interpretations of this passage, however, fail to see its place in Socrates' larger argument.

[24] I offer further remarks on the Greek conception of happiness in Blössner 2002, pp. 11–27. For an English-language discussion of the issue, see Kraut 1979.

generation of their freedom and pushes them to behave in undignified ways (562e–563b); the omnipotence of one tyrant enslaves the
citizen-body (e.g., 569b–c).

Knowledge, by contrast, is a good that can be shared. Not only can
knowledge (unlike rank, wealth, freedom, and power) be shared without being lessened, but under normal circumstances it will actually
be increased by sharing. Experience of this truth, which is common
to all who teach (hence the proverb *docendo discimus*, "by teaching,
we learn"), is in the final analysis the root of Socratic dialogue. And it
is on account of this unselfish ideal of happiness that the philosopher
is also the emblematically just man, while the four defective types
represent archetypally unjust ways of life and mistaken conceptions
of happiness.

Here the connection to the overarching theme of the dialogue
becomes clear. In the context of Glaucon's and Adeimantus' demand
for a protreptic argument in favor of the just life, Socrates also brings
four significant alternatives to the just life into view. After all, the
choice that Glaucon and Adeimantus see themselves as faced with
(358b–367e) is not merely a choice between justice and injustice, but
between justice and quite distinct forms of injustice. Were Socrates
merely to demonstrate that it does not pay to become a tyrant, he
would not yet have shown that there are no alternatives to justice
at all that one should pursue. That is why he eventually fills out in
concrete detail, here in Book 8, the four types of unjust life that he
first named as worthy of mention in Book 4.[25]

In short, behind the terminology for the types of soul and behind
the very concept of soul type in the *Republic*, we find a debate over
happiness. The psychology that Plato fashioned for this debate is
original, and was evidently developed with a view to the *Republic*'s
overall argument and in particular to the analogic reasoning it contains (see above, section III). The individual types portrayed in the
Republic have nothing in common with the "characters" we find in
comedy or in Theophrastus. Their faults or weaknesses are not there
to provoke or amuse us. Even the psychological taxonomies that we
find in other dialogues of Plato, for all their many verbal echoes of
the *Republic*, are actually knit together in a different way.[26]

---

[25] See 445c, with Blössner 1997, pp. 49–55.
[26] See Blössner 1997, pp. 183ff. and 240ff.

It is a mistake, then, to combine statements in the *Republic* concerning the "tyrannical man" with statements about the young and educable tyrant who bulks large in the *Laws*. In the *Republic*, "tyrannical" designates a type of soul; in the *Laws*, it designates a political position, without regard to psychology.[27] Combining statements taken out of context on grounds of nothing more than verbal similarity, an all too common procedure in the study of Plato, would produce in this instance not insight but confusion (see below, section IX).

VI. THE CONCEPTION OF THE CITY

To bring the individual into analogy with the city, Socrates, as we have seen, sketches a "political" conception of the soul – a conception according to which forces within the soul work with or against each other in the same way as social groups do within the city. Correspondingly, he represents social classes in such a way that their characteristic traits will turn up again in the soul; otherwise, the analogy would fail to go through. This constraint poses considerable problems when it comes to the representation of political conditions in the proper sense of the word.

When the Greeks theorized about politics they distinguished a regime primarily by the number of those in its ruling class: one, few, or the entire citizenry. A secondary criterion sometimes adduced was whether the ruling class was above the law or bound by its constraints. (Aristotle's sixfold constitutional schema in the *Politics* is constructed from the combination of these two criteria.) Characteristic laws and institutions also played a role in distinguishing political systems, as did the powers and responsibilities of office holders, the manner in which they were selected, and the rights and duties of citizens.[28]

Political considerations of this sort are at best marginal to the analysis of the various types of regime that we find in the *Republic*. Laws are seldom mentioned; institutional arrangements, never.[29]

---

[27] See further Blössner 1997, pp. 147–49.

[28] See, e.g., Pindar, *Pythians* 2. 87–88; Herodotus, 3.80–82; Plato, *Rep.* 338d; Aristotle, *Politics*, 1279a–b.

[29] In the case of oligarchy, one important law is described (551a–b); otherwise, although there is mention of laws in the inferior regimes (see 548b, 550d, 555c, 556a, 563d), we learn nothing of their content (with the possible exception of 547b–c).

There is vagueness about how offices get filled. The number of rulers is deemed irrelevant to the best regime (445d–e) and even for the inferior regimes does not serve as a marker of primary importance; otherwise it would not be possible for timocracy and oligarchy to stand in sharp contrast to each other (550e) despite their both being "oligarchies" in the sense of being ruled by few. (Both timocracy and oligarchy are characterized by the rule of a privileged group, in fact by the rule of what is largely the very same group, at least at the outset, 550d–551b.) Clearly, the *Republic* conceives of its political regimes in an unorthodox fashion.

In fact the analogy would simply not have worked had Plato applied standard political criteria. In the *Republic*'s psychology, for example, each type of soul has only a single ruler – that is, one ruling soul part – at any one time; but if the number of rulers is not a distinctive criterion of soul types, then it cannot distinguish types of city either. Likewise with the other traits of Socrates' supposedly "constitutional" or "political" analyses. The soul as Socrates describes it offers no analogue for the selection of rulers, their offices and responsibilities, or for the city's legal code or institutional arrangements. Socrates' descriptions of each type of city anticipate and eliminate those aspects that cannot be mapped onto the soul. So the "constitutions" portrayed in Books 8 and 9 can hardly be the historical statements or political analyses that many scholars have made them out to be.[30]

If any further support for this claim is needed, it can be found, for example, in the fact that the most prominent of all constitutional types discussed in the ancient debate over constitutions, monarchy, does not figure in the *Republic*, at least not in its standard form. ("Philosopher-kings" are not, properly speaking, kings, because they do not exert power. Instead, they alter ways of thinking. That is why it does not matter how many of them there are: see 445d–e).[31] Also, what Plato presents to his readers with "timocracy" (a word coined for the occasion, see 545b)[32] is a constitutional type

---

[30] For a full discussion of these traditional interpretations and their internal inconsistencies, see Blössner 1997, pp. 106–51. See also Frede 1997; Annas 1999, pp. 77–78.

[31] See further Trampedach 1994, pp. 186–202; Brunt 1993, ch. 10.

[32] Unfortunately, the new punctuation of 545b7–8 in Slings' "Oxford Classical Text" of the *Republic* obscures this point.

that simply did not exist in its own right.[33] Nor do Socrates' inter-locutors treat his account of the defective political systems as an excursus into history or political theory. Rather, they leave no doubt that they see it as part of his argument for the benefits of justice (544a, 544e–545b).

Finally, semantic analysis of concepts leads to the same conclu-sion. Let us take as our starting point (as any conceptual analysis should) Plato's use of words here. The defective constitutions are introduced as four standard types of human vice (kakia, 445c–e). Socrates' purpose in bringing them up is eventually to give an account of the most unjust man and so achieve clarity on the ques-tion of whether justice pays (544a, 545a–b). They are distinguished by appeal not to different ways of organizing political power but to different arrangements of the parts of the soul (544d–e). It is on the basis of psychological rather than political data, then, that Socrates establishes his typology of political regimes.

So in 544e–545b we find three political terms (oligarchic, demo-cratic, tyrannical) ranged alongside two psychological terms (victory-loving, honor-loving – the timocratic qualities) as if they were of equivalent application. The way in which this part of the dialogue is formulated leaves the reader in no doubt that the terms "timo-cratic," "oligarchic," "democratic," and "tyrannical" are intended to sum together as the conceptual foil to the term "just." Conclusion: Socrates' descriptions of the different cities associate not political systems but varieties of injustice.

In effect, Socrates in Books 8 and 9 of the Republic is evoking vari-eties of injustice for which the Greek language had no established terms; hence he must create his own terminology. That he adapts political concepts to this purpose finds some support in the usage then current, which identified the tyrant as the extreme case of the unjust man (see, e.g., 344a–c). When the extreme case of injustice can be associated with a political concept, analogous associations with milder forms of injustice follow naturally. The analogy itself provides another, more immediate justification for his practice: for

---

[33] See further Blössner 1997, pp. 76–85, which analyzes the ingenuity and suggestive-ness with which Plato connects this nonexistent constitutional type to empirical reality, in the shape of the Cretan and Spartan regimes.

if he is already projecting the attributes of the various political systems onto the soul, why not also their names?[34]

To put these political concepts to their required use Socrates must alter their sense; but such semantic shifts are attested in practically all of the dialogues.[35] Plato sometimes draws explicit attention to those he contrives in the *Republic* (e.g., at 550c).[36] Socrates' maneuver is facilitated by the fact that concepts such as *polis* and *politeia* have greater semantic breadth than the modern terms by which they are typically rendered (e.g., "republic," "constitution"). The ancient *polis* is not merely a political community but also has important social, legal, economic, religious, and military features. Whereas the modern state is set over its citizens as a separate entity, the *polis* is nothing over and above the organized citizen body in its various dimensions. And as a result, the concept of *politeia* – a word that designates the "system" or "organization of the *polis*" – involves the citizens of a *polis* in customs and traditions, in values and norms, in patterns of education and ways of living. It is not a concept that can be reduced to its constitutional aspect. Likewise in Plato's "*Republic*" – a conventional translation that can only partially match the Greek title *Politeia* – what is in question is not the rule of law and the rights of citizens but rather the behavior and attitude proper to those citizens, their justice; and these are attributes of individuals rather than of a political system. Accordingly, when Socrates begins (from Book 9 onward) to apply the term *politeia* not only to the orderliness and organization of the city, but also to that of the soul,[37] the title of Plato's work acquires a surprising new dimension.

This semantic shift is also apparent in the content of Socrates' descriptions of the various constitutional types, not just in his use of words. Socrates begins on each occasion with familiar political considerations, but proceeds to give his concepts a new, psychological twist. (The connection to empirical reality inspires trust and

---

[34] Further, partly tactical reasons for the choice of names are discussed in Blössner 1997, pp. 201–5.

[35] This has long been recognized and has been well documented (see Classen 1959). For examples in the *Republic*, see sections II, IV, and VII of this chapter. Further examples are in Blössner 1997, pp. 258–61 and 288 n. 822.

[36] On which, see Blössner 1997, p. 190 n. 520.

[37] See 579c, 590e–591a, 591e, 605b.

facilitates the agreement of the interlocutors.) So the timocracy is at first the rule of military men (547e–548a), but is later described as domination by "the spirited element" (the *thumoeides*, 548c). Oligarchy is introduced as rule by the rich (550c–d); but what then comes in for criticism is not their wealth but their greed (e.g., 551a), which is also seen as responsible for the regime's demise (555b).[38] Similarly, democracy is at the outset "rule by the poor" (557a), but its cardinal fault, which will be its undoing (562b–c), is the excessive desire for freedom. (Notice that such a criticism would fail if directed at the political system of Plato's Athens, whose citizens were no adherents of unlimited freedom.) And with the description of tyranny the political system falls even further from sight; in its place we get an account of the various constraints and compulsions, both psychological and external, that affect the tyrant himself.

In these "constitutional" critiques, then, political considerations are no more than points of entry. The target of Socrates' critique is not the political system: he is not condemning the fact that single individuals or the entire citizen body are in charge, nor that the city is ruled by soldiers, or by the rich, or by the poor. What he condemns is the overweening pursuit of honor, unappeasable greed, the excessive impulse for freedom, the unchecked drive for power. He denounces the false values and goals of individuals, not the defects of political systems. Socrates betrays only a modest interest in the legal structure of constitutions. What in a political or historical analysis would be the nub of things is mostly peripheral to the *Republic*.

Let us note that the connection between the familiar and the novel in Socrates' treatment of political concepts is purely associative. To be sure, the desire for glory is well suited to a militaristic society, the desire for wealth to an oligarchy, the desire for freedom to a democracy, and the desire for power to the tyrant; but these attributions are not inescapable. After all, the same desires can be found in other political systems. (Socrates himself makes a point of the greed both of democratic politicians and of the tyrant: 564e–565b; 568d–e.)

Because these desires are directed toward goods that cannot be shared, they are in essence unjust (see above, section V). Only those

---

[38] This is the decisive point for the analogy: see, e.g., 554a. The semantic shift was already noted by Aristotle (*Politics* 1316a–b, on which see Blössner 1997, pp. 139–49).

who have power and influence in the city can hope to satisfy such desires. Only the powerful can realize the unjust life, a life that will inevitably bring itself into conflict with the larger community.

As delimited by Socrates' argument, a tyranny will for the most part fail to realize these goals.[39] Timocratic pleasures must elude the tyrant when each victory is attributed more to his position than to his performance – not just in the eyes of his contemporaries but in the judgment of posterity. This excludes the possibility of genuine, lasting fame. Thus, no Roman emperor ever achieved lasting honor as a worthy athlete, however many victories at Olympia he won. (See also 578a.) Nor can the tyrant enjoy the (oligarchic) pleasure of increasing his wealth – not when profligacy is imposed on him by his reputation; not when he is compelled to satisfy each of his appetites (573c–574a), to start wars (566e–567d), and to hire mercenaries to fight them (577d); not when Socrates is able to describe him as a man who must forever spend whatever resources are at hand or come his way (568d–e, 573d–574a; cf. 577e–578a). Still less can this tyrant act on his whims (see, e.g., 577d–e, 579b–c). He is clasped in a tight corset of external and internal constraints;[40] none is further than he from the democratic man's ideal of happiness. And besides, the very notion of a timocratically (oligarchically, etc.) oriented tyrant would seriously disrupt the typology according to which the timocratic man is one distinct character type, the tyrannical quite another (see section V above).[41]

Socrates' purpose in selecting distinct types of constitution is to demonstrate how egoistic desires develop if left unchecked, and what the consequences are for city and for soul. In the context of this thought-experiment, names that would otherwise stand for political systems become ciphers for mistaken ways of life, led by mistaken ideas of happiness. What Socrates gives us here is no political critique but rather a critique of four ways of life that compete for attention with the just way of life that he recommends. (At certain points in the dialogue this shift of meaning is made explicit, e.g., at 557d.)

If happiness did indeed reside in the enjoyment of goods such as honor, money, freedom, or power, then it would best be achieved

---

[39] For a different view, see Ferrari 2003, p. 82.

[40] External constraints: e.g., 565d–e, 566a, 566e–567a, 567b–c, 567d, 568d–e, 579b–c. Internal constraints: e.g., 572e–573b, 574d, 574e, 574a, 574e–575a, 575c, 577c–d.

[41] See further Blössner 1997, pp. 204ff.

where these blessings were most available. Socrates' thought-experiment provides a counterdemonstration. He imagines people to a large extent succeeding in satisfying their desires, that is, achieving at least their superficial goals, in a society that is weighted toward those goals. If happiness resided in such things as they desire, then they would have to be happy. Yet this is not the case, as Socrates shows. His descriptions bring out how the defects of the lives they have chosen prevent these people from being happy. And they are defects that result not from the failure to achieve important goals in life but from the mistaken desire to achieve those goals in the first place.

The insatiable desire of the ruling elite in a city for (supposed) goods that cannot be shared also detracts from the happiness of the city as a whole, because these goods have only limited availability. When one group cannot keep its appetite in check, goods will be taken from other, weaker groups. So for example if the elite cannot restrain its greed for wealth, instability and conflict will inevitably erupt, which over time will detract from the happiness of all citizens, including the elite itself. Within the soul, meanwhile, this mistaken sort of striving betokens "unnatural" rule by a part of the soul that is quite incapable of satisfying all the parts together, in a balanced way, attending to all the needs of the individual (see above, section III).

The *Republic*'s narrative of the decline of constitutions, then, is neither political analysis nor a thesis in the philosophy of history nor a simple historical account. It is a critique of ways of life and of the mistaken conceptions of happiness that lie behind them. Socrates shows how those who pursue selfish notions of happiness fail to achieve the happiness that is their ultimate goal, and fail to do so precisely when they succeed in achieving their superficial goals (honor, wealth, freedom, power). Thrasymachus is not wrong to believe that the selfish often become more famous, more wealthy, more powerful than the just; he is wrong to believe that these goods will truly give these people the happiness that they ultimately seek.

VII. THE FORMATION OF CITY BY SOUL

On precisely two occasions the workings of the city-soul analogy are supplemented with the claim that attributes of the city are to be traced to attributes of their inhabitants – a claim that is presented as buttressing the analogy. Only in these two passages, and nowhere else in the dialogue, is a causal relation posited between the individual who represents the analogue for the city and the individual living in that city (see above, section V). For it is the individual *in* the city who forms the city, and it is the individual *analogous* to the city whose character is argued on the basis of the city's attributes. From this one can infer only a similarity between the two individuals, not an identity.

In the first passage, Socrates claims that characteristics such as warrior-spirit, intellectualism, or materialism, which come to be ascribed to a city, inevitably derive from corresponding characteristics of the citizens of that city. And he adds: they derive from the characteristics of each individual citizen in that city (435d–436a).

Now, it is clear enough that this claim is incorrect. The courage of a city could as well be explained by reference to the courage of its soldiers alone; and Socrates himself has shortly before this explained the wisdom of the best city with reference to the wisdom of its rulers alone (428b–429a). But it is not a claim that Socrates could avoid making; for without it he would not be able to produce a model of the soul that is valid for every individual. The claim serves Socrates' purpose of introducing the three parts of the soul, thereby making the analogy possible. It is an element in the rhetoric required by the workings of the analogy (see above, sections I, II, and IV–VI).

In the second passage, Socrates proposes that civic constitutions are to be traced back to those character types that are decisive for the city (544d–e). This is a claim that can make sense only because Socrates has already shifted the meaning of the names conventionally attributed to those constitutions (above, section VI). An oligarchy in the conventional sense of the term does not require oligarchic soul types; by contrast, a materialistic city naturally presupposes materialistic citizens.

What the claim achieves is to remove an objection to the analogy that would otherwise lie close to hand. Immediately before this, Glaucon had recalled Socrates' announcement in Book 4 (445c–d) that he planned to follow discussion of the just city with a discussion of four inferior types of city – types of city to which Socrates has now given specific names (543c–544d). By the rules of the analogy, then, there would have to be the same number of soul types, that is, five in all. But how is this possible, when there are only three parts of the soul and when each type of soul is constructed on the basis of the dominance of only one of these three parts? The answer that Socrates gives in 558d–559c and 571a–572b is not one that he can anticipate here. Instead, he finesses the difficulty with an improvised argument, so that the analogy can continue to seem valid until the fuller explanation comes along.

In both places, then, the assertion of a causal relation between city and (analogous) soul serves to secure his interlocutor's belief in the validity of the analogy. For without his interlocutor's agreement Socrates could not further develop his argument within the rules of elenctic discussion. On the other hand, agreement for no apparent reason would have spoiled the realism of the conversation (see below, section IX, point 3). In both places, then, it serves Socrates' purpose to finesse rhetorically the fact that the city does of course also have attributes that in no way derive from those of its citizens. (For example, a political regime is not stable or unstable because its *citizens* are stable or unstable.)[42] For this reason it would be naïve to count these two passages as straightforward Platonic doctrine.

Even apart from this rhetorical framework, the analogy does gain some plausibility from the assertion that a city's attributes stem from the souls of its citizens. But this causal relation is not a logical precondition for the analogy.[43] This is clear enough even at the most superficial level, from the fact that the analogy has already been established before the assertion of a causal relation crops up in the text for the first time (see above, section II).

VIII. THE INFLUENCE OF CITY ON SOUL

Causal relations that run in the opposite direction, from city to soul rather than soul to city, similarly play only a subordinate role in the workings of the analogy. It is only natural, however, that they should play a more important role in Socrates' general argument; for any city will influence the souls of those who inhabit it. This happens both

---

[42] That Plato was aware of the logical truth that attributes of wholes need not derive from attributes of their components is clear, since he makes it explicit in the *Hippias Major* (300b–302b). (There is, however, some dispute over the authorship of this dialogue.)

[43] Ferrari 2003, pp. 37–53, explains this clearly. His targets are the arguments of Bernard Williams (Williams 1973) and of Jonathan Lear (Lear 1992).

by deliberate plan, through laws and educational measures, as well as in an unplanned way, through exposure to exemplary values, norms, and modes of behavior. Both types of influence are given plenty of attention in the *Republic*, with more attention falling on deliberate measures for education and upbringing in the case of the just city (education of the soldier-guardians, education of the philosophers, censorship of poetry, establishment of a civic ideology, etc.), while in the defective cities attention falls more on unplanned and sometimes unwelcome ways in which the city molds its citizens (see, e.g., 548b–c, 550e–551a, 556b–c, 563d–e, 572c). Through such influences the citizens acquire their goals in life and their individual conceptions of happiness.

The city is not only where those goals in life are acquired but also where they must be fulfilled if they are to be fulfilled anywhere. Whether fulfillment is facilitated or impeded will depend on the particular type of city. A good example of this is provided by the "career" of the potentially tyrannical man, who in the oligarchic city remains a "drone" and leads the life of the idle rich, or of a beggar, or a criminal (552b–d). In the democratic city he is a politician or a fellow-traveler (564b–565c); in the tyrannical city, a mercenary or an actual tyrant (575b–d).

Political systems based on different social values offer different opportunities for the realization of personal goals in life and personal conceptions of happiness. In his descriptions of the four defective political systems Socrates makes sure that only one kind of desire or striving is given most room for development. But if even the enormous prestige attainable in a timocracy and the correspondingly great wealth, freedom, and power attainable in an oligarchy, democracy, or tyranny fail to deliver happiness, then these objects of desire must have been the wrong goals to have (see above, section VI).

There are two ways, then, in which the city influences the happiness of its citizens: It builds the structure of their souls and their goals in life; and it either creates the conditions for reaching these goals or impedes their development.

IX. METHODOLOGY

The interpretation offered here diverges in some respects from what has for some time been the more conventional view of the *Republic*. The innovations derive, however, not from a striving for originality, but from the attempt to apply in a thoroughgoing fashion certain methodological insights that have emerged in the scholarship of recent years. These insights center on (1) the significance of the dialogue form, (2) the relevance of context to argument, and (3) consideration of the whole range of constraints that arise from the task of presenting a particular argument in a particular fictional mode.

(1) Plato never speaks for himself in the *Republic*. Each sentence of the dialogue is uttered by a fictional character. The dialogue has no preface in which the author addresses the reader in his own voice (as, for example, Aristotle and Cicero do), nor does the author appear as a speaking character in his own dialogue.

Even the habitual protagonist of the dialogues, Socrates, is not designated as an authority to be uncritically followed. His characteristic irony and claim of ignorance (e.g., 506c–d), and above all his obviously rhetorical maneuvers in argument, cause a critical distance to open between himself and the reader.[44] This is what we should expect, provided we pay attention to the fact that as a general rule the Platonic dialogues adopt a skeptical and ironic tone toward "authorities" (as opposed to arguments).[45] But it is difficult to square with the claim that Socrates functions in the *Republic* as Plato's mouthpiece, directly transmitting Plato's philosophic beliefs to the reader.

The truth of the "mouthpiece" theory cannot be conclusively shown by pointing to any particular passage of the *Republic*. Some passages, however, conclusively contradict it: those passages where Socrates is obviously adopting a rhetorical strategy or is using an argument that he (and Plato) must know to be false. There are many other reasons too to take the view that Socrates plays a more complex role in this work than that of mere proxy.[46] Nor is mouthpiece theory required to explain the striking fact that in the *Republic* Socrates does not merely ask questions but provides answers, does not merely examine and refute the claims of others but emphatically advances a claim of his own. This fundamental trait of the dialogue, which has often been found "doctrinal" or "dogmatic,"

---

[44] For examples of rhetorical strategies adopted by Plato's Socrates and criteria for identifying them, see the comprehensive account in Blössner 1997, pp. 246–88. Examples are also given in sections II, IV, and VII above. See further point 3 of the current section.

[45] See Frede 1992; also Heitsch 1997, pp. 248–57 (and 237–41).

[46] See Blössner 1998a.

in fact derives naturally and necessarily from the crucial relation between the character Socrates (who is the paradigmatic just man, whose whole life *shows* his preference for justice) and the fact that examining the value of justice means in itself to *decide* about the goals of one's own life (cf., e.g., 545a–b). Since the subject matter is relevant for life, Socrates has given an answer long before: his life *is* the answer. But if Socrates already has a definite answer, Plato could not make him "ask questions" concerning this point; he only could give him an *argument* for his conviction that justice pays. The "dogmatic" trait of the dialogue, then, is required by the relation between subject and character. [47] (And an analogous explanation seems to me possible for other dialogues where interpreters meant to find "Plato's mouthpiece.")

It is significant that Socrates clearly marks his own argument as an improvisation (e.g., 368a–c). Nowhere does either the author or his fictional character make a claim of settled truth for the argument of the *Republic*. It is Plato's interpreters who have imposed the idea that Socrates is transmitting fixed "doctrine".

The text of the *Republic* offers no support, then, for the claim that Plato uses it to put his own views before the readers. What Plato is doing is rather to stage a dramatic discussion in which the character Socrates fictionally interacts with various partners in various ways, yet always in ways that are appropriate to the particular addressee and the particular situation. The type of discourse in which Socrates engages in the *Republic* is precisely the one that the *Phaedrus* (271a–278b, esp. 270b–272b) classifies as the communicative ideal. The reader is not the addressee but the witness of this discourse. What Plato intends to show him is not identical with what Socrates says to his interlocutor. Rather, Plato's staging transforms philosophic assertion into a dialogic "play," whose meaning results not just from the sum total of the statements contained in the text, but also from the drama in which those who utter these statements are involved.[48]

There are just two avenues of interpretation open to the reader of the *Republic* who pays attention to the text in all its complexity: He can confine his interpretation strictly to the level of the fictional

---

[47] See Blössner 1997, pp. 32–45.

[48] On this point there is agreement between current Platonic scholarship (e.g., Press 2000) and modern literary theories of dialogue (e.g., Hempfer 2002).

characters and to what they have to say. In that case what Plato himself thought or intended would be no part of his account. Alternatively, he can attempt to reconstruct Plato's views and convictions on the basis of the dialogic drama, by asking the following two questions: First, what must Plato have known in order to be able to present precisely those facts and problems that are actually presented in his text, in precisely the way that they are presented? And second, what is Plato likely to have intended by staging the dialogue in precisely this way and no other? (The second question cannot lead to conclusions as secure as can the first.) The goal of such a reconstruction would be to test various possibilities and so arrive at those assumptions that best explain why Plato wrote what he did.

(2) It is a basic rule of literary hermeneutics that statements can be properly understood only in their context. But when it comes to the interpretation of Plato's dialogues, the rule is often ignored.

From Book 2 of the *Republic* onward, Socrates develops a coherent and connected argument directed at promoting a conviction in his interlocutors, the conviction that it is indeed true that "justice pays." Much of what is subsequently said in the conversation on the subject of city and soul, education and poetry, metaphysics, as well as on other topics, is not a mere expression of Plato's opinion, then, but a component of a larger argument. In other words, what is said on these topics is directed at certain argumentative goals that may be presumed to determine the content of what is said in fundamental ways; and it is also directed at the interlocutor's level of understanding, since it is he whom the argument must convince, and convince in such a way that the argument continues to look realistic. But given that the argument develops and the level of the interlocutor's understanding varies as the dialogue progresses, a correct understanding of what is said in the dialogue must attend at every point to the context of these utterances and to the argumentative goal at which they aim.

Often enough, however, this is not in fact the practice of Plato's interpreters; in many cases context and the argumentative purpose of Socrates' statements are quite ignored. Assertions of the fictional character Socrates are taken out of context and read as if they were communications from the author, and intended to apply not just to a particular argument and a particular level of understanding, but quite generally. In such interpretations it does not matter whether an assertion comes from Book 2 or Book 9, or even from another dialogue; what level of understanding it is adapted to fit; what argumentative goal is serves in context. It is as if every assertion were more or less of equal value, including even those that Socrates makes only provisionally and later explicitly takes back (e.g., 419b–421a vs. 465e–466b).[49] Occasionally, the approach that isolates assertions from context will go beyond local misunderstandings (which are frequent)[50] and obscure one's view of entire sections of the dialogue. An example would be the misinterpretation of Books 8 and 9 as a political or historical critique. (See Section VI above). The psychology propounded in 435e–441c would be another.[51]

The design of the dialogue gives the impression that Plato himself also thinks it important that the reader should pay attention to the Socratic argument as a connected whole. There are about fifty places in the *Republic* where the interlocutor (and thereby the reader) is reminded of how what is currently being said relates to other parts of the dialogue. Repeatedly, the goal and structure of the whole argument on behalf of justice comes explicitly to the fore.[52] Plato could scarcely signal more clearly that everything being said is being said as part of an organic and purposeful whole. Readers who come to their understanding of the dialogue through excerpts or "key passages," however, are overlooking these indications.

(3) When an author sets himself goals, he is implicitly also going to make constraints for himself. These constraints will arise, for example, from the conventions of his chosen genre (consider, in Plato's case, his choice of the elenctic dialogue, on which more below); or from the readers' expectations and (restricted) knowledge, which the author tries to meet and to which he adapts; or they may be logical constraints of argument. We must take them all into account if we are to measure the author's room for maneuver and to recognize or reconstruct (point 1, above) the intentions with which he framed his work.

[49] More examples in Blössner 1997, pp. 261–64, 284–88.
[50] Examples in Blössner 1997, pp. 8–10.
[51] See further Blössner 1998b.
[52] E.g., 357b–368c (esp. 367a–e), 368c–369b, 371e–372a, 372d-e, 374e–375a, 376c–e, 392c, 399e, 403c, 412b–c, 414a–c, 427c–428a, 434d–435d, 444a–449b, 450c–451c, 457b–458b, 461e–462a, 471c–473b, 473c, 544a, 545a–c, 545d, 547a, 547c, 548c, 548d, 549b–c, 550b–d, 551b–c, 552e–553a, 553e–554a, 555b, 557a–b, 558c, 558d, 559d, 561a, 562a, 566d, 569a, 571a, 573c, 576b–c, 577c, 580a–d, 583b–c, 588b, 612a–e.

We have seen such constraints in action when examining how the workings of the analogy determined the particular ways in which city and soul were represented (above, sections V and VI). Also, the often remarked "doctrinal" quality of the *Republic* can be interpreted instead as a constraint for the author. Consider this too: there can be no question that Socrates must achieve his argumentative goal. It would be unthinkable that Thrasymachus' position should triumph in the end; unthinkable that Socrates should give up on the task of providing young men with the argument in favor of the just life that they so urgently request of him.

To this list of constraints we must add the rules of the special "elenctic" type of conversation that Socrates uses, a type of conversation in which the argument needs to be convincing not just in the end but also at each step along the way. Unlike the protagonists of a Ciceronian dialogue, for example, Socrates gives no speeches whose plausibility is only discussed after the speech has been delivered; instead, he is constantly assuring himself of his interlocutor's agreement.

At 347e–348b there is an acknowledgment within our text that this is the genre of conversation in which Socrates is engaged, and of how it differs from the "antilogical" type of dialogue (based on speeches pro and con).[53] In such a conversation, Socrates could not move forward in his argument were his interlocutors not in agreement with each step. (Passages such as 372c–d or 449b–451a illustrate this point.) If the argument demands that a certain step should follow next, but the real reasons for this step cannot be given (e.g., because of the currently restricted level of knowledge of either the interlocutor or the reader or both), and if, further, the conversation is intended to seem realistic, then a constraint results. It may be that a persuasive strategy must take the place of an explanation that the interlocutor (and the reader) would not properly be able to understand. (Examples have been given above in sections I, II, IV, and VII, and their number might easily be increased.)[54]

Remarkably, many of these passages not only contain rhetorical ploys, but also are scripted in a way that makes the arbitrary and

---

[53] Cf. Stemmer 1992, pp. 124–27; also Blössner 1997, pp. 251–56.

[54] At one point Socrates' tricky manner of leading discussion is made the object of express criticism: 487b–c.

fallacious elements of Socrates' argument leap to the eye – at least, to the eye of the viewer who does not insist on treating Plato's text as authoritative on its surface and on seeking to protect it from all critique. If we suppose Plato to have been of the opinion that a text that "offends" to some degree is especially apt to evoke critical thought (cf. 523a–524d), then we can appreciate how the author would have taken what was for him a standing constraint – Socrates' argument must succeed – and brilliantly turned this constraint to didactic advantage.

This striking fact about the design of the dialogue – that not only does Socrates' argument indeed contain fallacious elements, but the reader is also given the hints required to see them – also underlines the message that Socrates' argument on behalf of the just life is a provisional one, for which neither the author nor his character claim definitive truth. As long as Socrates does not claim to have certain *knowledge* of the Form of the Good, he is not able to (and, in fact, does not) claim such knowledge about whether it is really good to be just – despite the fact that he is deeply convinced of it. (But to be convinced of something is not to know it.) That is the deeper reason for the fact that the Socratic argument is (and can only be) provisional.

But this provisionality is not only a tricky invention found in a literary text. It reflects the real condition of human life. Not being philosopher-kings, who alone would *know* the Good, real people make their decisions on the basis of beliefs and convictions about what is good – without really knowing whether or not it *is* good.

Given this fact, we can conclude that the complexity of Plato's text reflects the complexity of human life. The *Republic* does not pretend to contain or to give final truths, and it does not intend to absolve the reader from the effort to make his *own* decision and to make his own sense of his life. This is the surprising message to which the author's use of Socratic rhetoric in the *Republic* amounts in the end.

X. SUMMARY

The analogical reasoning that takes us from city to soul is introduced in Book 2 with reference to a single attribute of both, namely, justice (section I), but in Book 4 the reference is significantly broadened.

Where before there was just the assumption that city and soul are alike on a single point, now a firm assertion emerges that they are entirely analogous in their structure and in their operations. (See section II.)

This larger claim enables Socrates to develop a new model of the soul. Familiar traits of earlier Greek psychology are suggestively woven into his tapestry, as are well-chosen snippets of "empirical evidence." But despite this, Socrates' model of the soul is cut to fit the cloth of the larger argument that he develops in the *Republic*. (See section III.)

The analogy between city and soul gives rise to a rich variety of metaphors that render the portrait of the soul more vivid and colorful. Indeed, the analogy provides a suitable terminology for many processes and states of the soul for which the Greek language had up to that point lacked words. The parallelism in how city and soul develop gives rise to contrapuntal contrasts of great elegance and poetic power. But throughout, Socrates carefully omits to mention that the analogy has its limits. (See section IV.)

The psychology that the analogy supports serves the *Republic's* larger argument about happiness. The parts of the soul and the different character types represent different conceptions of happiness, several of which are consonant with justice, while others, those that strive for goods that cannot be shared, are fundamentally unjust and selfish. Socrates presents us with four main types of selfish desire and attempts to demonstrate that the selfish person most completely loses his chance of happiness when he most fully attains the goal for which he strives. (See section V.)

Just as there are constraints on how the soul can be represented, so too with the different political constitutions. These had to be described in such a way as to enable the mapping onto corresponding types of soul, whose characteristics would then support the larger argument on which Socrates is engaged. And this constraint suffices to show that Books 8 and 9 cannot amount to the political analysis that some have taken them to be, nor a constitutional critique, nor a contribution to the philosophy of history. Conceptual analysis helps to confirm this claim, showing how the political terminology ("democratic," "tyrannical," etc.) acquires a quite new meaning in the context of Socrates' argument. (See section VI.)

In strict logic, the analogy operates independently of the assumption that the qualities of the city derive from those of its citizens. Nevertheless, this assumption has its rhetorical purpose within the elenctic conversation (section VII). Moreover, it is important for Socrates' argument that the city shapes the souls of its citizens and their conceptions of happiness and that it creates the framework within which those conceptions are either easier or more difficult to realize (section VIII).

To the extent that this interpretation differs from the established view of the city-soul analogy, that would be because it cleaves to some relatively simple maxims of interpretation more closely than is the general practice. Biographical approaches that would directly convert Socrates' critique of democracy in Book 8 into an undemocratic stance of Plato's ignore the distinction between author and fictional character. Precise attention to the Greek terminology also helps to clarify the situation here. Close attention to the principle that statements are to be understood in relation to their context restores whole sections of the dialogue to their proper place in Socrates' argument – sections that have often been interpreted in isolation or used as bricks in the construction of "Plato's psychology" or "Plato's political theory." New light can be shed on fundamental traits of the dialogue, including its supposedly doctrinal character, if we attend to the constraints that imposed themselves on its author when he wrote the dialogue – constraints arising partly from his subject, partly from his argumentative goals and from the logic required to reach them, and partly from the rules of elenctic discussion. Even Socrates' most rhetorical maneuvers, which an older, more positivistic approach to the text tends to ignore, can acquire in this way a meaning that is at once understandable and surprisingly philosophic. (See section IX.)

Among the constraints that Plato had to master are those thrown up by the analogy itself: the transformation of one "constitution" into another had to be consistently described on two levels at once, not just political but also psychological. In addition, familiar concepts from Homeric psychology as well as empirical data needed to be incorporated in order to bolster the analogy's plausibility. And the whole arrangement had to be so constructed as to allow Socrates to employ it to demonstrate the truth of his fundamental contention about justice. Only if we recognize the amazing complexity of this task can we appreciate the bravura performance that Plato gives in acquitting himself of it. If instead we simplify things by reducing the context-bound statements of fictional characters to straightforward declarations by their author, not only will we fail to understand the goals and the task that Plato set himself, we will also seriously undervalue his achievement as a writer.

WORKS CITED

Andersson, T. J. 1971. *Polis and Psyche: A Motif in Plato's* Republic. Stockholm.

Annas, J. 1999. *Platonic Ethics, Old and New*. Ithaca, N.Y.

Blössner, N. 1997. *Dialogform und Argument: Studien zu Platons "Politeia."* Stuttgart.

Blössner, N. 1998a. "Dialogautor und Dialogfigur. Überlegungen zum Status sokratischer Aussagen in der *'Politeia.'*" In *The* Republic *and the* Laws *of* Plato: *Proceedings of the First Symposium Platonicum Pragense*, ed. A. Havlíček and F. Karfík (Prague).

Blössner, N. 1998b. "Kontextbezogenheit und argumentative Funktion. Methodische Anmerkungen zur Platondeutung." *Hermes* 126: 189–201.

Blössner, N. 1999. *Musenrede und geometrische Zahl. Ein Beispiel platonischer Dialoggestaltung.* Stuttgart.

Blössner, N. 2001. "Sokrates und sein Glück, oder: Weshalb hat Platon den 'Phaidon' geschrieben?" In *Proceedings of the Second Symposium Platonicum Pragense*, ed. A. Havlíček and F. Karfík (Prague).

Blössner, N. 2002. *"The Encomium of a Noble Man": Anmerkungen zu Eric Voegelins Politeia-Interpretation.* Occasional Papers des Eric-Voegelin-Archivs an der Universität München XXI.

Brunt, P. A. 1993. *Studies in Greek History and Thought.* Oxford. Ch. 10: "Plato's Academy and Politics."

Classen, C. J. 1959. *Sprachliche Deutung als Triebkraft platonischen Philosophierens.* Munich.

Ferrari, G. R. F. 2003. *City and Soul in Plato's* Republic. Sankt Augustin. Rpt. Chicago 2005.

Frede, D. 1997. "Die ungerechten Verfassungen und die ihnen entsprechenden Menschen (Buch VIII 543a-IX 576b)." In Höffe 1997.

Frede, M. 1992. "Plato's Arguments and the Dialogue Form." In *Methods of Interpreting Plato and His Dialogues*, ed. J. C. Klagge and N. D. Smith, *Oxford Studies in Ancient Philosophy* supplementary vol. (Oxford).

Heitsch, E. 1997. *Platon:* Phaidros. *Übersetzung und Kommentar.* Göttingen.

Hempfer, K. W. 2002. "Lektüren von Dialogen." In *Möglichkeiten des Dialogs*, ed. K. W. Hempfer (Stuttgart).

Höffe, O., ed. 1997. *Platon:* Politeia. Berlin.

Irwin, T. 1977. *Plato's Moral Theory: The Early and Middle Dialogues.* Oxford.

Klosko, G. 1988. "The 'Rule' of Reason in Plato's Psychology." *History of Philosophy Quarterly* 5: 341–56.

Kraut, R. 1973. "Reason and Justice in Plato's *Republic.*" In Lee 1973.

Kraut, R. 1979. "Two Conceptions of Happiness." *Philosophical Review* 88: 167–97.

Lear, J. 1992. "Inside and Outside the *Republic.*" *Phronesis* 37: 184–215. Rpt. in J. Lear, *Open Minded: Working Out the Logic of the Soul* (Cambridge, Mass., 1998), and in *Essays on Plato's Psychology*, ed. E. Wagner (Lanham, Md., 2001).

Lee, E. N., A. P. D. Mourelatos, and R. M. Rorty, eds. 1973. *Exegesis and Argument. Phronesis* supplementary vol. 1. Assen.

Press, G. A., ed. 2000. *Who Speaks for Plato? Studies in Platonic Anonymity.* Lanham, Md.

Stemmer, P. 1988. "Der Grundriss der platonischen Ethik." *Zeitschrift für Philosophische Forschung* 42: 529–69.

Stemmer, P. 1992. *Platons Dialektik. Die frühen und mittleren Dialoge.* Berlin.

Stemmer, P. 1998. "Tugend." In *Historisches Wörterbuch der Philosophie*, ed. J. Ritter and K. Gründer, vol. 10: 1532–48. Basel.

Trampedach, K. 1994. *Platon, die Akademie und die zeitgenössische Politik.* Stuttgart.

Weinert, F. E., C. F. Graumann, H. Heckhausen, and M. Hofer, eds. 1947. *Fischer Funk-Kolleg Pädagogische Psychologie*, vol. 1. Frankfurt.

Williams, B. A. O. 1973. "The Analogy of City and Soul in Plato's *Republic.*" In Lee 1973. Rpt. in *Plato 2: Ethics, Politics, Religion and the Soul*, ed. G. Fine (Oxford, 1999); in *Essays on Plato's Psychology*, ed. E. Wagner (Lanham, Md., 2001); and in B. A. O. Williams, *The Sense of the Past: Essays in the History of Philosophy* (Princeton, 2006).

14 The Unhappy Tyrant and the Craft of Inner Rule

I

At the antipodes of Plato's account of virtue stand the just and the tyrannical souls. The former, of course, is ruled by reason endowed with wisdom; and the latter is ruled by a kind of *erōs*, which we will call erotic passion. The point of the contrast is to have a better understanding of the just soul. First, however, we need an understanding of the tyrannical. The tyrannical soul is the last in a declining series, from the philosophical through the timocratic, oligarchic, and democratic souls. At last, the tyrannical soul is the culmination of pathology in the appetitive part of the soul, the *epithumētikon*. To explain the various maladies arising in the appetitive part, Socrates introduces a generous variety of new kinds of appetites. In Book 8, he says the appetitive part has both necessary and unnecessary appetites (558d–559b). Using these notions, he explains the oligarchic and the democratic souls. In Book 9, Socrates introduces two more refinements in order to explain the tyrannical soul. First are the outlaw appetites, a subdivision of the unnecessary appetites (571b–d). Second is the erotic passion, itself a particularly intense sort of *erōs* (572e–573a). As there is a degradation in the kinds of civic rule, from oligarchy through democracy to tyranny, so there is a degradation in the forms of psychic rule associated with these various types of appetites. To understand the rule of erotic passion, we need to begin with the distinction between necessary and unnecessary appetites.

The first thing to understand about the role that these two types of appetites play in Socrates' story is that they are dispositions. We recognize a difference between my desire for this cup of cold water – an occurrence, even if not expressed in behavior – and my appetite for chocolate – a disposition. In English, the word "desire" seems to cover both occurrence and disposition. I can refer to my desire for this particular glass of wine and my desire for wine. My desire for this glass of wine might have sprung up when I spotted it on the table; my desire for wine is longstanding and is expressed in such occurrences as the latter. By contrast, it sounds a little odd to talk about my appetite for this particular glass of wine. However, I can talk about my appetite for wine and describe how long I have had it and how it has changed. The Greek word *epithumia* is translated both as desire and as appetite; but we need to be aware of the difference.

The idea that appetites are dispositions appears in the account of the oligarchic man in Book 8. This sort of person indulges the necessary appetites; he does not indulge the spendthrift appetites but enslaves them (554a). Necessary appetites are necessary because satisfying them allows us to live and is beneficial for health (558d–e).[1] When Socrates gives as examples the appetites for bread and relishes (559a–b), we are reminded of the fare in the simple city, the city of pigs: bread, barley cakes, and moderate amounts of wine. Relishes include salt, cheese, and olives (372c). Unnecessary appetites, then, are such that one can get rid of them, if one is trained from a young age. Moreover, dwelling in the soul, they do no good and some of them are harmful (559a). Since they are appetites for things beyond simple fare, one thinks of all the delicacies that characterize banqueting in the luxurious city: couches, tables, courtesans, myrrh, incense, and pastries (373a). In fact, back in Book 8, Socrates adds to this assessment when he says that they are not only harmful for the body but also harmful for the soul in respect of moderation and sound judgment (559b).

There is another dimension to the contrast between necessary and unnecessary appetites that will be important for understanding the unhappy tyrant. Socrates says that necessary appetites are profitable because they are useful for functioning. His example is the appetite to eat just up to the point of health and well-being (559a–c). The description means that the satisfaction of this appetite has an internal limit. It is not that one eats to a certain point and decides to

---

[1] I here adopt James Adam's reading of this disputed passage. See Adam 1963 [1902], vol. 2, p. 239.

quit; rather, the appetite itself is calibrated to be satisfied at a certain point. Still, it is not necessary to assume that the appetite aims at health or well-being, only that the point at which it is satisfied is consistent with health and well-being. Later, Socrates will characterize such general appetites as hunger and thirst as emptinesses (585a–b). They naturally seek to be filled. Empty they are painful; filled they are in a neutral or peaceful state (583c). Necessary appetites seem to build on this description; they are calibrated to seek the filling up of hunger or thirst. However, unnecessary appetites seem not to fit this description. They consume whatever is available because they are not just hunger or thirst but desires for unnecessary things. What counts as filling them up is not clear. So they have a tendency to become more and more demanding. Finally, as we shall see, some of these appetites become insatiable.

We can see, then, why the unnecessary appetites are called spendthrift. Socrates is comparing them to those people in the oligarchic city who spend whatever is available and make no contribution. Once reduced to poverty, these men are like drones in the beehive. Drone bees are either winged or wingless; the wingless may or may not have stingers. In the city, the wingless drone-like men are beggars or evildoers (552b–d). The sinister and lawless character of the latter is represented by their having stingers. Socrates recalls these drone-like men when he introduces a new kind of unnecessary appetite. He says that the drone-like appetites of the beggarly and evildoing variety arise in the oligarchic man because of his lack of education. However, he controls (katechomenas) them by force because of his concern for money (554b–c). So this oligarchic man has an appetite for criminal acts; if he could avoid getting caught, he would just as soon acquire money by stealing as by honest labor. Usually repressed, these evildoing appetites will show themselves in his dealings with orphans where he will have the opportunity to commit injustice. In other circumstances, when he must preserve the appearance of honesty, the oligarchic man restrains the bad appetites by force, not by persuading that it is not better to do something evil nor by taming them through reason, but through necessity and fear, trembling for his possessions.[2] Again, when it comes to spending

---

[2] This characterization suggests that it is possible to persuade these appetites and to tame them by reason. Of course, the oligarchic man lacks the education that

the money of others, his drone-like, spendthrift appetites will show themselves (554c–d). Finally, he avoids those expenditures that provide public honor because he is afraid of arousing the spendthrift appetites (555a).

Now we can see how necessary and unnecessary appetites are dispositions. In Book 4 Socrates characterizes the appetite of thirst as in itself neither for hot nor for cold drink; something like cold weather has to be added to determine it to be thirst for hot drink (437d–e). Of greater significance for the moral psychology of the *Republic*, in themselves appetites are not for what is beneficial – nor, by implication, for what is harmful (438a). However, in Book 8 we have appetites that are beneficial and appetites that are harmful. So there must be an assumption at work that distinguishes between what is said about appetites in Book 4 and in Book 8. The distinction seems to be that in Book 4 Socrates is talking about the basic appetites for food and drink; in Book 8 he is talking about the different ways these appetites are expressed as dispositions or tendencies to seek more specific kinds of food and drink. Roughly, necessary appetites are good habits and unnecessary appetites are risky or bad habits. However, necessary appetites are not intentional desires for what is beneficial for the body. Socrates says that it is their satisfaction that is beneficial. So, it is sufficient for Socrates' purpose that the necessary appetites are dispositions to seek what turns out to be beneficial. Something analogous holds for the unnecessary appetites. When he says that, dwelling in the soul, they are harmful, he is referring to the consequences of having these appetites. Thus, these appetites seek what each is an appetite for; it is the job of reason to deal with what is beneficial and harmful.

Neither type of appetite is an episodic desire simply determined by circumstance – like the thirst for hot drink. Each is a reliable disposition to go after specific kinds of things. When Socrates says that the oligarchic man is afraid of arousing the spendthrift appetites, he means that the oligarchic man is afraid of having a standing appetite

---

would provide him with the arguments and reasoning that would persuade and tame appetites. Besides, no one can persuade evildoing appetites that it is better not to do evil. By definition they are appetites for doing evil. So, in addition, the oligarchic man does not persuade his appetites and tame them by reason because he has the wrong kind of appetites. Thus, Socrates suggests that there are other kinds of appetites that can be persuaded.

that will waste money. What wastes money is not the occasional desire for pastry but the pastry-eating disposition. He is worrying about the kind of appetite that makes one look for pastry shops, plan on buying pastries, and daydream about pastries. Along with the idea of appetites as dispositions, Socrates also introduces what we might call repression. The oligarchic man must deal with these dispositions that, if allowed free rein, would waste money. He must keep them from expressing themselves, although they are still present, ready to do so if given the chance. So, the very phenomenon of repression reflects that these appetites are dispositions. The oligarchic man has a tendency to steal that expresses itself in criminal acts when he is not afraid of being caught. He also has an appetite for expensive delicacies that expresses itself if someone else is paying. A source of behavior, these dispositions are quasi-agents in the soul. In turn, they pose a risk of taking over.

Socrates' story about the liberation of the unnecessary appetites backs up this idea. When the son of an oligarchic father falls in with a flashy and exotic crowd that help him discover the delights of the unnecessary appetites, his father reclaims the youth – for a while. But the damage has been done (559a–560a). Secretly indulging the forbidden appetites, the youth discovers he has no good reasons for resisting a life of sensuality. His lack of education means that he is susceptible to other kinds of beliefs – at once bold and false – that purge his soul of the oligarchic "virtues." He comes to believe that a sense of shame is stupidity, that self-control is lack of manliness, and that measuredness and orderly expenditure are boorishness and lack of freedom. In the next phase, the oligarchic habits are replaced by the opposite vices. Again, the bold and false beliefs reorient the youth as they lead into his soul's acropolis, brightly crowned and accompanied by a chorus: arrogance, lack of control, dissoluteness, and shamelessness. All the while, they praise them, calling arrogance cultivation, lack of control freedom, dissoluteness magnificence, and shamelessness manliness (560a–561a). His reason now filled with such opinions, the youth believes that, for example, dismissing the opinions of his father and even looking down on him as a miser should not be described as arrogance since that name implies something objectionable. Rather, acting in these ways shows a praiseworthy attitude – cultivation, a kind of larger view of the world and the way it works. In this way, these beliefs have liberated the unnecessary appetites in the youth's soul and put aside the upbringing in the necessary appetites.

There are two periods in the life of the democratic man. The first, youthful phase just described is also characterized as bacchic, tumultuous, and in some sense abandoned to the vices introduced from without (561a–b). In Book 9 Socrates says the youth is led to every form of outrageous behavior and lawlessness (572c–e). However, in both Books 8 and 9, there is a second phase, clearly distinct from the first. While the second is marked by equality among appetites, the first is imbalanced toward the excessive. There is, so to speak, a revolutionary era and a postrevolutionary era. Still, the former lasts for some time, until this person grows older and the tumult subsides – as we shall see.

Two features are striking about the account of the youthful phase. First, the liberation of the unnecessary appetites leads to their being dominant in the soul. Socrates has said the vices have taken over the acropolis of his soul. Although they are not the only appetites that he satisfies, they are the focus of his life. Second, their taking over is the effect of his adopting certain beliefs. These two features might seem to be contingencies in the story that Socrates is telling. While in his story the unnecessary appetites come to dominate, it is not clear that they have to. It seems possible to have another story in which the oligarchic youth develops some bad habits that clash with his basic oligarchic nature. In this story, the youth does not adopt another set of beliefs that justify the unnecessary appetites taking over in the soul. Rather, having these appetites just flies in the face of his oligarchic beliefs. Even though he believes that measured expenditure is the best policy, he is capable of spending sprees that just conflict with his beliefs.

While this second story is possible, it is not the one Socrates tells. We can understand the difference between the two stories if we recognize that Socrates' is about character formation or a kind of constitution in the soul (cf. 590e–591a; 591e). Having a certain character or constitution implies having not just dispositions but also beliefs about the value of having those dispositions.[3] In Socrates' story, the false and bold beliefs are necessary and sufficient for having the kind of character in which the unnecessary appetites rule. They are

---

[3] Cf. Irwin 1995, pp. 284–87.

necessary because they purge the soul of the oligarchic "virtues." Unless this young man comes to reject the oligarchic "virtues" of shame, self-control, and measuredness in expenditure, the unnecessary appetites cannot displace the rule of necessary appetites. Once the oligarchic "virtues" are purged, then the false and bold beliefs are sufficient for establishing the kind of character in which the unnecessary appetites rule over and subordinate the rest of the soul. In Socrates' story, when the youth believes that, for example, dissoluteness is magnificence, then the unnecessary appetites take over in his life through the vices of arrogance, lack of control, dissoluteness, and shamelessness. For this constellation of vices to be one's character, he must believe that arrogance is cultivation, and the rest.

But then this excessive phase is righted by another change in his beliefs. Socrates says that if the youth is fortunate and not too far gone in bacchic frenzy, he will mature into a more balanced way of living. Then a kind of equality of pleasures sets in and rule in the soul is passed around as it falls out, as though by lot. Each kind of pleasure rules until it is sated (561a–b). Of more importance, there is a corresponding change in this man's thinking. He will accept no opinion as true that holds that some pleasures come from good and fine appetites and others from bad, or that some should be fostered and honored and others restrained and enslaved. Denying all such opinions, he claims all these appetites are the same and should be honored equally. There is even room for the pleasures of philosophy, to some extent at least (561b–d).

These passages, then, are a suggestive sketch of the way in which someone's character is formed.[4] In Socrates' account, having a character entails an integration of appetitive dispositions and beliefs about having those dispositions. In the democratic soul, in both of its phases, which appetites dominate or how appetites share in dominating depends on an ideology, a justification for the arrangement. Of course, one might object that any arrangement of appetites, with

---

[4] Cf. Annas 1999, p. 129: "No adequate account of the progress from virtue to vice can be produced just by citing dominance of one or another part of the soul; the progress looks more like a person making a series of increasingly catastrophic decisions as to which kinds of motivation to prefer." My interpretation goes beyond the notion of "kinds of motivation" to that of character types.

or without an ideology, should count as a character type. Socrates, however, seems to think that true character types – or, anyway, the clear types he is interested in – incorporate a view about the appropriateness of the different types of appetitive rule. In its way, this account mirrors the character formation of the philosopher, whose highly theoretical knowledge serves as the justification for the way his soul is arranged (500b8–c7). Of course, the democratic man, in both of his phases, has no knowledge to justify his psychological profile; he has only beliefs. And while his appetites and beliefs are integrated, the falsity of the latter has a price that the philosopher does not have to pay.[5]

While the false and bold beliefs are necessary and sufficient for the character type in which the unnecessary appetites rule, what they cannot guarantee, apparently, is the permanence of that rule. In his youth, the bold and false beliefs backed up the rule of the unnecessary appetites; now his new beliefs about the equality of appetites back up his variegated life of extremes. Still, for all of his inconstancy, the democratic man has a kind of ideology about his life. His life is not just a confused welter of competing appetites.[6] He holds fundamental beliefs that justify the way he lives. Of course, like the false and bold beliefs, they do not appear to be the product of systematic thought. In fact, they may be nothing more than rationalization for his life of extremes. But at least they show some attempt to conceive of his life from a general perspective and an attempt to present it to himself in a positive light. Even the democratic man has addressed the issue, to some extent, of what sort of person he wants to be.

---

[5] Christopher Gill makes a distinction between the prereflective and postreflective virtuous person in the *Republic*. The former has true beliefs about virtue but not knowledge. See Gill 1996, p. 200. Following this analysis, we could say the vicious person has false beliefs about virtue. Where these beliefs come from is not clear. In the case of the democratic youth they seem to be the sort of superficial opinions, urged by bad companions, that an empty-headed person would be susceptible to adopting without much critical thinking (559b).

[6] Cf. Scott 2000, pp. 29–34. While the democratic man's view of his life is not based on a full-scale rational process, still it is based on beliefs, however poorly acquired. So his life is not *just* a random series, or jumble, of desires. Reason still has a job – foreshortened and somewhat pathetic – to offer justification for a life in which the strongest desires dominate in turn. The role of reason in the soul is not totally lost but rather debased.

II

The figure of the tyrant haunts the *Republic*. Throughout, he is the foil for the just ruler. From the moment that Thrasymachus introduces the notion that justice is the advantage of the stronger, the tyrant is always threatening to make an appearance (338c). Then Thrasymachus says the most thoroughly unjust are those who subject cities and peoples to themselves (348d). These hints recall other occurrences of the tyrannical figure in the *Gorgias*. Polus lovingly describes the nefarious deeds of Archelaus of Macedonia (471a–d) to illustrate the idea that unimpeded power is obviously and clearly happiness. However, it is Callicles who adds a dimension to the idea of the tyrant that sheds light on the tyrant in *Republic* 9. Having claimed that it is right by nature for the better to have the advantage of the worse and the most powerful of the least powerful (483d), Callicles tries to counter Socrates' attempts at refutation by refining his idea of the powerful or the strong. He finally says that the stronger are those who are intelligent and brave about the affairs of the city; and they should rule (491c–d). To get Callicles to be more candid, Socrates asks the pregnant question: should these people rule over themselves? He is, of course, referring to self-control or moderation. This carefully chosen question provokes Callicles into a frank reply. The one who wields this political power will lead a life of sensuality. He will allow his appetites to be as great as possible and not discipline them. He will be able to serve them, as great as they are, through his intelligence and bravery and to fill up the appetite with what it needs. Finally, luxury, lack of discipline, and freedom – if they are backed up by force – are virtue and happiness (491d–492c).

However, we should not think of the tyrant as simply devoted to bodily appetites.[7] The tyrant is one who cultivates whichever kind of appetites he wants. The basic point is that, with respect to those appetites, he brooks no opposition; his pleasures come from his grandly satisfying them. Thus, Callicles has linked political power and sensuality in a remarkable way. Unimpeded rule in the city is the means to lead a truly unimpeded life of extravagant indulgence of appetites. This figure in the *Gorgias* is reflected in the image of

---

[7] Cf. Rudebusch 1999, p. 37.

the tyrant in *Republic* 9. The latter is an unbridled sensualist who comes to exercise tyrannical rule in the city; tyrannical rule is the full flowering of the tyrannical appetite in his own soul. To explain this tyranny, Socrates introduces two new kinds of appetites: the outlaw appetites and a kind of erotic obsession.

He begins Book 9 by saying that the idea of the unnecessary appetites needs to be refined. Within this category, we find the outlaw appetites. We are all probably born with these outlaw appetites, though in some these appetites are disciplined by law and the better appetites along with reason so that they are altogether rooted out or remain few in number and weak. In others, these appetites are strong and numerous. These outlaw appetites are awakened while we sleep. When reason, which tames and rules, is asleep, the wild and beastlike part, filled with food and strong drink, springs up, repelling sleep, and seeks to go forth and satisfy itself according to its nature. As though freed from all shame and sound judgment, it will dare to do all manner of things. It will not shrink from attempting to have sexual intercourse with a mother, as it thinks, or with any other of gods, men, or beasts (571b–d). Socrates also mentions, among shameful and foolish activities, blood pollution and eating forbidden food.[8]

While confined to the dreams of decent people (572b), the outlaw appetites come into their own in the tyrannical soul. The young man, who has been raised by a father with a democratic soul, follows in his father's pattern. At first he engages in all lawlessness, in the name of freedom. His father tries to bring him back to the middle way. However, the analogue to the father's seducers, a group of men now called *magoi* – mages – wants to keep the young man for themselves and their political plans for tyranny. They contrive to implant in him a kind of *erōs* as the protector of the idle appetites – a great winged drone. Socrates says that this *erōs* is surrounded by the other unnecessary appetites, filled with the pleasures of incense, myrrh, crowns, wine, and other unrestrained pleasures of this sort (572d–573a). Since these pleasures describe a milieu of banqueting, the *erōs* in question seems to be sexual, although it is hard to say what the object of this *erōs* is. While it might be focused on an exotic and beautiful

---

[8] Adam says that Socrates is referring to such things as parricide and cannibalism: see Adam 1963 [1902], vol. 2, pp. 319–20.

individual, the context makes it more likely to be an intensely pleasurable form of free-ranging sexual experience.[9] Its function, however, is clear; it is an erotic fixation that subjects everything else to
itself. Without this *erōs*, the democratic youth might fall back to a
constitution in his soul that would give all appetites an equal share
in ruling. Such a young man would never have the drive needed to
be a tyrant. Like Callicles' truly strong man, the tyrant must be a
sensualist. Unlike Callicles' sensualist, the tyrant has, in addition
to his other appetites, one that is supreme. It may seem odd that,
in Socrates' story, the mages would put forth as the candidate for
tyranny someone who is in the grip of sensuality. Still, they seem to
think that the drive toward tyranny is based on one appetitive need so
great that it will finally encompass absolute political power. Socrates
means to fascinate and horrify us with the specter of a tyrannizing
erotic drive.

At first, however, this *erōs* is not so sinister. It is a winged – and,
thus, stingless – drone (552c). It protects the idle appetites by keeping
them dominant in the soul of this young man, now besotted with an
individual or obsessed by a kind of sexual experience. In this way,
the erotic passion sustains the style of life in which arrogance, lack
of control, dissoluteness, and shamelessness are still thought of as
virtues. So the youth, undeterred by moral considerations or even by
jaded satiety, continues to live the life of a sensualist. But it will not
last. The dramatic change into the fully tyrannical soul comes with
madness. When the mages implanted an *erōs* in his soul, the young

[9] In an earlier passage, 402e–403a, Socrates describes a clearly sexual desire in terms
similar to the ones used later in this passage, 573b–c. While these descriptions
tempt one to think that this erotic passion is one of the outlaw appetites, it is distinct from the latter because it is implanted, whereas they are innate. The mystery
of this *erōs* is heightened by our not knowing exactly how it fits with what Plato
writes about *erōs* in the *Symposium* and *Phaedrus*. Both dialogues allow different
forms of *erōs*, a lower and a higher. The lower form is sexual and bodily. Cf. *Phaedrus* 250e–251a, 253d–254e, and *Symposium* 181b, 183e. It is usually portrayed as
promiscuous because its sole aim is the pleasure of sexual satisfaction. Cf. Halperin
1985, pp. 170–73. Socrates says of the grand erotic passion that it is a type of *erōs*
(572e); presumably, it is of the lower sort. There is a rich body of philosophical commentary on Platonic *erōs*. However, it is largely focused on the higher forms of *erōs*;
insofar as it deals with the lower, it explicates how this form is an aberration of the
higher or an imperfect expression of it. As a consequence, it has little to say about
the particular nature of *erōs* in this passage. For a helpful taxonomy in which this
erōs can be located, see Santas 1982.

man presumably experienced something exhilarating and intense – but not insane. Then, Socrates says, whenever the unrestrained pleasures magnify and feed the drone-like *erōs*, they bring about in it the sting of longing. Goaded by this sting, the erotic protector of the soul acquires a bodyguard of madness and goes raging through the soul. It seizes any belief or appetite that might be thought useful or capable of shame and kills and throws it out, until the soul is purged of moderation and filled with an alien madness (573a–b).

The erotic passion becomes tyrannical with the advent of madness as its bodyguard, a significant step in the analogous development of tyranny in the city (566b). However, in the soul this dramatic change is marked by the phenomenon of insatiability, that is, the sting of longing. Later, when Socrates says that hunger, for example, is an emptiness, he is suggesting that it is a natural imbalance; eating is aimed at restoring balance or equilibrium.[10] However, unnecessary appetites do not aim at restoring equilibrium. Thus, they consume whatever is available; and they are closely related to criminality because they demand more and more. As a consequence, these appetites are liable to becoming insatiable. Hunger, for instance, that does not aim at restoring equilibrium can become gluttony. No matter how much one eats, he still wants more. He cannot experience complete satisfaction; the pain of hunger never fully ceases. Something like this happens in the tyrannical soul (579e). Within the sybaritic banqueting life, the unrestrained indulgence of the grand erotic passion makes it insatiable. So much more profound an appetite than any of the others, still this *erōs* cannot be completely satisfied; its pain never fully ceases. The sting of longing, in fact, intensifies the pleasure and drives the youth mad. While wild parties may bring on the madness of erotic passion, from this point forward the tyrannical soul is driven by insatiable appetites (573d).

This rampage of the erotic passion and its mad bodyguard is a literary device as striking as the triumphal procession of the false and bold beliefs leading into the soul the vices of arrogance, lack of control,

---

[10] Gosling and Taylor 1982, pp. 118–20. The authors criticize Plato for confusing righting an imbalance with filling a deficiency. The confusion makes it difficult to think of gluttony as righting an imbalance. However, the confusion is avoided by the distinction between necessary and unnecessary appetites. Necessary appetites are righting an imbalance; unnecessary appetites are not. Thus, the latter can become insatiable.

dissoluteness, and shamelessness. It is also striking that madness has a dramatic role analogous to that of the false and bold beliefs. While the false and bold beliefs lead the procession of the vices into the soul, madness accompanies the erotic passion as its bodyguard. Whereas the false and bold beliefs exile the oligarchic "virtues," the erotic passion, accompanied by its bodyguard, kills and throws out useful appetites and beliefs and purges the soul of moderation. The parallels between madness and the false and bold beliefs show that they have analogous psychological functions. The function of the false and bold beliefs is to offer ideological justification for the rule of the unnecessary appetites. From their point of view, the oligarchic "virtues" are just silly. Madness is also a point of view, but it is portrayed as one that goes beyond falsity and even boldness. Possessed by *erōs*, the tyrannical man is like someone drunkenly arrogant. Moreover, in the grip of madness, he is like someone who expects to be able to rule over not only men but gods as well – and actually tries to do so (573b–c).

If Socrates sketched a theory of character formation in his account of the democratic man, here he is extending it boldly. The ideological justification for the democratic youth's excesses were false and bold beliefs; but false beliefs can at least clash with true beliefs. There is no ideological justification for the rampage of erotic passion. Rather, it is protected from the need for justification by madness – a view of one's own soul and of its milieu that is out of touch with reality. The difference is crucial; the intensity of the erotic passion is matched by the depth of its failure to grasp what is really happening. In trying to understand this phenomenon, we cannot rely on ordinary experience as a guide. Ordinary people, by definition, do not experience the type of tyrannical *erōs* that makes one mad. Rather, we must look to drama, film, and literature to find examples of character types defined by an all-powerful passion that is itself protected by grandiose delusions.[11]

The syndrome of madness, drunkenness, and erotic obsession plays itself out in the way this erotically obsessed youth leads his life. His devotion to the unnecessary and spendthrift appetites means

---

[11] It is also worth noting that these scenes from Socrates' narrative are strongly reminiscent of our contemporary portrayals of addiction, replete with erotic ecstasy, delusion, chaos, and regret – e.g., Stahl 1995.

they multiply and become more and more demanding. After using up his own resources, he turns to those of his mother and father, tricking them or stealing from them by force. This squalid picture is complete when this man brings his love object to live in the paternal household. For the sake of his newly acquired girlfriend, a harlot and unnecessary, he would rain blows down on his once beloved and necessary mother. Or for the sake of his newly acquired beloved boy, in the bloom of youth and unnecessary, he would do the same to his elderly and necessary father, the oldest of his friends. In fact, he would make his mother and father serve his new lover as though they were slaves (573d–574c). As shocking as this picture is to us, it would be even more so to a culture in which the structure of the family was clearly drawn. To fail to see – within the very household – beating his mother and father as monstrous, to fail to see the enslavement of his mother and father to his lover as outrageous, the tyrannical man must be drunken and mad.

Later in this passage, Socrates refers again to this bodyguard of the erotic passion. Now the bodyguard consists of newly liberated beliefs. These beliefs were formerly freed in sleep, when, under the control of his father and the laws, the youth had a democratic soul. In describing these beliefs Socrates is clearly associating them with the outlaw appetites; once these beliefs are liberated this man goes on to do in his waking life what he formerly did in sleep (574d–575a). This shift between appetites and beliefs seems less odd if we keep the idea of liberation in mind. First of all, these beliefs are analogous to the liberated slaves who become members of the tyrant's bodyguard in the tyrannical city (567e). In turn, the liberation of the beliefs seems to mean the conscious or waking acceptance, as good and appropriate, of such things as having sex with one's mother or with any man, beast, or god. In his arrogant phase, the democratic youth may have done outrageous and lawless acts under the guise of freedom. But now a new depth has been reached with the normalization of outlaw appetites by means of these liberated beliefs. Thus, we can see why this bodyguard of outlaw beliefs was previously called madness. To believe that it is good and admirable to live a life that incorporates, as stable dispositions, appetites capable of such things as murder and cannibalism is not arrogance; it is madness. Finally, these outlaw beliefs are fit to serve as a bodyguard to the erotic passion. Insofar as one has descended, goaded by erotic obsession, to the depths of believing such things, there is not much hope of dislodging the obsession. So just as the combination of false and bold beliefs plus unnecessary appetites defined the character of the democratic youth, so the combination of madness and erotic passion defines the tyrannical character.

Yet the combination of madness and erotic passion makes this man miserable. The soul of the man who is like the tyrannical city will be filled with much slavery and lack of freedom. The best parts will be enslaved, while the small, wretched, and mad part will be the despot (577c–d). In referring to parts of the soul, Socrates recalls the division into reason, spirited part, and the appetitive part, that is, *epithumētikon*. The small, wretched, and mad part is the erotic obsession. The other and best parts would then be reason and the spirited part, as well as the better desires of the *epithumētikon*. The consequences of slavery for reason and the spirited part are next explored. Just as the tyrannical city does least of all what it wishes, so the tyrannical soul would do least of all what it wishes, if one thinks of the soul as a whole, that is, if one thinks of the parts of the soul other than erotic passion. Being violently dragged around by madness, this soul is filled with confusion and regret. Next Socrates establishes that the tyrannical soul must be needy and insatiable. Finally, Socrates says that both the city and the man of this sort are filled with fear. In fact, one would not find more wailing, moaning, lamenting, and grief than in the tyrannical city. One will find the same thing in the tyrannical man possessed by the madness of appetites and erotic passions (577d–578a).

The intensity of this scenario seems melodramatic. Still, there is some plausibility in this picture. On the one hand, his soul is needy and insatiable because he has cultivated insatiable appetites. So his fear is rooted in a worry about being able to fill what continually demands to be filled. On the other, confusion and regret are linked to reason and the spirited part, that is, parts of the soul that have a broader view of one's life.[12] As we shall see, each has its own kind of desires and its own kind of pleasure (580d). The spirited part desires honor and respect. Reason desires truth and learning. When the erotic passion rules, they are forced to pursue false and alien pleasures (587a). Socrates' story suggests, then, that, while these parts of

---

[12] Cf. Irwin 1995, pp. 214–16.

the soul do not do what they wish, they continue to be dissatisfied so that their frustration is still felt. Because they are still present but frustrated, the tyrannical man, at some point or at some level, can feel this disappointment, which arises from some vestigial sense that his life has turned out badly. If so, although erotic passion, accompanied by madness, purges the soul of moderation, reason still seems able to regret what happens to it. Even though madness extirpates any beliefs or appetites, held over from a democratic past, that are capable of shame, the spirited part still seems able to feel regret over the loss.

How regret is possible can be seen if we think of another life, one devoid of regret. In this other kind of life, the erotic obsession could become so dominant in the soul that it could thoroughly debase reason and the spirited part. In such a person there is no sense that things have gone wrong psychologically. The man thus dominated by the erotic passion would be thoroughly corrupted. As a consequence, he would no longer be capable of regret or remorse about the state of his soul or his standing with others. If Socrates is ignoring the possibility of complete corruption, he might seem naïve. Still, his account of character formation is based on the notion that one's beliefs articulate as good what the appetites aim toward as satisfying; these beliefs can be false and even mad. Realizing that one's beliefs are false could lead to regret. However, madness, even more than false beliefs, opens the door to regret if madness cannot totally mask the underlying psychological disaster. In the ancient world, madness, like possession, is episodic; in moments of lucidity one feels remorse and regret.[13] While Socrates does not exploit the episodic nature of madness, this feature does show that part of the suffering of madness is the contrast with lucidity.

Finally, Socrates may seem less naïve if we focus on the role of reason. Reason is capable of having a view of the soul's welfare that is independent of what the appetites may or may not desire.[14] Reason's

---

[13] In her study of madness in ancient Greek tragedy, Ruth Padel recounts that madness is a possession of divine origin that comes from the outside and attacks what she calls the victim's innards – bodily organs identified with psychological functions. In turn, the consequence is grave, external harm. In most cases the madness happens once; in others, madness can recur (Padel 1995, esp. chs. 3 and 4.) The temporary or episodic character of madness allows the return of lucidity – an integral part of the curse, as in the *Bacchae*, for instance.

[14] Cf. Cooper 1999, pp. 124–25.

ability to grasp the truth is not confined to discerning which appetite is the strongest; its decisions are not restricted to catering to that appetite. Reason has its own aspirations for the soul. Even if in Book 4 Socrates holds that appetites are not basically for what is beneficial, still he holds that reason can know what is good for the soul and desire to achieve it. If reason – in spite of everything – is still able to discern and seek what is good for the soul, Socrates can continue to maintain that one does not willingly err when it comes to the welfare of one's soul (589c). Since this ability cannot be taken away from reason, perhaps its vestige can be seen in the episodic or underlying regret in the tyrannical soul.[15] Although degraded, reason still has some sense that the soul is not what it should be. As a consequence, we are not the unwitting victims of appetitive forces; they may drag us about but we can still be tragically aware of what is happening. Even if it is false, it is still a philosophically significant claim to say that reason can have some grasp of what is good, independently of whichever appetites may dominate in the soul.

Socrates does not believe, however, that the man with the tyrannical soul is the most miserable. He would be even worse off if he did not live a private life but were unfortunate enough to become himself a tyrant in actuality (578b–c). This development may seem puzzling given the miserable condition of this man's soul.[16] Yet it is not altogether unexpected; the mages were grooming him for tyranny from the beginning. Later in this account, Socrates says that the city whose majority are tyrannical souls will change the city into a tyranny, choosing the one with the most tyrannical soul as the actual tyrant. The mages and this majority believe that tyranny in the soul fits one to be a tyrant in the city. The tyrant treats his homeland in the way that, under the influence of erotic passion, he treated his parents. This citywide tyranny is the final goal of his appetite (575c–d). This tyrant is different from Callicles' ideal. In the *Gorgias* he was a sensualist whose drive for tyrannical power appeared to be a means to an end. In the *Republic* the tyrant is the full realization of the tyrannical *erōs*. This powerful and insatiable appetite is grandiose. It is so insatiable that it consumes everything in one's private life. Still its grandiosity has an even more powerful dynamic. Without

[15] Cf. Ferrari 1992, p. 265.
[16] Cf. Annas 1981, pp. 304–5.

any sense of limit, the tyrannical *erōs* would take over an entire city. Everything within its ken should feed its ever-expanding needs. Still, for all its totalitarian brutality, it cannot silence everything in the soul nor control everything in the city.

To illustrate this idea Socrates gives a series of images. The first is an allegory in which the tyrant is compared to a rich man who owns many slaves. Ordinarily, he does not fear the slaves because he can count on support from his fellow citizens. However, if a god were to transport him, his family, and his slaves to a desert place, the rich man would have to fear for his life and that of his family. He would have to free some slaves and fawn over them in order to be protected (578d–579a). In this allegory, the tyrant, far from being all-powerful, is a flatterer of servants. In the second image, the tyrant is portrayed as a prisoner in his own house – like a woman. Afraid to go out, he cringes behind the shutters, envying ordinary citizens the common pleasures of going abroad and looking at the sights (579b–c). Although the most sensual of men, he cannot fulfill this simplest of desires. The final image is the most vulgar. The tyrant, having no control over himself, must try to rule others. He is like someone with a sick and uncontrolled body who does not live privately but is forced to spend his life contending and fighting in bodily combat (579c–d). The shocking image implies that the tyrant is an object of disgust, soiling himself in public. As a private citizen, the man with a tyrannical soul suffers fear, longing, and regret. If he becomes an actual tyrant, to these are added the ills of such a public life. Now he must fear for his survival, flatter his servants, renounce the ordinary pleasures of the common free man, and become the object of disgust.

III

One of the most striking contrasts between the unhappy tyrant and the philosopher is of the role of violence in the soul of the former. One way to explain this violent imagery is to say that it assumes a story about integration among parts of the soul. When a part of the soul other than reason rules, what it takes to be good for itself is established as the focus and goal of the whole soul.[17] Since this narrowly conceived good cannot accommodate the other parts, they must be

[17] Cf. Irwin 1995, pp. 290–91.

forced to submit to nonrational rule. In the oligarchic, democratic (in its first phase), and tyrannical soul, the rulers are appetites. To these appetites are subjected, in more or less violent ways, the other parts of the soul, that is, reason and the spirited part. However, besides these permanent parts of the soul there are other elements, such as specific kinds of appetites, beliefs, habits, and virtues, that are also subjected to violence. Thus the oligarchic man, having decided that making money is the most important goal in life, pushes the spirited part and its love of honor off the throne in his soul; in its place he seats the appetitive part and its love of money, making it a great king. Not allowing reason to do anything but calculate how to make more money out of less nor honoring anything other than money and those who are rich, he is ambitious for nothing other than the possession of money and anything that will lead to it (553b–d). Elements in his soul, such as unnecessary appetites in general and a subset of these – the drone-like beggarly and evildoing appetites – are enslaved and repressed by force (554a–c).

However, the rule of reason in the philosopher's soul is not based on violence. It presents an alternative form of government, based on the virtue of moderation. Beginning in Book 4, with the definition of moderation, we find the idea that the parts of the soul can agree that reason should rule. This agreement is based, in some way, on the idea that reason knows what is beneficial for the parts and for the whole (442c–d). So, a fundamental contrast between the philosopher and the unhappy tyrant is that the rule of reason can secure agreement of the other parts, without force, because it knows about and seeks what is beneficial for the other parts. It can, so to speak, see beyond its own welfare and conceive of the welfare of the other parts and the welfare of the whole. By contrast, in the soul of the oligarchic man the good of the other parts is subordinated to what seems good to the appetite for money. Yet, as we shall see, there is something problematic about the notion that agreement in the soul is based on reason's knowledge of what is beneficial. To see the problem, we can begin with the charter for the rule of reason, the definitions of wisdom and moderation in Book 4.

According to the definition of wisdom in Book 4, reason rules in the soul with the knowledge of what is beneficial for each of the parts as well as what is beneficial for the whole formed by the three (442c). Since the definition of wisdom – like all the definitions – is based on the parts of the soul, reason knows what is beneficial for the appetitive part. In turn, it is concerned about the welfare of the appetitive part. However, after Books 8 and 9, we also know that the appetitive part can contain all sorts of appetites. It does not follow from the definition of wisdom that reason is concerned about the welfare of each of these kinds of appetites. In the appetitive part, we can distinguish between, on the one hand, the basic, nonspecific appetites for food, drink, sex, money, and gain, and, on the other, their specific expressions as appetites for more determinate kinds of things.[18] These basic desires can be expressed in various ways, as necessary appetites, as unnecessary appetites, as outlaw appetites, and as erotic passion. Knowing what is beneficial for the appetitive part does not mean knowing what is beneficial for each of these kinds of appetites – even if there is something that counts as what is beneficial for each. Finally, indulging any of these appetites is pleasurable but not necessarily beneficial. Even though there may be a sense in which any pleasure seems good from the perspective of the appetitive part, from the perspective of reason what is beneficial for the appetitive part is not pleasure as such but the underlying condition, which, in turn, results in pleasure or is pleasurable. Reason has knowledge about that condition.

In Book 4, the definition of moderation holds that someone is moderate because of the friendship and harmony of the parts, when the part that rules and the two parts that are ruled share a common belief (*homodoxōsi*) that reason should rule, and the two others do not raise faction against it (442c–d). There are two sections to this definition: (1) the two parts of the soul that are ruled and the part that rules share a common belief that reason should rule, and (2) the two parts that are ruled do not raise faction against reason. This passage is susceptible to at least two interpretations. In the first interpretation, (1) and (2) are different. (1) says that the two parts have a certain belief and (2) says that they act in a certain way. In the second, (2) gives the meaning of (1). (1) does not mean literally that, for example, the appetitive part holds the belief that reason should rule. Rather, the meaning of (1) just is that the appetitive part does not raise faction against the rule of reason. In this interpretation, the appetitive part

[18] Cf. John Cooper, "Plato's Theory of Human Motivation," at pp. 126–28 of Cooper 1999.

believes that reason should rule in the sense that it goes along with the rule of reason.

The problem with the first interpretation is that it can lead to a mistaken view of agreement. If other parts of the soul have beliefs about the propriety of the role of reason, then one might be tempted to think these beliefs come by way of calculation. It is as though the appetitive part thought to itself: "Reason knows what is best for me so I should agree to follow reason." However, establishing the basis for this kind of calculation would entail attributing to the appetitive part an improbably complex ability to conceive of its overall welfare and to grasp some relation between its welfare and the rule of reason – even though it cannot share in the knowledge that reason has about its welfare.[19] Moreover, in Book 4, Socrates argues that appetite as such is not for what is beneficial (439a). It is hard to see how appetite as such can care about what is beneficial for itself, as opposed to getting its immediate object. Finally, it would be fallacious to argue that, just because reason knows what is beneficial for the appetitive part and the appetitive part agrees that reason should rule, the appetitive part agrees that it should rule for the reason that it provides what is beneficial.[20]

[19] It has been argued that the appetitive part is capable of means-end reasoning because of the way that Socrates characterizes it as money-loving – see, e.g., Annas 1981, pp. 129–30. At 580e–581a Socrates says that (a) the appetitive part is called money-loving because it is by means of money that the appetites for food, drink, and sex are satisfied. But this passage does not necessarily attribute any reasoning capacity to the appetitive part. In the first place, (a) is ambiguous. On the one hand, it could be saying that the appetitive part desires money for the reason that money is a means for satisfying the other appetites. Even at that, (a) would imply only that the appetitive part desires money as a means; nothing need be implied about means-end reasoning by the appetitive part. Moreover, the appetitive part's desiring money as a means is a far cry from having a general conception of its own welfare. On the other, (a) also might be saying that, because money is a means of satisfying the other appetites, the nature of the appetitive part has been fashioned to be money-loving. Then the appetitive part need not desire money for the reason that it is a means to satisfying the other appetites, although the love of money would serve as such a means.

[20] Christopher Bobonich argues that the spirited and appetitive parts have beliefs about their welfare and that these beliefs are the basis for their agreement with reason (Bobonich 2002, pp. 242–45). This is not the place to engage these important arguments in the detail they deserve. A general comment will have to suffice. Like others, Bobonich does not seem to recognize the difference between the moral psychology of Book 4 and that of Books 8 and 9 – or at least the one being maintained in this article. In Book 4, Socrates is talking about parts of the soul in a general way;

How to avoid this kind of problem is not clear until the end of Book 9. In the last part of this book, Socrates and Glaucon conduct a mock contest to see whether the life of the philosopher or that of the tyrant is the best of all the lives. Then they sum up the argument of the central books of the dialogue with a new image of the tripartite soul. The latter two of these contests deal with the way the philosopher understands pleasure in general and bodily pleasure in particular. Once we see the philosopher's approach to the pleasure of the appetitive part, we will have a way of understanding agreement in the soul. It is the philosopher who can bring about in the spirited and the appetitive parts agreement about the rule of reason. But the philosopher's understanding of pleasure is essential to this task, as we shall see.

Coming as it does just after the description of the tyrant's life, the first contest is easy for Glaucon to judge. The kingly soul – that is, that of the philosopher – is the happiest, and the tyrannical the most unhappy (580b–c). The next two contests show the philosopher's point of view about pleasure. In the first of the two, Socrates announces that each part of the soul has its own kind of desire and its own kind of pleasure. Each kind of man – philosophical, honor-loving, gain-loving – thinks the corresponding pleasure to be the best. For instance, the philosopher thinks the pleasures of learning are the best pleasures. So if there were a contest about pleasures, each would pronounce his specific pleasures the best. However, only the philosopher knows the pleasures of the other parts from his own life, whereas, for example, the gain-loving man would have no experience of the pleasures of learning. So only the philosopher is in a position to render a well-founded judgment about which pleasure is best. Finally, when he says the pleasures of learning are best, only his judgment is competent (580d–582e). From this section we learn how the philosopher thinks about pleasure; he makes a comparative judgment on the basis, in part, of his experience of the different sorts of pleasure.

In the final contest, Socrates presents an argument that reflects the way the philosopher would experience pleasure. For our purposes,

and in Books 8 and 9 he is talking about character formation, including establishing dispositions in the appetitive part. Once the distinction is appreciated, we can explain agreement among the parts – at least up to a point – without an elaborate account of the capacities of the appetitive part.

the important part of this argument contrasts the pleasures of the appetites with the pleasures of learning. Hunger and thirst are emptinesses in the makeup of the body. Ignorance and lack of sense are emptiness in the soul. Both kinds of emptiness admit of filling up. The latter is more truly a filling because what is filled is more real and what it is filled with is more real. In saying that reason is more real than the appetitive part and that truth is more real than food, Socrates is using his usual criterion of reality, that is, what remains the same always. Presumably, we are to think that truth remains the same always but such things as food and drink do not. Because they come and go, being filled with them is not as real a filling up as being filled with truth, which does not come and go. Finally, the truer filling up affords the truer pleasure (585a–e).

This argument will be unconvincing unless one accepts the distinction between the comparative untruth of the filling up of bodily appetites relative to the filling up of ignorance. However, the argument presumes that the philosopher already holds this distinction. The philosopher is able to appreciate that the pleasures of the bodily appetites are less real than the pleasures of learning. On the whole, she will find learning more satisfying than eating and drinking. In fact, the intense pleasures of the banqueting life are the least real, and are even illusory (586a–c). However, this perspective does not mean that she dismisses the pleasures of the appetitive part. Socrates refers to particular kinds of appetite that follow knowledge and reason and that belong to the victory-loving and gain-loving parts. As we shall see, the appetites that follow knowledge and reason are the tame appetites. When these appetites pursue pleasure under the guidance of knowledge and reason and partake of those pleasures that the wisest part prescribes, they will enjoy the truest pleasures possible for them. These pleasures are the ones most proper to each, if what is best for each is what is the most proper. By contrast, if another part of the soul dominates, even that part will not discover its proper pleasure, and it forces the other parts to pursue an alien and false pleasure (586d–587a).

So reason has a role to play in prescribing pleasures. How it goes about this task is addressed in the culminating image of the tripartite soul. At the heart of the image is a new analogy for the way the philosopher cares for his soul – one that depends on the craft (*technē*) of farming.[21] Socrates compares the *epithumētikon* to an animal that has many heads, some tame and some wild (588c). To this animal there is added a lion, to represent the spirited part, and a man, to represent reason. In the soul of the just person, the man exercises care for the appetitive part, for the many-headed animal. Like a farmer, he nurtures and domesticates the tame parts of the animal and prevents the wild parts from growing (589b). The farming *technē* works on two levels, then. The first level corresponds to what we have called character formation. Reason – the analogue of the farmer – includes the tame appetites as dispositions in the appetitive part; and it excludes the wild appetites. At the outset, it is tempting to think that tame appetites are necessary and wild appetites are unnecessary appetites. Unfortunately, matters are not so clear. On the one hand, tame appetites surely include all necessary appetites. On the other, the wild appetites include some unnecessary appetites. The outlaw appetites are called wild (572b). And, by implication, the evildoing appetites would seem to be wild. Wild appetites cannot be domesticated by reason; the evil appetite, for example, for thievery, reason cannot persuade nor tame (554c–d). However, the classification of the unnecessary appetites that are not antisocial – for example, for incense, myrrh, harlots, and pastries – is unclear, even if prospects for domesticating them do not seem very bright. Finally, *erōs* itself is left in an ambiguous state. Even if there is an *erōs* distinct from the tyrannical erotic passion, is it tame or wild?

In spite of all this unclarity, we now have a way of understanding what is beneficial for the appetitive part. While the appetitive part consists basically of the general appetites for food, drink, and sex, it becomes specified by certain appetitive dispositions. At least part of what is beneficial for the appetitive part is to shape it by including some appetites as stable dispositions and excluding others. One should promote, as stable dispositions, the tame appetites for, for example, bread, cheese, olives, salt, and moderate amounts of wine. One should exclude those dispositions that come under the heading

---

[21] In *Republic* 4, Socrates makes an analogy between the craft of ruling and justice in the soul. In Parry 1996 I speculated that the craft of justice would be expressed in the building up of dispositions in the appetites (90–104). The farming *technē* expands on that theme.

of wild appetites because they lead to conflict and frustration (cf. 588e–589a). These include such unnecessary appetites as the outlaw and the evildoing appetites as well as grand erotic passion. Thus, Socrates has repaired the damage of Book 4, so to speak. There he argued that, basically, appetites are not for what is beneficial. But now we see that one can overcome this indifference by cultivating the *epithumētikon* so that it has only those appetitive dispositions that are docile to reason and, insofar as they are necessary, are beneficial. These are the appetites that Socrates has already identified as the ones that follow reason and, under its guidance, provide the truest pleasures (586d–e). While these pleasures are not the most intense – because the most intense are illusory – they are what is best for the appetitive part.

We can also distinguish a second level in the job of the farmer. He domesticates the appetites that he has selected; reason treats them as part of the household. It has a day-to-day job of dealing with the tame appetites. Here we seem to have a place for an idea that Socrates suggested in the account of the oligarchic man. When this man confronts evil appetites, he contains them by force, not by persuading them that it is not better to desire something nor taming them by reason (554c–d). This description suggests that some appetites can be persuaded and tamed by reason. Of course, it is hard to tell what Socrates means by persuading the appetites by reason. Perhaps he is thinking about such things as delayed gratification. When one's appetite for cheese is expressed as a particular desire for a particular piece of cheese, it can be persuaded to wait.[22] Insofar as the tame appetites include the necessary appetites, they seem reasonable candidates for this kind of treatment. In themselves, appetites for bread, cheese, olives, and salt are not so intense and demanding that delayed gratification would seem harsh. Thus, these appetites are more easily persuadable than those for incense, myrrh, fancy foods, and prostitutes.

---

[22] One might object that "persuading appetites" is metaphorical language for deciding not to indulge an appetite. However, persuading an appetite could mean causing the occurrent desire to cease. This account attributes to the appetites a capacity to react to the difference between present and future gratification, when it is presented. Even though, at this moment, one may desire this piece of kefalotyri, on consideration, its attraction would cease at the prospect that eating this piece – or another piece of cheese – at another time would be more gratifiying. Cf. Irwin 1995, pp. 219–20.

Still, one might wonder whether all tame appetites can be persuaded by promises of delayed gratification. Assuming that there is a tame form of sexual appetite (cf. 372b–c), it may be expressed as desire for a particular person – no substitutes allowed. And delayed gratification of sexual desire seems much more complicated than delayed gratification for cheese.[23]

In spite of such difficulties, now we have a way of understanding how the appetitive part shares in the belief that reason should rule, that is, how it expresses the virtue of moderation. Agreeing to the rule of reason fits with the second of the two interpretations of 442c–d, given above. The appetitive part agrees that reason should rule in the sense that it does not raise faction against it. This sense of agreement does not attribute a great deal of rationality to the appetitive part.[24] In the first place, the virtue of moderation depends on reason's allowing only tame appetites into the appetitive part of the soul. Thus, reason, so to speak, does not have to explain to the tame appetites that it is better, in general, to agree. Nor do the tame appetites figure it out on their own.[25] Rather, tame appetites are just the sort of appetites that, by their nature, fit into the regime of reason's ruling. In general, what they want coincides with what reason sees is beneficial. So, by definition, they are not the sort to raise faction against reason. In particular cases, where reason contravenes a particular desire for a particular object, tame appetites can be persuaded to forgo or to postpone. But they need not agree to a general proposition about the benefit of rational rule. All that is required is that, on each such occasion, the appetite in question be persuaded to follow reason. Here agreement to the rule of reason is piecemeal and due to the nature of a tame appetite. So, consisting as it does of tame appetites, the appetitive part has no cause to raise faction against reason.

Socrates has achieved his account of agreeing to the rule of reason, then, by the tactic of excluding all the appetites that could cause

---

[23] In the *Phaedrus*, sexual appetite is finally tamed, but through a series of violent confrontations with reason and the spirited part (254d–255a). Of course, the image of the charioteer is designed to be more violent than that of a farmer since the former does not choose his team whereas the latter cultivates only certain kinds of appetites.

[24] On the rational capacity of appetite, compare the present interpretation with Annas' Stoic reading of the tripartite soul. Cf. Annas 1999, p. 124.

[25] Cf. Irwin 1995, pp. 220–22.

trouble. In some ways it seems like too easy a victory. He seems not to have reflected on how difficult it might be to exclude the obstreperous appetites. If the natural state of the appetitive part consisted of just the basic appetites for food, drink, and sex, then keeping the wild appetites from growing would only be a question of not adopting bad habits. But in the tripartite image of the soul, the lowest part, the beast, has both tame and wild heads; it would appear that wild appetites are innate (588c). Outlaw appetites – a kind of wild appetite – are said explicitly to be innate. So wild appetites are already present, before one might adopt bad habits. Perhaps we have here a faint trace of the idea that the soul has a wild, bacchic urge incommensurable with the rule of reason. Embodied, for instance, in the conflict between Dionysus and Pentheus in Euripides' *Bacchae*, the idea is a potent challenge to the project of the *Republic*.

When Socrates introduced the outlaw appetites, he alluded to the possibility of getting rid of them entirely, or at least leaving the rest few and weak (571b–c). So far, how the wild appetites might be extinguished or weakened has been confined to the idea that the fundamental desire of the philosopher's soul is for the truth – that is, what reason wants. In turn, assimilating to reason, the bodily appetites will be satisfied with the truest pleasures. However, the truest pleasures are clearly not the most intense pleasures. So it appears that, since the philosopher seems to have no taste for the intense pleasures associated with the wild appetites, the latter just would not flourish, that is, would not grow. The weight that this idea must bear is clear if we think of a different and admittedly speculative possibility. Suppose that desire in the philosophical soul is not so easily diverted from bodily pleasure (cf. 485d–e). Nor is the appetite for the most intense pleasure just displaced by the prospect of having the truest pleasure. This philosopher, then, might have to repress the wild appetites – not in the way the oligarchic man does but more thoroughly. And if we allow this kind of repression of the wild appetites into the well-tended soul, then it seems only to be enkratic, in Aristotle's terminology. The enkratic person is in control of her appetites so that she does what she holds to be right although contrary desires are still present (cf. *Nicomachean Ethics*, 1151b–1152a). But surely agreement to the rule of reason should mean more than *enkrateia*.

Yet there is evidence that this possibility is more than speculative. While Socrates says that reason will make the other parts friendly to one another and to itself, in the same passage he also describes the relation between reason and the appetitive part in less friendly and more belligerent terms. What is fine is what subjugates the beast-like part of our nature to the human, or rather divine part, while what is shameful enslaves the gentle part to the wild (589b–d).[26] Later, the situation of the appetitive part in the best soul is compared to slavery (590c–d). Perhaps we should not make too much of this shift in terminology from making friends to subjugating. But it does show some sense that the appetitive part is not totally docile or malleable – as well as some ambivalence about the approach to the appetitive part. Finally, we have a promising idea for the project of achieving agreement in the soul – that is, the notion of furnishing the appetitive part with tame appetites as stable dispositions. However, in the notion of keeping the wild appetites from growing, we might not yet have an idea that can bear all the weight it is meant to.

WORKS CITED

Adam, J., ed. 1963 [1902]. *The* Republic *of Plato.* Cambridge.

Annas, J. 1981. *An Introduction to Plato's* Republic. Oxford.

Annas, J. 1999. *Platonic Ethics, Old and New.* Ithaca, N.Y.

Bobonich, C. 2002. *Plato's Utopia Recast: His Later Ethics and Politics.* Cambridge.

Cooper, J. 1999. *Reason and Emotion.* Princeton.

Ferrari, G. R. F. 1992. "Platonic Love." In *The Cambridge Companion to Plato*, ed. R. Kraut (Cambridge).

Gill, C. 1996. "Ethical Reflection and the Shaping of Character: Plato's *Republic* and Stoicism." *Proceedings of the Boston Area Colloquium in Ancient Philosophy* 12: 193–225.

Gosling, J. C. B., and C. C. W. Taylor. 1982. *The Greeks on Pleasure.* Oxford.

Halperin, D. 1985. "Platonic *Erōs* and What Men Call Love." *Ancient Philosophy* 5: 161–204.

Irwin, T. 1995. *Plato's Ethics.* Oxford.

Padel, R. 1995. *Whom the Gods Destroy.* Princeton.

Parry, R. D. 1996. *Plato's Craft of Justice.* Albany, N.Y.

Rudebusch, G. 1999. *Socrates, Pleasure, and Value.* Oxford.

---

[26] The article in LSJ on *poieō* (section IV) shows that the construction *hupo . . . poiounta* (589d), which we translate as "subjugate," comes from the context of war and conquest.

Santas, G. 1982. "Passionate Platonic Love in the *Phaedrus*." *Ancient Philosophy* 2: 105–14.

Scott, D. 2000. "Plato's Critique of the Democratic Character." *Phronesis* 45: 19–37.

Stahl, J. 1995. *Permanent Midnight*. New York.

15 What Is Imitative Poetry and Why Is It Bad?

Plato's argument against poetry in *Republic* 10 is perplexing. He condemns not *all* poetry, but only "however much of it is imitative [*hosē mimētikē*]" (595a). A metaphysical charge against certain works of poetry – that they are forms of imitation, "at a third remove from the truth" – is thus used to justify an ethical charge: that these works cripple our thought and corrupt our souls. Unfortunately, it is not at all clear how to understand the connection between the two charges. We can see how they are related in a loose way: imitators are concerned with images far removed from the truth about what they represent (596a–598b); many people are too foolish to distinguish imitation from reality and thus accept ignorant imitators as experts and guides (598c–602b); imitation appeals to and thereby strengthens an inferior part of the soul unconcerned with truth (602c ff.); worst of all, the charms of imitation can seduce even those who generally know better (605c–607a). But when we try to make Book 10's argument more precise, trouble ensues. Plato certainly never spells out the connection between the metaphysics of imitation and the charge of ethical harm. Moreover, he seems in the end (603c ff.) to abandon metaphysical considerations and give a straightforward argument against tragedy and the works of Homer based on their content – they represent people behaving immoderately – and psychological effect: as audience we weep and wail and behave as immoderately as the characters, and this undermines the order of our souls. This argument makes no mention of imitation or ignorance or removes from truth; what, then, is the relevance of the metaphysical charge, to which Plato devotes so much discussion?

The worry gains more force when we ask how the metaphysical charge *could* do any work in the argument – when we notice, that is, how difficult it is to apply Plato's definition of imitation to poetry. Plato illustrates what he means by "imitation" with a discussion of painting: the painter is an imitator because he copies material objects like beds instead of Forms, and copies them not as they are but "as they appear" (598a) – that is, as they *look*. What is the relevant analogy for the poet? What corresponds to the painter's bed? And in what sense can the poet, an artist working in a nonvisual medium, copy things "as they appear"? Plato's answers to these questions are far from clear, and thus it is hard to know what he means by calling poetry imitative.

Furthermore, even if we grant that poetry is somehow analogous to painting and that both are forms of imitation whose products are "at a third remove from the truth" (599d), why should this render poetry ethically harmful? After all, cannot something "third from the truth" be relevantly *similar* to the truth? A photograph of a person resembles the person to a high degree; a photocopy of the photograph resembles the person to a lesser degree. At each stage more detail and precision are lost; nonetheless, it is all a matter of degree – degree of resemblance – and although the photograph is a better likeness than the photocopy, common sense says that the photocopy is still most decidedly a likeness, and will do for many purposes in a fix. If this is right, then imitative poetry should be able to give us something relevantly like the truth about human affairs, and could therefore be a tool of moral education, not its enemy. And while such thoughts may be more natural to us with our modern tools of accurate reproduction than to the Greeks, Socrates himself seems to have suggested just this point in Book 3's discussion of poetry: "By making something false as similar to the truth as we can, don't we make it useful?" (382d).

There is, therefore, a major interpretative difficulty with Book 10: it is not at all clear how the ethical charge that certain works of poetry corrupt the soul depends on the metaphysical charge that these works are imitative.[1] To find a solution, we will have to give

---

[1] This problem has not been clearly identified as such in the many books and articles about Plato's critique of poetry, although insightful suggestions that might form the basis for a solution to it abound: see, in particular, Nehamas 1982; Ferrari 1989; Janaway 1995; Burnyeat 1999. These writers, however, either leave the connection between metaphysics and ethics at the level of suggestion or give unsatisfactory

a clear account of what Plato means by "imitative." In doing so, we will also be offering a solution to a related difficulty, one much discussed in the enormous body of literature on Book 10: that Plato licenses poetic imitations of one sort – imitations of virtuous people – in Book 3, but then condemns imitative poetry as a whole in Book 10.[2] To avoid contradiction, Plato must be defining "imitative" in Book 10 in a way that excludes faithful imitations of the virtuous. On the account I offer, he is doing precisely that: imitative poetry turns out to refer only to poetry that *misrepresents* human virtue in a dangerous way.

In coming to understand the relation between the metaphysical and ethical charges, then, we will gain a better understanding of the argument of *Republic* 10, and more generally of Plato's reasons for condemning the poetry he condemns. We will also discover an important series of parallels in the distinctions Plato makes between reality and appearances in various fields. These parallels will show Plato's attack on poetry to be intimately connected to his most central ethical and metaphysical views.

I. VISUAL APPEARANCES

Socrates begins Book 10 by congratulating himself on having excluded all imitative poetry from the ideal city, and proposes to explain why such poetry is dangerous by way of a general discussion of imitation (*mimēsis*). A large part of the ensuing discussion is concerned with *visual* phenomena: first mirror-reflections of the sun, plants, animals, and artifacts, then paintings of beds and bridles, then optical illusions. Although Socrates later warns against relying exclusively on the analogy with painting (603b), he clearly intends the discussion of painting and other visual phenomena to provide us with an understanding of imitation, and thereby to help in explaining

---

accounts of the connection (see section II below). The account that comes closest to doing the work I think needs doing is Belfiore 1983. I note points of comparison between her view and mine below.

[2] Book 3 clearly presents ethically beneficial poetry as engaged in imitation: the "unmixed imitator of the decent person" is admitted into the city (397d), and Plato uses cognates of *mimēsis* to refer to good poetry and art at 398b, 399a, and 401a.

what imitative poetry is and why it is dangerous. Let us consider the discussion with this point in mind.

The analysis of imitation begins with the premise that for each class of material objects there is a single immaterial Form, of which the many material particulars are likenesses;[3] thus a material bed is a likeness of the Form of the bed, which is the *true* bed, the bed that really is.[4] Then Plato considers a painting, a visual imitation, of a particular bed. The painting is a likeness of the material bed, itself a likeness of the *true* bed; therefore the painting is a likeness of a likeness of the original, thrice removed from "the nature" and "the truth" (597e). But it is natural to think, as I argued above, that a likeness of a likeness may still resemble the original; surely a painting of a bed, for example, captures something, although not all, of the nature of beds.

This, however, is decidedly not the way Plato thinks of imitation, and to understand why we must attend to a further ontological distinction that he makes, one far more central to the argument than has generally been noticed. This is the distinction between particular material objects, on the one hand, and their *appearances*, on the other.

The painter copies particular beds, not the Form of the bed. But "does he copy them as they are," Socrates asks, "or as they appear [*hoia estin ē hoia phainetai*]? For you must make this further distinction [*touto gar eti diorison*]" (598a).[5] He explains the distinction as follows: as one moves around a bed, viewing it from different angles, "the bed does not differ at all from itself, but it appears to be different" (598a). I propose that Plato's analysis of imitation makes most sense if we take this passage to distinguish not between two ways of considering one and the same object – as it is versus as it appears from any particular perspective – but rather between two

---

[3] The material bed is "something which is like [*hoion*]" the Form (597a); Plato suggests that perceptible things are likenesses or images of Forms throughout *Republic* 6–7.

[4] Does Plato really hold that there are Forms of artifacts like beds, or is his discussion here purely heuristic? My own view is that he posits the Form of the bed chiefly for the sake of the analogy with the ethical Forms at issue in poetry. I explain the analogy below.

[5] Translations tend to obscure the force of *touto gar eti diorison*: Grube/Reeve has "You must be clear about that"; Jowett has "You have still to determine this." Bloom translates as I recommend.

distinct objects, the bed itself and the appearance of the bed. The painter copies "not what is, as it is" – here referring not to the Form, but to the material bed, for this is within the scope of the "further distinction"[6] – but rather something different: "what appears [to phainomenon], as it appears." His painting is "an imitation of a phantom [phantasmatos]" rather than of the truth (598b); he captures "only a small bit [smikron ti]" of his subject, "and that a mere image [eidōlon]" (598b).[7] In other words, the appearance of a bed – what the painter paints – is nearly as far "removed from truth" as the painting of a bed: both are mere images of the particular bed (and therefore copies of copies of the Form). And indeed Book 10 makes no distinction in ontological level at all between appearance and artist's image. Plato refers to the appearances the imitator copies, as well as the images the imitator produces, as mere phantoms – phainomena, phantasmata, and eidōla.[8] (Is Plato here making a point only about what aspect of things the painter paints, or a more general point about what is available for perception? Some take him to be laying the ground for the theory of perception propounded by Russell and others in the last century: we see material objects like beds only indirectly, for between us and them intervenes a layer of sense-data, immaterial entities that are the direct objects of perception.)[9]

Thus far we have seen an argument that the appearance of a bed is ontologically distinct from the particular bed itself, and therefore

[6] Cf. Adam 1963 [1902], vol. 2, p. 394.

[7] Contrast eidōlon, which often connotes falsehood, with the more neutral eikōn, used to refer to images elsewhere in the Republic (e.g., Book 3, 401b ff.). As Halliwell points out, Plato abandons "the standard, non-prejudicial term" eikōn in Book 10 (Halliwell 1988, at p. 118).

[8] These words refer to the artist's work at 599a, 599d, 601b, and 605c, and to the thing imitated at 598b and 600e. As Nehamas puts it, this overlap of vocabulary "suggests that he is thinking of the object of imitation and of the product of imitation as being the same object – if not in number, at least in type. It almost seems as if he believes that the painter lifts the surface off the subject and transplants it onto the painting" (Nehamas 1982, p. 263).

[9] Note how close Russell is to Republic 10 in giving his case for the existence of sense-data: "Although I believe that the table is 'really' of the same colour all over, the parts that reflect the light look much brighter than the other parts. . . . [I]f I move, . . . the apparent distribution of colours on the table will change . . . [A] given thing looks different in shape from every different point of view"; and, in this connection, "[T]he painter has to . . . learn the habit of seeing things as they appear" (Russell 1912, at pp. 2–3 of the 1959 reprint); cf. Republic 598a, quoted above. For a defense of the idea that Plato was a proto-sense-data-theorist, see Paton 1921–22.

that in copying the appearance, the painter fails to copy the bed. But this by no means entails that the painter gets the bed *wrong*. After all, the appearance of a bed certainly looks like a bed, for a bed's "look" is precisely its visible aspect, its appearance. But Plato has shown us that the appearance is not only distinct but also qualitatively different from the bed: when viewed from different angles the bed itself remains the same, while the appearance of it varies (598a). Now compare this way of distinguishing the apparent bed from the material bed with the distinction Plato draws earlier in the *Republic*, and in other dialogues, between the apparent (i.e., perceptible) world as a whole and a reality of a higher grade:

The beautiful itself . . . remains the same and never in any way tolerates any differing (*alloiōsin*) whatsoever. . . . [but the many beautifuls] never in any way remain the same as themselves or in relation to each other.

(*Phaedo* 78d–e)[10]

The Form of beauty is intelligible but not at all perceptible. The "many beautiful things," on the other hand, are things that we see, things that are apparent. In this case, then, as in the case of the bed, what appears is varied, changing, and contradictory, while the real is stable, uniform, and consistent – the Form absolutely so, and the particular bed relatively to its appearance. (Here we have a concrete application of Plato's claim that the relation of the bottom two sections of Book 6's divided line to the top two is analogous to the relation of the bottom-most to the one above it: "as the opinable is to the knowable [i.e., as the perceptible realm is to the realm of Forms], so the likeness is to the thing that is like" (510a). As the many particular, perceptible beautiful things are to the beautiful itself, so is the shadow or reflection of a bed to the bed. And we have seen that Book

---

[10] Cf. the *Republic*'s first discussion of Forms, in Book 5: "The Form of Beauty itself . . . always remains the same in all respects [*aei men kata tauta hōsautōs ekhousan*]," but "of all the many beautiful things is there any one that will not appear ugly? Or any one of the just things that will not appear unjust? Or of the pious things that will not appear impious? . . . And the bigs and smalls and lights and heavies, will they be called any more what we say they are than the opposite?" (479a–b). The language is similar at *Symposium* 211a, where Plato offers a fuller explanation of how it is that each beautiful thing (for example) is in some way ugly. It is noteworthy for our purposes that each of these passages, among the most explicit we have in Plato about the difference between Forms and particulars, takes *to kalon* (the beautiful or fine) as its example.

10, by treating the appearances of material objects like images, adds them to the lowest level of the line alongside shadows and reflections.)[11] The distinction between the material bed as it is and as it appears is thus part of a general theory: appearances are qualitatively different from the realities that underlie them, in that appearances are varied and contradictory, while realities are stable and uniform.

What are the consequences of this theory for visual art? Plato tells us that the painter copies the appearance of material objects, not the reality. Why does the painter do so? Because he paints what he sees, what appears. To put it another way, he wants to make his paintings *look like* what they represent, and what looks like a bed is the "look" of the bed, its appearance. But if this is not only distinct from but also qualitatively different from the bed itself, then "realistic" painting, painting that looks like what it represents, must in a deeper sense *misrepresent* its subjects. That is, if a viewer is foolish enough to take the painting to show not merely how a bed looks, but what a bed is really like, the painting will give him false ideas about beds. The point is perhaps clearer in the case of the optical illusions Plato discusses later in Book 10: if two men of the same height stand at different distances from a viewer, the further one appears smaller. He isn't smaller, of course, but that is how he looks from that particular point of view. A realistic painter must portray the men "not as they are but as they appear" (598a), copying not the truth (that they are roughly the same size), but the appearance or *phantasma* that the further one is smaller. If he tries to paint the men as they are and not as they appear, his painting will be "unrealistic": it will not *look like* what it represents.[12]

---

[11] Cf. Paton 1921–22, p. 85. Note also that appearances are similar to shadows and reflections in being variable: as one walks around a bed, its shadow or reflection changes just as much as its appearance.

[12] The *Republic* thus anticipates the *Sophist's* distinction between "likeness-making" (*eikastikē eidōlopoiikē*) and "phantasm-making" (*phantastikē eidōlopoiikē*). Likeness-makers preserve the proportions and colors of what they represent, but as for those "who sculpt or draw very large works, if they reproduced the true proportions of their beautiful subjects . . . the upper parts would appear smaller than they should, and the lower parts would appear larger, because we see the upper parts from farther away and the lower parts from closer. . . . So don't these craftsmen say goodbye to truth, and produce in their images the proportions that seem to be beautiful instead of the real ones?" (*Sophist* 235a–e, trans. Nicholas P. White). Phantasm-making corresponds to what *Republic* 10 calls imitative art; as for likeness-making, *Republic* 10 does not explicitly discuss it, but according to

The discussion of painting, then, has illuminated what Plato means by "imitative" art: art that manages to be compelling and realistic by copying the way things appear, at the cost of misrepresenting the way things are. This charge, and the particular way Plato draws the distinction between realities and appearances – stable and uniform on the one hand, varied and contradictory on the other – will have significant consequences when we turn to the case of poetry and the *ethical* appearances in which it trades. First we must follow the case of painting, to see what power Plato attributes to art that copies appearances and leaves realities aside.

II. DECEPTION

Book 10's paradigm of the imitative artist is a man with a mirror, and we are clearly to understand the painter as one who emulates the mirror-holder, copying things exactly as he sees them – exactly as they appear. Of course Plato writes about realistic painting (and not about abstract, nonrepresentational, cubist, or expressionist art) because this is what he knew.[13] But we miss the point of his discussion of painting if we overlook the more philosophical reason for his interest in realistic painting. Plato wants to make the point that realistic painting has a certain power over us that makes it, on his view, significantly like (although far less dangerous than) poetry: the power to *deceive*.

[A] painter can paint us a cobbler, a carpenter, or the other craftsmen, even though he knows nothing about these crafts. Nevertheless, if he is a good painter, when he has painted a carpenter and displays his painting from far off, he might deceive children and foolish people by its seeming to be a real carpenter.[14]   (598b–c)

the argument I shall offer, the poetry that survives censorship in Books 2 and 3 and the hymns to gods and eulogies of good men that survive in Book 10 would fall under this category.

[13] Greek painters of the time were masters of realism, even of trompe l'oeil: witness the story that birds pecked at Zeuxis' painting of grapes, while Zeuxis tried to lift the painted curtain from Parrhasius' canvas. For a good discussion, see Keuls 1978.

[14] Here I follow the translation of Burnyeat 1999, p. 302. The standard translations have it that the painter deceives the children and fools "into thinking that it is a real carpenter." Both translations are in principle open to either what I will call the implausible reading or the reading that I will suggest, following Burnyeat and also Belfiore 1983; but Burnyeat's translation is overall preferable.

On the surface, Plato is making the implausible claim that people are often tricked into believing that the painter actually creates the three-dimensional objects he merely represents. We need to look beyond this interpretation, however, if we are to find a plausible view, and one that is in any way relevant to poetry. We can take our clue about how to do so from the objects of artistic imitation Plato chooses for his example – craftsmen, knowledgeable experts with the tools of their trades, as opposed to ordinary people or objects – and from the conclusion he draws from the example:

> Whenever someone announces to us that he has met a man who knows all the crafts and everything else that anyone knows, and that there's nothing that he doesn't know more exactly than anyone else, we must suppose that. . . . [the deceived person] is not able to distinguish between knowledge, ignorance and imitation. (598c–d)

The generalization we are to draw from the case of the painted carpenter is not, then, that imitators deceive us into thinking that they create actual people or tools instead of mere images, but rather that they deceive us into thinking them *experts* in all sorts of subjects. But why precisely does being an imitator – where that is defined as one who copies things as they appear instead of as they are – afford one a reputation for near omniscience? To see the connection we must turn to Plato's distinction among users, makers, and imitators (601b ff.).

The passage is a strange one: the relation of its threefold division to the earlier one (among maker of the Form, craftsman, and imitator) is problematic, and it is difficult at first to see how the passage connects to the overall argument. To interpret it aright, we must keep in mind that it forms the link between the discussion of painting and the discussion of poetry. It does so, I shall argue, by applying the appearance/reality distinction to matters of *value*.

For each thing, Plato says, there are three types of craftsmen: the one who uses it, the one who makes it, and the one who imitates it. The user is the true expert, for he alone knows what makes for a *good* thing of that kind: "Are not the excellence [or virtue, *aretē*], the fineness [or beauty, *kallos*], and the correctness of each implement, living creature, and action related to nothing but the use for which

each has been made or begotten?" (601d).[15] The maker, guided by
the knowledgeable user, has "right opinion" about whether what
he makes is "fine or bad" (601e). The imitator, on the other hand,
"will neither know nor have correct belief regarding the fineness or
badness of the things he imitates" (602a). Why not? We have learned
that the imitator copies the mere appearances of things. If he can do
so successfully in total ignorance of the value of his objects, it must
be that value does not *appear*.

The function of a carpenter's lathe (what it is for) does not meet the
eye, but must be understood. Since value is dependent on function
(601d), it is also the case that much of what makes for a genuinely
good lathe does not meet the eye (certainly not the eye of the lay-
man). But if genuine value is nonapparent, there is something related
that does meet the eye: apparent excellence or fineness, the quality
of appearing, not being, excellent or fine. And this, it seems, the
imitator does know, for

nevertheless he will imitate, not knowing in what way each thing is bad
or good [*ponēron ē khrēston*]. But the sort of things that appear to be
fine/beautiful to the ignorant many, this, it seems, he will imitate. (602b)

The true value of a lathe is nonapparent, but a lathe might *look*
to be a good one if it is shiny, or big, or has a dramatic shape. The
point is more compelling in the case of a complicated machine like
a car: one can, with no knowledge of how a car works or what makes
for a genuinely good car, know just what would make a car look fast
or tough to ignorant children – and can therefore make a picture of
what will look to them like an excellent car. (And the children will
assume, Plato implies in the passage on the painting of the carpenter,
that the person who can make such a picture knows all about cars.)

Thus the user/maker/imitator argument, like the discussion of
the painted bed, relies on the distinction between reality and appearances, but with an important difference: there Plato distinguished
what is really a bed from the appearance of a bed; here he distinguishes what is really excellent or *kalon* (fine or beautiful) from what
appears excellent or *kalon*.[16] In both cases, the imitator copies the

---

[15] Plato has already argued that excellence is dependent on function at *Republic*
1.352d ff.

[16] Belfiore interprets Plato as distinguishing between a true standard of the *kalon*,
function or usefulness, and a false, apparent standard: (aesthetic) pleasure. "The

appearances instead of the reality (the painter paints what appears to be a fine or good lathe, knowing nothing about what sort of lathe *is* fine or good); and in both cases by so doing the imitator makes work that is "realistic" – persuasive, compelling, and even deceptive. A painter who knows the truth about lathes could choose a genuinely good one as the subject of his painting, but if the lathe he portrays lacks the qualities that make lathes appear excellent to the ignorant, his viewers will not recognize it as a good lathe, and therefore will not think him an expert in carpentry. His painting will be unpersuasive, as "unrealistic," although in a different sense, as the painting that ignores perspective and copies the bed as it is instead of as it appears, or makes the further man look as big as the near.

Let us represent the analogy between the bed case and the carpenter case as follows:

Form	2nd remove	3rd remove (a)	3rd remove (b)
Form of bed	Material bed	Appearance of bed	Painting of bed
Form of lathe?[17]	*Kalon* lathe	Apparently *kalon* lathe	Painting of carpenter

With this schema in front of us, we notice one very marked *dis*analogy between the two cases. The appearance of a bed supervenes on and is caused by a particular actual bed; an apparently good

correct standard by which to judge the virtue and beauty of an artefact is that of function. . . . The imitator, however, and the children and fools he deceives, judge beauty by the standard of appearance, believing that those shapes and colors that give pleasure are beautiful. . . . Thus, the pleasingly-shaped hammer made by the imitator will appear to have a beautiful shape to children and fools. But a true craftsman will be able to see that such a shape is really not beautiful, for it would be awkward to handle" (Belfiore 1983, p. 46). I am sympathetic to her conclusions, although the identification of pleasure with the false standard of beauty and goodness needs more argument than she provides.

[17] No Form is mentioned in the user/maker/imitator argument, and while in the discussion of the bed Plato told us that the maker – the carpenter – looks to the Form, this would hardly be compatible with the present claim that the maker has only "correct belief" about what he makes, while it is the user who has knowledge (601e). It may be stretching the analogy further than Plato intended to put any Form here corresponding to the Form of the bed; perhaps, however, the relevant Form is the Form of beauty (the *kalon*) or of excellence. This would take better account of the fact that, as I have emphasized, what is really at stake in this argument is knowledge of *value*; it would also provide more continuity with the analysis of poetry as I understand it.

lathe, however, floats quite free of any genuinely good lathe. Something can appear to be good without actually being good; in fact, Plato implies here as so often, the two qualities rarely coincide.[18] Compare two very different senses of "apparent" in English: "an apparently good lathe" may refer to a good lathe that is manifestly good, or instead to a lathe that appears to be but is not in fact good. In his talk of apparent value, Plato clearly has the latter sense in mind.[19]

This disanalogy notwithstanding, we have very good reasons to take it that Plato does intend to draw an analogy between bed and apparent bed, on one hand, and *kalon* tool, and apparently *kalon* tool on the other. First, given Plato's general disparagement of appearances, the distinction between these two senses of "apparent" is not so sharp for him – the appearance of bed *is not* a bed, any more than a merely apparently good lathe is a good lathe. Second, as I show below, this reading makes the example of the carpenter and the distinction among user, maker, and imitator form a link between the discussion of painting and the discussion of poetry.

Moreover, if we depart from the immediate context and look to Plato's thoughts about the *kalon* more generally, we find a strong and surprising point of analogy between the two sorts of appearance. For look how Plato characterizes the difference between genuine and apparent cases of *kallos* – beauty or fineness – in *Republic* 9:

[The democratic city] would seem . . . to be the most beautiful [*kallistē*] of the constitutions. Just like a multicolored cloak embroidered [*pepoikilmenon*] with every ornament, so this city, being embroidered with every character, would appear to be most beautiful. And probably many people would judge it most beautiful, just as children and women do when they look at multicolored things [*ta poikila*].   (557c4–9)

The disordered, motley, multicolored democratic city is not beautiful or fine, any more than a cloak of many different colors. But *poikila* – multicolored or variegated – things *appear* beautiful and

---

[18] Cf., e.g., *Gorgias* 464a on the divergence between the good condition (*euexia*) of a thing and its *seeming* (*dokousa*) good condition.

[19] The Greek language has the resources for clearly marking the distinction between these two senses: *phainesthai* with a participle means is manifestly, while *phainesthai* with an infinitive means merely appears to be. In the relevant passages from *Republic* 10 Plato either uses an infinitive (602b) or uses forms of *phainesthai* on their own, relying on context or contrasts with forms of *einai* ("to be") to show that he intends the latter sense (see, e.g., 596e, 598a–b, and 602d–e).

fine to people as ignorant as women or children. Below we will see that this term *poikilon* has a great deal of ethical significance. If multicolored, variegated things are not truly beautiful, however, what is? Restricting ourselves for now to visual beauty, we find an answer at *Philebus* 51b–c: pure colors and simple shapes.[20] The genuinely beautiful is simple and uniform; the apparently beautiful is varied and contradictory. Thus, apparently *kala* things differ from genuinely *kala* things in just the same way that the appearance of a bed differs from the material bed – and in just the same way that the Form of beauty differs from the many beautifuls. (Here again, however, we must remember that the analogy is only an analogy: while the Form of beauty is absolutely stable and uniform, a genuinely beautiful cloak is only relatively so. Relative to an apparently beautiful cloak it is stable and uniform; relative to the Form of beauty it is varied and full of contradictions.) We can represent the analogy as follows:

Uniform reality	Varied appearance
Form of beauty	Many beautifuls
Material bed	Appearance of bed
Kalon object	Apparently *kalon* object

In the visual realm it is not perhaps plausible that only what is varied, and contradictory will appear *kalon*: it is hard to see why the painted lathe, for example, should fit this description. We will see below, however, that the objects of poetic imitation must be "multicolored," varied, and contradictory, in order to appear *kalon* or otherwise excellent to the audience. Let us turn to poetry now, after taking stock of the conclusions we have drawn from Plato's discussion of painting.

[20] "By the beauty of a shape, I do not mean what the many might presuppose, namely that of a living being or of a picture. What I mean . . . is rather something straight or round and what is constructed out of these with a compass, rule, and square, such as plane figures and solids. Those things I take it are not beautiful in a relative sense as the others are, but are by their very nature forever beautiful by themselves. . . . And colors are beautiful in an analogous way" (*Philebus* 51c–d, trans. D. Frede; the colors in question are described as "pure" at 51b.) Here too Plato distinguishes between what is truly beautiful and what appears beautiful to ordinary people; the latter is something more complex and varied, like a picture or a person.

- Even within the "realm of becoming" appearances are distinct from reality.
- Appearances differ from realities, being varied and contradictory, while realities are stable and uniform.
- Therefore, imitative art – that is, realistic, persuasive art that copies appearances – necessarily *misrepresents* those subjects.
- Therefore, one who lacks the knowledge that imitators copy mere appearances (one who lacks the antidote Plato mentions at 595b) will be deceived, believing both that things truly are as the imitator presents them and that the imitator is an expert about his subjects.

III. ETHICAL IMITATION

Now we must determine how to apply Plato's analysis of imitation to poetry. The painter is an imitator because he copies a material bed, not the Form of the bed, and copies the bed as it appears, not as it is; doing so allows him to deceive foolish people into thinking him an expert. How can we construct an analogy for poetry? Plato defines the object of poetic imitation as follows: "human beings doing actions under compulsion or voluntarily, and believing that as a result of acting they have done well or badly, and in all this either feeling pain or enjoyment" (603c). So as the painter is to the bed, the poet is to human action. But what could it mean to say, as we must to complete the analogy and apply the analysis of imitation, that the poet copies human action as it *appears* and not as it is? And how does this enable him to deceive his audience? Plato gives us no explicit answer to these questions. We need to find an interpretation that not only fits with Plato's characterization of poetry, but also allows us to make sense of the argumentative structure of Book 10. That is, as I stressed in the Introduction, we need an interpretation on which it will come out that poetry corrupts *because* it is a form of imitation, copying appearances instead of reality – an answer that connects the metaphysical charge against poetry to the ethical.

One might think that Plato has in mind the following parallel: just as the painter captures the visible aspect of objects at rest, so the poet captures the visible and audible aspects of humans in motion (humans acting), and thus just as the painter tricks us into thinking that there is a real carpenter on his canvas, so the poet tricks us into thinking that there is a real king grieving or giving orders on the stage. This, however, is hardly a plausible view about poetry's powers; the Greek audience was savvier than that. More significantly, the interpretation fails to connect the metaphysical charge to the ethical: why should it be corrupting to present the illusion of someone walking around, especially if it is not particularly corrupting to present the illusion of someone standing still, as painters do?[21]

A second interpretation, fairly widespread, holds that the poet captures the appearance and not the reality of human action in that he captures only "the words and actions" of his characters; he "does not express, for he does not understand, the principles which underlie those appearances and which constitute reality," and thus captures "only the external, not the inner meaning" of human action.[22] This interpretation may capture some of Plato's thoughts about poetry, but it cannot explain what he means by calling poetry imitative. First, it is not quite a fair characterization of poetry: tragedians write soliloquies revealing their character's inner thoughts and motivations, and Homer uses narrative to convey the same information. Second, like the first interpretation we considered, this one too fails to connect the metaphysical charge against poetry to the ethical. Poets who can accurately copy the appearance or "feel" of behavior can at least in principle produce convincing copies of *good* behavior, and thereby present good role models for the citizens; why should it matter whether they understand what motivates such behavior? Surely, the passages of Homer that Plato lets stand in Book 3 fall under just this description, and perhaps so too will the hymns to the gods and eulogies of good men that he prescribes in Book 10.

In what follows I offer a very different interpretation of "copying action as it appears," one that is in line with the work of Belfiore and Nehamas. In doing so I answer the questions with which we began in the Introduction: how the analysis of imitation as working at a third remove from the truth, as well as the discussion of painting, prove relevant to the charge that poetry corrupts the soul. The

---

[21] Book 3 in fact recommends censorship and supervision of all the arts, but it is clear that Plato regards poetry as the most dangerous of all.

[22] Tate 1928, p. 20. Cf. Ferrari: poets "convey the feel of human behaviour, without being possessed of the understanding from which such behaviour would arise in life" (Ferrari 1989, p. 129).

account is this: Just as the painter copies what appears to be, but is not, a bed, the poet copies what appear to be, but are not, instances of human excellence: the appearance of excellence, *apparent* excellence.[23] Furthermore, apparent human excellence is not only distinct from genuine human excellence, but also differs from it in a way that precisely parallels the difference between the apparent bed and the material bed, or between the many beautiful things and the Form of beauty: varied, contradictory characters appear excellent, while true human excellence lies in stability and uniformity of soul. But to be varied and contradictory in character is in reality to be *vicious*. Therefore imitative, "realistic" poetry persuades us to take ignorant poets as experts in human affairs, presents vicious characters as role models, and thereby corrupts our souls.

The first point to make in defending this interpretation is that on Plato's view the chief business of poetry is to present images of human excellence. Just after drawing his conclusions from the carpenter case about imitation's power to deceive, Socrates says,

> After this we must consider both tragedy and its leader, Homer, since we hear from some people that these men know all the crafts, all human things concerned with excellence and vice, and the divine things too.   (598d–e)

As we read on, it becomes clear that the second of these areas of alleged expertise, "all human things concerned with excellence and vice," is the main focus of his criticism. Socrates moves to pass over a discussion of the crafts, generalizes his claim against Homer by saying that he is "third from the truth about excellence" (599d), and concludes that imitative poets imitate "images [*eidōla*] of excellence and the other things they make poems about" (600e), the other things now being an afterthought. (Indeed, the other two areas of expertise are closely related to this one: knowledge of crafts is one form of human excellence, and in Book 2 Socrates has described stories about the gods as "stories told with a view to excellence" (378e).) In general, poetry is concerned not merely to represent certain ways of acting, but to represent certain ways of acting as *good* (and others as bad).

---

[23] I follow both Belfiore and Nehamas in arguing that Plato complains about poetry because it presents characters who are in fact vicious but seem excellent to the ignorant audience; I want to show more clearly than these writers do how this aspect of poetry's *content* (the kind of character it represents) is connected to the fact that such poetry is imitative in form.

This idea underlies the entirety of the *Republic*'s discussion of poetry. The censorship of poetry about gods and heroes, in Books 2 and 3, was premised on the idea that we take poetry's heroes as role models: we admire and strive to emulate them.[24] (This is just as Protagoras describes the effect of poetry in the *Protagoras*: children "learn by heart the poems of good poets, in which there are many . . . praises and encomia of the good men of old, so that the child is eager to imitate them and desires to become like them" (*Prt.* 325e–326a).) Book 10's denigration of poetry is a response to "praisers of Homer who say that this poet educated Greece, and that it is worthwhile to take up his works for study regarding management and educating in human affairs, and to live having *arranged one's whole life* in accordance with this poet" (606e, emphasis added): Socrates compares Homer to the Sophists (600c) because he too is viewed as an expert in human excellence who can teach us how to live.[25]

There is a wealth of evidence outside the *Republic* that Plato's contemporaries thought of poetry in this way as well. Aristotle's *Poetics* gives us an explicit (and uncritical) statement of the view that poetry's characters are examples of human excellence: the characters in Homer and the tragedies are *better* than we are (*Poetics* 2.1488a11, 15.1454b9), and tragedy (in contrast with comedy) represents *kala* actions of *kala* characters (*Poetics* 4.1448b25, cf. 15.1454b9). Aristotle also quotes Sophocles as saying that he depicted people "as they ought to be" (*Poetics* 25.1460b33). Perhaps the most explicit statement of Plato's worry comes from Xenophon, where Niceratus brags,

---

[24] "Nor is it suitable at all to say that gods war and fight and plot against other gods . . . if indeed those who will guard our city should consider it most shameful to hate one another easily" (378b–c); cf. 391e. Conversely, if a poem presents a character as base, we tend to disdain his behavior: "We would be right to censor the lamentations of renowned men, handing them over to women and not good women either, and to all the bad men, so that those whom we say we are raising to guard the country will be disgusted by acting like those people" (387e–388a). In Books 2 and 3 the claim that we think good, admire, and emulate poetry's heroes is a crucial (although implicit) premise of censorship: the young guardians should not for the most part imitate – play the parts or speak the words of – worthless characters, because by doing so they will come to be like them; if they do ever imitate bad characters they must do so disdainfully and only "in play" (396e).

[25] For relevant passages in other dialogues, see *Charmides* 157e, *Laches* 191b, and *Menexenus* 239b, all cited in Halliwell's commentary on Book 10; Halliwell says that Plato "takes it that one of the oldest and most basic functions of poetry is to bestow praise on figures who are viewed as paragons of humanity in some significant respect" (Halliwell, 1988, pp. 122–23).

"My father, concerned that I should become a good man, forced me to learn all of Homer by heart" (*Symposium* 3.5, cf. 4.6–7).[26]

We can best understand this view of poetry, and Plato's criticism of it, if we read phrases like Aristotle's "better than us" very broadly. Poets sometimes present their characters as paragons of the standard virtues (Odysseus is prudent, Achilles brave, Nestor wise), but Plato is complaining about a more general feature of poetry: that it holds up even its obviously immoral characters as subjects of awe and admiration. Homer and the tragedians present characters we would call "larger than life." We think that in creating them the authors have distilled something of the essence of human nature. And while we may not easily recognize ourselves in Plato's description of poetry's audience,[27] perhaps this way of thinking is not after all so alien to us: we might praise a truly fine work of fiction by saying that it shows us, in some way, who we are. If the poets are thought to be experts in human excellence, it is in part because they seem to be experts more generally in human nature, or human affairs.

The object of poetic imitation, then, is human action, and in particular *excellent* human action. The tragedians and Homer are "imitators of images of excellence and the other things they write about" (600e). The word translated as "image" here is *eidōlon, mere* image, the very word that Plato has used earlier in Book 10 to refer to the appearance of the bed in contrast to the bed itself (598b). This should indicate that Plato does not mean to say that poets imitate genuine human excellence as it appears to us or insofar as it is apparent (as Tate would have it). Rather, just as the painter imitates the appearance of the bed and not the bed itself, the poet imitates *eidōla* of excellence instead of genuine excellence. But this is just to say that the poet imitates *apparently* excellent characters and actions – that is, whichever characters and actions appear excellent to the ignorant many.

---

[26] Burnyeat comments rightly that the comic context should be taken into account here (Burnyeat 1999, p. 306), but the other evidence I cite shows that while Niceratus' claim may be meant as parody, it by no means misses its mark.

[27] The works of Homer and Hesiod and the tragedians were not objects of study for the elite; they were instead popular entertainment, and could plausibly be credited with (or blamed for) influencing and forming popular values and the popular view of human nature. See Murphy 1951; Havelock 1963; Burnyeat 1999; and the comparisons between Plato's attack on poetry and contemporary attitudes toward television in Nehamas 1988.

Now we see in what sense poets imitate the appearance of human action, and we understand the analogy between painting and poetry:

Form	2nd remove	3rd remove (a)	3rd remove (b)
Form of bed	Material bed	Appearance of bed	Painting of bed
Form of lathe?	*Kalon* lathe	Apparently *kalon* lathe	Painting of carpenter
Forms of virtues?	Excellent character	Apparently excellent character	Poem about character

Very few people know the truth about human excellence or virtue, *aretē* – the preceding nine books of the *Republic* have made this point abundantly clear. Book 10 has told us that the excellence of any living thing, like that of any tool, is related to its *function* (compare again *Republic* I, 352d ff.); without knowledge of the function and nature of the soul, no one can know what real excellence is, nor whether a particular person is excellent or not. But humans, like tools, can *appear* excellent or *kalos* without really being so, and what makes for apparent excellence is precisely the province of the imitator. It is the poet more than the painter that Plato has in mind when he says that the imitator "will imitate . . .the sort of things that appear to be fine or beautiful to the ignorant many" (602b, quoted above). The poet does not really know what makes for a skilled doctor, a wise general, a brave soldier, or a just king, but he knows just what sort of behavior will *seem* skilled, wise, brave, and just to popular opinion. This is how a poet such as Homer gains his reputation for knowing "all the crafts and all human things concerned with excellence and vice" (598d–e). Because his portrayal of a doctor healing a patient impresses the ignorant audience as capturing precisely what a good doctor would do, they think that Homer himself knows all about medicine; because he portrays behavior that seems to the audience to exemplify bravery, justice, wisdom, piety, and self-control, they think him an expert in human excellence, a fit teacher to guide them in living their lives.

The poet, then, presents characters and actions that appear *kalon* and excellent to the audience. He does so by imitating the appearance, not the reality, of human excellence. Being faithful to the appearances, his art is imitative in Plato's special sense – "realistic," plausible, and persuasive – and therefore he too can deceive his audience. They think him an expert about human excellence because he produces images so like what they take to be the real thing.

None of this, however, is enough to show that poetry is ethically harmful. If the appearance of excellence is relevantly *like* the reality – if Homer's Achilles acts more or less as genuinely brave men would – then imitative poetry may deserve a place in the ideal city, and cannot be accused of corrupting the soul.[28] Is this so? Does poetry present faithful images of excellence? Or is imitative poetry, like painting, "realistic" and persuasive at the cost of misrepresenting the reality?

Long before we get to Book 10 we already know that poetry praises people who are in fact vicious: in Book 2 Adeimantus tells us that poets "account happy and honor vicious [*ponērous*] people who have wealth and other kinds of power" (364a); Book 9 tells us that poets "praise tyranny as godlike" (568b). In the same Book 2 passage Adeimantus accuses poetry of perpetrating the very view about morality that the *Republic* is concerned to disprove: that injustice is more profitable than justice (364a). This is certainly how things *seem* to people, but it is not, Plato argues, how things are.

Now notice how Plato characterizes the difference between genuine human excellence and the traits admired by the many and praised by the poets, apparent excellence. Virtue, as defined in Book 4, is a harmonious ordering of the soul, in which there are no conflicts or tensions. In Book 10 Plato emphasizes that such a state is stable and uniform: the virtuous character is "prudent and peaceful, remaining always nearly the same as itself [*phronimon te kai hēsukhion ēthos, paraplēsion on aei auto hautōi*]" (604e). This should remind us of the description of the material bed, in contrast to its appearance, as "differing in no way from itself" (598a), and the description of the Form of beauty as "remaining always the same in all respects" (479a).[29]

---

[28] That Plato thinks faithful images of genuinely good characters do deserve *some* place in the ideal city is clear from Books 2 and 3. Such images contribute to moral education; how they do so is an important question, but one that lies outside the scope of this chapter. See Malcolm Schofield's chapter 6 in this volume.

[29] It is important to note that the virtuous character is only *paraplēsion* to itself – nearly the same, very similar – while the unchanging unity of the Form is absolute. As Plato says later in Book 10, our souls are never perfect when embodied (611b ff.). The virtuous soul is as good, as uniform, and as stable as an embodied soul can be, but nonetheless falls far short of the ideal.

Book 10 describes the genuinely virtuous character in this way only to add that it does not lend itself to poetic imitation:

> [T]he wise and peaceful character, remaining always nearly the same as itself, is neither easily imitated nor easy to understand when imitated, especially not by a motley crowd gathered at the theater. For the imitation would be of an experience alien to them [*allotriou . . . pathous*].   (604e)

In what sense is genuine virtue an "alien experience" to most people, and thus not an easy subject of imitation? It cannot be merely that most people have not had the experience of being prudent and peaceful, for neither have they had the experience of being a general or a king or Electra, and it is imitations of these characters that they most enjoy. Rather we should hear "alien" in something closer to the Brechtian sense. A story whose hero is quiet and imperturbable, reacting to fortune's blows not with passion and drama but with calm reasoning and utter self-control, leaves the mass audience as cold as would an abstract painting of a bed. The peaceful character simply does not "look like" a hero – someone "better" than us, *kalos*, larger than life, admirable, exciting, worth watching – any more than a painting that tries to copy the reality of a bed by ignoring perspective and foreshortening will look like a bed. Poetry that copies the reality instead of the appearance of virtue will leave the audience puzzled, distanced, bored, and in no way inclined to think the author an expert in human excellence. The claim that the virtuous character is difficult to imitate, then, must rest on the view that the reality of human excellence is very different from the appearance.

What then, is apparent excellence like – what sort of character appears excellent? It must be the one Plato contrasts to the genuinely virtuous character by describing as *eumimēton*, easily imitated – the kind of character people admire, enjoy watching, and consider a plausible hero. This character Plato characterizes as "irritable and multicolored [*aganaktētikon te kai poikilon*]" (605a5) – stormy, passionate, emotional, full of inner conflict, subject to varied moods and changing desires. Such a character is in fact the very contrary of the virtuous character – it is vicious.[30] But this is precisely the kind of character Homer and the tragedians choose as their heroes: hotheads, lamenters, passionate lovers, wily plotters, wrathful avengers.

---

[30] The democratic character type, second in vice and misery only to the tyrannical, is called *poikilon* at 561e; the *Laws* refers to vicious characters as "multicolored and base [*ēthē kai poikila kai phaula*]" (*Laws* 704d).

Looking back to the discussion of poetry and music in Books 2 and 3, we find Plato making much the same charge. Genuine excellence is stable and uniform, or as Plato here puts it, "simple" (*haploun*), and art should represent it as such.[31] Popular art, however, tends to represent gods and heroes as changeable, varied, full of contradictions and multicolored variety.[32] Here Plato applies this criticism to the style as well as content of representation: the style of narrative suitable for representing a virtuous person has "little variation," but people much prefer hearing the style that has "motley forms of variation" 397b–c; later he contrasts meters and rhythms appropriate to an "orderly and courageous life" to ones that are multicolored (*poikilous*) and varied (*pantodapas*) (399e–400a). In general, "simplicity [*haplotēs*] in music and poetry" is beneficial (404e), but variety conforms to popular taste.[33]

Genuine excellence and the beneficial art that copies it is "simple" (*haploun*); the character that appears excellent, and thus the art that copies apparent excellence, is "multicolored" (*poikilon*). This latter word echoes throughout the *Republic*: in the passages from Book 3 quoted above, in Book 10 where both the "easily imitated" character and the poet's imitations of him are multicolored (604e, 605a), and in Book 9 where Socrates tells us that women and children foolishly think multicolored things beautiful or fine (557c, quoted above). It is worth noting that poets used this very word to characterize their heroes: Hesiod's Prometheus is *poikilos*, as is Aeschylus'; Euripides uses the same word for his Odysseus, while Homer's Odysseus is *poikilomētēs* – "multicolor-minded."[34] Indeed Homer's Odysseus is a paradigm of a varied and contradictory character presented as hero: he is the man of many wiles and many tricks, *polutropos*, *polumēkhanos*, *polumētis*, anything but *haplous*.

---

[31] The just person is called *haploun* at 361b, a god at 380d; for passages describing good art as *haploun*, see below.

[32] Poetry represents gods as appearing in many shapes, but in reality a god retains one and the same shape, being simple (*haploun*, 380d). Poets represent Achilles (a hero and the son of a goddess) as full of turmoil (391c), but a true god-like hero is stable and calm.

[33] Even "polyharmonic or multistringed instruments" – the flute first among them – are ruled out in favor of simple ones (399c).

[34] Hesiod's *Theogony* 511, Aeschylus' *Prometheus Bound* 310, Euripides' *Iphigenia at Aulis* 526, Homer's *Iliad* 11.482 and *Odyssey* 3.163.

Plato's criticisms imply, then, that appearances in the realm of human affairs differ from reality in just the same way that we have seen appearances differing from reality throughout. Let us add this to our chart as follows:

Uniform reality	Varied appearance
Form of beauty	Many beautifuls[35]
Material bed	Appearance of bed
Kalon object	Apparently *kalon* object
Excellent character	Apparently excellent character

Now we see the ethical payoff of the discussion of painting, and the relevance of the user/maker/imitator argument. We also have a solution to the problem that has vexed many commentators as to whether Plato contradicts himself by allowing poetry that imitates virtuous characters in Book 3, but condemning all imitative poetry in Book 10. Imitative poetry is "realistic" poetry: it copies things as they appear, not as they are. In particular, it copies virtue as it appears, that is, *apparent* virtue, presenting varied, contradictory, dazzling heroes. Poetry that copies the reality of virtue (i.e., presents images of stable, uniform characters) – like the passages of Homer that survive censorship in Book 3, and the "hymns to gods and eulogies of good men" allowed into the city in Book 10 (607a) – may well include imitations of characters, but it is not "imitative" in the technical sense Book 10 defines: it copies things as they are, not as they appear.[36]

---

[35] *Timaeus* 50d calls the entire realm of becoming, the perceptible realm, multicolored – *poikilon.*

[36] Contra Adam (see his note on 607a) and the many who agree with him that Plato defines *all* poetry, and indeed all art, as imitative. I thus side with Tate, Ferrari, Janaway, Nehamas, and others who allow Books 3 and 10 to be consistent by arguing for a distinction between imitation, on the one hand, and imitativeness, on the other, and stressing that Plato condemns only *imitativeness*. Each, like me, defines imitativeness in such a way that poets (or actors) who imitate only good characters are not thereby imitative: Ferrari, Janaway, and Nehamas argue that to be imitative is to enjoy imitation for its own sake or to enjoy imitating anything whatsoever, regardless of its worth; Tate argues that to be imitative is to copy what is at a second remove from truth instead of the Forms. I prefer my solution in that it is more closely tied to the metaphysical analysis of imitation and the discussion of painting. My solution does still leave us with an inconsistency: *imitation* is defined

Now we are also, almost, ready to answer the question with which we began: what is the relation between the metaphysical charge that imitative poetry is at a third remove from the truth and the ethical charge that it "puts a bad constitution" in the soul? To complete the answer – and to get a full view of *Republic* 10 – we need to put in place the psychological side of the story.

IV. CORRUPTING THE SOUL

Poetry that encourages us to admire and emulate vicious characters surely does no ethical good. But Plato's accusation is more specific: imitative poetry harms us by "putting a bad constitution" into our souls (605b) – that is, by strengthening an inferior part of the soul and thereby weakening or overthrowing the rule of reason. If this charge is to stand, Plato must show that *just insofar as poetry is imitative*, it targets and gratifies an inferior part of the soul. But here the argument of Book 10 may seem to involve a serious non sequitur.

Socrates asks over what part of the soul imitation exerts its power at 602c; he begins his answer by examining a class of visual appearances that stand out as mere appearances: optical illusions. A person can know how things really are and yet still experience an illusion: a submerged stick looks bent even when one knows it is straight. Plato takes this to show that two distinct parts of the soul are at work in such cases: the rational part, whose beliefs are sensitive to reasoning and calculation, and some other part, unreasoning and base,[37] that believes that things are as they appear.[38] Because painters show things as they appear (the painter paints the submerged stick as bent, and the more distant man as smaller), he concludes that visual

in Book 10 as copying things as they appear, not as they are, but in Books 2 and 3 is indiscriminate between copying appearances and copying realities. This seems to me a blatant, but not very problematic, inconsistency in Plato's text: we can allow that Plato introduces a technical sense of "imitation" in Book 10, while using the term more broadly in the earlier books; after all, the more technical sense relies on metaphysical distinctions not introduced until Books 5–7.

[37] It is one of the base (*phaula*) things in us (603a); it is "far from wisdom" (*phronēsis*, 603a), and it is "thoughtless" (*anoēton*, 605b).

[38] 602c–603b. The conclusion is established by an application of the principle of opposites, the same principle Plato used to establish the division of the soul in Book 4. The argument relies on some questionable presuppositions, in particular that when the stick looks bent, one (in part) *believes* that it is bent.

imitation appeals to this inferior, appearance-receptive part of the soul.

Then he turns to poetry. The discussion makes no overt reference to appearances or illusions of any kind: instead, it describes the kind of characters and situations imitative poetry tends to represent. Socrates even warns his interlocutors not to rely on the analogy with painting in determining what part of the soul poetry affects (603b). He proceeds to describe our responses to poetry as appetitive and emotional, in ways strongly reminiscent of his earlier characterization of the appetitive and spirited parts of the soul.[39] But the conclusion he draws at the end of the discussion is that imitative poetry affects the very part of the soul that is taken in by optical illusions:

> The imitative poet instills a bad constitution in the private soul of each person, gratifying the part of the soul that is thoughtless and doesn't distinguish the bigger from the smaller, but supposes that the same things are at one time large and another time small. (605b–c)[40]

How does Plato reach this conclusion, and what does it mean? How is watching a tragedy or listening to Homer psychologically parallel to experiencing an optical illusion; how, for example, is "hungering for weeping and wailing" parallel to seeing a submerged stick as bent? The connection has seemed to most interpreters obscure or absurd.[41] But the account developed above resolves the mystery: in

---

[39] Most explicitly: "concerning sexual desires and anger [thumou] and all the appetitive desires and pains and pleasures in the soul . . . poetic imitation . . . nurtures these things, watering them although they should wither, and sets them up to rule in us although they should be ruled" (606d). Plato also describes this part of the soul as one that "*hungers* for the satisfaction of weeping and sufficiently lamenting, being by nature such as to have *appetites* for these things [epithumein]; this is the part that is satisfied and delighted by the poets" (606a, emphasis added); he describes the type of character naturally akin to poetic imitation as "irritable and multicolored" (605a), where previously he has used such terms to characterize spirit and appetite, respectively. Commentators have wished to resist the conclusion that spirit or appetite is at issue here, because they think it improbable that either of these parts could be involved in optical illusions. The argument I give in what follows should make Plato's strong implication that appetite and spirit are intended far more palatable.

[40] The illusion-believing part of the soul first sees a man close by and believes that he is large, then sees him at a distance and believes that he is small.

[41] Nehamas speaks for many here: "Why should our *desire* tell us that the immersed stick is bent?" (Nehamas 1982, p. 265). He goes on to argue that some hitherto unmentioned subdivision of reason is intended. The basis for this reading (shared

describing the passionate, dazzling, varied, conflicting characters and actions imitative poetry represents, Plato takes himself to be showing that such poetry imitates ethical *appearances*. A straight stick submerged in water appears bent; likewise a multicolored character appears *kalon* and excellent to us, human affairs appear important (604d), and an event such as the death of a son appears obviously bad (603e ff.; Plato calls such events "*seeming* evils" (*dokounta kaka*) at 613a). A passage from the *Phaedo* (69b) is helpful here: what most people think of as virtue (and thus what imitative poetry represents) is in fact only a *skiagraphia* of virtue – a shadow-painting, something akin to trompe l'oeil. Plato classes *skiagraphiai* with optical illusions at *Republic* 602d.[42] Imitative painting trades in visual illusions, imitative poetry in ethical illusions. Thus the passionate emotions provoked by imitative poetry are to be understood as responses to vivid appearances of things as good or bad, wonderful or terrible. Hence Plato's sharp contrast between indulging these emotions, on the one hand, and rational calculation, on the other: weeping and wailing at the death of one's son, like believing that a submerged stick is bent, means assenting to the way things appear instead of using rational calculation to determine how things really are.[43]

by Burnyeat 1999 and others) is a difficult passage at 602e that seems to imply that the stick appears bent to the *rational* part of the soul; there are readings of 602e, however, that avoid this unpalatable conclusion (see, e.g., Adam 1963 [1902], vol. 2, p. 408 and 466–67). For fuller discussion of this passage, *Republic* 10's argument, and the connection between appearances and the nonrational soul, see Moss 2006.

[42] See also *Republic* 586b–c, where Plato describes the impure pleasures of the many as shadow-painted images (*eidōla eskiagraphēmena*) of the true pleasures of the philosopher, and *Laws* 663c where ordinary, corrupt notions of justice and injustice are like shadow paintings viewed from a flawed perspective.

[43] The reason-led person is "measured" in his grief (603e) and holds back from lamentation because he follows "calculation" (604d); note that measurement and calculation are precisely the tools that reason employs in combatting optical illusions (602d–603a). Ethical "calculation" includes the thought that "it is unclear what is good and bad in such things [e.g., the death of one's son]" (604b): although the death of a son certainly *appears* to be bad, just as the stick in water appears to be bent, reason does not simply accept this appearance. The rational man also calculates that "human affairs are not worth great seriousness" (604b–c): here reason puts his or her pains into perspective, just as it corrects for effects of distance in matters of sight. Nussbaum argues that one of Plato's main complaints against tragedy is that it represents good people genuinely suffering from the blows of fortune, while on the Socratic view, a good person cannot be harmed (Nussbaum 1986): we can understand this as the complaint that poetry fails to distinguish what merely *appears* bad (human misfortune) from what is genuinely bad. For good discussion of

Thus realistic, imitative poetry caters to the appearance-responsive, nonrational soul, while poets who present "quiet and moderate" characters, like painters who present true proportions, fail to present things as they appear and thus fail to engage this part of the soul. Now that we have the psychological side of this story in place, we can see why imitative poetry is so worrisome to Plato – that is, why on his account it has such influence and power. First, it is this nonrational part of the soul that tends to dominate in most people. The earlier books of the *Republic* showed us that reason rules the souls only of the few (the virtuous, the philosophic): most people are ruled by appetite or spirit. However precisely Plato intends to identify Book 10's "inferior part of the soul" (603a) with appetite or spirit, here too he holds that most people are ruled not by reason but by the irrational passions, desires, and prejudices that oppose it. Second, this "hungering," "insatiable" part of the soul (604d, 606a) feels intense *pleasure* when gratified. Poetry that caters to its desires for emotional release is thus called "the poetry aiming at pleasure and imitation," where these seem to be equivalent descriptions (607c).[44] The intense pleasure imitative poets provide, along with the persuasive realism that makes them seem to be experts, puts ordinary people fully in their sway. (That emotional responses are so vivid, powerful, and pleasurable should help to explain why imitative poetry is so dangerous, while painting, although it targets the same part of the soul, is less so.)

Most worrisome to Plato – the "greatest charge" against poetry – the pleasures of imitative poetry are so strong that they threaten to upset the order even of a "decent" person's soul (605c). Here it is crucial to recognize that, as we have shown, the pleasures poetry offers us are not the cheap thrills of pulp fiction or "trash." Imitative poetry offers us compelling portraits of human affairs and human excellence – compelling because they are realistic, that is, they capture these things as they appear. In so doing, such poetry gives

the parallels between visual perception and emotional reactions, see White 1979; Belfiore 1983; and Ferrari 1989.

[44] Cf. "If you let in the pleasurable muse in lyric or epic poetry, pleasure and pain will be kings in your city" (607a). The *Gorgias* puts the point very clearly: tragedy is a form of flattery, for it aims "only to gratify the spectators," has no qualms about "saying something pleasant and gratifying to them but corrupting," and refuses to say what is "unpleasant but beneficial" (*Gorgias* 502b).

us the emotional satisfaction of identifying, grieving, and rejoicing with its heroes. When we understand Plato's criticisms we see how closely they apply to the very features that make us value Homer and Sophocles, and Shakespeare and Dostoevsky too. Recall the distinction above between simple (excellent) and multicolored (apparently excellent) characters, and the corresponding distinction between simple (nonimitative) and multicolored (imitative) art. What we call "great literature" is rarely simple: it is complex and varied, rich in detail, in subtlety and even in contradictions. It presents characters who undergo change (think of the charge that a book lacks "character development"), who hold our interest by feeling deep conflict and struggling over what to do, whose human weaknesses allow us to learn from them and whose passions let us sympathize with them. In the visual realm Plato leaves us pure colors and simple shapes (*Philebus* 51b–c, quoted above); in literature, as he makes quite clear in Book 3, he leaves us steady, quiet characters persuading each other with reason, and enduring calmly in the face of trials.[45] Imagine an *Iliad* cast only with Nestors, or a sane, dispassionate Hamlet with no taste for revenge. Or imagine a protagonist who accepts imminent death calmly, and spends his last hours engaged in quiet, rational persuasion. This last makes for excellent Platonic dialogue – but does it give even the most highbrow among us what we want from art?[46]

V. CONCLUSION

Now at last we have our solution to the problem with which we began. How is the metaphysical charge against poetry, that it is a form of imitation and thus at a third remove from the truth, related to the ethical charge, that it corrupts the soul? Imitative art copies

---

[45] See 389e–390d.

[46] Burnyeat holds out hope that the "hymns to the gods and encomia of good men" allowed into the city at 607a will include "engaging narratives" and "adventure stories" (Burnyeat 1999, p. 278). This may be right, but Plato clearly recognizes that the poetry he countenances lacks the pleasures of the poetry he condemns: "the more poetic and pleasing" poems are, "the less they should be heard" (387b); the multicolored style is most pleasant (397d), but the simple one is more beneficial (398a); the poet who will be admitted to the ideal city is "more austere and less pleasure-giving" than the poets who will be expelled (398a–b). The question of whether Plato means his own dialogues to be poetry of a sort is an important one: see the discussion of "anti-tragic theatre" in Nussbaum 1986.

appearances instead of realities, and therefore is "realistic" – persuasive and compelling, able to deceive the audience into thinking the artist an expert in his subjects. Imitative poetry copies appearances of human affairs, and of human excellence in particular. But these appearances differ drastically from the reality: being varied and contradictory instead of stable and uniform, the apparently excellent character is in fact a model of vice. The audience is deceived by the "realistic" portrayal: they admire and emulate the hero as a paragon of excellence, and take the author to be an expert in human excellence, an expert about how one should live. The spell is all the stronger and more pernicious in that poetry's appearances influence and gratify the nonrational part of the soul, a part that experiences powerful and disruptive pleasure. By gratifying this part of the soul poetry strengthens it; thus the audience's rational thought is crippled, and their souls are harmed.

Last, we have seen that Plato's argument against poetry in *Republic* 10 is far more substantial than it first appears. He is not merely making the complaint that various influential poets happen to write ethically harmful poetry. Rather, he has presented an argument, based on metaphysical and psychological theory, that *only* ethically harmful poetry – poetry that reflects and reinforces the flaws in popular morality – can compel us and move us with its portrayal of human affairs. Persuasive, pleasing, *poikilon* (multicolored) poetry has what beneficial but austere *haploun* (simple) poetry lacks: the power over ordinary people that makes poetry a matter of such concern to Plato in the first place, and the power over even a Plato or a Socrates that make them wish it could be redeemed.[47]

WORKS CITED

Adam, J., ed. 1963 [1902]. *The* Republic *of Plato*. Cambridge.
Belfiore, E. 1983. "Plato's Greatest Accusation against Poetry." In *Canadian Journal of Philosophy*, suppl. vol. 9: *New Essays on Plato*, ed. F. J. Pelletier and J. King-Farlow (Guelph, Ontario).

[47] See the lover's farewell to poetry at 607c–608a, Socrates' avowal of love for Homer at 595b, and Plato's frequent quotation of Homer and other poets throughout the dialogues.

For valuable comments, criticism, and discussion concerning the issues in this chapter, I am grateful to Cian Dorr, John Ferrari, Alexander Nehamas, Ron Polansky, Nicholas Rescher, Nick Zangwill, and audiences at the University of Pittsburgh and University College Cork.

Burnyeat, M. F. 1999. "Culture and Society in Plato's *Republic*." *Tanner Lectures in Human Values* 20: 215–324.

Ferrari, G. R. F. 1989. "Plato on Poetry." In *The Cambridge History of Literary Criticism*, vol. 1, ed. G. A. Kennedy (Cambridge).

Halliwell, S., trans. and ed. 1988. *Plato: Republic 10*. Warminster.

Havelock, E. A. 1963. *Preface to Plato*. Cambridge, Mass.

Janaway, C. 1995. *Images of Excellence*. Oxford.

Keuls, E. C. 1978. *Plato and Greek Painting*. Leiden.

Moss, J. 2006. "Pleasure and Illusion in Plato." *Philosophy and Phenomenological Research* 72, no. 3.

Murphy, N. R. 1951. *The Interpretation of Plato's* Republic. Oxford.

Nehamas, A. 1982. "Plato on Imitation and Poetry." In *Plato on Beauty, Wisdom and the Arts*, ed. J. M. E. Moravcsik and P. Temko (Totowa). Rpt. in A. Nehamas, *Virtues of Authenticity: Essays on Plato and Socrates* (Princeton, 1999).

Nehamas, A. 1988. "Plato and the Mass Media." *The Monist* 71: 214–34.

Nussbaum, M. C. 1986. *The Fragility of Goodness*. Cambridge.

Paton, H. J. 1921–22. "Plato's Theory of *EIKASIA*." *Proceedings of the Aristotelian Society* 22: 69–104.

Russell, B. 1912. *The Problems of Philosophy*. New York. Rpt. Oxford, 1959.

Steven, R. G. 1933. "Plato and the Art of His Time." *Classical Quarterly* 27: 149–55.

Tate, J. 1928. "'Imitation' in Plato's *Republic*." *Classical Quarterly* 22: 16–23.

Tate, J. 1932. "Plato and 'Imitation.'" *Classical Quarterly* 26: 161–69.

White, N. 1979. *A Companion to Plato's* Republic. Indianapolis, Ind.

16 The Life-and-Death Journey of the Soul

Interpreting the Myth of Er

> *Puis elle commençait à me devenir inintelligible, comme après la métempsycose les pensées d'une existence antérieure.*
>
> Proust

The story of Er, a Pamphylian soldier who died in battle but several days later returned to life on his funeral pyre and reported what his soul had seen and heard in the world beyond, brings the *Republic* to a close in a visionary mode whose complexity tests the limits of understanding. For three (overlapping) reasons, the narrative raises more questions than it can answer: first, because it undertakes the profoundly ambitious task of presenting a symbolic perspective on the whole of reality, a figurative equivalent of Book 6's theme of "the contemplation of all time and all being" (486a); second, because its densely allusive texture yields a surplus of possible meanings that cannot be adequately encompassed by any single interpretation; and third, because it stands in a kind of challenging counterpoint, combining harmony and dissonance, with the rest of the *Republic*. Plato weaves into the account of Er's experience numerous strands from the materials of Greek philosophy, science, religion (not least, mystery religion), poetry, historiography, and even visual art. This fascinating multiplicity of sources and associations is not my primary concern here, though some pointers will be provided parenthetically as I proceed. I do, however, want to explore the character of the passage as an elaborate piece of philosophical *writing*, rather than as the vehicle for a set of putative authorial beliefs. While the myth's overall significance as an ultimate (i.e., cosmic and eternal) vindication of justice looks clear enough at first sight, it leads us, I shall contend,

445

into realms of irreducibly difficult interpretation. That, indeed, may be part of its raison d'être. The myth can fruitfully be thought of as inviting a "cyclical" reading in conjunction with the preceding dialogue, a reading that forms a hermeneutic parallel to the existential cycle of life and death pictured in Er's account, but one that Plato's text itself does not supply the means to bring to a definitive conclusion.

The story comprises three main sections, enacting in turn the three great ideas of eschatological judgment, cosmological necessity, and reincarnation or metempsychosis, though this sequence is interrupted more than once by comments that Socrates makes in his own voice. In the first section (614c–616a), Er's soul, having left his body, travels with other souls to the site of postmortem judgment, where it observes their consignment to a millennium of rewards/punishments in (or above) the sky and below the earth. Er does not follow these souls further but hears others, returned from the sky or earth, recounting their experiences during the previous millennium, including what those who went below had witnessed of the horrific punishment of tyrants. In the next phase (616b–617c), seven days later, Er travels onward with the group of returning souls. On the fourth day of their journey, they see ahead a column of intense light binding together the universe. Inside the light hangs the spindle of Necessity, Ananke, the eight segments of whose hemispherical whorl correspond to an astronomical configuration of sun, moon, fixed stars, and five (known) planets. On the rims of the spindle's segments sit eight Sirens, emitting the notes of an octave (and thus giving expression to a music or harmony of the spheres), as well as three Moirai or Fates (Lachesis, Klotho, Atropos), the daughters of Necessity. In the final part (617d–621b), a priest of Lachesis tells the returning souls that they must choose their next incarnate lives and take full responsibility for their destinies. The souls make their choices, with an extraordinary range of results: not least, many of those who have come down from the rewards of the sky now paradoxically condemn themselves to bad, unhappy lives in the next period of earthly existence. The choices are confirmed; each soul is accompanied by the *daimōn* ("spirit") that it implicitly chose. These new persons then drink the waters of the river Heedless (*Ameles*), in the plain of Forgetting (*Lēthē*), thus erasing (some of the) memories of their previous lives. They sleep, but are roused by thunder and an earth tremor before being released into their next embodied lifespan. Er reawakes on his funeral pyre.

Er's soul journey, though a *muthos* (as Socrates himself calls it, 621b) qua act of storytelling, is neither a replication of a culturally canonical narrative nor a total invention of Plato's. Like its relatives in *Gorgias* and *Phaedo*, it traverses some familiar terrain of traditional Greek underworld mythology, recalling in part the visits to Hades of heroes such as Odysseus, Orpheus, and Heracles. But affinities with *Phaedrus* underline its combination of the story patterns of both descent and ascent, *katabasis* and *anabasis*.[1] It is, in effect, a reinvented myth, and as such one contribution to Plato's larger project of (re)appropriating the medium of myth for his own philosophical purposes. This was a project for which, of course, there were pre-Socratic precedents, not least in Parmenides and Empedocles, but also in Pythagorean myths, now lost, relating specifically to metempsychosis.[2] It was also an enterprise that involved Plato in a larger arena of intellectual competition over the uses of myth with Sophists, historians, and others. Above all, the myth of Er is a quasi-poetic piece of writing, as Socrates acknowledges at the start, with studied ambiguity, when he contrasts what he is about to relate, but thereby also prompts comparison, with Odysseus' "tale told to Alcinous" in the *Odyssey* (614b).

On one level the myth can be read as a philosophically transfigured *Odyssey*, with the soul's quest for eternal happiness, and the many dangers that imperil it, replacing the hero's quest for home. Odyssean motifs reinforce the point: the integration of (eight) Sirens into a model of cosmic harmony (617b), for instance, rewrites their status as (two) seductive but destructive demons in *Odyssey* 12, and the catalogue of figures at 620a–c contains several Odyssean echoes, including a refiguring of Odysseus himself as a soul that has learnt the futility of human honor seeking (*philotimia*).[3] The myth's

---

[1] Albinus 1998 broaches some relevant themes.

[2] Pythagorean myths of metempsychosis: Aristotle *De Anima* 1.3, 407b21–3; cf. Plato *Grg.* 493a (note 19 below). Morgan 2000 investigates Plato's relationship to pre-Socratic myth.

[3] The Sirens may be a Pythagorean borrowing: see Iamblichus, *De Vita Pythagorica* 82, but this could equally reflect a subsequent Pythagoreanizing of Plato's own text. Odysseus's search for an inconspicuous life (620c–d) echoes both the philosophical repudiation of *philotimia* (cf. 545a–55a, 581b–86c) and the war-weary home seeking of his Homeric persona.

gestures of competition with the *Odyssey* remind us, more broadly, of the "ancient quarrel" between philosophy and poetry invoked earlier in Book 10 (607b), as well as the extensive critique of poetic "mythology," including the mythology of Hades, in Books 2 and 3. The implied contest with poetry is rendered more acute by the fact that at 2.365e Adeimantus cited the poets as a primary source of culturally entrenched convictions about the afterlife, while at 10.596c Socrates mentioned the depiction of Hades (together with "things in the sky," also pertinent to the myth) as one aspect of what he provocatively called mimetic art's aspiration to "make everything." Nor should we overlook, given Book 10's specific analogy between poetry and painting, that the myth is also a rival to visual art, especially to Polygnotus's great panoramic vision of the underworld, his *Nekuia*, in the Cnidians' meeting-hall at Delphi.[4] But to speak of rivalry prompts a hard question. If poets and painters cannot be trusted in their portrayals of Hades, why should Socrates himself (or Plato) expect to be? Why should Er be a more credible witness than Odysseus? The terms of the question are perhaps too blunt. A nuanced conception of rivalry must allow for some overlap of goals, not sheer antagonism. In the *Gorgias*, Socrates actually cites Homer more than once in support of parts of his own eschatological myth.[5] We should be prepared to read the myth of Er, then, as a philosophical recomposition, not an outright rejection, of poetry.

In certain respects, however, Er's soul journey could equally be said to have an *anti*mythological and antipoetic slant. For one thing, the hero Odysseus, despite his cameo appearance in the story, is displaced as narrator by an apparently ordinary barbarian soldier, though a "valiant" one (*alkimos*, 614b, a poetic term found nowhere else in Plato). We are told nothing about Er himself other than his non-Greek name, patronymic, and ethnic identity, onomastic details in which it may be tempting to detect etymologizing puns.[6] Furthermore, Socrates speaks from the outset with quasi-historical immediacy,

---

[4] Polygnotus's *Nekuia*, itself a "rival" to poetry, is described by Pausanias 10.28–31. Figures common to the painting and Plato's myth are Agamemnon, Ajax, Orpheus, Thamyras/-is, Thersites.

[5] *Grg.* 523a, 525d–e, 526d.

[6] Er (for which both Iranian and Semitic roots have been proposed) might suggest "spring" (*ēr*) in Greek; more remotely, Armenius (attested as a real name at Athens in the fourth century) could evoke *ērmenos*, "raised up." Pamphylian means "of the whole [human] race": a hint of universalism? See further in Halliwell 1988,

as though chronicling a factual report received from a "messenger" (614d, 619b; cf. 619e). There are even some stylistic touches, such as the mannered verbal repetition at 614b ("he came back to life, and coming back to life . . ."), that remind us of Herodotus and help to create a kind of veneer of historicity, but at the same time an impression of artfully calculated narrative. It may be no coincidence that Herodotus' work contains the story of Aristeas of Proconnesus, a shaman-like messenger of the divine who supposedly made soul journeys while under trance and who possibly had Pythagorean connections.[7]

Also germane to the pseudo-historiographical impression is a striking literary trait, though one almost inevitably lost in translation. After the initial, scene-setting announcement at 614b, most of the account is couched in indirect speech. This feature makes the passage an exceptionally sustained piece of "foregrounded" *oratio obliqua* (as opposed to the background *oratio obliqua* of, for instance, the *Symposium*), offset only by three pieces of quoted direct speech (615d–616a, 617d–e, 619b) and by Socrates' comments on the myth. If we compare this technique of writing with the tripartite scheme of diegetic modes established by Socrates in Book 3 (392c–398b), we find that the telling of Er's story stretches and complicates the categories of that typology. In that earlier context, narrative (*diēgēsis*) was classified in three forms: "pure" or "simple," that is, entirely in third-person, descriptive mode; "narrative through mimesis," that is, direct speech or verbally dramatised enactment; and the alternating combination of these two, as in Homeric epic. The discussion in Book 3 illustrated the possible inclusion of indirect speech within a passage of "simple" narrative (393d–394a), but it did not anticipate the use of *oratio obliqua* to provide a complete framework of narration. The myth of Er thus has an intricacy of layering, including narrative within narrative (and even indirect discourse within indirect discourse),[8] which exceeds the terms of Book 3's schema.

---

pp. 170–71, with references on p. 169 for the larger question of the myth's non-Greek affinities.

[7] Herodotus 4.13–16 (with a possible allusion to reincarnation, 4.15).

[8] In addition to the "embedded" narrative of 615a–616a, there is implicit indirect speech *within* indirect speech at 614c–d, 619c, 620d; at 616d Socrates assimilates an element of his own conjecture into Er's report. On other aspects of the myth's relationship to Book 3's typology of narrative, see Bouvier 2001.

True, the form of the myth is consistent with Socrates' earlier anxieties about the allure of dramatized, "mimetic" storytelling and
its capacity to imprint destabilizing patterns of feeling on the mind
(394e–398b). But the point of this form is not only to keep the narrative "austere" (398a). The protracted use of indirect speech (not
paralleled in scale by any other Platonic myth) is strangely obses-
sive.[9] It is equally readable as a marker of transcription, purporting to
transmit a message with total fidelity, or as a constant reminder that
this is someone else's version of events. Its narrative point of view,
moreover, is simultaneously that of the faceless character Er and yet,
in a certain sense, that of the cosmos itself, beyond the subjectivity
of a human eye. To make matters more elaborate still, all this is fil-
tered, as it were, through Socrates' own poetic-authorial voice. There
is consequently a sort of diegetic ambiguity to the myth, leaving it
suspended between testimonial confidence and imagined distance,
between an air of plain truth telling and of exotic fiction. All in all,
the presentation of Er's story makes its status deliberately puzzling:
ostensibly factual yet astonishingly bizarre; quasi-historiographical
yet shot through with traces of the poetic; redolent of traditional
Greek myths (in its underworld topography and most of its cast of
named individuals; Ardiaeus, 615c–e, is an exception), yet with a
putatively non-Greek origin that lies beyond reach of verification.

Despite these narrative ambiguities, all of which feed into
hermeneutic problems I address below, one feature of Plato's engagement with the traditions of poetry remains salient. The "greatest
charge" brought by Socrates against poetry earlier in Book 10 focused
on the powerful psychological appeal of tragic emotions in both
Homer and Attic drama. Socrates spoke there (605c–606b) of the
pleasure of "surrendering" sympathetically to the passionate grief
expressed by heroic characters, and thereby vicariously absorbing a
tragic evaluation of life and death. The myth of Er, by contrast, places
human life against a background of cosmic order and eternal justice.
By the *Republic*'s own criteria, it offers an antitragic vision of the
world. That vision crystallizes in the choice of "the greatest tyranny"
by the foolish, greedy soul at 619b–c. On realizing the "destiny"
(*heimarmenē*) that follows from its choice, this soul collapses into

---

[9] See Tarrant 1955; but her judgment on the myth of Er ("the impression of tidings
from afar," p. 223) is vague.

a self-pity exhibited by profuse wailing and breast beating. Those gestures are precisely reminiscent of the description of tragic heroes earlier in Book 10 (605d); they are also linked to Book 9's claim that the tyrannical soul is especially susceptible to "regret," *metameleia* (577e), an emotion symptomatic of the internal psychic conflict of injustice (352a). Undone by his own ignorance into picking a life that condemns him to eat his own children (a horror that pointedly recalls the experience of Thyestes, subject of several known tragedies), the future tyrant indulges in a display of self-exculpation that is almost parodic of a tragic figure – Oedipus, let us say – who indignantly externalizes responsibility for his fate. The myth, in other words, echoes the psychological tones of tragedy in order to negate them with the force of a kind of cosmic irony.[10]

But there may be more than that to say about the relationship of this self-deludingly forlorn character – this parodic Oedipus, as it were – to the phenomena of tragedy. We can use his case to probe some of the issues that underlie the myth's place in the thematic architecture of the *Republic*. We learn that this soul (or person: see below) had previously lived in a well-regulated state and with a degree of virtue (*aretē*), but "without philosophy." After its judgment, it had been rewarded with a thousand years in "heaven." In one regard, this episode exemplifies the point, made twice at the start of Book 9 (571b–572b), that the lawless desires that flourish in the tyrannical soul are present in *every* soul, though in most people kept in check by law, "better desires," or reason. But the doom of the rash figure in the myth seems to give a pessimistic twist to that principle. Not only does its previous existence count for nothing; the same is true for its millennium of beatitude in the presence of a transcendent beauty. Now, this soul had in some measure *been* just; it could not otherwise have been sent up to the sky by the judges (see 614c). Its justice and virtue were, for sure, incomplete, because lacking in truly philosophical understanding; but that only seems to compound the ineffectiveness of the long period it has spent contemplating "visions indescribable in their beauty" (615a, echoing the form of the good, 509a). In the *Phaedrus* myth, souls that have been in the vicinity of the spectacle of true being, but have failed actually to "see" it, can at the worst fall back down into the life

[10] See Halliwell 2006.

of a tyrant (248c–e). But the *Phaedrus* also states that living justly leads to improvement in the soul's destiny (248e), whereas the future tyrant in the myth of Er has been deemed (partially) just, yet still falls into the most evil and unhappy of human conditions – unlike, one should also note, the comparably virtuous but unphilosophical souls mentioned by Socrates in the *Phaedo*, outside the myth.[11] The *Republic* elsewhere certainly allows for the corruption of good, even philosophical natures, both individually and collectively. But while such corruption occurs *within* human life, the soul's choice of tyranny in the myth appears to introduce an element of failure into the cosmic apparatus of justice. If a rewarded soul can regress so catastrophically, would not some form of suffering in the world beyond have made better sense? On the most pessimistic reading, this soul, having previously lived a life of some justice, may now fall into the category of the "incurable," and thus become eternally unredeemable.[12]

Grappling with such problems encourages us to reflect on interpretative strategies toward the philosophical and literary character of Platonic myths, which constitute a complex class of compositions. Plato's own usage of *muthos* and its cognates must of course be consulted, but that usage, itself embedded within dramatized speech, cannot do all the work of interpretation for us. Within the *Republic*, *muth-* terms are applied to a diverse spectrum of materials: the folktale parable of Gyges' ring, the subject matter of poetry, everyday storytelling, traditional mythology, the "noble lie," the scenario of the dialogue's hypothetical city building, and, by implication at least, the triform image of the soul at the end of Book 9.[13] But if Books 2–9 are framed as a thought-experiment that in its entirety can be called a *muthos* by Socrates, then the application of the same term to the story of Er (621b) cannot justify a clean split between

---

[11] *Phd.* 82a–b: reference to "habit" (*ethos*) and the phrase "without philosophy" (*aneu philosophias*) both parallel *Rep.* 619c.

[12] Incurables: *Rep.* 615e, *Grg.* 525c–6b, *Phd.* 113e. The Neoplatonist Proclus refused to take this concept (like much else of the myth) literally: see Kroll 1901, pp. 178–79. On the paradoxically bad choices made by previously rewarded souls, cf. Annas 1982, at p. 135, but she overstates the position: 619d (reference misprinted in Annas) does not say that "most" of the souls from heaven made bad choices, but, more indeterminately, that "in rough terms, just as many" of those ensnared in bad choices had come from heaven as from below the earth.

[13] 359d, 377d–98b passim, 350e, 376d, 377c, 415a–c, 501e, 565d, 588c.

logos and *muthos*. The dialectical creation of the ideal city and the recounting of the myth of Er both involve narrative-cum-imaginative perspectives from outside ordinary experience. Indeed, when introducing the subject of the guardians' education at 2.376d, Socrates speaks of the exercise simultaneously as one of "storytelling" (*muthos, muthologein*) and of "discussion" or "argument" (*logos*); similarly, he refers later to "the regime whose story we are telling in argument/discussion" (*muthologoumen logōi*, 6.501e). *Muthos* and *logos* are, it seems, in some sense intertwined throughout the *Republic*.

Contrary to what is sometimes claimed, no simple, unqualified *muthos/logos* dichotomy is presupposed in Plato's work.[14] The juxtaposition of the two terms, when it does appear, has contextual not overarching force and can be used to draw more than one distinction. Thus, in different settings and for different purposes (and in the mouths of different characters), it can appeal to a contrast between poetic story forms and nonpoetic statements (*Phd.* 61b), between narratives and speeches/dialogue (*Prt.* 320c, 324d, 328c), between fiction and history (*Ti.* 26c–e), or between a "mere tale" and a seriously credited contention (*Grg.* 523a, 527a, but contested by Socrates there). Since *logos* can mean "discourse" in the broadest sense, it is not surprising that *muthos* is often subsumed under *logos*, and the situation is complicated further by the fact that Plato sometimes uses *muth-* terms in an archaizing sense of "speech" or "utterance."[15] Within the *Republic*, Socrates' critique of poetry in Books 2 and 3 classifies all *muthoi* (stories, mostly poetic) as *logoi* (376e–7a), pieces of discourse, or speech acts, whose significance and acceptability are to be judged by reference to the underlying convictions or values they are capable of conveying to their audiences. This helps to suggest why something might count as a *muthos*, qua discourse with a narrative dimension, yet still form part of the larger "argument" or *logos* of a dialogue: consider how, for instance, the myth of

---

[14] For critiques of the *muthos/logos* distinction, see Annas 1982, pp. 120–22; Murray 1999; Edmonds 2004, pp. 161–71. Brisson 1998 offers a full but somewhat overschematized account.

[15] *Muthos* subsumed under *logos*: e.g., *Rep.* 376eff., 398b, 522a, 565d–e, *Phdr.* 237a, 241e, *Ti.* 29d, 30b, 55d, 56a; cf. *Ti.* 59c (*muthos* as medium of *dialogizesthai*). *Muthos* as "utterance" (Homeric usage, e.g., *Rep.* 389e, 390d): *Laws* 773b, 790c, 812a.

the *Politicus* impinges on the direction of the overall discussion, checking one line of analysis while broaching another. We need, therefore, to beware the pitfall of equating a formal dialogue/myth distinction with a functional argument/myth distinction. The latter cannot be altogether clear-cut, if only because there is no uniform model of "argument" in Plato's writings as a whole: whatever may be *said* about philosophical method, the dialogues (not least, the *Republic* itself) stage discussion that proceeds through a blend of claims both tested and untested, inferences both deductive and inductive, analogies and similes, images, examples, and anecdotes. The philosophical role of Platonic myths or narratives varies with the thematic and dramatic counterpoint in which they stand to their compositional settings. Myths, for example, that occur within an ongoing conversation, like those in *Phaedrus* and *Politicus*, have a rather different dialogic dynamic from those, including *Gorgias* and *Republic*, that sound the final note of a work. Nor does it make much sense to draw a sharp dividing line between narratives, like that of Gyges' ring, that are called *muthoi* in Plato's text, and those, such as the cave in *Republic* 7 (itself, notice, evocative of Hades: 521c), that are not.

The myth of Er actually constitutes the last part of Socrates' "argument" for the external rewards of justice, the part dealing with posthumous rewards from the gods (612b–c, 614a), although within the main vista of the story those rewards as such are largely out of sight (only alluded to at 615a).[16] The myth is therefore an extension of the case for justice that has been made since Book 2; it is a component of the *Republic*'s overarching *logos*, the cumulative organization of its discussion. The fact that the credentials of Er's narrative are not exposed to scrutiny distinguishes it to some extent, but not absolutely, from the procedures of argument followed elsewhere in the work, procedures that incorporate many other unexamined (even highly counterintuitive) propositions. One further, crucial consideration, to which I shall soon return, is that Socrates interposes into the myth interpretative statements of his own, finding in it a moral (in every sense) for life, treating it as material for reflective

---

16 Ferrari 2008 deftly situates the myth in relation to the *Republic*'s theme of the "rewards" of justice.

reasoning (denoted by the verbs *analogizesthai* and *sullogizesthai*), and taking it as grounds for belief (*doxa*) of varying strengths.[17] So the myth could be said to involve a sort of shadow dialectic, conducted by Socrates with himself in his two "voices" as detached summarizer of Er's account and as explicator or exegete of that account.

In the light of what has already been indicated about both the terminology and the variable uses of *muthos* in Plato's dialogues, we should not expect to find a definitive key to the reading of any Platonic myth. Instead, we should accept the existence of multiple levels of significance within such philosophically framed narratives, levels that can accommodate elements of the literal, the metaphorical, the personificatory, the symbolic, the allegorical (i.e., systematically symbolic), the speculative, and, ultimately, the mystical (a category definable in terms of intrinsic resistance to rational interpretation). Technical classifications in this area, both ancient and modern, are labile. We may choose, for example, to call the fullest surviving ancient reading of the myth of Er, that of Proclus, substantially "allegorical," even though Proclus's own language is always that of "symbolism" (*sumbolon*, etc.) and "enigma" or "hidden meaning" (*ainissesthai*, etc.), never of *allēgoria*. Such technicalities need not detain us here. Plato's own dialogues abound, in fact, in acknowledgments of the availability of numerous kinds of oblique, veiled, and cryptic discourse. Such acknowledgments open up more options than they close down; we should not adduce them selectively to construct a pure paradigm of Platonic myth. It is unwarranted, for instance, to treat the Socrates of the *Phaedrus*, who at one point belittles rationalizing interpretations of traditional myth (229c–e), as ruling out allegorical interpretation per se, especially when, for example, the Socrates of the *Theaetetus* can just as easily commend a philosophical allegory (155d, involving Iris, with her correlate symbol the rainbow, which happens to appear in the myth of Er, 616b). It is equally mistaken, though commonplace, to extract a general repudiation of allegory from *Republic* 2's dismissal of subtextual meaning

---

[17] *Analogizesthai*, 616c (cf. 524d), *sullogizesthai*, 618d (cf. esp. 516b, 517b, 531d); see note 29 below. The myth warrants *doxa* of "adamantine" strength at 619a, but at 619e Socrates talks in terms of probability or likelihood (*kinduneuein*).

(*huponoia*, "underthought") as a defense of ostensibly immoral stories about the gods: that passage targets its point only at what the young are capable of grasping.[18] Other Platonic passages – among them the hypothetical Aesopic fable by which Socrates expresses the perplexing relationship between pleasure and pain in the *Phaedo*, an esoteric construal of the "mud" of Hades in the same dialogue, and the water-carriers section of the *Gorgias* – appeal to the potentially positive use of symbolism and allegory: to do so, they sometimes employ the terminology of *ainittesthai* (to encode meaning in cryptic form), which we know was current in Plato's day in the interpretation of various texts, including Orphic writings, as the Derveni papyrus shows.[19] A full Platonic typology of kinds of discourse, if such a thing were feasible (and it has certainly never yet been attempted), would have also to include the zone of speculative thought inhabited by such things as the "likely story" of the *Timaeus*, or the sort of quasi-Hesiodic plausibility (making fictions or falsehoods that "resemble the truth") that is invoked as valuable at the end of *Republic* Book 2 and put hypothetically into practice in the case of the noble lie.[20]

Interpreting Platonic myths, then, is an exercise in tracing the relationships among shifting layers of meaning, both literal and non-literal. With the story of Er, the most obvious illustration of both the possibilities and difficulties of decoding allegorical modes of discourse is the spindle suspended in the lap of Necessity (616c–617c). The methodically itemized list of the spindle's immediate properties – the order and size of its rims, their varying luminosity – makes it coherently intelligible as a mathematical model of celestial bodies in a spherical, geocentric cosmos, whether or not we posit the specific impact of Eudoxus' contemporary astronomy of concentric spheres (though, in fact, Parmenidean rings may be at least

---

[18] Lear 2006 pursues this point in relation to the work as a whole. Brisson 1998, pp. 122–27, unwarrantedly maintains that Plato repudiates allegorical interpretation per se.

[19] See *Phd.* 60b–c, 69c (cf. the metaphor at *Rep.* 533d), *Grg.* 493a–d. The early development of Greek ideas of allegory, including the Derveni papyrus, is discussed in Ford 2002, pp. 67–89.

[20] "Likely story": *Ti.* 29d, 59c, 68d. Falsehoods that "resemble the truth": *Rep.* 2.382d (cf. Hesiod *Theogony* 27), with the noble lie at 3.415a–c.

as important an inspiration).[21] It is also easy to construe a connection between the spindle and the *Republic*'s own ideal of astronomy, adumbrated at 528d–530c (with the parallel template for harmonics, 530d–531c), as dealing not with the visible cosmos in its own right but with the perfect patterns of reality and beauty that inform and underlie it. Nor, given the defined instrumentality of a (real) spindle, can we doubt the status of its holder, Ananke herself (an inheritance, in part, from the systems of Parmenides and Empedocles), as the personification of a principle of cosmic purposiveness, rather than a materialist, Anaxagorean conception of necessity of the kind deprecated in the *Phaedo*, *Timaeus*, and *Laws*. Yet the larger apparatus of symbols associated with the spindle (its partly "adamantine" material, Necessity's knees, the singing Sirens and Fates) involves a density of figuration that defeats secure interpretation. It is not so much that there are problems of "visualization," such as the spindle's position vis-à-vis the column of light at 616b–c (or, indeed, the position of Ananke vis-à-vis the world): disputed details of this kind belong to a visionary mode that deliberately thwarts transparent exegesis. More substantively recalcitrant is the synthesis or fusion of cosmology and morality, with the interplay of order and disorder it entails. In narrative terms, Ananke's spindle provides a quasi-mystical experience for the souls soon to be reincarnated; the necessity she represents has consequences for those souls, as later references to the necessity of their own destinies confirm.[22] But how do we get from an astronomy that is under Ananke's total supervision, via her daughters, the Fates, who participate in a choreographed cosmic design yet place (through Lachesis) on individual souls the burden of choosing their destinies, to the internal inescapability of those choices themselves? What is the relationship between the seemingly "adamantine" (616c) machinery of cosmic governance and the free choices made by souls in transition from one life to the next? Moreover, taken with the rest of its context, the spindle exploits but also refashions imagery from several sources: traditional-cum-Homeric mythology (including the Sirens and Lachesis), mathematical astronomy,

---

[21] On Eudoxus's system see Dicks 1970, pp. 151–89, with pp. 109–14 on the myth of Er. Parmenides' cosmic wreaths/rings (*stephanai*) fit "on/against one another," *epallēlous* (A37 DK): Morrison 1955 offers one reconstruction.

[22] 617e, 618b, cf. 621a.

Pythagorean motifs (the harmony of the spheres), and the esotericism of Bacchic-Orphic mystery religion (as affinities with funerary gold lamellae confirm).[23] This sheer multiplicity of resonances, but accompanied by the myth's lack of a consistent alignment with any of those sources, makes the scope of allegory fraught with uncertainty.

That uncertainty bears heaviest on the myth's controlling themes of soul immortality, eschatological judgment, and reincarnation. These daunting ideas, all of which lie in the outer reaches of what can be thought or imagined, throw up a central hermeneutic challenge. With them, no ready-made alternative to literalism, no correspondence of the spindle-cosmos variety, is available. Yet literalism itself, so I shall suggest, seems to threaten the myth with incoherence. The crux is the understanding of immortality (survival of the soul), which is in turn presupposed by postmortem judgment and transmigration.[24] Plato had reason to expect that some otherwise sympathetic readers of the *Republic* would find immortality hard to believe. He mirrors that expectation in the text, just as he does, to poignant effect, in the *Phaedo*. When, earlier in Book 10 (608d), Socrates asked Glaucon, "Haven't you realised that our soul is immortal?" Glaucon looked him in the eye and exclaimed with amazement, "I most certainly haven't!" Socrates' ensuing attempt to establish the immortality of the soul by deductive reasoning does not lay claim to impregnability; it carries a touch of provisionality at 610a–b. The myth itself could count as an "argument" for belief in immortality, but only if Er's testimony is treated as authoritative, which, on the face of it, Socrates takes for granted but can do nothing to validate. But there is, in any case, a deeper level of difficulty here. Socrates' preceding argument for immortality, like those in *Phaedo*, posits a rigorous dualism of body and soul, allowing precisely for the separability of the latter, in its "pure" state, from the former (611b–612a). The myth itself sets out from the supposition of the soul's

---

[23] See Edmonds 2004, pp. 29–110, for a recent reappraisal of the gold lamellae, with 51–52, 88–91 for affinities with the myth of Er; cf. note 40 below. The attachment of "signs" of judgment round the necks of the just at *Rep.* 614c may evoke the placing of gold leaves on the chests of the dead.

[24] The myth of Er never contemplates the technical possibility, registered at *Phd.* 87d–8b, that a soul might survive more than one body yet eventually cease to exist and therefore not be unconditionally immortal (*athanatos*, immune to death).

survival of bodily death. But in keeping with the traditions of poetic and artistic mythology, and like Plato's other eschatological myths, Er's report proceeds to picture souls as embodied, spatiotemporally enduring entities (indeed *persons*, as we shall see). Literal acceptance of this aspect of the myth would be self-contradictory, collapsing the nonmaterial into the material. Yet the narrative seems to go out of its way to accentuate the quasi-personal continuity of souls on their trajectory from this world to (and through) the afterlife. How, then, are we to discern a stable significance in the representation of the disembodied as, so to speak, phantoms of embodiment?

As a preliminary move, this interpretative challenge can usefully be contextualized in relation to the work's earlier citations of prevailing attitudes to the afterlife. The following is a necessarily summary catalogue of the most pertinent passages. In Book 1 (330d–e), Cephalus remarked that inherited myths of Hades are ridiculed by most adults but arouse anxieties in the minds of those close to death. In Book 2, appealing for a defense of justice's nonconsequentialist value, Adeimantus mocked Orphic and kindred images of an afterlife in which the just enjoy a perpetual symposium, while the unjust are mired in mud (363c–d); later on, he described widespread skepticism about the idea of postmortem punishment for injustice (366a). In the censorship of poetry at the start of Book 3, Socrates himself objected to depictions of Hades as a place of terrors: how could future guardians develop courage, he asked, if they believed things that inculcate fear of death (386b)? In Book 4, Socrates referred all the ideal city's religious regulations, including the treatment of the dead, to the Delphic oracle, with the categorical statement that "about such matters we ourselves possess no knowledge" (427b). Differently, but equally pertinently, in Book 7 Socrates at one point equated arrival in Hades, for the soul that lacks philosophical knowledge, with "falling perfectly asleep" (534c–d): the language of this brief passage may be tinged with irony, but the conception of death as eternal sleep was a historical option and is in fact one of the two possibilities considered by Socrates, noncommittally, at the end of the *Apology* (40c–e). By contrast, at several junctures in the *Republic* Socrates permits himself to anticipate a positive afterlife for deceased guardians or philosophers. In Book 5 he borrowed from Hesiod to suggest that some guardians might become earth-roaming spirits (*daimones*) after death (468e–9a); in Book 6, he spoke of the fine "hope" with which the uncorrupted philosopher will depart from this life (496e, echoing some of Cephalus' language at 1.330e–331a; cf. 498c); while in Book 7 he posited an afterlife in the "isles of the blest" for deceased guardians (540b–c), adding that they might be worshipped by their former communities as *daimones* if the Delphic oracle approved, but, if it did not, then as "happy and godlike." Finally, as I mentioned earlier, Socrates' critique of mimetic art in the first part of Book 10 cited the unfounded pretensions of poets and painters in depicting the domain of Hades (596c).

No integrated structure of beliefs emerges from these passages. On the contrary, uncertainty about an afterlife – uncertainty tempered by hope – is the predominant impression, even where Socrates is concerned. Nor does Book 10's formal argument for the immortality of the soul bridge the gap between that cumulative impression and the myth itself, since it provides no source of insight into what a discarnate soul is capable of experiencing, a point Socrates himself highlights by his contrast between the "impaired" soul of earthly existence (for which the barnacle-encrusted seagod Glaucus stands as analogue) and the "pure" soul whose nature could only be contemplated on a more elevated plane of thought (611b–612a). Given the *Republic*'s wavering images of the afterlife, Er's story appears out of nowhere, professing to carry an eschatological authority that the *Republic* had not previously envisaged. Moreover, despite its putatively non-Greek origin, the story unmistakably assimilates certain traditional motifs of Greek underworld mythology, not least the gruesome torture of the exceptionally evil. No wonder, then, that Epicurus's disciple Colotes accused Plato of hypocrisy in this respect, complaining that the myth peddled the same pernicious and "tragic" mythology that the *Republic* attacks the poets for propounding.[25] But the matter is less straightforward than Colotes may have been disposed to recognize. In Book 3, it is the evaluation of death as an intrinsic evil, therefore as something terrible even for good people, that Socrates repudiates; in that same context (386b–387c), it is only certain components of traditional underworld topography (and their generalized prospects for the fate of souls) that he censors, components that happen *not* to reappear in Er's account. Some of the work's other eschatological references, too, such as the "isles of the

---

[25] Colotes' view is recorded by Proclus, in Kroll 1901, pp. 105–6.

blest,"[26] are compatible with the myth, especially if we keep in mind Socrates' indication that he offers a selective summary of Er's report (615a). Even so, a discrepancy remains between Er's story and some of Socrates' own earlier conjectures about the afterlife. There seems a world of difference, for example, and not only at the level of the literal but also in metaphorical or symbolic import, between eternal "sleep" for unphilosophical souls (534c–d) and the traumatic destiny of the figure in the myth, already considered, who had lived justly but "without philosophy." Most fundamental of all, how can an idea as far-reaching as reincarnation be held back till so late a stage of the inquiry into what it means for humans to lead just, good lives?[27] Is this a glaring flaw in the design of the *Republic* or an inducement to return to the start (the process of "cyclical" reading that I posited earlier) and rethink everything afresh?

The myth of Er was written for readers who might have held an allegiance to any one of several conceptions of the afterlife (Homeric, Eleusinian, Orphic, and others) or, like the skeptical Glaucon, no allegiance at all. What does the myth invite those readers to make of the nature and experiences of disembodied souls? Er's account begins with a statement of how his soul "left him" and "journeyed" to an "awesome" (*daimonios*) location (614b–c). In what follows Er's soul continues to behave entirely like an incarnate person, listening to and watching everything that confronts it. So, rather vividly, do all the souls in the myth: among other things, they enter and leave the place of judgment, wear their verdicts round their necks, convene in encampments like festival crowds, and make use of language. Prima facie, then, the souls possess bodies: Ardiaeus and the other tyrants even have their hands, feet, and heads shackled before being flayed (615e–616a). Matters are complicated by the fact that Er's account oscillates between talk of "souls," *psuchai* (with corresponding feminine pronouns and gender-inflected participles/adjectives), and talk of persons (masculine grammatical forms, plus references to named individuals), switching between, and even merging, the two idioms

---

[26] The isles of the blest appear in the *Gorgias* myth (523b, 524a, 526c); cf., less determinately, Socrates' anticipation at *Phd.* 115d, with *Smp.* 179e, 180b for the traditional motif.

[27] For one problematic hint of reincarnation prior to the myth, see note 32 below. At 498e, to Glaucon's ironic amusement, Socrates had envisaged reincarnation for Thrasymachus and others.

without qualm. At 617d–e, for example, the priest of Lachesis starts with the language of souls, then moves to that of persons. Likewise at 620d–e, the Greek shifts in quick succession from souls to persons, back to souls, then finally back to persons, where we stay for the final sentences of the account (621a ff.).[28] The interest of this observation is more than linguistic. It reflects the way in which the myth juxtaposes, or rather superimposes, two models of the soul: that of a notionally disembodied set of capacities for ethical reasoning, desire, and emotion and that of the self-conscious identity of a person, built around memory of, and continuity with, a personal history. More radically, we might say that it seems to fuse together immortal and mortal, a paradox not lost on the priest of Lachesis, who solemnly addresses those preparing for reincarnation with the oxymoron, "souls that last only a day" (*psuchai ephēmeroi*, 617d).

Just before embarking on the myth, Socrates spoke of the things that "await each person after death" (614a), and the myth bears him out. The souls persist in being, or at any rate remembering, the persons that they were. This is so until at least the point at which, having chosen new identities (which they assume in a manner somewhat like actors donning masks and costumes), they pass beneath the throne of Necessity – perhaps even till they drink from the river Heedless (621a–b). That last moment, when some souls drink more than required (and therefore forget more deeply), evidently insinuates the possibility of subsequent *anamnēsis*, recollection, by embodied souls of their preexistence, even though that notion has played no prior part in the *Republic* and, what is more, is conspicuously absent from Socrates' comments on the myth. It is worth reflecting, however, that drinking from the river also serves to obliterate the new person's *advance* knowledge of what its life holds in store, the concealment from the soul itself, as it were, of its own "destiny." Despite that break in the thread of consciousness, Er's narrative offers no explicit clue to whether or how souls might cease to be the souls of (successive) persons, or at any rate of animals (620a–d). It concentrates on the sequential experiences of the soul as, at every significant stage, the repository of a personal identity and the locus of ethical agency. If Socrates' remarks at 611b–612a might have created

---

[28] At 620e–21a, moreover, there is a sort of merging of *daimones* into persons: the subject of the sentence passes, silently as it were, from the former to the latter.

an expectation that the myth would project an image of the "pure" soul, disentangled from the body (Glaucus without the barnacles), it leaves us after all with souls that apparently have much the same features as those posited elsewhere in the dialogue, whether or not we think of them as tripartite.[29] But that psychological continuity with the rest of the work brings us up against an awkward question. What is to stop us from circumventing all those old doubts about Hades by treating the myth not as making claims about a literal "beyond" but as an allegory of embodied life itself?

We can best pursue that question by turning to the two main comments (and, in due course, also the third) that Socrates adjoins to his telling of Er's story.[30] The first and longest, at 618b–619a, is given dramatic emphasis by interrupting the speech of Lachesis's priest to the souls (619b follows on from 617e). It is also given a stylistically marked emotional intensity, with one of the longest sentences anywhere in Plato and a vocative phrase, "O dear Glaucon," which Socrates also uses to lend feeling to a number of major pronouncements elsewhere in the *Republic*, including the introduction of philosopher-rulers (473d) and a warning in Book 7 about the ineffable nature of ultimate truth (533a). But what is most striking about the passage is how Socrates translates the gravity of the soul's choice in Hades (his term, 619a) into an imperative for "each of us" to seek ceaselessly for knowledge – indeed, strictly, for a *teacher* – of the difference between good and bad lives, and "to choose the better life, within our range of possibilities, always and everywhere" (618c). His prefatory statement that at the moment of prenatal choice lies "the whole danger for a human being [*anthrōpos*]" (618b) is at first sight incongruous, since the choosing souls in the story are not strictly people at all, though we have seen Er's account picturing them extensively as persons. Part of Socrates' point, it is tempting to say, is that we must practice or "rehearse" in life for the choice that, in the myth's own dramatic terms, we will face *between* lives: he says as much at 619a, though there too he talks, climactically,

---

[29] Nowhere in the myth do the terms *logistikon, thumoeides, epithumētikon*, or their close cognates, occur. More loosely *thumos*-related words are found at 613a, 619b; on the verbs *analogizesthai, sullogizesthai*, see note 17 above.

[30] There are also brief interventions in Socrates' own voice at 615a, 615c–d. In the *Gorgias* myth too we find comment (524b–d etc.) mixed with narrative (523a–4a etc.), but in that dialogue *both* are delivered in Socrates' voice.

of what is at stake as the happiness of a human being (*anthrōpos*) not a discarnate soul. But in the very act of stressing the ubiquitous importance of moral learning and choice ("always and everywhere"), and thereby extrapolating back from the myth to incarnate existence, Socrates brings into play an instability between the mythic narrative and his commentary on it. In Er's own account, the choice of a new identity involves an antenatal fixing of what one's life will hold in store, in terms not just of physical endowment and social status but also of ethical character. That is implied by the words of the priest of Lachesis, and Er himself reports that a soul's "order" or "orderliness" (*taxis*) followed of necessity (Ananke *internalized* in the soul) from the choice of externally defined life type.[31] This sense of sealing one's fate, morally as well as socially, is further corroborated by subsequent episodes of the myth, especially by the description of the future tyrant's "fate" or "destiny" (*heimarmenē*, 619c) to eat his own children and by the language of fulfillment and irreversibility at 620d–e. Yet Socrates' comment, in keeping with the *Republic* as a whole, clearly presupposes that life is not ethically predestined from the outset. It uses the language of practicing strenuously, learning, seeking, discerning, and choosing, in order to reinforce its message that moral agency must be exercised at every moment to maintain the commitment of a life.

Socrates' first and fullest comment on the myth, then, gives rise to a conundrum. It interprets an image of definitive, once-for-all choice (productive of a "destiny") as communicating a vitally recurrent imperative ("always and everywhere") to be a moral "seeker and learner." What is more, within the myth prenatal choices are themselves formed partly on the basis of *previous* existences, so that, on this scenario, the individual may be paying the price (or reaping the rewards) of the life of, in a sense, someone else, as a passage earlier in Book 10 seemed, anomalously, to hint.[32] Far from simply

---

[31] I.e., the same life type could be chosen for morally different reasons (as the examples at 620a–d tend to suggest); if that were not so, it would make no sense to say that the lives did not contain an "order" of soul. I take 618c–d, where Socrates speaks in terms of complex interplay (or "mixing") of external and ethical features of life, to bear out that reading. For *taxis* of soul, see 577d and *Grg.* 504b–d; cf. *taxis* of life at 561d (587a is also pertinent).

[32] 613a implies reincarnation, but also the possibility (contrary to the later myth) of punishment in life for the mistakes of previous lives.

illuminating the myth by extending its significance back from the other world to the present, Socrates' comment deepens the difficulties that face Plato's readers, especially since in this regard the myth threatens the *Republic*'s entire vision of how individuals can be morally formed in the course of their passage through the educational, social, and political settings of their lives. But Socrates himself betrays no sign of difficulty or incongruity, aligning the idea of choice "in this life" and "in the whole of the hereafter" with eloquent assurance.

Socrates' second, much shorter comment (619d–e), unlike the first, is interposed unobtrusively into the flow of Er's account, with the change of syntax from indirect to direct speech conveying a confident change of voice from reporter to exegete of the myth. However, the ease with which Socrates makes that adjustment belies a further strain between exegesis and narrative. The second comment extrapolates from the scenario in Hades to the conduct of an embodied life, and, like the first, purports to configure the two things – the worlds of "here" and "there" – in a pattern of matching results for those (Socrates here speaks the language of persons, not souls) who journey between them. But not only does this duplicate the earlier tension between an all-determining life selection and the aggregative choices that determine the unfolding of a life from within. Now there is an additional puzzle. Er's account has just described the fate of the figure who had lived a life of some virtue but "without philosophy" and who, despite the reward of a millennium in the sky, was then driven by blind greed (*laimargia*, 619c: the only occurrence of this term in the *Republic*) to choose the greatest tyranny. But this was not a unique case; many of those returning from the sky, and therefore deemed just by the underworld judges, made similarly bad choices of their next life. Er's narrative intimates three possible reasons for their regression: first, as exemplified by the future tyrant, a lack of philosophical knowledge of good and evil; second, a lack of sufficient exposure to suffering and toil, *ponoi* (619d, a tacit admission that their "rewards" have actually weakened their judgment); and third, the "luck of the draw" in the order of choosing (619d).

That last factor has caused disquiet, even doubts about the text, on the part of some interpreters. But it is picked up directly by Socrates, who says: "if each time someone arrives in this earthly life, he philosophizes soundly and his place in the lot does not fall among the last, he would be likely not only to be happy here," but also to enjoy a "smooth, heavenly journey," in both directions, between this world and that (619e). Yet the disquiet is not wholly misplaced. The priest of Lachesis had told the souls choosing their next lives that even the one who drew last place in the order of choice need not despair: "even for the last to come forward there is a desirable, not a bad, life, if he chooses wisely and lives strenuously" (619b). It is not enough to try to harmonize Socrates' comment (and Er's general report) with the priest's pronouncement by saying that the "lot," symbolizing all the external circumstances over which a person has no control, can have some effect on, but need not destroy, the goodness of a life. The priest stresses that even for the last to choose (and choice there will always be, 618a), there is a good life still available and, by impli- cation, a good destiny for the immortal soul that leads such a life. Socrates himself, for sure, wishes to affirm that true happiness, and a "smooth, heavenly journey" between this world and the next, will belong to one who philosophizes soundly. But not only does he qual- ify the affirmation, in contrast to the priest's hieratic confidence, with a degree of eschatological tentativeness (using the language of likelihood: the verb *kinduneuein*, 619e).[33] He also hints that the very possibility of a philosophical life might be blocked by sheer contingency (a late place in the lot). In other words, while the priest implies that (ethical) understanding (*nous*, 619b) can always prevail over the external or material conditions of a life (because "virtue has no master," 617e), Socrates implies that even philosophical wisdom cannot sustain itself independently of external circumstances. In the course of his positive construal of the myth's moral meaning, a subtle note of reservation creeps almost inadvertently into Socrates' tone of voice.

The two comments with which Socrates interrupts the report of Er's experiences intensify the challenge of the myth, turning it into an exercise in which narrative and reasoning become entwined in a dialectic of their own. At the heart of this challenge lies the

---

[33] The conditional sentence as a whole at 619d–e, if taken *au pied de la lettre*, would entail that even *possession* of philosophic wisdom could not guarantee the "heav- enly road," i.e., a verdict of justice, in the other world. To avoid that devastatingly extreme consequence, one should (as John Ferrari points out to me) treat the second part of the conditional (relating to the lot) as modifying the first (i.e., the possibility of a life of sound philosophy).

paradoxical idea of self-chosen destiny. That paradox lurks, on closer inspection, in the very words of the priest who, on behalf of Lachesis ("Allotter"), tells the souls that they will choose their own *daimōn*, (life) spirit, and will *not* have one "allotted" to them (*lēxetai*, 617e, from the verb *lankhanein*, origin of Lachesis's own name). The myth here positions itself, in a manner hard to decode, in relation to a variety of earlier Greek ideas about souls and *daimones*. It seems to fall somewhere in between three different versions of a *daimōn*: the agent of an individual's fortune (in traditional/popular thought), an entity underlying successive incarnations (Empedocles), and that which is self-constituted by an individual's life (Heraclitus, Democritus).[34] Given the strongly antitragic thrust of the myth to which I previously drew attention, it is remarkable that the motif of self-chosen destiny has some kinship with the psychologically dark and troubled world of Greek tragedy itself, where the extent and workings of human responsibility are always, at best, incompletely intelligible, and sometimes opaque. The chorus and protagonist of Sophocles' *Oedipus Tyrannus*, for example, share the mysterious sense that in blinding himself Oedipus was both doing the work of a *daimōn* and acting on a terrible impulse of his own (1327–33). The correlate of such intractable uncertainty in the myth of Er is the triangular relationship between the priest's emphatic assertion of a doctrine of absolute moral agency ("responsibility belongs to the chooser; god is without responsibility," 617e), the demonstration, in Er's report, that even moderate virtue (virtue "without philosophy") and its post-mortem rewards are no protection against a lapse into the greatest evil, and, finally, the hint in Socrates' commentary that even the very possibility of philosophy might be undone by a drastic impairment of the external conditions of a life (drawing a lot "among the last"). Plato's text provides no explicit resolution of the problems raised by this sequence of ideas. But we can at least attempt some

---

[34] See, e.g., Hesiod *Works and Days* 314 (cf. 122–23), Theognis 161–64, pseudo-Lysias 2.78 (with the verb *lankhanein*), Empedocles fr. 115 DK (also with *lankhanein*), Heraclitus fr. 119 DK, Democritus fr. 171 DK. At *Phd.* 107d–e (cf. 113d), unlike the *Republic*, the *daimōn* is allotted to the soul (*lankhanein* once more); at *Ti.* 90a–c it is a metaphor or symbol for (part of) the soul itself. The relationship between *daimones* and souls in the Derveni papyrus is uncertain: see discussion in Betegh 2004, pp. 85–9. On later Platonist "demonology," see Dillon 1996, pp. 31–32, 317–20.

clarification by placing them in relation to the tension between literal and allegorical interpretations of the myth's fundamental theme of reincarnation.[35]

If we take that concept literally, then at the moment of prenatal choice each soul has an opportunity to discern and evaluate in advance the externals of the life it selects, applying the kind of moral calculus that Socrates outlined in his first comment (618c–d). Whatever its place in the lot, the soul has a chance to commit itself to the ethically best life open to it; in that sense, there are no constraints on the exercise of virtue ("virtue has no master," as we have been told, 617e), even though the element of chance (tuchē) in the range of lives available may mean that a choice made for the best reasons will still unavoidably lead to morally imperfect action. Equally, however, the very fact of a prenatal choice appears to determine the entire course of a life, as the future tyrant so grievously discovers. It turns that life into the playing out of an unalterable role: ironically, given the ethical momentum of the Republic as a whole, the sheer weight of responsibility placed on the soul prior to incarnation cancels the scope for active responsibility in the individual decisions and episodes of life. Moreover, the cycle of reincarnation brings with it further layers of complexity in the psychological causation of a life choice, since each soul, at the moment of choice, is still potentially influenced by its memories both of its previous existence and of the rewards/punishments subsequently assigned to it. The workings of such causation, as reported by Er, are too convoluted to be reduced to either optimism or pessimism. The narrative illustrates that, over a series of lives, a degree of justice can nevertheless be followed by severe regression, while some cases of injustice can be counteracted by a fresh impulse toward virtue: as each cohort of souls choose their next lives, most experience "a reversal [metabolē] between bad and good" (619d). On the most thoroughgoing literalism, the fluctuating outcomes of metempsychosis lead into impenetrable obscurity. What, for example, are the future prospects of just souls that choose reincarnation as tame animals (620d)? Will the circumstances of their animal lives enhance or impede their possibilities of moral progress

---

[35] Positions on this issue are polarized: Annas 1982, pp. 129–38, unpicks the myth in almost entirely literal terms (despite "symbolic," p. 137); Thayer 1988, esp. pp. 377–79, explicitly discards literalism. Cf. note 12 above.

when the next cycle of existence comes round? If Er's own reactions to the mass spectacle of reincarnation are any guide, no overall inference can be drawn from the process; its mixed results encompass the pitiful, the ridiculous, and the amazing (620a), lending a tragicomic aura to the cosmic scene. One thing alone seems clear. Er's observations and Socrates' comments converge on the idea that, whatever the partial impact of other factors, the exclusive hope of happiness lies in the choice of justice for its own sake. Thus *belief* in this model of reincarnation, while it may theoretically limit the ethical autonomy of the embodied soul, can orientate the aspirations of that soul in only one direction: acting as though nothing other than justice matters (618e).

But how different is that upshot from a reading of reincarnation as an allegory of the life of the soul in *this* world? If, with some prompting from Socrates' comments at both 618b–19a and 619d, we focus on a this-worldly reading of the myth, the motif of a prenatal life choice can be interpreted as a stark emblem of the inescapably self-forming consequences of ethical agency, a magnified image of how at every moment ("always and everywhere") the individual soul/person is intrinsically responsible for what matters most about its existence.[36] Every action, we might thus say, brings with it its own "afterlife." Every choice makes us what we are; when we choose, we activate (and become) something, and therefore cannot simply pull back from *ourselves*, as the greedy soul would like to do – a graphic exemplification of Book 9's idea of the tyrant as peculiarly enslaved by, and imprisoned in, his own desires (577d–e, 579b). The emphasis placed by such an interpretation on this-worldly moral agency can help, among other things, to underscore a major difference between the myth and the premises of Greek mystery religion, some of whose symbolism undoubtedly colors Er's story. While mystery religion offers an essentially ritualized route (i.e., initiation) to postmortem happiness (and the same was probably true for the practices we call Orphism, belittled by Adeimantus in Book 2), Plato's myth, as reinforced by Socrates' exegesis, suggests that the soul's salvation – at any and every point of its existence – is to be found nowhere else than inside its capacity to determine its own ethical

---

[36] *Rep.* 519c mentions the idea of unifying an entire life by a single "aim" or vision (*skopos*); but such unity is something only certain lives possess.

self by choosing between good and evil. Insofar as this capacity is fulfilled most authentically in "philosophy," we can call philosophy itself the true form of initiation, but initiation from within, as the *Phaedrus* intimates (249c–d). In broader terms, a this-worldly reading of the myth of Er supports the cumulative moral case made by the entire *Republic* for the identification of a good and happy life with a just life, even though, as I earlier stressed, such a reading must still acknowledge, in line with Socrates' second comment, an element of "chance" or circumstantial contingency that can in extreme cases occlude the possibility of philosophy itself.[37]

But a dilemma remains, a dilemma that the myth creates but cannot by itself resolve. An exclusively this-worldly reading of the myth would discard precisely what occasioned its telling in the first place, the tenet of the soul's immortality. As such, it would dislocate the myth from its structural position in the work, as well as rendering opaque Socrates' own repeatedly *dual* perspective on the here-and-now and the hereafter in his comments on Er's story. On the other hand, the more strictly we press the notion of a defining, preincarnational life choice, the more we are confronted with a determinism that imperils the psychological, ethical, and political coherence of the rest of the *Republic*, which presupposes at almost every turn (including, ironically, Socrates' first comment on the myth) the aptitude of souls to be educated, to learn and practice the difference between justice and injustice, and to shape the goodness of their embodied lives by an incremental series of chosen actions. The dilemma remains right to the end. When, in his final remarks on the myth, Socrates speaks of how "it could save us, if we are persuaded by it" (621c), the verb *peithesthai*, with *muthō* as its indirect object, might suggest belief, trust, or reliance of more than one kind, as too, for comparison, might the similar wording of Socrates' hope that the inhabitants, and even the rulers, of the ideal city might come to "be persuaded" by the *muthos* of the noble lie (415c). In such cases, acceptance of a story's literal veracity (cf. *Phaedrus* 229c) is not the only option; confidence in its normative authority must also be reckoned with.[38] If we look for illumination outside the *Republic*, we find

---

[37] *Tuchē* is glimpsed only in the margins of the *Republic*: see esp. 492a–c, 579c, 592a, 603e.

[38] Note here the traditional poetic phraseology of *peithesthai muthōi*, which involves taking advice, not assimilating information: see, e.g., Homer *Iliad* 4.412 (quoted at *Rep.* 389e; cf. note 15 above), Theognis 437 (quoted at *Meno* 96a).

that the myth that underwrites the soul's immortality in the *Phaedo* needs to be "repeated as incantation" (*epaidein*): that is, employed as a nonepistemic, partly self-persuasive device, used by Orphics, among others, for dealing with recurrent fears or problems.[39] On that analogy, the mythic epilogue to the *Republic* invites a trust that might be as much *affective* as rational. In view of my earlier contention that Er's story is presented with a diegetic ambiguity that leaves it strangely suspended between truth and fiction, it is apt (and, one might add, in keeping with the rich tradition of ancient interpretations of the passage) to conclude that the myth does not permit its readers to settle on a definitive either-or adjudication between literalism and allegory. Appropriately, in a work whose fabric is threaded with many metaphors of journeying (through life, dialectic, and the quest for justice), each reader is left with the prospect of a continuing, upward journey (621c), which is also a choice of how far to follow Socrates in the moral imagination along the cyclic path between this world and the other (619e).[40]

But if one test of the myth's persuasiveness can be only affective, we are bound, on a dramatic level, to wonder about the person to whom it was directly addressed: Glaucon. He, we recall, was originally amazed that Socrates should expect him to believe in the soul's immortality, though he was nonetheless eager to hear a story of the afterlife (614b). Has *he* been "persuaded"? The work fades out, as it were, without telling us. That makes it a specimen of one kind of ending cultivated by Plato.[41] *Gorgias* provides the most direct comparandum, but there is also an oblique affinity of atmosphere with the finale of *Phaedo* and with Socrates' (and Plato's) rehearsals, as it were, for that finale in the *Apology* and *Crito*. In keeping with the life-and-death focus of all those works, the absence of a response from

---

[39] *Phd.* 114d7; cf. 77e–8a. Orphic incantations: Euripides, *Cyclops* 646, and perhaps the Derveni papyrus col. 6.2 (Betegh 2004, p. 14).

[40] Other metaphors of journeying: e.g., 328e (with my final paragraph), 364d–5b, 420b, 435d, 445c, 452c, 504c, 515e, 532b–e. The idea of the soul's journey after death was older than Plato: see, e.g., Pindar, *Olympian Odes* 2.70; it is also found on some funerary gold leaves (cf. note 23 above). On the myth's own interpretative "afterlife" in antiquity, Untersteiner 1966, pp. 210–17, 236–38 (notes), provides an overview. Note the general idea of the myth of Er (with others) as symbolic/allegorical at Clement, *Stromata* 5.9.58.

[41] *Parmenides, Politicus, Timaeus,* and *Laws* also finish without signaling what happens "next." Some dialogues stage the breakup of the gathering: *Cratylus, Euthyphro, Laches, Meno, Phaedrus, Symposium,* and, most portentously, *Theaetetus.* Sometimes, as in *Philebus,* the possibility of continuation is mooted.

Glaucon to the visionary perspective of the myth, together with the lack of any gesture of mundane or veristic closure of the kind some dialogues allow themselves, forms a subtle piece of counterpoint to the trope (or, if one prefers, the hope) of the soul's onward, unfinished journey. We have been asked to contemplate a prospect beyond the horizon of death, yet the destination of the "upward journey" of which Socrates speaks (621c), echoing the imagery of the cave, is not and cannot be in sight. The unfinished journey recalls, and is an extension of, the journey of life at 1.328e, a further indication of the difficulty of disentangling this-worldly and other-worldly readings of the myth. Despite the almost vatic tone in which Socrates anticipates the soul's eternal well-being, the work's denial of a final reaction to Glaucon functions as a signal of its own philosophically incomplete status. The end of the *Republic*, I submit, enacts a silence that is both dramatic and metaphysical.[42]

WORKS CITED

Albinus, L. 1998. "The *katabasis* of Er." In *Essays on Plato's* Republic, ed. E. N. Ostenfeld (Aarhus).

Annas, J. 1982. "Plato's Myths of Judgement." *Phronesis* 27: 119–43.

Betegh, G. 2004. *The Derveni Papyrus*. Cambridge.

Bouvier, D. 2001. "Ulysse et le personnage du lecteur dans la *République*: réflexions sur l'importance du mythe d'Er pour la théorie de la *mimēsis*." In *La philosophie de Platon*, ed. M. Fattal (Paris).

Brisson, L. 1998. *Plato the Myth Maker*. Chicago.

Dicks, D. R. 1970. *Early Greek Astronomy to Aristotle*. London.

Dillon, J. 1996. *The Middle Platonists*, rev. ed. London.

Edmonds, R. G., III. 2004. *Myths of the Underworld Journey: Plato, Aristophanes, and the "Orphic" Gold Tablets*. Cambridge.

Ferrari, G. R. F. 2008. "Glaucon's Reward, Philosophy's Debt: The Myth of Er." In *Plato's Myths*, ed. C. Partenie (Cambridge).

Ford, A. 2002. *The Origins of Criticism*. Princeton.

Halliwell, S. 1988. *Plato: Republic 10*. Warminster.

Halliwell, S. 2006. "Plato and Aristotle on the Denial of Tragedy." In *Oxford Readings in Ancient Literary Criticism*, ed. A. Laird (Oxford).

Kroll, W. ed. 1901. *Procli Diadochi in Platonis Rem Publicam Commentarii*, vol. 2. Leipzig.

---

[42] I am grateful to my fellow participants in the *Republic* conference held at Berkeley, and above all to John Ferrari, for helpful comments on this chapter.

Lear, J. 2006. "Myth and Allegory in Plato's *Republic*." In *The Blackwell Guide to Plato's Republic*, ed. G. Santas (Oxford).

Morgan, K. A. 2000. *Myth and Philosophy from the Presocratics to Plato*. Cambridge.

Morrison, J. S. 1955. "Parmenides and Er." *Journal of Hellenic Studies* 75: 59–68.

Murray, P. 1999. "What Is a *Muthos* for Plato?" In *From Myth to Reason?*, ed. R. Buxton (Oxford).

Tarrant, D. 1955. "Plato's Use of Extended *Oratio Obliqua*." *Classical Quarterly* 5: 222–24.

Thayer, H. S. 1988. "The Myth of Er." *History of Philosophy Quarterly* 5: 369–84.

Untersteiner, M. 1966. *Platone:* Repubblica *Libro X*. Naples.

FURTHER READING

Babut, D. 1983. "L'unité du livre X de la *République* et sa fonction dans le dialogue." *Bulletin de l'Association Guillaume Budé* 42: 31–54.

Moors, K. 1988a. "Muthologia and the Limits of Opinion: Presented Myths in Plato's *Republic*." *Proceedings of the Boston Area Colloquium in Ancient Philosophy* 4: 213–47.

Moors, K. 1988b. "Named Life Selections in Plato's Myth of Er." *Classica et Medievalia* 39: 55–61.

Richardson, H. 1926. "The Myth of Er (Plato, *Republic*, 616b)." *Classical Quarterly* 20: 113–33.

Schils, G. 1993. "Plato's Myth of Er: The Light and the Spindle." *Antiquité Classique* 62: 101–14.

Smith, J. E. 1985. "Plato's Myths as 'Likely Accounts,' Worthy of Belief." *Apeiron* 19: 242.

Stewart, J. A. 1960 [1905]. *The Myths of Plato*, ed. G. R. Levy. London.

Villani, A. 2001. "Le fuseau et le peson. Note sur la colonne lumineuse de *République* 616b." In *La philosophie de Platon*, ed. M. Fattal (Paris).

BIBLIOGRAPHY

This is intended as a contemporary working bibliography for a serious student of the *Republic* whose principal language is English. Accordingly, its emphasis falls on the more recent scholarly literature produced in English; but earlier studies and those written in other languages are also a substantial presence here.

An annually updated bibliography of scholarly work on Plato has been online since 2000 and is accessible from the home page of the International Plato Society, at www.platosociety.org. It is compiled by Luc Brisson with the assistance of Frédéric Plin, both of the CNRS, Paris. Previous editions of the bibliography have appeared at five-year intervals (on the decade and half-decade) in the journal *Lustrum*.

I have made liberal use of the full and thematically organized bibliographies on the *Republic* to be found in vol. 2 of item 77 below (bibliography compiled by Annie Larivée), and in the relevant section of Richard McKirahan's *Plato and Socrates: A Comprehensive Bibliography, 1958–1973* (New York, 1973). Larivée's bibliography is a particularly useful supplement to what follows for work written in languages other than English.

General studies of Plato often contain particular chapters on the *Republic*. Some of the most important are listed in section III.A. A more discursive but much briefer and more elementary guide to further reading about the *Republic* can be found in my edition of Tom Griffith's translation of the work, [19] below; a guide of similar type by Rachana Kamtekar can be found in [22].

The bibliography is divided into the following categories, which from section IV onward are intended to correspond approximately to

474

the sequence in which the chapters of this book present topics from the *Republic*.

JOURNAL ABBREVIATIONS

AGP	*Archiv für Geschichte der Philosophie*
AJP	*American Journal of Philology*
AP	*Ancient Philosophy*
APA	*Proceedings and Addresses of the American Philosophical Association*
APQ	*American Philosophical Quarterly*
BACAP	*Proceedings of the Boston Area Colloquium in Ancient Philosophy*
CP	*Classical Philology*
CQ	*Classical Quarterly*
CR	*Classical Review*
HPQ	*History of Philosophy Quarterly*
HPT	*History of Political Thought*

JHP   *Journal of the History of Philosophy*
JHS   *Journal of Hellenic Studies*
JP   *Journal of Philosophy*
OSAP   *Oxford Studies in Ancient Philosophy*
PAS   *Proceedings of the Aristotelian Society*
PPR   *Philosophy and Phenomenological Research*
PR   *Philosophical Review*
REG   *Revue des Études Grecques*
RM   *Review of Metaphysics*
RMM   *Revue de Métaphysique et de Morale*
TAPA   *Transactions and Proceedings of the American Philological Association*

ABBREVIATED REFERENCES TO EDITED COLLECTIONS

Dixsaut, *Études 1*   M. Dixsaut, ed., *Études sur la* République *de Platon*, vol. 1: *De la justice: éducation, psychologie et politique*, A. Larivée, co-editor. Paris, 2005.

Dixsaut, *Études 2*   M. Dixsaut, ed., *Études sur la* République *de Platon*, vol. 2: *De la science, du bien et des mythes*, F. Teisserenc, co-editor. Paris, 2005.

Fine, *Plato 1*   G. Fine, ed., *Plato 1: Metaphysics and Epistemology*, Oxford Readings in Philosophy. Oxford, 1999.

Fine, *Plato 2*   G. Fine, ed., *Plato 2: Ethics, Politics, Religion and the Soul*, Oxford Readings in Philosophy. Oxford, 1999.

Höffe   O. Höffe, ed., *Platon*: Politeia. Berlin, 1997.

Kraut   R. Kraut, ed., *Plato's Republic: Critical Essays*. Lanham, Md., 1997.

Ostenfeld   E. N. Ostenfeld, ed., *Essays on Plato's* Republic. Aarhus, 1998.

Santas   G. Santas, ed., *The Blackwell Guide to Plato's* Republic. Oxford, 2006.

Vegetti   M. Vegetti, ed., *Platone: La Repubblica* (Naples, 1998–) Vol. 1 (1998): Book 1; vol. 2 (1998): Books 2–3; vol. 3 (1998): Book 4; vol. 4 (2000): Book 5; vol. 5 (2003): Books 6–7.

Vlastos, *Plato 1*   G. Vlastos, ed., *Plato 1: Metaphysics and Epistemology*. Garden City, N.Y., 1971. Rpt. Notre Dame, 1978.

Vlastos, *Plato 2*   G. Vlastos, ed., *Plato 2: Ethics, Politics, and Philosophy of Art and Religion*. Garden City, N.Y., 1971 Rpt. Notre Dame, 1978.

I. EDITIONS, COMMENTARIES

I.A. Comprehensive editions and commentaries

The most recent and authoritative edition of the Greek text of the *Republic* is

[1] Slings, S. R., ed. *Platonis* Respublica, Oxford Classical Texts. Oxford, 2003.

The critical notes supporting Slings' edition have been collected as

[2] Slings, S. R. *Critical Notes on Plato's* Politeia, ed. G. Boter and J. M. van Ophuijsen. Leiden, 2005.

See also

[3] Boter, G. *The Textual Tradition of Plato's* Republic. Leiden, 1988.

The standard comprehensive commentary in English remains

[4] Adam, J. ed. *The* Republic *of Plato*, 2 vols. Cambridge, 1963 [1902].

Note that the second edition of 1963 adds only an introduction by D. A. Rees but is otherwise a reprint of the first edition of 1902.

An important new comprehensive commentary in Italian is ongoing:

[5] Vegetti, M., ed. *Platone: La* Repubblica, multiple vols. Naples, 1998–.

Five volumes have appeared so far, covering Books 1–7. Each contains Italian translation, notes by Vegetti, and thematic commentary by Vegetti and other Italian scholars. For a review of its contents in English, see G. R. F. Ferrari, "Vegetti's Callipolis," *OSAP* 23 (2002): 225–45. The thematic essays in the commentary section (listed individually in the topic categories below) are not only original contributions in their own right, but also provide exceptionally full synthesis of the scholarly literature in a wide variety of languages and scholarly traditions.

A three-volume translation with running commentary in German is due to appear in the series

[6] Heitsch, E., and C. W. Müller, eds. *Platon: Werke, Übersetzung und Kommentar*, Akademie der Wissenschaften und der Litteratur zu Mainz. Göttingen, 1994–.

The editors are to be P. Stemmer (Books 1–4), A. Schmitt (Books 5–7), and N. Blössner (Books 8–10).

Earlier comprehensive commentaries are

[7] Jowett, B. A., and L. Campbell, eds. *Plato's* Republic: *The Greek Text, with Notes and Essays,* 3 vols. Oxford, 1894.

[8] Stallbaum, G., ed. *Platonis* Politeia, 2 vols. London, 1868. Greek text with commentary in Latin.

I.B. Partial editions and commentaries

Recent work in English:

[9] Halliwell, S., trans. and ed. *Plato:* Republic *10*. Warminster, 1988.

[10] Halliwell, S., trans. and ed. *Plato:* Republic *5*. Warminster, 1993.

Both books have Greek text, facing-page translation, and commentary.

[11] Murray, P., ed. *Plato on Poetry*, Cambridge Greek and Latin Classics. Cambridge, 1996. Greek text of *Ion* and *Republic* 376e–398b, 595–608b, with commentary.

[12] Rose, G. P., ed. *Plato's* Republic Book *1*, Bryn Mawr Commentaries. Bryn Mawr, Pa., 1995 [1983]. Greek text with commentary. Note that the commentary addresses only grammatical and syntactic issues that arise for the learner of Greek.

Earlier work in English:

[13] Allan, D. J. *Plato:* Republic *I*. London 1993 [1940]. Greek text with still useful commentary.

[14] Warren, T. H. *The* Republic *of Plato: Books 1–5, with Introduction and Notes.* London, 1888. Greek text with brief commentary.

I.C. Ancient commentaries

The Neoplatonist commentary of Proclus is available as

[15] Kroll, W. *Procli Diadochi in Platonis Rempublicam Commentarii,* 2 vols. Leipzig, 1899–1901. Rpt. Amsterdam, 1965.

While no English translation exists, there is an annotated French translation:

[16] Festugière, J., trans. *Proclus: Commentaire sur la* République, 3 vols. Paris, 1970.

For a translation of 12th-century Arabic philosopher Averroes' commentary on the *Republic*, see

[17] Lerner, R. *Averroes on Plato's* Republic. Ithaca, N.Y., 1974.

II. TRANSLATIONS

The principal contemporary English translations of the *Republic* are

[18] Bloom, A., trans. *The* Republic *of Plato*. New York, 1991 [1968]. Contains long interpretive essay.

[19] Griffith, T., trans., and G. R. F. Ferrari, ed. *Plato: The* Republic, Cambridge Texts in the History of Political Thought. Cambridge, 2000.
Note that versions printed since 2002 contain modifications to the translation.

[20] Grube, G. M. A., trans. *Plato's* Republic. Indianapolis, Ind., 1974.

[21] Grube, G. M. A., trans. *Plato's* Republic, revised by C. D. C. Reeve. Indianapolis, Ind., 1992. Rpt. in J. Cooper, ed., *Plato: Complete Works* (Indianapolis, Ind., 1997).

[22] Lee, H. D. P., trans. *Plato: The* Republic. Harmondsworth, 1987 [1955]. Rpt. 2003 with new bibliography by R. Kamtekar.

[23] Reeve, C. D. C., trans. *Plato:* Republic. Indianapolis, Ind., 2004.

[24] Sterling, R. W., and W. C. Scott, trans. *Plato: The* Republic. New York, 1985.

[25] Waterfield, R., trans. *Plato:* Republic, Oxford World's Classics. Oxford, 1993.

A contemporary French translation with full and very useful introduction, notes, and bibliography is

[26] G. Leroux, trans. *Platon: La* République. Paris, 2002.

The following modern German and Italian translations have been reissued with editorial material provided by contemporary scholars:

[27] Rufener, R., trans. *Platon, "Der Staat" (Über das Gerechte).* Introduction, notes, and bibliography by T. A. Szlezák. Düsseldorf, 2000 [Zürich, 1950].

[28] Sartori, F., trans. *Platone: La* Repubblica. Introduction by M. Vegetti, notes by B. Centrone. Rome, 1997 [1966].

Earlier English translations of note are

[29] Cornford, F. M., trans. *The* Republic *of Plato.* Oxford, 1941.

[30] Jowett, B., trans. *The* Republic *of Plato.* 3rd ed. Oxford, 1888. Available in various reprinted and amplified editions.

[31] Lindsay, A. D., trans. *Plato: The* Republic, Everyman's Library, introduction by A. Nehamas, notes by R. Bambrough. New York, 1992 [1906].

[32] Shorey, P., trans. *Plato: The* Republic, Loeb Classical Library, 2 vols. Cambridge, Mass., 1937 [1930]. Facing-page Greek text; full but idiosyncratic annotation.

III. COMPREHENSIVE STUDIES

III.A. Books, chapters of books, articles

[33] Annas, J. *An Introduction to Plato's* Republic. Oxford, 1981.

[34] Annas, J., *Platonic Ethics, Old and New.* Ch. 4, "The Inner City: Ethics without Politics in the *Republic*." Ithaca, N.Y., 1999.

[35] Baracchi, C. *Of Myth, Life, and War in the* Republic. Bloomington, Ind., 2002.

[36] Benardete, S. *Socrates' Second Sailing: On Plato's* Republic. Chicago, 1989.

[37] Bloom, A. "Interpretive Essay." In [18].

[38] Blössner, N. *Dialogform und Argument: Studien zu Platons "Politeia."* Stuttgart, 1997.

[39] Bosanquet, B. *A Companion to Plato's* Republic. London, 1925 [1895].

[40] Brann, E. *The Music of Plato's* Republic*: Socrates' Conversations and Plato's Writings.* Philadelphia, 2004.

[41] Brumbaugh, R. S. "A New Interpretation of Plato's *Republic*." *JP* 64 (1967): 661–70.

[42] Craig, L. H. *The War-Lover: A Study of Plato's* Republic. Toronto, 1994.

[43] Crombie, I. M. *An Examination of Plato's Doctrines.* London, 1962 Vol. 1, ch. 3, "The *Republic*."

[44] Croiset, M. *La République de Platon.* Paris, 1946.

[45] Cross, R. C., and A. D. Woozley. *Plato's* Republic: *A Philosophic Commentary.* London, 1964.

[46] Dorter, K. *The Transformation of Plato's* Republic. Lanham, Md., 2006.

[47] Ferrari, G. R. F. *City and Soul in Plato's* Republic. Sankt Augustin, 2003. Rpt., Chicago, 2005.

[48] Friedländer, P. *Plato,* trans. H. Meyerhoff, vol. 3: *The Dialogues, Second and Third Periods.* Princeton, 1969. Ch. 22, "*Republic*."

[49] Gigon, O. *Gegenwärtigkeit und Utopie: Eine Interpretation von Platons "Staat,"* vol. 1. Zürich, 1976. Only the first volume appeared, covering Books 1–4.

[50] Grote, G. *Plato and the Other Companions of Sokrates.* London, 1885. Vol. 4, chs. 35–37.

[51] Guthrie, W. K. C. *A History of Greek Philosophy,* vol. 4: *Plato: The Man and His Dialogues, Earlier Period.* Cambridge, 1975. Ch. 7, "The *Republic*."

[52] Howland, J. *The* Republic: *The* Odyssey *of Philosophy.* New York, 1993. Rpt., Philadelphia, 2004.

[53] Irwin, T. *Plato's Ethics.* Oxford, 1995. Chs. 11–17.

[54] Joseph, H. W. B. *Essays in Ancient and Modern Philosophy.* Oxford, 1935. Chs. 1–5.

[55] Kahn, C. H. *Plato and the Socratic Dialogue: The Philosophical Use of a Literary Form.* Cambridge, 1996. Chs. 10 and 11.

[56] Krämer, H. J. *Arete bei Platon und Aristoteles.* Heidelberg, 1959. Ch. 1, secs. 1 and 3.

[57] Mitchell, J. *Plato's Fable: On the Mortal Condition in Shadowy Times.* Princeton, 2006.

[58] Murphy, N. R. *The Interpretation of Plato's* Republic. Oxford, 1951.

[59] Nettleship, R. L. *Lectures on the* Republic *of Plato.* 2nd ed. London, 1901.

[60] Ophir, A. *Plato's Invisible Cities: Discourse and Power in the* Republic. Savage, Md., 1991.

[61] Pappas, N. *Routledge Philosophy Guidebook to Plato and the* Republic. London, 1995.

[62] Ranasinghe, N. *The Soul of Socrates.* Ithaca, N.Y., 2000. Ch. 1, "Glaucon's Republic."

[63] Reale, G. *Toward a New Interpretation of Plato,* trans. J. R. Catan and R. Davies. Washington, D.C., 1997. Part 3, ch. 11, "The Nature and Solution of the Major Metaphysical Problems of the *Republic* Left Unsolved in the Traditional Paradigm."

[64] Reeve, C. D. C. *Philosopher-Kings: The Argument of Plato's* Republic. Princeton, 1988. Rpt., Indianapolis, Ind., 2006.

[65] Reeve, C. D. C. *Women in the Academy: Dialogues on Themes from Plato's* Republic. Indianapolis, Ind., 2001.

[66] Roochnik, D. *Beautiful City: The Dialectical Character of Plato's* Republic. Ithaca, N.Y., 2003.

[67] Rosen, S. *Plato's* Republic*: A Study.* New Haven, Conn., 2005.

[68] Sayers, S. *Plato's* Republic*: An Introduction.* Edinburgh, 1999.

[69] Schleiermacher, F. *Schleiermacher's Introductions to the Dialogues of Plato,* trans. W. Dobson. Cambridge, 1836. Part 3, "*Republic*." Rpt., Bristol, 1992.

[70] Sprague, R. K. *Plato's Philosopher-King.* Columbia, S.C., 1976. Chs. 5 and 6.

[71] Strauss, L. *The City and Man.* Chicago, 1964. Ch. 2, "On Plato's *Republic*."

[72] Szlezák, T. A. *Platon und die Schriftlichkeit der Philosophie.* Berlin, 1985. Ch. 18, "*Politeia.* Den Philosophen nicht loslassen."

[73] Taylor, A. E. *Plato: The Man and His Work,* 2nd ed. New York, 1936 Ch. 11., "*Republic*."

[74] Trabattoni, F., *Platone.* Rome, 1998. Chs. 10 and 11.

[75] Voegelin, E., *Order and History,* vol. 3: *Plato and Aristotle* [*The Collected Works of Eric Voegelin,* ed. D. Germino, vol. 16]. Columbia, S.C., 2000. Ch. 3, "The *Republic*."

[76] White, N. P., *A Companion to Plato's* Republic. Oxford, 1979.

Of these works, the following can be classified either as introductory treatments or as surveys: [33], [37], [39], [43]–[45], [50], [51], [59], [61], [68], [69], [73], [74], [76]. Leo Strauss in [71] inaugurated a tradition of interpreting the

Republic that continues to be represented in [36], [37], [40], [42], [52], [66], and [67]. [56], [63], and [72] apply to the *Republic* the approach to Plato associated with the "Tübingen school," which emphasizes the relevance of Plato's "unwritten teachings."

III.B. Collections of articles

[77] Dixsaut, M., ed. *Études sur la* République *de Platon,* vol. 1: *De la Justice: Éducation, Psychologie et Politique* (A. Larivée, co-editor); vol. 2: *De la Science, du Bien et des Mythes* (F. Teisserenc, co-editor). Paris, 2005. Twenty-eight new articles, all in French but written by an international variety of scholars. An important collection, ranging over all aspects of the *Republic.*

[78] Höffe, O., ed. *Platon:* Politeia. Berlin, 1997. Sixteen new articles, one-third of which are in English, the remainder in German. The roster is less varied than that of [77] but its quality is high.

[79] Kraut, R., ed. *Plato's* Republic: *Critical Essays.* Lanham, Md., 1997. Thirteen reprinted articles.

[80] Ostenfeld, E. N., ed. *Essays on Plato's* Republic. Aarhus, 1998. Eight new articles, all in English. An interesting, small-scale collection.

[81] Santas, G., ed. *The Blackwell Guide to Plato's* Republic. Oxford, 2006. Thirteen new articles, all in English. An important collection, complementary to this volume in several respects.

[82] Zuckerman, E., ed. *Four Essays on Plato's* Republic, *St. John's Review* special double issue 39.1–2 (1989–90). Four new articles in the tradition of Jacob Klein and Leo Strauss; one is an earlier version of [40].

Individual chapters from each of these works are listed separately in the appropriate subsections below. (The reprinted articles in [79] are already listed in their own right; and chapters in [77] have not been listed if written in French by English speakers, when those writers have written on the same topic elsewhere in English.)

IV. STUDIES OF PARTICULAR TOPICS

IV.A. The Republic *as Literary Dialogue*

Many comprehensive treatments of the *Republic* pay sustained attention to its writerly qualities, and some offer methodological prologues — notably [38], [42], [46], [52], [60], [66], [67]. Several collections of articles have also appeared in recent years on the topic of Platonic dialogue form in general, some of which are the source for individual pieces in this section. See further the works cited in chapters 1, 2, 3, and 13 in this volume.

[83] Ausland, H. "Socrates' Argumentative Burden in the *Republic*." In *Plato as Author: The Rhetoric of Philosophy*, ed. A. N. Michelini (Leiden, 2003).

[84] Blondell, R. *The Play of Character in Plato's Dialogues*. Cambridge, 2002. Ch. 4, "A Changing Cast of Characters: *Republic*."

[85] Blössner, N. "Dialogautor und Dialogfigur. Überlegungen zum Status sokratischer Aussagen in der '*Politeia*.'" In *The* Republic *and the* Laws *of Plato: Proceedings of the First Symposium Platonicum Pragense*, ed. A. Havlíček, and F. Karfík (Prague, 1998).

[86] Canino, L. L. "La battaglia." In Vegetti, vol. 1. Topic: the imagery used for dialectical debate.

[87] Canino, L. L. "La belva." In Vegetti, vol. 1. Topic: the use of hunting imagery.

[88] Clay, D. "Reading the *Republic*." In *Platonic Writings, Platonic Readings*, ed. C. Griswold (University Park, Pa., 2002 [New York, 1988]).

[89] Cohn, D. "The Poetics of Plato's *Republic*: A Modern Perspective." *Philosophy and Literature* 24 (2000): 34–48.

[90] Gallagher, R. L. "Protreptic Aims of Plato's *Republic*." *AP* 24 (2004): 293–319.

[91] Gifford, M. "Dramatic Dialectic in *Republic* Book 1." *OSAP* 20 (2001): 35–106.

[92] Gutiérrez, R. "En torno a la estructura de la *República* de Platón." *Apuntes Filosóficos* 22 (2003): 39–47.

[93] Hyland, D. "Taking the Longer Road: The Irony of Plato's *Republic*." *RMM* (1988): 317–36.

[94] Kahn, C. H. "Proleptic Composition in the *Republic*, or Why Book 1 Was Never a Separate Dialogue." *CQ* 43 (1993): 131–42.

[95] Rosenstock, B. "Rereading the *Republic*." *Arethusa* 16 (1983): 219–46.

[96] Rowe, C. J. "The Literary and Philosophical Style of the *Republic*." In Santas.

[97] Rutherford, R. B. *The Art of Plato: Ten Essays in Platonic Interpretation*. Cambridge, Mass., 1995. Ch. 8, "The *Republic*."

[98] Seery, J. "Politics as Ironic Community: On the Themes of Descent and Return in Plato's *Republic*." *Political Theory* 16 (1988): 229–56.

[99] Smith, P. C. "Not Doctrine but 'Placing in Question': The 'Thrasymachus' (*Rep.* 1) as an *Erōtēsis* of Commercialization." In *Who Speaks for Plato? Studies in Platonic Anonymity*, ed. G. A. Press (Lanham, Md., 2000).

[100] Stella, M. "*Prooimion e nomos*." In Vegetti, vol. 1.

[101] Stella, M. "Socrate, Adimanto, Glaucone: racconto di ricerca e rappresentazione comica." In Vegetti, vol. 2.

[102] Stokes, M. C. "Adeimantus in the *Republic.*" In *Justice, Law and Method in Plato and Aristotle,* ed. S. Panagiotou (Edmonton, 1987).

IV.B. The Republic *in its political context*

[103] Adkins, A. W. H. "*Polupragmosunē* and 'minding one's own business': A Study in Greek Social and Political Values." *CP* 71, no. 4 (1976): 301–27.

[104] Barker, E. *Greek Political Theory: Plato and His Predecessors.* London, 1918. Ch. 11, "Plato and the States of Greece."

[105] Brunt, P. A. *Studies in Greek History and Thought.* Oxford, 1993. Ch. 10, "Plato's Academy and Politics."

[106] Cartledge, P. "The Socratics' Sparta and Rousseau's." In *Sparta: New Perspectives,* ed. S. Hodkinson and A. Powell (London, 1999).

[107] Davidson, J. *Courtesans and Fishcakes: The Consuming Passions of Classical Athens.* London, 1997. Chs. 1 and 9.

[108] Ferrari, G. R. F. "Introduction." In [19], pp. xi–xxii.

[109] Field, G. C. *Plato and His Contemporaries.* London, 1948 [1930].

[110] von Fritz, K. *Platon in Sizilien und das Problem der Philosophenherrschaft.* Berlin, 1968.

[111] Gouldner, A. *Enter Plato.* New York, 1965.

[112] Howland, J. "Plato's Reply to Lysias: *Republic* 1 and 2 and *Against Eratosthenes.*" *AJP* 125, no. 2 (2004): 179–208.

[113] Klosko, G. *The Development of Plato's Political Theory.* New York, 1986. Ch. 1, "Plato and Greek Politics."

[114] Lee, H. D. P. "Translator's Introduction." In [22], secs. 1 and 2.

[115] Ludwig, P. *Eros and Polis: Desire and Community in Greek Political Theory.* Cambridge, 2002.

[116] Monoson, S. S. *Plato's Democratic Entanglements: Athenian Politics and the Practice of Philosophy.* Princeton, 2000. Esp. chs. 5 and 6.

[117] Nails, D. *The People of Plato: A Prosopography of Plato and Other Socratics.* Indianapolis, Ind., 2002.

[118] Ober, J. *Political Dissent in Democratic Athens: Intellectual Critics of Popular Rule.* Princeton, 1998. Ch. 4, sec. D, "A Polis Founded in Speech: *Republic.*"

[119] Schuhl, P. M. "Platon et l'activité politique de l'académie." *REG* 59 (1946): 46–53.

[120] Trampedach, K. *Platon, die Akademie und die Zeitgenössische Politik.* Stuttgart, 1994.

Of these works, [108], [113], and [114] are intended as introductory. [105] is primarily historical; [111], [115], [116], and [118] are primarily sociological;

[109] and [120] combine something of both approaches. See also [294] and [332] below.

IV.C. Justice, happiness, and the human good

[121] Annas, J. "Plato and Common Morality." *CQ* 28 (1978): 437–51.
[122] Barney, R. "Socrates' refutation of Thrasymachus." In Santas.
[123] Bobonich, C. *Plato's Utopia Recast: His Later Ethics and Politics.* Cambridge, 2002. Ch. 1, "Philosophers and Non-philosophers in the *Phaedo* and *Republic.*"
[124] Butler, J. "Justice and the Fundamental Question of Plato's *Republic.*" *Apeiron* 35 (2002): 1–17.
[125] Campese, S. "Cefalo." In Vegetti, vol. 1.
[126] Chappell, T. D. J. "The Virtues of Thrasymachus." *Phronesis* 38 (1993): 1–17.
[127] Chappell, T. D. J. "Thrasymachus and Definition." *OSAP* 18 (2000): 101–7. Responds to [137].
[128] Coby, P. "Mind Your Own Business: The Trouble with Justice in Plato's *Republic.*" *Interpretation* 31, no. 1 (2003): 37–58.
[129] Cooper, J. M. "The Psychology of Justice in Plato." *APQ* 14 (1977): 151–57. Rpt. in J. M. Cooper, *Reason and Emotion.* (Princeton, 1999).
[130] Cooper, J. M. "Two Theories of Justice." *APA* 74.2 (2000): 5–27. Rpt. in J. M. Cooper, *Reason and Emotion* (Princeton, 1999).
[131] Dahl, N. O. "Plato's Defence of justice." *PPR* 51 (1991): 809–34. Rpt. in Fine, *Plato 2.*
[132] Demos, R. "A Fallacy in Plato's *Republic?*" *PR* 73 (1964): 391–95. Rpt. in Vlastos, *Plato 2.*
[133] Devereux, D. "The Relationship between Justice and Happiness in Plato's *Republic.*" *BACAP* 20 (2004): 265–305.
[134] Dixsaut, M. "Le plus juste est le plus heureux." In Dixsaut, *Études 1.*
[135] Donovan, B. "The Do-It-Yourselfer in Plato's *Republic.*" *AJP* 124, no. 1 (2003): 1–18.
[136] Dorter, K. "Socrates' Refutation of Thrasymachus and Treatment of Virtue." *Philosophy and Rhetoric* 7 (1974): 25–46.
[137] Everson, S. "The Incoherence of Thrasymachus." *OSAP* 16 (1998): 99–131.
[138] Friedländer, P. *Plato,* trans. H. Meyerhoff, vol. 2: *The Dialogues, First Period.* Princeton, 1964. Ch. 3, "*Thrasymachus (Republic* Book 1)."
[139] Gastaldi, S. "*Dikaion/ dikaiosynē.*" In Vegetti, vol. 1.
[140] Gastaldi, S. "Polemarco." In Vegetti, vol. 1.
[141] Gastaldi, S. "*Sōphrosynē.*" In Vegetti, vol. 3.

[142] Gosling, J. C. B., and C. C. W. Taylor. *The Greeks on Pleasure.* Oxford, 1982. Ch. 6, "*Republic.*"

[143] Hall, R. W. "The Just and Happy Man of the *Republic*: Fact or Fallacy?" *JHP* 9 (1971): 147–58.

[144] Hall, R. W. "Plato's Political Analogy: Fallacy or Analogy?" *JHP* 12 (1974): 419–35.

[145] Hall, R. W. "Platonic Justice and the *Republic.*" *Polis* 6 (1986): 116–26.

[146] Hellwig, D. Adikia in Platons "Politeia": Interpretationen zu den Büchern 8 und 9. Amsterdam, 1980.

[147] Hemmenway, S. R. "The *tekhnē*-analogy in Socrates' Healthy City: Justice and the Craftsman in the *Republic.*" *AP* 19 (1999): 267–84.

[148] Heinaman, R. "Plato's Division of Goods in the *Republic.*" *Phronesis* 47 (2002): 309–35.

[149] Irwin, T. *Plato's Ethics.* Oxford, 1995. Chs. 11, 12, 14, 15, and 17.

[150] Kamtekar, R. "Imperfect Virtue." *AP* 18 (1998): 315–37.

[151] Kamtekar, R. "Social Justice and Happiness in the *Republic*: Plato's Two Principles." *HPT* 22 (2001): 189–220

[152] Kirwan, C. A. "Glaucon's Challenge." *Phronesis* 10 (1965): 162–73.

[153] Klosko, G. "*Dēmotikē aretē* in the *Republic.*" *History of Political Thought* 3 (1982): 363–81.

[154] Kraut, R. "Reason and Justice in Plato's *Republic.*" In *Exegesis and Argument*, ed. E. N. Lee, A. P. D. Mourelatos, and R. M. Rorty (*Phronesis* supplementary vol. 1). Assen, 1973.

[155] Kraut, R. "Two Conceptions of Happiness." *PR* 88 (1979): 167–97.

[156] Kraut, R. "The Defence of Justice in Plato's *Republic.*" In *The Cambridge Companion to Plato*, ed. R. Kraut (Cambridge, 1992).

[157] Kraut, R. "Plato's Comparison of Just and Unjust Lives (Book 9.576b–592b)." In Höffe.

[158] Lee, E. N. "Plato's Theory of Social Justice in *Republic* 2–4." In *Essays in Ancient Greek Philosophy 3*, ed. J. Anton and A. Preus (Albany, N.Y., 1989).

[159] de Luise, F., and G. Farinetti. "L'infelicità del giusto e la crisi del socratismo platonico." In Vegetti, vol. 2.

[160] de Luise, F., and G. Farinetti. "Infelicità degli *archontes* e felicità della *polis.*" In Vegetti, vol. 3.

[161] Lycos, K. *Platon on Justice and Power: Reading Book 1 of Plato's Republic.* Albany, N.Y., 1987.

[162] Mabbott, J. D. "Is Plato's *Republic* Utilitarian?" In Vlastos, *Plato* 2. Revised version of 1937 original.

[163] Mohr, R. D. "A Platonic Happiness." *HPQ* 4 (1987): 131–45.

[164] Moors, K. F. *Glaucon and Adeimantus on Justice: The Structure of Argument in Book 2 of Plato's Republic.* Washington, D.C., 1981.

[165] Morrison, D. "The Happiness of the City and the Happiness of the Individual in Plato's *Republic.*" *AP* 21 (2001): 1–24.

[166] Muller, R. "La justice de l'âme dans la *République.*" In Dixsaut, *Études 1.*

[167] Neschke-Hentschke, A. "Justice socratique, justice platonicienne." In Dixsaut, *Études 1.*

[168] Nussbaum, M. C. *The Fragility of Goodness.* Cambridge, 1986. Ch. 5, "The *Republic*: True Value and the Standpoint of Perfection."

[169] Ostenfeld, E. N. "*Eudaimonia* in Plato's *Republic.*" In Ostenfeld.

[170] Parry, R. *Plato's Craft of Justice.* Albany, N.Y., 1996.

[171] Pigler, A. "La justice comme harmonie de l'âme dans la *République* et dans les *Ennéades.*" In Dixsaut, *Études 1.*

[172] Reeve, C. D. C. "Socrates Meets Thrasymachus." *AGP* 67 (1985): 246–65.

[173] Rist, J. "The Possibility of Morality in Plato's *Republic.*" *BACAP* 14 (1998): 53–72.

[174] Sachs, D. "A Fallacy in Plato's *Republic.*" *PR* 72 (1963): 141–58. Rpt. in Vlastos, *Plato 2*, and in Kraut.

[175] Santas, G. *Goodness and Justice.* Oxford, 2001. Chs. 3 and 4.

[176] Santas, G. "Methods of Reasoning about Justice in Plato's *Republic.*" In Santas.

[177] Schiller, J. "Just Men and Just Acts in Plato's *Republic.*" *JHP* 6 (1968): 1–14.

[178] Schütrumpf, E. "Konventionelle Vorstellungen über Gerechtigkeit: Die Perspektive des Thrasymachos und die Erwartungen an eine philosophische Entgegnung (Buch 1)." In Höffe.

[179] Scott, D. "Metaphysics and the Defence of Justice in the *Republic.*" *BACAP* 16 (2000): 1–20.

[180] Shields, C. "Plato's Challenge: The Case against Justice in *Republic* 2." In Santas.

[181] Singpurwalla, R. "Plato's Defense of Justice." In Santas.

[182] Sparshott, F. "Socrates and Thrasymachus." *The Monist* 50 (1966): 421–59.

[183] Stauffer, D. *Plato's Introduction to the Question of Justice.* Albany, N.Y., 2001.

[184] Stokes, M. C. "Some Pleasures of Plato, *Republic* 9." *Polis* 9 (1990): 2–51.

[185] Teloh, H. "A Vulgar and a Philosophical Test for Justice in Plato's *Republic.*" *Southern Journal of Philosophy* 13 (1975): 499–510.

[186] Thayer, H. S. "Models of Moral Concepts and Plato's *Republic.*" *JHP* 7 (1969): 247–62.

[187] Vegetti, M. "Trasimaco." In Vegetti, vol. 1.

[188] Vegetti, M. "Glaucone." In Vegetti, vol. 2.

[189] Vegetti, M. "Grammata." In Vegetti, vol. 2.

[190] Vlastos, G. "Justice and Happiness in the *Republic*." In Vlastos *Plato 2*. Rpt. in G. Vlastos, *Platonic Studies* (Princeton, 1981 [1973]).

[191] Vlastos, G. "The Theory of Social Justice in the *polis* in Plato's *Republic*." In *Interpretations of Plato*, ed. H. F. North (Leiden, 1977).

[192] Vlastos, G. *Socrates: Ironist and Moral Philosopher*. Cambridge, 1991. Additional note 2.1: "The Composition of *Republic* 1."

[193] Waterlow, S. "The Good of Others in Plato's *Republic*." *PAS* 73 (1973): 19–36.

[194] Weingartner, R. H. "Vulgar Justice and Platonic Justice." *PPR* 25 (1964–65): 248–52.

[195] White, F. C. "Justice and the Good of Others in Plato's *Republic*." *HPQ* 5, no. 4 (1988): 395–410.

[196] White, N. P. "The Classification of Goods in Plato's *Republic*." *JHP* 22 (1984): 392–421.

[197] White, N. P. *Individual and Conflict in Greek Ethics*. Oxford, 2002. Ch. 5, "Individual Good and Deliberative Conflict through the Time of Plato."

[198] Williams, B. A. O. "Plato against the Immoralist (Book 2.357a–367e)." In Höffe. Rpt. in B. A. O. Williams, *The Sense of the Past: Essays in the History of Philosophy* (Princeton, 2006).

[199] Williams, B. A. O. "Plato's Construction of Intrinsic Goodness." In *Perspectives on Greek Philosophy: S. V. Keeling Memorial Lectures in Ancient Philosophy 1991–2002*, ed. R. W. Sharples (London, 2003). Rpt. in B. A. O. Williams, *The Sense of the Past: Essays in the History of Philosophy* (Princeton, 2006).

Several studies in this section focus on Book 1: [122], [125], [126], [127], [137], [138], [140], [161], [172], [178], [182], [183], [187]. For bibliography on the question whether the philosopher-king sacrifices happiness by returning to the cave, see section IV.F, "Philosopher-Kings." For bibliography on the Form of the Good, see section IV.G, "Metaphysics, Epistemology, the Forms."

IV.D. Psychology

[200] Allen, D. "Envisaging The Body of the Condemned: The Power of Platonic Symbols." *CP* 95, no. 2 (2000): 133–50.

[201] Anagnostopoulos, M. "The Divided Soul and Desire for the Good in Plato's *Republic*." In Santas.

[202] Andersson, T. J. *Polis and Psyche: A Motif in Plato's* Republic. Stockholm, 1971.

[203] Bobonich, C. *Plato's Utopia Recast: His Later Ethics and Politics.* Cambridge, 2002. Ch. 3, "Parts of the Soul and the Psychology of Virtue."

[204] Brown, E. "A Defense of Plato's Argument for the Immortality of the Soul at *Republic* 10.608c–611a." *Apeiron* 30 (1997): 211–38. Rpt. in *Essays on Plato's Psychology*, ed. E. Wagner (Lanham, Md., 2001).

[205] Brown, G. "The Character of the Individual and the Character of the State in Plato's *Republic.*" *Apeiron* 17 (1983): 43–47.

[206] Burger, R. "The Thumotic and the Erotic Soul: Seth Benardete on Platonic Psychology." *Interpretation* 32, no. 1 (2004–5): 57–76.

[207] Calabi, F. "*Andreia/ thymoeides.*" In Vegetti, vol. 3.

[208] Campese, S. "*Epithymia/ epithymētikon.*" In Vegetti, vol. 3.

[209] Carone, G. "*Akrasia* in the *Republic*: Does Plato Change His Mind?" *OSAP* 20 (2001): 107–48.

[210] Cooper, J. "Plato's Theory of Human Motivation." *HPQ* 1, no. 1 (1984): 3–21. Rpt. in Fine, *Plato 2*, and in *Essays on Plato's Psychology*, ed. E. Wagner (Lanham, Md., 2001).

[211] Cornford, F. M. "Psychology and Social Structure in the *Republic* of Plato." *CQ* 6 (1912): 246–65.

[212] Ferrari, G. R. F. "*Akrasia* as Neurosis in Plato's *Protagoras.*" *BACAP* 6 (1990): 115–39.

[213] Frede, D. "Die ungerechten Verfassungen und die ihnen entsprechenden Menschen (Buch 8.543a–9.576b)." In Höffe.

[214] Gerson, L. "A Note on Tripartition and Immortality in Plato." *Apeiron* 22, no. 1 (1987): 81–96.

[215] Gigon, O. "Die unseligkeit des Tyrannen in Platons *Staat* (577c–588a)." *Museum Helveticum* 45 (1988): 129–53.

[216] Gill, C. *Personality in Greek Epic, Tragedy, and Philosophy: The Self in Dialogue.* Oxford, 1996. Ch. 4, "The Personality Unified by Reason in Plato's *Republic.*"

[217] Gosling, J. C. B. *Plato.* London, 1973. Ch. 3, "Admiration for Manliness."

[218] Graeser, A. *Probleme der Platonischen Seelenteilungslehre. Zetemata*, vol. 47. Munich, 1969. Ch. 1, "Die Seelenteilungslehre der *Politeia.*"

[219] Harrison, E. L. "The Origin of *thumoeides.*" *CR* 3 (1953): 138–40.

[220] Hobbs, A. *Plato and the Hero: Courage, Manliness, and the Impersonal Good.* Cambridge, 2000. Chs. 1, 2, 7, and 8.

[221] Höffe, O. "Zur Analogie von Individuum und Polis (Buch 2.367e–374d)." In Höffe.

[222] Hoffman, P. "Plato on Appetitive Desires in the *Republic.*" *Apeiron* 36, no. 2 (2003): 171–74.

[223] Irwin, T. *Plato's Ethics*. Oxford, 1995. Ch. 13, "*Republic* 4: The Division of the soul."

[224] Irwin, T. "The Parts of the Soul and the Cardinal Virtues (Book 4.427d–448e)." In Höffe.

[225] Jaeger, W. "A New Greek Word in Plato's *Republic*: The Medical Origin of the Theory of the *thumoeides*." *Eranos* 44 (1946): 123–30.

[226] Kahn, C. "Plato's Theory of Desire." *RM* 41 (1987): 77–103.

[227] Kenny, A. J. P. "Mental Health in Plato's *Republic*." *Proceedings of the British Academy* 55 (1969): 229–53. Rpt. in A. J. P. Kenny, *The Anatomy of the Soul* (Oxford, 1973).

[228] Klosko, G. *The Development of Plato's Political Theory*. New York, 1986. Part 2, "The Moral Psychology of the Middle Dialogues."

[229] Klosko, G. "The 'Rule' of Reason in Plato's Psychology." *HPQ* 5, no. 4 (1988): 341–56.

[230] Larivée, A. "Malaise dans la cité: eros et tyrannie au livre 9 de la *République*." In Dixsaut, *Études 1*.

[231] Lear, J. "Inside and Outside the *Republic*." *Phronesis* 37, no. 2 (1992): 184–215. Rpt. in Kraut; in J. Lear, *Open Minded: Working Out the Logic of the Soul* (Cambridge, Mass., 1998); and in *Essays on Plato's Psychology*, ed. E. Wagner (Lanham, Md., 2001).

[232] Leroux, G. "La tripartition de l'âme: politique et éthique de l'âme dans le livre 4." In Dixsaut, *Études 1*.

[233] Lesses, G. "Weakness, Reason, and the Divided Soul in Plato's *Republic*." *HPQ* 4, no. 2 (1987): 147–61.

[234] Loraux, N. "L'âme de la cité. Réflexions sur une *psuchē* politique." *L'Écrit du Temps* 14–15 (1987): 35–54.

[235] Lorenz, H. "Desire and Reason in Plato's *Republic*." *OSAP* 27 (2004): 83–116.

[236] Lorenz, H. "The Analysis of the Soul in Plato's *Republic*." In Santas.

[237] Maguire, J. "The Individual and the Class in Plato's *Republic*." *CJ* 60, no. 4 (1965): 145–50.

[238] Miller, F. D., Jr. "Plato on Parts of the Soul." In *Plato and Platonism*, ed. J. M. van Ophuijsen (Washington, D.C., 1999).

[239] Miller, M. "A More 'Exact Grasp' of the Soul? Tripartition in *Republic* 4 and Dialectic in the *Philebus*." In *Truth*, ed. K. Pritzl (Washington, D.C., forthcoming).

[240] Moline, J. *Plato's Theory of Understanding*. Madison, 1981. Ch. 3, "*Epistēmē* and the Psyche."

[241] Moreau, J. "La cité et l'âme humaine dans la *République* de Platon." *Revue Internationale de Philosophie* 40 (1986): 85–96.

[242] Mulgan, R. G. "Individual and Collective Virtues in the *Republic*." *Phronesis* 13 (1968): 84–87.

[243] Neu, J. "Plato's Analogy of State and Individual: The *Republic* and the Organic Theory of the State." *Philosophy* 46 (1971): 238–54.

[244] Patterson, R. "Plato on Philosophic Character." *JHP* 25, no. 3 (1987): 325–50.

[245] Penner, T. "Thought and Desire in Plato." In Vlastos, *Plato 2*.

[246] Price, A. W. *Mental Conflict*. London, 1995. Ch. 2, "Plato," secs. 4–7.

[247] Repellini, F. F. "La trottola." In Vegetti, vol. 3.

[248] Robinson, R. "Plato's Separation of Reason and Desire." *Phronesis* 16 (1971): 38–48.

[249] Robinson, T. M. *Plato's Psychology*. Toronto, 1995 [1970]. Ch. 3, "The *Republic*."

[250] Rosen, S. "The Role of Eros in Plato's *Republic*." *RM* 18 (1965): 452–75. Rpt. in S. Rosen, *The Quarrel between Philosophy and Poetry: Studies in Ancient Thought* (New York, 1988).

[251] Scott, D. "Plato's Critique of the Democratic Character." *Phronesis* 45 (2000): 19–37.

[252] Shields, C. "Simple Souls." In *Essays on Plato's Psychology*, ed. E. Wagner (Lanham, Md., 2001).

[253] Shiner, R. "Soul in *Republic* 10.611." *Apeiron* 6 (1972): 23–30.

[254] Smith, N. D. "Plato's Analogy of Soul and State." *Journal of Ethics* 3 (1999): 31–49. Rpt. in *Essays on Plato's Psychology*, ed. E. Wagner (Lanham, Md., 2001).

[255] Stalley, R. F. "Plato's Argument for the Division of the Reasoning and Appetitive Elements within the Soul." *Phronesis* 20 (1975): 110–28.

[256] Stella, M. "Freud e la *Repubblica*: l'anima, la società, la gerarchia." In Vegetti, vol. 3.

[257] Stocks, J. L. "Plato and the Tripartite Soul." *Mind* 24 (1915): 207–21.

[258] Szlezák, T. A. "Unsterblichkeit und Trichotomie der Seele im zehnten Buch der *Politeia*." *Phronesis* 21 (1976): 31–58.

[259] Thein, K. "Justice dans la cité et justice en l'âme: une analogie imparfaite." In Dixsaut, *Études 1*.

[260] Thyssen, H. P. "The Socratic Paradoxes and the Tripartite Soul." In Ostenfeld.

[261] Vegetti, M. "*Sophia/ logistikon*." In Vegetti, vol. 3.

[262] Weiss, R. *The Socratic Paradox and Its Enemies*. Chicago, 2006. Ch. 6, "*Republic* 4: 'Everyone desires good things.'"

[263] Williams, B. A. O. "The Analogy of City and Soul in Plato's *Republic*." In *Exegesis and Argument*, ed. E. N. Lee, A. P. D. Mourelatos and R. M. Rorty, *Phronesis* supplementary vol. 1 (Assen, 1973). Rpt. in Kraut; in Fine *Plato 2*; in *Essays on Plato's Psychology*, ed. E. **Wagner** (Lanham, Md., 2001); and in B. A. O. Williams, *The Sense of the Past: Essays in the History of Philosophy* (Princeton, 2006).

[264] Wilson, J. R. S. "The Argument of *Republic* 4." *Philosophical Quarterly* 26 (1976): 111–24.

[265] Woods, M. "Plato's Division of the Soul." *Proceedings of the British Academy* 73 (1987): 23–48.

For discussion of the city-soul analogy in particular (a topic that overlaps considerably with sections IV.C and E), see, within this section, [202], [205], [211], [221], [231], [237], [242], [243], [254], [259], [263], and [264]; see also [38], [47], and [66]. The topic of the *thumos* or spirited part of the soul is the focus of [200], [207], [217], [219], [220], and [225]; that of *erōs* or passionate desire is the focus of [230], [250] (see also [115]); both are the topic of [206].

IV.E. Politics

[266] Allen, D. S. *The World of Prometheus: The Politics of Punishing in Democratic Athens*. Princeton, 2000. Ch. 10, "Plato's Paradigm Shifts."

[267] Annas, J. "Plato's *Republic* and Feminism." *Philosophy* 51 (1976): 307–21. Rpt. in Fine, *Plato 2*.

[268] Annas, J. "Politics and Ethics in Plato's *Republic* (Book 5.449a–471c)." In Höffe.

[269] Arends, F. "Plato as Problem-solver: The Unity of the *polis* as a Key to the Interpretation of Plato's *Republic*." In Ostenfeld.

[270] Ausland, H. "Plato's Ideal Cosmopolitanism." In *Polis and Cosmopolis: Problems of a Global Era*, ed. K. Boudouris, Proceedings of the 14th Conference of the International Association for Greek Philosophy, vol. 1 (Athens, 2003).

[271] Bambrough, R., ed. *Plato, Popper and Politics*. Cambridge, 1967.

[272] Barker, E. *Greek Political Theory: Plato and His Predecessors*. London, 1918. Chs. 8–10.

[273] Barney, R. "Platonism, Moral Nostalgia, and the 'City of Pigs.'" *BACAP* 17 (2001): 207–27.

[274] Beltrametti, A. "L'utopia dalla commedia al dialogo platonico." In Vegetti, vol. 4.

[275] Bloom, A. "Response to Hall." *Political Theory* 5, no. 3 (1977): 315–30.

[276] Bluck, R. S. "Is Plato's *Republic* a Theocracy?" *Philosophical Quarterly* 5 (1955): 69–73.

[277] Bluestone, N. H. *Women and the Ideal Society: Plato's* Republic *and Modern Myths of Gender*. Amherst, Mass., 1987.

[278] Brown, L. "How Totalitarian Is Plato's *Republic*?" In Ostenfeld.

[279] Burnyeat, M. F. "Sphinx without a Secret." *New York Review of Books* (May 30, 1985): 30–36. Review of L. Strauss, *Studies in Platonic Political Philosophy*.

[280] Burnyeat, M. F. "Utopia and Fantasy: The Practicability of Plato's Ideally Just City." In *Psychoanalysis, Mind, and Art*, ed. J. Hopkins and A. Savile (Oxford, 1992). Rpt. in Fine, *Plato 2*.

[281] Calabi, F. "La nobile menzogna." In Vegetti vol. 2.

[282] Campese, S. "*Misthōtikē*." In Vegetti, vol. 1.

[283] Campese, S. "Nudità." In Vegetti, vol. 4.

[284] Campese, S. "La prima ondata: il 'dramma femminile.'" In Vegetti, vol. 4.

[285] Campese, S. "La seconda ondata: la comunanza di donne e figli." In Vegetti, vol. 4.

[286] Campese, S., and L. L. Canino. "La genesi della *polis*." In Vegetti, vol. 2.

[287] Canto, M. "Le livre 5 de la *République*: les femmes et les platoniciens." *Revue Philosophique de la France et de l'Étranger* 114 (1989): 378–84.

[288] Canto-Sperber, M., and L. Brisson. "Zur sozialen Gliederung der Polis (Buch 2.372d–4.427c)." In Höffe.

[289] Coby, P. "Why Are There Warriors in Plato's *Republic*?" *HPT* 22 (2001): 377–99.

[290] Cornford, F. M. "Plato's Commonwealth." In F. M. Cornford, *The Unwritten Philosophy and Other Essays*, ed. W. K. C. Guthrie (Cambridge, 1967 [1935]).

[291] Crossman, R. H. S. *Plato Today*. London, 1937.

[292] Dawson, D. *Cities of the Gods: Communist Utopias in Greek Thought*. Oxford, 1992. Ch. 2, "The Platonic Utopia: A City without the Household."

[293] Devereux, D. "Socrates' First City in the *Republic*." *Apeiron* 13, no. 1 (1979): 36–40.

[294] Due, B. "Plato and Xenophon: Two Contributions to the Constitutional Debate in the 4th Century B.C." In Ostenfeld.

[295] Farinetti, G. "Il confronto di Marx con Platone (attraverso Hegel)." In Vegetti, vol. 4.

[296] Ferrari, G. R. F. "Strauss' Plato." *Arion* 5, no. 2 (1997): 36–65. Responds to [279].

[297] Fortenbaugh, W. W. "On Plato's Feminism in *Republic* 5." *Apeiron* 9, no. 2 (1975): 1–4.

[298] Frede, D. "Platon, Popper und der Historismus." In *Polis und Kosmos: Naturphilosophie und politische Philosophie bei Platon*, ed. E. Rudolph (Darmstadt, 1996).

[299] Gadamer, H.-G. *Dialogue and Dialectic*, trans. P. C. Smith. New Haven, Conn., 1980. Ch. 4, "Plato's Educational State."

[300] Gadamer, H.-G. "Platons Denken in Utopien." *Gymnasium* 90 (1983): 434–55.

[301] Gaiser, K. "Zur Kritik an Platons Staatsutopie." In K. Gaiser, *Gesammelte Schriften*, ed. T. A. Szlezák (Sankt Augustin, 2004).

[302] Gastaldi, S. "L'allegoria della nave." In Vegetti, vol. 5.

[303] Gastaldi, S. "La guerra della *kallipolis*." In Vegetti, vol. 4.

[304] Gastaldi, S. "*Nomos* e legislazione." In Vegetti, vol. 3.

[305] Giorgini, G. "Leo Strauss e la 'Repubblica' di Platone." *Filosofia Politica* 5 (1991): 153–60.

[306] Griswold, C. L., Jr. "Platonic Liberalism: Self-perfection as a Foundation of Political Theory." In *Plato and Platonism*, ed. J. M. van Ophuijsen (Washington, D.C., 1999).

[307] Gutiérrez, R. "The Logic of Decadence: On the Deficient Forms of Government in Plato's *Republic*." *New Yearbook for Phenomenology and Phenomenological Philosophy* 3 (2003): 85–102.

[308] Hahm, D. E. "Plato's 'Noble Lie' and Political Brotherhood." *Classica et Mediaevalia* 30 (1969): 211–27.

[309] Hall, D. "The *Republic* and 'The Limits of Politics.'" *Political Theory* 5, no. 3 (1977): 193–313.

[310] Hays, D. "An Examination of Popper's Criticisms of Plato's *Republic*." *Dialogos* 19 (1984): 81–90.

[311] Helmer, É. "Histoire, politique et pratique aux livres 8 et 9 de la *République*." In Dixsaut, *Études I*.

[312] Hourani, G. F. "The Education of the Third Class in Plato's *Republic*." *CQ* 43 (1949): 58–60.

[313] Hyland, D. A. "*Republic* Book 2 and the Origins of Political Philosophy." *Interpretation* 16 (1989): 247–61.

[314] Hyland, D. A. "Plato's Waves and the Question of Utopia." *Interpretation* 18 (1990): 91–109.

[315] Isnardi-Parente, M. "Motivi utopistici — ma non utopia — in Platone." In *La Città Ideale nella Tradizione Classica e Biblico-cristiana*, ed. R. Uglione (Turin, 1987).

[316] Jenks, R. "The Machinery of the Collapse: On *Republic* 8." *HPT* 23 (2002): 22–29.

[317] Kamtekar, R. "What's the Good of Agreeing? *Homonoia* in Platonic Politics." *OSAP* 26 (2004): 131–70.

[318] Keyt, D. "Plato and the Ship of State." In Santas.

[319] Klosko, G. "Provisionality in Plato's Ideal State." *HPT* 5 (1984): 171–93.

[320] Klosko, G. *The Development of Plato's Political Theory*. New York, 1986. Part 3, "Platonic Politics."

[321] Klosko, G. "The 'Straussian' Interpretation of Plato's *Republic*." *HPT* 7 (1986): 274–93.

[322] Kochin, M. S. *Gender and Rhetoric in Plato's Political Thought*. Cambridge, 2002.

[323] Kytzler, B. "Platonische Unorte." In *Utopie und Tradition: Platons Lehre vom Staat in der Moderne*, ed. H. Funke (Würzburg, 1987).

[324] Laks, A. "Legislation and Demiurgy: On the Relationship between Plato's *Republic* and *Laws*." *Classical Antiquity* 9 (1990): 209–29.

[325] Lesser, H. "Plato's Feminism." *Philosophy* 54 (1979): 113–17.

[326] Leys, W. A. R. "Was Plato Non-political?" *Ethics* 75 (1965): 272–76. Rpt. in Vlastos, *Plato* 2.

[327] de Luise, F. "La *kallipolis* di Rousseau." In Vegetti, vol. 4.

[328] de Luise, F., and G. Farinetti. "La *technē antilogikē* tra *erizein* e *dialegesthai*." In Vegetti, vol. 4.

[329] de Luise, F., and G. Farinetti. "Il filosofo selvatico." In Vegetti, vol. 5.

[330] Mattei, J.-F. "Platon et Karl Popper: l'idée de démocratie." In *La Philosophie de Platon*, ed. M. Fattal (Paris, 2001).

[331] McKeen, C. "Swillsburgh City Limits (the 'City of Pigs': *Republic* 370c–372d)." *Polis* 21 (2004): 70–92.

[332] Menn, S. "On Plato's *Politeia*." *BACAP* 21 (2006): 1–55.

[333] Natali, C. "L'élision de l'*oikos* dans la *République* de Platon." In Dixsaut, *Études 1*.

[334] Neschke-Hentschke, A. "Politischer Platonismus und die Theorie des Naturrechts." In *Polis und Kosmos: Naturphilosophie und politische Philosophie bei Platon*, ed. E. Rudolph (Darmstadt, 1996).

[335] Neumann, H. "Plato's *Republic*: Utopia or Dystopia?" *Modern Schoolman* 44 (1967): 319–30.

[336] Okin, S. M. "Philosopher-Queens and Private Wives: Plato on Women and the Family." *Philosophy and Public Affairs* 6 (1977): 345–69.

[337] Page, C. "The Truth about Lies in Plato's *Republic*." *AP* 11 (1991): 1–33.

[338] Pinotti, P. "La *Repubblica* e Dumézil: gerarchia e sovranità." In Vegetti, vol. 3.

[339] Planinc, Z. *Plato's Political Philosophy: Prudence in the* Republic *and the* Laws. London, 1991. Ch. 1, "*Phronesis* and the Good in the *Republic*."

[340] Popper, K. R. *The Open Society and Its Enemies*, vol. 1: *The Spell of Plato*. London, 1966 [1945].

[341] Pradeau, J.-F. *Plato and the City: A New Introduction to Plato's Political Thought.* Exeter, 2002. Ch. 2, "The Political Psychology of the *Republic.*"

[342] Rankin, H. D. "*Paradeigma* and Realizability in Plato's *Republic.*" *Eranos* 63 (1965): 120–33.

[343] Reeve, C. D. C. "Women." In C. D. C. Reeve, *Women in the Academy: Dialogues on Themes from Plato's* Republic (Indianapolis, Ind., 2001).

[344] Rosenstock, B. "Athena's Cloak: Plato's Critique of Democracy in the *Republic.*" *Political Theory* 22 (1994): 363–90.

[345] Said, S. "La *République* de Platon et la communauté des femmes." *L'Antiquité Classique* 55 (1986): 142–62.

[346] Sartorius, R. "Fallacy and Political Radicalism in Plato's *Republic.*" *Canadian Journal of Philosophy* 3 (1974): 349–63.

[347] Sauvé-Meyer, S. "Class Assignment and the Principle of Specialization in Plato's *Republic.*" *BACAP* 20 (2004): 229–43.

[348] Saxonhouse, A. W. "The Philosopher and the Female in the Political Thought of Plato." *Political Theory* 4 (1976): 195–212. Rpt. in Kraut.

[349] Saxonhouse, A. W. *Fear of Diversity: The Birth of Political Science in Ancient Greek Thought.* Chicago, 1992. Ch. 6, "Callipolis: Socrates' Escape from Tragedy."

[350] Schofield, M. "Plato on the Economy." In *The Ancient Greek City-State,* ed. M. H. Hansen (Copenhagen, 1993). Rpt. in M. Schofield, *Saving the City: Philosopher-Kings and Other Classical Paradigms* (London, 1999).

[351] Schofield, M. "Approaching the *Republic.*" In *The Cambridge History of Greek and Roman Political Thought,* ed. C. J. Rowe and M. Schofield (Cambridge, 2000).

[352] Scolnicov, S. *Plato's Metaphysics of Education.* London, 1988. Chs. 10–12.

[353] Skemp, J. B. "How Political Is the *Republic?*" *HPT* 1 (1980): 1–7.

[354] Sparshott, F. E. "Plato as Anti-political Thinker." *Ethics* 77 (1967): 214–19. Rpt. in Vlastos, *Plato* 2.

[355] Spelman, E. "Hairy Cobblers and Philosopher-Queens." In E. Spelman, *Inessential Woman: Problems of Exclusion in Feminist Thought.* (Boston, 1988). Rpt. in N. Tuana, ed. *Feminist Interpretations of Plato.* (University Park, Pa., 1994).

[356] Stefanini, L. *Platone,* 2nd ed. Padova, 1949. Vol. 1, part 2, ch. 6, "L'idealismo politico della *Repubblica.*"

[357] Taylor, A. E. "Decline and Fall of the State in *Republic* 8." *Mind* 48 (1939): 23–38.

[358] Taylor, C. C. W. "Plato's Totalitarianism." *Polis* 5 (1986): 4–29. Rpt. in Fine, *Plato* 2.

[359] Vegetti, M. "Ricchezza/povertà e l'unità della *polis*." In Vegetti, vol. 3.

[360] Vegetti, M. "*Beltista eiper dynata*: lo statuto dell'utopia nella *Repubblica*." In Vegetti, vol. 4.

[361] Vegetti, M. "La razza pura." In Vegetti, vol. 4.

[362] Vlastos, G. "Does Slavery Exist in Plato's *Republic*?" *CP* 63 (1968): 291–95. Rpt. in G. Vlastos, *Platonic Studies* (Princeton, 1981 [1973]).

[363] Vlastos, G. "Was Plato a Feminist?" *Times Literary Supplement* 4485 (March 17–23, 1989): 276, 288–89. Rpt. in N. Tuana, ed., *Feminist Interpretations of Plato* (University Park, Pa., 1994), and in Kraut.

[364] Waldron, J. "What Plato Would Allow." *Nomos* 37 (1995): 138–78.

[365] Wallach, J. R. *The Platonic Political Art: A Study of Critical Reason and Democracy*. University Park, Pa., 2001. Ch. 6, "The Constitution of Justice (*Republic*)."

[366] Wender, D. "Plato: Misogynist, Paedophile, and Feminist." *Arethusa* 6, no. 1 (1973): 75–90.

Studies intended as introductory: [272], [320], [341], and [351]. Discussions of whether the *Republic* promotes totalitarianism: [271], [278], [291], [298], [310], [330], [340], and [358]. Studies of feminism in the *Republic*: [267], [277], [284], [285], [287], [322], [325], [333], [336], [343], [345], [348], [355], [366]. Studies of the *Republic*'s utopianism: [274], [280], [292], [300], [301], [314], [315], [323], [335], [342], and [360]. Discussion of Leo Strauss' influential (and controversial) interpretation of the *Republic*: [275], [279], [296], [305], [309], [321], and see also [66]. Studies of the noble lie: [281], [308], [337].

IV.F. Philosopher-kings

[367] Aronson, S. H. "The Happy Philosopher — A Counterexample to Plato's Proof." *JHP* 10 (1972): 383–98.

[368] Beatty, J. "Plato's Happy Philosopher and Politics." *Review of Politics* (1976): 545–75.

[369] Brickhouse, T. C. "The Paradox of the Philosopher's Rule." *Apeiron* 15 (1981): 1–9. Rpt. in *Plato: Critical Assessments*, vol. 3, ed. N. D. Smith (New York, 1998).

[370] Brown, E. "Justice and Compulsion for Plato's Philosopher-Rulers." *AP* 20 (2000): 1–17.

[371] Brown, E. "Minding the Gap in Plato's *Republic*." *Philosophical Studies* 117 (2004): 275–302.

[372] Cambiano, G. "I filosofi e la costrizione a governare nella *Repubblica* platonica." In *I filosofi e il potere nella società e nella cultura antiche*, ed. G. Casertano (Naples, 1986).

[373] Davies, J. "A Note on the Philosopher's Descent into the Cave." *Philologus* 112 (1968): 121–26.

[374] Dorter, K. "Philosopher-Rulers: How Contemplation Becomes Action." *AP* 21 (2001): 335–56.

[375] Kraut, R. "Egoism, Love, and Political Office in Plato's Psychology." *HPQ* 5 (1988): 330–34.

[376] Kraut, R. "Return to the Cave: *Republic* 519–521." *BACAP* 7 (1991): 43–62. Rpt. in Fine, *Plato* 2.

[377] Mahoney, T. "Do Plato's Philosopher-Rulers Sacrifice Self-interest to Justice?" *Phronesis* 38 (1992): 265–82.

[378] Nightingale, A. W. *Spectacles of Truth in Classical Greek Philosophy: Theōria in its Cultural Context.* Cambridge, 2004. Ch. 3, "The Fable of Philosophy in Plato's *Republic.*"

[379] Schofield, M. *Saving the City: Philosopher-Kings and Other Classical Paradigms.* London, 1999. Ch. 2, "The Disappearing Philosopher-King."

[380] Spaemann, R. "Die Philosophenkönige (Buch 5.473b–6.504a)." In Höffe.

[381] Vegetti, M. "Il regno filosofico." In Vegetti, vol. 4.

[382] Vegetti, M. "I filosofi a scuola e la scuola dei filosofi." In Vegetti, vol. 5.

[383] Vernezze, P. "The Philosophers' Interest." *AP* 12 (1992): 331–49.

[384] White, N. P. "The Ruler's Choice." *Archiv für Geschichte der Philosophie* 68 (1986): 22–46.

The question whether the philosopher sacrifices personal happiness by returning to the cave is a topic also addressed by many of the comprehensive treatments of the *Republic* in section III.A, particularly those in English. See also sec. 9 of [165].

IV.G. Metaphysics, epistemology, the Forms

[385] Baltes, M. "Is the Idea of the Good in Plato's *Republic* Beyond Being?" In M. Baltes, Dianoēmata: *Kleine Schriften zu Platon und zum Platonismus,* ed. A. Hüffmeier, M.-L. Lakmann, and M. Vorwek (Stuttgart, 1999).

[386] Baltzly, D. "'To an unhypothetical first principle' in Plato's *Republic.*" *HPQ* 13 (1996): 149–65.

[387] Baltzly, D. "Knowledge and Belief in *Republic* 5." *AGP* 129 (1997): 239–72.

[388] Cambiano, G. "La méthode par hypothèse en *République* 2." In Dixsaut, *Études* 2.

[389] Cherniss, H. "On Plato's *Republic* 10.597b." *AJP* 53, no. 3 (1932): 233–42.

[390] Cooper, N. "Between Knowledge and Ignorance." *Phronesis* 31 (1986): 229–42.

[391] Cunningham, S. "On Plato's Form of the Good" *Gnosis* 12, no. 3 (1984): 94–104.

[392] Demos, R. "Plato's Idea of the Good." *PR* 46 (1937): 245–75.

[393] Dixsaut, M. "Encore une fois le bien." In Dixsaut, *Études* 2.

[394] Ebert, T. *Meinung und Wissen in der Philosophie Platons*. Berlin, 1974. Ch. 4, "*Doxa* und *Epistēmē* in den mittleren Büchern des 'Staates.'"

[395] Ferber, R. *Platons Idee des Guten*. Sankt Augustin, 1987 [1984].

[396] Ferber, R. "Did Plato Ever Reply to Those Critics, Who Reproached Him for 'the emptiness of the Platonic Idea or Form of the Good?'" In Ostenfeld.

[397] Ferber, R. "L'idea del bene è o non è trascendente? Ancora su *epekeina tēs ousias*." In *Platone e la Tradizione Platonica: Studi di Filosofia Antica*, ed. M. Bonazzi and F. Trabattoni (Milan, 2003).

[398] Ferejohn, M. T. "Knowledge, Recollection and the Forms in *Republic* 7." In Santas.

[399] Ferrari, F. "Conoscenza e opinione: il filosofo e la città." In Vegetti, vol. 4.

[400] Ferrari, F. "Teorie delle idee e ontologia." In Vegetti, vol. 4.

[401] Ferrari, F. "L'idea del bene: collocazione ontologica e funzione causale." In Vegetti, vol. 5.

[402] Fine, G. "Knowledge and Belief in *Republic* 5–7." In Fine, *Plato 1*.

[403] Gadamer, H.-G. *The Idea of the Good in Platonic-Aristotelian Philosophy*, trans. P. C. Smith. New Haven, Conn., 1986. Ch. 3, "The *Polis* and Knowledge of the Good."

[404] Gaiser, K. "Plato's Enigmatic Lecture 'On the Good.'" *Phronesis* 25 (1980): 5–37.

[405] Gallop, D. "Image and Reality in Plato's *Republic*." *AGP* 47 (1965): 113–31. Rpt. in T. Irwin, ed., *Plato's Metaphysics and Epistemology* (New York, 1995).

[406] Gonzalez, F. J. "Propositions or Objects? A Critique of Gail Fine on Knowledge and Belief in *Republic* 5." *Phronesis* 41 (1996): 245–75. Responds to [402].

[407] Graeser, A. "Plato on Knowledge and Opinion (*Republic* 5)." *Synthesis Philosophica* 5 (1990): 407–17.

[408] Gosling, J. C. B. "*Republic* 5: *ta polla kala*." *Phronesis* 5 (1960): 116–28.

[409] Gosling, J. C. B. "*Doxa* and *dunamis* in *Republic* 5." *Phronesis* 13 (1968): 119–30.

[410] Hitchcock, D. "The Good in Plato's *Republic*." *Apeiron* 19 (1985): 65–92.

[411] Horn, C. "Platons *epistēmē-doxa*-Unterscheidung und die Ideentheorie (Buch 5.474b–480a und Buch 10.595c–597e)." In Höffe.

[412] Irwin, T. *Plato's Ethics*. Oxford, 1995. Ch. 16, "*Republic* 5–7."

[413] Joseph, H. W. B. *Knowledge and the Good in Plato's* Republic. Oxford 1948.

[414] Krämer, H. J. "*Epeikeina tēs ousias*: zu Platon, *Politeia* 509b." *AGP* 51 (1969): 1–30.

[415] Lachterman, D. "What Is 'The Good' of Plato's *Republic*?" *St. John's Review* 39, nos. 1–2 (1989–90): 139–71.

[416] Lafrance, Y. *La Théorie Platonicienne de la* Doxa. Montréal, 1981. Ch. 5, "La République."

[417] Lafrance, Y. "Les entités mathématiques et l'idée du Bien en *Republique* 6.509d–511e." *Diotima* 14 (1986): 193–97.

[418] Miller, M. "Platonic Provocations: Reflections on the Soul and the Good in the *Republic*." In *Platonic Investigations*, ed. D. J. O'Meara (Washington, D.C., 1985).

[419] Mittelstraß, J. "Die Dialektik und ihre wissenschaftlichen Vorübungen (Buch 6.510b–511e und Buch 7.521c–539d)." In Höffe.

[420] Parry, R. "The Uniqueness Proof of Forms in *Republic* 10." *JHP* 23 (1985): 133–50.

[421] Paton, H. J. "Plato's Theory of *EIKASIA*." *PAS* 22 (1921–22): 69–104.

[422] Penner, T. "The Forms, the Form of the Good, and the Desire for Good, in Plato's *Republic*." *The Modern Schoolman* 80 (2002–3): 191–233.

[423] Penner, T. "Plato's Theory of Forms in the *Republic*." In Santas.

[424] Rawson, G. "Knowledge and Desire of the Good in Plato's *Republic*." *Southwest Philosophy Review* 12 (1996): 103–15.

[425] Robinson, R. *Plato's Earlier Dialectic*, 2nd ed. Oxford, 1953. Ch. 10, "Hypothesis in the *Republic*."

[426] Santa Cruz, M. I. "La dialectique platonicienne d'après Plotin." In Dixsaut, *Études 2*.

[427] Santas, G. "The Form of the Good in Plato's *Republic*." *Philosophical Inquiry* (Winter, 1980): 374–403. Rpt. in *Essays in Greek Philosophy 2*, ed. J. Anton and A. Preus (Albany, N.Y., 1983), and in Fine, *Plato 1*.

[428] Santas, G. "Knowledge and Belief in Plato's *Republic*." In *Greek Studies in the Philosophy and History of Science*, ed. P. Nicolacopoulos (Dordrecht, 1990).

[429] Santas, G. *Goodness and Justice*. Oxford, 2001. Ch. 5, "Plato's Metaphysical Theory of the Form of the Good."

[430] Shorey, P. "The Idea of Good in Plato's *Republic*." *Studies in Classical Philology* 1 (1885): 188–239.

[431] Silverman, A. *The Dialectic of Essence: A Study of Plato's Metaphysics*. Princeton, 2002. Ch. 3, sec. 2, "The Emergence of Forms: The *Republic*, Book 7."

[432] Smith, N. D. "Knowledge by Acquaintance and 'Knowing What' in Plato's *Republic*." *Dialogue* 18 (1979): 281–88.

[433] Stemmer, P. "Das Kinderrätsel vom Eunuchen und der Fledermaus: Platon über Wissen und Meinen in *Politeia* 5." *Philosophisches Jahrbuch* 92 (1985): 79–97.

[434] Stemmer, P. *Platons Dialektik: Die Frühen und Mittleren Dialoge.* Berlin, 1992. Ch. 4, "Entfaltungen des elenktischen Verfahrens."

[435] Stokes, M. "Plato and the Sightlovers of the *Republic*." In *The Language of the Cave*, ed. A. Barker and M. Warner (= *Apeiron* 25.4 [1992]).

[436] de Strycker, E. "L'idée du Bien dans la *République* de Platon." *L'Antiquité Classique* 39 (1970): 450–67.

[437] Szlezák, T. A. *Die Idee des Guten in Platons* Politeia: *Beobachtungen zu den mittleren Büchern.* Sankt Augustin, 2003.

[438] Thein, K. "Les Formes dans la *République*." In Dixsaut, *Études* 2.

[439] Trabattoni, F. "Il sapere del filosofo." In Vegetti, vol. 5.

[440] Vegetti, M. "*Technē*." In Vegetti, vol. 1.

[441] Vegetti, M. "Glaucon et les mystères de la dialectique." In Dixsaut, *Études* 2.

[442] Vegetti, M. "Dialettica." In Vegetti, vol. 5.

[443] Vegetti, M. "*Megiston mathēma*: l'idea del 'buono' e le sue funzioni." In Vegetti, vol. 5.

[444] White, F. C. "The *Phaedo* and *Republic* 5 on Essences." *JHS* 98 (1978): 140–56.

[445] White, F. C. "The Scope of Knowledge in *Republic* 5." *Australasian Journal of Philosophy* 62, no. 4 (1984): 339–54.

[446] White, N. P. *Plato on Knowledge and Reality.* Indianapolis, Ind. 1976. Ch. 4, "The *Republic*: Forms, Hypotheses, and Knowledge."

[447] Wieland, W. *Platon und die Formen des Wissens.* Göttingen, 1982. Sec. 10, "Die Idee des Guten und ihre Funktionen."

[448] Williamson, R. B. "*Eidos* and *agathon* in Plato's *Republic*." *St. John's Review* 39 (1989–90): 105–37.

The following studies in this section focus on or importantly involve the Form of the Good: [385], [386], [391]–[393], [395]–[396], [401], [403], [404], [410], [414], [415], [418], [422], [424], [427], [429], [430], [436], [437], [443], and [448].

IV.H. Sun, line, and cave

[449] Austin, J. L. *Philosophical Papers*, ed. J. O. Urmson and G. J. Warnock. Oxford, 1979. Ch. 13, "The Line and the Cave in Plato's *Republic*."

[450] Barnes, J. "Le soleil de Platon vu avec des lunettes analytiques." *Rue Descartes* 1 ["Des Grecs"] (1991): 81–92.

[451] Brunschwig, J. "Revisiting Plato's Cave." *BACAP* 19 (2003): 145–74.

[452] Burnyeat, M. F. "Platonism and Mathematics: A Prelude to Discussion." In *Mathematics and Metaphysics in Aristotle*, ed. A. Graeser (Stuttgart, 1987).

[453] Calabi, F. "Il sole e la sua luce." In Vegetti, vol. 5.

[454] Campese, S. "La caverna." In Vegetti, vol. 5.

[455] Casertano, G. "La Caverne: entre analogie, image, connaissance et praxis." In Dixsaut, *Études* 2.

[456] Couloubaritsis, L. "Le caractère mythique de l'analogie du Bien dans *Republique* 6." *Diotima* 12 (1982): 71–80.

[457] Dewincklear, D. "La question de l'initiation dans le mythe de la Caverne." *Revue de Philosophie Ancienne* 11 (1993): 159–75.

[458] Dixsaut, M. "L'analogie intenable." *Rue Descartes* 1 ["Des Grecs"] (1991): 93–120. Rpt. in M. Dixsaut, *Platon et la question de la pensée: Études Platoniciennes I* (Paris, 2000).

[459] Ferber, R. "Notizen zu Platons Höhlengleichnis." *Freiburger Zeitschrift für Philosophie und Theologie* 28 (1981): 393–433.

[460] Ferguson, A. S. "Plato's Simile of Light, Part 1." *CQ* 15 (1921): 131–52.

[461] Ferguson, A. S. "Plato's Simile of Light, Part 2." *CQ* 16 (1922): 15–28.

[462] Fogelin, R. G. "Three Platonic Analogies." *PR* 80 (1971): 371–82.

[463] Gaiser, K. "Das Höhlengleichnis." In K. Gaiser *Gesammelte Schriften*, ed. T. A. Szlezák (Sankt Augustin, 2004).

[464] Goldschmidt, V. "La Ligne de la *République* et la classification des sciences." In V. Goldschmidt, *Questions Platoniciennes*. (Paris, 1970).

[465] Hackforth, R. "Plato's Divided Line and Dialectic." *CQ* 36 (1942): 1–9.

[466] Hall, D. "Interpreting Plato's Cave as an Allegory of the Human Condition." *Apeiron* 14 (1980): 74–86.

[467] Hamlyn, D. W. "*Eikasia* in Plato's *Republic*." *Philosophical Quarterly* 8 (1958): 14–23.

[468] Jackson, H. "On Plato's Republic 6.509d sq." *Journal of Philology* 10 (1882): 132–50.

[469] Karasmanis, V. "Plato's *Republic*: The Line and the Cave." *Apeiron* 21 (1988): 147–71.

[470] Krämer, H.-J. "Die Idee des Guten: Sonnen- und Liniengleichnis (Buch 6.504a–511e)." In Höffe.

[471] Lafrance, Y. "Platon et la géométrie: la construction de la Ligne en *République* 509d–511e." *Dialogue* 16 (1977): 425–50.

[472] Lafrance, Y. "Platon et la géométrie: méthode dialectique en *République* 509d–511e." *Dialogue* 19 (1980): 46–93.

[473] Lafrance, Y. *Pour Interpréter Platon I: La Ligne en République 6.509d–511e. Bilan Analytique des Études (1804–1984)*. Montréal, 1986.

[474] Lafrance, Y. *Pour Interpréter Platon II: La Ligne en République 6.509d–511e. Le Texte et son Histoire.* Montréal, 1989.

[475] Lizano-Ordovás, M. A. "*Eikasia* und *Pistis* in Platons Höhlengleichnis." *Zeitschrift für Philosophische Forschung* 49 (1995): 378–97.

[476] Malcolm, J. "The Line and the Cave." *Phronesis* 7 (1962): 38–45.

[477] Malcolm, J. "The Cave Revisited." *CQ* 31 (1981): 60–68.

[478] Morrison, J. S. "Two Unresolved Difficulties in the Line and Cave." *Phronesis* 22 (1977): 212–31.

[479] Oakeshott, M. *On Human Conduct.* Oxford, 1975. Pp. 27–31. Discussion of the cave.

[480] Pontificia Universidad Católica del Perú. *Los Similes de la República 6–7 de Platón.* Lima, 2003.

[481] Repellini, F. F. "La linea e la caverna." In Vegetti, vol. 5.

[482] Robinson, R. *Plato's Earlier Dialectic,* 2nd ed. Oxford, 1953. Ch. 11, "The Line and the Cave."

[483] Schuhl, P.-M. *La Fabulation Platonicienne.* Paris, 1968. Ch. 2, sec. 2, "Autour de la Caverne."

[484] Smith, N. D. "Plato's Divided Line." *AP* 16 (1996): 25–46. Rpt. in *Plato: Critical Assessments,* vol. 2, ed. N. D. Smith (New York, 1998).

[485] Smith, N. D. "How the Prisoners in Plato's Cave Are 'Like Us.'" *BACAP* 13 (1997): 187–204.

[486] Stocks, J. L. "The Divided Line of Plato *Rep.* 6." *CQ* 5 (1911): 73–88.

[487] Strang, C. "Plato's Analogy of the Cave." *OSAP* 4 (1986): 19–34.

[488] Sze, C. P. "*Eikasia* and *Pistis* in Plato's Cave Allegory." *CQ* 27 (1977): 127–38.

[489] Szlezák, T. A. "Das Höhlengleichnis (Buch 7.514a–521b und 539d–541b)." In Höffe.

[490] Wieland, W. *Platon und die Formen des Wissens.* Göttingen, 1982. sec. 12, "Beiträge zur Deutung der Drei Gleichnisse."

[491] Wilson, J. S. "The Contents of the Cave." In *Canadian Journal of Philosophy,* supplementary vol. 2: *New Essays on Plato and the Pre-Socratics,* ed. R. Shiner and J. King-Farlow (Guelph, Ontario, 1976).

IV.I. Mathematics and the sciences

[492] Burnyeat, M. F. "Plato on Why Mathematics Is Good for the Soul." *Proceedings of the British Academy* 103 (2000): 1–82. Rpt. in *Mathematics and Necessity,* ed. T. Smiley (Oxford, 2001).

[493] Cattanei, E. "Un nouveau pouvoir pour les mathématiques: quelques remarques sur le cursus d'études du livre 7 de la *République*." In *La Philosophie de Platon,* ed. M. Fattal (Paris, 2001).

[494] Cattanei, E. "Le matematiche al tempo di Platone e la loro riforma." In Vegetti, vol. 5.

[495] Cherniss, H. "Plato as Mathematician." *RM* 4 (1951): 393–425. Rpt. in H. Cherniss, *Selected Papers* (Leiden, 1977).

[496] Cornford, F. M. "Mathematics and Dialectic in the *Republic* 6–7." In *Studies in Plato's Metaphysics*, ed. R. E. Allen (London, 1965).

[497] Ehrhardt, E. "The Word of the Muses." *CQ* 36 (1986): 407–20.

[498] Fowler, D. H. *The Mathematics of Plato's Academy: A New Reconstruction.* Oxford, 1999 [1987].

[499] Gaiser, K. "Platons Zusammenschau der mathematischen Wissenschaften." In K. Gaiser, *Gesammelte Schriften*, ed. T. A. Szlezák (Sankt Augustin, 2004).

[500] Hare, R. M. "Plato and the Mathematicians." In *New Essays in Plato and Aristotle*, ed. R. Bambrough (London, 1965).

[501] Lloyd, G. E. R. "Plato as a Natural Scientist." *JHS* 88 (1968): 78–92.

[502] Meriani, A. "Teoria musicale e antiempirismo." In Vegetti, vol. 5.

[503] Miller, M. "Figure, Ratio, Form: Plato's Five Mathematical Studies." In *Recognition, Remembrance, and Reality*, ed. M. McPherran (= *Apeiron*, 32.4 [1999]).

[504] Mourelatos, A. P. D. "Plato's 'Real Astronomy': *Republic* 527d–531d." In *Science and the Sciences in Plato*, ed. J. P. Anton (Delmar, N.Y., 1980).

[505] Mourelatos, A. P. D. "Astronomy and Kinematics in Plato's Project of Rationalist Explanation." *Studies in the History and Philosophy of Science* 12, no. 1 (1981): 1–32.

[506] Mueller, I. "Ascending to Problems: Astronomy and Harmonics in *Republic* 7." In *Science and the Sciences in Plato*, ed. J. P. Anton (Delmar, N.Y., 1980).

[507] Mueller, I. "Mathematical Method and Philosophical Truth." In *The Cambridge Companion to Plato*, ed. R. Kraut (Cambridge, 1992).

[508] Repellini, F. F. "Astronomia e armonica." In Vegetti, vol. 5.

[509] Robins, I. "Mathematics and the Conversion of the Mind, *Republic* 7. 522c1–531e3." *AP* 15 (1995): 359–91.

[510] Sigurdarson, E. S. "Plato's Ideal of Science." In Ostenfeld.

[511] Taylor, C. C. W. "Plato and the Mathematicians." *Philosophical Quarterly* 17 (1967): 193–203.

[512] Vegetti, M. "Medicina." In Vegetti, vol. 2.

IV.J. Poetry, culture, the arts

[513] Annas, J. "Plato on the Triviality of Literature." In *Plato on Beauty, Wisdom and the Arts*, ed. J. M. E. Moravcsik and P. Temko (Totowa, N.J., 1982).

[514] Babut, D. "L' Unité du livre 10 de la *République* et sa fonction dans le dialogue." *Bulletin de l'Association Guillaume Budé* 42 (1983): 31–54.

[515] Barker, A. *Psicomusicologia nella Grecia Antica*. Naples, 2005. Sec. 1, "Musica e carattere nella *Repubblica* di Platone."

[516] Belfiore, E. "The Role of the Visual Arts in Plato's Ideal State." *Journal of the Theory and Criticism of Visual Arts* 1 (1981): 115–27.

[517] Belfiore, E. "Plato's Greatest Accusation against Poetry." In *Canadian Journal of Philosophy* supplementary vol. 9: *New Essays on Plato*, ed. F. J. Pelletier and J. King-Farlow (Guelph, Ontario, 1983).

[518] Brancacci, A. "Musique et philosophie en *République* 2–4." In Dixsaut, *Études 1*.

[519] Brancacci, A. "A Theory of Imitation in Plato's *Republic*." *TAPA* 114 (1984): 121–46.

[520] Brisson, L. "Les poètes, responsables de la déchéance de la cité: aspects éthiques, politiques et ontologiques de la critique de Platon." In Dixsaut, *Études 1*.

[521] Brunschwig, J. "*Diēgēsis* et *mimēsis* dans l'oeuvre de Platon." *REG* 77 (1974): 17–19.

[522] Burnyeat, M. F. "Culture and Society in Plato's *Republic*." *Tanner Lectures in Human Values* 20 (1999): 215–324.

[523] Collingwood, R. G. "Plato's Philosophy of Art." *Mind* 34 (1925): 154–72.

[524] Demand, N. "Plato and the Painters." *Phoenix* 29 (1975): 1–20.

[525] Dyson, M. M. "Poetic Imitation in Plato's *Republic* 3." *Antichthon* 22 (1988): 42–53.

[526] Elias, J. A. *Plato's Defense of Poetry*. London, 1984.

[527] Else, G. "The Structure and Date of Book 10 of Plato's *Republic*." *Abhandlungen der Heidelberger Akademie der Wissenschaften, Philosophisch-historische Klasse* (1972), Abhandlung 3.

[528] Else, G. *Plato and Aristotle on Poetry*. Chapel Hill, N.C., 1986.

[529] Ferrari, G. R. F. "Plato and Poetry." In *The Cambridge History of Literary Criticism*, vol. 1: *Classical Criticism*, ed. G. A. Kennedy (Cambridge, 1989). Secs. 4 and 5.

[530] Ford, A. *The Origins of Criticism: Literary Culture and Poetic Theory in Classical Greece*. Princeton, 2002. Ch. 9, "Literary Culture in Plato's *Republic*: The Sound of Ideology."

[531] Gadamer, H.-G. *Dialogue and Dialectic*, trans. P. C. Smith. New Haven, Conn., 1980. Ch. 3, "Plato and the Poets."

[532] Gastaldi, S. "*Paideia/ mythologia*." In Vegetti, vol. 2.

[533] Gill, C. "Plato and the Education of Character." *AGP* 67, no. 1 (1985): 1–26.

[534] Gill, C. "Plato on Falsehood – Not Fiction." In *Lies and Fiction in the Ancient World*, ed. C. Gill and T. P. Wiseman (Austin, Tex., 1993).

[535] Giuliano, F. M. *Platone e la Poesia*, International Plato Studies, 22. Sankt Augustin, 2005.

[536] Golden, L. "Plato's Concept of Mimesis." *British Journal of Aesthetics* 15 (1975): 118–31.

[537] Gould, J. "Plato and Performance." In *The Language of the Cave*, ed. A. Barker and M. Warner (= *Apeiron* 25.4 [1992]).

[538] Greene, W. C. "Plato's View of Poetry." *Harvard Studies in Classical Philology* 29 (1918): 1–75.

[539] Grey, D. R. "Art in the *Republic*." *Philosophy* 27 (1952): 291–310.

[540] Griswold, C. "The Ideas and the Criticism of Poetry in Plato's *Republic*, Book 10." *JHP* 19 (1981): 135–50.

[541] Halliwell, S. "The *Republic's* Two Critiques of Poetry (Book 2.376c–3998b, Book 10.595a–597e)." In Höffe.

[542] Halliwell, S. *The Aesthetics of Mimesis: Ancient Texts and Modern Problems*. Princeton, 2002. Chs. 1–4.

[543] Havelock, E. A. *Preface to Plato*. Cambridge, Mass., 1963. Ch. 1, "Plato on Poetry."

[544] Janaway, C. *Images of Excellence*. Oxford, 1995. Chs. 4–6.

[545] Kardaun, M. "Platonic Art Theory: A Reconsideration." In *The Winged Chariot: Collected Essays on Plato and Platonism in honour of L. M. de Rijk*, ed. M. Kardaun and J. Spruyt (Leiden, 2000).

[546] Keuls, E. C. *Plato and Greek Painting*. Leiden, 1978.

[547] Kuhn, H. "The True Tragedy: On the Relationship between Greek Tragedy and Plato." *Harvard Studies in Classical Philology* 52 (1941): 1–40; 53 (1942): 37–88.

[548] Lear, G. R. "Plato on Learning to Love Beauty." In Santas.

[549] Levin, S. B. *The Ancient Quarrel between Poetry and Philosophy Revisited: Plato and the Greek Literary Tradition*. Oxford, 2001.

[550] de Luise, F., and G. Farinetti. "*Hyponoia*: l'ombra di Antistene." In Vegetti, vol. 2.

[551] Marcos de Pinotti, G. E. "*Mímēsis* e ilusiones de los sentidos en *República* 10: observaciones a la crítica de Aristóteles a la *phantasia* platónica." *Methexis* 18 (2005): 53–66.

[552] Moravcsik, J. "On Correcting the Poets." *OSAP* 4 (1985): 35–47.

[553] Moss, J. "Pleasure and Illusion in Plato." *PPR* 72, no. 3 (2006).

[554] Moutsopoulos, E. "Platon, promoteur d'une psychologie musicale (*République*, 3.398c–405d)." In Dixsaut, *Études 1*.

[555] Muller, R. "La musique et l'imitation." In *La Philosophie de Platon*, ed. M. Fattal (Paris, 2001).

[556] Murdoch, I. *The Fire and the Sun: Why Plato Banished the Artists*. Oxford, 1977.

[557] Naddaf, R. A. *Exiling the Poets: The Production of Censorship in Plato's* Republic. Chicago, 2002.

[558] Nehamas, A. "Plato on Imitation and Poetry." In *Plato on Beauty, Wisdom and the Arts*, ed. J. M. E. Moravcsik and P. Temko (Totowa, N.J., 1982). Rpt. in A. Nehamas *Virtues of Authenticity: Essays on Plato and Socrates.* (Princeton, 1999).

[559] Nehamas, A. "Plato and the Mass Media." *The Monist* 71 (1988): 214–34.

[560] Osborne, C. "The Repudiation of Representation in Plato's *Republic* and Its Repercussions." *Proceedings of the Cambridge Philological Society* 33 (1987): 53–73.

[561] Partee, M. H. "Plato's Banishment of Poetry." *Journal of Aesthetics and Art Criticism* 29 (1970): 209–22.

[562] Rohatyn, D. "Struktur und Funktion in Buch 10 von Platons *Staat.*" *Gymnasium* 82 (1975): 314–30.

[563] Rubidge, B. "Tragedy and the Emotions of Warriors: The Moral Psychology Underlying Plato's Attack on Poetry." *Arethusa* 26 (1993): 247–76.

[564] Smith, N. D. "Images, Education, and Paradox in Plato's *Republic.*" *Apeiron* 32 (1999): 125–41.

[565] Stanford, W. B. "Onomatopoeic Mimesis in Plato *Rep.* 396b–397c." *JHS* 93 (1973): 185–91.

[566] Tate, J. "'Imitation' in Plato's *Republic.*" *CQ* 22 (1928): 16–23.

[567] Tate, J. "Plato and 'Imitation.'" *CQ* 26 (1932): 161–69.

[568] Teisserenc, F. "*Mimēsis* narrative et formation du caractère." In Dixsaut, *Études 1.*

[569] Urmson, J. "Plato and the Poets." In *Plato on Beauty, Wisdom and the Arts*, ed. J. M. E. Moravcsik and P. Temko (Totowa, N.J., 1982). Rpt. in Kraut.

[570] Verdenius, W. J. *Mimesis: Plato's Doctrine of Imitation and Its Meaning for Us.* Leiden, 1949.

[571] White, J. "Imitation." *St. John's Review* 39, nos. 1–2 (1989–90): 173–99.
Commentaries particularly relevant to the issues in this section are [9] and [11].

IV.K. Myth and religion

[572] Albinus, L. "The *katabasis* of Er." In Ostenfeld.

[573] Annas, J. "Plato's Myths of Judgement." *Phronesis* 27 (1982): 119–43.

[574] Bouvier, D. "Ulysse et le personnage du lecteur dans la *République*: réflexions sur l'importance du mythe d'Er pour la théorie de la *mimēsis.*" In *La Philosophie de Platon*, ed. M. Fattal (Paris, 2001).

[575] Brisson, L. *Plato the Myth Maker.* Chicago, 1998.

[576] Brisson, L. "La critique de la tradition religieuse par Platon et son usage dans la *République* et dans les *Lois.*" In *Cosmos et Psychè: mélanges offerts a Jean Frère,* ed. E. Vegleris (Hildesheim, 2005).

[577] Calabi, F. "Gige." In Vegetti, vol. 2.

[578] Campese, S., and S. Gastaldi. "Bendidie e Panatenee." In Vegetti, vol. 1.

[579] Cerri, G. *Platone Sociologo della Comunicazione.* Milano, 1991. Ch. 3, "Platone inventore di miti: persuadere narrando."

[580] Chatelain, F. "'Le récit est terminé,' Platon, *République* 612b." *Revue de Philosophie Ancienne* 5 (1987): 95–98.

[581] Couloubaritsis, L. "Le statut du mythe de Gygès chez Platon." In *Mythe et Politique,* ed. F. Jouan and A. Motte (= *Bibliothèque de la Faculté de Philosophie et Lettres de l'Université de Liège* 257 [1990]).

[582] Des Places, É. "Les derniers thèmes de la *République* de Platon." *Archives de Philosophie* 19 (1956): 115–22.

[583] Druet, F.-X. "Les niveaux de récit dans le mythe d'Er: Platon *Rép.* 10.613e–621d." *Les Études Classiques* 66 (1998): 23–32.

[584] Ferrari, F. "*Theologia.*" In Vegetti, vol. 2.

[585] Ferrari, G. R. F. "Glaucon's Reward, Philosophy's Debt: The Myth of Er." In *Plato's Myths* ed. C. Partenie (Cambridge, 2008).

[586] Frutiger, P. *Les mythes de Platon: Étude Philosophique et Littéraire.* Paris, 1930.

[587] Hall, R. W. "On the Myth of Metals in the *Republic.*" *Apeiron* 1, no. 2 (1967): 23–32.

[588] Hartman, M. "The Hesiodic Roots of Plato's Myth of Metals." *Helios* 15 (1988): 103–14.

[589] Howland, J. "Raconter une histoire et philosopher: l'anneau de Gygès." In Dixsaut, *Études* 2.

[590] Janka, M., and C. Schäfer, eds. *Platon als Mythologe: Neue Interpretationen zu den Mythen in Platons Dialogen.* Darmstadt, 2002. An important collection, although it contains no chapter on myth in the *Republic* in particular.

[591] Johnson, R. R. "Does Plato's Myth of Er Contribute to the Argument of the *Republic*?" *Philosophy and Rhetoric* 32, no. 1 (1999): 1–13.

[592] Lear, J. "Myth and Allegory in Plato's *Republic.*" In Santas.

[593] Lieb, I. C. "Philosophy as Spiritual Formation: Plato's Myth of Er." *International Philosophical Quarterly* 3 (1963): 271–85.

[594] Lincoln, B. "Waters of Memory, Waters of Forgetfulness." *Fabula* 23 (1982): 19–34.

[595] Mattéi, J.-F. "Du mythe hésiodique des races au mythe homérique des Muses dans la *République*: une interprétation 'économique' de la politique platonicienne." *Diotima* 19 (1991): 13–21.

[596] McPherran, M. "The Gods and Piety of Plato's *Republic*." In Santas.

[597] Moors, K. "Muthologia and the Limits of Opinion: Presented Myths in Plato's *Republic*." *BACAP* 4 (1988): 213–47.

[598] Moors, K. "Named Life Selections in Plato's Myth of Er." *Classica et Medievalia* 39 (1988): 55–61.

[599] Morgan, K. A. *Myth and Philosophy from the Presocratics to Plato.* Cambridge, 2000. Ch. 7, "Plato: Myth and the Soul."

[600] Morgan, M. L. *Platonic Piety: Philosophy and Ritual in Fourth-Century Athens.* New Haven, Conn., 1990. Ch. 5, "Education, Philosophy, and History in the *Republic*."

[601] Morrison, J. S. "Parmenides and Er." *JHS* 75 (1955): 59–68.

[602] Richardson, H. "The Myth of Er (Plato, *Republic* 616b)." *CQ* 20 (1926): 113–33.

[603] Schils, G. "Plato's Myth of Er: The Light and the Spindle." *Antiquité Classique* 62 (1993): 101–14.

[604] Schubert, P. "L'anneau de Gygès: réponse de Platon à Hérodote." *L'Antiquité Classique* 66 (1987): 255–60.

[605] Schuhl, P.-M. *La Fabulation Platonicienne.* Paris, 1968. Ch. 3, secs. 1 and 2. Topic: the myths of Gyges and of Er.

[606] Segal, C. "'The myth was saved': Reflections on Homer and the Mythology of Plato's *Republic*." *Hermes* 106 (1978): 315–36.

[607] Smith, J. "Plato's Use of Myth in the Education of the Philosophic Man." *Phoenix* 40 (1986): 20–34.

[608] Stewart, J. A. *The Myths of Plato*, ed. G. R. Levy. London, 1960 [1905].

[609] Thayer, H. S. "The Myth of Er." *HPQ* 5 (1988): 369–84.

[610] Vegetti, M. "*Katabasis*." In Vegetti, vol. 1.

[611] Vegetti, M. "Adimanto." In Vegetti, vol. 2.

[612] Vernant, J.-P. *Myth and Thought among the Greeks.* London, 1983. Ch. 4, "The River of *Amelēs* and the *Meletē Thanatou*."

[613] Villani, A. "Le fuseau et le peson. Note sur la colonne lumineuse de *République* 616b." In *La Philosophie de Platon*, ed. M. Fattal (Paris, 2001).

IV.L. History of the reception of the Republic

[614] Abbate, M. "Il Bene nell'interpretazione di Plotino e di Proclo." In Vegetti, vol. 5.

[615] Calabi, F. "Aristotele discute la *Repubblica*." In Vegetti, vol. 4.

[616] Funke, H., ed. *Utopie und Tradition: Platons Lehre vom Staat in der Moderne.* Würzburg, 1987. Eight essays, six of them in German; the English-language contribution is J. Glucker, "Plato in England: The Nineteenth Century and After."

[617] Höffe, O. "Vier Kapitel einer Wirkungsgeschichte der *Politeia*." In Höffe.

[618] O'Meara, D. J. *Platonopolis: Platonic Political Philosophy in Late Antiquity*. Oxford, 2003.

[619] Press, G. A. "Continuities and Discontinuities in the History of *Republic* Interpretation." *International Studies in Philosophy* 28, no. 4 (1996): 61–78.

[620] Stalley, R. F. "Aristotle's Criticism of Plato's *Republic*." In *A Companion to Aristotle's Politics*, ed. D. Keyt and F. D. Miller, Jr. (Oxford, 1991).

[621] Vegetti, M. "La critica aristotelica alla *Repubblica* nel secondo libro della *Politica*, il *Timeo* e le *Leggi*." In Vegetti, vol. 4.

[622] Vegetti, M., and M. Abbate, eds. *La* Repubblica *di Platone nella Tradizione Antica*. Naples, 1999.

Press' very useful article [619] gives references at n. 16 to the extensive literature on the history of the reception of Plato's dialogues in general, which of course includes that of the *Republic*. To his list can now be added:

[623] Demetriou, K. "The Development of Platonic Studies in Britain and the Role of the Utilitarians." *Utilitas* 8, no. 1 (1996): 15–37.

[624] Glucker, J. "The Two Platos of Victorian Britain." In *Polyhistor: Studies in the History and Historiography of Ancient Philosophy*, ed. K. A. Algra, P. W. van der Horst, and D. T. Runia (Leiden, 1996).

[625] Kobusch, T., and B. Moysisch. *Platon in der Abendländischen Geistesgeschichte: Neue Forschungen zum Platonismus*. Darmstadt, 1997.

[626] Neschke-Hentschke, A., ed. *Images de Platon et Lectures de ses Oeuvres: les Interprétations de Platon à travers les Siècles*, A. Étienne, co-editor. Louvain, 1997.

[627] Tarrant, H. *Plato's First Interpreters*. Ithaca, N.Y., 2000.

INDEX OF PASSAGES

Note: The editor is grateful to Agnes Gellen Callard for preparing the two indexes to this volume.

INDEX OF NAMES AND SUBJECTS